THE AUSTRALIANS IN NINE WARS

Also by Peter Firkins
STRIKE AND RETURN

THE AUSTRALIANS IN NINE WARS

WAIKATO to LONG TAN

PETER FIRKINS

McGRAW-HILL BOOK COMPANY

New York   St. Louis

San Francisco

Library of Congress Cataloging in Publication Data

Firkins, Peter C
    The Australians in nine wars.

    1. Australia--History, Military. I. Title.
DU112.3.F57   1972   355'.00994   72-3444
ISBN 0-07-021065-9

Published in Australia.1971 by Rigby Limited. Wholly designed
and set up in Australia. Printed by Lee Fung Printing Co. Ltd.,
Hong Kong. Published in U.S.A. 1972 by McGraw-Hill Book Company.

For

Elizabeth, Rosemary,

and Caroline

ACKNOWLEDGMENTS

I should like to express my very deep appreciation to the following distinguished gentlemen for their most helpful advice and comments during the preparation of this book, without which my task would have been immeasurably more difficult:

Lieutenant-General the Honourable Sir Edmund F. Herring, K.C.M.G., C.B.E., D.S.O., M.C., E.D.; Lieutenant-General Sir Henry Wells, K.B.E., C.B., D.S.O.; Lieutenant-General Sir Ragnar Garrett, K.B.E., C.B.; Major-General S. C. Graham, D.S.O., O.B.E., M.C.; Major-General R. A. Hay, M.B.E.; Major-General P. A. Cullen, C.B.E., D.S.O., E.D., F.C.A.; Brigadier A. W. Buttrose, D.S.O., E.D.; Brigadier G. P. Hunt, C.B.E.; Brigadier P. Masel, O.B.E., E.D.; the late Mr Gavin M. Long, O.B.E., B.A. (editor of the official history of Australia in the second World War, who kindly read and commented upon the first draft of the manuscript); The Honourable C. T. Cross, American Ambassador to Singapore.

I am most grateful to the Director and staff of the Australian War Memorial, Canberra, for their help in numerous ways, and to the Board of the Australian War Memorial for permission to reproduce photographs, paintings, and excerpts from volumes of the Australian Official History of the second World War; also to Messrs. Angus & Robertson Pty. Ltd. for permission to reproduce excerpts from *General Monash's War Letters*, edited by F. W. Cutlack, and *Tobruk*, by Chester Wilmot. Finally, my sincere thanks go to Misses Andrea Keddie, Heather Bruce, and Gay Whitby, for the many long hours they have voluntarily spent on preparing the manuscript for publication.

CONTENTS

BOOK III

The Fight for the Homeland

BOOK IV

The Uncertain Years

ILLUSTRATIONS

Note :   *All illustrations in this volume are reproduced by kind permission of the Board of the Australian War Memorial, Canberra.*

MAPS

FOREWORD

by His Excellency the Governor-General of Australia, The Right Honourable Sir Paul Hasluck, G.C.M.G., G.C.V.O., K. St. J.

This book does not raise arguments about why wars started and how Australia came to take part in them. That is another part of Australian history.

The author accepts as his starting point that on nine different occasions in a little over a century Australians were under arms and engaged in war, and he recounts what they did. This is essentially a book that honours the fighting man by telling of the conditions in which they served, the engagements in which they took part, the losses endured and the victories won. It is a book about the proving of Australian manhood in the test of battle.

The author seems to me to have achieved two ends. He has put the role of Australian troops in perspective with the role of the other Imperial or Allied troops with whom they served and re-established for them the credit and honour that has sometimes been obscured in other narratives. He has also brought clearly and proudly before the reader the quality of the Australian soldier.

Because he has done this I commend the book and trust that the reading of it will remind the old and teach the young how bravely and well our soldiers have fought and how honourably they have served the nation in times of trial and danger.

Our people would be lacking in freedom and intelligence if they did not argue about the causes and consequences of wars; they will be lacking in vision if ever they are unable to recognise and to honour courage and devotion to duty.

Paul Hasluck

Government House
Canberra
May, 1971

AUTHOR'S NOTE

The wars which usually are begun by politicians have to be fought and won by soldiers. In this book, I have not attempted to detail the political background to the nine occasions on which Australians have been committed to action overseas, nor the way in which the fighting men have been backed up — or otherwise — by those who remained at home.

My concern, in this volume, has been with the soldiers themselves. In a companion volume, I hope to tell the story of Australian sailors and airmen.

In order to produce a book of manageable proportions, it has been necessary to omit individual mention of most of the thousands of deeds of personal gallantry which are woven into the saga of the Australian fighting man. In most cases I have dealt with the action of military formations rather than those of individuals, but the reader will realise that such terms as battalions, regiments, brigades, divisions, and armies are simple collective nouns for various numbers of men. Each man is a vital part of the whole. His skill, bravery, and devotion are the essentials of military success.

Some readers may query the use of the term "war" to cover some of the military operations in which Australians have been engaged. Korea, for example, has sometimes been given the odd euphemism of a "police action." But to the men engaged in it, it was war — whether declared or not.

When referring to specific units, I have used the adjectives British or Australian purely for convenience, to indicate that the formation was predominately of men from Great Britain or Australia.

Far too often the Australian, Canadian and New Zealand contributions to the world's conflicts have been disguised in contemporary military history under the vague cloak of British or Allied, and this book is a modern attempt to help place the role of the Australians, at least, in better perspective.

BOOK I

Years of Youthful Glory

❋ ❋ ❋ ❋ ❋ ❋

"*The nation that wishes to defend its land and its honour must spare no effort, refuse no sacrifice and make itself so formidable no enemy will dare assail it. A League of Nations may be an instrument for the preservation of peace, but an efficient army is a far more potent one.*"

GENERAL SIR JOHN MONASH

1

MAORIS, DERVISHES, AND BOXERS

THE LEGEND OF THE AUSTRALIAN FIGHTING MAN, WHICH BLOSSOMED into full flower on the bloody razorback ridges of Gallipoli during 1915, was indeed far distant when 1,475 volunteers embarked for the Maori Wars during 1863; a campaign in which the British had been engaged intermittently since 1845.

Formed into four regiments, the Australian contingent was given the name of the Waikato Militia, because by that time the fighting was concentrated in the Waikato area in the neighbourhood of Auckland. A high percentage of New Zealand's 56,000 Maoris had their tribal territories in this fertile region, and, as in Australia, the white settlers had steadily encroached upon the most productive soil. The fierce Maori warriors, whose Polynesian ancestry gave them skill and delight in the arts of war, reacted a good deal more vehemently than most of the Australian Aboriginal tribesmen. Many of them had firearms acquired from early traders, but even with their traditional weapons they were a dangerous foe.

Fortunately for the settlers, the tribes were to some extent divided by hereditary tribal areas, customs, and antagonisms. If they had united, under an abortive alliance known as the Maori King Movement, they might have prevented settlement of their lands for much longer. Even as it was they constituted an increasing menace to the settlers, and as the danger mounted the British Government was compelled to reinforce the regular troops and citizen forces already fighting the Maoris.

Major-General Pratt, Commander-in-Chief of the Imperial Forces in Australia, sent much of his garrison across the Tasman, and the Victorian Government sent its entire navy; the steam corvette *Victoria*, of 580 tons.

3

By 1861 there were six British battalions in New Zealand, under the command of Lieutenant-General Duncan Cameron, a Crimea War veteran whom the British Government had despatched to subdue the Maoris.

The first four regiments of the Waikato Militia, augmented by a further 1,200 men raised and despatched in 1864, had few opportunities of aspiring to the noble heights suggested by the London *Times*, which on 4 September 1864 declared: "The sentiment of the Australian colonies is now almost universally enlisted in the cause of the New Zealand settlers, and there is hardly any sacrifice which would not be made to promote the complete establishment of the Queen's authority."

This was not because the Maoris had been overawed by the display of British strength. In fact one of the leaders of the angry Waikato tribes, Wiremu Tamihana, proclaimed: "I have consented to attack the whole town (Auckland). I shall spare neither unarmed people nor property. This is how it will be; the unarmed people will not be left." But General Cameron forestalled him, by crossing the Maungatawhiri River into the Waikato country and leading his force of British regulars through the dense bush to attack the strongly fortified Maori *pas*. The main battle was on 20 November 1863, when they assaulted Rangariri. Four officers and thirty-eight men were killed, and over 100 wounded, before the Maoris surrendered.

The Australian troops did not take part in this attack, but were used to protect the settlers against marauding war parties between Auckland and the Waikato front. As Cameron pushed slowly on from Rangariri, he employed the Australians in scouting and flanking operations around his main force. 10,000 men, including the New Zealand militia and the Australian volunteers, were under his command by the time he faced the Maoris for the last engagement of the campaign; at Te Ranga on 21 June 1864. This was the first pitched battle in which Australians took part; men of the 1st Regiment of Waikato Militia, under Captain Moor, were used in the assault on the Maori defences. It was a victory for the British, and the Australians were praised for the dash and enthusiasm with which they joined in the attack.

After this, the main fighting was against a fanatical Maori terrorist movement, the Hau-Haus. The last skirmish with them was in February 1872, when they were defeated and dispersed at the headwaters of the Urewera River.

Before this, a good many of the Australians had gone home. A scheme to settle and protect the country had envisaged the manning of redoubts around which civilisation would spread in safety, and the 1st Regiment of Waikato Militia was stationed at Tauranga, the 2nd at Alexandria, the 3rd at Cambridge, and the 4th at Hamilton. The troops were, in effect, to become soldier-settlers, but when their terms of engagement expired most of the Australians either sold or abandoned the land which they had taken up. For most of them, it had been a somewhat unglamorous adventure. They suffered a few casualties during brushes with Maori war parties, but most of their time was spent in tedious garrison or patrol duties.

* * *

Australia's very modest contribution to a colonial war certainly caused no ripple in the world's diplomatic capitals of that period, and eleven more years were to pass before the young colonies had another opportunity of stirring any of their dormant martial aspirations. On 26 January 1885, Khartoum fell to the fanatical troops of the Mahdi after 317 days of siege, and General Gordon was reported to have been "betrayed and massacred." This dealt a severe blow to British prestige, and when news of the tragedy reached Sydney on 11 February the acting Premier of New South Wales, Mr W. B. Dalley, immediately called a Cabinet meeting after conferring with his military commander. Acting swiftly upon his Government's support, he cabled the New South Wales Agent General in London to say: "The Government offer to Her Majesty's Government two batteries of the Permanent Field Artillery with ten 16-pounder guns, properly horsed, also an effective and disciplined battalion of infantry 500 strong; the artillery will be under the command of Colonel Roberts R.A., the whole force under the command of Colonel Richardson the Commandant, and undertaking to land the force at Suakin within 30 days from embarkation."

The British Government accepted the offer "with much satisfaction." The Colonial Governments of Victoria, Queensland, and South Australia made similar offers but these were declined, as the British Government desired to avoid further delay.

Britain was sorely in need of friends, and the *Daily Telegraph* said, "It seemed as if at one stride Australia had taken her place as a Power that must be reckoned with." Political correspondents in Berlin reported that the offer had made a "tremendous and deep impression in the German capital," and a similar reaction was reported from Rome.

The New South Wales contingent was raised and despatched in less than two months; a remarkable achievement for a young nation with such little military background. When its 750 men marched through the streets of Sydney on 3 March 1885, singing, "The girl I left behind me," and other popular ballads of the period they were received by demonstrations of wild enthusiasm and patriotism, culminating in a tumultuous farewell as they embarked on the troopships *Iberia* and *Australasian*. 200,000 citizens were jammed around Circular Quay, whilst over a hundred small boats jostled for position in the harbour. Then the two ships carrying Australia's first expeditionary force steamed through Sydney Heads, but it is unlikely that the troopers aboard realised that they were establishing an historical milestone.

They reached Suakin, on the Red Sea, on 29 March, and were delighted to find on arrival that they were to be brigaded with the elite of the British Army: the Brigade of Guards. Within twenty-four hours of disembarkation they were advancing on Tamai, as part of a 10,000 man force which marched for sixteen hours under a broiling sun before reaching its objective. At Tamai, the Australians came under fire for the first time, and three men were slightly wounded. The expedition cleared the village of Osman Digna's Arab guerrillas, then made the gruelling return march to Suakin, which took thirteen and a half hours to accomplish. The operation was no great feat of arms, but was a severe test for men who had barely landed from their troopships, and who had been civilians only twelve weeks before.

Colonel A. J. Bennett, who was a member of the contingent and later served in the South African War and first World War, remarked that he never experienced worse physical conditions than in the six weeks of the Suakin campaign. He said, "Intense heat, dust, insects, thirst, and stench from bodies of dead Arabs and animals provided sufficient horrors of war, with dysentery and sunstroke claiming tremendous toll. A few skirmishes and many weary marches provided much sweat, but little glory."

The rest of their time in the Sudan was mainly spent on railway fatigue work, although fifty men were temporarily attached to the Camel Corps.

The campaign, which did not settle the Sudan situation for very long, ended in May, and the Australians were disappointed that they had not seen more action. The New South Wales Government offered them for service in India or on a Mediterranean station, but this was turned down by the British Government after protracted negotiations.

The men were repatriated in the troopship *Arab* on 17 May 1886, and encountered the greatest hazard of their adventure when an epidemic of "fever" broke out in the crowded troop decks. Six men died of it during the voyage. The remainder disembarked in Sydney on 23 June, receiving the same adulation to which they had departed. They were awarded two decorations; the Queen's Egyptian medal in silver, with the clasp "Suakin," and the Khedive of Egypt's bronze star.

No great feats of military endeavour were performed by the expeditionary force, and none of its members qualified for the award of twenty guineas a year for five years should he have won the Victoria Cross. But it was a modest milestone in Australia's military heritage, and, most significantly, it had established a precedent. From then on, it was taken for granted that Britain's far flung outposts should render military assistance to the mother country in time of conflict.

*   *   *

Fourteen years passed before Australia had another opportunity to show the mettle of her fighting men. This time, they joined in two separate campaigns on two different continents. While troopers of the Mounted Infantry were beginning to earn an enviable reputation in the South African War, a small force was raised to help the Allied troops engaged in fighting the Chinese in the Boxer Rebellion.

On 28 June 1900, the Colonial Office cabled the Premier of New South Wales, Sir William Lyne, to suggest that units of the Australian naval squadron should be despatched to China. The response was immediate. The *Wallaroo* left Port Jackson early in July, and the gunboat *Protector* sailed from Sydney on 11 August. On 8 August, a Naval Brigade of 200 men from Victoria and 260 men from New South Wales left for China.

They landed at Tientsin, where a detachment of 300 was placed under the command of General Lorne Campbell and deployed for attack against the Pehtang forts, but the forts were captured by German troops before the rest of the Allied forces could be brought into position.

In September, a detachment of the Victorian force was attached to a punitive expedition of four nationalities, under the command of General Alfred Gaselee, which was to attack Pao-Ting-Fu. But on arrival before the city, the columns were met by the Chief Magistrate and other officials, who conferred with General Gaselee and allowed the town to be occupied in four zones; British, French, German, and Italian.

Towards the end of October 1900 the British troops were withdrawn from North China. Winter saw 230 men of the New South Wales contingent established at Peking, whilst the Victorians formed part of the Tientsin garrison. Their duties during the bitter Chinese winter were not exactly military. They policed the cities, and were called upon for a variety of odd jobs which included manning the fire brigade and acting as guards and ticket collectors on the railways. Such tasks gave scant opportunity for glory, but when the Australians were withdrawn in March 1901, they received many messages of commendation from army and civil authorities for their performance, plus a more practical token of appreciation in the form of $1,500 given by the Council of Tientsin to be divided among the men who served in the city's police and fire brigade.

2

SOUTH AFRICA

HALFWAY ACROSS THE WORLD, A LARGER FORCE OF AUSTRALIANS WAS
engaged in more desperate business than fighting fires and collecting
tickets, as part of the British armies which were making heavy
weather of battling against the determined Boer commandos.

When negotiations finally broke down between the British Government
and the South African Republic, in October 1899, Australia was still a
continent divided into six separate colonies, each one guarding its autonomy
with considerable jealousy. Included among each colony's responsibilities
was the organisation of defence forces, which up until Federation was not a
national responsibility.

Australians had observed, with keen and partisan interest, the lengthy
diplomatic manoeuvring before the break between the British and South
African Governments. As early as July 1899, the Government of Queensland
had offered a contingent of 250 mounted infantry with machine guns if war
was declared. This was shortly followed by similar offers from New South
Wales and Victoria, and as soon as the news that war had broken out was
received in Australia the nation erupted into patriotic fervour.

War was declared on 11 October 1899, but its coming had been so obvious
that a conference had been convened in Melbourne by the various military
commandants on 28 September 1899. They decided to raise a joint contingent consisting of 2,500 men of all arms, of whom more than half were
to be mounted.

But the British War Office, to which the military value of Colonial troops
was an unknown factor, had different ideas. The notion that Australian
volunteers could be as efficient as British regular soldiers was regarded as

8

heresy, and War Office acceptance of the Australian offer was a demonstration of Empire unity rather than a consideration of military competence. However, Empire unity was an important element in face of the hostile reaction of France and Germany to Britain's intentions at that time.

Australia's offer of 2,500 men, mostly mounted, was changed following a cable from the Secretary of State for War, Lord Lansdowne. This stated, among other things: "Firstly, units should consist of 124 men, secondly may be infantry, mounted infantry or cavalry. In view of numbers already available, infantry most, cavalry least serviceable."

The Colonial Governments reluctantly assented to the British proposals, and their military commandants began to arrange for the organisation and embarkation of their units.

During the first year and half of the war 2,900 regular troops were sent to South Africa, plus "Citizen Bushmen" contingents totalling 3,637 men. Most of the latter were equipped by public subscription and raised from untrained sources, although generally they were officered by men with previous military experience. A total of 6,771 horses was despatched with the troops.

Most of the Australian contingent was divided into small units which were attached to larger British formations, but they had not been in South Africa long before their skill was felt by the Boers and noted by the British. The competence of the Australian mounted soldier was quickly recognised, and the priorities indicated in Lord Lansdowne's rather condescending telegram were rescinded. Ultimately, all Australian infantry was mounted, and this provided Lord Roberts with nearly double the number of mounted troops previously at his disposal. This in turn enabled the wide flanking movements which were the determining factor in the relief of Kimberley and the subsequent advance upon Bloemfontein and Pretoria.

Lord Roberts, who was the most widely experienced British commander of his era, said: "All the colonials did extremely well, they were very intelligent and they had what I want our men to have: more individuality. They could find their way about the country far better than the British cavalryman could do."

This compliment from the British Commander-in-Chief was significant, because it expressed for the first time what is perhaps the basic difference in the character of the Australian soldier from that of any other nationality. His individuality and initiative have revealed themselves so often in so many campaigns that they are recognised as fundamental to his military make-up.

In the Boer War, he certainly had an advantage over his British comrades. The South African veldt, with its vast horizons and great empty plains, was very similar to the Australian bushland which he knew so well. A large percentage of the Australian contingent was made up of bushmen, from

wealthy squatters to the roughest of stock riders, so it is little wonder that
they had an eye for the country and could match the skill and bushcraft
of the enemy. For the most part, the Boers outthought, outfought and out-
witted the regular British Army, which still suffered the agonies of extreme
conservative orthodoxy. Still trained to fight in tight, compact units under
the direction of officers carrying out staff directives, the British soldiers
were slaughtered by enemies whom they rarely even sighted.

The first notable action in which the Australian contingent was engaged
was fought soon after the arrival of the Queensland Mounted Infantry, late
in 1899. On New Year's Day, 1900, they took part in an attack on Boer
positions at Sunnyside. Taking full advantage of the natural cover offered
by the veldt, they stalked the Boers in the same way as the Boers had stalked
the British. Advancing on three sides in an outflanking movement, they
captured the laager and took forty prisoners.

A correspondent wrote: "The dexterity of the Queenslanders was
remarkable; they stalked the enemy as a sportsman would stalk a deer,
criticizing their own fire and the fire of the foe with coolness and interest."

This action was an historic affair in another sense too, in that it was the
first occasion on which Australians and Canadians had fought together in
war. A hundred Canadians and two hundred of the Duke of Cornwall's
Light Infantry supported the Queenslanders in their attack on Sunnyside.

During the following month, on 9 February 1900, another brisk skirmish
was fought out at Cape Colony, when Captains Cameron and Salmon led
a patrol of fifty Tasmanians on reconnaissance from Rensburg.

This encounter was recorded by Louis Creswick, the War's most notable
historian, who appreciated and understood the qualities of the men from the
Antipodes. He wrote: "The Australians cleverly took shelter and returned
an active fusillade, but the Boers seemed to be everywhere in overwhelming
numbers. The Australians with great gallantry took possession of a kopje
and held it for a good hour and a half, but the numbers opposing them were
too great and when the Dutchmen worked round to the rear and fired on
their horses they thought it high time to come down, mount, and retire,
amid a hurricane of lead. The same action was repeated, the holding of
another kopje and the evacuation of it in consequence of the arrival, in the
rear, of the Boers, and finally a retirement had to be effected across open
plains exposed to fierce volleys from the pursuing enemy. Strange to say,
very few of the colonials were wounded, though they held their ground
during the day with wondrous pluck and tackled the Boers with dexterity
equal to their own. Indeed the coolness and courage of Captain Cameron
were reflected by his men and Captain Salmon, whose baptism of fire this
was, made a remarkable display of gallantry in the field. Of grit and gallantry
there was no end."

On the same afternoon, another skirmish involving the Australians took place near the British camp at Slingersfontein, which the Boers began shelling. Captain Moor and his men took up positions on a hill near the Boer guns, and were attacked by large numbers of Boers who called on the Australians to surrender. But according to Creswick "they fixed bayonets and yelled defiance."

Moor's men held their ground until dark, when they made their way out through the encircling Boers and reached the safety of the British camp with a loss of one killed and three wounded.

The unconditional surrender of Pretoria was hastened by a hard driving force of Australians under Colonel de Lisle; and Lieutenant W. W. Russell Watson, who took part in the attack, acted as emissary for Lord Roberts. He entered the city with a white handkerchief tied to his whip, and demanded to see General Botha. After preliminary discussions with city officials he was escorted to the great Boer leader's residence, and extended generous courtesy from General Botha and other Boer generals. After an hour's conference they agreed to the terms of unconditional surrender, and Lieutenant Watson rode out of the city to rejoin his unit. With Colonel de Lisle, he reported to Lord Roberts at his headquarters some miles away, and informed him of the Boer leaders' decision.

The Battle of Diamond Hill, on 12 June 1900, was a victory for the New South Wales Mounted Rifles, the 6th Mounted Infantry Battalion, and the 1st West Australian Mounted Infantry.

The New South Wales Mounted Rifles and 6th Mounted Infantry were ordered to attack the hill with fixed bayonets by Colonel de Lisle despite a furious fusillade from the Boers, who just before darkness retired to a second position 1,200 yards away. They were routed out of these positions by the West Australians, and their force of 4,000 retreated in disorder across Bronkhers Spruit. They suffered heavy casualties and left a trail of wagons and guns.

Members of the South Australian contingent made a name for themselves at about the same time. Under the command of Captain J. R. B. O'Sullivan, a hundred of them made an early morning march to capture a convoy carrying six months' supplies to General de Wet's force. They captured the convoy, but then had to face an attack by 400 Boers, who were fought off after an action lasting four hours.

During the whole of the South African campaign, the most memorable Australian action centred around five acres of flat plain near a boulder covered kopje, and encircled by high ground which not only overlooked the ground to be held but also the watering point half a mile distant.

This desolate site was a ford on the Elands River at Brakfontein, to which a force under Colonel Hore was despatched, in mid July 1900. Lord Roberts had ordered Hore to secure the crossing and keep it open for the movement of supplies.

Colonel Hore commanded 100 men of the Queensland Mounted Infantry under Major Tunbridge, 100 men of the New South Wales Bushmen under Captain Thomas, 50 Victorian Bushmen under Captain Ham, and 150 Rhodesians. Other than rifles, their weaponry comprised only one 7-pounder gun and two Maxim machine guns.

The Australian leader and his troops maintained that aggressive spirit which had so characterised their achievements in the campaign thus far. While preparing their defences, they pushed out patrols to engage a force of between 2,500 and 4,000 Boers, who had swarmed up to beseige the outpost as soon as they saw the force begin to dig in.

On 19 July, Major Tunbridge and a squadron of his Queenslanders escorted a supply convoy into the post, and Colonel Hore retained it there because of the tenuous situation. The Boers brought up artillery, and from early August pounded the defences with a merciless barrage. On one day alone 1,500 shells were fired into the camp, killing five men, wounding twenty-seven, and causing great damage to all sections including the hospital. But the defenders stuck grimly to their task. They used the timber from smashed wagons to cover their trenches, and sent men to the river for water under cover of darkness.

A correspondent wrote a graphic description of the scene. "But these fellows were not to be bombarded with impunity. They examined their resources, looked ruefully at their one gun, a muzzle loader which before long jammed. The Boers' fire was too hot and snipers too numerous to make repairs to their position, so they had to wait for night. Then they set to work with a will, brawny arms and knowing heads, to build trenches and shelters which would defy the Boers."

The constant bombardment provoked a young Queenslander, Lieutenant Amant, into leading twenty-five of his men on a night raid to destroy the "pom pom" rapid fire gun that was causing most havoc to the Australian positions. They crept up on the Boer post, and killed the crew and destroyed the gun in a few minutes of savage fighting. But as they withdrew to the Australian lines the Boers opened up with a tremendous barrage in retaliation, and Amant was killed. Ironically, his was the only Australian death that night.

Creswick recorded the effect of this casualty on the morale of the defenders when he reported that: "The valiant lieutenant, though he knew it not, had struck the keynote of victory. His comrades swore with tremendous oath that they would die rather than give in and that the white flag would never float over those five acres."

Two major attempts were made to relieve the beseiged post. Firstly General Carrington with 1,000 men was despatched from Zeerut. He had orders to push on at all costs, but after a minor skirmish with the Boers his force retreated seventeen miles, much to the displeasure of Lord Roberts.

SUDAN AND SOUTH AFRICA. *Top:* Sudan War. New South Wales infantrymen marching from the camp at Suakin. *Bottom:* South African War. Australians and New Zealanders charge the Boer guns during the attack on Babington's convoy near Klerksdorp, 24 March 1901.

Three days later General Baden-Powell set out with a relief force, but when within twenty miles of the post he was informed that the Australians had surrendered, and withdrew.

On 8 August, the Boer leader General De la Rey sent a messenger to the Australian post. He invited them to surrender, saying that two other posts in the area had been taken, that Carrington had been repulsed, and that the Boers would soon be in command of the entire country. He promised them all the honours of war, including retention of their arms and a safe conduct to the nearest British post, but warned that if they did not surrender they would be blown to pieces by his heavy artillery.

Colonel Hore replied that even if it were his personal wish to surrender, and it wasn't, he was commanding Australians who would cut his throat if he acceded to the Boers' demands. He concluded his reply with, "I don't expect that your artillery will change the minds of these men," and asked De la Rey not to shell the hospital. This request was honoured by the Boers, although they fully implemented their threat so far as the remainder of the fort was concerned.

Heavy fighting erupted again as soon as Hore's refusal to surrender was received. Shells howled and crashed around the trenches, and there were vicious duels between Boer and Australian snipers. The enemy held the initiative during daylight by virtue of their numbers and higher positions, but the Australian night raids were deadly. They crept to within feet of the Boer positions, to destroy their guns and crews. But when the Boers tried to infiltrate the Australian lines they were usually located and beaten off by the forward scouts.

On the night of 10 August, an Australian scout was despatched through the Boer lines to Mafeking, which he reached on the thirteenth. His mission was to seek relief for the garrison, but heavy fighting continued until the fifteenth. It died away during the night, and the following morning was strangely quiet. Patrols were sent out to reconnoitre the Boer lines, and they found them abandoned. The Boers had given it up as a bad job, and pulled out during the night. Their feelings were summed up by a Boer historian in 1905, who when describing the "Elands River affair" wrote: "For the first time in the war we were fighting men who used our own tactics against us. They were Australian volunteers and though small in number we could not take their positions. They were the only troops who could scout into our lines at night and kill our sentries, while killing or capturing our scouts. Our men admitted that the Australians were more formidable opponents and far more dangerous than any British troops."

In five weeks fighting, 1,379 of the 1,540 horses in the camp had died or been killed, but the defenders' casualties had been surprisingly light in view of the intensity of the action. Only five were killed, seven died of wounds, and thirty-eight were wounded.

HEROES OF THREE WARS. *Top:* Tom Derrick, V.C., D.C.M., receiving badges of rank after being commissioned. *Bottom:* Two Simpsons. *Left*, Simpson and his donkey, Gallipoli. *Right*, WO2 Ray Simpson, V.C., in Vietnam.

Lord Kitchener rode into the camp on the afternoon of 16 August, and said "You have had a hot time, but have made a remarkable defence. Only Colonials could have held out and survived in such impossible circumstances."

The defenders marched out of their fort under Lord Methuen and after a rest in Mafeking, they went on to Pretoria where they were inspected by Lord Roberts. News of the action spread through South Africa, especially since it was one of the few occasions, up to then, in which the Boers had been worsted. It may perhaps be seen as the first major contribution to the Australian military tradition.

The correspondent of a Cape Town newspaper observed, "Once again Australian troops, this time supported by Rhodesians, showed that the Boer can be confused and even stopped by enterprising men. Outnumbered by more than ten to one and completely outgunned, the Colonials must have enraged the Boers who knew from experience that it is easy to overwhelm small British garrisons. The Australians have brought an intellectual appreciation to warfare."

Creswick recorded "Every soldier who saw the place afterwards expressed surprise that they could have held out so long, and it is therefore, the more creditable to them to have done so when every hope of relief seemed entirely cut off."

The South African War was still being fought when, on 1 January 1901, the Federation of the Australian States was effected and the Commonwealth Government began the task of unifying Australia's defences. This altered the status of the Australian contingents serving in South Africa. Instead of being a collection of units representative of individual colonies, they were welded together and designated the Australian Commonwealth Horse. As such, they continued to render excellent service until Lord Kitchener and General Botha signed the peace treaty on 31 May 1902.

Australia had contributed a total of 16,175 men, of whom 518 were killed in action or died of wounds and 882 were wounded. Fifteen years later, such a casualty list could be run up in one morning on the Western Front. The Boer War was the last of the "gentlemanly" wars of the nineteenth century; regarded by the public as enthusiastically as though they had been sporting fixtures, and blundered through by staff officers who also regarded war as a kind of aristocratic sport.

Six Victoria Crosses were awarded, one being to Lieutenant F. W. Bell of the 5th West Australian Contingent, who won his decoration at Brakpan on 16 May 1901. When his unit was retiring through heavy fire, Bell noticed one of his men dismount, and returned to pick him up. Bell's horse could not carry both men, so he put the wounded trooper in the saddle, covered his retreat, and then calmly withdrew himself.

The campaign initiated numerous aspects of military practice which are regarded as fundamental today, but in South Africa they were unique. One was the high standard set by the New South Wales Field Ambulance Corps. One of its medical staff, Captain Neville (later Sir Neville) Howse, won the first Victoria Cross at Vredesort in July 1900, and Lord Roberts was so impressed with the efficiency of the unit that he recommended it as a pattern for the British Army.

Another innovation introduced by the Australians was the attachment of chaplains to most units, a practice not followed by the British Army until after the Boer War.

After three years of campaigning the Australians left South Africa with an extremely fine reputation, particularly in the roles of scouting, reconnaisance and sniper activity. These were the warlike crafts for which their background had equipped them well.

The Australians developed a healthy respect for the bravery of the individual British soldier, but had nothing but disdain for the British leaders at almost every level. In fact, it was not until the British command realised that the Boers could only be defeated by unconventional methods that they began to achieve worthwhile successes in the field.

The British command fell into even deeper disfavour when four Australian officers were court martialled by the British Army and sentenced to death for the alleged killing of Boer prisoners of war. The death sentence was carried out on two of the officers, one of whom was the well-known bushman poet "Breaker" Morant. The executions caused a great deal of resentment in Australia, and soon afterwards the Commonwealth Parliament passed an Act which entrusted the discipline of Australian troops to their own command. Australian courts-martial are forbidden to impose the death penalty upon any Australian soldier unless he "traitorously delivers up a garrison or traitorously corresponds with the enemy."

3

FOUNDER OF THE A.I.F.

THE MAULING RECEIVED BY THE BRITISH ARMY IN SOUTH AFRICA compelled radical changes in military thinking, which included the establishment of a General Staff controlled by an Army Council. This comprised the Secretary of State for War, the heads of the chief departments of the General Staff, and certain civil members. Even before Georges Clemenceau made his immortal comment that, "War is too important to be left to generals," the rulers of Britain had become uneasily aware that some of their own generals left much to be desired.

A Committee for Imperial Defence had been formed, and Imperial Conferences were held in London in 1902 and 1907. The British Government invited the Dominions to apply to the Committee for advice and guidance on all matters of domestic defence.

During this period, the old "defence forces" of the pre-Federation colonies were being re-organised into the Army of the Commonwealth of Australia. This process was supervised by an outstanding British soldier: Major-General Sir Edward Hutton. He was one of the "rebels" who occasionally appeared amongst the conformist British officers of that era — which perhaps is why he was dispatched to Australia.

He had distinguished himself in command of a mounted brigade in South Africa, including the earlier Australian contingents in that war. A man of particularly strong personality and character, he had the reputation of being a difficult subordinate; a trait not particularly encouraged in the British Army. His ultimate career is thought to have been prejudiced by such incidents as his outspoken criticisms of General Sir John French and others when conducting manoeuvres at Aldershot.

16

He had keen foresight in military matters, and fought for his opinions against those who held political power in Australia. During a previous tour of duty in New South Wales, he had pressed for the integration of the Colonial defence forces, and for the institution of a military college along the lines of West Point in the United States and Kingston in Canada.

These ideas, and others, were rejected; usually on the grounds of lack of finance. But Captain J. W. Niesigh, a well known Sydney military critic, wrote in 1904: "Those who care to look through later records will find how all those ideas have since been adopted and placed to the credit of others."

Like many others of strong and forthright personality, Hutton could also be a man of great charm. He insisted that, "By going to church on Sundays I always play cricket better for the rest of the week."

In 1903, a man of equally outstanding personality was appointed to Hutton's staff as Assistant Quartermaster-General. This was William Throsby Bridges.

Bridges was born at Greenock, Scotland, on 18 February 1861: the son of a Royal Navy captain. His mother was a daughter of Charles Throsby, of Moss Vale in New South Wales. He was educated at the Royal Navy School at New Cross, London, a school for the sons of Royal Navy and Royal Marine Officers, and was still at school when his father retired from the navy and took his family to Canada, where his own father, the Rev. George Bridges, had lived for many years.

William Bridges continued his education at Trinity College, Port Hope, and in 1877 was enrolled at the Royal Canadian Military College, Kingston. The College had been formed in the previous year, and Bridges, as one of its first students, was registered as Number 25 on the College roll. The *College Review* of 1946 recalled him as, "A tall, thin student, with long legs, and a slight stoop, who did not play games, nor was he prominent in his studies, but spent much of his spare time reading in the smoke room."

While he was at Kingston, his father lost money through a bank failure. In 1879 he brought the remainder of his family to Australia, leaving William in Canada to complete his military studies. When he graduated he followed his family to Sydney, and since there was no vacancy in the defence forces he obtained a position with the Department of Roads and Bridges as an inspector. He worked for this Department until 1885, the year in which Gordon was killed and the Government of New South Wales offered a contingent of men to fight in the Sudan. This seemed to be an ideal opportunity for a trained soldier, but the rush of enthusiasts left no room for Bridges. Soon afterwards he heard of a vacancy in the New South Wales Permanent Artillery. He was appointed to that unit, and began the long and distinguished career in the service of Australia which was to be concluded with tragic prematurity.

His first command was the coastal batteries on Middle Head in Sydney

Harbour; a somewhat uninspiring appointment which lasted until the Government decided to transform the battery site into a gunnery school in 1891. Bridges was sent to England to attend a long course of gunnery at Woolwich and Shoeburyness. He also took a firemaster's course.

Bridges' return to Australia with these qualifications, and the rank of Major and Chief Instructor in Artillery, was the real beginning of his military career. The outbreak of the South African War gave him a second opportunity to gain experience in the field, and this time he was more successful. He volunteered for service overseas, and as a major of artillery rode with Major-General John French's cavalry division in its swift relief of Kimberley and attack against Paardeberg. But like many other soldiers in this ill-prepared campaign he contracted typhoid, and was invalided back to Australia towards the end of 1900.

His return to Australia coincided with Federation, and he soon became involved in the work which was being led by Hutton; that of integrating the colonial defence forces into a single Australian Army.

Bridges, in his capacity as Chief of Intelligence, was regarded by those who knew and worked with him as being a man of great intellectual capacity. His stature grew rapidly within the ambit of Australian defence staff work, and in June 1905 he urged that, as no officer in Australia had had any experience of mobilization, someone should be sent to England to confer with the British officers reviewing Australia's military structure. He also urged that this officer concerned should attend the Swiss Army manoeuvres of 1906. By that time, a scheme of universal military training had been suggested, with the aim of creating a trained "citizen army" which could be mobilised in case of need. Bridges pointed out that no Australian staff officers had any experience of the problems which might be connected with such mobilisation, and that, as Switzerland also had a citizen army, its organisation of mobilisation could provide helpful guidance.

His views were supported by the Minister for Defence, J. W. McCay; a lawyer and distinguished citizen soldier who was to render outstanding service in the Great War and become Major-General Sir J. W. McCay, with command of the 5th Division in France. The Military Board recommended Bridges as being the right officer to follow through his own ideas, and he left Melbourne for London in early January 1906. Besides maps, plans, and other information, he carried with him the specific instruction "Not to furnish opinions."

One of his major tasks was to be the revision of the Australian war establishment tables, and these were actually prepared by Bridges in conjunction with officers of the General Staff, and approved by the Mobilisation Committee.

On 7 June he received the Committee's full report, which dealt with principles and not details, and then for the next three weeks devoted himself to completing a memorandum to the Minister for Defence in Australia, outlining the changes involved and the steps necessary to give effect to them.

By the end of June he was free to observe the Swiss manoeuvres, and then attended British military establishments including an exercise in Scotland where he passed the examination for "Tactical fitness for command." In mid-August he was about to return to Australia via Canada, where he proposed to visit Kingston College, but he was asked by the British War Office to travel via Hong Kong and furnish them with a report. While on this mission he took the opportunity to observe the manoeuvres of the Japanese Army, which treated him as a particularly distinguished guest.

On arrival in Australia he set to work on the task of drafting a defence scheme for the Commonwealth. Normally this would be the function of a General Staff, but the Australian defence establishment still did not provide for such a group.

Bridges had to work without a precedent to guide him. Unlike the British Army, which expected to fight its wars on foreign soil and relied on the Navy to keep invaders out of Britain, he was concerned only with home defence. The Australian Government did not plan to send its citizen army overseas.

One of Bridges' proposals included the Scheme which had been suggested by General Hutton some years before, for the establishment of an Australian military college. At the Imperial Conference of 1907, Prime Minister Deakin had supported such a project, but had indicated that it was not yet justified by the size of Australia's military forces. However, Deakin returned to Australia determined to increase the size of the Army, and the establishment of a suitable college was included in his plans.

Unfortunately Deakin's Government was defeated before the Bill was passed, but his successor, Prime Minister Andrew Fisher, supported the proposals with some modifications. They became law at the end of 1908. The New Zealand Government also showed interest, but the scheme was temporarily deferred. This was mainly because too few young Australians and New Zealanders showed enough interest in becoming career officers in their countries' infant armies.

In 1909, Bridges was selected as Australia's representative on the Imperial General Staff in London. Now with the rank of colonel, he is reputed to have made the profound observation during a meeting of the General Staff that: "Your training manuals are as much use to the Australians as the cuneiform inscriptions on a Babylonian brick."

While he was in London, Lord Kitchener was invited to visit Australia. Kitchener was regarded as the British military genius, and had just completed the re-organisation of the Indian Army. The main purpose of the invitation was to obtain his opinion on the scheme for "universal training," which had been prepared by an outstanding Australian staff officer; Colonel J. G. Legge.

Kitchener not only endorsed Colonel Legge's proposals, but also made a strong plea for the establishment of a military college with similar ideals to that of West Point in the United States, where the training was "severe and thoroughly military."

The Minister for Defence, Joseph Cook, revitalised the proposal which had been deferred for so long, and appointed Colonel Bridges as Commandant of the Royal Australian Military College with the rank of brigadier general.

When the appointment reached Bridges in England, he seized the opportunity to inspect the British colleges at Woolwich and Sandhurst, then went to West Point and finally to his own old college at Kingston. On his return to Australia, he presented his plans to the Minister for Defence, with the observation that he admired West Point, a college which he described as being primarily for the formation of character, but that in military subjects the teaching should follow the pattern set by Sandhurst and Woolwich. He also advised that the College should be set in 1,000 acres of open ground and not be near to a large city.

The vicinity of Canberra, which only recently had been chosen as the site for the Federal capital, seemed to be ideal, and Bridges visited the pastoral country on which the capital was to be laid out. He selected the old Campbell homestead of Duntroon, which was separated from the city site by a wooded hill, Mount Pleasant, and looking down on the plain traversed by the Molonglo River. In less than a year, the homestead and 370 acres of the property had been leased from its owner, Colonel J. E. Campbell, and the house was being renovated to provide the officers mess and school headquarters while other buildings were constructed, thus providing Australia with a military college of which it can be justifiably proud.

On 21 June 1911, forty-two Australian and New Zealand cadets were inducted into the college, and on 27 June it was officially opened by the Governor General, Lord Dudley.

It was proposed that Duntroon should provide the headquarters staffs and area officers required for Australia's citizen army, which had been divided into 224 army areas, and become responsible for the training and administration of the units in each area.

Bridges commanded Duntroon for nearly three years, until he left to become Inspector-General of the Australian Military Forces in May 1914. During his three years as Commandant, he established a standard which earned for Duntroon the reputation of being second to none. Sir Ian Hamilton, when Inspector-General of the British Army's overseas forces, visited the college in 1914. After Gallipoli, where he commanded the British forces, he wrote that: "I recognised the wonderful work being done for Australia by the devoted and single minded General Bridges and his staff, but it was not until the bitter fighting and terrible trials at the

Dardanelles that I fully realised the priceless value of what had been done at the Royal Military College."

There were 147 cadets at Duntroon when Bridges left in May 1914, and by the end of the year seventy-one of them were on active service. Of these, seventeen lost their lives at Gallipoli, and thirty-four were wounded. General Bridges was to die with the cadets whom he had trained.

4

THE GREAT COMMANDERS

BRIDGES DIED TOO EARLY IN THE FIRST WORLD WAR FOR HIS FULL potential to be realised. If he had survived the sniper's bullet which killed him on Gallipoli, he may have established himself among the most eminent leaders during that war. Instead, the Australians were led to victory by three men who also played various parts in the creation of the Australian Army. They were Brudenell White, John Monash, and Harry Chauvel.

All three of them were to be knighted and to attain field rank, and two of them came from somewhat similar backgrounds. White was the son of an Irish ex-officer; Chauvel the grandson of an Indian Army officer. Monash, the son of a German Jewish migrant to Australia, came from a family with no known military connections.

White was born on 23 September 1876, in the small Victorian country town of Saint Arnaud, seventy miles north-west of Ballarat. He was the seventh child of John Warren White and his wife Mysie, who represented the very finest of Australian pioneering stock.

John White was an Irishman from County Clare, whose forebears had included Sir Dominick White, later Baron and Count D'Albi and Marquis D'Alberville during the reign of the Stuarts. The titles originated from the days of the Holy Roman Empire. His own father had been a barrister and was known in Ireland as the "father of the Irish Bar."

White, like so many Irishmen, joined the British Army. It was fairly natural that he should become an officer in the Rifle Brigade; one of the elite formations of the Army. But after service in Canada he resigned his commission in 1850 and migrated to Australia to join the gold rush, arriving in the sailing ship *Lightning*. Seven years later he met a newcomer from Ireland; Mysie (Maria) Gibton who had just come from County Dublin in 1857. After a comparatively short courtship they married, and lived in various country districts in Victoria. John White became closely associated with the land and during these early years was a stock agent; buying and selling farms and sheep as well as taking an interest in community affairs, for he was at one time mayor of Saint Arnaud.

Six feet three inches tall, he possessed all the better characteristics of the "country gentleman;" good looks, high ideals, aristocratic bearing, and expert horsemanship. His wife was the personification of the gentle, deeply religious Irishwoman, and together they raised a large and loving family. This devoted family background had a profound effect on all the children, but particularly on the son whom they named Cyril Brudenell Bingham White. Though his doting parents could hardly have anticipated the illustrious career that lay ahead of him, nor that he would be described by his great contemporary, General Sir John Monash, as "Far and away the ablest soldier Australia has ever turned out."

The White family moved from Victoria to Queensland, where John White owned several station properties during the years spent there. They experienced all the vicissitudes of early Australian country life, from great wealth to comparative poverty, but whatever their circumstances they were always surrounded by animals; particularly horses and dogs. Brudenell White later recorded that he was "practically brought up on horseback."

He was educated at various schools in Brisbane, but with his father's fortunes on the ebb became a clerk with the Australian Joint Stock Bank at the age of fifteen.

Determined that his future should not suffer because of this, he began to study law in his spare time, with the intention of qualifying as a barrister.

He became disenchanted with banking very early in his career, but jobs were difficult to obtain and he drove himself to study until late at night and again in the early morning, before riding to the bank on horseback.

Soon, fate took a guiding hand. An older bank official, Richard Dowse, was adjutant of the Queensland Volunteer Rifles, and he invited young White to a week-end exercise. This experience, as White wrote long afterwards, "Gave me my first idea of soldiering."

But the law remained his paramount ambition, and he continued to study it for another three long years, until the bank transferred him to Gympie and he came under the influence of two other men who were also keen citizen soldiers. One was Captain C. B. Steele, commander of the Wide Bay Infantry Regiment, and White made the decision that was to profoundly influence his life when in 1897 he was commissioned as a junior officer in the Regiment.

In the same year, he was transferred by the bank to Charters Towers, but the opportunity soon arose for him to escape the chains of banking. Applications were called for the appointment of officers to the Queensland Permanent Artillery, although he had only three weeks to prepare for the examinations that normally required twelve months study. He told his mother that there just wasn't time for him to cover the syllabus, but she encouraged him to try. With coaching from his old headmaster, Major A. J. Boyd, and Captain J. J. Byron of the Permanent Artillery, he sat for the examination and passed top of the list. From then on, his career never flagged.

The various Colonies were about to have their permanent forces integrated into the Commonwealth defence forces, so he was an officer of the Queensland Permanent Artillery for a very short period before becoming a member of the Australian Army. In 1902 he went to South Africa as a subaltern in the Commonwealth Horse, and fought in the final stages of the war with the mobile columns under Major-General Ian Hamilton.

The greatest test of his leadership qualities came aboard the troopship *Drayton Grange*, during the voyage home. More than 1,000 time expired Australian troops had been bundled on to the ship at Durban because the authorities were afraid to keep them ashore any longer. Even allowing for the accepted troopship standards of the day, the conditions on board were exceedingly poor, and not long after the vessel had put to sea the troops staged an open mutiny.

White was ship's Adjutant, and was called on by the mutineers to listen to their grievances. When going below deck he was threatened with being tossed in a blanket, but not only avoided this fate but also managed to pacify the men's grievances, which for the most part probably were fairly justified.

Shortly after returning to Australia he was appointed A.D.C. to General Hutton in his task of supervising the re-organisation of the Australian Army. Hutton's soldierly and gentlemanly qualities had a profound influence on the character of the Australian forces and on the officers who served under him, particularly upon a man who was so close to him as his A.D.C.

As they travelled throughout Australia, during this critical phase of its Army's development, they established a friendship which was to endure until Hutton's death after the first World War. Hutton took a paternal interest in his *protégé* as White gradually climbed to success, particularly during the war years when his reputation and stature grew as steadily as those of the A.I.F. Late in life, White recalled that "Curly" Hutton was "one of the finest and greatest soldiers I have ever known."

In 1905, White married Ethel Davidson, the daughter of a Victorian grazier, and was selected to be the first Australian officer to attend the British Staff College. With his wife and baby daughter, he spent 1906-7 at Camberley. Here he met two British Army officers who were to render distinguished service with the 1st A.I.F. Duncan Glasford, a Scottish officer who transferred to the A.I.F. and played a gallant role during the first days on Gallipoli, and was later killed in action as a brigadier at the Somme battle in 1916, was one. John Gellibrand, a Tasmanian, who was destined to command the 3rd Australian Division and become one of Australia's great leaders, was the other.

While he was at Camberley, White attracted the favourable attention of its Commandant, Brigadier Henry Wilson; later to be Chief of the Imperial General Staff during the latter period of the first World War. Wilson once told him, "If there are any more like you in Australia, young man, send them over here. We can do with them."

White finished the course at Camberley with great distinction. Wilson's final report on him stated in part: "With a lack of soldiering experience as compared with his companions, the results have been eminently satisfactory and he promises to be an excellent staff officer. His opinion carries weight with the other students and he deserves great credit in passing out so high. He will do well either in the field or in an office, and I recommend him for an appointment on the General Staff."

While he was on his way back to Australia, the War Office communicated with the Defence Department in Melbourne, suggesting that, if the Australian authorities agreed, White should be appointed "General Staff Officer, third grade, at headquarters with colonelcy pay of £500 per annum."

The Australian Minister for Defence concurred, with the provision that the War Office should send out a General Staff officer as a substitute for White. So in October 1908 he was on his way back to Britain with his family, to begin a four year appointment. The next three years were spent training and lecturing to regular British Army divisions stationed in Great Britain and Ireland.

He was recalled to Australia in 1911 to assist in the implementation of the Kitchener scheme. He was appointed to one of the key positions in the Australian Army, as Director of Military Operations and Chief Assistant to the Chief of the General Staff Brigadier J. M. Gordon, but suffered a drop in rank from colonel to major.

His new appointment gave him the opportunity of living with troops in camp again, as he travelled around Australia guiding the training of Australia's expanding citizen army. He was a most strenuous advocate of the "part-time army" principle, and his enthusiasm for Australia's citizen soldiers was a significant feature of his military career. At Gallipoli he told the official Australian war historian, Dr C. F. W. Bean, "With the cadet drills we have, if every part of the time is properly used on essentials, and with, say, ten days continuous camp for the men, we can produce troops fit to be sent abroad like the Australians at Gallipoli."

Besides his responsibility for supervising the training of Australia's citizen army, during these years he also saw Australia's need for a blueprint not only for mobilisation but also for the despatch of an expeditionary force in case of war between Britain and Germany. Bridges had drawn up a plan for mobilisation, but successive Ministers for Defence rejected White's proposals to plan for the despatch of a substantial contingent to aid Britain at short notice. Perhaps they did not care to consider this eventuality, though it is obvious that White, like some other military men, could foresee the forthcoming clash.

However, a compromise was reached as a result of an approach by General Godley, who had been lent to New Zealand by the British Army, backed up by General Gordon, Chief of the Australian Staff. In 1912 they suggested to the Australian Minister for Defence, Senator G. F. Pearce, that a joint Australian and New Zealand plan should be adopted in case either country was invaded. At a subsequent meeting it was agreed that the proportion should be based on the number of troops which each country had sent to the South African War, so that the proposed division would consist of 12,000 Australians and 6,000 New Zealanders.

Senator Pearce instructed White to draw up secret plans for the necessary organisation, and thus forged a vital link in Australia's defence preparedness. Soon afterwards, in July 1914, General Gordon retired as Chief of the Australian Staff and returned to England. Major White, at the age of thirty-eight, was appointed his successor in an acting capacity.

In that same month, Gavril Princep fired the shot that sparked off Europe's powder-keg, and it was soon apparent that Britain would be drawn into the war. On 1 August, Major White, Colonel V. C. M. Sellhein, the Adjutant General, and the Secretary of the Naval Board attended a Cabinet meeting, to discuss what aid Australia could offer to Britain.

Prime Minister Cook asked White if Australia had any plan for the despatch of forces overseas. Ironically, he was talking to the only man in the country who had given the subject any professional consideration, and was in a position to answer with conviction and clarity. He guaranteed that a force of 12,000 men could be raised and dispatched in six weeks. But, as Canada had offered 30,000 men, the Prime Minister enquired if a force of 20,000 men could be organised in the same time. White replied that in his opinion there was a very fair chance of the additional men being enlisted, armed and dispatched within six weeks, and as a result of these assurances Cook authorised the offer of 20,000 men.

When war was declared on 4 August 1914, General Bridges was selected to lead the Australian division and White was promoted to lieutenant-colonel and appointed its Chief of Staff. Colonel J. G. Legge returned to Australia a few days later and assumed the role of Chief of the General Staff.

White's service under Bridges was the beginning of his role as Chief of

Staff to a succession of Australian field commanders, each of whom he served with distinction, loyalty and self effacement. He admired Bridges' great intellect, judgement, and honesty, and found his death to be a grievous loss. His successor, General H. B. Walker, was a British army officer who did not have Bridges' capacity for administration; a lack which compelled White to spend more of his time at headquarters.

His next chief was General Sir W. R. Birdwood, the General Officer Commanding the A.I.F. Except for a short period during the latter stage of the Dardenelles campaign, White was to stay with him until the end of the war. Birdwood was a fine commander of men, and was immensely popular with the front line troops. He was one of the very few senior British officers who had sufficient insight to understand the Australian character. He and White developed a good working partnership, though it is no slight to Birdwood's reputation to say that White had become the tactical and administrative leader of the team by the time Birdwood was appointed commander of the British 5th Army.

* * *

John Monash was born in Melbourne on 23 June 1865, the son of Louis and Bertha Monash. Louis Monash first arrived in Australia as a young man of twenty-three; one of many thousands attracted to this country by the gold rush. As he stepped ashore from the vessel *Julius Caesar* in 1853, his picture of the new life lying ahead could hardly have held space for the notion that the name of Monash would find honour in the Australian military pantheon. Especially since that honour would be found in fighting against his own homeland, where he was born of German Jewish blood in Krotoschin, Prussian Poland.

Louis Monash wasted little time in gold-seeking. He established an importing firm in Melbourne, and prospered to an extent that enabled him to return to Germany in 1862. He intended to see his family in Stettin and buy merchandise for his business, but while in Prussia he met and married Bertha Manasse; ten years his junior and the sister of his brother's wife.

John Monash went to school at Saint Stephens' on Dockers Hill, where his ability in drawing and English were first noticed. At nine, his family moved to the country town of Jerilderie, where Louis opened a general store. His son took to country life with such ardour that he spent countless hours walking in the nearby bush, where kangaroos still thronged in hundreds. He learnt to ride, and walking and riding became the only forms of exercise which he ever enjoyed.

He soon outstripped the capacity of the local school, and the headmaster, William Elliott, encouraged his parents to take him back to Melbourne to give him the opportunity of higher education. With true Jewish respect for culture, they accepted the necessary expense and inconvenience. Bertha took young John and her two little girls to Melbourne while Louis remained in Jerilderie to keep the store.

John was enrolled in Scotch College, Melbourne, in 1877, when he was twelve. He blossomed under the influence of better teachers and educational facilities, won the English Essay prize each year, and matriculated at fourteen. Too young to go on to Melbourne University, he stayed on at Scotch for another two years and in 1881 finished there as dux in mathematics, equal dux of the school, and winner of a £25 Exhibition in Mathematics. This was a help, because his father's success had lost its initial impetus and the family finances were strained by keeping two households and paying for his education.

As Dr C. E. W. Bean says in *The Official History of the Great War*, the University, "Opened for him a field of marvel and delight," when he enrolled in the Faculty of Arts in 1882, as the first step towards qualifying as a Civil Engineer. Bean continues: ". . . for two years, his omnivorous mind roamed at will, taking in little that would help him to answer examination questions, but vast quantities of the amazingly deep and general knowledge that afterwards stored that immense repository, giving him interests in and some degree of power over most men, and things that he met, enabling him to pass a valuable judgement upon almost any problem that life presented to him."

During his first year, he complained of the lectures being attuned too much to the duller pupils. Often he would miss his own, and attend those at the other faculties. While this helped to assuage his thirst for knowledge, it did not help to satisfy the drier demands of his examiners. He failed the first year examinations, and his parents were distraught until he compensated for this first failure by the intensive study which enabled him to pass the supplementary exams, early in 1882.

His second year was hampered by lack of finance. To help pay for his studies he coached private students for the matriculation, and despite the extra work completed a brilliant second year in Arts. He was elected to the Council of Students, and his keen interest in military history prompted him to join the University Rifles. But the money ran out, and he had to leave the University at the end of 1884.

It was at the time when Melbourne was growing fast. New building was going on everywhere, and his lengthy walks were now taken with the aim of watching the various engineering techniques involved. He had studied surveying at the University, and soon found a job with the engineers who were building Prince's Bridge. As they moved on to other contracts he was given more responsible work, and continued his studies in his spare time.

As a part-time student, he continued working towards his target of a career in civil engineering. He obtained his Bachelor's degree in this faculty in 1891, and his Master's in 1893. Still this was not enough. He decided that

COMMANDERS, 1914-1918. *Top left*, W. T. Bridges. *Top right*, H. G. Chauvel. *Centre left*, William Birdwood. *Centre right*, Brudenell White. *Bottom:* John Monash (seated) with his staff at the Australian Corps headquarters, Bertangles, France, in 1918.

a knowledge of law would help him in his profession, so continued his studies and became a Bachelor of Laws in 1895. He obtained his Bachelor of Arts degree in 1895 also, and in the same year qualified as a water supply engineer, patent attorney, and municipal engineer.

The fact is that he was that rare and vital combination of the born student and man of action. Even though working during the day and studying at night, he still found time for military training. In 1887, the University militia company in which he had served for three years, rising to the rank of colour sergeant, was disbanded for lack of support, so he applied for a commission in the Garrison Artillery, a volunteer unit. A note which he wrote at that time gives an interesting forecast of his future, because he said, "The undercurrent of my thoughts has been running strongly on military matters. Yesterday things came to a finality. I have been attached to Major Goldstein's battery. A combination of military and engineering professions is a possibility that is before me."

Sir Ernest Scott, who was Professor of History at Melbourne University from 1913 to 1936, described him as "not only . . . a great soldier and a masterly engineer, but also a tireless student in many branches of knowledge. Only those who knew him well were aware, for instance, that the general who had planned the successful operations which gained the Australian victory of 8 August 1918 could have sustained an argument with any musical expert on the interpretation of the symphonies of Beethoven, but he knew those great works as well as he knew the strategic doctrines of Gneisenau or the tactical methods of Moltke."

An anecdote illustrating his grasp of many subjects was told during the war. After an interview with Monash, his new Deputy Assistant Director of Medical Services was asked how he got on with "the old man." The doctor said, "Got on? I don't know. I've just had the stiffest ten minutes *viva voce* in my own profession that I've ever been through. Dammit, I began to wonder whether I knew anything at all about medicine."

His mind, like a computer, stored every item of information which he fed into it during a lifetime of gaining new knowledge on a huge variety of subjects. The organisation of his life was almost mechanically methodical. He indexed every letter, cross-catalogued all his books and papers, and mapped out a programme of work for each day, allowing himself ten minutes leeway for every project so that he could make up misjudged time or relax for a few minutes before continuing his schedule. Because of these things it would be easy to think of him almost as a robot, but the letters written to his wife during the war reveal him as having an intense humanity and a continuous concern for the men whom he had to send into battle.

He married in 1891, and in 1893 was appointed assistant engineer and chief draftsman to the Melbourne Harbour Trust; his first executive employment. The future must have looked particularly promising, because

GALLIPOLI, 1915. *Top:* This photograph of Table Top (*top left*) was taken from No. 1 Outpost, and shows the rugged country which is typical of the Gallipoli Peninsula. *Bottom:* Near Quinn's Post.

Victoria was enjoying the most buoyant period of its history. Money was plentiful, land prices were high, and many large building projects were under construction in Melbourne, but the boom collapsed soon after Monash joined the Harbour Trust. Tens of thousands were thrown out of work, and people who had enjoyed varying degrees of prosperity became paupers overnight.

Monash also suffered, when the Harbour Trust cut down staff in 1894, but he had developed enough confidence in his own abilities to open his own practice; a bold step in a time of such depression and especially because he was now responsible for his two sisters besides his wife and baby daughter. But it was the right decision, and after the first frugal years his reputation became established. His services as a consultant were sought for such major engineering projects as the Bundaberg-Gladstone railway, the Mullewa-Cue railway line in Western Australia, the Kelly Basin-Gormanston railway line in Tasmania, and the King River bridge on the Burnie-Zeehan line, which was built to his design. From 1896 onwards he specialised in the construction of reinforced concrete, and was an Australian pioneer in this field.

He also received commissions as an expert witness in law suits involving engineering contracts, in which his legal studies were invaluable. His mathematical skill, analytical insight, judicial objectivity and tremendous powers of exposition also distinguished him in such cases, and many of his contemporaries regarded his capacity for lucid explanation as his greatest quality. It was a power which was illustrated many times in both war and peace, and Major General Sir H. V. Cox, a popular British commander of the Australian 4th Division, once said that he always attended Monash's brigade conferences for the sheer pleasure and edification of listening to his expositions.

As Victoria emerged from its economic depression, Monash's practice expanded and his personal fortunes improved, but he did not lose interest in military affairs. He was promoted to major in 1897, lieutenant-colonel in 1908, and colonel commanding the new 13th Infantry Brigade in 1913. He did not volunteer for the South African War because he was so heavily involved in his work, and rightly did not consider it a national emergency.

1912 brought fresh laurels with election as President of the Victorian Institute of Engineers and appointment to the Council of Melbourne University.

His command of the 13th Infantry Brigade presented him with a challenge that he accepted with his customary vigour. Early in 1914, its manoeuvres were observed by General Sir Ian Hamilton during his visit to Australia as Inspector General of British Overseas Forces. He was sufficiently impressed to recall the event more than two years later, after the Gallipoli campaign which he commanded and in which Monash served with distinction. Hamilton wrote: "He is a very competent officer. I have a clear memory of his standing under a gum tree at Lilydale, near Melbourne, holding a conference after a manoeuvre, when it had been even hotter than it is here now. I was prepared for intelligent criticisms but thought they would be so wrapped up in cotton wool of politeness that no one would be very much impressed. On the contrary, he stated his opinions in the most direct, blunt, telling way. The fact was noted in my report and now his conduct out here has been fully up to sample."

When war broke out in 1914, Monash was appointed Deputy Chief Censor in the Department of the Chief of the General Staff. Soon afterwards he succeeded Colonel McCay as Chief Censor, when McCay was appointed to command one of the first A.I.F. brigades. Monash hoped that he too would receive an early appointment for overseas service, but tackled his present task with his usual thoroughness. One of his first duties was the internment of several German scientists who had just arrived to attend a conference of the British Association for the Advancement of Science; an unhappy experience, because Monash had looked forward to meeting them in his capacity as a leader in Australian engineering, and had been scheduled to give them an official welcome to the conference.

Any fears that he may have felt of being overlooked for an important field command were dispelled on 15 September 1914, when he was appointed to lead the 4th Infantry Brigade of the Australian Imperial Force. The brigade landed in Egypt at the end of January 1915, and became part of the composite Australian and New Zealand division under Major-General Sir Alexander Godley.

With a leader like Monash, the troops of the 4th Brigade were trained to the highest degree of fighting efficiency. Their quality reflected that of their commander, under whom they were to undergo the test for which they had all volunteered and spent long months in preparation. They formed part of the spearhead for the greatest amphibious operation in the history of warfare up to that time, and were landed on the Anzac beachhead of Gallipoli on the first day of the campaign. Except for a short respite in September/October, when they were withdrawn for a rest on one of the Aegean Islands, Monash and the survivors of the 4th Brigade saw the whole bloody business through from 25 April until the withdrawal on 19 December 1915.

* * *

Henry George Chauvel was the third in the trio of brilliant leaders produced by Australia during the first World War; a remarkable contribution in view of the comparatively short history of Australian arms.

Chauvel was born in 1865, on a cattle station owned by his grandfather at Tabulam on the Clarence River in New South Wales. He grew up, like many of his contemporaries, in the harsh conditions of the Australian bush, which among other qualities bred a keen eye for country, expert horsemanship, and the type of independence and initiative which are found only in men who are bred to fend for themselves under the most arduous circumstances.

His grandfather was a retired Indian Army officer, and his influence helped to mould Chauvel from a very early age towards the military personality of the man who was to lead the Desert Mounted Corps in an unbroken line of success.

Chauvel was educated at Toowoomba and Sydney Grammar Schools, where he was a corporal in the Cadet Corps. In direct contrast to Monash, he showed no particular aptitude for study apart from avid reading of military history. But he was a keen and successful sportsman, and his small and wiry build made him an ideal horseman. Even as a boy he was much sought after as a jockey for amateur and picnic race-meetings in the country of New South Wales and Queensland, where he rode many winners.

From sport to soldiering is a very narrow gap, and later in life, after his forces had occupied Damascus and he was nearing the end of his long and triumphant campaign in Palestine and Syria, he mentioned that the two historical heroes of his boyhood were J. E. B. Stuart, the great cavalry leader of the American Civil War, and Saladin, who led the Muslims against the Crusaders. "I never thought in those days that I should take part in a cavalry operation greater than anything undertaken by them," he said.

He began his military service in 1886, by joining the Upper Clarence River Light Horse as a 2nd lieutenant. He transferred to the Queensland Mounted Infantry Regiment in 1890, with the rank of lieutenant, and was promoted captain in the following year. Except for a brief period as a sub-inspector in the Queensland Mounted Police, in 1894-95, his life was devoted to professional soldiering.

When the South African War broke out he volunteered for service at once, and went overseas as major and adjutant of the Queensland Mounted Infantry. Later, he became commander of a composite mounted force which included Queensland, British, Canadian, and South African horsemen; his first opportunity to reveal a rare capacity for handling men of many different types, temperaments, and backgrounds. This quality, together with an outstanding tactical ability, was the main reason for his promotion to command of the Desert Mounted Corps in the first World War. It comprised Australians, New Zealanders, British Yeomanry, Indian Cavalry, and Spahis and Barbs from French North Africa, in one of the most complex corps commands ever assembled. His success in handling it may be thought remarkable in that he possessed none of the flamboyant qualities traditionally attributed to "leaders of men." In fact, his personality was somewhat converse to that of most Australian military leaders of his era. He possessed an extraordinary reserve, which revealed little depression at a reverse nor elation at a victory.

He fought right through the South African campaign, taking part in the relief of Kimberley and many other notable engagements, and rose to the rank of lieutenant-colonel in command of the 7th Battalion, Australian Commonwealth Horse. His service was recognised by the C.M.G., the Queen's Medal with four clasps, and a mention in dispatches.

On returning to Australia from the South African War he was appointed Staff Officer to the Light Horse in South Australia. During the next few years, he held numerous administrative posts in the slowly expanding Australian military forces. Between 1904-11 he also acted as A.D.C. to the Governor General, and in 1911 was appointed Adjutant General; a post which he held through his promotion to colonel in 1913 until 1914, when he succeeded Colonel J. G. Legge as Australian representative on the Imperial General Staff at the War Office.

When war was declared he was still en route to London, and on arrival asked for employment in France. Instead, he was informed of Australia's intention to recruit a division of infantry and a brigade of Light Horse for deployment overseas, and that he was to command the Light Horse.

Before proceeding to take up his new appointment he inspected Salisbury Plain, where the Australians were to be sent for final training. His adverse report on the winter training conditions there was largely responsible for the A.I.F. being diverted to Egypt.

On Salisbury Plain, he may have met Captain Thomas Blamey, who was to become the commander of Australian military forces during the second World War and Australia's first field-marshal. At that time, Blamey had been an army officer since 1906, and recently had spent two years at the British Staff College at Quetta, in India, from which he graduated at the top of the entrants. He was posted to England to gain experience with British units, and when the war broke out was serving at the headquarters of the Wessex Territorial Division on Salisbury Plain. In November, he sailed from London to join the 1st Division A.I.F. at Mena, just outside Cairo, and was promoted to major and appointed G.S.O. III (Intelligence) under the division's Chief of Staff: Colonel Brudenell White. This began an association which was to have a profound effect upon Blamey's military career.

Chauvel arrived in Egypt soon after the 1st Light Horse Brigade had landed, and with his wide experience in handling mounted infantry from both the South African war and long peacetime service he was the ideal director of their training. But when he led them into action it was as a dismounted formation. The three regiments of the Brigade landed at Gallipoli in May 1915, and remained on the Peninsula for the rest of the campaign. He was not to lead mounted troops in action until the battle of Romani, in 1916.

5

ANZAC

O N 4 AUGUST, 1914, LESS THAN THREE MONTHS AFTER GENERAL BRIDGES had left Duntroon, Great Britain declared war on Germany. The response by every Dominion and Colony of the British Empire was enthusiastic and immediate. The Commonwealth of Australia declared war on Germany on 5 August 1914, and offered to Britain "A force of 20,000 men, of any desired composition, to any destination desired by the Home Government, the force to be at the complete disposal of the Home Government."

The British "gratefully accepted the offer," and the Australian government gave Bridges the task of raising the force for overseas service. Soon afterwards he was given command of the force; the first division of those which were to form the 1st Australian Imperial Force, and to lay the corner-stone of Australia's recognition as a power to be reckoned with.

Bridges himself suggested that General Sir Edward Hutton, who had just retired from the British Army, should lead the A.I.F., but the Australian Government had no doubts that Bridges was the right man for the job.

Bridges was the only "colonial officer" to be given command of his country's fighting force, since Canada and New Zealand chose British Army officers to lead their contingents, but the wisdom of the decision was shown in the almost incredible speed with which Bridges mobilised his force. By 21 September, the work of raising, arming, officering, training, clothing, and shipping 20,000 men had been completed. The years of preparation had come to fruition.

Bridges designated his force as the 1st Division and 1st Light Horse Brigade of what he personally named the Australian Imperial Force, and no commander can have ever led such a magnificent body of men away from their homeland. The young Australian men who clamoured to join the A.I.F. came from all walks of life, and represented the widest possible cross section of Australian manhood, but they all had two things in common. They had a zest for adventure which startled even their most ardent supporters, and a physical fitness which was unsurpassed by any other army in the world. Indeed their medical examinations were so absurdly rigorous that many of those rejected for the first force were accepted for service within six or nine months, when the standards for entry into the A.I.F. had been slightly lowered.

Most of them had had some military training, under the citizen army scheme introduced by Colonel Legge, but Legge himself did not go with them. He was then the newly appointed Chief of the Australian General Staff, and was organising a smaller force of 2,000 men whose objective was to "Seize and destroy the German wireless stations in the south-west Pacific, at Yap, Nauru, and in the region of New Guinea."

This task had been given to them as the result of an urgent request from the British Government, received in Australia on 7 August 1914. To retain command of the seas, it was imperative for Britain to hunt down the German ships operating in the Pacific out of such bases as Wei-hai-wei in China, and destruction of their communications had first priority.

For this purpose a mixed force was formed, and named the Australian Naval and Military Expeditionary Force. It consisted of a battalion of 1,000 men specially raised in Sydney, a body of 500 naval reservists and ex-seamen to serve as infantry, and 500 citizen soldiers from Queensland. The force was commanded by Colonel W. Holmes, a militia officer who had served in the South African War.

The 2,000 men, comprising the fifth expeditionary force to be sent by Australia to take part in foreign wars, sailed to Port Moresby, where it was briefed and regrouped for the attack and sent on to Blanche Bay, site of the German capital, Rabaul, on 11 September. The Queensland contingent had to be left at Moresby, because the stokers of their troopship chose that moment to go on strike.

Parties of naval reservists were landed at Herbertshohe and Kabakaul, followed by other naval men and then the infantry. The first shots ever fired by Australians against a European enemy resounded in some brief but bloody skirmishes in the jungle, causing numerous casualties on both sides. They were severe enough to cause the German officers to ask for surrender terms on 14 September, and on 17 September the German Governor agreed to sign an armistice. His troops surrendered on 21 September, the day on which units of the 1st A.I.F. sailed from Sydney. Colonel Holmes granted them full military honours, and the Governor was allowed to return to Germany on parole not to take any further part in the war. Civilians who swore an oath of neutrality could stay in their homes, but those who refused were interned in Australia. The native constabulary was transferred to the new administration.

The other German possessions named by the British Government were gradually occupied by Colonel Holmes' detachments, usually in captured German vessels. New Ireland, the Admiralty Islands, Western Islands, Bougainville, New Guinea, Nauru, and the German Solomon Islands were all brought under Australian administration until their future could be decided at the end of the war. Their occupation was in marked contrast to that experienced twenty-eight years later when Japanese possession of these territories threatened, for the first time, the integrity of the Australian continent and resulted in some of the bitterest fighting endured on any warfront during World War II.

With one successful campaign recorded to Australian arms, the people of Australia looked almost worshipfully at the young men of General Bridges' A.I.F. Newspapers, public speakers, parsons, and members of parliament all vied with each other in praise of the troops, which with some justice were regarded as being the "cream of the nation." Those were the days in which every country engaged in the war was caught up in the same insane fever of enthusiasm, which would be cooled only by the brutal casualties of a new kind of warfare, as yet only vaguely glimpsed by a few dismal prophets who hardly dared to make themselves heard.

At least the 1st A.I.F. was fortunate in having extremely competent leaders. General Bridges had selected Colonel C. G. Brudenell White to be his Chief of Staff. His brigade commanders were Colonel Henry MacLaurin, a Sydney barrister and militia officer who was destined to be killed on 27 April 1915, twenty-four hours after landing on Gallipoli; Colonel James Whiteside McCay, a Melbourne barrister, militia officer, and former Federal Minister for Defence; and Colonel E. G. Sinclair-MacLagan, a former British Army officer who had transferred to the Australian Army some years before the war, and had assisted Bridges in establishing Duntroon. The command of the 1st Light Horse Brigade was given to Colonel Henry George Chauvel, who at the time was Australia's representative on the Imperial General Staff in London.

Under their leadership, the formation and fitting out of the twelve battalions of infantry, three regiments of Light Horse, and the artillery and ancillary units proceeded with expert speed. A great variety of ships, including passenger liners which had been in Australian ports at the outbreak of war, were requisitioned as transports, and by 21 September 1914 all contingents were ready to sail.

By 24 October, the ships had begun assembling in the quiet beauty of King George Sound, at Albany in Western Australia. They sailed in from the Eastern seaboard ports, and for the next week replenished supplies and waited for their naval escorts and the ships carrying the New Zealand Brigade.

On 1 November, at 8.55 a.m., the first ship weighed anchor, and the majestic convoy of thirty-six transports and three cruisers began to steam out of the Sound. The rolling downs and hills which faded behind them would be, for many of the troops, the last that they ever saw of their homeland. Two days later they picked up two more transports and the Japanese cruiser *Ibuki* and steamed on with them to the battlefronts of the world. One of their escort cruisers, the *Sydney*, was detached as they steamed through the Indian Ocean, and went off to fight Australia's first naval battle in which she destroyed the *Emden*.

Originally it was expected that the A.I.F. would go to the Western Front, in France. (Incidentally it is strange that the term "Western Front" became generally accepted, because it was the western front of the Germans, and not of the Allied troops.) But while the vast troop convoy was two days out of Aden, General Bridges received a signal advising him that Turkey had entered the war, and that his force was "To train in Egypt and go to the front from there."

The 1st A.I.F. arrived in Egypt in time for the 1st Division to spend Christmas in camp at Mena, under the shadows of the Pyramids, while the Light Horse was based at Maadi on the other side of Cairo.

These troops, together with the New Zealand Brigade, were formed into the Australia-New Zealand Corps and placed under the overall command of General Sir William Birdwood, an Indian Army cavalry officer with a distinguished record of service and the reputation of being an understanding leader of fighting men. One of the numerous legends about the way in which the acronym ANZAC came into being credits Birdwood with its invention. In some versions, he is said to have seen the initials lettered on the side of a packing case addressed to the A(ustralia) N(ew) Z(ealand) A(rmy) C(orps). In others, he is supposed to have seen them used by a signaller.

During February 1915 two more brigades of Australians arrived; one under the command of Colonel John Monash, lawyer, engineer and militia officer, and the other under Colonel G. deL. Ryrie, a tough pastoralist, politician and one time pugilist. They were to form a composite New Zealand and Australian Division under the command of Major-General A. J. Godley.

General Bridges and Colonel White directed the training of the Australians and they were relentless in their drive for perfection. While their troops sweated on route marches or mock attacks through the dust and flies of Egypt, the war on the Western Front of Flanders and France had reached a stalemate. The British regular army had been almost destroyed in the fighting of the autumn and winter, and Kitchener's "New Army" was being prepared for its blood-baths at Loos and on the Somme. The French and

Germans were busily building up the gigantic armies which would maul each other into extinction at Verdun. For the moment, there seemed no way in which the existing forces could break the deadlock of trench warfare.

Churchill, then First Lord of the Admiralty, was characteristically impatient of warfare which so far had produced little but enormous casualties. He conceived a bold amphibious operation which would thrust into what he termed, in the second World War, the "soft underbelly of Europe." This would compel the Germans to switch troops away from the Western Front, and meet a request from the Russians to relieve the German pressure on their front by attacking the Turks. Lord Kitchener, feeling that he was unable to spare troops from France to assist the Russian ally, concluded that if a demonstration was made it would have to be carried out by the Royal Navy alone. After consultation with Churchill and senior Naval officers, plans were laid to attack Turkey by bombarding the forts on Gallipoli, which guarded the narrow entrance to the Dardanelles. Once they had been reduced, the ships could sail through to Constantinople and threaten the city with their guns. A simple and savage scheme, which, had it succeeded, could have changed the course of the war. Unfortunately, it did not.

A British fleet, consisting mainly of old battleships, with a French squadron, was dispatched to the Dardanelles in February 1915. The forts at the entrance to the Dardanelles were smashed by the huge naval guns, but a narrow minefield laid about ten miles up the Dardanelles put a swift end to the planned triumphal procession up the Straits. Several ships were lost, and the remainder retreated. Weeks passed with no change in the situation, and late in March these operations were halted and the warships recalled. It had been a bitter failure, whose only result had been to alert the Turks to the Peninsula's vulnerability. If Churchill's complete operation had been carried out, with a force landed in Turkey in those first vital weeks, the result might have been very different. As it was, the story of Gallipoli was to be one of tragic blunders and heroic failures.

However, at the beginning of the attacks, in anticipation that they would succeed and the forts require army occupation, the British and French Governments appointed General Sir Ian Hamilton in command of an army for this purpose. It consisted of the British 29th Division, part of the Royal Naval Division, and a French Division. When the Navy's attempt failed, the decision was made to give the task to the Army. The Australia-New Zealand Army Corps was added to Hamilton's force, and was on its way towards immortality in military history.

On 1 April all leave was stopped at the 1st Division's camp. The New Zealand and Australian Division followed suit, and by 3 April camp was struck and the troops began to move. Elated and excited at the thought of action after the dreary months in Egypt, they boarded troopships in Alexandria and sailed for the islands, which was the jumping-off port for the entire attack. On 9 April 1915, General Bridges embarked with his staff in the troopship *Minnewaska*.

The vast armada of 200 warships and transports packed into Lemnos harbour set sail for their respective operational destinations on the evening of 24 April, beginning the largest and most ambitious seaborne invasion that the world had known until then. The Anzacs had been allocated a beachhead, which became known as Anzac Cove, about a mile north of the Gaba Tepe promontory. The British 29th Division was to land at the southernmost tip of the Peninsula, at Cape Helles. Colonel Sinclair-MacLagan, commander of the 3rd Brigade, had been selected to lead the Australian assault. When he bid farewell to General Bridges, shortly before sailing, Bridges said, "Well, you haven't thanked me yet."

"Yes, sir, I do thank you for the great honour of having this job to do with my brigade," replied MacLagan. "But if we find the Turks holding those ridges in any strength, I honestly don't think you'll ever see the 3rd Brigade again."

"Oh, go on with you," Bridges said, laughing.

At 3.30 a.m. on the morning of Sunday, 25 April, the first troops boarded rowing boats. These were to be towed by steamboats over the two and a half

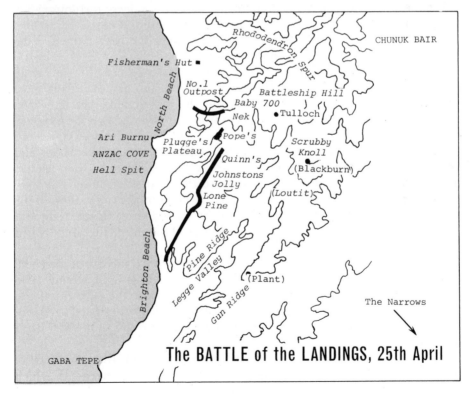

The BATTLE of the LANDINGS, 25th April

miles to shore. At 4.29 a.m. the boats grounded, and the Australians leapt ashore into a torrent of fire poured down by rifles and machine-guns in the Turkish emplacements, sited hundreds of feet above the beach on a precipitous hill which rose almost sheer from the sea.

The Anzacs raced over the shingle beaches to the cover of the cliff, and then found that the contours of their landing beach were very different from those in which they had been briefed. They had in fact been deposited about a mile north of their correct point, and were on a section of the coast described by General Birdwood and his senior Australian officers as impossible for an attempted landing when they had scanned the area from a warship a few days before the invasion.

For sheer courage, it would be hard to better the spirit of those men who lay at the bottom of a 300-foot cliff, their dead and wounded smothering the beach and sprawling in the water behind them. After a brief rest they dropped their packs, fixed bayonets, and began to swarm up the steep, rocky gullies into the storm of fire from the hidden positions above them. By dawn, they had reached the top of the hill, after taking every trench and emplacement which tried to stop them. It was a feat which spoke volumes for the physical fitness of the Australians as well as for their courage.

From the hill top, the Australians looked out over a deep, tortuous valley which rose to a second ridge 600 yards away. Beyond that again was a third ridge, joining the main ridge of Chunuk Bair. This had been named as the principal objective of the brigade that morning.

In the valley beneath them, the Australians could see the retreating remnants of the Turks who had survived the initial assault. They gave immediate chase, determined to carry out the instructions that had been drummed into them by all their leaders from Birdwood down for a month previous to the landing: "Keep going at all costs—go as fast as you can."

As a result of the confusion caused by the landing errors, the troops had been split into comparatively small parties. When reformed by their leaders on the beaches, they had thrust forward in these same formations, despite the opposition, the denseness of the undergrowth and the ruggedness of the country and its ridges. They conquered the second ridge in strength, and some small parties reached the prime objective of the third ridge and looked out over the Dardanelles.

Colonel MacLagan, who came ashore with the second wave of his Brigade, quickly assessed the dangers inherent to his own Brigade in having been landed a mile too far north of the correct point, and also the vulnerability of the whole Anzac front. He made two immediate decisions designed to restore the position, and these had a profound effect on the result of the first day's operations.

The first was based on the fact that his troops were far from that part of the third ridge they had been ordered to seize, or the southern half which extended for two miles north of the strongly held Gaba Tepe. So he sent his brigade major, Major C. H. Brand, up from the beach to control the troops who were pushing in that direction. It was known that substantial Turkish reserves were being held on the lower country inland of Gaba Tepe, and the Australian leaders expected the first and strongest Turkish counter attacks to come from this direction.

Brand, on reaching the forward troops, looked out towards the wide expanse of the third ridge. Its jagged spurs were a magnificent but threatening spectacle. He pondered the advice which he and his superiors had drummed into the troops during the previous weeks, to go forward at all costs, but when he looked on the stark terrain ahead he decided that to push on with the limited forces at his disposal would only increase the likelihood of their being cut off and annihilated. He sent a runner back to Colonel MacLagan, expressing these views and giving his opinion that he should retire with his men to a position on the second ridge at 400 Plateau, where two battalions could be seen digging in.

MacLagan's reply ordered Brand to keep his advanced parties forward to cover the two battalions, apparently in the hope that when the 2nd Brigade was landed it should come up on his right, and that if conditions were suitable the advance could be resumed. In the meantime, he had climbed to the top of another ridge, named Plugges Plateau, and looked out over the mile and a half of crumpled folds and slopes of the second ridge. He realised that the four miles expanse of the third ridge, hidden beyond it, would be most difficult for his scattered companies to reach and retain, which confirmed the view expressed by Brand.

MacLagan also felt, on his observation point, that a defensive position could be held on the second ridge until the overall position had been clarified.

His second major decision was that his brigade would have to secure the northern flank and the 2nd Brigade the southern flank. This was contrary to the Battle Orders, which specified the reverse roles of action for the two brigades.

The 2nd Brigade, under Colonel McCay, landed at about 7.30 a.m., and MacLagan asked McCay for his support in altering the battle plan. McCay replied that he was being asked to disobey orders before he had even engaged the enemy, and suggested that he should inspect the position himself. MacLagan told him that there wasn't time to do so, and assured him that the northern flank had been secured. McCay then agreed, and the change was confirmed by General Bridges when he was informed of it shortly after landing with his staff at 7.30 a.m.

While these developments were unfolding, neither MacLagan nor any of the other leaders knew that two groups had actually reached the third ridge. These looked out from a prominent hump known as Scrubby Knoll, nearly a mile north east of 400 Plateau, on to the ultimate prize of the whole operation; the waters of the Narrows. The first two to reach this position were Lance-Corporal P. deQ. Robin who was killed three days later, and Private A. S. Blackburn who was destined to win the Victoria Cross at Pozières. They were followed soon after by Lieutenant N. M. Loutit and two companions. A mile further south, another group had reached the crest of the third ridge and could gaze upon the same spectacle. This party was led by Lieutenant E. C. P. Plant.

But the parties at Scrubby Knoll were soon pushed back by the Turks, who were now moving up from this direction. Shortly afterwards a furious engagement took place between them and the advance parties of Australians who were beyond 400 Plateau. A little later a group of Turks estimated to be between 2,000-3,000 men appeared from the southern end of the third ridge, complete with mules and guns. At about 9 a.m. MacLagan judged that a powerful counter-attack was developing.

However, he could see units of the 2nd Brigade moving up on his southern flank and he was confident of his positions being held, although insufficient reinforcements were coming up to allow him to press the intended advance on to the third ridge. Because of this he discarded any intentions of achieving this objective at about 10 a.m.

When he returned to his headquarters in mid-morning he observed a critical fight taking place to the north on a feature named Baby 700 Hill, beyond Monash Valley and the second ridge. These were troops of the 11th and 12th Battalions who had been landed north of Ari Burnu on a beach surrounded by a semi-circle of almost sheer gravel cliffs, 250-400 feet high and heavily defended by the Turks. The Australians suffered heavy casualties during this landing and lost many of their officers, but with typical dash and determination they rallied and climbed the feature, which became known as Russell's Top. They pushed northwards along the top of the height until it began to narrow to a neck, afterwards known as The Neck. About 150 yards wide, narrowing to seventy, it had steep gullies descending to the sea on the left and Monash Valley on the right. The saddle of these ravines led straight up to the long open feature of Baby 700, and it was along this feature that the Australians advanced as the Turkish defenders withdrew.

By 9 a.m. by means of a series of rushes against the Turkish position, the Australians had reached Baby 700. Beyond this rose the inland shoulder of the next summit, Chunuk Bair, which was the most important height of the whole range on the Australian front.

The Turks hurried up reinforcements, and the struggle for Baby 700 grew in intensity. Both sides captured, lost, and recaptured the same positions numerous times, with casualties mounting at every assault and the bodies of khaki-clad Australians lying among those in the dun, shabby uniforms of the Turks.

MacLagan saw the latter stage of this engagement when he returned to his headquarters. Knowing the importance of these heights to the Australian bridgehead, he immediately directed reinforcements to the area, but many of the fresh troops which he ordered towards Hill 700 were diverted en route to plug other critical gaps on the front.

As the sun rose higher in the sky, hot and parching even though it was only the Turkish spring, the intensity of the battle mounted to a fury that filled the harsh gullies with rolling clouds of dust and smoke and the echoing staccato of rifles and machine-guns, punctuated by the soul-curdling shriek of shell fragments from the airbursts overhead and crash of shells exploding on the rocky hillsides.

From dawn onwards, men on the warships watched the landing points and ridges through binoculars, trying to see what was happening. They were cheered by seeing the Australians in apparent control of the ridges, and impressed by their casual postures during lulls in the fighting; an attitude which since then has become familiar on many battlefields.

The Turks opposing the Australians in this battle, were the 19th and part of the 9th Divisions under Lieutenant-General Mustafa Kemal: a fine tactician who later became a general and the President of Turkey. By a quirk of fate he had decided to exercise his troops that morning over the very ground which the Australians were to attack, and thus thwarted what otherwise might have been the crucial stroke of the whole Gallipoli campaign.

For the rest of the morning and most of the afternoon, this battle swayed back and forth across the height, until, at 4 p.m., the Turks finally drove in the Australian line. In the later stages, when all the reserves of the 1st Australian Division had been employed, this had been reinforced by New Zealanders. But when the reserves ran out the position became untenable. The Turks penetrated The Neck and actually reached Russell's Top, which was behind the northern end of the Australian line on the second ridge.

While this action was being fought on Baby 700, an equally vicious battle had developed a mile to the south on 400 Plateau. Here, the Australians had made a grim day-long defence against the Turkish 27th and 77th Brigades, who preceded their repeated charges with cries of "Allah, Allah." Men of the 2nd Brigade who had taken Pine Ridge, the furthermost spur from 400 Plateau, were completely cut off from their comrades and still fighting at dusk. Four years later the Australian Historical Mission discovered the scene of their last stand, and found the men's remains still there in the crescent shaped groups in which they had fought it out, the battalion colours still visible on their sleeves.

By nightfall, the Anzac front was critically poised. Instead of driving inland on a front of four miles wide, the Australians and New Zealanders were precariously perched on a bridgehead a mile wide and half a mile deep, with only one ridge between them and their landing place.

The British 29th Division had landed at Cape Helles, and was even further from its objectives than the Australians and New Zealanders at Gaba Tepe; a fact as yet unknown to the Anzacs. Although the British had encountered heavier opposition, the southern section of the peninsula was much flatter ground than that at Anzac Cove and therefore easier country in which to operate.

16,000 men, including the 1st and 4th Brigades under MacLaurin and Monash, and great quantities of stores had been landed during the day at Anzac, but casualties had also been extremely heavy. A steady stream of wounded had been brought down to the beaches, where they waited to be ferried out to the hospital ships anchored off shore among the great fleet of warships and transports.

Just before nightfall, a string of messages from the front indicated that the left flank was driven in and the right badly shaken. General Bridges, with Colonel Brudenell White, had landed at Anzac Cove at 7.30 a.m. on 25 April with the headquarters staff of 1st Division, which included Major Thomas Blamey. White was Chief of Staff, and Blamey, as his G.S.O. III, already had commenced to model himself upon a man whom he described as "a noble character."

MacLagan went down to the beach to this headquarters, and Bridges asked him, "Well, old pessimist, what have you got to say about it now?"

"I don't know, sir," he replied. "It's touch and go. If the Turks come on in mass formation on the left, I don't think anything can stop them."

His view was shared by Colonel McCay, and also by Major-General Godley of the New Zealanders. He and Bridges felt that General Birdwood should be advised of the gravity of the situation, and sent a message to the *Minnewaska*, asking him to come ashore at once. When he landed, the two Anzac commanders advised him that they thought the wisest move would be a withdrawal of their troops and an attack somewhere else. Birdwood was shocked, but he had learned to trust Bridges' judgement. He returned to the ship, and told General Hamilton who was on board *Queen Elizabeth* of the views of Bridges and Godley. However, this had no effect.

Admiral Thursby, who commanded the ships and landing boats, said he doubted whether the troops could be re-embarked without being caught on the beaches and slaughtered by the Turks, and had told Bridges that he would "rather stay and die there in the morning than re-embark."

After a brief conference, General Hamilton told Birdwood: "You have got through the difficult business. Now you have only to dig, dig, dig, until you are safe."

This settled the issue. The Anzac force had to be retained on Gallipoli because it could not be taken off. So they followed their Commander-in-Chief's suggestion, and "dug, dug, dug," until history was made.

6

AFTERMATH

THE "MASS FORMATION" OF TURKS, WHICH COLONEL MACLAGAN HAD feared, did not appear during that night. They, like the Australians and New Zealanders who had fought them from dawn until long after dusk, were so exhausted that they slept where they fell. The two armies had fought each other to a standstill, and General Bridges and his staff saw the sun rise next morning with a sense of overwhelming relief. The Anzacs had not entirely succeeded in their assault, but they certainly had not failed. They had a toehold from which it would now be difficult to dislodge them.

During the next few days, the only break in the lull came when the Turks attempted to capitalise on their position on the northern flank by attacking down The Neck, but were repulsed with heavy losses from the accurate gunfire of the warships standing offshore.

On 3 May, General Hamilton asked Birdwood for as many troops as he could spare from the Anzac front in order to launch an offensive in the Cape Helles sector, in the hope of taking the key position of Achi Baba peak before the Turks had time to strengthen their position in that area. The New Zealand Brigade and the 2nd Australian Brigade, which had been the least heavily involved in the fighting on the Anzac front, were transferred south. They took up positions between the British 29th Division and the French Division, both of which attacked in broad daylight. This was contrary to the advice of General Hamilton, who had suggested a night attack in order to minimise losses. But General Hunter-Weston, commander of the British Division, claimed that with the loss of so many of his officers he dreaded the confusion of night operations. The first attack won only about half a mile, and paid for it with many dead and wounded. The New Zealand Brigade, attached to the 29th Division, participated in the second assault. Its orders arrived late and again little ground was won, but General Hunter-Weston had no more constructive plan than to order a similar attack in the afternoon. "Casualties? What do I care for casualties?" he demanded when an officer ventured to say that the impending attack was sure to cause heavy losses.

This unimaginative and purposeless leadership was the first of numerous occasions in which Australian troops suffered under British Army commanders, in the campaigns of both World Wars.

Hunter-Weston's remark exemplified the destitute mentality of much British Army leadership. This was based principally on the theory of artillery barrage followed by frontal infantry attacks. If this failed, it was usually repeated until either it achieved its objective or there were no infantry remaining to carry on. This had worked perfectly in such battles as Omdurman, when hordes of undisciplined tribesmen flung themselves against trained British and Egyptian troops, but was useless against a defence which was barbed with all the weapons of modern warfare. Since Waterloo, the British Army's experience had been largely gained in minor Colonial wars against inferior opposition, interspersed by such disasters as Afghanistan, Balaclava, Isandhlwana, and Colenso. Its feats had been popularised by the British press, basking in the reflection of that golden Victorian era which supposed that the sun would never set on the Empire. Even the sagging fortunes of the British Army during the South African War were bolstered by press fabrications, to quieten a home population which was beginning to wonder why the superior strength of its army took so long to crush the small Boer forces.

It is only fair to state, however, that the callous lack of military imagination displayed by all too many British commanders was suffered just as much by their own troops as by the "colonials" who were unlucky enough to serve under them. The seventy magnificent divisions raised for Kitchener's "New Army" were flung away in the battering-ram attacks on the Western Front, and it was only the courage and stoicism of the British private soldiers and junior officers which held the line for so long. The weakness of the British military system lay in the caste snobbery with which the entire British social system was permeated. In 1914, it was only forty-four years since officers had been able to buy their commissions. Promotion was still a matter of "who you knew" as well as "what you knew." Intrigue and influence, which occasionally came to the surface in such vicious power-struggles as that between Kitchener and Lord Curzon over the Indian Army, played as much part in running the Army as did professional training and competence. Haig's oft-quoted comment that "The machine-gun is a much over-rated weapon" exemplifies the backward-looking attitude of most senior officers, many of whom were cavalrymen still entranced by the notion that war was an occupation for gentlemen, and could not bend themselves to the realisation that it was a matter for experts.

Many millions of men had to suffer until their leaders learnt their lessons. Among these were the Australians and New Zealanders whom Hunter-Weston killed in three days of useless attacks which gained no worthwhile ground. In fact, the main Turkish positions had not even been seen by the attacking troops. At last, General Hamilton decided to take direct control of the situation, though he was still of the opinion that if the Turkish lines could be breached, the whole front would collapse. For this vital assault, he deployed the 2nd Australian Brigade, who were digging in for the night when orders arrived for them at 4.55 p.m. By 5.05 p.m. they were on the move, as part of a general advance supported by heavy bombardment from the warships.

The four Australian battalions fixed bayonets and advanced into a murderous small arms fire, trotting forward with heads down as though running into a thunderstorm. They reached some forward trenches, where they rested for several minutes to recover from the speed of their advance, and then Colonel McCay jumped up on to the parapet and shouted, "Now then Australians! On, Australians!"

Line after line of the Brigade followed him towards the enemy; dodging, running, or crawling into the murderous fire which was hitting more than one man out of three. Within an hour, 1,000 men had been killed or wounded, which reduced the strength of the Brigade to 1,900.

They had advanced 1,000 yards, and were within 400 yards of the main Turkish position, but their lines were now so thin that they were unable to press home their attack. As the darkness thickened they were ordered to retire, and the survivors were sent back to their own front.

On the Anzac front, Colonel Monash's 4th Brigade and the New Zealand Brigade attempted to recapture Baby 700 but were repulsed with heavy losses.

Colonel Monash vividly described this period of fighting in a letter to his wife. "Apart from many things which cannot be written about yet, the thing above all others which stands out uppermost in the terrible fighting which has been incessant since our landing on 25 April is the magnificence of our Australian troops. I have had plenty of opportunity of comparing them with the troops of British regular units and Territorials, and the British officers are the first to admit that for physique, dash, enterprise and sublime courage, the Australians are head and shoulders above any others. Throughout the whole of the fighting there has never been a murmur of complaint, in spite of the hardships and privations and continuous hours and hours of toil and deafening clamour. The men are as docile and patient and obedient and manageable as children, yet they are full of the finest spirit of self-devotion. For the most perilous enterprises whenever volunteers are called for every man in sight offers instantly, although often it means certain death to many of them. They are always cheerful, always cracking jokes, always laughing and joking and singing, and as I move among them and ask 'Well lads how are you getting on?' the invariable answer is 'First rate, sir' or 'Ryebuck,' or 'We're ready for another go.'

"During an attack a few nights ago on a ridge in front of us (which did not succeed owing to an accident) one of the machine-gun detachments suffered badly and left the gun and equipment on the slope of the hill. I called for volunteers to rescue the gun, and a selected party went out in the dusk, under a hot fire, and after three attempts succeeded in recovering the gun and tripod and all its parts. The night before last the 15th Battalion and a squadron of the 1st Light Horse were ordered to send out an assaulting party to clear out some Turkish trenches in front of one of the posts we are holding. Sixty men went out cheerily in the face of a murderous fire and only fifteen got back after accomplishing their task.

"The 14th Battalion on the day of landing were sent to seize a hill, and did so with the loss of twelve officers and two hundred men, without faltering or wavering. Among those killed was Captain Hoggart who won my shield at Williamstown two years ago—which you presented to him. Among the seriously wounded was Gordon Hanby. He was hit through the chest while trying to drag a wounded soldier into safety.

"The 16th Battalion on 1 May, at dusk, charged the 'Razor Ridge' singing 'Tipperary,' and 'Australia will be there.' Personally I have come through unscathed, although several men have been hit, and some killed close beside me. General Birdwood, General Bridges, and General Trotman have all been hit while in my section of the position; and about a dozen of my headquarters personnel have been killed and wounded. I hear McCay has been hit.

"In spite, however, of our heavy losses (a total of over half the brigade) the men, as I say, are cheerful, not to say jolly, and are only too eagerly awaiting the next advance. I am convinced that there are no troops in the world to equal the Australians in cool daring, courage and endurance."

The mention of Bridges being hit was written the day after the General received a wound which was to prove fatal.

Bridges and his staff had been ashore since 7.30 a.m. on the day of the landing, and for the rest of that day and during the following three weeks he toured every section of the precarious front, directing operations with complete indifference to his own safety.

On the morning of Saturday 15 May, he set out from his headquarters with two of his staff, to visit Colonel Chauvel's sector. They came to a casualty station in a precipitous indentation on the right side of a valley adjacent to a feature known as Steele's Post, and after talking to some of the medical staff Bridges dived around the protective barricade in order to continue his tour. Immediately, those in the medical post heard shouts and a call for stretcher bearers.

General Bridges had been mortally wounded, but when he was brought into the post he whispered to Captain Thompson, the medical officer of the 1st Battalion, "Don't have me carried down. I don't want to endanger any of your stretcher bearers." Thompson replied, "Nonsense, sir. Of course you've got to be carried down." He continued to protest, but finally submitted and was taken to the hospital ship *Gascon*. His last instruction to Colonel N. Howse, Director of Army Medical Services was "Please convey my regrets to the Minister for Defence that my dispatch concerning the landing is not complete . . . I am too tired now."

On urgent representation to King George V by General Sir William Birdwood, General Bridges was appointed a Knight Commander of the Order of the Bath on the day before he died. This was the first such award to the Australian services, and Bridges was also the first Kingston graduate to receive the honour, as well as being its first cadet to command a full division in the field.

He died of his wound on 18 May, and his last words were: "I have commanded an Australian Division for nine months."

His body was brought back to Australia. On 3 September 1915, it was buried on the hill overlooking the Duntroon Royal Australian Military College. On his tomb are the words "A gallant and erudite soldier." His charger Sandy, which followed the gun carriage at the funeral, is reputed to be the only horse returned to Australia out of the 121,324 sent overseas during the first World War. Today, his head is proudly displayed in the War Memorial at Canberra.

The value of General Bridges' leadership was summed up by Dr C. E. W. Bean in the Australian *Official History*, in which he wrote, "Bridges' habit of exposing himself to danger, had made it from the first unlikely that he would survive many months of fighting. Had he done so, it is probable that he would have emerged the greatest of Australia's soldiers, as he was certainly the most profound of her military students. His powerful mind and great knowledge were supported by outstanding moral and physical courage, and also by a ruthless driving force, rare in students. Only in Haig and Allenby did the Australians meet any commander whose forcefulness equalled that of Bridges. His defect as a leader, the inability to display those qualities which would make the ordinary man love and follow him, was finding its compensation in the conspicuous bravery with which, since the Landing, he had won the admiration of the troops."

On the very day that Bridges died, Australians were put to a supreme test when their positions were attacked by four Turkish divisions; a total of 42,000 men. From 3.30 a.m. onwards, wave after wave of the enemy came from the direction of Wire Gully in front of 400 Plateau. They outnumbered the 17,500 Anzacs, all that there were to oppose them in the whole bridge-head, by more than three to one. The Turks screamed "Allah, Allah," as they advanced into the terrible fire of the Australian defenders who yelled back bits of slang they had picked up in Egypt: "Saida," "Backsheesh," and "Eggs-a-cook."

The Turkish formations were shredded by the storm of fire. Only a few men reached the parapets of the Australian trenches and they were dealt with by the bayonet. At Courtney's Post, the Turks forced their way into one bay by the use of bombs, and several attempts to drive them out were repelled until Lance-Corporal Albert Jacka leapt into the trench. Single handed, he killed seven, shooting five and bayoneting two. For this epic he received the first Victoria Cross to be awarded to an Australian soldier in that war.

The crippling losses suffered by the Turks compelled them to call off the attack. After about two hours fighting, over 4,000 of them lay dead and 7,000 wounded in front of the Australian lines. The defenders themselves had suffered 628 casualties. An informal truce was called next day to recover some of the Turkish wounded, and several days later a formal truce was arranged in order to bury the dead and succour those few wounded who had endured until then.

The protracted truce negotiations, between senior Turkish officers and General Birdwood in Anzac headquarters, were conducted in an atmosphere of strained formality. The enemy delegates were impeccably dressed in gold laced uniforms, and the Australian and British staff officers were equally correct. Neither side wished to give the impression of desiring the armistice; an absurd situation which had to be resolved because of the obvious health hazards to both sides. It was reduced to the ludicrous when an Australian soldier, quite unperturbed by the proceedings, lifted the dugout flap and with typical Australian disregard for protocol shouted, "Have any of you bastards got my kettle?"

This battle had a profound effect on the Australian soldiers, who up until then had rather despised the Turk as a dirty and cruel fighter. Henceforth, they developed a great admiration for "Johnny Turk," because of the courage shown during the terrible carnage of those two hours.

The Turks did not attempt any further frontal attacks of that scale on the Australian and New Zealanders' bridgehead, and the Anzac front sim-mered down to less savage activity until the end of June, when Mustafa Kemal launched an attack from The Neck with a fresh and well trained brigade. He was fiercely repulsed by dismounted men of the 3rd Light Horse, and suffered heavy losses.

In the June-July period, the British and French at Cape Helles launched several abortive offensives, and the Anzacs staged diversionary attacks, sorties and concentrations on their front to deceive the Turks into maintaining reserves on this sector instead of throwing them in against the main action further south.

The battle had become one of endurance against fearsome conditions as much as that against the enemy. When Field-Marshal Viscount Slim was Governor-General of Australia, he recalled that his most lasting memory of Gallipoli was "the stench." Thousands of unburied or part-buried bodies decayed in the sun, breeding billions of flies who inflicted such diseases as dysentery and hepatitis on the troops living in trenches and dugouts hacked from the dry, dusty soil. Water had to be brought up under fire; rations were mostly semi-liquid canned meat and hard biscuits. Small scratches and grazes refused to heal, and became infected sores. By the end of July, the 25,000 men at Anzac were being depleted by a sick list of 200 a day, but the spirit of the troops—some of whom were in trenches only fifteen yards from the enemy—remained as light-heartedly determined as ever.

Both in and out of battle, the Australians were forging the "Anzac tradition" which comprised so many things: raw courage in adversity, endurance of the worst that fate could offer, a jovial gallantry, and a concern for one's mates that was exemplified by Private Simpson and his donkey Murphy, who between them rescued countless wounded from the exposed gullies and ravines until Simpson also fell, and Murphy cropped the coarse grass around his corpse as though oblivious to the carnage which men had created.

7

WITHDRAWAL

AFTER THE FAILURE OF THE OFFENSIVES FROM CAPE HELLES, GENERAL Hamilton developed a plan to break the deadlock that now gripped the Dardanelles campaign. The Anzac front was to be reinforced with a British division and brigade and an Indian brigade, and a breakout assault would be launched. To assist this, he proposed landing two British divisions at Suvla Bay, a flat section four miles north of Anzac which was defended by only three weak Turkish battalions.

The Anzacs were to feint an attack towards the strong positions at Lone Pine, on the southern and larger half of the 400 Plateau, whilst the British and French were to stage a diversionary action on the Cape Helles front.

Unfortunately, there was nothing radical in Hamilton's concept. It was designed to grind the Turks by a succession of battles, in much the same pattern that Field Marshal Haig was to develop on a much larger scale during the last two years of the war on the Western Front. It ignored the fact that in warfare of that era, before the full development of tanks and aircraft as fighting machines, the defence was stronger than the attack — as had been proved when the 17,500 Australians held off four Turkish divisions.

The 1st Australian Brigade was to attack Lone Pine at 5.30 p.m. on 6 August, following a heavy bombardment by howitzers which had been in operation intermittently for three days previously. News of this fresh offensive had galvanised the Anzacs into new life. They hoped that at long last it would bring some relief to the overall situation, even though they had become fatalistic enough to realise that still heavier casualties than those of previous battles must be the inevitable result of such a large-scale assault.

52

Tunnels, about 500 yards long, were dug towards the Turkish lines, and as the sun sank behind them, the Australians swarmed out of these like ants. They wore white armbands, and had calico squares sewn on their backs, to assist identification in the gathering dark. The first line of attackers rushed the Turkish trenches, but to the unbelieving eyes of the succeeding troops they seemed to bunch up on top of the trenches. As each wave of men went over, it joined what had virtually become a queue. The delay was caused because the Turkish trenches had been covered with heavy pine logs, so that the Australians could not get at the enemy and were at first compelled to shoot and stab down between chinks in the logs. But one by one they were wrenched aside, and the Australians leapt into the trenches to engage the Turks in savage hand to hand fighting. By 6 p.m. the Turkish positions at Lone Pine had been taken, but their reserves began moving up immediately and for the next three days and nights they counter attacked continually. They attempted to drive out the Australians by intensive hand bombing, but the Australians repeatedly caught the bombs and threw them back— until the Turks grew wise and shortened the fuses. Finally the only effective counter was to smother the wick with half filled sand bags. Twice, the Turks set fire to the logs which the Australians had replaced over the trenches, but the fires were extinguished. Heaps of Turkish dead littered the parapets from the repeated charges, but the Australians managed to evacuate wounded and buried their own dead as quickly as possible. Their spirit was indomitable, and the brigade reserves were so anxious to get in the fight that they were offering five pounds to be given the chance of beating off the next Turkish charge. Their courage and physical strength endowed them well for this type of fighting, which had all the ingredients of back alley brawling, rioting, mayhem and massacre.

By 10 August the fighting at Lone Pine had died down, and by then the Australians had lost 80 officers and 2,197 men and the Turks over 5,000 dead. Men of the 1st Australian Brigade were awarded seven Victoria Crosses for this battle; the greatest number ever won by Australian troops in a single engagement.

Shortly after the tremendous fight at Lone Pine began, the formations were assembling for the main attack into the rugged country north of Anzac, in the hope of creating the breakout for which this whole enterprise had been mounted. At 8.30 p.m. on 6 August, four unmounted regiments of the New Zealand Mounted Rifles attacked a series of strong Turkish posts in the foothills, with "Old No. 3 Post," which was the strongest point, as the immediate objective. "Old No. 3 Post" was rushed after a devastating bombardment by the Navy at 9 p.m.; a practice that had been in operation for the past six weeks and which had the effect of driving the Turkish garrison into shelter.

When the bombardment ceased on that night, the Turks found their opponents on top of them. The precipitous slopes had been climbed under cover of the noise, and the New Zealanders strictly observed their orders that only bayonets were to be used. They overwhelmed post after post in deadly silence, and continued their stealthy advance until, by one o'clock, they completed a brilliant operation by capturing the strongly held position of Bauchopes Hill.

While they were fighting their way up the ridges, a British brigade marched northwards along the foreshore to guard the left flank and captured the seaward end of the spur north of Bauchopes. This cleared the foothills, and allowed the three columns which were forming up behind to prepare for their attacks on the main ranges by way of the deep, pitch black gullies which led to them.

The New Zealand infantry brigade was to attack up the second gully, the Chailek Dere, on to Rhododendron Spur, and then move along to the main objective of the offensive: Chunuk Bair. The 29th Indian Brigade would work up the third gully, Aghye Dere, and then work along to the twin summits north of Chunuk Bair, known as Hill Q and Koja Chemen Tepe. The third force, Brigadier Monash's 4th Australian Brigade, would thread a further branch of Aghye Dere, cross a gully beyond it, and follow the crest of Abdel Rahman Bair, with a view to attacking the highest summit of the main range: Hill 971.

The British IX Corps was to land four miles further north, at Suvla Bay. Its objective was the next range of hills, north of Hill 971.

But when the sun rose on 7 August, the New Zealand Brigade was still 1,000 yards short of its objective of Chunuk Bair. The Indian Brigade was still in the gullies, one mile short of its twin objectives of Hill Q and Koja Chemen Tepe. Monash's brigade also was well short of its objective, having taken a ridge it assumed to be Abdel Rahman Bair but which in fact was the second ridge south of that point.

According to General Birdwood's plan, the hour of dawn should have heralded the final breaking of the Turkish positions, on the main range north of Anzac. This, however, was on the assumption that the New Zealanders would have taken Chunuk Bair. From that foothold they would have attacked downwards along the ridge towards the Anzac front at Russell's Top, where a series of trenches had barred the way across The Neck and Baby 700. These were to be attacked simultaneously by the 3rd Australian Light Horse Brigade. However, it was soon realised that, as the main operations during the preceding night had not achieved their objectives, the Light Horse assault would be performed unaided, with the Turks alerted and without benefit of the intended distractions at the rear of the Turkish positions.

The Australian Light Horse units were probably the cream of the 1st A.I.F. formations, because men clamoured to join them and it was possible for the very best of Australian manhood to be chosen for their ranks. They were superb horsemen, mostly from country districts, and General Birdwood had in fact considered mounting the 3rd Brigade for a cavalry charge into the rear of the Turkish lines, in similar fashion to the Light Brigade at Crimea. Fortunately, perhaps, the idea did not materialise.

When the ridges above them had not been taken as planned, they decided to press on with the attack. At 4.23 a.m., the 8th Light Horse Regiment scrambled from their positions, following an intense bombardment of the Turkish lines by artillery and naval guns.

The Turkish front trench was only twenty to sixty yards from the Australians. As the first wave of Light Horsemen went over the top, on a front seventy yards wide, they were met by a torrent of fire. It cut them to ribbons, and not a single man was able to run more than ten yards towards the Turks without being killed or wounded.

The second line, waiting in the trench, listened to the hell above them. They knew that they too must face the same storm, but when the whistle blew at 4.33 they leapt out instantly. Most of them fell only a few yards beyond the bodies of the first wave, but a few Light Horsemen reached the Turkish parapet and planted red and yellow flags to mark their position.

The third wave was to be made up from men of the 10th Light Horse Regiment. When they filed into the trenches, their commander questioned the wisdom of continuing the attack, but the brigade major said that some of the previous wave had reached the Turkish lines and insisted that they must be supported. So, at 4.45 a.m., they charged, and were cut down like the others. The final wave was delayed for half an hour, while a decision was made as to whether the assault should continue. One can only imagine the feelings of the men who waited for the decision to be made, but when the command came they went over the top as unflinchingly as their predecessors —and met the same fate. Out of 1,000 men who took part in these attacks, 800 were killed or wounded; the flower of a nation uselessly slaughtered.

Meanwhile, the New Zealanders had continued their advance up Rhododendron Spur, and had reached a point 300 yards from the southern shoulder of Chunuk Bair. With Gurkhas in support they pressed home their attack, but were swept away by the Turkish fire which enfiladed them from adjacent ridges. The New Zealanders continued their attacks until midmorning, when their own exhaustion and strong Turkish reinforcements forced them to halt. Although none of the summits had been attained, good progress had been made, particularly on Rhododendron Spur. The positions captured at least provided a sound base from which further attacks could be launched if they could be resumed before the Turks brought up more reserves. All three assaulting columns were to take part: the New Zealanders, Monash's 4th Brigade, and the Indian Brigade.

As dawn broke, the New Zealanders could be seen scaling the rugged heights. Apparently there was no opposition, as for some reason the Turks had withdrawn. The New Zealanders looked down over the Straits, and in the distant valleys to the right could see the worn paths and ledges behind the Turkish lines. They were not allowed much time in which to admire the view, because a sudden roar of small arms fire from nearby crests sent a blizzard of bullets through the New Zealanders. They suffered heavy casualties, and with supporting British troops were eventually driven from the heights by elements of two Turkish divisions.

By nightfall, New Zealand counter-attacks had regained much of the ground, and despite heavy casualties they clung precariously to their positions a few yards from the crestline. A final attack was ordered for the following morning. Monash's brigade would stand fast whilst the Indian Brigade would form the left of the attack from its positions 150 yards from Hill Q and 90 feet below. On the right, the New Zealanders would seize the crest, whilst in the centre, a British brigade of five battalions, forming up close behind the New Zealanders, would attack northwards and seize Chunuk Bair.

The attack went in at dawn after a heavy naval bombardment, but the New Zealanders, after their forty-eight hours of terrible punishment, faltered mainly because the flanking support they were expecting from the British brigade did not appear.

The 6th Gurkhas, and a South Lancashire battalion of the Indian Brigade, rushed the neck between Hill Q and Chunuk Bair and could see down towards the Straits. But the British brigade, which at that moment should have been advancing over Chunuk Bair, had been thwarted in its movement to its start lines, because of the wounded and other traffic coming down from the New Zealand positions. Taking an alternative but more tortuous route, the brigade finally made its assault about three hours late, but was repulsed with heavy casualties.

The Gurkhas and South Lancashires took a final look at the Straits and retired to their start positions, thus ending the last hope of breaking the Turkish stranglehold on the Anzac bridgehead and forcing a decision at Gallipoli. The worst aspect of the situation was that the courage, effort, and sacrifices of the men involved were nullified by the lassitude and incompetence of British leadership during the landings four miles further north, on the beaches of Suvla Bay. The failure of the British commander to seize his opportunity can have few parallels in the history of war.

The British force, of two fresh divisions, was landed in three echelons on the night of 6 August. The first 7,000 were unopposed as they landed at 9.30 p.m., almost without getting their feet wet, and the rest landed at various times during the night. But, by dawn, they were in complete confusion. Instead of pushing inland to take the hills, the troops were still milling around the beaches and had merely seized the two arms of the bay.

Their only opposition was three weak Turkish battalions, which with the exception of two small posts were entrenched in hills three miles inland. At the end of the first twenty-four hours, these 1,500 Turks had inflicted 1,600 casualties on the British divisions, which now had 20,000 men ashore and were barely two miles in from the beaches.

The operation was commanded by Lieutenant-General the Honourable Sir Frederick Stopford, who had never been on active service and whose sole recommendation for command was his seniority in the British Army hierarchy. He remained on board his headquarters ship *Jonquil* until 5 p.m. on 8 August; nearly two days after the first of his men had landed. This gave plenty of time for order and counter order to add to what Admiral Hayes described as the "ghastly inertia" ashore.

General Hamilton, at his Lemnos headquarters, waited impatiently for news of the landing. The first came at mid-day on the seventh, when Stopford reported: "As you see, we have been able to advance little beyond the beach."

Twenty-four hours later, he reported: "I consider Major General Hammersley (commander of 2nd Division) and troops under him deserve great credit for result attained against strenuous opposition and great difficulty. I must now consolidate."

Hamilton, now quite beside himself with anxiety, hurried across to visit Stopford on board the *Jonquil*, arriving in the afternoon of 8 August. He asked, "Where are your troops and why aren't they in the hills?"

"The men are exhausted. They must have more artillery to support them. After a night's rest they will attack in the morning," Stopford told him.

"Why not tonight?"

"Well, for one thing, Hammersley is all against a night attack."

"But we must occupy the heights at once," Hamilton said. "It is imperative we get to Ismail Oglu Tepe and Tekke Tepe now."

Hamilton was known as a gentlemanly general. Most of his photographs show him with a charming if somewhat spinsterish smile. Perhaps he was not rough enough with Stopford's evasions and excuses, but in any case he went ashore and directed the landing force to commence its advance, despite opposition from Hammersley for the same reasons given by Stopford.

At 6.30 p.m. that night, the troops were moving forward. But it was too late. The Turks had had forty-eight hours in which to bring up reinforcements, and by 4 a.m. next morning the British had been repulsed in the foothills and had suffered heavy losses. This caused Stopford to signal Hammersley: "Do not try any more today, unless the enemy gives you a favourable chance."

By 10 August, the Suvla expedition had crumbled into disaster. The troops had been dislodged from any heights they had taken, and a few days later Stopford and his divisional generals were all replaced by younger men.

During the four days of this saga of senile impotence the Anzac front had continued to press forward against the bitterest opposition, as the New Zealand, Australian, Indian and British brigades fought and clambered their way to the peaks of their objectives. The New Zealanders had reached Chunuk Bair, and British and Indian troops had captured the neck between Q and Chunuk Bair, before Turkish reinforcements pushed them all back on 9 August. The Anzac offensive came to a standstill because there were no more reserves to use. 12,000 Australian, New Zealand, Indian and British casualties had been suffered in those four days, and the Turks had also been dealt crippling losses, but they still held the heights.

In one of Monash's letters to his wife, he described this phase of the campaign, saying: ". . . we also had Cox's Indian Brigade. The job was the complete conquest of the Sari Bair Range, but we succeeded only in getting a lump of it, and a fair lump too—but not all. The Turks have contested our advance inch by inch, and have fought with the greatest bravery and skill—but we steadily gained ground every day. The Turkish losses have been enormous, but our losses have been heavy too—so heavy that we can now do no more than hang on to what we have gained and wait for reinforcements. As an index of our losses, I marched out of Reserve Gully on 6 August with 3,350. My parade state today is 1,037. I have left in the whole brigade, two lieutenant-colonels, five majors, three captains, and twenty-two lieutenants (out of a total of 136 officers) —of course many of these are lightly wounded or sick, and will rejoin later.

"Much of the fault with the British troops lay in the leadership; the officers do not mix with the men as we do, but keep aloof, and some senior officers appeared chiefly concerned in looking after themselves and making themselves comfortable. It only shows how hard it is to make an army after a war has been started. I hope Australia will learn the lesson, and England too, and that the lesson will not prove a bitter one. But the Australians are uniformly splendid. I suppose I have now only about 300 of those who left Melbourne with me. All the rest are reinforcements not nearly so well trained, yet the right spirit is there and they are so adaptable that in a week or two they are almost as good as the old hands."

Among the reinforcements which had arrived by that time was the 2nd Australian Division, with Major Blamey as its Assistant Adjutant and Quartermaster-General. After about three months on Gallipoli, he had been sent back to Egypt with other officers as the nucleus of the staff of the new division as it was being formed.

Another offensive was prepared, and launched from Suvla on 21 August. It crashed like a breaking wave against the Turkish defences, and like a breaking wave it simply ebbed away. The Allied armies retired to their old positions, and settled into an uncomfortable waiting for something to happen. General Hamilton reckoned up his losses, and telegraphed Lord

Kitchener that to have any hope of early success he would require reinforcements totalling 100,000 men. But Gallipoli had lost its glamour. Gradually, over the next few months, the decision to evacuate took shape, and Hamilton was replaced by General Sir Charles Monro. On 8 December 1915, the British Government decided to withdraw all troops.

Local fighting had continued on all three fronts. At Anzac, the Australians used their expertise in mine tunnelling to dig under the enemy lines, and made a number of successful raids, but the net result was only to increase the number of killed and wounded on both sides.

The troops at Anzac and Suvla were withdrawn on the nights of 18 and 19 December, under a plan drawn up by Brigadier Brudenell White, the Australian Chief of Staff to Birdwood, which is described in the British *Official History* as a "model of precision and clear thinking." The men at Cape Helles were withdrawn on 8 January 1916.

Brudenell White had been Bridges' co-architect of the landing at Gaba Tepe, and his tremendous capacity for detail, quickness of grasp, lucidity, high spirit, patriotism, and great sense of duty set an inspiring example to the other members of the staff.

The Australian story of this tragic campaign is equally Brudenell White's, for he was deeply involved from start to finish. His outstanding service during the bitter eight months was capped by his ingenious plan for the withdrawal; one which surely has few equals in the history of warfare.

When it was decided that the forces at Suvla and Anzac were to be withdrawn simultaneously, White perceived that the rugged terrain of Anzac posed special problems for the troops there. At Suvla, however, the ground was comparatively flat, and a withdrawal could be performed on the traditional lines of successive rearguards passing through established lines of defence. This was impossible at Anzac, because the Turks were always on higher ground. There was no hope of the routine withdrawal procedure being carried out without tempting a disastrous assault.

So White instructed that the fire at Anzac should be progressively slackened. This would accustom the Turks to periods of inactivity, and in fact for two days from 24 November no infantry or artillery guns were used at all.

When final plans were called for, White's draft was based on deceiving the Turks up to the last moment, with the withdrawal being completed on both fronts in two nights. Strong opposition was encountered from the Royal Navy staff, which claimed they would have to move their ships in daylight in order to get into position for the night operations. Their objections were supported by all the Army commanders concerned, but the most serious opponent of White's plan was General J. Byng, the commander of the British forces at Suvla. He considered that the chances of deceiving the Turks were so remote as to be impracticable.

White, however, argued that his plan was the only means of pulling out the troops with minimum losses. He spoke so convincingly to Birdwood, who was then the senior commander, that Birdwood finally agreed and then impressed his wishes upon Byng. With great reluctance, the British general assented, but White soon discovered that he still intended to withdraw his troops from Suvla long before the Anzac Corps withdrawal on the last night. This would have left the Anzacs in a most vulnerable position. White protested to Birdwood about this piece of arrogant perfidy, and Byng was ordered to comply with his plan.

The proof of his arguments came when 80,000 men were withdrawn from Suvla and Anzac on the final two nights, for a loss of six men wounded.

The *Official History* analysed White's contribution to this phase of the campaign when it recorded that: "He had exercised almost single handed control over the movement at Anzac. It was White whose vision, combined with an unfailing sense of proportion and power of lucid explanation and courteous insistences in conference, influenced probably more than any other human agency the tactics by which the evacuation, not only at Anzac and Suvla, but also at Helles was carried out."

But 10,100 Australians and New Zealanders were left behind, in their shallow graves on the Peninsula; some 20,000 had been wounded. And, in eight months of endurance, the men of Anzac had forged a reputation which was a source of fierce pride to their descendants, and which had placed Australians squarely amongst the finest fighting men in the world.

8

TO THE WESTERN FRONT

IT WAS NOT ONLY THE REPUTATION OF THE AUSTRALIAN FIGHTING MAN that was forged on Gallipoli. His leaders also showed that they could apply themselves to modern warfare with the same dogged ability to overcome difficulties, and flexibility in finding a way around them, which characterised a stock that had pioneered a rugged new country. McCay, Chauvel, Monash, and Brudenell White had all shown themselves worthy of the troops who followed them.

Their qualities were quickly recognised by the Australian Government, during the reorganisation which followed the withdrawal from Gallipoli. The troops had been returned to Egypt, and the intention was that the 1st and 2nd Divisions, encamped at Tel-el-Kebir, and the Australian component of the New Zealand and Australian Division based at Moascar, should become part of an army of twelve infantry and two cavalry divisions to defend Egypt. They were being reinforced by large numbers of men arriving from Australia. To begin with, it was expected that they would be put into action against a Turkish army of a quarter of a million men who would attack Egypt in an attempt to cut the Suez Canal, but for the time being the Turks were licking their wounds after Gallipoli. It soon transpired that the Australians would be needed more urgently on the Western than on the Eastern front.

Major General A. J. Godley, temporarily in command whilst General Birdwood was still solemnising the last rites of the Gallipoli campaign, recommended that four Australian divisions be formed from the two evacuated from Gallipoli and the 30,000 reinforcements then unallotted in Egypt. Godley proposed to the British War Office that these troops should be joined with a full New Zealand division to form two Anzac Corps which would make up an Australian and New Zealand Army. The Australian Government had also promised another division, with artillery, which would raise the A.I.F. strength to five divisions.

The War Office gave their blessing to the proposal of two Anzac Corps, but opposed their grouping into an Anzac Army.

In addition to these corps there would be an Anzac cavalry division, consisting of the Australian Light Horse Brigades and New Zealand Mounted Rifles Brigades.

The expansion of the Australian divisions from two to four was achieved by splitting the veteran battalions returning from Gallipoli in two, and making up the numbers from the recruits who had just landed in Egypt. Whilst the reinforcements were raw and untrained troops, they were nevertheless splendid material who, when blended with the veterans, formed a magnificent basis for the new army. The expansion also gave an opportunity for promotions. Battalion commanders who had distinguished themselves at Gallipoli would be raised to brigade commanders, and so on down the ranks.

In the great task of re-organisation, Brudenell White was the driving force and co-ordinator, and his completion of the work, with all its myriad details, so that the 1 Anzac Corps was ready to sail to France at the end of March 1916, was a stupendous accomplishment. White had followed his tactical success of the Gallipoli withdrawal with an equally important administrative success; two of the most solid achievements by any Australian soldier until then. He was promoted to brigadier-general and appointed Chief of the General Staff of the corps. Both he and Birdwood considered that his talents would be better employed in that capacity, rather than as commander of one of the new divisions, and he voluntarily relinquished his greatest ambition of commanding an Australian division in the field. A tremendous sacrifice on his part, but one which was to be to the enduring benefit of the A.I.F.

His old chief, General Sir Edward Hutton, heard much praise of White's work at Gallipoli, and wrote from England to say: "Go on as you have begun. Oblivious for yourself and of your own future, do what you know to be right and shame the devil."

When the greater part of the A.I.F. moved from Egypt to France, White and Birdwood had to fight a major administrative battle; firstly with General Sir Archibald Murray, Commander-in-Chief in the Middle East, and then with General Sir Douglas Haig, British Commander-in-Chief in France. Both these men wanted direct control over the Australian forces in their respective commands, without the Australian leaders having the right of formal access to their Government. But this was directly against the policy laid down by General Bridges before the Australians sailed for overseas, endorsed by their Government, and jealously guarded by commanders in the field. Both Haig and Murray were compelled to accept it, and it has been rigidly adhered to, in every theatre of war in which Australian troops have been engaged since then—much to the vexation of British and American leaders during both World Wars.

Chauvel was the only one of the three commanders, now moving towards their place in history, who remained in the East. So far, he had had no opportunity to manoeuvre his Light Horse regiments with the sweep and dash of his cavalry heroes, and in fact many of his splendid troopers had been massacred in useless infantry attacks ordered by the higher command. But he had led his brigade with a distinction which confirmed the promise of his South African days, and for the last six weeks before that withdrawal had been in temporary command of the 1st Australian Infantry Division.

Gallipoli gave little scope for senior commanders to display their talents, especially in the tormented 400 acres of Anzac, but was a tremendous test of command personality. Generals and brigadiers virtually lived with their men, who learned to know their officers intimately. Any weakness became cruelly evident, and the successful commanders were those who gave a continuous example of courage, military expertise, and a willingness to share the hardships of their men.

Chauvel's quiet and reserved character won the respect rather than the affection of the troops in his command, but General Birdwood was conscious of his power of leadership and was keen to offer him one of the infantry divisions bound for the Western Front. But when Chauvel learnt that the Light Horse regiments were to be remounted for service in the Egyptian theatre, he applied to stay with them. His story becomes that of the campaign against the Turks, while White and Monash took on the Germans.

After Monash's inspired leadership at Gallipoli, for which he was awarded the C.B., the Australian Minister of Defence, Senator Pearce, urged that either he or Brudenell White should be given command of the new 4th Division. But General Birdwood offered it to Major-General H. V. Cox, an Indian Army officer who commanded one of the Indian brigades in action at Gallipoli. He made White his Chief of General Staff, and gave divisional commands to McCay and to H. A. Lawrence, who later became Chief of Staff to the British General Staff in France.

Naturally Monash was disappointed, but continued without complaint in his work of training his brigade for service in France. Probably he realised that his opportunity for divisional command would not be long in coming, and in July 1916 he was offered command of the new 3rd Division being raised in Australia. He was promoted to major-general, and sailed for England, where he supervised the final training programme of the 3rd Division on Salisbury Plain. Wartime expediency had swept aside Chauvel's objection to that bleak upland as a training ground for Australians.

While the expansion and training of the Anzac divisions in Egypt were being pressed on, the pattern of the war was changing. 1916 had brought a new savagery to the Western Front, where the Germans were mounting massive attacks against the French at Verdun, and the British had been asked to renew pressure on their sector of the front. Kitchener's "New Army" was taking shape, and there was high confidence that the Allies could mount a massive offensive and break the German Army.

On 29 February 1916, General Birdwood received orders that 1 Anzac Corps under his command and comprising 1st and 2nd Australian Divisions and the New Zealand Division would begin moving to France within a fortnight; more urgently than originally had been planned. 2 Anzac Corps under General Godley, and comprising the 4th and 5th Australian Divisions, would for the time being remain in Egypt. Major Thomas Blamey was on the staff of the 2nd Division, and had played a vigorous part in the moulding of the new Anzac Corps in Egypt during the reorganisation after Gallipoli.

*   *   *

When 1 Anzac Corps arrived on the Western Front during March-April 1916, the ground had been fought over during twenty months of warfare of a savagery undreamed of when hostilities began. So far, none of the combatant commanders had seen any of their plans work out. The little Belgian Army had been shredded by the Germans, but their victory had brought them nothing but the occupation of a hostile country and had presented a powerful propaganda weapon to the Allies, who used it to play on American sympathies. The German drive on Paris, planned for so long and coming so near to success, had been smashed by the French — who nevertheless had not been able to drive the enemy out of their country and now faced them across their section of the line of trenches which stretched from the English Channel to Switzerland. The finely trained British Expeditionary Force, whose skilful musketry had made the Germans think that they possessed the machine-guns denied to them by their commanders' conservatism, had worn away its strength at Mons, Ypres, Le Cateau, and other battles in which together with its reinforcements it had fought with a courage which unfortunately was not equalled by the tactical ability of its generals.

The offensives of Neuve Chapelle, Loos, and Festubert had done nothing but add more names to the war memorials which eventually would be erected in hundreds of British towns. Such refinements as poison gas, introduced by the Germans in April 1915, had added yet another dimension to the sufferings of men on both sides of the front lines. So far, no general on either side seemed able to think of any other military technique beyond increasingly massive bombardments of the enemy followed by increasingly huge infantry attacks which resulted in more and more killed and wounded. Even when the British developed the tank (the 1912 invention of an Australian, L. E. de Mole), they used it so unskilfully that the one weapon which could have ended trench warfare was frittered away as an infantry support or wasted in its unsupported success at Cambrai.

The Anzac Corps took over a section of the British front line, extending south east of Armentières from II British Corps, just as another huge offensive was being planned — the one which the British General Staff was confident would roll the Germans back to the Rhine. Australian veterans of the Gallipoli campaign considered that trench warfare on the Western Front was more comfortable and less tense than conditions on the Peninsula, and appreciated such comforts as regular hot meals, civilian towns immediately behind the lines, better amenities, and more modern arms. All these things were more re-assuring than the desolation of Gallipoli.

At first, the Anzacs' routine was confined to active patrolling and sniping, with particular emphasis on increased trench raiding during the latter half of June. The aim of these was to discover what enemy formations and defences would oppose the great Somme offensives planned by the British and French high commands, to atone for the failure of those launched in September-October 1915 and to deal a fatal blow at the Germans.

Two and a half months later, 2 Anzac Corps arrived in France. They took over the line held by 1 Anzac Corps just before the new attack was launched. It began on 1 July, preceded by an artillery bombardment which was heard in England. The British and French infantry then rose out of their trenches to make the first sacrifices of what was to be known as the Battle of the Somme; in reality a series of battles in which, once more, the defence proved stronger than the attack, and which petered out in the mud of winter. After a fortnight of confused fighting which breached the enemy front over a two-mile length, the British had fed twenty-five divisions into the battle and suffered 100,000 casualties; killed, wounded and missing. Some of the more depleted divisions were transferred to other parts of the front and fresh divisions brought in to replace them, but it was discovered that the Germans were doing likewise. On 13 July, British intelligence ascertained that some of the enemy reinforcements had been shifted from the Lille sector.

This recalled a recent suggestion for a British attack on the Sugar Loaf salient, south of Armentières between Fromelles and Aubers and adjacent to the town of Lille. Lieutenant-General R. Haking, commander of XI British Corps which lay immediately south of the Anzac sector, had been urging that a combined attack from his and the Anzac fronts should be made on Sugar Loaf salient with the objective of taking the Aubers ridge, against which the British had made two costly and unsuccessful attempts in 1915.

This plan was at first rejected, on 12 July. But next day, staff officers from G.H.Q. hurried to discuss it with the 1st Army Commander, on the grounds that an artillery demonstration might deter the Germans from transferring more troops from the Lille district to the more critical front further south.

They suggested artillery because they were opposed to an infantry attack, but found that the 1st Army Commander was adamant in his support for General Haking's proposals to employ three infantry divisions with the aim of capturing Aubers Ridge and thus straightening out the line. It was proposed that Haking should command the operation, using the 61st British Division and 5th Australian Division, which had only just entered the line.

He proposed to soften up the German positions with a three-day artillery bombardment, to "give the impression of an impending offensive operation on a large scale." Haking's conviction that the salient could be taken and held was apparently undeterred by the costly failure of a similar attack which he had launched against the Boars Head salient, four miles further south, only a short time before.

Haig's staff remained doubtful, especially after one of them visited the line and decided that there was considerable risk of disaster if the attack was made. But Haking was emphatic that he had sufficient artillery, and that it would be "bad for morale" if the operation was cancelled. So at 6 p.m. on 19 July 1916, after several delays, the British and Australian divisions attacked, following the prescribed three day bombardment which—as usual—had warned the enemy of the impending assault and caused them to heavily shell the areas of assembly.

The 8th and 14th Australian Brigades quickly crossed No Man's Land, which at this point was only 150-250 yards wide, despite the heavy casualties inflicted on the 8th by German shelling while the men were still in their trenches, waiting for the order to "go over the top." Many more Australians were killed or wounded on the way across, but the German front trenches were quickly cleared by the first wave of troops while the second, third and fourth waves pressed on through the German defences and out into the open country beyond, firing at the fleeing enemy as they went.

But as the scattered parties of infantry pressed further on they were bewildered by being unable to find the third trench, that they were supposed to seize and hold as their own new front line. After crossing several watery ditches, and exchanging fire with Germans who had settled in shellholes, the Australians realised that some staff officer had made a mistake. Either the third trench was non-existent, or it must be one of the ditches.

They decided that all they could do was to occupy one of them. They filled sandbags with mud, and tried to clear the ditch of the water that was over their boots and in some places even deeper. Darkness fell after three hours' fighting, and the two Australian brigades held a makeshift front line along the ditches while the battalion commanders established their headquarters in what had been the German front line. On their right flank was the 15th Brigade, which had had to attack directly opposite the salient across the widest strip of No Man's Land, about 500 yards. They had met withering fire from the 6th Bavarian Division, which caused heavy casualties. The Brigade Commander, Brigadier "Pompey" Elliott, one of the outstanding fighting leaders of the 1st A.I.F., judged that his troops had reached their objectives when the enemy fire had died away. But when his brigade reinforcements went forward, they found No Man's Land littered with their dead and wounded comrades. They ran into a fresh torrent of machine gun and rifle fire from the Bavarians, who were now standing on their parapets and firing at everyone who moved. The same fate befell the extreme right flank of the 14th Brigade.

The British 61st Division had attacked the other side of the salient, and also had been caught by the German fire as they crossed No Man's Land, which on their sector was comparatively narrow. Only one of their battalions reached the enemy trenches, and was quickly driven out again. The only material success had been gained by the 8th and 14th Brigades of the Australian Division, who between them had captured over 1,000 yards of the enemy lines.

The Germans still held their positions, so the right flank of the 14th Brigade was critically exposed. To relieve them, General Haking ordered the 61st Division to make another attack at 9 p.m., with support from the 15th Brigade. The remnants of the 15th, despite the crippling losses in their first advance went forward with great gallantry, once again being subjected to the full fury of the German defences. In the meantime the 61st Division had cancelled its attack, and been ordered to retire to their old front line; a decision of which the Australians had not been informed.

Despite this lack of support, the 15th Brigade captured a small section of the German trenches on the 14th Brigade's right flank. Bitter fighting continued all through the night, as the Germans brought up more reinforcements. The Australian carrying parties, instead of retiring for more supplies, stayed with their beleaguered comrades to fight it out.

The Germans counter-attacked on both flanks of the Australian position, where hand to hand fighting and bombing went on all through the night. Gradually the overwhelming German strength began to tell as they worked their way behind the Australians. By 5.45 a.m. the 8th Brigade had been forced out of the German trenches, and had to charge German units who were established in No Man's Land, in order to regain their original lines.

The position of the 14th Brigade was now desperate, and at 8 a.m. orders were given for it to retire across No Man's Land through a communication trench dug during the night. Captain N. Gibbins, of the 55th Battalion, was ordered to cover the withdrawal of his brigade: in a dogged rearguard action, he and his men succeeded in doing so. Gibbins was the last man to regain the Australian lines, but was killed as he jumped over the parapet.

Even as the embers of this bitter engagement died away, Australian parties hopelessly cut off behind the German lines were still fighting at 9.20 a.m.

During the withdrawal of the two brigades, General Haking had been endeavouring to get the 61st Division into attack again in order to support the Australians, but they were unable to do so.

In twenty-seven hours fighting, the 5th Australian Division had lost 5,533 men. An informal truce was made with the Germans, to bring in the wounded who still littered No Man's Land. This was made possible through the humanity of a Bavarian officer, who challenged an Australian batman looking for his dead officer near the enemy lines.

Two years later, when details of the German defences came into British possession, it was found that the "third trench," which was to have been the Australian objective in this battle, had in fact been non-existent.

The Australian Chief of Staff, Brudenell White, had forecast the tragedy of Fromelles two days before it took place, and had been appalled by the lack of preparation and planning on the part of the British Corps to which the Australians were attached. When Haig was challenged on the score that some of his staff work was sadly lacking in this instance, he rejected the implication—even though he had been opposed to the use of infantry. If his original intention, of using nothing but an artillery demonstration, had been enforced, the shattering losses to the 5th Division would never have occurred. The performance of the British 61st Division in this action served to confirm the impression which was growing in the A.I.F.; that the British "New Armies" lacked both fighting capacity and leadership.

For the Australians, the Fromelles battle was a bitter introduction to the chaotic savagery of warfare on the Western Front. But even worse was soon to follow. The greatest test in their four years of campaigning took place during the next few days, in which the 1st, 2nd and 4th Australian Divisions played a vital and urgent role in the Battle of the Somme. Their entry to the battle has been described by a British historian as a "powerful accession of strength to Haig's army and a potent new weapon."

They were flung into combat with little warning. While the 1st Division was marching through Picardy to the Albert area, its commander, Major-General H. B. Walker, was sent for by General Sir Hubert Gough, commander of the 4th British Army. Gough's first words were: "I want you to go into the line and attack Pozières tonight."

Walker protested. He said that the order gave far too little time for preparation by his headquarters, which had not yet established itself in the forward area, and by the troops themselves. Birdwood and Brudenell White backed him up, and the order was rescinded for twenty-four hours.

The task given to the 1st Division, with its two sister divisions in reserve, was to seize the summit of the long ridge behind the village of Pozières. Along this ridge lay the second line of German defences, known as the old German second line system of trenches (OGS2). Known to the Germans as Hill 160, it was one of the highest points on the battlefield and gave a great tactical advantage. It had a clear, gently graded field of fire in all directions—including Pozières village, which lay on an open plateau projecting from the ridge. On the summit stood the remains of Pozières Windmill.

After the capture of Pozières, it was planned to turn northwards and thrust behind the heights of Thiepval, on which rested the northern end of the German battlefront. Pozières was part of a double assault, in the centre and on the right, by the British 4th and 5th Armies. It was integral to Field Marshal Haig's policy of a "wearing out battle, carried out methodically and without haste, trench by trench." So far it had been attacked four times by British infantry between 13-17 June, but each attack had failed. Because of these failures, the High Command was determined on success and relied on the Australians to do the job.

A heavy bombardment of the village and the old German second lines was methodically carried out for two days, and the 3rd and 1st Brigades of the 1st Division attacked half-an-hour after midnight on 23 July.

The assault followed standard Western Front tactics. The German front opposite to the Australians was blanketed by an intense field artillery bombardment, to cut the remaining wire, break down the parapets, and force the German machine-gunners to keep under cover. The moment the

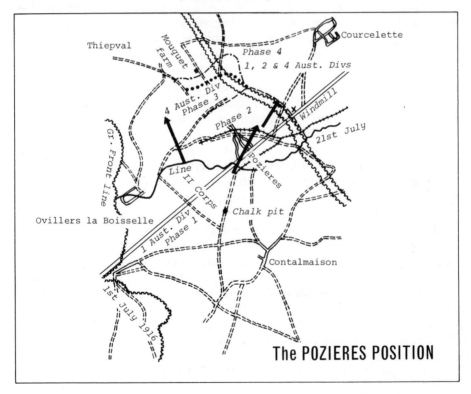

The POZIERES POSITION

barrage lifted, the Australians charged across and took the German front line almost immediately. The advance was continued at half-hour intervals over the succeeding stages. The second stage took the troops to the hedges behind the village, and the third on to the main road through Pozières.

The area was defended by the German 117th Division, which was severely mauled. Many of its men were killed or captured, and the remainder retired to the northern end of the village or into communication trenches beyond. They counter-attacked at dawn, but were sharply repulsed with heavy casualties. The first objective, "old German line number one," was captured, but ground had been so torn up by the artillery bombardments that it was difficult to ascertain the line of O.G.2. Beyond the new Australian positions, the enemy still held their trenches and were able to fire into the open flank of Australians attacking the eastern end of Pozières. For a short time, the Australian line had to be adjusted accordingly.

During daylight of 23 July the Australians consolidated their newly won ground, deepened their trenches, and pushed out patrols which captured a number of dugouts and other minor positions, while enjoying the fruits of victory in the form of cigars and other luxuries found in the deep and well stocked German dugouts.

On their left, the British 48th Division had taken part of the communication trenches west of the village, but the advance by the whole of the 4th Army on the right flank had ground to a halt without gaining new territory.

"I can just hear the low burst of guns up beyond Pozières. Pozières is ours, captured alone by our division," Major Thomas Blamey wrote in a letter home shortly after the battle. "We are all very proud of the feat. Our plan, which was chiefly mine, led to a brilliant success. We took the job after the British had failed in three separate efforts. We carried the covering position, the western flanking position, and the village in great style, not all in one operation, but still we did it. It was the most brilliant exploit since the opening days of this most terrible battle. The hostile bombardment on our poor lads during the battle is said to have been as bad as Verdun—our men are in my opinion, the finest fighting men in all the world."

The comment about the plan being "chiefly mine" referred to his recent promotion to G.S.O.I. of the 1st Division; a post previously held by Brudenell White. Almost his first task on taking up the appointment in early July was to plan the 1st Division's operations in the Somme offensive, in which they assumed the spearhead and pivotal roles at Pozières.

But the Germans could see Haig's intention as well as he could himself. They knew the vital importance of Pozières to their whole defensive system, and were determined to regain it. After three attempts had been defeated on 23 July, they began the systematic bombardment of the village which earned it the reputation of the "hell of Pozières."

The Australian advance had gained the only ground in the whole of the seven mile front of Haig's offensive, so the German IV Corps, in whose area Pozières lay, switched the greater part of its artillery bombardment onto the crest of Pozières ridge. Soon, it became obvious that the rest of the front was to remain dormant, while the main German effort was to be directed against the Australians.

At first, the bombardment was methodical rather than intense. The German howitzers dropped about four shells a minute onto the trenches dug on the southern side of the old Roman road, in a systematic pounding which killed or buried many of the Australians manning the line. Their comrades dug frantically in an effort to save them, but as soon as one shocked and gasping man had been rescued several more would have become victims of the remorseless shells. By evening, relieving troops could not distinguish some sections of the trench from the mass of shellholes around it. The bombardment was even more intense on the south west entrance to the village, where the main approach road was so lined with dead that it became known as Dead Man's Road.

Meanwhile, General Gough was pressing the Australian leaders to resume their advance. He explained that his intention after seizing Pozières was to capture the "Old German Lines," and then press on a mile towards Mouquet Farm, where the ridge dipped northwards to the River Ancre. His opinion was that the German defences around Pozières were lightly held, and that if the Australians moved quickly they could cut off Thiepval; the original objective of the attack.

On the night of 24 July, the Australians took their first step in their effort to satisfy Gough. They attacked two trench systems along the western edge of Pozières, and after savage fighting all through the night they seized their objectives at dawn. They had to fight off a counter attack from the 18th German Division, which had been thrown into the battle, and endure the continuous artillery bombardment against the narrow entrances to the village. As well as furious hand to hand fighting, a tremendous bombfight developed during the night, and one Australian described the action as: "Bombs at the double, machine guns at the double—carriers at the double—more bombs at the double—strings of men going up."

On 25 July the intensity of the German bombardment increased; an obvious prelude to an attempt to retake the village. At 4.30 p.m. the Germans could be seen massing for the counter-attack, which included a fresh regiment brought into the line. But a furious British artillery barrage broke them up before they even began to move forward.

Next day, the 1st Division were establishing posts and trenches facing the O.G. Lines, as a prelude to an attack on the main German positions. Once again the enemy deluged the area with a bombardment of such intensity that the Australians began to expect a major assault, and called for more help from the British artillery. The answer to this was a massive deluge of shells onto the German positions, including the full weight of the heavy guns of neighbouring British corps. This holocaust continued for six hours, until midnight, when mercifully for the troops the uproar subsided into almost complete silence. After this, the staff realised that the 1st Division was not fit for further offensive action. For three days it had withstood a bombardment of a fury that was not even exceeded in the Battle of Verdun, and during those seventy-two dreadful hours had suffered 5,285 casualties.

The sheer hell of this battle was described in a letter home from Lieutenant J. A. Raws, later to be killed in action. He wrote: "Nothing but a charred mass of debris with bricks, stones and girders and bodies pounded to nothing, and forests! There are not even tree trunks left, not a leaf or a twig. All is buried, and churned up again and buried again. The sad part is that one can see no end of this. If we live tonight, we have to go through tomorrow night and next week and next month. Poor wounded devils you meet on stretchers are laughing with glee. One cannot blame them—they are getting out of this. We are lousy, stinking, ragged, unshaven, sleepless. I have one puttee, a dead man's helmet, another dead man's gas protector, a dead man's bayonet, my tunic is rotten with other men's blood, and partly spattered with a comrade's brains."

General Haig took a careful interest in the Australian introduction to Western Front warfare at Pozières, and on 20 July wrote in his diary: "The Australians went in last night opposite Pozières. I told Gough to go into all details carefully, as 1st Australian Division had not been engaged in France before and possibly overlooked the difficulties of this kind of fighting."

On 22 July he wrote: "I visited Gough after lunch to make sure that the Australians had only been given a simple task," followed by the entry of 27 July, which reads: "The Australians are in great spirits. One regiment began the fight with 900 men and finished up with 1,300. This was due to men joining up from other units which had been ordered to withdraw for a rest."

After the 2nd Division's introduction to battle he wrote: "I think the cause of failure was due to lack of preparation. During the day I visited 1 Anzac Corps H.Q., where I met Birdwood and his Chief of Staff General Brudenell White who is already revealing himself as another great Australian soldier . . . some of their divisional generals are so ignorant, and like many Colonials so conceited that they cannot be trusted to work out unaided the plans of attack."

There is a strange and arrogant irony about this remark, because if Gough had had his way the "Colonials" would have been committed to battle with even less preparation. And, in fact, at the time of Pozières there was only one Australian general in command of an Australian division. The rest were British, on loan from the British Army. But even if they had all been Australian, Haig's attitude was somewhat absurd after the Australians' experiences on Gallipoli, at Fromelles, and now again at Pozières. In all three actions, they had poured out their blood at the behest of British commanders whose sole tactical inspiration seemed to be that of flinging masses of men against artillery and machine guns, in the hope that they would somehow overcome them by sheer weight of numbers.

The 2nd Division, under Major-General J. G. Legge, who as colonel had played such a prominent part in the pre-war citizen army training scheme, relieved their exhausted comrades. Those who watched the survivors of the 1st Division come out described them as, "drawn and haggard and so dazed that they appeared to be walking in a dream and their eyes looked glassy and starey."

General Legge's men had fought on Gallipoli with distinction, but so far had no experience of fighting a pitched battle. Together with the inexperience of Legge and his staff in dealing with the scale of operations to which they were now committed, this was not helped by General Gough's pressure on them to resume the attack.

The scene of desolation around Pozières was hardly conducive to comfort. The chalky parapet of O.G. rimmed the horizon 500-700 yards away to the north and east, with a belt of wire entanglements and iron stakes. The Germans looked down on the Australian positions, over the falling crest that once had been turnip fields but was now a dusty shell torn chaos, towards the gaunt remains of village hedges near which the Australian lines were dug. The village itself was unrecognisable. The debris of buildings and their contents had been pounded into ash, and was spread six feet deep over the surface. Apart from vague tree stumps, there was no indication that a village had ever existed. Everywhere lay dead and decaying bodies or fragments of bodies, rags of clothing, papers, weapons, odds and ends of equipment, and rusting fragments of steel. It was like a gigantic rubbish dump.

By 27 July the 2nd Division had completed its task of taking over the line, and General Legge advised that he would be ready to launch a major attack on the following night. In the meantime, two diversions somewhat interfered with his programme. During the whole afternoon and evening of 27 July the 5th Brigade, which was on the right flank of the division's front, became voluntarily involved in a tremendous bomb fight in support of an attack by the 23rd British Division, and expended much of its ammunition and energy in the engagement. And, throughout the day, the Australian preparations had been frustrated by a bombardment almost as heavy as the one of the previous day. Their trench digging was continually disrupted, and they suffered heavy casualties. Nevertheless forward posts were finally established in some areas, and, where it was not possible to prepare trenches for the assault, an old railway track that skirted the village was used as an assembly point.

At nightfall on 28 July the three brigades took up their position in the forward area, and something had been learnt from experience. Their assault was not to be preceded by a gigantic artillery duel, lasting days or hours and warning the enemy that an attack was planned, but by only three minutes of rapid gunfire immediately before the attack.

However, the Germans had detected the preparations—as from their positions on the ridge they could hardly fail to do. Although they also withheld their artillery, they were ready for the assault when it came. The 5th Brigade, attacking south from the Bapaume road, was heavily engaged by enemy machine gunners when the advance began shortly after midnight. The 7th Brigade, struggling through uncut wire entanglements, wrenched at the iron stakes and tried to evade the obstructions, but they too were slashed by machine gun fire. They still managed to capture a part of O.G.1., and advanced close to the objective of O.G.2. One battalion overran its objective; a road which was so disfigured from shellfire that they failed to recognise it. But their gains were lost when the Germans counter-attacked. The only territory retained was on the 6th Brigade's sector, where it managed to hold the ground which it had seized on the northern flank.

These paltry gains cost the 2nd Division 3,500 men; killed, wounded, or missing during the two days of building up to the attack and the fury of the night itself. At a post-mortem on the battle, Haig was once more extremely critical of the way in which it had been conducted. He regarded the failure as being mainly due to lack of proper preparation, and went so far as to tell Birdwood and Brudenell White that, "You are not fighting bashi-bazouks (Turks) now."

Apparently this was intended to imply that the Gallipoli campaign had been a picnic, and that the vaunted Australians were not proving themselves in action against European soldiers. It was too much for White. He agreed that some of the 2nd Division's preparations had been incomplete, but told Haig that Gough had not allowed enough time for the battle to be properly planned and carried out. Instead, he had pressed Major-General Legge and his staff into action before they had had a chance to familiarise themselves with the battlefield.

Then, pointing at the map, he dissected each of the supposed blunders in turn, and showed that in every case the actual course of events had been quite contrary to the information given to Haig by the British staff officers. The British officers expected Haig to explode at this presumption from a "colonial," but when White had finished his exposition, Haig laid his hand on White's shoulder and said mildly, "I dare say you are right, young man." (White, at that time, was forty.)

But the battle still had to be won. General Legge was keenly conscious of his Division's failure, and despite its heavy losses he asked for another chance. After several postponements, during which the Germans bombarded the

Australian front almost continually and caused many casualties as well as churning up the trenches which they dug and dug again, the 2nd Division was ordered to attack again at 9.15 p.m. on 4 August; the beginning of the third year of the war.

The German positions were smothered with shellfire for three minutes, and the three brigades rose out of their torn-up trenches.

The men of the 7th Brigade charged so furiously that they were on top of the Germans almost as soon as the last shell burst. The Germans had no time to man their machine guns, and in many cases were trapped in their dugouts. O.G.1 was captured and secured, and the Australians smashed their way forward through the German defence system. The impetus of their attack took them through O.G.2 and onto Pozières crest, whence they looked over the wide shallow valley behind the German second line. They could see the treetops and roofs of Courcelette in the foreground, and the woods of Bapaume stretching away beyond.

The loss of Pozières was a major threat to the German battlefront, and an order from their High Command demanded that "Pozières plateau must be recovered at any price." General von Below issued a special Order of the Day, which stated: "Attacks will be made by successive waves eighty yards apart. Troops which first reach the plateau must hold until reinforced whatever their losses. Any officer or man who fails to resist to the death will be immediately courtmartialled."

The 2nd Australian Division was depleted and exhausted by the epic capture of Pozières and incapable of carrying out Gough's demands that they should now push north to Mouquet Farm and on behind Thiepval. They lost 6,848 men, with two battalions losing between 600 and 700 men each, during their twelve days on the Pozières sector.

On the night of 5 August they were relieved by the 4th Division, which had been waiting in reserve, despite a German barrage which was even more intense than those which had been experienced until then. The Australians had created a major bulge in the German defence system, so the enemy was able to shell them from almost every direction.

On the morning of 7 August, the Germans mounted a counter-attack on a front of 400 yards, retaking some of the scantily held Australian positions, and might have driven the Australians right off the ridge if it had not been for the astounding courage of one man. He was Lieutenant Albert Jacka, V.C., who had won his award at Gallipoli. Jacka was commanding the southern platoon of the 14th Battalion at O.G.1, and during a tremendous German bombardment he decided to take cover in a dugout with the eight or nine men remaining from his platoon. Soon afterwards a German rolled a grenade down into the dugout entrance, and Jacka was left with only seven men. He gathered them together, and they charged up into the open to see the Germans marching a column of Australian prisoners to the rear.

They attacked and killed the escort with hands and bayonets, helped by the prisoners who were quick to turn on their guards. They seized the guards' rifles, and the whole group began to fight its way back to Pozières through the rear of the advancing Germans.

Shooting at point blank range, and still using their hands and bayonets or clubbing the enemy with rifle butts, they created such havoc that the Germans still on their feet surrendered to them. Jacka, who had led and inspired this savage fight, was seriously wounded but managed to regain his own lines. Through his supreme courage, the German efforts to re-take Pozières were frustrated, and the Australians secured their hold on the position. From then on, the men of the 4th Division referred to themselves proudly as "Jacka's Mob."

The 4th Division was anxious to capitalise on the advance of its two sister divisions, and on 8 August resumed the advance towards Mouquet Farm. Behind a creeping barrage, its 4th Brigade fought its way along the ridge and captured several trenches. On the next night they consolidated these gains by further advances, and in fact progressed so far that they escaped the German bombardment but were threatened by their own.

General Gough, in planning the drive to Thiepval, had set the Australians an almost impossible task. They had to advance along a narrow salient, which the Germans barraged with their usual efficiency. Not only did their shells kill the Australian infantry, but also the supply carriers who had to struggle along the same route.

On the night of 10 August, patrols established posts in the valley south of what remained of Mouquet Farm, and at a sunken road east of the farm. Mouquet Farm lay about a mile north-west of Pozières, where the ridge began to dip northwards to the River Ancre. General Gough's original plan had envisaged the Germans at Thiepval being cut off if the Australians had seized the farm quickly after their attacks on 24/25 July, but Gough had not made any allowance for the extraordinary difficulties faced by the men who had to make the assault. They were forced to drive along a narrow salient behind the one held by the Germans at Thiepval.

The only way in which the Australians could reach their new front, except in ones or twos, was by a long route up to Pozières and then northwards through the almost impassable chaos of trenches pounded into holes and hillocks by the bombardment. These ran beside the ridge and over two undulations, and every man who rose to the skyline of these could be seen by the Germans. They fired from front, flank, and rear at every movement, and could enfilade the northern ends of the trenches with machine guns. Yet reinforcements, ration parties, and ammunition carriers somehow managed to get through to the rubble that was Mouquet Farm.

The Germans counter-attacked twice on 11 August, using fresh troops of the XIX Saxon Corps which had relieved IX Corps, but were beaten off by

General Bridges and his Staff (*Australian War Memorial painting by George Coates and Dora Meeson*). This painting portrays senior officers of the 1st A.I.F. watching training operations near one of the Pyramids. Major-General Bridges and Lieutenant-Colonel Brudenell White are seated; others are Howse, Talbot-Hobbs, Patterson, McCay, Sinclair-MacLagan, and MacLaurin.

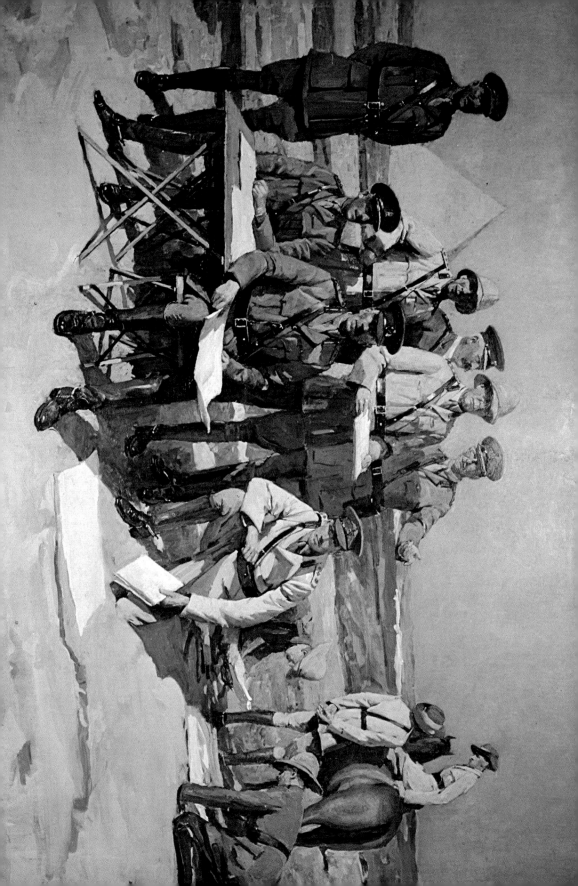

the Australians. In company with II British Corps, who were on the Australians' left flank, preparations were made to attack the German positions around the farm, but another German attack recaptured the ground recently taken by the British. This caused the Australians to modify their plan of attack, but in any case it was foreseen by the Germans who loosed another terrible storm of shells onto their positions.

The C.O. of the 51st Battalion reported to the Brigade Commander, Brigadier-General T. W. Glasgow, that it would be a mistake to press on with the offensive in that salient, but his advice was ignored. The attack went on, and the Australians captured a quarry near the farm and part of the German "Fabeck Trench" north-east of the farm.

Attack after attack was made by the 1st and 4th Divisions for another month, but they gained no more ground. In its first tour of duty, the 4th Division lost 4,649 men.

When they were at last relieved by the Canadian Corps, the Australians had suffered 23,300 casualties after seven weeks fighting around Pozières; more than the total losses at Gallipoli. When the last of them came out, an observer reported "The way was absolutely open to shellfire and others were bending low and running hurriedly. Our men were walking as if they were in Pitt Street, erect, not hurrying, each man carrying himself as proudly and carelessly as a British officer."

The tradition of Anzac had certainly been upheld, although the Australians felt they had been shockingly mishandled by the High Command. General Gough, by ordering attacks which obviously could not succeed, was mainly responsible, but for eight weeks the only substantial advances by the British Army had been made through the efforts of the Australians at Pozières. As the Australian *Official History* rightly claims: "The Pozières windmill site is more densely sown with Australian sacrifice than any other place on earth." To commemorate the battle, the Australian War Memorial Board purchased the site of the windmill, where a small memorial was erected to perpetuate the valour of those men.

The Australians were taken out of the line to restore their shattered divisions with fresh troops from home, but returned in November to take part in the final stages of the Somme battle under vastly different conditions. The dusty desolation of Pozières was swamped by the rains of approaching winter, and on 14 and 16 November, under appalling conditions, they attacked at Gueudecourt and Flers.

In a subsequent action at Gueudecourt, on 4/5 February 1917, the Victoria Cross was won by the most decorated Allied soldier of the first World War; Captain Harry Murray, a former gold miner. The London *Times* reported: "Commanding the right flank company, Captain Murray's skill and courage resulted in the position being quickly captured. Very severe fighting followed and three heavy counter-attacks were driven off,

The Landing at Anzac (*detail from Australian War Memorial painting by G. Lambert*).

all these successes being due to Captain Murray's inspired leadership. Throughout the night the company suffered severe casualties through concentrated shellfire and once the gallant band was forced to give ground for a short way. Murray rallied his command and saved the situation by sheer valour. He encouraged his men, led bombing parties, led bayonet charges and carried wounded men to safe places. From first to last he was a glorious example and constant inspiration."

Small gains were made, but the Battle of the Somme was slowly drowning in the mud. Both sides settled into comparatively static postures; the Germans to build up their defences, and the British to plan yet another assault designed to breach them. Apart from sniping, patrolling, or occasional trench raids, the main concern of the front-line soldier was to keep himself alive while existing in sub-human conditions of mud, rain, snow, and sleet, among the remains of five months of carnage.

The Somme had "destroyed a generation;" had killed scores of thousands of men on both sides, left many more of them physically or spiritually maimed, and then thundered away into extinction like a great storm fading into the distance, without any of the brave hopes of 1 July 1916 being realised.

9

ROMANI

WHILE THE FOUR AUSTRALIAN INFANTRY DIVISIONS ON THE WESTERN Front were winning themselves a reputation for reckless valour, their comrades of the Light Horse were also creating a legend in their own right.

Earlier that year, on 29 April 1916, the Turks had decisively defeated and captured a strong Anglo-Indian force at Kut-al-Amara on the River Tigris in Persia. This followed their victories in the same month, in which they had overwhelmed a British mounted brigade at Oghratina and Katia, thirty miles east of the Suez Canal. It was time for a counterblow, and General Sir Archibald Murray, the British Commander-in-Chief, ordered the Light Horse into the forward zone and placed Chauvel in command of all operations. It was the first phase in a campaign which was to earn him the reputation of being the finest leader of mounted troops in modern warfare, and probably he was the last of the great cavalry commanders.

When Chauvel had decided to remain in the East, instead of taking a Western Front command, it was a fortuitous moment for the Allies in that area. When his pennant was hoisted at Anzac Mounted Division headquarters in March 1916, he must have looked into the future with confidence and satisfaction. Most of his officers and N.C.O.'s had served at Gallipoli as infantry, and more than half his men had been through the same trial.

His force consisted of the 1st, 2nd, and 3rd Australian Light Horse brigades and the New Zealand Mounted Rifle Brigade. He chose his staff with great care, and it was almost a prerequisite that they should have served on Gallipoli with distinction. Most members of the brigade staffs had been through the same campaign, and a number had served as Light Horse in South Africa. Right from the start, the newly formed division was built upon a firm foundation of tough, experienced, and enthusiastic officers and men.

When he was ordered to undertake his first offensive operation, after the British defeat at Oghratina and Katia, he took the Light Horse to these two positions. But they found that the Turks had withdrawn, and Chauvel, after thoroughly reconnoitring the whole area, recommended to General Murray that a strong garrison should be placed at Romani, to meet the renewed Turkish threat at the Suez Canal.

Romani lay astride the northern route, twenty-three miles from the Canal. It was near to the sea and surrounded by great sandhills which extended inland for about six miles. The three most prominent of these were given the names of Mount Royston, Mount Meredith, and Wellington Ridge. They created a natural defensive position, dotted with palm clumps which provided the only shade. Inland from Romani was the dry and forbidding Sinai Desert, over which no unmechanised army could travel to attack the Canal. Chauvel thus hoped that the Turks would be forced to fight on ground of his own choosing, because they could not afford to leave this menace on their flank.

General Murray accepted Chauvel's plan, and a brigade of Light Horse was sent to Romani. They were reinforced, a few weeks later, by the New Zealand Mounted Rifle Brigade, and when the railway had been pushed through the 52nd Scottish Division was also stationed there.

The Light Horse, besides maintaining its garrison role, quickly pushed out reconnaissance patrols into the surrounding desert. These included two notable efforts in scorching heat; one to Bir el Abd and the other to Bir el Bayud, which were situated between twenty and thirty miles east of Romani. These forays offered excellent training for troops operating in country that hitherto had been regarded as impossible for mounted troops.

General Murray was quick to appreciate the value of the Anzacs, and in writing to the War Office said: "I am assuming that you are leaving the three Australian Light Horse Brigades and the New Zealand Brigade with me otherwise I shall be deprived of the only reliable mounted troops that I have."

This was a far cry from a memorandum which he had sent only a few months previously, shortly after taking up his Middle East command, in which he damned the Australians as being "most backward in training and discipline" and not fit for service in France.

Murray was the personification of the pompous "Colonel Blimp" type of British staff officer. He was something of a curiosity to the Australians, who treated him with considerably less than the quivering respect to which he was accustomed from British troops. He and his staff, who were cast in the same mould, issued many instructions designed to bring the Australians to heel. These included the saluting of officers, but the Australians were accustomed to judging their officers by their personal qualities and not by their badges of rank, and paid little attention to Murray's orders in this respect.

But after the patrol to Bayud he wrote: "I do not think any other troops could have undertaken the operation successfully in the present weather." and at the end of May he reported: "Any work entrusted to these excellent troops is invariably well executed."

The old wells and pools at Wadi Muksheib, fifty miles south of Romani, accumulated large supplies of water after a sudden storm, so the 3rd Light Horse Brigade spilled and sealed them. This was to make the central route across the desert impassable, and increase the chances of forcing the Turks to battle along the northern route.

On 18 July, four formations of Turkish troops totalling about 8,000 were observed plodding across the desert, and the 2nd Light Horse Brigade harassed them continually in hit-and-run style. But they moved steadily closer to Romani, and the Australians awaited the coming battle with keen expectation. It was obvious that the Turks were being drawn into the trap that Chauvel had methodically planned.

He expected the enemy to attempt to envelop the southern end of the Romani defences, and then to seize the camp and railway, so he placed his resting 1st Light Horse Brigade on a line extending southwards from the Scottish Division. Two Light Horse regiments were lined out south of the camp, in front of the main sandhills south-west of the Romani defences. The 1st Light Horse Regiment was kept in reserve while the 2nd Brigade was out harassing the Turks, and the 3rd Brigade, which had been part of the Canal defences, was ordered to move up to Romani. The New Zealand Mounted Rifle Brigade was in reserve ten miles away.

By 1 a.m. on 4th August, a total of about 14,000 Turks had been brought up to Romani, and began their attack against the Australian screen. Screaming their customary "Allah, Allah," they thrust in a direction which would take them past the Scottish flank to the long sandhill called Wellington Ridge which flanked the camp and railway behind the Scots. They intended to attack them from the rear and front at dawn.

But they ran head on against the two Light Horse Brigades, who between them had 1,600 rifles, though only two regiments with about 500 rifles held the three mile screen. The desert night flickered and crackled with musketry until just before dawn, when 8,000 Turks made a determined charge up the sandhill known as Mount Meredith. This was lightly held by Light Horse men, but they resisted fiercely before retiring gradually to Wellington Ridge, south of the camp, in accordance with Chauvel's plan of battle.

He now brought the 2nd Light Horse Brigade into line on the left flank of the 1st. The 2nd Brigade was commanded by a South African; the great cavalry leader Brigadier J. R. Royston. He galloped from one sector of the front to another, cheering on his men, and although he was nearly sixty he rode fourteen horses to a standstill in a few hours. He swept through the heavy Turkish fire with a bloodstained bandage streaming behind him like a battle pennant, yelling, "Keep moving, gentlemen; keep moving! Stick to it, lads; stick to it! You are making history today! We're winning now, they're retreating in hundreds!"

Later, a Light Horseman remarked, "When Galloping Jack told us that, I poked my head over the top. Retreating? The bastards were advancing in thousands!"

The 52nd Scottish Division supported the Light Horse by firing a steady artillery barrage into the advancing masses of Turks, but the Australians were being gradually pressed back. Chauvel had thrown his immediate reserves into the battle, and could see now that the Turks were fully extended and that their attack was beginning to flag. It was time for a vigorous counter-attack, but the only troops now available were still back in the Canal Zone. This was despite General Murray's instruction to the British commander concerned, Major-General H. A. Lawrence, to move his headquarters from Kantara or to delegate authority to an officer in the forward area. Lawrence had done neither, because he feared that the Turks would bypass Romani and strike at the Canal. So the battlefront and reserves were virtually under three separate commands; Chauvel, Lawrence, and Murray.

But Lawrence's fears were proved groundless after the return of a reconnaissance by the 5th Light Horse, which he had sent out on the night before the attack. They confirmed that the Turks were not advancing on the Canal, so he ordered the New Zealand Mounted Rifles and 5th Yeomanry Brigade to move forward. At about noon on 4 August, the weary Australians holding Mount Royston against 2,000 Turks, on the exposed flank of the British line, saw the vanguard of the New Zealand columns. In the early afternoon the New Zealanders and Yeomanry attacked the Turks, and later in the day a brigade of Lawrence's infantry reserve, from the 42nd Lancashire Division, took over the right flank from the mounted troops. By early evening, the exhausted Turks were surrendering in large numbers.

During the day, the Turks had also massed further east for an advance on Wellington Ridge, but they were broken up by artillery followed by a Light Horse attack, which took many prisoners.

After their hurried desert march in blazing heat, and an afternoon of fighting, the relieving troops were also exhausted by nightfall. Chauvel realised that the remainder of the Turks must be in the same condition, so rested his men until 4 a.m. on 5 August. Then, the 1st and 2nd Light Horse Brigades, together with British infantry, attacked from Wellington Ridge. The Turks in the central sector opposite the ridge resisted strongly until they were rushed by the tired, hungry, and angry Light Horsemen, and by

5 a.m. more than 1,000 were prisoners. The enemy remnants could be seen retiring in disorder towards Katia, and by 6.30 a.m. all the Turks in the area had been routed.

Romani had been a tactical triumph for Chauvel. He had drawn the Turks into his trap, and, despite the absurd division of command which had delayed his reserves, he had launched his counter-attack at the vital moment which gained the victory he had anticipated. It was a stroke made possible by his keen eye for terrain and ability to forecast enemy reactions.

He followed up immediately, by moving against the Turks at Katia. The New Zealanders, Yeomanry, and 3rd Light Horse marched off at 10 a.m., and by 4 p.m. the Light Horsemen were attacking the southern flank at Katia, capturing 425 men, just as the other mounted troops were approaching from the front. But the frontal attack was beaten off, because the horsemen were not backed up by the anticipated infantry support. The 52nd Division arrived too late to participate, and the 42nd British Division completely broke down with heat and exhaustion during the slogging march from Romani to Katia across loose sand or burning, hard-packed soil. The Anzacs and British were temporarily withdrawn, not knowing at first that the Turks were abandoning Katia from the other side. After a pause for

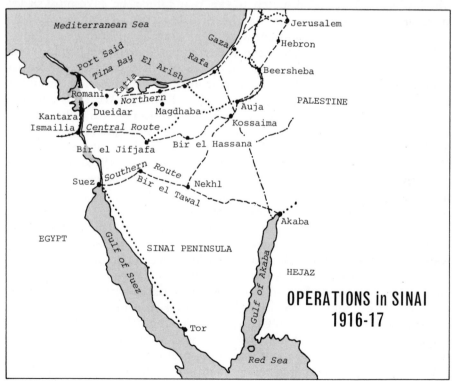

breath, the Light Horse followed them and attacked the remains of the 6,000 Turkish force at Bir el Abda, on 9 August.

The Turks were able to hold the Australians at bay, but still fell back; this time to their base at El Arish. During five days of fighting, they had lost half their force; about 5,250 being killed and wounded and 4,000 captured. British casualties totalled 1,130, of whom all but a few hundred were men of the 5,000 Light Horsemen who had fought in the battle.

Throughout the first major action fought under his command, Chauvel had shown himself to be a master of strategy. He had foreseen the Turkish movement, led them towards his own choice of ground, beaten them in a pitched battle, and followed it up so vigorously that they were driven back to their base. The only flaw on the victory was the lack of drive in the infantry support. If they had been led with any purpose, the whole Turkish force could have been annihilated. Fortunately, Chauvel's handling of his men had kept the Anzac Mounted Division largely intact. If it had been broken up by the enemy, it is unlikely that the British infantry and yeomanry would have been able to keep the Turks out of the Suez Canal Zone.

Not many of the Allied commanders in the field, at that moment in the first World War, could boast of so decisive a stroke. Yet when General Murray sent his official dispatch to the War Office, he gave most of the credit for the Romani victory to the British infantry—and most of his recommendations for decorations were in favour of British officers and men.

It can only be surmised that this was in order to maintain the morale of the British public and of his own troops in the field, because the British ·infantry—as distinct perhaps from their artillery—can hardly be said to have behaved with any great distinction at Romani. Murray's action is even harder to understand in view of a cable sent to the War Office shortly before the battle, in which he said: "I have indisputable proof that Birdwood has been trying to get GHQ in France to agitate to have some of my Anzac Mounted Division reinforcements. The Anzac troops are the keystone of the defence of Egypt, and I am at this moment arranging to form all reinforcements into camel corps. I know I can rely on your help in this matter, which is of vital importance to the defence of Egypt."

Perhaps the problem was that Murray, like the Western Front generals, "led from the rear," without personal knowledge of the conditions under which they ordered their men to fight and relying upon sycophantic staff officers to keep them advised. Some months after Romani, he visited the battlefield for the first time, and went over it in detail with senior officers of the Light Horse and the British infantry. After this, he admitted that his dispatches had been unfair to Chauvel and his Light Horsemen.

But it was too late, and to their resentment of his autocratic pomposity the Australians had added a loathing for his prejudice.

By that time, Murray had made good use of the Australian victory at

Romani. He planned to drive the Turks out of Palestine, and in mid-September the three Light Horse brigades attacked the Turkish positions at Mazar, about half-way to El Arish. After a series of minor actions Mazar was taken in November, and finally the Turks fell back beyond El Arish. It was entered by the Light Horse, New Zealanders, and Camel Brigade in December. After months in the desert, they thought that the squalid village was a "pleasant, civilised town."

10

WESTERN FRONT: 1917

AFTER THE BATTLE OF THE SOMME, THE BRITISH HIGH COMMAND MIGHT WELL have felt like the Roman general who said "Another such victory will destroy us" when he looked upon the heaps of slain after he had conquered Carthage. Instead, they prepared to make 1917 a year of even greater offensives, in which Australian soldiers were destined to be the spearheads.

There was, however, some ground for cautious optimism. The Russians and Italians were pressing the Austrians on two fronts; the Turks had been defeated in Sinai and had failed to follow up their victory at Kut; some progress was being made against the Bulgarians at Salonica; the French, under General Nivelle, had regained much of the ground lost in the gigantic battle of Verdun; the carnage of the Somme had forced the Germans back into the huge series of defences ultimately to be known as the Hindenburg Line.

But the Germans, too, had had successes. On their Eastern Front, their armies under Hindenburg and Ludendorff had dealt the Russians the blows which soon would lead to their complete collapse and withdrawal from the war. Field-Marshal Hindenburg had been appointed Commander-in-Chief of the German Army, with General Ludendorff as his Chief of Staff, and in August 1916 they took over from General Falkenhayn on the Western Front.

This appointment was to render more difficult the Allied objective of a huge and devastating attack to be delivered in the south by the French and around Arras by the British. After surveying the condition of the Western Front during and after the Somme, the new commanders ordered the construction of a defence line to the rear of the "bulge" driven into the

German front from Arras to near Laon. This bulge had been created by British and French defences on the Somme, and offered a flank which favoured a British attack. By withdrawing to this new line, first called the Siegfried Stellung and later the Hindenburg Line, the Germans reduced the vulnerability to attack at Arras and would need fewer men along their front.

The Hindenburg Line is probably the most famous defence system in the history of warfare. When they retreated to the sanctity of its shelter, the Germans laid waste the zone between it and their old front line. Towns and villages were destroyed, forests and orchards cut down, in order to give the maximum fields of fire and observation. The Line itself, though strictly speaking it was not continuous, hinged on the British front near Arras and ran through St Quentin; a total distance of about forty-five miles.

It consisted of three distinct lines of trenches, with fifty yards or more of barbed wire in front of each line, cut across a defence zone which in some places was four miles deep. Concrete emplacements were built for machine-guns, a network of railways was laid to keep troops and supplies flowing steadily in from the rear, and any gaps in the line were covered by huge concentrations of artillery. The German High Command believed that the Line was impenetrable, and proposed to stand on the defensive behind it while they used the zone as a "rest" area for divisions cut up in battle. More battleworthy troops could be deployed for use on other fronts, and it was also hoped that by holding up the Allied advance it would buy time in which the U-boat campaign could inflict a decisive defeat on British shipping.

If Hindenburg and Ludendorff had any interest in the Australians who were to attack this new line, they would have looked in vain for any mention of them in Sir Douglas Haig's dispatch to the War Office summarising the Battle of the Somme—though he referred to the "cool and sound judgement, thorough knowledge of the profession, tact and determination" of Sir Hubert Gough. But the Germans no doubt read with great interest the report submitted by General Sixt von Arnim, Commander of the IV German Corps, in which he said: "The frontal attacks over open ground against a portion of our unshaken infantry, carried out by several English cavalry regiments which had to retire with heavy losses, give some indication of the tactical knowledge of the (British) Higher Command."

General von Arnim also said: "It was most striking how the enemy assembled and brought up large bodies of troops in close order into our zone of fire. The losses caused by our artillery fire were consequently large."

He praised the British artillery and the tenacity of English infantry in defence, but reported that: "Commanders . . . in difficult situations, showed that they were not yet equal to their tasks," and made a remark which might very well have applied to Gough's handling of the Australians at Pozières: "Insufficiently prepared attacks and counter-attacks nearly always fail through being too hurried."

On New Year's Day 1917, Brudenell White was promoted to major-general, though his modesty at first forbade him to wear the badges of his new rank. He continued to wear a brigadier's insignia, because none of his corps Chiefs of Staff were above that rank, until he was persuaded that he would win more recognition for the A.I.F. by displaying his new rank with the pride which it justified.

General Monash also was in France by this time. He had arrived on 26 November 1916 with his 3rd Division, which immediately was named the "Larkhill Lancers," after their headquarters on Salisbury Plain, or "The Neutrals," from their delay in getting into the war, by the battle-hardened men of the three Australian divisions already in France. They had heard something of Monash's training methods during the 3rd Division's stay in England, which had produced a somewhat less exuberant body of troops than those of its sister formations. His patient planning, tirelessly careful organisation, and generally gentle methods of training were designed to produce a body of men who knew exactly what they were doing, and who would win battles by building one success upon another.

Monash also had introduced some innovations which aroused the scorn of his contemporaries. One of these was an insistence that men of the 3rd Division should wear the brims of their Digger hats turned down all round, instead of being looped up on the left-hand side like those of the other Australian troops already in France.

Monash made his headquarters at the Chateau de la Motte, near Steen-werck, and the 3rd Division was posted to a comparatively quiet sector of the front near Armentières. They were to stay there for nearly six months, with the men being "blooded" on trench raids which earned them a reputation for vigorous action. Their comrades in the other Australian divisions were being far more actively employed.

Plans for the new offensive against Arras, to be made by Gough's 5th Army of which 1 Anzac Corps was a part, were well under way. But German prisoners mentioned the immense defence line being prepared behind their present front, and orders were given for probing assaults to be made to find out the facts. Australian patrols confirmed that the Germans were with-drawing on most of their front, leaving a thin screen of posts to cover their retirement, although the German positions further south were for the moment unchanged.

From 26 February 1917 the Australians exerted constant pressure on the German withdrawal, with harassing attacks against the lightly held enemy positions. These yielded Warlencourt, Le Barque, and Ligny Thilloy, at the foot of the Bapaume heights. Early attempts to take Bapaume were repulsed, but it was finally seized on 17 March, together with Sunray Trench on the southern sector of the Australian front.

The villages of Grevillers, Fremicourt, Delsaux Farm, Lebucquiere,

Velu, Vaulx-Vraucourt, Morchies, and Beaumetz, all fell to the 5th Division in early March, despite a strong German counter-attack against Beaumetz. The 2nd Division took a number of villages on the approaches to the Hindenburg Line, though they had a hard fight to capture Lagnicourt. On 2 April the 4th Division relieved the 2nd, and seized Noreuil, in the valley north of Lagnicourt, after another fierce contest. Only one important village, Hermies, remained to be taken by the Australians on their sector, and this was successfully invested on 9 April, together with the neighbouring hamlet of Demicourt, despite spirited German resistance.

On the same day, the British 3rd Army began the offensive at Arras. At first, all went well. The Canadians at last conquered Vimy Ridge, and the British gained their objectives further south, but the early promise was not sustained. General Allenby, the Army commander, failed to follow up his preliminary successes, and consequently was relieved of his command.

On 1 Anzac Corps front, preparations were begun for an early attack against the Hindenburg Line east of the village of Bullecourt. The Australians were to attack on the eastern side of the village while the V British Corps attacked on the west. The objective, once the Hindenburg Line had been breached, was to wheel eastwards and capture a second line of German defences; the Wotan Line. This had been prepared as a hurried stopgap, in case the British should break through on the Arras sector.

Bullecourt was a vital point in the Hindenburg Line, and one of its most heavily defended. Wire entanglements had been placed in wide double belts, boldly patterned with angles intended to divide attacking troops and cause them to crowd into spaces murderously covered by machine-guns.

The attack was ordered for 10 April, just twenty-four hours after the first blows against Arras, but on 8 April both Generals Birdwood and Brudenell White protested to General Gough that the German entanglements had not been sufficiently cut by artillery. It was their opinion that the attack should be postponed until enough barbed wire had been cleared away to open the German position to attack.

On 9 April, the leader of the Royal Tank Corps company attached to 5th Army suggested to Gough that his tanks should make a surprise assault on the Hindenburg Line. They would crush a way through the wire entanglements, and then call up the infantry. He told General Gough that his tanks were ready to advance immediately, so Gough agreed to the idea and ordered that the main assault should still be carried out at dawn on 10 April.

Birdwood and White were still sceptical, but reluctantly agreed to the plan after senior Tank Corps officers had assured them that the wire would be broken before the infantry went in. This tactic, of mass attack ahead of the infantry instead of being used as infantry supports, had long been proposed by the Tank Corps as the proper role for their weapon.

The 4th Australian Division was to follow twelve tanks into a deep gulf in the Hindenburg Line, with Bullecourt standing out on one side and a gentle rise on the other, on which a loop of the German line ran around Quéant.

On reaching the Hindenburg Line, four tanks were to turn westwards towards Bullecourt, followed by an Australian battalion which would seize the village. After this, the 62nd British Division was to move up and occupy Bullecourt, and then follow the tanks in an attack on the westward side of the Hindenburg Line. When this operation was complete, the Australian and British divisions were to advance a further mile to the villages of Riencourt and Hendecourt, west of the Wotan Line.

This was the plan, but it did not work out. Although it was Easter, it was extremely cold, with snow falling heavily. The two brigades of the 4th Division were assembled with considerable haste during the night, and moved up to their forward positions. They lay out on the snow-covered ground, waiting anxiously for the tanks to arrive, but the time slipped by without sight or sound of them. Until, just before dawn, one of the tank officers telephoned divisional headquarters from Noreuil, which was about a mile behind the front line, to say that due to the extreme blizzard conditions they could not bring their tanks up in time for the attack. The Australian infantry brigades had to be withdrawn as dawn was breaking, but luckily a snow squall screened them from the Germans who were sitting behind their powerful defences a few hundred yards away.

That day, Birdwood and White heard that the British had not succeeded with their attack at Arras, and once again Birdwood and White protested to Gough against the attack on Bullecourt being made with so little preparation. But Gough insisted, and now said that General Haig considered it to be more necessary than ever. He hoped that it would help to relieve the pressure on the Arras front.

So a fresh attempt was ordered, for 4.30 a.m. the following morning, but with a slight modification. It was now known that a small section of the German wire had been cut, so the infantry were to follow fifteen minutes behind the tanks without waiting for signals.

The two Australian brigades, still weary from the previous night of sleepless cold and tension, moved up again during darkness and once more lay out on the freezing ground. The thousands of men waited silently between their own front line and the massed thickets of the German barbed wire, knowing that if the enemy suspected their presence he would deluge them with shells and machine-gun fire. The rumble and clank of tank engines and tracks made them tense into preparation to advance, but by 4.30 a.m. only three tanks had reached the 4th Brigade on the right, and none had arrived to spearhead the 12th Brigade drive on the left. The three tanks churned forward, and as ordered the infantry followed fifteen minutes later.

But the two leading battalions caught up with the tanks before they had even reached the wire entanglements, and by that time the Germans had been alerted. They opened up with a ferocious torrent of fire, and the situation that Birdwood and White had foreseen now came to pass. The Australians were caught in the open in front of the wire. Either to retreat or to stay where they were would have been disastrous, so they charged forward through the narrow gaps in the wire. With a courage that carried them through the storm of bullets they reached their objectives, and took the first two German trenches.

The 12th Brigade had had to wait until fifteen minutes after zero hour for the first of their tanks to appear, and when it arrived it added insult to injury by firing into a trench full of Australians. But at 5.15 a.m. the leading battalion began to advance, and like the 4th Brigade it also seized the enemy's two first lines of trenches. The 4th Division had thus achieved its objectives without any assistance from the tanks, none of which even reached the German wire defences. In fact, by 7 a.m., they all had been destroyed.

Nevertheless, faulty reports from air and artillery observers said that they could be seen leading the Australians into Hendecourt, thus inspiring two errors which had far reaching results on the battle.

Firstly, Gough ordered the 4th British Cavalry Division to pass through the Australians, in order to attack the "retreating" Germans, but these troops ran into strongly entrenched enemy positions and were badly cut up before being finally withdrawn. Secondly, artillery support was withheld for several hours, despite repeated Australian requests. Captain Harry Murray of Pozières fame was once more in the thick of the fighting, and sent back a message saying, "With artillery support we can keep the position till the cows come home." This put the situation in its true perspective, but Gough still would not permit supporting barrages to be fired against the Germans.

The enemy was thus left free to move and fire almost as they pleased, and by 8 a.m. the re-entrant behind the Australians was practically closed off to supplies and reinforcements by the intensity of the German machine-gun fire. Soon, with all their usual courage and vigour, the Germans counter-attacked in divisional strength, and forced both the 4th and 12th Brigades back along the trenches. By 11.30 a.m., in was apparent that the 4th Brigade would have to break off the attack and retire to their own lines—if they could. The German fire across No Man's Land was deadly, and Murray told his men that it was either "be captured or go into that." He was one of the very few to get back.

The 12th Brigade had also been engaged in bitter trench fighting, and when the British artillery was at last permitted to fire, later in the morning, its first barrage fell on the Brigade troops when they were battling for existence against savagely determined German attacks. They too began to withdraw, and the 48th Battalion was the last out of German lines. Its men proudly picked their way back through the defences, helping along the walking wounded and followed by their officers.

The 4th Division had achieved an almost incredible feat, by capturing part of the Hindenburg Line without artillery or effective tank support, but paid a heavy price. Out of 3,000 men in the 4th Brigade, 2,339 were killed, wounded, or captured. The 12th Brigade lost 900.

After their disastrous experiences at Fromelles and Pozières, the first battle of Bullecourt gave the Australian soldier even less confidence in the High Command. It was a long time before he could be persuaded to accept the tank as a reliable weapon. Equally, the Australian generals were stunned by the lack of perspicacity shown by the British Army commanders. Despite their comparative inexperience in the higher direction of war, Brudenell White and others had constantly pointed out weaknesses in the British plans of attack. Just as constantly, they were ignored.

The withdrawal from Bullecourt was quickly followed by a German thrust against the 1st Australian Division, which was holding a front of 13,000 yards in accordance with Haig's directions that the front lines must be lightly manned, but in great depth. General von Moser, commander of the German XIV Corps, believed that a counter-stroke against the lightly held Anzac front might keep the British from transferring reserves to the critical Arras offensive. So, on 15 April, the Germans unleashed the greater part of four divisions, comprising twenty-six battalions, against the 1st Division's positions in the Lagnicourt area, which were held by four battalions.

This meant that a force of approximately 16,000 was attacking positions held by 4,000 Australians. Even though the Australians had the advantage of firing from their defensive positions against troops advancing across the open, it was still very long odds. Afterwards, the Germans reported that the Australian machine-gun positions were "cleverly emplaced and bravely fought," but the Germans were equally brave in the attack. Seemingly endless waves of men in muddy grey uniforms and coalscuttle helmets rose out of their positions and tried to reach the Australian trenches, and eventually they adopted what one Australian officer called the "school of seals" formation, with groups of up to a hundred taking cover in a shellhole and then, on their leader's command, diving over its rim into another crater a little closer to the Australians.

The Australians, standing along the firing-step of their trenches, held them off with a hammering barrage of rifle and machine gun fire and showers of bombs thrown by hand or projected from trench mortars. But sometimes a charge of the enemy would break through into a section of trench, for a brief and frenzied struggle with bayonets, rifle butts, and rifles and pistols fired almost touching the antagonist's tunic. The Germans would die there, or perhaps drive the Australians along the trench for a few minutes until they rallied for a charge heralded by a shower of bombs.

Romani (*detail from Australian War Memorial painting by G. Lambert*).

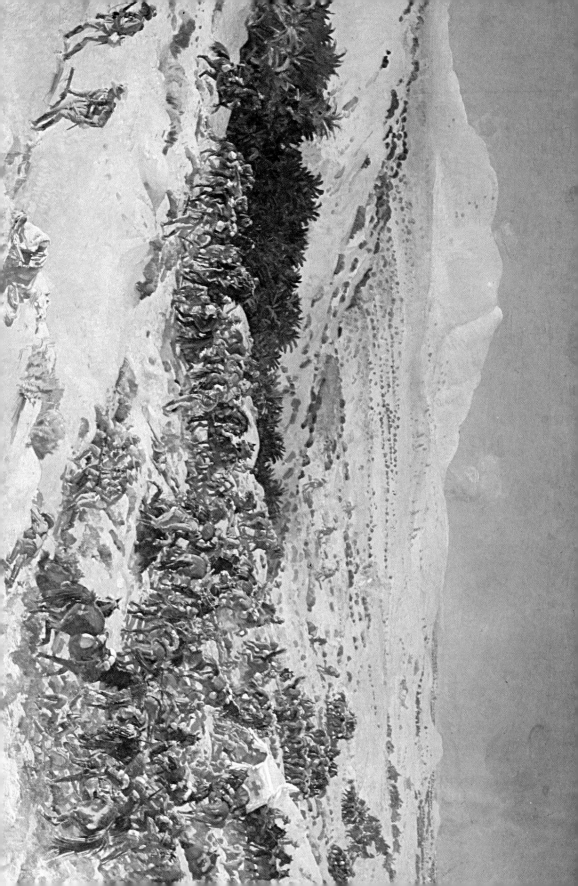

The sandbags along the Australian parapets were shredded by bullets, the firing-steps were almost covered with empty cartridge cases which clinked under the men's boots, the bottoms of the trenches were a litter of equipment among which the dead and wounded lay, sometimes trampled on by a rush of the living. The combatants' throats were dry with frantic effort, and their ears filled with the sound of rifles which rose to a continuous crackling roar when some fresh rush had to be beaten off, the noise of machine-guns which seemed to rise to a metallic scream, the punching slam of bombs and the yells, oaths, and shrieks of men fighting and dying.

Slowly the impetus of the German attack faded away, until towards the end of the day the Australians realised that no more of them were struggling towards their trenches. Both sides, then, looked out across a fearful sight: No Man's Land of the Western Front after an attack. The Germans lost 2,313 men during the day, and many of them were lying in heaps only a few yards from the Australian parapet. Many more were scattered among the torn up wire and the debris of battle. As the sun set, a dreadful sound rose from the men too badly wounded to drag themselves back to their own lines; "like a cattle market," as a British soldier on another occasion described the sobbing moans and wails which slowly died away as life ebbed during the night.

Out of their 4,000 men, the Australians suffered 1,010 casualties during what was to become known as the Lagnicourt counter-attack; another incident in the war which dragged on without apparent progress.

On the following day, the French Army under General Nivelle opened a major offensive in the Aisne region. He urged the British to launch complementary assaults on their own sector, so fresh attacks were launched at Arras on 23 and 28 April. They had little success, but the next British offensive was to be a huge assault by fourteen divisions on a front of sixteen miles. On the extreme left, the Canadians would attack from the Vimy region. On the right, the I Anzac and V British Corps would again tackle the Hindenburg Line in the Bullecourt area, and if possible go on to seize the Wotan switch.

Ample artillery was provided, to pound Bullecourt and adjacent sections of the Hindenburg Line in support of the 2nd Australian and 62nd British Divisions. The plan for the 2nd was very similar to that made for the 4th Division's earlier attacks on Bullecourt, except that there would be no tanks and two brigades would advance behind a creeping barrage. The 62nd Division would be assisted by ten tanks, in its attack on the western side of the village.

At 3.45 a.m. on 3 May, the troops went over behind a massive barrage. Twenty minutes later, German flares of all colours could be seen rising and falling above the smoke of the barrage, and some observers thought that they included the "success" flares of the two Australian brigades.

Operation Bulimba, Alamein (*detail from Australian War Memorial painting by Ivor Hele*).

In fact, the 5th Brigade had been pinned down in front of the wire entanglements by deadly cross fire from the German machine-guns. The 6th Brigade had been able to seize a few bays of the Hindenburg trenches, but were now in an extremely vulnerable position. They had suffered badly as they went through the Hindenburg Line on a narrow front, and were now subject to attack on both flanks. But they clung grimly to their gains, and even launched furious bombing attacks on the Germans. They captured part of the 5th Brigade's objective, which was lost and then won again in bitter hand to hand fighting.

Meanwhile the 62nd British Division, attacking the west side of the village, had also been frustrated, although some of its troops reached the Hindenburg Line. Reports filtered back that they had taken Bullecourt, and were believed even though Brigadier Gellibrand, commander of the Australian 6th Brigade, could see that they were not breaking through and had sent a message back to that effect. When 5th Army headquarters finally realised the truth, they ordered him to send one of his reserve battalions to attack Bullecourt. This was directly against the advice which he had submitted as the "man on the spot," and when he saw the first wave of this battalion being killed he immediately broke off the attack.

But his brigade fought doggedly on towards their own objectives, supported by the 7th Brigade. At the end of the day these Australian troops, together with the Canadians in the extreme north, were the only ones to reach their objectives out of all the British troops engaged in the offensive.

Early on 4 May, the 1st Australian Division went forward to relieve the 6th Brigade, and continued the advance begun by their comrades. The Germans counter-attacked continually on both flanks, often with flame throwers, but were always repulsed, and the Australians gradually extended their hold on the German trenches behind the Hindenburg Line.

Up to 7 May, attempts by both the 62nd and 7th British Divisions had failed to take Bullecourt, but the 1st Brigade of the 1st Australian Division, with their trench mortars and rifle grenadiers, had won over 400 yards of the Hindenburg Line on the right and 200 yards on the left.

The French Army offensive had been a disastrous failure, and the Arras effort was fading rapidly, so Bullecourt now became the focus of action on the whole Western Front. On 6 May, the Germans delivered an eighteen hour bombardment of the Australian positions, which was described as being even worse than at Pozières. During the day, they launched their sixth general counter-attack, spearheaded by the 3rd Guards Division with flame throwers, but this was also beaten off. The singlehanded courage of Corporal G. J. Howell was instrumental in throwing the Germans further back than their starting point in one sector. It was a feat that won him the Victoria Cross, for which the citation read: "Seeing a party of the enemy who were likely to outflank his battalion, Corporal Howell, on his own initiative, single-handed and exposed to heavy bomb and rifle fire, climbed on to the top of the parapet and proceeded to bomb the enemy, pressing them back along the trench. Having exhausted his stock of bombs, he continued to attack the enemy with his bayonet, and was severely wounded. The prompt action and gallant conduct of this N.C.O. in the face of superior numbers was witnessed by the whole battalion and greatly inspired them in the subsequent attack."

On 17 May, the 5th Australian Division relieved the 1st. They began a vigorous push which extended the Australian hold on the west of the Hindenburg Line, and linked with Scottish troops of the British 7th Division who had finally seized the eastern side of Bullecourt some days before. The Germans launched another massive counter-attack against both the Australians and the British on 15 May, but were severely repulsed. After this failure they decided to withdraw from Bullecourt.

From 5 to 17 May the Bullecourt fighting was mentioned in the British news bulletins on every day except one, and on many occasions was the headline item. One French journalist reported laconically: "The Australians have again captured the British communique."

The second battle of Bullecourt cost the Australians 7,000 casualties. Their feat of winning an impossible position in the Hindenburg Line, and holding it against seven general counter-attacks and a dozen minor ones, delivered "by the very cream of the Prussian Army," was rewarded to some extent by Haig's comment in his dispatch; that it ranked "Among the great deeds of the war."

1 Anzac Corps was withdrawn from the line, to rest, refit, and build up its strength from reinforcements.

11

BLOODY PASSCHENDAELE

NORTH OF BULLECOURT, II ANZAC CORPS WAS BEING PREPARED FOR A
new offensive on the Messines-Wytschaete front, as part of General
Sir Herbert Plumer's 2nd Army.

"The Plum," as he was known, was widely regarded as the most competent
of the British commanders on the Western Front. His slogan was "trust,
training, and thoroughness," and he did in fact plan his operations with a
thoroughness that was noticeably absent amongst his contemporaries. He
earned the respect and affection of those whom he sent into battle by his
feeling and understanding for the troops; again, a quality which was rarely
found among commanders in those campaigns.

Yet he was far from being the physical picture of a great soldier, as was
Haig with his noble features or Gough with his tough cavalryman's mask.
Sir Philip Gibbs, the British war correspondent, said that, "In appearance
he was almost a caricature of an old time British general, with his ruddy,
pippin cheeked face, with white hair and a fierce little white moustache, and
blue, watery eyes, and a little pot belly and short legs."

The Ypres salient, which was part of the sector he had commanded since
the spring of 1915, had always been a critical tactical liability to the British
Army. It was overlooked by the enemy on three sides, and had only a narrow
communications line through the cruelly shattered old city of Ypres.

It was hoped that the newly planned offensive in Flanders would break
the deadlock and allow the British Army to sweep along to the Belgian coast,
where they could seize the bases built for the German submarines which
were sinking so many of the ships on which Britain relied.

Once the original salient had been captured, Haig's intention was to push along the ridge northwards and northeastwards through Passchendaele, and down through Roulers and Thourent. But to secure these objectives the Messines-Wytschaete ridge would first have to be enveloped, and the Battle of Messines was in fact the first stage of "Third Ypres" or what has gained tragic immortality as Passchendaele.

The importance of the Messines ridge, which had been held by the Germans since they captured it in 1914 and was one of their principal ramparts on the Western Front, was summarised in a German order which read: "The unconditional retention of the independent strong points, Wytschaete and Messines, is of increased importance for the domination of the whole Wytschaete salient. These strong points must therefore not fall even temporarily into the enemy's hands."

By that time, the British Army was the only Allied force on the Western Front which was capable of mounting an effective offensive. After the chaotic failure of General Nivelle's offensive, many units of the French Army had mutinied. It was being reorganised by General Pétain, but its overall morale had sunk to an alarmingly low degree.

The 2nd Army attack was to be launched by II Anzac Corps, under General Godley, and the British X and IX Corps. II Anzac Corps was a

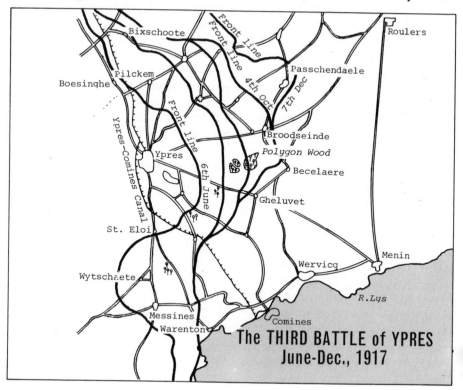

The THIRD BATTLE of YPRES
June-Dec., 1917

composite formation, comprising the New Zealand Division, the 25th British Division, and the 3rd Australian Division, which for the coming attack had been reinforced by the 4th Australian Division.

For Major-General John Monash and his 3rd Division, Messines was to be their first great trial by battle. Since arriving in France in the previous November, their duties had been the comparatively unexacting ones of manning the front on a quiet sector, enlivened by a series of carefully planned and successful raids on the German trenches. They were very conscious of being under the keen and somewhat cynical regard of the other four Australian divisions, which had covered themselves with battle honours, and anxious to justify the lengthy and careful training with which Monash had brought them to fighting pitch. When Haig reviewed them on Salisbury Plain, shortly before it sailed for France, he put his hand on Monash's shoulder and said, "I wish you all the best, old man. You have here a very fine division."

Monash had planned their part in the battle as carefully as Plumer had planned the overall operation. His instructions were issued in no less than thirty-six successive circulars, one of them in seven parts, but even as his officers read them the battle was secretly under way. Tunnelling companies of British and Australian miners were digging nineteen tunnels under the German lines and into Messines Ridge, and they packed a total of 957,000 pounds of explosives into the chambers at their ends. At 3.10 a.m. on Thursday 7 June 1917, after a week of heavy bombardment, the mines were exploded.

Before the eyes of the horrified Germans behind the lines: "Nineteen gigantic roses with carmine petals, or enormous mushrooms rose up slowly and majestically out of the ground and then split into pieces with a mighty roar, sending up multicoloured columns of flame mixed with a mass of earth and splinters into the sky."

II Anzac Corps was to attack the summit facing its sector. The 3rd Australian Division, the New Zealand Division, and the 25th British Division were to attack side by side, and the 4th Australian Division was to carry out the final phase of the Corps attack after the summit had been captured.

All through the night preceding the assault, the Germans bombarded the whole British sector with gas shells. About 500 men of the 3rd Division were put temporarily out of action when their assembly point in Ploegsteert Wood was saturated with gas. But the advance went on with perfect co-ordination, and by 5.30 a.m. Messines had been brilliantly captured by the New Zealanders with the 3rd and 25th Divisions in their correct positions on the flanks. The main heights along the battlefront had been taken except in the extreme north, where British X Corps was operating near Ypres.

The battle plan was for the attack to be resumed at 1 p.m., when on the Anzac front the 4th Australian Division was to take over from the New Zealanders and 25th British. Because of the hold up of British X Corps, this next stage was postponed until 3 p.m., but when that time came the centre corps, IX British, was not in position. But both II Anzac and X British went forward, and the former captured some of the objectives allocated to the missing British Corps.

The 4th Australian Division fought its way to the main German defences on the Oostaverne Line, beating off enemy counter-attacks, which temporarily regained some of the ground, and as the battle developed half of the front was held by Australian troops. The extended left flank of the 4th tried to cover the area allotted to the missing British Corps, and because of this a gap opened in the centre. It took four days and nights of bitter fighting for this gap to be closed and the Oostaverne Line secured.

But by the evening of the first day, Plumer's Anzac troops had gained a tremendous success. The German salient south of Ypres was now eliminated, and the way was open for the more important offensive which was planned to be delivered in July. Besides the front-line troops who had fallen during the battle, the Australians sustained an unhappy loss in the death of General Holmes, the popular and capable commander of the 4th Australian Division. He was mortally wounded by a chance salvo some time after the main battle had finished while he was showing the ground won by his troops to Mr W. A. Holman, the Premier of New South Wales.

The success of Messines was only the beginning of nearly half a year of sacrificial warfare, which was to rank Passchendaele with the Somme as two of the bloodiest battles ever fought. With astounding courage and devotion, the British and Dominion soldiers flung themselves again and again onto the enemy defences, and died in their thousands.

Haig, who was keen to consummate the success at Messines, pressed ahead with his plans to take Passchendaele and allotted the task to Gough's 5th Army and Plumer's 2nd Army. The campaign was to be divided into three separate and distinct phases, the first by the 5th Army with the battles of Pilckem Ridge on 31 July, Gheluvelt Plateau on 10 August, and Langemarck on 16 August. All these were fought under the general direction of 5th Army. The second phase, to be conducted by 2nd Army, was distinguished by the battles of Menin Road Ridge on 20 September, Polygon Wood on 26 September, and Broodseinde on 4 October. The third and final stage, also under 2nd Army, were the battles of Poelcappelle on 9 October, Passchendaele I on 12 October, and Passchendaele II on 26 October.

On 31 July, fourteen British and two French divisions, on a seventeen mile front, began the last grand scale set piece assault conducted by the British Army in the first World War. The attack was preceded by a two weeks' bombardment, and supported by over 2,000 cannon.

On the left of the 5th Army's front, good progress was made. The German second line, and in some places their third line, of trenches were seized. But the attack broke down in the vital centre sector, where five British divisions were assaulting the Gheluvelt Plateau. Very small gains were made, at the cost of heavy casualties. The Germans employed their standard tactics, of counter-attacking with fresh divisions brought up from reserve, to great effect. By mid-afternoon, the British attack had been reversed into a state of desperate defence. On this first day, the only Dominion troops used were the New Zealand and 3rd Australian divisions, but they played little more than diversionary roles.

To add to the problems of the battle, heavy rain fell during the afternoon and turned the battlefield into a quagmire; the first of the almost continuous rains which were to make the battleground a place of even greater torment for the soldiers. Gough, who as usual wanted to maintain an offensive regardless of casualties, hoped to keep up the momentum of his pressure against the Germans, but Haig told him to: "Have patience and do not put in our infantry attack until after two or three days of fine weather, to enable our guns to get the upper hand and to dry out the ground."

This of course was the proper decision, even though a memorandum from G.H.Q. asked rather oddly, "Do we take into consideration the physical capacity of the infantry?"

In most cases, the key to the situation soon slipped out of Gough's grasp, as the Australians had already discovered in earlier battles.

The rain continued with monsoonal devastation, and the battle, having failed to achieve its most important first day objectives, was bogged down into a stalemate until 10 August. On that day, the British troops assaulted Gheluvelt Ridge again, but were unsuccessful because of the "undiminished strength of the German artillery concentration on and behind the plateau." They did in fact take the German forward zone, which was some 800 yards deep, but were driven out by six counter-attacks. A main feature of the German defence system was the *mebus* or "pill box;" circular structures of reinforced concrete with walls four feet thick. The machine-gunners within them were hardly affected by anything less than a direct hit by an eight-inch shell, or by brave men who wriggled through the mud to drop a bomb through a loophole.

The third attack was launched against Langemarck on 16 August. The rain still fell, and the advance was slowed to a plodding forward in thick mud, into which men were shot down in hundreds — many of them actually drowning in the slime if they were unable to rise. The only ray of sunshine on the whole sorry front was offered by the Canadians, who gained ground at Lens on 15 and 23 August.

So far, the offensive had been another man-killing failure. The French Army, under Pétain, had moved cautiously. Instead of launching a major counter stroke from Verdun, to draw the enemy strength away from Passchendaele, they had made a limited assault on 20 August. It had gained them important ground, and inflicted heavy casualties on the Germans, but had made no difference to the British situation.

Out of twenty-two British divisions engaged so far, fourteen had been forced to withdraw for refitting and reinforcement. Even their weapons were affected by the mud. Casualties totalled 68,000; not many more than were suffered in the first day of the Somme, but the terrible conditions under which these later battles were fought was beginning to sap the morale of the British fighting men. Many of them had been physically and mentally drained by months or even years of Western Front service, or were men of a lower physical category than those who had been flung away so profligately on the Somme.

While they had been battling against fearful weather and a German defence of apparent invincibility, the decision was taken on 26 August to put fresh troops into a new main offensive, against Westhoek Ridge. The men chosen for the task were the four Australian divisions of I Anzac Corps, who had had three months rest since their ordeal on the Somme concluded with the second battle of Bullecourt.

Their depleted ranks had been filled by reinforcements, and their training had probably reached the highest peak attained by the A.I.F. during the first World War—since "rest" did not imply that the men sat around and did nothing. They were kept in vigorous training but were rested from actual combat. The divisions were a solid blending of veterans with the magnificent material still volunteering from Australia. Every Australian serviceman, in that war, was a volunteer.

The 1st and 2nd Divisions took over the section of the front, opposite Westhoek Ridge, which was known as Glencorse Wood. The 4th and 5th Divisions were in reserve behind them.

General Harrington, Plumer's Chief of Staff, left the planning of this stage of the battle to General Birdwood and his own Chief of Staff; Brudenell White. The weather had now eased somewhat, and the ground in this area had dried superficially except for water-filled shell holes. They planned the battle to be a succession of limited offensives, like blows from a sledgehammer, at intervals of a few days. And, because of the failure of the battle so far, the Australians also planned to attack with much greater concentration than the British had employed. One division would be used for about 1,000 yards of front.

At 5.40 a.m. on 20 September, after a five days bombardment, the two Australian Divisions formed the centre of the offensive, with the Scottish 9th Division on their left. For the first time in history, two Australian divisions attacked side by side, which sent them forward with surging confidence. Not only did they have greater faith in themselves than in other troops, but the attack had been planned by their own generals, whom they trusted more than they did those of the British Army.

This action, the Battle of the Menin Road, was a solid success, and vindicated the Australians' confidence in themselves and their leaders. The Germans bombarded their assembly point a few minutes before they began the assault, and they lost some men, but the infantry closed ranks and followed their own barrage with perfect battle discipline. They swarmed all over the first objective, half a mile away; paused for an hour, and then surged on another 500 yards, to take their second objective. The third assault carried them irresistibly towards their final task, another 200 yards deeper inside the German defences. The first three "blows from the sledge-hammer" had been struck, and had crushed the Germans beneath them.

By mid-day the Australians were digging in, and waiting for German counter-attacks. These were broken up before they could take effect, by the storms of shellfire from the Australian and British artillery.

The Australians were justifiably elated, because they had won the first victory in the Passchendaele campaign. They had suffered some 5,000 casualties, and it was estimated that the Germans had lost about the same amount. The British divisions supporting the Australian spearhead had also taken their objectives with one or two minor exceptions.

General Birdwood reported: "Our own artillery barrage was magnificent —quite the best the Australians had ever seen. Creeping forward exactly according to plan, the barrage won the ground, while the infantry followed behind and occupied all the important points with a minimum of resistance. Three lines of objectives had been laid down, and the third of these was reached by 10.15 a.m., our men being in great heart. At 3.15 p.m. came the expected German counter-attacks, but so effective was our artillery fire that by 7 p.m. the attack had been killed."

The second "step by step" thrust was the Battle of Polygon Wood, which began at dawn on 26 September. This time the spearheading divisions were the 4th and 5th Australians, who had relieved the 1st and 2nd. On the previous day, the Australian positions had been jeopardised by a German counter-attack which drove back the northern flank of the X British Corps, and exposed the line from which the Australians were to begin their advance along the ridge. Brigadier "Pompey" Elliott, whose brigade was to make the advance from that point and whose flank was now threatened, decided to help the British to clear the position. After a day's heavy fighting by one of his battalions, the starting line was secured.

The two Australian divisions advanced behind a "copy-book" barrage, and swept over the German positions to a depth of 1,200 yards. They captured all their own objectives quickly, and Elliott's brigade not only reached its own targets but also captured some of those allotted to X British Corps, which had not kept up with the Australians.

Like Menin Road, Polygon Wood was another triumph for the staff work of Birdwood and Brudenell White. In his memoirs, Ludendorff commented: "The 26th proved a day of heavy fighting, accompanied by every circumstance that could cause us loss. We might be able to stand the loss of ground, but the reduction of our fighting strength was again all the heavier."

Now, the Australians faced Broodseinde Ridge, and for the first time in history four Anzac divisions fought side by side. II Anzac Corps was brought into line beside I Anzac Corps, and this powerful force comprised the 1st, 2nd, 3rd Australian Divisions against Broodseinde Ridge, with the New Zealand Division opposite Abraham Heights, which joined the main ridge at Broodseinde. As support for these formations, eight British divisions were to attack on a total front of 8,500 yards.

At 5.20 a.m. on 4 October, after a night of steady rain and forty minutes before the Australian advance was to begin, the Germans commenced a tremendous bombardment of the Australian line, which caused heavy casualties among the forward positions. But promptly at the zero hour of 6 a.m., the Australians rose and advanced behind their own artillery barrage. As the mass of troops moved forward, they glimpsed an almost unbelievable sight between and beyond the spouting earth and rolling smoke clouds of their barrage. An equal mass of German soldiers was advancing to meet them, instead of trying to beat off the assault from their trenches and pill boxes.

By one of those coincidences which no planning can foresee, the Germans had planned an attack for precisely the same moment as the Australians, in an effort to recapture some of their ground lost between Polygon Wood and Zonnebeke. As they advanced, they were first caught by the Australian and British artillery and then the Australian infantry. The collision of the two forces was almost like a nineteenth century battle, in which the opposing armies met on open ground, but the Germans were badly shaken by the barrage which had caught them in the open.

Despite this, they stood and fought, in a series of savage hand to hand conflicts and bombing fights, but the Australians drove them back and crashed through the German defences. There was deadly fighting around the pill boxes, but the Australians gradually overwhelmed these too. The advance rolled on, and Broodseinde Ridge was theirs.

Monash's 3rd Division had the furthest to go, but had proved itself to be as battleworthy as its more experienced countrymen in the other divisions. Monash reported proudly: "Our success was complete and unqualified. Over 1,050 prisoners and much material and guns. Well over 1,000 dead enemy counted, and many hundreds buried and out of reach. We got absolutely astride of the main ridge. Both Corps and Army declare there has been no finer feat in the war."

Ludendorff wrote: "The battle of 4th October was extraordinarily severe, and again we only came through it with enormous losses." A German official report spoke of it as, "the black day of October 4th." General Plumer described it as "the greatest victory since the Marne." (In which the French smashed the German drive on Paris in August-September 1914).

As Monash said, the victory was indeed "complete and unqualified." For the first day since May 1915, the British Army could look out over the green Flemish lowlands as far as Keiberg, which was an extension of the ridge on the Australian left. But it was a bitter victory, because it persuaded Haig that the German line was about to crack. Despite the continued bad weather, and the approaching winter season, he determined to press on to the ultimate prize: Passchendaele.

Although the Germans had been severely shaken, they brought up fresh reinforcements opposite the Anzac front. On 9 October, II Anzac Corps, which had two British divisions in support, began another advance. The day's objective was the next section of the main ridge in front of Passchendaele, but only a small amount of ground was taken, and at heavy cost. Nevertheless, the higher command believed that sufficient progress had been made to launch a direct assault on Passchendaele.

Once again the spearhead was to be II Anzac Corps, with the 3rd Australian, New Zealanders, and 4th Australian Divisions and five British divisions on their left.

They went in at dawn on 12 October, and after bitter fighting in the driving rain and deep mud the 3rd Division reached the outskirts of Passchendaele. The 4th Division reached Keiberg, but ultimately they and the New Zealanders had to fall back from the ground they had won. "The Australians," General Gough told Haig, "were determined to put their flag on the ruins of Passchendaele." But the ambition was beyond them. They had carried the brunt of the battle for nearly a month, and were exhausted by heavy casualties and the demoralising effect of living in trenches that were crumbling ditches, with the men exposed to almost constant icy rain and fighting through deep, clinging mud that held them trapped like flies on flypaper.

The Canadians were brought in to relieve II Anzac Corps, and were given three stages to capture Passchendaele; a task which the Australians and New Zealanders had tried to perform in one. On 6 November, they succeeded, and the Australians were withdrawn from the Ypres battlefield.

*   *   *

On 15 October, with the events of the battle still fresh in his mind, General Monash described it in a letter to his wife. He wrote: "Just in the degree that the battle of 4 October was brilliantly successful, so were the operations of 12 October deeply disappointing, although the 3rd Australian Division did magnificently under the most adverse circumstances.

"It is bad to cultivate the habit of criticism of higher authority, and therefore, I do so now with some hesitation, but chiefly to enable you to get a correct picture of what the situation was.

"You will remember that the division was relieved in the line by the 66th Division, and, from the point which we had reached, viz some 2,300 yards from Zonnebeke towards Roulers on the Zonnebeke-Roulers railway, this division was to divide with us the further advance to and inclusive of Passchendaele; each division having about a mile to go in depth. Moreover, the plan was to steadily shorten the interval of time between the successive blows. As you know, the first blow was on 20 September, the second on 26 September, the third on 4 October. Then came the necessary pause while army and corps divisional boundaries were changed, leading to the fourth blow on 9 October, and a fifth and final blow on 12 October.

"I am inclined to believe that the plan was fully justified, and would have succeeded in normal weather conditions. It could only have succeeded, however, in the hands of first-class fighting divisions whose staff work was accurate, scientific and speedy. My own division and the New Zealanders had proved their ability to march for five successive days, and then go into a complex battle with only three days' preparation on the ground, and you must understand that each division has to make all its own preparations in regard to roads, tracks, pushing forward its guns, supplying its ammunition dumps, burying its telegraph cables, establishing its numerous headquarters, aid-posts and report-centres, and a thousand and one other details. We did it, as you know, with complete success and perfect co-ordination in the period between 10 a.m. on 1 October and daybreak on 4 October, and the operation was a complete and perfect success. Under normal conditions, we might, and probably would have, done it again in a period of forty-eight hours. But the Higher Command decided to allow us only twenty-four hours, and even under these circumstances with normal weather conditions, we might have succeeded.

"However, a number of vital factors intervened, and I personally used every endeavour to secure from the corps and army commander a twenty-four hours' postponement. The Chief, however, decided that every hour's postponement gave the enemy breathing time, and that it was worth taking the chance of achieving the final objective for this stage of the Flanders battle.

"Considerable rain began to set in on 6 October. The ground was in a deplorable condition by the night of 8 October, and, in consequence, the 66th and 45th Divisions who had taken up the role of the 3rd Australian and the New Zealand Divisions, failed to accomplish more than about a quarter of a mile of their projected advance. Even in the face of this the Higher Command insisted on going on, and insisted, further, that the uncompleted objectives of this fourth phase should be added to the objectives of our fifth phase; so that it amounted to this, that Russell and I were asked to make a total advance of $1\frac{3}{4}$ miles.

"The weather grew steadily worse on 10 and 11 October. There was no flying and no photographing, no definite information on the German redispositions, no effective bombardment, no opportunity of replenishing our ammunition dumps; and the whole of the country from Zonnebeke forward to the limits of our previous captures was literally a sea of mud, in most places waist deep. Even in spite of all these difficulties, I might have succeeded in accomplishing the goal aimed at but, most unfortunately, the division on my left (the New Zealanders) had in the first stage of their advance to cross the Ravebeek, which not only proved physically impossible, but the banks of it had been strongly wired on the enemy's side. Consequently, the N.Z. Division could obtain no footing upon the Bellevue Spur, and the left flank of my advance was, therefore, fully exposed to the enfilade fire of a large number of concrete forts scattered over the spur.

"At the end of the day's operations we had accomplished only about another three-quarters of a mile of our advance, being pulled up by the exhaustion of our men within 1,000 yards of the village. My casualties have been rather heavy, and will, I fear, exceed 2,000, but the display of gallantry and self-devotion of the troops was altogether beyond praise. We captured 351 prisoners and did a lot of successful bayonet fighting, but on this occasion I doubt if the Boche casualties were any severer than ours. I think they were at least as severe, judging from the fact that his stretcher-parties are still at work all along our front, while our wounded have all been got in twenty-four hours ago, and the conditions of the ground which he occupies is much better than ours."

Passchendaele, as it became known in general usage, or the Third Battle of Ypres as it was termed in official histories, had at last been won by the British Army. But at enormous cost. The true number of British casualties in the hell of Passchendaele may never be known, because a variety of figures had been reported until as late as 1948. It seems probable that they were in the region of a quarter of a million. Eleven major attacks had been made, of which the two Anzac Corps had spearheaded five, the British two, and the Canadians the final four.

And for this incredible total of human suffering and death, the gains had been negligible. An advance of about nine thousand yards, and possession of part of the ridge, was all that Haig and his staff could place in the balance. The hoped-for aim of the attack—possession of the German submarine bases—had long since been washed away by the rains of that dreadful autumn.

12

FROM GAZA TO JERUSALEM

EVEN BEFORE BIRDWOOD AND WHITE HAD HAD TO SUFFER FROM GENERAL Gough's bull-at-a-gate tactics, and long before Monash's feelings after the slaughter of his 3rd Division had broken through his disciplined reluctance to "criticise higher authority," their fellow-general in the Middle-East had been suffering from British leadership.

After Romani, General Chauvel was in overall command of the Anzac Mounted Division and the Imperial Mounted Division. The latter comprised two Australian Light Horse brigades and the British Yeomanry, and was led by an Englishman.

The two divisions were part of the force with which General Murray, the British Commander-in-Chief, planned to drive the Turks out of Palestine. Also at his disposal were the 53rd and 54th British divisions of infantry, the Camel Brigade, which was two-thirds Anzac, and a New Zealand light motorised unit.

Murray's first objective was Gaza, where the Turks were strongly entrenched two miles from the sea and just across the Sinai-Palestine border. Since falling back on this position after their expulsion from Sinai, they had been preparing for the inevitable British assault.

The plan of attack called for a three-pronged assault. The infantry would attack from the south and south-east, while the Anzac Mounted Division, led by Brigadier Ryrie's 2nd Light Horse Brigade, would roll up Turkish resistance as it outflanked Gaza from the north. The New Zealanders and British Yeomanry were to cut off the town on the east, while the New Zealanders and the Camel Brigade acted as a barrier to prevent the Turks from bringing in reinforcements on the outer flanks.

It was a well-knit plan, and after their success at Romani the troops were confident that they could give the Turks another solid push. The main problem was water—especially for the hundreds of horses. Everyone concerned knew that the battle must be won quickly, so that men and animals parched by violent action over the harsh terrain could reach the wells at Gaza.

The troops moved into position during the night of 25-26 March, and as the desert sky was lit by sunrise they began to move forward against the Turkish trenches. The Turks put up their usual stubborn resistance, so that the net closed very slowly, but by nightfall the British infantry had taken the heights of Ali Muntar. The New Zealanders and the Yeomanry had stormed the heights on their own front, and the Light Horse had entered the northern suburbs of Gaza.

A Turkish general was amongst the many prisoners who had been captured, and the attacking troops could feel that the defence was cracking. Then, to their utter disbelief, they were ordered to withdraw. Some units of the Light Horse already had found water, and Chauvel himself questioned the order. But it was repeated, and they had no option but to pull out of the city which was almost in their hands.

The reason for the order has never adequately been explained, especially since Murray wrote to the War Office that the first battle of Gaza had been "a most successful operation, and had filled our troops with enthusiasm." The trouble may have been that he commanded from far in the rear, from luxuriously equipped headquarters in the Savoy Hotel in Cairo. In his *Memoirs*, Lloyd George wrote that the failure to take Gaza was ". . . the most perfect example exhibited on either side in any theatre during this Great War of that combination of muddleheadedness, misunderstanding and sheer funk which converts an assured victory into a humiliating defeat."

Murray and his Eastern Force commander, Lieutenant-General Sir C. M. Dobell, then prepared to fight the battle again, in order to gain the victory which the troops had been prepared to place in their hands. They ordered a new offensive for 19 and 20 April, and once more the British infantry trotted across the desert towards the Turkish emplacements. They were met by a storm of fire which shredded the advancing formations.

The Turks had made good use of Murray's delay, and had brought up substantial reinforcements. Murray lost the battle, and lost his command. The War Office replaced him with General Allenby, for whom they had been seeking a conveniently distant command since the failure of his part of the offensive at Arras on the Western Front.

The combat troops knew little of such manoeuvrings in high places, and were impressed by the fact that the new broom began sweeping extremely clean. Allenby was a cavalryman, and his large physique and fiery, impulsive and driving temperament had earned him the nickname of "The Bull."

His impact on the British command in Egypt was somewhat similar to that of Montgomery in the second World War. He gave it a ruthless shake-up, including the transfer of headquarters from the Savoy Hotel to Kelat, just behind the front in Sinai.

Sir Philip Chetwode was sent out to replace Dobell, and the latter's Eastern Force command was abolished by Allenby. When fresh infantry divisions arrived at the end of July 1917, he reorganised his force into two army corps of infantry, XX of four divisions under Chetwode and XXI of three divisions, under another newly-arrived commander: Lieutenant-General E. S. Bulfin. The "Desert Columns" of mounted troops were reformed into the Desert Mounted Corps. This consisted of three divisions, including all the Light Horse, the Camel Brigade, and British and New Zealand mounted troops. Command of the Corps was given to Chauvel, now promoted to lieutenant-general; the first Australian soldier to reach that rank. He handed over command of the Anzac Mounted Division to Major-General E. W. C. Chayter, the New Zealand leader.

With his weapon now formed, Allenby lost no time in using it against the Turks. He accepted a plan prepared by Chetwode for the capture of southern Palestine, by breaking through the inland flank of the Turkish line at Beersheba and then outflanking Gaza. A strong presence would be retained before Gaza in order to make the Turks think that another frontal assault was brewing.

Seven infantry divisions and three mounted divisions would be employed, and the key to success would be speed. As a German general was to say in the second World War: "The desert is heaven for the tactician, and hell for the quartermaster." The problems of supplying huge columns of troops moving across a waterless waste were enormous, and any delay or repulse could cause a disaster.

Besides this, Allenby was even more insistent that Beersheba must be seized on the first day of the attack, because failure to do so would enable the Turks to reorganise their defences and upset the plan to roll up their line and outflank Gaza. For this reason, the action of the Australian Light Horse was to be particularly important. They had the task of sweeping round the south and south-east of Beersheba and storming it from the rear, while the infantry attacked from the west.

The offensive began on 27 October 1917, with ponderous naval shells arching in from warships off the coast, and falling on the defences around Gaza while the artillery in front of it commenced a steady barrage. As the gunflashes flared through the desert night of 30 October, the infantry and mounted troops plodded through the sand to take up their positions around Beersheba.

The ancient Biblical town lay in a saucer in the Judean Hills, with high ground to the north, east, and south-east. The infantry attack began with a dawn bombardment of the Turkish positions on the lower ground west of Gaza, and by noon the troops of General Chetwode's XX Corps had seized their objectives. It was hoped that this operation would draw the Turks away from their eastern defences, but there was no slackening of their fire against men of the Anzac Mounted Division as they fought their way up the hills. Early in the afternoon they rushed the strongly held hill of Tel el Saba, a formidable rocky outcrop covering about three acres and rising to 250 feet, and took it by 3 p.m.

But the battle was falling behind schedule. The Turks were fighting with their usual tenacity, and unless their defences could be pierced by a sudden and irresistible blow then the night might fall with the British still outside the town. General Chauvel brought up the 4th Light Horse Brigade, which had been held in reserve, and gave the necessary orders to their leader, Brigadier Grant. The brigade was to ride down out of the hills and break through the Turkish defences on the south of the town.

Strictly speaking, the Light Horse were mounted infantry. They used their horses for mobility, to take them to places where they might dismount and drive home the attack at close quarters. Their weapon was the rifle and bayonet; not the sword or lance of the cavalryman. But now, for the first time, they were to be used as cavalry—and it is absurd that many Australians know more about the "Charge of the gallant six hundred" which were thrown away against the guns of Balaclava than they do about the charge of 500 of their own countrymen which ended in victory.

The Light Horse men moved off at the trot, to that strange and thrilling symphony which may never be heard again; the drumming hooves, clinking metal, and creaking leather of a cavalry brigade going into action. As each troop rode to the top of a ridge and looked down a long, shallow valley towards Beersheba, they knew that the main Turkish defences lay in front of them and that the fate of the battle was in their hands.

They rode forward at the same steady trot until they could see the main Turkish trenches and the first bullets cracked overhead from rifles and machine guns along the sloping sides of the valley. Then the pace quickened, with each man leaning forward like a jockey and urging his horse into the gallop. The tight formations were becoming strung out now, and the thunder of galloping hooves seemed to be echoed by the roar of rifle and machine gun fire as the horseshoe of trenches ahead of them and along the slopes on their flanks exploded into action. Horses and men went down in kicking tangles on the hard, dusty ground, but as the pace increased the Turkish fire became wild and high.

First to reach the Turkish lines were the two ground scouts, Troopers Healy and O'Leary, who had been about eighty yards ahead of the Brigade when it began to charge. O'Leary jumped clean across all the trenches and charged on alone towards Beersheba, but paused to take on a gun and its crew single-handed and forced them to surrender. Healy leapt off his horse into the first trench, and took on its occupants with his bayonet.

He was followed almost immediately by the thundering mass of men and horses. The Turks cowered into their trenches as the horses jumped over them, and had hardly put their heads up again before they were attacked by the dismounted troopers, who scrambled off their horses and charged with rifle and bayonet from the rear. Impelled by the frenzied excitement of the charge, the Light Horse troopers plunged into the trenches and shot and bayoneted the demoralised Turks until the remnants threw down their weapons and yelled for mercy.

As though the Light Horse had broken open a dam, the rest of the besieging force poured through the gap which they had made. The 12th Light Horse Regiment trotted into Beersheba just in time to prevent the Turks from blowing up the vital wells, while the enemy tumbled back into the hills in complete disorder. The 4th Light Horse Brigade alone captured thirty-eight officers and 700 men; far more than their own number.

Later, a Turkish signal was intercepted in which their commander said that his troops had broken because "They were terrified of the Australian cavalry," and a captured German officer, one of those attached to the Turkish Army, said: "I have heard much about the fighting qualities of the Australian soldiers. They are not soldiers at all. They are madmen."

With Beersheba secured, Allenby's forces quickly rolled up the line between the city and Gaza, and on 6 November Gaza itself fell. Allenby then switched the main attack from the right flank to the left, and his troops advanced steadily up the coastal plains. The Light Horse regiments took part in numerous skirmishes, but on the whole the operation was spearheaded by the infantry and Jerusalem was captured on 9 December; a much-needed fillip for British morale. The Turks attempted a counter-attack on 27 December, but this too was defeated by the British infantry.

Chauvel's operations in Sinai and during subsequent campaigns are of particular interest because, by 1918, the cavalry force in the area comprised the largest body of mounted troops ever to be used in modern warfare. They included Australians, British, New Zealanders, and Indians, with some units of French colonial cavalry. A great deal of the tactical responsibility for this force fell upon Chauvel.

It had developed out of the 1916 mounted formations in the Middle East; Chauvel's own Anzac Mounted Division, which consisted of the 1st, 2nd, and 3rd Light Horse Brigades and the New Zealand Mounted Rifles; and the Imperial Camel Corps, consisting of two battalions of Australians, one of Australians and New Zealanders, and one of British troops. Many of these men originally were infantry, and were trained for the Camel Corps in Egypt.

These two formations were known as the Desert Column. Early in 1917, the Imperial Mounted Division was formed. This was made up from the 3rd and 4th Light Horse and the 5th British Yeomanry Brigade, but in July, 1917 its name was changed to the Australian Mounted Division and, when the Camel Corps was disbanded in 1918, the Australian elements of that corps joined the division as the 5th Light Horse. From 12 August 1917, all the formations mentioned above comprised the Desert Mounted Corps, under Lieutenant-General Sir H. G. Chauvel.

The 5th Indian Cavalry Division landed in Egypt in March 1918, and the 4th British Cavalry Division, formerly the Yeomanry Mounted Division which was formed in August 1917, was organised in July 1918.

13

THE SAVING OF AMIENS

WHEN THE SULLEN DAWN OF NEW YEAR'S DAY 1918 BROKE OVER THE Western Front, it had been a battlefield for nearly thirty-nine continuous months, ever since the Germans dug in on the Aisne after withdrawing from their defeat on the Marne. On each day of those thirty-nine months, hundreds and sometimes thousands of men had died.

The Allies looked forward to 1918 with mixed feelings. The Americans had now joined in the war, but so far had not had the opportunity to make their presence felt. Against that gain, there was the loss of Russia, whose collapse had freed thirty-five German divisions and 2,000 guns to fight on the Western Front. Italy had suffered a disastrous defeat at Caporetto, and her armies were being bolstered up by British troops withdrawn from the Western Front. Britain had armies fighting in France, Salonika, Italy, and Palestine, and was obliged to maintain a military presence in such places as India, Aden, East Africa, and Persia. She was pouring forth the money accumulated during a century of mercantile eminence, and the blood of her peoples, at a rate whose true consequence would not be realised until the end of yet another war.

The war itself had become all-engulfing. The Western Front itself was like a gigantic industry, which trained, fed, and equipped men for what they themselves referred to as "the sausage machine." Apart from the combatant troops, there were hundreds of thousands of men employed in every conceivable capacity behind the lines, from bootmakers to butchers; from mechanics to tailors.

The wild-eyed patriotic frenzy with which every nation had entered the war had long since disappeared—except, perhaps, in the United States.

Countless people on both sides had ceased to believe in the war, but fought and worked on in a mood of grim resignation. There had been some severe cracks in morale. The French Army had mutinied en masse, but gradually had been patched together again. The British Army had mutinied at their huge base at Etaples, but their discipline was strong enough to prevent it from becoming serious. The Easter Rebellion in Dublin, in 1916, had sent an ominous tremor through the seeming monolith of the British Empire.

Many politicians, such as Lloyd George in England and Clemenceau in France, had lost faith in their own generals. The generals, however, had not lost faith in themselves, and persisted in their theory that all they needed was more men, more equipment, bigger guns, in order to achieve the break-through which none of them, so far, had attained. Only one general, Ludendorff, had begun to think that there might be some way of opening the door apart from trying to smash it down.

The combatant European nations were running desperately short of men. In Germany, youths of the 1920 conscription class were being called up. Some English battalions were composed of lads of no more than eighteen or nineteen. The civilian populations were being combed through relent-lessly. Wounds counted for nothing. A man had to be crippled before he could be sure of exemption from the firing line, and those who survived any lesser wounds were patched up as quickly as possible.

In such circumstances, the Australian troops were eminent for their strength, vigour, and high spirits. They were all volunteers; in the front line because they wanted to be there, not because they had been herded there like cattle. Conventional British officers looked down on them for their lack of discipline and their free-and-easy way towards senior ranks; a cartoon in the soldiers' magazine *Aüssie* of 1918 depicts a "Pommie officer" asking a lounging digger, "Why do you not salute?" to which the answer is, "Well, y'see, we've quite given it away."

This very quality was envied by the British lower ranks; hidebound by a discipline which sent them mutely forward to the deaths inflicted upon them by the incompetence of their generals. If they faltered, they still had to die, because they were subject to the death penalty which was no longer permitted by the Australian Government. Yet the Australians were impelled by stronger forces; pride, self-confidence, and the knowledge that they must not let down their mates.

"They were rough beggars," an old man who had served as sergeant in a London regiment said in 1970. "Do anything for a drink. I remember a terrible row when an Aussie battalion pulled the labels off a heap of jam tins, and made the French civilians believe that they were Aussie pound notes. They had all the plinkety-plonk (*vin blanc*=white wine) they wanted, but by the time the Frogs found out the Aussies had gone up the line again. Probably half the poor buggers were dead by that time."

They were called rough, uncontrollable, drunken, undisciplined, uncouth —but no one ever questioned their fighting qualities. Under their own staff and their own field officers, they gave respect to men who earned it and fought with controlled skill and fiery courage. And, as the war continued, their British overlords slowly and reluctantly began to realise that they were at their best when left to fight in their own way.

When the year began, the Australians on the Western Front were being "rested" on a quiet sector, following their losses at Passchendaele. In November 1917, a longstanding ambition of the Australian Government and Army had been achieved, with the decision to form an Australian Corps of four divisions with one in reserve. As long before that as 1916, the Australian Prime Minister "Billy" Hughes had promised a sixth Australian Division to General Haig if he would constitute an Australian Army, but Haig was reluctant to agree. He said that six divisions hardly justified the formation of an Army.

This opinion was technically correct, but there were occasions during 1918 when the Australian Corps was numerically stronger than some of the armies to which it was attached. However, the most important result of the decision to satisfy Australian aspirations was to weld all the individual divisions that comprised the A.I.F. in France into the most potent instrument of war on the Western Front.

During the bitter engagements of 1917, the Australians together with the four Canadian divisions and the New Zealanders had established themselves as the finest troops in the line. Consequently, they were frequently committed to carrying a disproportionate share of the burden. Their part in the battles of 1917 had been successful because of their outstandingly superior leadership and the greater moral and physical strength of the troops themselves.

While the Australian Corps was being organised, there were ominous indications that the Germans were preparing for a major offensive. They were steadily building up their strength with men from the Russian front, and concentrating their vast military ability towards striking a massive blow before the American strength could back up the Allied line. By contrast to their single-minded preparations for victory, there was a simmering dispute between the British and French High Commands, as to their respective responsibilities, and also between Haig and the British Prime Minister, David Lloyd George. These two men, different in every conceivable way, had a longstanding distrust of each other. Such feelings were hardly conducive to the solidarity and co-operation required to meet the impending German threat, and when the blow finally fell it faced the British and French with the greatest crisis of the war.

The British Third and Fifth Army lines were stretched to their limits, and the commanders had attempted to make up for shortage of men by a defence system consisting of a forward line, which was nothing more than a series of outposts which would give the alarm and fall back, and a defence line of a series of strong points 2,000 yards apart, connected by trenches and dense wire entanglements. Behind this again was a defence zone, which was incomplete when the battle began.

The idea was that the enemy would be allowed to enter the spaces between the strong points, then checked by the wire, and slaughtered by machine-gun crossfire and barrages from field gun batteries and heavy artillery.

The German concentration of troops behind the lines was seen by scouting aircraft, and trench raids discovered that many fresh German divisions had arrived at the front. Interrogation of prisoners showed that Thursday, 21 March 1918, would be the day of the attack, and the British were ordered to stand to at 4.30 a.m. on that morning.

The German plans were favoured by a dense fog, and throughout the night they had brought up thirty-seven divisions to within less than two miles of the front. The men in the British outposts, straining their eyes into the muffling fog, could not see or hear anything. All they could do was sense that something was about to happen.

At 4.45 a.m., all the German batteries opened fire with what seemed like a single gigantic crash. Their shells fell as far back as twenty miles behind the lines, and blanketed the British forward and defence zones, artillery positions, headquarters, and communications. Behind the lines the area was drenched with gas shells, and the gas mingled with the fog and clung near the ground. Attempts to reply to the barrage were almost useless, because the artillery observers could not see anything through the fog.

While the shells were falling, Ludendorff's new tactics were under way. Instead of the expected mass attack, he was using the same tactics which had brought about the massive defeat of the Italians at Caporetto, in 1917; "flying wedges" of machine-gunners, constantly reinforced from the rear, which cut their way through the wire and wiped out the front line troops. This opened the way for the general advance, which began at different times along the front. Its initial success was due to the combined effect of the monstrous barrage, which had smashed up many of the British strong points, and the dense fog which continued for several more days. In many cases, the Germans were well past the strong points before the surviving defenders even knew that they had got through. Exactly the same thing happened to the field artillery batteries, who found themselves being attacked at close quarters before they had had a chance to open fire.

By the end of the day, Ludendorff had committed sixty-four divisions to the battle; more than the total strength of the British Army in France. In a desperate resistance hampered by the fact that no one really knew what was happening, the British lost thousands of men and were steadily forced backwards in what began to seem like the "breakthrough" that every general had lusted after so ardently for so long. The line of the 3rd Army held, but Gough's 5th Army was beaten so far back that it was only by a series of hurried withdrawals that he prevented himself from being completely encircled. This would have broken the line to an extent that might never have been repaired.

This enormous success was beyond Ludendorff's most optimistic expectations, and in order to take full advantage of it he changed his plan. Now, he decided on a three-stage operation, designed firstly to separate the British and French armies, secondly to drive the British into the Channel, and thirdly to defeat the French. Originally his intention had been to attack the British front with two armies, while holding one in preparation to beat off any French intervention.

Keyed up for action, the Australian divisions heard the news of the British reverses, and waited in their Flanders billets for the call that they knew must come. Almost incredulously, they heard of the loss of Péronne, Bapaume, Pozières, Mouquet Farm, Thiepval, and those other heaps of rubble which once had been villages, for which so much of their blood had been shed on the Somme battlefield.

The orders came at last, and by 25 March the 3rd and 4th Divisions were under way in train or bus; their bands playing "Colonel Bogey" and the

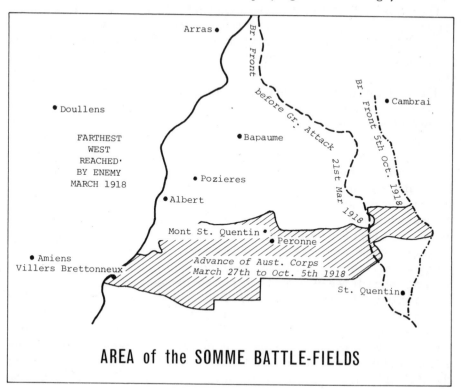

AREA of the SOMME BATTLE-FIELDS

other familiar marching songs as they journeyed south to a battle which was being described as "the worst crisis of the war." The 4th Division, under Major-General E. G. Sinclair-MacLagan, took up positions around Hebuterne, south west of Arras.

They encountered a swarm of refugees, hurrying westwards with their pathetic loads of household goods, but by this time the French civilians were wise in the ways of the war. Where they recognised the free, confident swing of the marching battalions, they called out "*Les Australiens!*" and began to turn their carts to follow them. When a soldier asked one of them why he had changed his mind, the answer was: "*Pas necessaire maintenant. Vous les trendez!*" ("No longer necessary. You will turn them!") Monash described their reaction when he wrote: "You can hardly picture the delight of the French population during the three weeks when the 150,000 Australians arrived on this front to cover Amiens. They knew it meant for them safety and a retention of their homes and property. It was the same story when the 1st Australian Division was sent hastily back to Flanders and stopped the Boche advance west of Bailleul."

*   *   *

The 4th Brigade of the 4th Division dug in at Hebuterne, but its two other brigades, instead of being held in reserve, were rushed south to Albert. Here, a British division had been withdrawn from the front by mistake, thus bringing an already grave situation to an unnecessary and unexpected crisis.

The first German wave smashed against Hebuterne on the morning of 27 March, and was followed by a succession of determined assaults on the 4th Brigade defences. But the Germans received almost the first check to their triumphant advance. Instead of giving ground, the Australians beat them off and even began advancing into the German front. The other two brigades held a line from the Western outskirts of Albert, across the Ancre River at Dernancourt, and then across to the beginning of the 5th Army sector on the Somme River.

Meanwhile the 3rd Division, under Major-General John Monash, had detrained at Doullens and been taken in buses to the old Roman highway to Bapaume, which now formed the road between Amiens and Albert. Together with the rest of the Australian troops coming south, they were the only ones heading towards the enemy. They moved through retreating columns of British troops, mingled with the inevitable refugees. Men in the disorganised British units yelled such comment as: "You're going the wrong way, Digger!" "Jerry'll souvenir you and your bloody band too!" "You Australians think you can do anything." But one British officer gazed admiringly at the confident Australians, and later recorded: "They were the first cheerful stubborn people we had met in the retreat." Once again, the refugees were cheered up by the sight of the slouch-hatted soldiers, and called, "*Fini* retreat—*beaucoup d'Australiens ici!*"

In many areas, it was a complete panic. "Wild-eyed Tommies," as Monash called them, were mingled with civilian refugees amidst a chaos of vehicles of every type. Many of them had become separated from their units, and had lost or thrown away their weapons. "It was really amusing to see the Tommy transport galloping wildly all over the adjacent fields," he wrote, and he ordered his military police to round up the straggling British privates and form them into bodies "suitable for employment if required."

The wholesale confusion was summarised in a letter to his wife, in which he wrote: "I found that the whole headquarters (comprising a total personnel of about 500) had cleared out of Corbie in the late afternoon in a great hurry, abandoning most of their papers and kit, and found them sitting very disconsolately in a dark building, practically wringing their hands, as all the divisions of the corps had been biffed badly that day. The only men in the crowd who seemed to have their wits about them were the Corps Commander, Lieutenant-General Congreve, and his Chief of Staff Officer, Hore-Ruthven. Both these men are V.C.s. They were seated at a little table with their maps spread in front of them, examining them by the light of a flickering candle. As I stepped into the room General Congreve said, 'Thank heaven, the Australians at last.' Our conversation was of the briefest. He said, 'General, the position is very simple. My corps at four o'clock today was holding the line from Bray to Albert, when the line broke, and what is left of the three divisions in the line after four days' heavy fighting without food or sleep are falling back rapidly. German cavalry have been seen approaching Morlan-court and Buire. They are making straight for Amiens. What I want you to do is to get into the angle between the Ancre and the Somme as far east as possible and stop him.'

"This constituted the whole of my orders. I got them to place a small room at my disposal and give me the use of a telephone and from there worked all night to make the necessary arrangements.

"During the night of 28 March I pushed my line out 2,000 yards eastwards until they were in actual contact with enemy patrols. In the afternoon the expected happened, and he attacked me in considerable force—the 3rd German Naval Division on the right or north, the 13th Prussian Division in the centre, and the 18th Schleswig-Holstein Division on the left or south. Overnight I had got all my artillery into position behind my line and the battle was a walkover for us. We simply slaughtered the enemy wholesale, both with machine-gun fire and with artillery. After an hour the whole attack had petered out, and this up to the time of writing is the end of the German attempt to capture Amiens by direct approach. We captured prisoners from all three divisions opposite us; one of them carried an autograph photo of the divisional commander (Major-General Bloch von Blottwitz).

"Most of the villages in the neighbourhood had, of course, been hurriedly evacuated by the inhabitants, and I have been at great pains to try and have gathered up all the fowls, pigs, cattle, and sheep and have had them driven back to concentration camps. I quickly had all the villages policed with good stout Australians and we rapidly restored order.

"On the night of 29 March General MacLaglan's troops came into the line on my immediate left and had several brushes with the enemy which were all in our favour. The 5th Australian Division meanwhile also arrived and came in north of MacLagan, linking up with the New Zealanders, so that we now present a strong united front over a frontage of some twelve miles and the enemy will batter himself against it in vain.

"The main disaster to the British front in this part arose through the failure of the Fifth Army which held the line south of the Somme. Fifth Army has been practically pulverised into fragments and its commander (General Gough) has been sent home. The French immediately took over the defence of the line south of the Somme, but have moved slowly and for several days the situation on my right flank was very obscure.

"From conversation with German prisoners I learned that they had had no idea that the Australians were in this part of the world. Our press correspondents are forbidden even to mention the fact that Australians are in this vicinity, and several long cables which I know are ready to go to Australia have been held up in consequence. The full story, therefore, of what Australians and New Zealanders have done to entirely retrieve the situation will probably not be known to the world at large until the news has become stale."

*   *   *

By the night of 27 March, the two Australian divisions with the remnants of the British 35th Division were entirely responsible for the 3rd Army's flank. Early the following morning, the 12th Brigade of the 4th Division was heavily attacked by the German 50th Reserve Division along its entire front between Dernancourt and Albert, but the Australians stopped the Germans dead, who withdrew, leaving hundreds of dead and wounded.

Ludendorff's offensive was now beginning to lose its momentum, although a fresh attack was launched along a wide front on 30 March, in an attempt to split the British 5th Army from the French 1st Army. On the extreme northern flank of the front, the Germans launched fresh divisions against Monash's 3rd Division. They were beaten back, with what one of their own regimental histories described as, "The worst miscarriage in its history."

But the drive to separate the French and British armies continued, and the line was pushed in as though by a blunt wedge as the Germans fought their way towards Amiens. To hold them back, the British 12th Lancers and an Australian infantry battalion were ordered into the line. The infantry were commanded by Lieutenant-Colonel L. J. Morshead, who was to achieve considerable eminence in the second World War. Amongst the commanders in that war, probably he was the one who was most inspired by the example of Monash.

The combined force launched an aggressive counter-attack, and although this did not regain as much ground as was hoped for it gave the Germans a bloody nose. The French 1st Army counter-offensive was beginning to get under way, and it soon became clear that the German onslaught would eventually meet the fate of all other attempted breakthroughs.

But Ludendorff's armies had driven so close to Amiens, and its vital road and railway junctions, that he was not going to give up too easily. He re-organised his lines of communication, stretched to their limit by ten frenzied days of effort, and had more guns and ammunition brought up to the front.

On 4 April he attacked with fifteen divisions on a front of twenty-one miles, with two-thirds of his effort directed towards the French and the remainder against the British 5th Army, which by now had readjusted its front lines. This stroke was directed at Amiens and the railways south of the city, and if successful was to be followed by a series of attacks between the Somme and Arras.

The 9th Brigade of the 3rd Australian Division covered Villers-Bretonneux, whose northern and southern flanks were held by two British divisions. They seemed to be holding the Germans until the British 14th Division caved in and lost Hamel. In mid-afternoon, the British 18th Division broke on the Australian's southern flank, and the whole line was forced to retire to the outskirts of Villers-Bretonneux.

The fate of this position appeared to be sealed, and the Germans surged steadily closer to the ruined village. Then, a battalion of the 9th Brigade stormed out of a hollow in which they had been waiting. With bayonets glinting in the declining sun, they charged straight for the enemy. In a series of savage encounters with bombs, bayonets, and bullets, they smashed the Germans back from the outskirts of the village and forced them to retire to their trenches, a mile away. The 15th Brigade was brought across the Somme, to hold and restore the northern flank of the town, and Villers-Bretonneux was saved.

Meanwhile, south of the village, the Germans had seized Hangard Wood and Moreuil. They drove the French back beyond the Avre and entered Senecot Wood, from which they could observe Amiens. The 4th Australian Brigade and the New Zealand Division, still holding the front at Hebuterne, were heavily attacked by two German divisions, but once more beat them back with heavy casualties.

The 12th and 13th Brigades of the 4th Division were holding the railway embankment and cuttings in the Dernancourt sector, and learnt from prisoners that the Germans were going to launch their main attack on Amiens right through the Brigades' areas. At dawn on 5 April, this attack began with an intensive artillery and trench mortar bombardment, and then three and a half German divisions assaulted the Australians along the three-mile curve of the railway line between Dernancourt and Albert.

The Germans swarmed forward regardless of losses, looming out of the early morning mists until they were right on top of the Australian positions. The outnumbered Australians met them in furious hand-to-hand fighting, and grimly defended their positions, but the Germans slowly forced their way under the bridge and captured the flank and rear neighbouring posts on top of the embankment. But the Australian brigades had been told that they must hold their positions "at all costs." They did so; fighting doggedly throughout the day, and falling back only when the threat of encirclement became a reality. In late afternoon, the last Australian reserves were thrown in, and battled up to the brow of the embankment against the most intensive fire. The Germans also had suffered heavy losses, and were exhausted and demoralised by a day of fighting against an enemy which refused to surrender to overwhelming odds. This fresh assault by snarling, bayonet-wielding young men in the prime of their strength was too much for them. They tumbled back from the railway, and Amiens was saved.

On 4 and 5 April the Australians lost about 1,800 men. The Germans lost half as many again, and had been defeated on the most vital sector of their offensive. When the 2nd Division relieved the men of the 12th and 13th Brigades, their officers were so proud of them that they could not speak of them without emotion.

Ludendorff had staked most of the remaining men, resources, and pride of the German Army on his huge offensive, whose initial successes had been greeted with paeans of triumph in Germany. He was not going to give in yet, and switched his operations to the northern front of the British lines, south of Armentières, which was held by the Portuguese Corps. The Portuguese wilted very quickly, and the Germans outflanked Armentières. They drove through the British defences at Messines and reached the approaches to Hazabrouck; twenty miles beyond their starting point, and an important rail centre in the north as Amiens was in the south.

Haig immediately ordered the 1st Australian Division, which had just reached Amiens to join the Australian Corps, to move north to cover Hazebrouck. Despite being shelled and bombed whilst re-training at Amiens, they reached the threatened area next day; in time to relieve British troops including the 4th Guards Brigade.

They helped to stabilise the line against intensive German attacks urged on by personal messages from Hindenburg and the Kaiser, and with a French detachment and the British 5th Division brought the Germans to a stand-still.

An "Order of the Day," issued by a junior Australian officer to his section on the Hazebrouck front, and found on him and the bodies of his men, emphasises the spirit of the Australians. It read:

1. This position will be held and the section will remain here until relieved.
2. The enemy cannot be allowed to interfere with this programme.
3. If the section cannot remain here alive it will remain here dead, but in any case it will remain here.
4. If any man through shell shock or other cause attempts to surrender, he will remain here dead.
5. Should all guns be blown out, the section will use Mills grenades and other novelties.
6. Finally the position as stated will be held.

The position was held.

During the period of respite in which Ludendorff was attacking the Armentières area, the British front which covered Amiens was completely reorganised. General Rawlinson had taken over the 5th Army after Gough's dismissal, and it had been renumbered as the 4th Army. For one period, this army's entire front was held by the Australian Corps, with three divisions in line and one in reserve. They held a total of seventeen miles. The British III Corps relieved half the Australian front in mid-April, including the portion covering Villers-Bretonneux, whilst the Australians maintained the Somme position, though Haig ordered that one Australian division should be held in reserve to retake Villers-Bretonneux if the British were forced into another withdrawal.

He could see that the Germans were massing for yet another attack on the vital hinge of Amiens, and they opened a new offensive with gas-shell bombardment of the Villers-Bretonneux area. This bombardment, throughout 17 and 18 April, drenched the area with mustard gas and put many of the Australian and British troops out of action. On 24 April, the Germans made their first large-scale tank attack, and the machines clanking forward through the early morning fog were followed closely by masses of infantry. They broke through the line held by the British Corps at every point of their attack, drove the British out of Villers-Bretonneux, Abbey Wood, Hangard Wood and village, and reached the junction of the Rivers Avre and Luce. The morning's fighting included the first tank battle in history. Machines of the Royal Tank Corps engaged the German tanks and knocked many of them out of action; a success which helped to stabilise the line. Apart from this, the British attempts to organise a counter-attack during the morning were not successful.

In mid-afternoon, the commander of the British III Corps ordered a counter-attack along each side of Villers-Bretonneux, by the 12th and 15th Australian Brigades and a composite British brigade. He ordered the attack to be made in daylight and from the south, but obviously did not understand the type of man with whom he was dealing. The two Australian brigadiers, Glasgow and Elliott, who were outstanding fighting leaders of the A.I.F., flatly rejected his instructions. They insisted that the attack should be made at night, and eastwards; not across the German lines as he had planned.

"If God Almighty gave the order, we couldn't do it by daylight," Brigadier Glasgow said bluntly. After a certain amount of argument, the Corps Commander agreed that the attack would go in at 10 p.m., by surprise and without previous bombardment. His initial order had been another example of the lack of judgement and sagacity shown by British commanders in the field.

General Hunter Weston's remark at Gallipoli, of "Casualties? What do I care for casualties?" was very much a reflection of the stratification of British society; the belief that one class had been created to give orders, and another class created to obey them—no matter what the cost might be. It was in direct contrast to the real concern shown by the Australian and other Dominion leaders for the welfare of men under their command; a difference which also was apparent during the second World War. Apart from being lamentable in itself, the professional incompetence of a large section of British Army leadership imposed a critical burden on the operational efficiency of that Army.

At Villers-Bretonneux, the Australians duly attacked on their own terms. As their advance swept past the woods they were met by very intense machine-gun fire, which threatened to delay the 13th Brigade until Lieutenant Sadlier detached himself from his platoon and ran into the woods with his platoon sergeant. He crept up on six machine-gun posts of the 4th German Guard Division, and destroyed them one after another by bombing; a feat which earned him the Victoria Cross. It enabled the brigade to continue a southern pincer movement.

From the north, Brigadier Elliott's men of the 15th Brigade rushed the village in bright moonlight, during the early hours of Anzac Day. Cheering wildly, they stormed through the ruined streets, and routed the Germans out of their positions at bayonet point. By dawn the village was in Australian hands again, and a dangerous situation averted. Monash commented later that: "In my opinion this counter-attack at night, without artillery support, is the finest thing yet done in the war by Australians or any other troops."

In order to secure a firm junction with the French Army, which now extended its front to the southern edge of Villers-Bretonneux, Haig now reversed the positions of the Australian Corps and the III British Corps.

LIGHT HORSE TROOPERS, 1916-1918. *Top:* Guarding Turkish prisoners captured at Es Salt, Palestine. *Centre:* The left flank outpost of the 5th Light Horse at Ghoraniyeh Bridgehead, Palestine, April 1918. *Bottom:* The 2nd Brigade passing through the village of Zernukah, Palestine.

The Australians now linked with the French and held the line from Villers-Bretonneux to the Ancre, while the British took over between the Ancre and Dernancourt. For the first time, the Australians were concentrated in their own Corps area, with the exception of the 1st Division. This was still retained in the north where the British commander refused to release them because of the unreliability of the other troops in the area.

THE WESTERN FRONT, I. *Top:* These barbed wire entanglements between Lormisset Farm and Mushroom Quarry were typical of Western Front defence systems. *Centre:* The August advance, 1918. Lieutenant Downes briefs his platoon of B Company of the 29th Battalion. *Bottom:* Brigadier H. G. Bennett and his staff in the headquarters dug-out near Hooge Crater.

14

MONASH TAKES COMMAND

L UDENDORFF'S OFFENSIVE HAD HAD ONE GOOD RESULT, IN THAT IT frightened the jealous Allied leaders into uniting under one commander, and for the rest of the war they fought under the leadership of Marshal Foch. And plenty of fighting lay ahead, because Ludendorff's repulse in the north did not deter him from making another determined thrust further south.

As the Somme sector simmered down, following the recapture of Villers-Bretonneux, a series of reports during May and June reveal Australian successes in what they laconically described as "peaceful penetration."

Basically, this consisted of very active patrolling of the German lines, in a manner so furtive that the enemy was losing whole sections in front line trench systems without being aware of it until several hours afterwards. As spring became summer, and the self-sown crops of cereals and grasses covered the battlefront which once had been farmland, so the opportunities for peaceful penetration improved.

The 1st Australian Division was the first to practice this new tactic. Stationed in Flanders, away from the Australian Corps, they exerted such pressure in May and June that German posts were taken daily. In one morning, they captured 1,000 yards of the German 13th Reserve Division's front, and took 120 prisoners, including 3 officers, and 11 machine-guns. Prince Franz of Bavaria, commander of the 4th Bavarian Division which had been relieved by the Reserve division in front of the Australians, told his troops that "This state of affairs was a disgrace to the division."

The other Australian divisions did not lag far behind the 1st. On 9 May, Haig noted that General Monash's 3rd Division, "During the last three days, advanced their front about a mile, and gained observation over the slopes to the east. The ground gained was twice as much as they had taken at Messines last June and they had done it with very small losses, some 15 killed and 80 wounded, and they had taken nearly 300 prisoners."

On 19 May, the 2nd Division at a cost of 40 casualties captured over 400 prisoners, and on 11 June seized the latest German front system at Morlancourt and took 325 prisoners. The German divisional commander reported that, "a complete battalion had been wiped out as with a sponge."

The commander of the 41st German division told his troops, "At 11 a.m. on 8 July, the enemy penetrated the forward zone of the 108th division by means of large patrols without artillery preparation, and at 10 p.m. on the same day with artillery preparation. He occupied the trench where our most advanced outpost lay and apparently captured the occupants comprising fifteen men. The larger part of the forward zone has been lost."

Haig's comment that the 3rd Division had taken twice as much ground as they had at Messines, and with very small losses, was revealing—though he did not point the moral to himself nor to anyone else. Messines had been a battle fought in usual Western Front style, with immense and tedious preparations including the laying of the great mines and with the enemy well aware that some kind of offensive was being planned, so that they were able to make their own plans to rebound against it. The 3rd Division's operation introduced completely new tactics, and showed that when the Australians were freed from the supervision of conventional generals trying to fight a conventional war in a conventional way—because they were too inflexible to try anything else—it was possible to make large gains for a small loss.

While Monash's men were putting an even finer cutting edge on their battle prowess in this way, he himself had been advised of a promotion which every Australian soldier would acclaim. On 14 May 1918, he wrote to his wife: "I expect within a few days to be appointed to the command of the Australian Army Corps . . . much the finest corps command in the British Army."

The appointment was confirmed, and with it his promotion to lieutenant-general. (One of the many oddities of the British military system is that a lieutenant-general is senior to a major-general). On 31 May he took up his new command, taking over from General Birdwood who had been relieved as commander of the A.I.F. and given command of the reconstituted British 5th Army.

There had been three candidates for command of the Australian Corps; Generals John Monash, Brudenell White, and Talbot Hobbs. The latter had been in command of the Australian 5th Division, and had led it with great distinction. Birdwood, as their senior officer, had the task of recommending his successor for Haig's approval.

He believed that Hobbs was fit for command of any Corps but that of the Australians, who in their country's interest needed a man of outstanding strength and personality. Birdwood was astute enough to know that the British High Command did not consider the best interests of the Australians when it came to choosing between them and its own troops, and considered that Hobbs was too gentlemanly a man to withstand the pressures which might be imposed upon him.

White had all the requisite qualities, but because of his own magnanimous decision to act as Birdwood's Chief of Staff, instead of taking a divisional command when the opportunity arose after Gallipoli, he was now junior to Monash and lacked his experience of direct command.

Birdwood's recommendation of Monash was accepted immediately. Haig had a great regard for Monash and a high opinion of his leadership, and had said of him, "He is a very capable man. He has made a great success of everything he has touched; a very solid man."

Lieutenant-General Sir W. N. Congreve, commander of the British VII Corps, under whom Monash had served when the Australians shored up the collapsing front at Amiens, described him as the finest divisional commander on the Western Front.

So Monash took over the Australian command, and White followed Birdwood when the latter went to command the British 5th Army. Birdwood thought so highly of White that he recommended his appointment as Haig's Chief of Staff. This recommendation was not accepted, due no doubt in part to what General Blamey later described cynically as the "Union of British Generals," and in part to the fact that Haig had grown somewhat testy with White. While Birdwood, whom Haig did not particularly like, was in command of the A.I.F., Haig had once asked White why the Australians had not appointed one of their countrymen to that post. White answered: "God forbid. General Birdwood has a position among Australians which is far too valuable to lose."

White served loyally under Birdwood for the rest of the war, on the comparatively quiet sector held by the British 5th Army between Bethune and Armentières. Further south, the Australian and Canadian troops were carrying the main burden of the British Army front, and he followed their fortunes with consuming interest and an increasing resentment at the wording of Haig's communiques. It was at the time when an Allied victory on the Western Front was at last becoming assured, and the Dominion troops were playing the vital part in the final struggle. Haig, however, reported that "French, Canadian, Australian, and British divisions had taken part" in the great victories; a wording which perhaps was technically correct but certainly did not give credit where it was due.

White's intense pride in the A.I.F. compelled him to say later that: "The position was that the British had to have a success. It was all-important for their army to have a victory, and in order to do so Haig had to make use of the only corps whom he could rely, but the value of the victory would be lost if it was made out as a victory for Canadian and Australian troops. There was not any fear that we should not get the credit for this, it was only the present credit that we had to contribute to the British Army. It was a sacrifice that we should make for the whole."

Not many generals were as magnanimous as White, in either of the two World Wars. The "sacrifice that we should make for the whole" certainly was not apparent when, during the second World War, the achievements of Australian, New Zealand, and other Commonwealth troops received an anonymous recognition by being made a part of the glory of the British Army as a whole.

When describing his new appointment, Monash wrote: "The Australian Corps is much the largest of any of the twenty army corps in France, for it contains all the five Australian divisions, and a very large number of corps troops, comprising a regiment of cavalry, a cyclist battalion, many brigades of heavy and super-heavy artillery, several battalions of tanks, corps, signal troops, ammunition parks, supply columns, mobile workshops, labour battalions, two squadrons of flying corps, and many other units. The total command, of course, fluctuates in accordance with locality and the military situation, but at present exceeds 166,000 officers and men. Moreover owing to the great prestige won by the corps during the last three months, it is much the finest corps command in the British Army."

He was now Sir John Monash, K.C.B., having been created a Knight of the Bath, and in a letter to his friend Dr Felix Meyer he remarked that it was, "A distinction to the magnificent division of which it has been my good fortune to be placed in command, in recognition of the series of brilliant victories achieved . . . during the spring, summer, and autumn campaigns of 1917."

He summarised his new command in another letter to his wife, in which he said, "My command is more than two and a half times the size of the British Army under the Duke of Wellington, or of the French Army under Napoleon Bonaparte, at the Battle of Waterloo. I have in the Army Corps, an artillery which is six times as numerous and more than a hundred times as powerful as that commanded by the Duke of Wellington."

Before the end of the war, he had even more men under his command, and by September 1918 the Australian Corps contained 200,000 men and was the largest corps on the Western Front though about 50,000 were not Australians. The corps included 1,000 American engineers, two batteries of Royal Horse Artillery, and two British infantry divisions. British troops were now serving under an Australian commander, instead of vice versa.

By that time, his own reputation and that of the Australian troops were at their zenith, and he was becoming the target of a certain amount of jealous sniping. Detractors remarked that he was becoming vain, though he could surely have been allowed a certain amount of vanity, and he also was criticised because he had not served in the front line as a junior officer. Though most of the British generals, including Haig, laboured under a similar disability, except for those who had served in colonial wars which had no relevance to the monstrous struggle on the Western Front. And Monash had at least served as an infantry colonel at Gallipoli.

But it was said that this lack of experience made it hard for him to assess the truth of reports from the front, and made him unable to distinguish between a genuine fighting leader and a parade ground leader. If this was so, then his overall capacity more than compensated for such disadvantages. He regarded war as a practical business to be won by practical means, and described his last victory against the Hindenburg Line as "simply a problem of engineering." Earlier, he said he had learnt that one of the ways to carry out the responsibilities of command was "to try and deal with every task and situation on the basis of simple business propositions, differing in no way from the problems of civil life, except that they are governed by a special technique."

This was a very different outlook from the "death or glory" attitude which still possessed many commanders on both sides of the front, but, as a contemporary British historian has said, Monash was probably the only first World War commander who would have been equally at home in the second World War. Perhaps his principal offence, in the eyes of his military detractors, was that he was a civilian. They may have been disturbed by the fact that he showed greater competence in the art of war than many professionals.

If so, they must have been equally upset by some of the other Australians in positions of high command at the time of Monash's elevation to command of the Australian Corps, because a number of these men were "citizen soldiers." One exception was Brigadier T. A. Blamey, whom Monash appointed as his Chief of Staff and who said later that Monash had "the most highly trained mind that I had to deal with in that war." Monash regarded him as an outstanding staff officer, with a mind cultured far above the average; widely informed, alert, and prehensile. It was an opinion that was to be proved correct during the second World War.

Four out of the five divisional commands were held by citizen soldiers, three of whom were appointed to their new responsibilities at the same time as Monash. The 1st Division was given to Major-General T. W. Glasgow, who had entered the war as a major in the Light Horse and taken part in the earliest stages of the Gallipoli campaign. He had commanded the 13th Brigade from the date of its formation and all through the Somme, Messines, and Passchendaele.

The 2nd Division went to Major-General C. Rosenthal; an architect in civil life. He was an artillery specialist, who had been a general of divisional artillery and commander of the 9th Brigade. A massive man, of great physical energy, he was incapable of recognising the possibility of failure and was regarded as the supreme optimist.

The 3rd Division was to be commanded by Major-General J. Gellibrand. A Tasmanian by birth, he had served in the British Army for a brief period as a young man, but had resigned in frustration at the orthodoxy and hidebound attitude of that service. A keen student, of philosophical outlook, he had commanded several brigades during 1916-1917 and was a man of great courage who was popular with his troops. His weakness appeared to be an administrative uncertainty.

The 4th Division was retained by Major-General Sinclair-MacLagan, who had held that command since 1917. British-born, and originally a British Army officer, he had been wholeheartedly Australian in outlook since he had assisted General Bridges in the establishment of Duntroon. He led the 3rd Brigade of the A.I.F. in the Gallipoli landing, and unlike Rosenthal was a complete pessimist and pragmatist.

The 5th Division command was retained by Major-General J. J. T. Hobbs, who also had been appointed to divisional command in 1917. Like Rosenthal, he was an architect and an artillery specialist, and as a citizen soldier had spent many years in training before the war. He had a great affection for the Australian soldier, and inexhaustible sympathy for those who were obliged to serve in subordinate roles.

On 18 June, Monash held his first Divisional Commanders' Conference, attended by the five major-generals and their Chiefs of Staff, and at its conclusion Hobbs pointed out that it was an occasion of historic significance in that it was the first time in the history of Australia that such a council of war had been held by Australian commanders. Together, they brought a new dimension to the prosecution of the war on the Western Front.

15

THE THEORIES ARE TESTED

I F MONASH FELT A CERTAIN VANITY IN HIS COMMAND OF THE AUSTRALIAN Corps, it was not based upon a desire for military glory of the conventional type. His sole aim, when engaging the enemy, was to beat him as quickly and cheaply as possible, in a businesslike style which saw no romance in heaps of mangled dead.

"I have formed the theory," he wrote, "that the true role of the infantry was not to expend itself upon heroic physical effort, not to wither away under merciless machine-gun fire, nor to impale itself upon hostile bayonets, nor to tear itself to pieces in hostile entanglements, but on the contrary to advance under the maximum possible protection of the maximum possible array of mechanical resources, in the form of guns, machine-guns, tanks, mortars, and aeroplanes; to advance with as little impediment as possible, to be relieved as far as possible of the obligation to fight their way forward, to march resolutely, regardless of the din and tumult of battle, to the appointed goal, and there to hold and defend the territory gained; and to gather, in the form of prisoners, guns and stores, the fruits of victory."

Such a theory may seem simple and obvious enough nowadays, but in 1918 it was regarded as revolutionary—especially by the "cavalry generals" who were responsible for most British strategy, and who for most of the war regarded the infantry's task as that of breaching the line so that the cavalry might ride through to triumph.

Ludendorff's March offensive had been the nearest so far to approaching Monash's dictum on the role of infantry in modern war, but the German general had been singularly fortunate in the weather which allowed his infiltrating parties to cut the wire and outflank the British strong points.

The operations which Monash planned and carried out, based firmly upon his novel theory, were to succeed with a brilliance which was not matched by any of his contemporaries on either side.

A little more than a month after taking command, Monash's theories were tested at the battle of Hamel, on 4 July 1918. In his planning for this battle, Monash set up a new role for the tanks. Tank tactics on the Western Front had developed into a stage in which they virtually replaced the artillery, by advancing well ahead of the infantry, but Monash insisted that they should advance with the infantry and be used as a tactical weapon under general control of senior infantry commanders on the spot. After the first battle of Bullecourt, in which the tanks had failed to fulfil their task, the Australians had become sceptical of their value. But improved machines and more experienced crews had become available since then, and Monash was prepared to give them another trial.

After this, he turned to the order of battle for his infantry, and set this out with the meticulous attention to every detail which characterised his command. "A perfected battle plan," he wrote, "is like nothing so much as a score for a musical composition, where the various arms and units are the instruments, and the tasks they perform are their respective musical phrases. Every individual unit must make its entry precisely at the proper moment, and play its phrase in the general harmony."

In his planning, he introduced the command system which became the standard pattern for the Australian Corps and then for the British Army for the rest of the war, and was accepted as fundamental by all armies in the second World War. It was based on making absolutely certain that every participant knew exactly what he had to do and was thoroughly conversant with every relevant detail of the plan.

He summarised the system when he wrote, "Although complete written orders were invariably prepared and issued, very great importance was attached to holding conferences, at which there assembled every one of the senior commanders and heads of departments concerned with the impending operation. At these conferences I personally explained every detail of the plan, and assured myself that all present applied an identical interpretation. The battle plan having been thus crystallised, no subsequent alterations were permissible, under any circumstances, no matter how tempting. This fixity of plan engendered a confidence throughout the whole command which facilitated the work of every commander and staff officer."

Monash was helped in the planning by Thomas Blamey, now a brigadier. Blamey's star as a staff officer had risen swiftly against the sombre background of war. As G.S.O.1 of the 1st Division he had requested a field command in order to gain experience in the trenches as well as behind the planning table, and late in 1916 took over command of the 2nd Battalion for three weeks and then temporarily led the 1st Infantry Brigade. But it was believed that his talents would be put to better use in planning the battles rather than fighting them, and he was recalled to his post as G.S.O.1. He held it through the bitter campaigning of 1917 and into 1918, when he was once more appointed to succeed Brudenell White, this time as Chief of Staff to General Monash when the latter was given command of the Australian Corps.

The brevity of Blamey's tenure of a fighting command during the first World War worried him a little during his later and even more distinguished career, and provided his critics with a convenient stick. But it did not worry Australia's military leaders, and Monash wrote of him that, "Nothing was ever too much trouble. I was able to lean on him in times of trouble, stress and difficulty, to a degree which was an inexpressible comfort to me."

Hamel was not only to test Monash's military theories, but also his strength of character. Eight companies of the 33rd American Division had been incorporated into the 4th Australian Division, in order to obtain fighting experience, but on the day before the attack the commander of the American Army, General Pershing, demanded that his troops should be withdrawn from the Australian battle.

Having planned their part in the battle, Monash resisted him. Even after

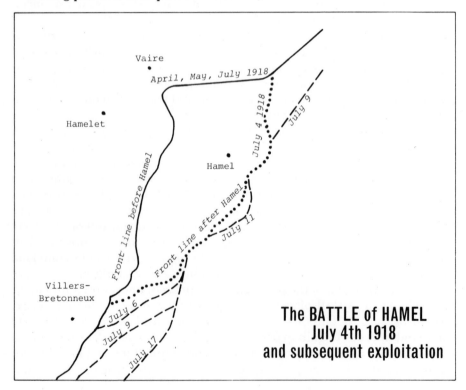

Pershing compromised by asking that only four companies should be withdrawn, he still stood firm. "I well know that the withdrawal of those Americans would result in untold confusion, so I resolved to take a firm stand and press my views as strongly as I dared; for even a corps commander must use circumspection when presuming to argue with an army commander," he wrote.

Both Haig and General Rawlinson supported his stand, and Haig said that he would answer to Pershing if it should be necessary. As it happened, there were no recriminations. The attack went in on 4 July, with sixty tanks going forward approximately 120 yards apart, followed closely by the Australians and Americans. The battle was a brilliant tactical success and was all over in 93 minutes, with a loss of 51 Australian officers and 724 other ranks and 6 American officers and 128 other ranks. Three tanks were damaged and thirteen men wounded in the tank crews. The Germans lost forty-one officers and 1,431 other ranks, together with considerable equipment.

Monash reported: "No battle within my previous experience passed off so smoothly, so exactly to timetable or was so free from any kind of hitch."

A nineteen-year-old signaller, Keith Phillips of Adelaide, was one of those who watched the battle from a ridge overlooking the trenches. Fifty-two years later, he said, "It was a sight I've never forgotten. It was like looking down on a set piece—like a model of a battle, with everything happening in order. Just before dawn we could see all the gun flashes and the shells exploding on the German trenches, and then when it got light enough we could see the lines of infantry all moving steadily forward."

The battle made a significant introduction to modern warfare, when Captain L. J. Wackett, of No. 3 Squadron Australian Flying Corps, developed a system of dropping supplies to the advancing troops. About 100,000 rounds of ammunition were dropped to the Australian machine gunners, establishing a precedent which would have a profound effect twenty-four years later. Their sons, fighting one of the grimmest battles of the second World War over the Owen Stanley Ranges in New Guinea, relied to a vital degree on supplies dropped from the air.

The striking success of Hamel became the model for almost every attack made by British infantry in conjunction with tanks for the remainder of the first World War. Shortly after the battle, G.H.Q. paid the Australian Corps the compliment of publishing to the whole British Army, a General Staff brochure containing the complete text of Monash's orders, with a detailed description of the battle plans and preparations and an official commentary. The last paragraph of the brochure tersely expressed the reason which the High Command saw behind the success of the Australians. It stated: "Last, but most important of all, the skill, determination and fine fighting spirit of the infantry carrying out the attack."

"Peaceful penetration" again became the vogue for the Australians for some weeks after the Battle of Hamel, and they stepped up their activities to such an extent that the Germans opposite them were reduced to a pitiably low morale. The German 2nd Army Commander, General von Marwitz, issued an order that: "Troops must fight. They must not give way at every opportunity and seek to avoid fighting, otherwise they will get the feeling that the enemy is superior to them."

A British staff officer wrote in the 4th British Army's war diary that the Australian Corps had, "in the preceding months, gained a mastery over the enemy such as has probably not been gained by our troops in any previous period of the war."

This ascendancy was due principally to the magnificent leadership of their own generals and the confidence which they gained from being a complete national formation, instead of being a mere part of another formation and with no sense of control over their own destinies.

The next major battle was planned for 8 August, when the Australian Corps would form the centre of a major attack. 4th Army, with British III Corps, would be on their left flank, and the Canadian Corps was brought down secretly from the Arras sector to form the right flank, with the French 1st Army flanking the Canadians.

Haig was most anxious that this attack should be an overwhelming success, and in his orders to General Rawlinson told him to advance as rapidly as possible and capture the old Amiens line of defence.

430 tanks were to lead the three-stage attack, and, if the infantry broke through, three British cavalry divisions would exploit their success.

The first blow was to be delivered on 8 August by the Australians, Canadians, and British III Corps, in conjunction with the French 1st Army further south. But, on 6 August, there was a setback on the British sector. The Germans reacted somewhat belatedly to one of the Australian exercises in peaceful penetration, carried out at Morlancourt on the night of 30 July. The Australians had captured three officers, 135 other ranks, thirty-six machine-guns, and two trench mortars, and were justifiably pleased with themselves as they vacated their positions to the British on the following day. But the Germans planned vengeance, brought up fresh troops, and the relieving British caught the full fury of their reprisal.

Consequently the British III Corps front was pushed back 800 yards less than two days before the Battle of Amiens was due to begin, but Haig gave them no respite. He instructed that, "General Butler (III Corps Commander) has now been told that, so far as his corps is concerned, the battle has begun, and he must carry out his orders as best he can, so as to cover the left of the Australian Corps when they advance on the 8th." Instead of resting on the day before the battle, the British had to spend it recovering the ground they had lost.

At 4.20 a.m. on 8 August, the artillery opened up with a creeping barrage, and the infantry followed the shellbursts forward. At first the troops moved through a dense Somme Valley fog made even thicker by a smoke screen, but it did not hinder their steady progress across the battlefield. Then, as the sun grew stronger, the fog rose and revealed the magnificence of the advance. Infantry in lines of hundreds of men, tanks, guns, artillery horse teams, cavalry and transport were all pressing forward across the German positions.

By 7 a.m. the Australians had reached their first objective, by 10.30 a.m. their second, and by 11 a.m. the Canadians were up beside them on the southern flank. At 1.30 p.m. the Australians and Canadians had occupied all their objectives, but the British III Corps had faltered in the advance. This had allowed the Australian north flank to be enfiladed by heavy fire from the Chipilly spur, and caused heavy casualties.

The co-operation of the Australians and Canadian Corps was superb and the blow they had struck was described by General Ludendorff as: "The black day of the German Army in the history of the war." In his memoirs, he wrote, "This was the worst experience I had to go through. Early on 8 August, in a dense fog that had been rendered still thicker by artificial means, the British, mainly with Australian and Canadian divisions and French attacked between Albert and Moreuil with strong squadrons of tanks, but for the rest with no great superiority."

The Australians captured 183 officers, 7,742 other ranks, and 173 guns, for a loss of some 3,000 men. The Canadians had been similarly successful, by capturing 114 officers, 4,919 other ranks, and 161 guns, for slightly greater losses than the Australians.

During the next few days, both these corps and the French further south continued to exploit their initial successes. By the middle of August they had reached the trenches of the old Somme battlefield, and came up against a strong German front running south from the Somme through the villages of Chuignes and Herleville.

The Australians and Canadians had advanced a total of twelve to fourteen miles and the Australian casualties for the whole offensive amounted to about 6,000. The Canadians were withdrawn from the Somme sector, and returned to their old stamping ground at Arras.

For the next several weeks General Monash's men continued intense offensive activity. This included the Battle of Chuignes, which was in support of a major offensive launched further north by the British 3rd Army, in what was better known as the Battle of Albert. In a succession of quick advances, the Australians reached the Somme near Péronne, where the river comes in sharply with a right-angled bend from the south. This, together with the marshes, formed an obstacle to the Australian advance. On the north bank of the Somme, the 3rd Australian Division had fought its

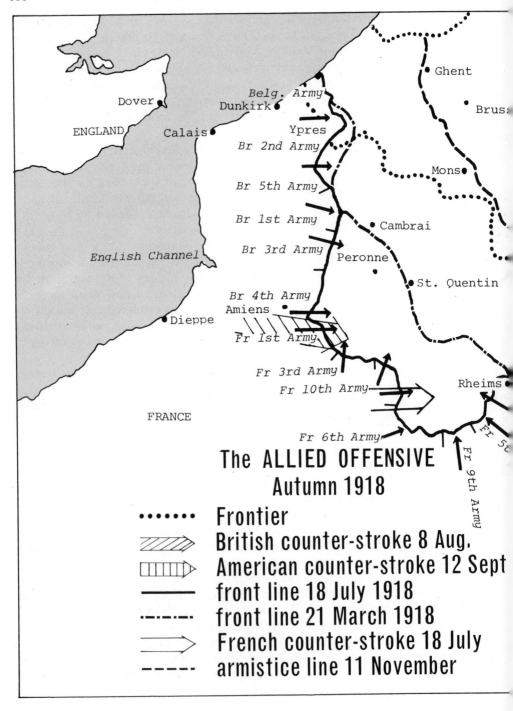

The **ALLIED OFFENSIVE**
Autumn 1918

·······	Frontier
▨▨▨▷	British counter-stroke 8 Aug.
▭▭▭▷	American counter-stroke 12 Sept
———	front line 18 July 1918
·—·—·—	front line 21 March 1918
⟹	French counter-stroke 18 July
------	armistice line 11 November

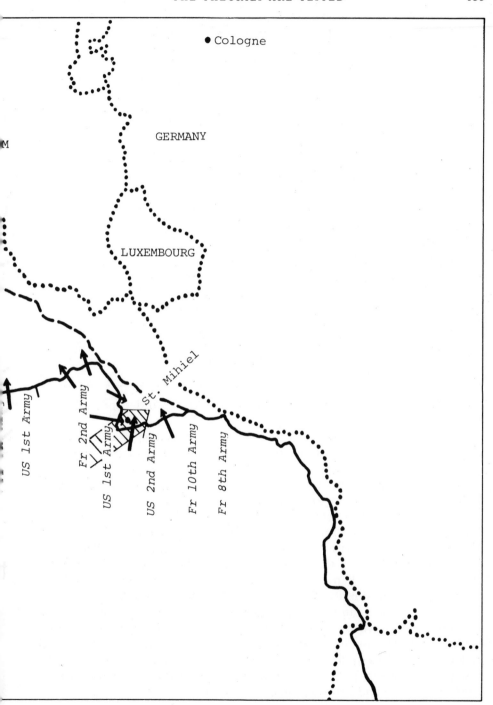

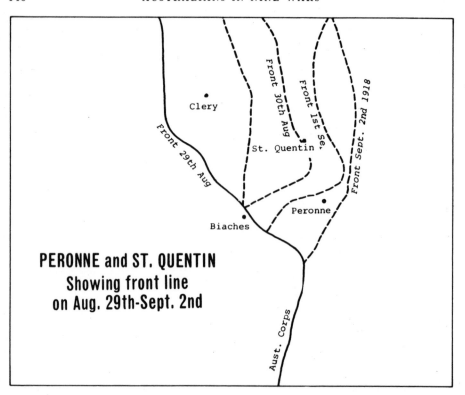

PERONNE and ST. QUENTIN
Showing front line
on Aug. 29th-Sept. 2nd

way along the slopes and valleys beside the river, and captured Bray, Susanne and Curlu.

These limited offensive actions by the Australians came to a climax with what various writers have described as the "finest feat of the war;" the capture of Mont St Quentin. This height, north of the Somme, had been called "a Gibraltar commanding the passages of the Somme and access to Péronne," and was the key to the whole region.

General Monash laid before his Army Commander, Rawlinson, plans to transfer his main strength to the northern side of the Somme and then rush Mont St Quentin with three battalions. Incredulously, Rawlinson demanded, "And so you think you're going to take Mont St Quentin with three battalions?" When Monash assured him that it could be done he replied, "What presumption! However, I don't think I ought to stop you! So go ahead and try, and I wish you luck!"

Monash must have spoken very convincingly, because in spite of his initial scepticism Rawlinson changed the direction of his Army's advance to conform to Monash's plan. The Germans, however, were well aware of the importance of Mont St Quentin, and had garrisoned it with troops which included the élite 2nd Prussian Guards Division.

THE WESTERN FRONT II. *Top:* Wounded being treated in an advanced dressing-station near Ypres, September 1917. *Bottom:* Gassed Australian soldiers lying in the open in front of an overcrowded aid post near Bois de l'Abbe. They had been gassed in the operations in front of Villers-Bretonneux.

Monash prepared the assault with his usual precision. He set his engineers to building new bridges over the Somme and repairing the old ones, and on 29 and 30 August the 3rd Division continued its advance along the northern bank of the Somme. They cleared the enemy from most of his positions covering the river bend, and towards the evening of 30 August the first men of the 2nd Division could be seen passing close around the bend.

The 3rd Division drove the Germans out of Clery and allowed the 2nd to pass through, but the enemy still retained their hold on a mile of ground from which the main attack was to be launched next day.

The 20th Battalion of the 5th Brigade, which was to support the three battalions to be used for the assault, had to clear the way. They hammered their way through the mile-deep trench system, and after nightfall finally reached the starting point for the coming attack. In this operation, the battalion took 120 prisoners and captured eleven machine-guns, but took heavy losses in the process.

The 17th, 18th, and 19th Battalions of the 5th Brigade moved into the positions cleared for them by the 20th Battalion; only seventy officers and 1,250 men in all, because the battalions had been badly knocked about in the previous days of fighting. But while the shell-fragments of their artillery barrage were still falling on the Germans, the Australians rose out of their trenches in the cold pre-dawn darkness; yelling like fiends and keeping up a rapid fire in order to make the Germans think that they were being attacked by a larger force. Monash wrote later that he had modelled the attack on the sudden onslaughts perfected by Stonewall Jackson during the American Civil War, following a swift turning movement during the night which had deceived the enemy as to the direction of the attack.

The Australians burst through the enemy defences and charged Feuilla-court and the main height, making up for the lack of numbers by the sheer speed and savagery of their attack. "It all happened like lightning, and before we had fired a shot we were taken unawares," the historian of the Guard Alexander Regiment wrote after the war.

On the right flank, the 19th Battalion encountered heavy opposition from enemy troops in a ruined sugar factory at St Denis, on the main road between Péronne and St Quentin, but by 7 a.m. the three battalions had overwhelmed the fortress. General Rawlinson was shaving before breakfast when Monash telephoned to tell him of the victory.

But the Prussian Guard was not to be defeated so easily. The Germans quickly reorganised and launched a savage counter-attack, which drove the Australians out of their thinly held positions in Mont St Quentin village, on the crest of the height. Reinforcements were hurried up to them as they held on grimly just below the summit, and at midnight the four battalions were relieved by the 6th Brigade. During that day they had taken a fortress, beaten off five separate counter-attacks, and taken 800 prisoners—

THE WESTERN FRONT, III. *Top:* Australians had to fight their way through country like this in their Passchendaele attacks on German concrete redoubts. *Centre:* German dead in their front line after its capture by Australians in the Menin Road Battle of the Passchendaele operations. *Bottom:* The band of the 5th Brigade marches through the smouldering ruins of Bapaume, on 19 March 1917.

but at fearful loss to themselves. Only eight officers and seventy-five men of the 17th Battalion were left to plod wearily back down the hill.

Next day, 1 September, the 6th Brigade assaulted the summit in a vicious close-quarters action, in which the bayonet was the weapon most freely used by both sides. General Monash was driving his troops to the utmost of his endurance, knowing that if he lost the initiative the "Gibraltar of the Somme" would have to be recaptured at far greater loss. He brought the 14th Brigade of the 5th Division around through Clery, and they drove the Germans out of the woods north of Péronne. Thrusting downwards, they charged across the moat and drove the Germans back in savage street-fighting. They captured the main part of the town, but when they tried to pass around it to the north they were stopped by withering fire from the ramparts.

Next day, the 2nd Brigade of the 2nd Division drove beyond Mont St Quentin, and the 15th Brigade of the 5th Division completed the capture of Péronne.

In an operation supreme in courage and tactical skill, the Australians had knocked the Germans completely off balance by a series of infantry attacks performed without the aid of artillery or tanks. During three days, they had captured the vital Mont St Quentin-Péronne complex of defences and communications, which the Germans had planned to hold at any cost, and the Australian victory was one of the major blows which forced the enemy to retire beyond the Somme to the Hindenburg Line.

The Australians won six Victoria Crosses during the three days of fighting, but lost 3,000 in killed and wounded. It was no wonder that the Germans were beginning to regard them as their major threat. Their cartoonists represented Lloyd George as climbing to victory on a heap of Canadian and Australian corpses, and, as Monash said later, made the British Government even more unwilling to acknowledge Australian successes because they were afraid that the Dominion troops would begin to believe the enemy propaganda.

General Rawlinson stated in an Order of the Day: "The capture of Mont St Quentin is a feat of arms worthy of the highest praise. The natural strength of the position is immense and the tactical value of it, in reference to Péronne and the whole system of the Somme defences, cannot be over estimated. I am filled with admiration for the gallantry and surpassing daring of the 2nd Division in winning this important fortress, and I congratulate them with all my heart."

Monash was equally quick to congratulate Major-General Rosenthal, the Commander of the 2nd Division, and wrote to him: "On the completion of the present series of operations by the 2nd Australian Division, I tender you my warmest thanks for the brilliant services which they have rendered. The performance of the Division since they have resumed duty in the line on 24 August have been on the highest plain of merit. While all troops and services of the Division have contributed to these great successes, no one will begrudge the singling out of the 5th Brigade for special praise. The capture of Mont St Quentin has evoked a chorus of praise throughout the Press of the world as the finest single feat of the war, and this high encomium is richly deserved. The subsequent decisive defence of that important key position by the 6th and 7th Brigades is not less noticeable."

Concurrent with the success of the Australian operations, the Canadians further north had made a vital break through on the Drocourt-Quéant switch line, thus forcing the withdrawal of the Germans behind the Sensee and the Canal du Nord. Most of the gains that the Germans had made on the British front, in the great offensive launched on 21 March had now been lost again, mainly through the relentless efforts of the Australians and Canadians.

Nor had he been any more successful further south. The reorganised French armies, together with the Americans who had fought their first major battle of the twentieth century at Chateau Thierry, had spoiled his thrust towards Paris. The brief weeks of feverish triumph which the Germans had enjoyed, and in which it had actually seemed for a while as though they might win on the Western Front, were at an end. But Ludendorff was not yet ready to give in.

On the British 4th Army sector, where the Australian Corps was employed, the Germans withdrew into the immensely strong defences of the Hindenburg Line. The ground in front of it was protected by a belt of wire "which nothing but a rat could get through." Up to a hundred yards wide, it was a dense maze of wickedly barbed wire strung on stout posts, pierced only by alleys designed to bunch the attackers so that they could be slaughtered by machine-gun fire.

In front of this were the three trench lines which had been dug and fortified by the British Army during its previous threat to the Line, and which had been captured by the Germans during the March offensive. The first of these was captured by the Australians on 11 September, using "peaceful penetration" tactics, but the other two were too strongly held to yield to anything but a full-scale assault.

Rawlinson obtained permission for such an attack, which began at dawn on 18 September in dense fog and heavy rain. The 1st and 4th Australian Divisions formed the spearhead of the ten divisions of the 4th Army, and both divisions reached their objectives during the day. Men of the 1st Division took the second and third German lines, while the 4th Division fought its way across the shallow valleys of the area right up to the dense wire protecting the Hindenburg Outpost Line, then worked round through the trenches captured by the 1st and finally bombed its way into the remnants of the enemy defences in front of the Line. By dawn on 19 September, the

Australians were in position along the St Quentin Canal, and could look over it to the main Hindenburg Line.

With a total assault strength of 5,900 men, the two Australian divisions captured 4,300 prisoners and 79 guns, out of the total of 12,000 prisoners taken by the 4th Army. But it was the last battle of these two divisions whose brilliant fighting career had begun three and a half years before: one on the cliffs of Gallipoli and the other in Egypt. The accumulation of heavy casualties, a slackening in the supply of reinforcements, and a system of well-deserved home leave for the veterans who had served since Gallipoli, had eaten away the fighting strength of the two famous divisions.

16

VICTORY EAST AND WEST

GENERAL ALLENBY HAD ENTERED JERUSALEM ON FOOT, WALKING through the Jaffa Gate to the Citadel in a manner which he deliberately made unceremonious as befitted the liberator of the Holy City. "I make known to you that every sacred building, monument, holy spot, shrine or place of prayer will be maintained and protected according to the existing customs and beliefs of those to whose faith they are sacred," he said in his proclamation to the citizens, and as an earnest of his intentions he kept most of his troops out of the city.

The final battle for Jerusalem had been won by British infantry of London regiments, who had advanced under bitter wintry conditions of mud and rain and stormed the ridges around the city. With Jerusalem secured, Allenby planned to consolidate his achievements so far by holding on to his northern front on one hand, and advancing across Jordan to link up with T. E. Lawrence's Arab troops on the other. For the time being, a further thrust towards Damascus and Aleppo was hampered by the winter rains which had caused considerable damage to road and rail communications.

But Lloyd George, in London, was seeking for some means of drawing the enemy strength away from the Western Front, and sought permission from the Joint Allied Staff at Versailles for an offensive in Palestine which would compromise the Turkish attitude towards the Germans and knock away the enemy props in the Balkans or Middle East. He was adamantly opposed to the sausage-machine strategy of the Western Front commanders, and in his *Memoirs* states that if the men wasted on the Somme had been used in Palestine, then Turkey might have been broken in time for the Allies to save

Roumania, equip Russia, and end the war two years earlier. "The military advisers who scorned the Palestine campaign as a futile and wasteful 'sideshow' have a heavy reckoning to settle," he wrote, and his opinion was justified by the fact that one of the reasons given by Ludendorff for seeking an armistice was the collapse of the Bulgarian Army, which meant that Roumania could be retaken by the Allies and its supplies of wheat and petrol denied to Germany.

In early 1918, Lloyd George sought an offensive designed to drive up to Aleppo, in Syria, but the estimate of troops and supplies required for such an offensive was gravely in excess of available resources. As a compromise, General Jan Smuts was sent to Palestine by the War Cabinet, and he recommended that British operations in Mesopotamia be halted and that two divisions and a cavalry brigade be transferred from that front to Allenby's in Palestine. If Allenby succeeded in reaching Aleppo, this would in any case cut the Turkish communications with Mesopotamia and force the Turks there to surrender.

While the War Cabinet was discussing this recommendation, Allenby was beginning to move. He commenced a campaign of active support for the Arabs who were harassing the Turkish garrison at Ma'an, sixty miles south of the Dead Sea and on the Pilgrims' Railway to Mecca, and decided to destroy the railway where it passed along the high plateau east of the River Jordan, at the town of Amman.

By February 1918, the British line had been pushed eastwards to the valley of the Jordan, nearly 4,000 feet below and to the west of the Dead Sea. In this movement the Anzac Mounted Division had outflanked the Turks, who withdrew from Jericho. This city was occupied on 21 February, thus establishing the line along the Jordan valley.

Smuts' plan was accepted by the Cabinet towards the end of February, and when Allenby launched his raid on Amman he believed that he was going to be reinforced for his drive towards Aleppo. The Light Horse columns marched across the Jordan Valley on 23 March, crossing the River Jordan and heading for the hills in which Amman and Es Salt lay on a plateau 4,000 feet above sea level.

The attack was to be made along three tracks, but the continuing winter rains had made two of them impassable to vehicles and the third nearly so. Despite this, the Light Horsemen made rapid headway, and captured Es Salt on the evening of 25 March.

Brigadier Ryrie's 2nd Light Horse Brigade, and the New Zealand Mounted Rifles, had taken a separate route towards Amman, and cut the railway north and south of the town. But, despite two days of stiff fighting by the Anzac force, they could not take Amman from the mixed force of Turks and Germans which held the defences.

On 30 March the Light Horse was ordered to withdraw, and crossed the

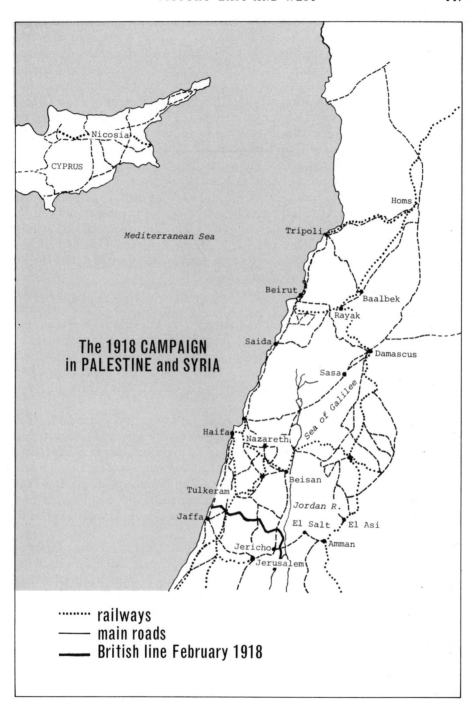

The 1918 CAMPAIGN
in PALESTINE and SYRIA

CYPRUS

Nicosia

Mediterranean Sea

Homs

Tripoli

Beirut

Baalbek

Rayak

Saida

Damascus

Sasa

Sea of Galilee

Haifa

Nazareth

Beisan

Tulkeram

Jordan R.

Jaffa

El Salt   El Asi

Jericho

Amman

Jerusalem

·········· railways
———— main roads
━━━━ British line February 1918

River Jordan again on 2 April. The Turks followed them down out of the hills, and on 11 April attacked at Ghoraniyeh, where a bridgehead across the Jordan had been established. They were beaten off with heavy casualties.

By mid-April, the Arab irregulars fighting against their ancient enemy had cut the Pilgrims' Railway in so many places that it had become useless to the Turks, but Allenby was conscious that his raid on Amman and Es Salt had not given them as much help as he wished. The Hedjaz Arabs gave him a grandiloquent promise that they would support his next attack on the Turks with "20,000 rifles," and he planned another blow for 30 April.

For this, which was to become known as the second battle of Es Salt, his objectives were the foothills of Shunet Nimrin and the town on the plateau above them. Chauvel launched the Australian Mounted Division and the 60th British Infantry Division into the attack, with the infantry assaulting Turkish positions in the foothills while the Light Horse crossed the Jordan at Jisr ed Damie ford. The 4th Light Horse Brigade remained at the ford, to hold off an attack from west of the river, while the 3rd Light Horse, under Brigadier Wilson, went on to Es Salt.

They clambered up the stony ridges and made a vigorous attack on the town, which fell to them during the night. But their success was shortlived, because the rest of the operation had failed. The Turks launched a savage assault on the 4th Light Horse at the Jordan crossing, and forced them to withdraw after hard fighting, while the Turkish positions along the foothills beat off the attempt to overrun them. Success had been dependent upon surprise, which had not been achieved, and the Hedjaz Arabs had not materialised.

A Turkish Army Corps hurried down the Jordan valley, crossed the river on a pontoon bridge, and placed themselves firmly across the supply and reinforcement route to the Allied forces. The men and horses of Allenby's divisions were cut off in hungry, mountainous country from which the waters of the winter rains had run away. With his troops in position, the German General Liman von Sanders, commander of the Turkish and German forces in the area, began a fierce counter-attack. It was designed to wipe out the trapped divisions.

At Chauvel's headquarters, well up towards the front, they saw a cloud of dust racing towards them across the desert, and soon Allenby's staff car pulled up near the Corps pennant. The "Bull" jumped out and strode across to Chauvel, who pointed out the exact situation on the map. The staff officers watched curiously as the English general, whose burly frame seemed compact with the smashing force and energy with which he had taken command of the situation in the Middle East, listened to the quiet voice of the wiry little Australian.

When Chauvel had finished, Allenby paced up and down in obvious agitation, clasping and unclasping his big hands behind his back. Then he stopped suddenly, and as though every word caused him pain jerked out, "Chauvel! Order general retirement! Retreat is deplorable—but capture would be a debacle!"

Chauvel smiled slightly, and said quietly, "Very good, sir. There will be no capture."

Allenby got back in his car and sped off to another sector, leaving Chauvel in charge of the situation. His achievement during the next few days has been described as a classic in rearguard fighting. Taking advantage of every weakness in the Turkish line, he was indefatigable in the direction of the most difficult military operation of all; extricating a force cut off from its main body from the grip of a superior enemy.

Unit by unit, almost man by man, his troops fought their way out. They withdrew from Es Salt on 4 May, and the troopers slithered down precipitous wadis on horseback, with every second horse of the rearguard carrying a wounded man as well as its own rider. When the line was firm again, Chauvel's first words were of praise for his men.

The repulse of this thrust showed that the Turco-German alliance still had plenty of sting in its tail, but it had the effect of making Liman von Sanders focus his attention on the inland flank, east of the Jordan, whereas Allenby planned to break through on the coastal plains.

His task was made harder by Ludendorff's massive offensive on the Western Front. Instead of Allenby's forces being built up, they were robbed of twenty-two British infantry battalions and most of his Yeomanry, which were converted to machine gun companies. A total of 60,000 men was hurried from Palestine to France to help to stem the German tide.

The remaining British infantry and cavalry were reorganised to become the nuclei of Indian divisions, though the 54th Division remained unchanged. Two new cavalry divisions, the 4th and 5th, resulted from this reorganisation.

The Australian Mounted Division now became completely Australian, when the 5th (British) Yeomanry Brigade was ordered to France and was replaced by the 5th Light Horse Brigade under Brigadier G. M. McArthur-Onslow, a New South Wales pastoralist. They had been serving with the Imperial Camel Brigade, which was now disbanded. Their fellow brigades in the Division were the 3rd Light Horse under Brigadier L. Wilson, a Queensland solicitor, and the 4th Light Horse under Brigadier W. Grant, a Queensland pastoralist. Officers and men of the Light Horse Brigades knew these commanders to be tough fighting men who shared their dangers, hardships, and triumphs to the full, but they were irritated by the fact that the division was commanded by Major-General H. L. Hodgson, a British cavalry officer. There were many brilliant Light Horse leaders who would have been ideal for the divisional command.

The Anzac Mounted Division was unaffected by the reorganisation, It still consisted of the 1st Light Horse Brigade, under Brigadier C. F. Cox; the

2nd Light Horse Brigade under Brigadier G. de L. Ryrie, a bluff Australian pastoralist, politician, and pugilist; and the New Zealand Mounted Brigade. The Division was commanded by Major-General Sir E. W. C. Chaytor, the great New Zealand leader.

These two magnificent divisions, battle-hardened and by this time well seasoned by the harsh conditions of the desert, were the iron core of the force which Allenby was building up for his drive towards Damascus. He needed all of his vast energy to create a new army out of the material which had been sent to him to replace the troops taken for the Western Front. Lloyd George says that the twenty-two battalions of Indian infantry which were hurried to Palestine were raw recruits who had seen no service. Many of them had not even fired their musketry courses, and they had hardly any signallers, few machine gunners, and no bombers. Most of their British officers were as raw as the rankers, and since the majority of them could not speak Hindustani they had great difficulty in communicating with troops who spoke no English.

While Allenby hammered them into shape, the Australians sweated out the summer and kept in trim for the next attack. Their main enemies were malaria, sandfly fever, heat, and boredom, but on 14 July they had to fight off a strong German attack on their positions in the Jordan valley, near the two prominent hills Mus Allabeh and Abu Tellul. They held the line, and the Germans retreated after suffering heavy casualties.

At last Allenby was ready to move, and at dawn on 19 September he began his move up the coast. He was faced by three Turkish armies with a stiffening of Germans; the 4th, 7th, and 8th. Their total strength was believed to be 103,090, though later reports revealed them to be considerably stronger. Disease, desertion, and the shortage of supplies which by that time was afflicting all the enemy nations had reduced them to a poor state of morale, but they were still capable of ruthless fighting in attack or defence. Allenby had a ration strength of 140,000, divided into three army corps, but many of them were still semi-trained troops who had yet to hear their first shot fired in anger.

On the morning of 17 September, General Allenby in company with Chauvel visited the divisional headquarters of the Australian Mounted Division, at which the divisional commander and all the brigade and regimental commanders were present. After greeting each officer present, Allenby said, "I have come, gentlemen, to wish you good luck, and to tell you that my impression is that you are on the eve of a great victory. Everything depends—well, perhaps not everything, but nearly everything, on the secrecy, rapidity, and accuracy of the cavalry movement."

The Battle of Sharon, or Armageddon as Allenby preferred to call it, was about to be launched. It culminated in the destruction of the Turkish 7th and 8th Armies, and together with the subsequent rout resulted in the capture of 75,000 Turkish and German prisoners and vast quantities of supplies and equipment.

By 9 a.m. on 19 September, General Chauvel was leading the Australian, Anzac, and Indian mounted divisions over the enemy's old trenches, while the infantry wheeled north-eastwards into the hills to attack Tul Keram and other positions. Allenby's two cavalry divisions drove parallel along the coast to cross the Carmel range, and before dawn emerged on the plain of Esdraelon, about thirty miles behind the Turkish front, just in time to prevent the enemy from blocking the Musmus Pass. They continued their drive to the north and captured Nazareth that evening, with General von Sanders and his staff narrowly escaping capture by the Indians.

While the Indians were driving the Turks out of Nazareth, Chauvel had sent his mounted brigades along a more easterly track through the Carmel range, detaching the 3rd Light Horse to attack Jenin in order to cut off the Turkish retreat in the centre of their line. They took 2,000 German and Turkish prisoners.

The 10th Light Horse Regiment, of the 3rd Brigade, wheeled southwards again, until they sighted elements of the enemy's main force. In a monumental feat of bluff they opened fire and attacked, deceiving the Turks into thinking that they were a much stronger detachment than they were. 3,000 Turks surrendered, more were rounded up, and by next morning the 3rd Brigade held a total of 8,000 prisoners at Jenin.

The divisional commander, Major-General Hodgson, said when visiting the regiment, "Well done, the Tenth. I suppose never before in the history of the world has such a number of prisoners been taken by so small a force as one regiment." Not only were 8,107 prisoners captured, but several divisional commanders as well.

Now that Allenby had the enemy on the run, he kept pressing them hard. Chauvel's mounted force of Australians, New Zealanders, Britons and Indians were constantly on the move. Their target was Damascus, and the Light Horsemen with their comrades hounded the enemy northwards. Beisan, through which the Turkish communications ran to the Jordan valley, was captured by the 4th Indian Cavalry, and Haifa, on the coast, fell to the 5th Indian Cavalry. The 5th Light Horse, in support of British infantry at Tul Keram, destroyed the railway line at Samaria, behind the enemy centre.

Overhead, the R.A.F., and Australian Flying Corps squadrons created havoc among the defeated and disorganised columns of retreating Turks and Germans along the Balata-Ferweh-Shibleh-Jordan road. This was the old Roman highway, with steep hills on the left and a sheer precipice into the Wadi Beisan on the right. The airmen began their attacks at dawn on 21 September, when aircraft caught the 7th Army transport pouring into Balata where 600 wagons and guns were crowded along the road. In

Khurbet Ferweh, and for a mile or two beyond, were another 200 horse-drawn wagons, and more long columns were approaching Ain Shibleh.

The terrible massacre continued all day, until the passes were completely blocked. The airmen were sickened by the slaughter they had caused, including men who were dragged over the precipice by the maddened animals.

Three days later, when Chauvel's cavalry passed along the road, they counted the terrible toll. 837 four-wheeled wagons, 87 guns, 55 motor lorries, 75 carts, 4 motor cars and scores of water carts and field kitchens had been smashed and abandoned, with the corpses of men and animals still lying among them. The air attack may be seen as the prototype of the "blitzkrieg" operation which the Germans used so devastatingly in the second World War.

Chauvel sent his tough mobile columns to deal punch after punch at the crumbling enemy front. With a masterly tactical stroke, he forestalled von Sanders' attempt to defend Damascus, and this resulted in one of the stiffest encounters of the whole campaign. Liman von Sanders planned to check the advance in the region of Lake Tiberias, by holding the Yarmuk Gorge, east of the southern end of the lake, and the country on the south and west of the lake. Chauvel decided to break through the defence line at Semakh, a little railway town on the southern end of the lake, and sent the 4th Light Horse Brigade to do the job.

On 25 September they came in sight of the town, and discovered that the enemy had built a heavily defended strong point which included the stone buildings of the railway station, a stationary train, railway engines, and other material dragged together to barricade the position. It was held by Turks and a strong detachment of Germans, including machine gunners, and a more cautious commander than Brigadier Grant might have decided to withdraw his horsemen and wait for artillery support. Instead, he led a hell-for-leather attack on the position, and the Australians broke through the defences and came to bayonet point with the enemy. It developed into a furious and bloody battle in which the Light Horsemen fought Turks and Germans in and around the railway station and even in the corridors and compartments of the train, but ended with what was left of the enemy running away or surrendering.

General von Sanders' line of defence was broken, and on the same day the Anzac Mounted Division had advanced out of the Jordan valley and assaulted Amman, capturing the town and taking the Turkish 4th Army's rearguard as prisoners; another 4,500 men to swell the great mob of defeated enemy which was being driven to the rear, while Lawrence and his Arabs snapped at the Turkish flanks.

Chauvel's handling of his three cavalry divisions was a dominating and dramatic feature of the great offensive. Despite the rugged country and the speed of the advance, he kept complete control over his scattered columns and synchronised their activities so exactly that they maintained a series of staggering blows on the rapidly disintegrating enemy, keeping them so constantly off balance that the Battle of Sharon was the ultimate success in an unbroken line of victory since Romani.

In 1919, Chauvel said that this period was the most interesting and important part of his service in the A.I.F., and remarked that the destruction of the Turkish armies at Sharon led indirectly to the surrender of Bulgaria. Turkey had promised to help Bulgaria, then being attacked by an Allied force from Salonica, with a reinforcement of seven divisions, but after Sharon it was obvious that Turkey was on the verge of collapse. The defeat at Sharon also led directly to the destruction of the 4th Turkish Army soon afterwards, and the surrender of Turkey. "As a demonstration of the value of cavalry in open warfare and the combination of all arms, including the Air Force, in defence, attack, and pursuit, these campaigns have been without parallel in modern history and an invaluable school for the Australian soldier," he said.

The 5th Light Horse entered Damascus at 5 a.m. on 1 October 1918, closely followed by the other units of the 3rd Brigade. It was a scene of incredible confusion, with the horsemen pushing their way through screaming throngs of Arabs celebrating the end of Turkish rule, and Lawrence with his desert sheikhs who already were beginning to squabble over the spoils of victory.

Next day, Australian detachments pursued remnants of the Turkish force fifteen miles north of Damascus, and rounded them up after some half-hearted skirmishes.

This was virtually the final operation of Australian troops on this front, though Chauvel himself, in command of the Indian cavalry divisions, continued with the northward push into Lebanon and Syria. They drove the Turks steadily before them, and at last Allenby captured Aleppo, the capital of Turkey-in-Asia. On 30 October the Turkish Government offered armistice terms which were almost unconditional surrender, and the war in the east was over.

* * *

"I commenced today a series of decisive battle operations," Monash wrote to his wife on 27 September 1918. He referred to the beginning of the attack against the Hindenburg Line. He had drawn up a detailed and elaborate plan for a breakthrough offensive, which had been accepted by Haig, and for six days had been holding a series of conferences at which he spoke with his customary lucidity, explaining each formation's exact task in relation to the whole order of battle.

Haig had allocated what he termed "the main attack" to the Australian Corps, which was to assault the Hindenburg Line at a point where the

St Quentin Canal ran in a tunnel beneath the hills between Bellicourt and Vendhuille. The land in fact formed a bridge over the subterranean canal. It was three and a half miles wide, and at a point where the enemy could be fairly certain of an attack.

Two major problems faced the Australians. The "tunnel sector," allocated to them for their vital spearhead role, was north of their recent gains in front of the Hindenburg Line. Despite several attempts by the British III Corps, the Hindenburg Outpost Line had not been captured in this sector, and consequently the start-line for the attack lay about half a mile in front of the British sector. As Monash wrote: "The best troops of the United Kingdom have long ago been used up and we now have a class of man who is without initiative or individuality. They are brave enough, but simply unskilful . . . Very few English divisions can today be classed as first-class fighting troops, relied upon to carry out the tasks set."

The second problem was depletion of Australian strength now that the 1st and 4th Divisions had been withdrawn from the line, and so the Australian Corps was reinforced by American II Corps, comprising the 27th and 30th Divisions under Major-General G. W. Read, who was insistent that his troops should be under the active command of Monash during the battle.

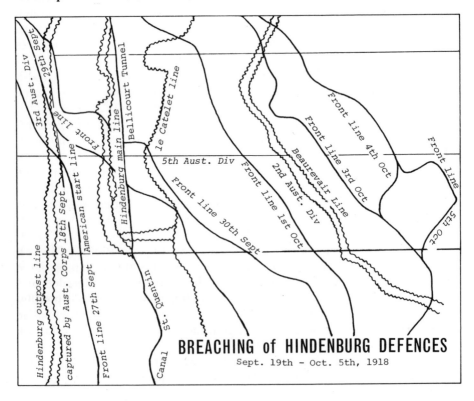

BREACHING of HINDENBURG DEFENCES
Sept. 19th – Oct. 5th, 1918

"These are strong divisions and the men are of a very fine quality, although the commanders and staff are quite inexperienced," Monash wrote, and he brought back 217 of his veteran officers and men from the 1st and 4th Divisions to give tactical advice to the Americans.

The 27th American Division took over most of the sector held by British III Corps on the left of the Australians, and the 30th American Division moved up on the right flank. Monash planned for the Americans to attack the main German line, on the ground above the tunnel, and the second, or Le Catelet line, a mile further east. The 3rd and 5th Australian Divisions were to pass through the gap which had been made, carry on the attack for about another three miles, and break through the last line of defences at Beaurevoir. He relied upon them to break through without the assistance of a creeping barrage, though it was proposed to use tanks in support of each divisional thrust. To screen the troops and guns attacking over the tunnel sector, the preliminary barrage was thickened by smoke shells, especially on the flanks. When the tunnel sector itself had been captured, the Allied troops would fan out to seize the north and south banks of the St Quentin Canal on the eastern side of the tunnel.

Soon after the American infantry of the 27th Division had been brought up to the front they attempted to advance across the half-mile between their trenches to a start-line which would be level with the rest of the attack. They achieved a partial success but could not hold on to their gains, and were driven back into their positions. Monash decided that they should make another attempt just before the main attack was due to go on, so that the whole advance would start on the same line.

They attacked without preliminary barrage but with the help of additional tanks, and on 29 September the whole American line was moving forward through thick mist and smoke. Their early success signals gave the impression that they were rolling the Germans before them, but when the Australians advanced at 11 a.m. they ran into strong German opposition between them and where the Americans were supposed to be.

Western Front veterans had learnt long before that not even the heaviest barrage, nor the first wave of the most determined assault, would wipe out every pocket of resistance. Always there remained survivors who emerged from deep dugouts or from somewhere beneath the wreckage, and with the customary tenacity and devotion of the German Army would fight their guns until further resistance was hopeless. The Australians had become used to mopping up such rearguards before reporting that a captured position was secure, but the wild charge of the enthusiastic but inexperienced Americans had overlooked this necessity. And, on this occasion, even stronger enemy formations than usual had been overlooked, because the Germans had kept reinforcements hiding in the tunnel.

Consequently the Australian 3rd and 5th Divisions found themselves confronted with the task of carrying out the American attack all over again, and saving a situation which was falling to pieces. It took them three days of fierce fighting to re-establish the plan of attack, without the support of the tanks and artillery which had cleared the way for the Americans.

The 5th Division found that the 30th Americans had captured part of its objective, which was the southern entrance to the tunnel at Bellicourt village, but had been stopped dead without entering the village. The Australians quickly summed up the situation and surged through the scattered American formations, carrying with them a considerable number of Americans who in the confusion of their first battle had been separated from their own units. The Germans fought back furiously, but in a fierce hand-to-hand encounter the Australians drove them back and swept forward through Bellicourt village, mopping up German pockets of resistance with bomb and bayonet.

The 5th Division made an equally determined attack, and by mid-afternoon both divisions were astride the Hindenburg Main Line; the 5th on the east and the 3rd on the west. During the next two days the Australians went through some of the fiercest fighting ever seen on the Western Front as the Germans battled desperately to hold the line, but the Australians consolidated their positions and captured Bony, Joncourt, and Le Catelet, which were three of the key points in the Hindenburg Line complex of defences.

On 1 October they were relieved; the 5th by the 2nd Australian Division and the 3rd by a British division. Two days later, the 2nd Division broke through the Hindenburg Line over the full width of the Australian Corps front from the strong Beaurevoir defences southwards, and on 5 October Monash sent the fresh 6th Brigade to capture Montbrehain. They succeeded in a brilliant operation which began with a bayonet charge against the German positions, and brought about the complete collapse of the Hindenburg Line.

The way was now open for final victory, but the Australians had fought their last battle on the Western Front. During the night of 5 October 1918 the Australian infantry handed over the line to II American Corps, and were withdrawn for a rest. Before they could be called into the line again, the hammer blows dealt by the American, French, and British armies under the overall command of Marshal Foch had forced the Germans to ask for an armistice.

17

PENALTIES AND REWARDS

From the moment when they first stormed Turkish positions on the heights of Gallipoli, the men of the 1st A.I.F. established a reputation for reckless valour which was enriched during subsequent actions on the Western and Eastern Fronts.

Between 1914 and 1918, Australia produced a fighting army that is unique in modern war. Every single man of the 331,781 who went overseas on active service was a volunteer, and an unusually high proportion of these saw action in the front line or in close support of the fighting troops. This, of course, was because the base facilities without which they could not have operated were provided by the British Army, together with the greater part of their weapons, ammunition, and other supplies. The Australian soldier's hands were left free for fighting.

In France, their contribution to the successes of the British Army was quite disproportionate to the numbers involved, and a considerable share of the glory assumed by that army derived from the efforts of the Australians, Canadians, and New Zealanders. Not until very late in the war did they, and the Australians in particular, receive due credit for their deeds. As late as 11 September 1918 Monash wrote to his wife that the English newspapers had attributed Australian successes to "other troops" who had failed in the same task. He protested about this to the war correspondent of the London *Times* and to General Rawlinson and the Chief of the Imperial General Staff, saying that unless the achievements of Australian troops received their proper public recognition he would not hold himself responsible for the maintenance of their fighting spirit.

"I put it plainly that they are by nature and instinct sportsmen, and that they would refuse to go on playing any game in which their scores were not put up on the scoring-board," he wrote. His protests were successful, and at long last the London press began to make specific mention of the Australian troops instead of lumping them together under such references as "our men in France."

From 27 March to 5 October 1918, the five divisions of the Australian Corps engaged a total of thirty-nine German divisions. On every occasion, they checked their assaults, captured their positions, or broke through their lines. They captured a total of 29,144 prisoners and 338 guns, and liberated 116 towns and villages.

In Monash's analysis of the Australian effort, he showed that although the Australian Corps represented only 9½ per cent of the total strength of the British Army engaged on the Western Front during this period, they captured 23 per cent of the prisoners taken and 23¼ per cent of the guns, and re-occupied 21½ per cent of the reconquered territory.

The cost was extremely high. Out of every six men engaged, at least one paid the penalty for Australian success by losing his life, suffering a wound, or being recorded as "missing in action"—which almost invariably meant that he had been buried or blown to pieces by a shell. The total casualty list was 25,000 during less than seven months.

By the end of the war, the Australian Corps was regarded as the supreme formation on the Western Front, for reasons which were obvious to unprejudiced observers. Brigadier-General Sir James Edmonds, the official British war historian, wrote in *Military Operations France and Belgium 1918* that: "The leading of the Canadian and Australian officers and N.C.O.'s was superior to that of the British regimental cadres, and no doubt for the reason that they had been selected for their practical experience and power over men and not for theoretical proficiency and general education." In the British Army, the old ways died hard.

The contemporary British historian John Terraine, in his book *The Western Front 1914-1918*, reached the same conclusion. He wrote: "The 4th Army included the Canadian Corps and the Australian Corps, which because of a more flexible system of training and discipline and of a more able and enterprising type of officer recruited from wider social backgrounds than the British were the most formidable troops in Haig's command." Such comments also have been made by other writers.

From the landing on Gallipoli onwards, the Australian troops were used as the spearhead of every attack carried out by the various British armies in which they served. For this honour, they paid a terrible price. 59,258 were killed. 166,815 suffered wounds. 4,084 became prisoners of war.

The *Encyclopaedia Britannica* states that the total casualties suffered by troops of the British Empire during the first World War amounted to 35.8 per cent of the forces mobilised for war service. The total Australian casualties, however, amounted to 68½ per cent of their armed forces; one of the highest percentages among the nations engaged in that war. And, bearing in mind the total Australian population at that time, which was less than five million, this is even more significant. Particularly since Australia was a nation which up to that time had only the slightest of military traditions. Unlike the British and European countries, in which war up to that time had been regarded as a romantic occupation for the aristocracy and which were tense with traditional feuds and enmities, Australia had had little disposition towards warfare. Even its military leaders had no greater ambition than to finish the job as quickly as possible—which is perhaps why they fought so efficiently. After the war, Monash said that from 1914 until 1918 he had never known a day which was free from "horror, loathing, and distress."

The penalties had been paid, but the rewards, except for victory itself, were few. As has been seen, overall recognition for the Australian effort was hard to come by. Chauvel, Brudenell White, and Monash all received knighthoods, but the first two find little place in most histories of that war. T. E. Lawrence, whose contribution to the victory is the subject of increasing dissent, is a household name, whereas Chauvel and his Light Horse, who did so much to break the spirit of the Turks, are virtually unknown outside Australia.

Monash received most recognition of all, as was no more than his due. He received the accolade of knighthood from King George V at Australian headquarters at Bertangles, behind the Western Front; the first time for nearly 200 years that a British monarch had knighted a commander in the field. It was a simple but moving ceremony, attended by a guard of honour drawn from all the units that had contributed to his success. After the Armistice, he was a guest at the State Banquet given at Buckingham Palace, and led 5,000 Australian troops in an Anzac Day parade through London in 1919.

The most emphatic tribute was paid to him by the British Prime Minister, David Lloyd George, who wrote in his *Memoirs* that Monash was "... according to the testimony of those who knew well his genius for war and what he accomplished by it, the most resourceful general in the whole British Army." And that: "Unfortunately the British Army did not bring into prominence any commander who, taking him all round, was more conspicuously fitted for the post. No doubt Monash would, if the opportunity had been given him, have risen to the height of it. But the greatness of his abilities was not brought to the attention of the Cabinet in any of the dispatches. Professional soldiers could hardly be expected to advertise the fact that the greatest strategist in the Army was a civilian when the war began, and that they were being surpassed by a man who had not received any of their advantages in training and teaching."

It is fair to note, however, that Lloyd George had developed an extra-ordinary antipathy towards Haig—which was mutual. Haig was always generous in praise of Monash and his work, but could hardly have been expected to recommend him as his own replacement.

Like most Australian soldiers, Monash was very conscious of the somewhat disdainful attitude adopted by Britons of that time towards "Colonials"—an attitude which was perfectly summarised in that popular novel of the period, *Peter Jackson*, in which Gilbert Frankau wrote: "For Peter had never foregathered with Australians, and, like most of his countrymen, was rather inclined to think of them as 'Colonials'—a vague term which formerly typified to the Englishman 'the kind of chap who can't make a living at home.'"

Monash was particularly irritated by sneering comments upon the Australian soldier's alleged lack of discipline, and wrote: "Very much and very stupid comment has been made upon the discipline of the Australian soldier. That was because the very conception and purpose of discipline have been misunderstood. It is, after all, only a means to an end, and that end is the power to secure co-ordinated action among a large number of indivi-duals for the achievement of a definite purpose. It does not mean lip service, nor obsequious homage to superiors, nor servile observance of forms and customs, nor a suppression of the individuality. The Australian is accustomed to teamwork. He learns it in the sporting field, in the industrial organisation, and in his political activities. The teamwork which he developed in war was of the highest order of efficiency. Each man understood his part and under-stood also that the part which others had to play depended upon the proper performance of his own."

Unfortunately, there were too many Britons of all classes to whom discipline *did* mean "obsequious homage to superiors and servile observance of forms and customs." To this type, the independence and individuality of the Australian soldier was an offence.

Other Britons had a different, though not entirely dissimilar, view of the Australians. The story is told that during the Victory Parade in London, someone in the crowd asked when the Australians would be passing by. A Cockney stepped out on the road, looked at the marching columns, and said, "'ere come the thievin' bastards now!"

With the fighting over and the French and British armies of occupation settling down along the Rhine, the Australian Government faced the task of repatriating the five Australian divisions together with such ancillary formations as the squadrons of the Australian Flying Corps. Prime Minister W. Hughes hoped that Brudenell White and John Monash would combine their great powers of administration to organise this as quickly as possible, and White travelled from France to London with a cadre of senior officers to assist in the task.

He called on Monash at Australian headquarters in Horseferry Road, but came away from the interview shocked and deeply hurt. For reasons which have never been divulged, Monash had suggested to him that he should return to Australia. Good soldier that he was, White did not attempt to fight against the obvious opposition of a superior officer, and Monash was appointed Director-General of Repatriation and Demobilisation while White returned home.

Some clue to Monash's action, which was out of key with all other descriptions of his generous and co-operative nature, may be found in the letter which he wrote to his wife on 25 June 1918. In this, he speaks of an intrigue of which he had been informed, in which "certain people strongly desire to displace Birdwood." (Birdwood was still Commander-in-Chief of the A.I.F. as a whole, even though Monash was in command of the Australian Corps.)

He summed up the intrigue by saying that those behind it realised that Birdwood could most easily be displaced by suggesting a more suitable man for his position. They had decided that Monash would have most appeal to those in the highest quarters. Their first problem, however, was to displace him from command of the Corps—since they feared that he would not be attracted to the superior post by offers of higher rank and prestige. Therefore they were "putting about propaganda" to the effect that Brudenell White, as a regular soldier, would be more fitted to the task of commanding the Australian Corps than Monash.

Monash does not even imply that he believed any of this, but it is possible that under the gruelling strain of his responsibilities he had come to see White as a participant in the intrigue.

Having been given the task of resettling the 180,000 Australians who were still serving overseas, he applied himself to it with his customary flair for organisation. Training courses were begun for those who had to wait in Britain while Monash and his staff struggled to obtain the necessary sea transport from the war-depleted merchant fleets, but the process slowly gathered momentum and in December 1919 Monash himself could return home for demobilisation.

During a press interview in Melbourne he said, "If I am needed in a national sphere, I am willing to place myself at the service of my country," but he made no attempt to exploit the tremendous reputation which he enjoyed. His book *The Australian Victories in France 1918* was published in 1920, and he submitted it to Melbourne University as a thesis for his Doctorate of Civil Engineering. This was awarded, to crown his long list of academic achievements.

In the concluding paragraphs of that book, he expressed his military philosophy in words which seem to have a particular relevance in our own days, when a certain section of the community tries to convince the rest that military service is a shameful imposition upon the rights of the individual.

He wrote: "It may seem appropriate to end this memoir on a personal note. I have permitted myself a tone of eulogy for the triumphant achievements of the Australian Army Corps in 1918, which I have endeavoured to faithfully portray. Let it not be assumed on that account that the humble part which it fell to my lot to perform afforded me any satisfaction or prompted any enthusiasm for war. Quite the contrary.

"From the far off days of 1914, when the call first came, until the last shot was fired, every day was filled with loathing, horror, and distress. I deplored all the time, the loss of precious life and the waste of human effort. Nothing could have been more repugnant to me than the realisation of the dreadful inefficiency and the misspent energy of war. Yet it had to be, and the thought always uppermost was the earnest prayer that Australia might forever be spared such a horror on her own soil.

"There is, in my belief, only one way to realise such a prayer. The nation that wishes to defend its land and its honour must spare no effort, refuse no sacrifice to make itself so formidable no enemy will dare assail it. A League of Nations may be an instrument for the preservation of peace, but an efficient army is a far more potent one.

"The essential components of such an Army are a qualified staff, an adequate equipment and a trained soldiery. I state them in what I believe to be their order of importance, and my belief is based upon the lessons which this war has taught me. In that way alone can Australia secure sanctity of her territory and the preservation of her independent liberties.

"Such a creed is not militarism, but is of the very essence of national self-preservation. For long years before the war it was the creed of a small handful of men in Australia, who braved the indifference and even the ridicule of public opinion in order to try and qualify themselves for the test when it should come. Four dreadful years of war have served to convince me of the truth of that creed, and to confirm me in the belief that the men of the coming generation, if they love their country, must take up the burden which these men had had to bear."

Also in 1920, Monash undertook the organisation of the first Anzac Day parade through Melbourne, in which 40,000 men marched to honour their fallen comrades, and in October of that year the Government of Victoria invited him to become General Manager of the newly formed State Electricity Commission: a challenge which he accepted with his usual zest.

He became the full-time Chairman of the vast scheme in 1921, and found that his powers of lucid administration and explanation were to be as valuable as his professional competence. The Commission was under fire from many critics, and he sought permission to address both Houses of the Victorian Parliament in order to explain the project. The politicians found themselves listening as attentively as the senior officers who had attended his conferences

on the Western Front, of which F. M. Cutlack said later: "In conference at
division headquarters each would be asked to deliver his views, and in the
end they would leave, each convinced that his own plan had been adopted,
yet each conscious that he had seen his scheme polished and perfected by
the General's own suggestions for its performance."

Monash convinced the critics that the scheme was viable, and continued
with the task of developing the Yallourn coal deposits, and building a giant
power station and a 120-mile transmission link between the Latrobe
Valley and Melbourne.

He maintained his interest in military affairs, and became a critic of the
way in which Australia's armed forces were being allowed to deteriorate.
He was appointed to the Federal Government's Council of Defence, and in
1929, together with Sir Harry Chauvel, was promoted to the full rank of
general. The two men were the first Australians to be thus honoured.

For nearly thirteen years after the Armistice he lived a full and useful
public life against the background of a contented home life, which included
a loving interest in his grandchildren. His son-in-law, the late Dr Gershon
Bennett, said, "He wished to teach my young sons to read, so first he taught
himself phonetics and all the latest teaching methods for small children, then
for a quarter of an hour, 9 to 9.15 every morning, he taught reading, and at
five years of age the boys had learnt to read."

He died at the age of sixty-six, on the morning of Thursday, 8 October
1931, after a short illness, and was accorded a State Funeral by the Federal
Government. Hundreds of thousands of Melbourne people, many of them
veterans of his divisions, watched silently as the cortege moved through the
streets towards Brighton Cemetery.

An equestrian statue of General Sir John Monash, G.C.M.G., K.C.B.,
C.B., V.D., was unveiled in 1950, in the Kings Domain of Melbourne near
the Shrine of Remembrance. It looks towards the city in which he was
educated, in which he established his reputation as a civil engineer, and
where he began the military career which was to make him Australia's most
famous soldier.

*   *   *

Brudenell White returned from France to the life of a serving soldier in
peacetime. Shortly before embarkation he was knighted as a K.C.M.G., and
his war record had been recognised by the awards of the D.S.O. in 1915, the
C.B. in 1916, and the C.M.G. in 1918, together with five foreign decorations.

He was not perhaps regarded as quite such a glamorous figure as either
Monash or Chauvel, but commanded considerable public respect which he
reciprocated by his pride in the Australian Army and its achievements.
Something of what he felt was reflected in his statement, "I would rather be
a corporal in the Australian Army than a field-marshal in any other," and
he, like Monash, understood perfectly the outstanding features of the

Australian soldier. "The Australian required of his officers three qualities; character, courage, and capacity," he wrote. "This is a deliberate statement, nowhere were there better officers. It is significant, this bent of democracy towards efficient leadership."

His comment that, "The success of the evacuation from Anzac was due to discipline," is interesting in the light of Monash's remarks upon the nature of discipline, and the whole character of the 1st A.I.F. is summed up by his: "In the A.I.F., what a man was fit for he was given the opportunity to become. This is real democracy, but before it could function as it should, man had to learn the need for service, sacrifice, fellowship and unselfishness."

Australian achievement was stated first-hand from his knowledge as a senior staff officer when he wrote: "In the attacks in Flanders in September and October 1917, Australian troops, there is no gainsaying it, converted the operations of those months from failure to success."

He returned to Australia at the time when Major-General J. G. Legge was Chief of the General Staff, and it was commonly thought that he would use his war-gained prestige to back up recommendations for Australia's regular forces to be made large enough to cover the Commonwealth's defence requirements. However, he maintained that the citizen army principle was the most suitable for Australia, and in 1919 advocated that a vote of two-thirds of both Federal Houses of Parliament should give a government the power to employ such a citizen force wherever it might be required to defend the nation.

But most of the world, and the democracies in particular, did not want to think about military problems. The nations engaged in the first World War had suffered a total of 22 million casualties, and with eager idealism it was hoped that the League of Nations would somehow find the way to avoid another such tragedy. The world economic situation was sliding down into a slump after the wartime boom, and by 1922 the Australian defence expenditure had been reduced to the barest minimum.

So the committee formed in August 1919 to bring in recommendations for re-organising Australia's citizen army, under the chairmanship of the Hon. George Swinburne and composed of Generals White, Legge, and McCay, found that no-one wanted to listen to their proposals. These were publicly known as Brudenell White's plan, and he said that he wanted to produce a citizen army that was "real and not a sham." His programme envisaged the training of all Australian youths, and their allocation into specific units which could be quickly mobilised. But it drew wide opposition from various sections of the community, for the usual mixture of selfish and well-intentioned reasons.

In 1920 he organised the arrangements for the Australian tour by the Prince of Wales, and on 1 June of that year he succeeded Legge as Chief of the General Staff, or "the Australian branch of the Imperial General Staff" as he preferred to call it. He was created a Knight Commander of the Victorian Order in the same year. In 1923, Prime Minister Bruce asked him to become Chairman of the Commission which had been formed to re-organise the Commonwealth Public Service.

He accepted the appointment, and wrote to his mother to say "I have laid down my sword and taken up my pen." He was forty-six when he left the Australian Army, disappointed that his plans for a citizen force had been pigeon-holed but still serving his country through his nomination to the Council of Defence, which comprised the Prime Minister, Defence Minister, the Treasurer, General Monash, and the chiefs of the three armed services.

The work of the Council of Defence was brought almost to a standstill by the impact of the Great Depression, but White was amongst the first to warn that a second World War was inevitable. He strove to make provision for Australia being exposed to Japan without the help of Britain.

In his new role as head of the Commonwealth Public Service he drew considerable criticism for his methods of re-organisation, especially since these provided for promotion on the basis of efficiency instead of seniority, but a senior public servant who assisted him wrote at the time, "From east to west and north to south, officers of the service regarded Sir Brudenell White's decisions as straightforward, just, and honest."

In 1926 he organised another Royal Tour of Australia, that of the Duke and Duchess of York. Lord Cavan, formerly a corps commander on the Western Front, accompanied the Royal couple, and later wrote to White, "I think you are the absolute world's champion organiser. Their Royal Highnesses are simply delighted with everything."

Behind his public duties and responsibilities, he had long cherished an ambition to return to the land, on which he had spent his boyhood. This was especially for the sake of his young family, from whom he had endured much separation, and by 1925 he had saved enough to buy a 2,000 acre farm outside Melbourne. At weekends he would travel home from his Melbourne office to work on developing the property. When the Federal Parliament was moved from Melbourne to Canberra in 1926, and many government departments went with it, he realised that for him to do likewise would sever him from his private life. Fortuitously he was offered an appointment as Chairman of the Australian board of the New Zealand Loan and Mercantile Agency and superintendent of its Australian business, and for the next eleven years became a leader of the Australian commercial community. For his services to the government, he was created Knight Commander of the Bath.

Once more, his unfailing courtesy and powers of organisation were his great strengths, especially as he had to guide his company through one of the worst depressions in world history. "He knew nothing about woolselling," a colleague said. "That of course he left to the experts. It was as an organiser that he was of so much value to us."

Station owners, seeking finance for their impoverished properties, left his office empty-handed, but one of them said, "I couldn't be disappointed. It rather made me feel foolish to have asked him."

Officially, he was out of the public eye for the first time in many years, but he still served on the Council of Defence and on seven important boards and committees including the Australian War Memorial Board.

In 1939, at sixty-three, he retired to the splendid property which he had developed with the help of his wife and sons, and which had been expanded by the purchase of neighbouring farms. A man with his experience of war and the world could hardly have doubted that fresh hostilities would be long delayed, but perhaps he hoped against hope that he would be left in peace to enjoy his retirement. The rest of his story must begin with the outbreak of the second World War.

*   *   *

As befits the man, the tale of Sir Harry Chauvel after his return to Australia in 1919 can be told simply and without decoration, though his honours included nine mentions in dispatches and C.M.G., C.B., K.C.M.G., K.C.B., and G.C.M.G. As a regular officer, he found like many of his contemporaries who had commanded large bodies of men in the field that there were very limited opportunities in a small and rapidly diminishing army.

From 1919 until his retirement in 1930 he served as Inspector-General of the dwindling Australian Military Forces, and from 1923 onwards combined this appointment with that of Chief of Staff; a post which he held in succession to Brudenell White.

After leaving the army he became a director of several important Australian companies, including the National Bank and the Colonial Mutual Life Assurance Co. Ltd., and took an active part in the commercial life of Sydney. In 1937 he returned briefly to his lifetime profession by taking command of the Australian contingent which attended the coronation of King George VI, and commanded all the Dominion and Colonial troops involved in the ceremonies.

He gradually faded into full retirement until 1942, when he was asked to form and organise a Home Guard, known as the Australian Volunteer Defence Force, to help to combat the threat of Japanese invasion. With the title of Inspector-in-Chief, he carried out this task with complete success. On 4 March 1945, still in the service of his country at the age of eighty, the old soldier died a few months before final victory.

*   *   *

Brigadier Thomas Blamey's contributions to the Australian victories had been recognised with the C.B., C.M.G., and D.S.O. During 1918, he had been Monash's right-hand man in planning the series of successes which had followed one another on an unprecedented scale, and paved the way for the capitulation of the German Army. One of his most memorable experiences came after the Australian triumph in the battle of Amiens, which Ludendorff described as "the black day of the German Army." Haig asked Monash to bring the Australian leaders to meet him at the Red Chateau at Villers-Bretonneux, and made an emotional speech of thanks in which he said with tears running from his eyes, "You do not know what the Australians and Canadians have done for the British Empire in these days."

After the Armistice, Blamey helped Monash with the repatriation of Australian troops. He returned to Australia in 1919 and was appointed Director of Military Operations at Army Headquarters in Melbourne, a post which he held until 1922 when he was posted to London as Colonel General Staff at the High Commissioner's Office in Australia House, and Australian representative on the Imperial General Staff. In those days, such appointments were undemanding. Interest in military affairs was at an anti-climax, and Blamey's duties were mainly those of liaison. He was unfavourably impressed, however, by the attitude of British Army officers towards the achievements of Dominion troops in the first World War; an attitude which no doubt hardened his own when, during the second World War, he became involved in a number of acrimonious disputes with British generals concerning their proposed use of Australians in the Middle East campaigns.

* * *

In the *Illustrated London News* of 29 August 1970 there is an article on the *kriegsspiel*, or war game, invented by a German officer in the nineteenth century and after that used by the German General Staff to aid in planning their campaigns and battles. The writer says that they used the *kriegsspiel* to plan Ludendorff's offensive of March 1918, and that the outcome of their "game" indicated a marginal victory for the Germans. It is most probable that the Australian counter-attacks during that offensive were the vital factor which tipped the scales towards an Allied victory instead.

BOOK II

The "Muddle East"

❋ ❋ ❋ ❋ ❋ ❋

"*I have, however, always considered from the very start that our participation in the operations in Greece was a definite strategic blunder. Our hands were more than full at that time in the Middle East, and Greece could only result in the most dangerous dispersal of force.*"

FIELD-MARSHAL VISCOUNT ALANBROOKE,
quoted in *The Turn of the Tide*, by
Sir Arthur Bryant

18

BACK TO THE ARMY AGAIN

L IKE MOST NATIONS ON 3 SEPTEMBER 1939, AUSTRALIA WAS ILL-PREPARED
for the war which was in fact no more than a resumption of the
hostilities which had ceased on 11 November 1918. There had
been plenty of storm warnings during the years in between. Japan had
been waging a savage imperialistic war against China for nearly ten years.
Mussolini's legions had been launched against the primitive troops of
Ethiopia, and that country had become an Italian colony. German and
Italian divisions had fought alongside Franco's troops in the Spanish Civil
War. Germany had re-occupied the Rhineland, and taken over Czecho-
slovakia and Austria in coups which the French and British had
countenanced with no more than token protestations. The two decades
since the great armies were demobilised in 1919 had seen little of peace and
prosperity. The sufferings of the great depression were only just fading into
history, memories of the first World War were stark in most adult minds,
and the average man had a half-despairing hope that he would be spared
the enormity of another war and allowed to enjoy a modest contentment.
This hope was encouraged by his leaders, who strove desperately for peace
until, almost too late, they realised that they must prepare for war.

Australia's armed forces had been allowed to deteriorate disgracefully.
Compulsory service in the militia had been suspended since 1929, and the
permanent army consisted of only about 3,000 men. There were however
six and a half divisions of volunteer militia, in various stages of training, but
these could not be obliged to serve overseas at that time.

In the late 1930s the Australian Government prepared to spend $86
million, a gigantic sum for the depleted economy of those days, on revitalising

the armed forces, but the decision had barely taken effect before war broke out.

As in 1914, Australia was quick to support Great Britain in her declaration of war against Germany. As before, there was a surge of volunteers, but the atmosphere was somewhat different this time. The young men had read books, seen films, and heard first-hand stories about modern war, so they had few illusions as to warfare being a kind of gallant picnic. Amongst them was a number of veterans of the 1st A.I.F., ready and able to train them in the craft of war. The almost frenzied enthusiasm of August 1914 was noticeably absent. Instead, there was a more subdued excitement, based on a realisation that a long hard task lay ahead. No one, at that time, had any idea of how long and hard it would be.

On 15 September 1939, it was announced that the 6th Division would be raised for service at home or overseas, and in November compulsory militia service was reinstituted, for men to serve only within Australia.

Except for the unfortunate Poles and for the men at sea and in the air, the second World War sagged swiftly into a strange anti-climax which an American journalist described aptly as "the phoney war." There was little offensive action on either side, so it was possible for the 2nd A.I.F. to be built up without any great feeling of urgency. The organisation was adminis-tered by the Chief of the General Staff, Lieutenant-General Squires, but he died on 3 March 1940. The Minister for the Army asked the Deputy Chief, Major-General John Northcote, to offer the position to Brudenell White.

White had been retired from the army for nineteen years, though he was still on the list of unattached officers, with the rank of lieutenant-general. He felt that he was somewhat out of touch, but his strong sense of duty obliged him to treat the request as an order that must be obeyed. "I feel like Cincinnatus called from his farm," he told a journalist from the Melbourne *Herald*, who found him in his paddocks looking like a typical farmer. "May I say that I much prefer being Cincinnatus at the plough, though I do appreciate the honour paid to me. I do want it to be realised however, that I am not taking up any appointment for a fixed term, but only to fill a gap. I do not want to act to the detriment of any permanent staff officer, and as soon as my services are unnecessary I want to return to the farm."

He was promoted to full general, the first serving Australian soldier to attain that rank, and from the placid ambience of his crops and flocks moved smoothly back into the huge machinery of the army, beginning to grind into gear again after its long stretch of neglect and minimal activity.

Preparations already were well advanced for the despatch of an Australian Corps overseas. By that time, it was expected that the 6th Division would serve in France, after completing its training in Palestine, and a brigade had sailed from Sydney in January. With vivid memories of his experiences at the hands of British commanders, White realised that the man chosen to

THE WESTERN FRONT, IV. A graphic illustration of the effect of constant shellfire on the French villages through which the front line ran. *Top:* is the village of Pozières, photographed just before the war. *Bottom:* is the site of the village as it appeared when the Australians were fighting at Pozières in 1916.

lead the 2nd A.I.F. overseas would have to be a man of exceptionally strong will, personality, and character. He would have to be able to stand up for the integrity of his force against the inevitable pressures exerted by the British Government and its army commanders, both strategically and tactically.

The man whom General Sir Cyril Brudenell White chose for this position was Lieutenant-General Sir Thomas Blamey; a somewhat unpopular choice at the time, but one which in the outcome proved to be correct.

Shortly before the war broke out, Blamey was perhaps at the nadir of his career. Certainly he could not have dreamed that Chamberlain's somewhat colourless tones, announcing the declaration of war against Germany, heralded his own eventual appointment as field-marshal. He was the first Australian soldier to achieve that rank, and the second Dominions commander, after Jan Smuts, to receive a field-marshal's baton.

He was a short, nuggety man, with the physical toughness of his Cornish father and the resilience of his pioneer-stock Australian mother. He had a ruthlessness which displayed itself when he refused to have anything to do with General Gordon Bennett after the latter's escape from Singapore, an emotional loyalty which led him into trouble during his civilian career, a highly perceptive intelligence which made him impatient with humbug and those who refused to see the error of their ways, and a bluntness of speech and action which caused him to tread heavily upon even the most revered toes. He was in fact very much of what is regarded as "a typical Australian," so it is strange that he was never truly popular with the Australian press, public, or government.

Blamey was born on 24 January 1884, on the property which his father had taken up on the Murrumbidgee River at Lake Albert, four miles from Wagga Wagga. He was the seventh child of his parents, who had spent the first six years of their married life in pioneering a cattle property in the Charleville district of Queensland. Drought had forced them to sell out in 1878, but with typical outback pluck they "gave it another go" on the Murrumbidgee. Fortune served them no better, and drought, bush fires, and low cattle prices obliged them to surrender the fine 5,000 acre property.

The effect on Blamey of these events, combined with his parents' stories of their earlier lives in the bush, was to breed in him a fierce national pride. It was a pride felt by many in those days, seeming to flourish in discouragement and adversity and taking strength from the very harshness of the land which was so hard to conquer. It impelled men to talk of Federation; of joining the colonies together and turning the scattered communities into a nation.

He was educated at the Superior Public School in Wagga Wagga; then a remote country town. An insatiable capacity for reading gave him horizons beyond the narrow limits of farmlands, chapel, and schoolyard, in which he was a formidable fighter despite his lack of height—or perhaps because

MEDICAL SERVICES. *Top:* The Matron and staff of the 1st Australian Stationary Hospital, Ismailia, Egypt, 1915. *Centre left,* Senior Sister E. Bray administers oxygen to a wounded soldier being flown out of New Guinea. *Centre right,* Exhausted stretcher bearers of 9th Field Ambulance sleep in the mud during the Passchendaele operations, 1917. *Bottom:* A wounded Digger being carried along the Kokoda Trail by Papuan bearers.

of it. But life was lived much in the open air in those days; horsemanship came almost as naturally as walking, and he was a keen player of Rugby and Australian Rules football. He was a member of the school Cadet Corps, but showed no particular leaning towards a military life until 1899, when with his eighteen year old brother Jim he presented himself at the recruiting office and tried to enlist for the Boer War. Though he stoutly maintained that he too was eighteen, the recruiting sergeant took one look at the fifteen year old boy and told him and his brother to go home and grow up.

Denied the opportunity to take potshots at the Boers, he joined the New South Wales Education Department as a pupil-teacher. His first post was at the Lake Albert school, in 1899, whence he was promoted to the South Wagga Public School in 1901.

The Cadet Corps at this school was organised on somewhat more serious lines than the one in which he served his own cadetship, and under the guidance of the very sergeant who had rejected him for Boer War service he began to feel the first stirrings of a martial instinct. But he still planned a career in education, and in 1902 sat for an Education Department examination to select twenty-five pupils for advanced training in Sydney. He came twenty-seventh on the list, but swallowed his disappointment and sought for a fresh opportunity. It came with an offer from a cousin, who was headmaster of Fremantle Boys' School in Western Australia. This was the glamour State in those days, with a fabulous goldmining boom that was attracting countless young adventurers.

Blamey arrived in Fremantle in July 1903, and at the Boys' School displayed the first signs of an aptitude for authority. He was given a class with a reputation for unruliness, but within a few days had tamed their larrikin behaviour so thoroughly that they became known as "Blamey's Lambs." He renewed his interest in Cadet Corps work, and took great pride in the achievements of a musketry team of five cadets which he trained. The team won the Western Australian Cup for musketry in a contest open to cadets between twelve and thirteen from all over the State.

Blamey had been brought up as a Methodist, with the fervent faith which was customary in those days, and during this period he confirmed his deep religious convictions by regular preaching at various suburban churches. He addressed the congregations to such effect that, early in 1906, the Methodist Church actually invited him to enter the ministry. He was offered a church at Carnarvon, with a stipend far in excess of his schoolteacher's salary, but chance was pulling him in a completely different direction. He had read a newspaper advertisement inviting applications for an examination to select young men for commissions on the Cadet Instructional Staff of the Australian Military Forces, and with his own successful background in such work decided that it would give him a satisfying career.

The first stumbling block was a lack of the necessary textbooks, which took so long to arrive from Sydney that he had only two weeks in which to prepare for the examination, instead of the five weeks available to candidates in the eastern States. He faced this challenge with a determination which gained him third place amongst candidates from all over Australia, but his pleasure in the achievement was marred by a letter from Army headquarters, Melbourne, notifying him that no post was available in Western Australia and that the four vacancies in the other States had all been filled by candidates in those States.

As he was to show on a number of occasions in later life, he was not to be rebuffed by mere officialdom. He wrote a polite letter of protest to the Army, and requested an early appointment, but when this was turned down he prepared a case that had all the appearances of a legal brief. He pointed out the moral obligation involved, since a candidate less successful than himself had been given an appointment, and ended with a veiled threat that he would take legal action if he did not receive an early commission.

The Army gave in, and ordered him to Melbourne for a ten day induction course. He sailed for the East again, having spent three years and four months in Western Australia; a period of success which had been marked by the impression which he had made in both educational and ecclesiastical circles. He had passed a teachers' examination in 1903 that gained special commendation from the Educational Department, and had made a wide circle of friends and colleagues. They were particularly intrigued by his ability to recite long poems or passages from books; a faculty which came to him through his extraordinarily retentive memory and extremely wide reading. This phenomenal memory and wide general knowledge, gained through his love for reading, were characteristics which he shared with Monash, and which in the same way were to aid him in his military career.

His early years in the Army were mainly occupied with the development of the school cadet system in Victoria, during the period in which the Australian Army was being created as a single entity out of the six small and incohesive colonial militia forces. During this time he had his first brush with the Bennett family. Mr George Bennett was the headmaster of a school whose Cadet Corps came under the jurisdiction of Lieutenant T. A. Blamey, and they fell out over a matter of administration. Mr Bennett's son Gordon was later to become Major-General Gordon Bennett, and the antipathy between him and Blamey extended over forty years.

In 1909, Blamey married Minnie Millard; the daughter of a well known Melbourne stockbroker and seven years his senior. The marriage culminated nearly three years of courtship which had originated from their mutual interest in the Methodist Church, and they had two sons; Dolf, who was killed at Richmond, New South Wales at the age of twenty, as a pilot in the R.A.A.F., and Tom, who saw much service with his father during the second World War.

Blamey's first promotion, to captain, was on 1 December 1910. In 1911 he began to prepare for an examination that would determine selection of an Australian officer for attendance at the Indian Army Staff College at Quetta. He applied himself to the task with unrelenting concentration, and passed the examination as top of the entrants in late 1911.

He left for India almost immediately, and with his young family arrived in Quetta in December 1911. During the next two years he was plunged into a life completely different from anything he had known before; the snobbish yet convivial existence of regular officers of the British and Indian Armies during the "last years of the old world." It says much for his adaptability that, as a man with the somewhat narrow and earnest background of a Nonconformist upbringing in the late nineteenth century, he was able to fit himself completely into his new surroundings, both at work and play. In fact he showed some of the first signs of relinquishing the strict code of his Methodist upbringing, and later commented, "The period abroad has taught me many things. The chief one is that life is not to be taken too seriously. Keep on smiling is about the best thing going."

He graduated from Quetta Staff College in December 1913, with high credits for his examination papers. The next step in his military experience was a posting to England to serve with British units, while his family returned to Melbourne. It was expected to be a short separation, but he arrived in England in June 1914 and did not see his family again for six years.

His service in the first World War, as mentioned in previous chapters, was largely that of a staff officer of increasing seniority under Brudenell White and John Monash, and this was followed by his appointment to the High Commissioner's Office in London. He returned to Melbourne in 1925 to take up the post of Deputy Chief of the General Staff, but a sequence of events were to sever his Army career and place him more blatantly in the public eye than all his military service had done.

In 1923 the Victorian Police Force had gone on strike because of unsatisfactory working conditions. A settlement had been patched up, and the men had returned to duty while a Royal Commission tried to unravel the causes of the upheaval. One of the Commission's findings was that the salary provided for a Police Commissioner was insufficient to attract a man of high calibre.

The State Premier, Sir Stanley Argyle, was desperate for a solution to the continuing discontent, and asked General Sir Harry Chauvel, then Inspector-General of the Australian military forces, to recommend an army officer who might be suitable for the position. Chauvel suggested Blamey, who accepted the position on 1 September 1925 at a salary of £1,500 ($3,000) per annum.

For the next eleven years, he devoted himself wholeheartedly to the task of improving the lot of the Victorian policeman. Some of his reforms had a lasting influence, whereas others were inevitably less successful. It was a difficult position affected by strong political undercurrents, and his appointment did not suit the Labour Party of the day. Had Blamey trod warily he might have survived, but he was betrayed by the strong sense of loyalty to subordinates and friends which became so apparent during the second World War.

The first occasion on which this brought him into disrepute was when the Superintendent of the C.I.B., Inspector J. O. Brophy, apprehended two masked and armed men and was wounded in a shooting affray. Brophy was accompanied by two women at the time, and in an attempt to protect his subordinate from the unsavoury implications of the case which were being ferreted out by journalists, Blamey issued a false press statement. It was an early example of his tactless handling of the Press.

The second occasion was when the police raided a brothel, and found that one of the men caught in a compromising situation was carrying Blamey's police pass. This, of course, was meat and drink to the journalists, who already had been offended by Blamey's bluntness. Blamey was able to show conclusively that he had been elsewhere at the time, and that he was not the culprit, but he did know the man involved. He refused to reveal this man's identity or to explain how he happened to be carrying the Police Commissioner's identity card, so the occurrence left large unanswered questions in the public mind. As Blamey said later, "If you throw enough mud, some of it is bound to stick."

The incidents provided leverage for his political enemies, and the Labor Party forced the Country Party Premier, Mr Albert Dunstan, to request Blamey to resign. He did so in July 1936.

This ended the unhappiest period of his life, and left him with a bleak outlook for the future. He was fifty-two, and with his integrity in shreds saw little likelihood of being able to obtain other employment. Since 1931 he had held command of the 3rd Division of the Australian Army, but this was little more than a spare-time appointment connected with militia training and expired on 31 March 1937. His name was placed on the list of retired Army officers.

He received a meagre pension from the Victorian Government, which he supplemented by a general affairs programme which he conducted over Radio 3UZ, Melbourne, under the pseudonym of "The Sentence." With Nazi Germany and Fascist Italy on the march in Europe and Africa, and Japan expanding her ambitions in Asia, there were plenty of international events for him to discuss—especially with reference to Australia's long-neglected defence establishment.

But these same events were to be the cause of his rehabilitation. In late

1938, as the Australian Government began to realise that the nation could not escape the disaster whose shadow was beginning to fall across the world, Blamey was appointed Chairman of the Manpower Committee, then Controller-General of Recruiting, and eventually, on 28 September 1939, General Officer Commanding the 6th Division, 2nd A.I.F. He raised the division, which in its early days was known as "Blamey's Mob," but when the government decided to form a second division for general service (the 7th) and the 1st Australian Corps was instituted, he was recommended for command of this Corps by Brudenell White.

There were many who criticised this recommendation; not only because of his controversial career as Commissioner of Police, but also because of his age. At fifty-five, he was said to be too old for the arduous duties of an overseas command, but he had two great allies in the Federal Parliament. Mr R. G. Menzies, when acting as a Minister in the Victorian Parliament, had formed a high opinion of Blamey's capabilities. Mr R. G. Casey had served with him during much of the first World War, and knew from personal experience that he was excellently suited for the command. Despite the critics, his appointment was confirmed in April 1940, and he took up the task with intense concentration and energy.

* * *

The days of the "phoney war" were over. Germany had begun to strike; first in Denmark and Norway, next in Belgium, Luxembourg, and France. As the pace of preparations speeded up, Brudenell White drew up a "charter" for service of the 2nd A.I.F. overseas. Ironically, it was virtually a replica of that which had been framed by himself and General Bridges before the first World War, and established four main principles:

1. That the A.I.F. should be recognised as an Australian force under its own commander, with the right of direct communication to its own Government and with no part of the force to be detached or employed separately without the commander's consent.
2. It would serve under the operational control of the commander-in-chief of the theatre in which it served.
3. Its control and supply would be the responsibility of the local commander-in-chief.
4. The administration of its "domestic" matters would be the prerogative of its own commander, subject only to the general control of the Australian Government.

White, no doubt recalling the clashes which he and Birdwood had had with the British command during such occasions as the first battle of Bullecourt, emphasised that these principles should be agreed to by the British Government, which had been disposed to ignore them during the previous conflict. The "charter" was to be put to the test even sooner than he expected.

With the collapse of France, the decisive defeat of the British armies in France, and the entry of Italy into the war, it was obvious that the Australian Corps would not be merely "training" in the Middle East in order to support the British, but would be fighting there. Containing the oilfields upon which Britain so largely relied, the area was an inevitable target for the Axis powers.

Elements of the 6th Division, under Major-General Iven Mackay, and the 7th Division, under Major-General J. D. Lavarack, already had arrived in Egypt or were en route there, though in June a convoy of 6th Division troops had been diverted to England to help defend that country against the expected invasion. By the end of 1940, the two divisions had almost completed their establishment in Egypt and another division, the 8th, was being trained in Australia.

White had urged that Blamey should proceed to Egypt as soon as possible, to make sure that the British adhered to the Australian Government's policy for control of the nation's troops. Blamey arrived to find that White's suspicions were well-founded. General Sir Archibald Wavell, the area commander, was planning to disperse the first A.I.F. brigades among British formations; a policy which Blamey resisted vigorously. In this first blunt confrontation, Blamey justified White's choice of him as the right man to command the A.I.F., and he was successful in ensuring that the Australian troops retained their complete national identity.

In Australia, the pressure of work upon Brudenell White was mounting every day. Italy's entry into the war had closed the Suez Canal route to Australia, and it was apparent that Australian production would have to be stepped up until the nation could supply its own requirements without depending upon imports. The shape of events overseas had made a profound impression upon the men of Australia, and volunteers flocked to the recruiting centres in such numbers that recruiting had to be suspended temporarily until the first applicants could be absorbed. White urged the Government to form another division, the 9th, and there was no lack of men to fill its ranks.

To assist in their training, White called upon many of the veterans of the 1st A.I.F.; men who were too old for field service but who were ready and able to recreate the spirit of the first World War contingents. During this time, it was suggested that one division of the 2nd A.I.F. should be sent to Malaya on a temporary basis, with the ultimate aim of joining the other Australian formations in the Middle East. White opposed the suggestion, on the grounds that Australians were not used to their best advantage as garrison troops, and with almost prophetic vision he feared that they would be cut off if hostilities developed in the Asian theatres. If he had still been alive in 1941, the history of the 2nd A.I.F. might have been very different.

But on 13 August 1940 he was called to Canberra for a Cabinet meeting, and took off from Melbourne in a Lockheed Hudson whose passengers included the Minister for the Army, the Hon. A. G. Street, who had been a staff officer in the 1st A.I.F.; Sir Henry Gullett, the Minister for Air, who had served with distinction in the Australian Flying Corps; Colonel F. Thornthwaite, one of White's colleagues from the 1st A.I.F.; and several other servicemen.

The flight to Canberra was made through a clear morning, and when the pilot arrived over the capital's airport he made a circuit before coming in to land. Apparently he misjudged the approach, and realising that he was too low to clear a hill he banked steeply. The aircraft stalled and crashed, and all aboard were killed.

The funeral service for White was held in St Paul's Cathedral, Melbourne, and was followed by a procession along St Kilda Road to the Shrine of Remembrance. His remains were taken to Buangor, where he was laid to rest four miles from the farm to which he had retired from public life.

His wife and family installed a memorial plaque in the old St John's Church at Canberra, with an inscription which ends with Milton's lines:

> *Servant of God, well done, well hast thou fought,*
> *The better fight.*

19

DESERT VICTORY—AND DEFEAT

IN DECEMBER 1940, GENERAL WAVELL STRUCK HARD AGAINST THE ITALIANS in North Africa. They had advanced into Egypt during the last four months, and by 9 December eight Italian divisions were deployed between Sidi Barrani and the fortress of Bardia. Against them, Wavell had an army which had to hold Palestine, Egypt, the Sudan, and Kenya, and was scattered across those areas. It consisted of an armoured division, two Indian and two Australian divisions (the 6th and 7th), a New Zealand division, two divisions of East African troops, and a cavalry division. The best-trained among them were the regular Indian troops and the armoured division, the remainder being in various stages of training and equipment.

In a three day battle between 9-12 December, the Italians received the first of the many disastrous defeats which were to result in Germany taking over operations against the British in North Africa. The 7th British Armoured Division and the 4th Indian division seized Sidi Barrani and drove the Italians back in disorder, taking 38,000 prisoners.

Wavell then turned his attention southwards, to his planned offensive against the Italian colonial empire of Abyssinia, Somaliland, and Eritrea. 91,000 Italian and 199,000 native troops were deployed throughout this area, and Wavell planned to attack them with a force whose backbone consisted of his Indian infantrymen with their British regular officers. They were first-class troops with a lengthy military tradition, and for the most part had been trained in India before the war.

When they were withdrawn to the south, their positions facing the Italians to the west of the Egyptian border were taken by the 6th Australian Division. Some senior British officers held no small reservations as to whether this

181

division, which was composed almost entirely of volunteers who had been civilians until quite recently, would be capable of maintaining the momentum generated by the Indian divisions.

The Australians themselves had no such fears. They were superbly fit, confident in their officers, conscious of the fact that they were the first men of the 2nd A.I.F. to be committed to battle, and determined to uphold the traditions created by the 1st A.I.F., and particularly by such men as those of the Light Horse, under conditions very similar to those being faced now.

Fortunately these qualities far outweighed their disabilities. They were still undertrained, and grossly ill-equipped by any standards, but particularly by those which were accepted as normal later in the war.

Their commander, Major-General Iven Mackay, had seen an exceptional amount of active service during the first World War; firstly on Gallipoli, and then as C.O. of infantry and machine-gun battalions during the bitter campaigns on the Western Front of 1916/17, ending the war as commander of the 1st Infantry Brigade. For these services he had been awarded the C.M.G. and D.S.O., and between wars, while pursuing his career as a schoolmaster, he had maintained a lively interest in the militia forces. He was commander of the 2nd (Militia) Division in 1939.

His front line service was an invaluable background to the distinguished leadership which he was to show in Libya, Greece, and in the South-West Pacific campaigns, although his modest personality tended to belie his capacity for shrewd appreciation of a tactical situation.

Under Mackay's command were the 16th, 17th and 19th Infantry Brigades, led by Brigadiers A. S. Allen, S. G. Savige, and H. C. H. Robertson. The artillery was commanded by Brigadier E. Herring. All four brigadiers had distinguished records of active service in the first World War.

Brigadier Allen, a chartered accountant by profession, was commissioned in the militia at the age of nineteen. Five years later he was leading a battalion in France after service on Gallipoli. He was the type of military leader that appeals to the Australian soldier; blunt in speech, honest, without affectation, and with a solid background of front-line service. His short stature and heavy build brought him the inevitable nickname of "Tubby," and for the six years previous to the outbreak of war he had commanded the 14th (Militia) Infantry Brigade.

Brigadier Savige had served as an N.C.O. on Gallipoli, was commissioned in France, and led a small independent force in Kurdistan in 1918; mainly upon the somewhat ironical task of protecting defeated Turks from massacre by the Arabs. He too was a friendly, practical leader of men. He was commander of the 10th (Militia) Infantry Brigade between the two wars, and he had established a successful agency business in Melbourne.

Brigadier Robertson, the only regular soldier of the three infantry brigade leaders, was thought by some people to have the outstanding tactical mind of Australia's second World War military leaders. Unfortunately he also gained the reputation of being a difficult subordinate, which eventually caused him to be relegated to less active commands. He had served with the Light Horse in Gallipoli and Palestine, and was regarded as an outstanding leader and trainer of troops, being possessed of a vigorous self-confidence and a fanaticism for physical fitness. Between the wars he had held, among other appointments, those of Chief Instructor of the Small Arms School and Director of Military Art at Duntroon.

Brigadier Herring was a Melbourne barrister, a former Rhodes Scholar, who had served with the British Army during the first World War on the Western Front and in Macedonia. He had joined the Australian militia in 1922, and had commanded various artillery regiments during the between wars period.

Each of them was to justify his appointment and show his fitness for command. Mackay, Savige and Herring were to become corps commanders; Robertson became commander of the British Commonwealth Occupation Forces in Japan; Allen ended the war as a divisional commander. Colonel G. A. Vasey, the Assistant Adjutant and Quartermaster General of the 6th Divison, also became a divisional commander.

The task of Mackay and his men was to drive the Italians out of Bardia, the fortress into which they had retreated; actually an 18-mile semi-circle of fortifications. As the Australians approached their start lines for the assault, on 3 January 1941, they were extremely conscious of their responsibility to continue the advance against Mussolini's legions and to uphold the reputation of Australian troops in the field.

Lieutenant-General R. N. O'Connor, commander of the Western Desert forces and the victor of Sidi Barrani, had left the planning of the assault to Mackay and his staff, and had placed the tanks of the 7th British Armoured Division under their command.

Bardia's perimeter was some eighteen miles in extent and defended by a continuous anti-tank ditch, plus numerous concrete blockhouses placed at strategic intervals and sunk almost to ground level, so that they were hard to locate and harder still to knock out by artillery. It would be a far harder nut to crack than any of the other defences so far encountered during the advance, and Mackay decided that its conquest would require operations similar to those conducted in France during 1916-18. Surprise was essential, and they would have to rapidly exploit any breakthrough. The garrison was estimated at 20,000 Italians; at least as many men as those in the attacking Australian force.

Mackay planned to attack with six battalions of the 16th and 17th Brigades under the command of Brigadiers A. S. Allen and S. G. Savige. The role of the 16th Brigade was to break into the perimeter, after which the 17th would follow them, wheel right, and advance from the Bardia-Capuzzo road against the right of the Switch line; a chain of posts which cut off the southern end of the fortress.

In the gloom before the desert dawn on 3 January, a battalion of the 16th Brigade moved silently into position 1,000 yards from the Italian perimeter. At 5.30 a.m., Herring's artillery let fly with a vicious bombardment of a narrow section of the line, while the infantry moved up as close as possible to the barrage. The moment it lifted they were on their feet in a charge which overcame the battered defences, broke through, and began to sweep in both directions. Like water pouring through a breach in a dam, two more battalions and a number of tanks followed them through, and by nine o'clock the 16th Brigade was four miles inside and ready to throw back a counter-attack by Italian armour.

A battalion of the 17th Brigade fared less well. They followed through the breach in the line and attacked towards the south, but were held up by artillery and machine-gun fire which cut down many of their effectives. They paused, reorganised, and made another determined attack, which secured their objectives by nightfall. The heaviest opposition was experienced at the southern end of the perimeter, which beat off an attack by one Australian battalion and caused considerable loss. Mackay had been instructed by O'Connor to hold Robertson's 19th Brigade in reserve, in readiness for the advance on Tobruk if Bardia should fall, but he launched them against the southern end of the perimeter on the following morning. They found that the resistance had faded away, and the 16th Brigade, advancing northwards towards the little township of Bardia, encountered nothing more formidable than gigantic crowds of surrendering Italians. The actual number who threw down their arms is uncertain to this day, but it is believed to be between 41,000 and 45,000; well over double the number estimated to be within the fortress.

The spoils of victory were enormous. One Australian soldier said long afterwards that the stacks of Italian rifles were "higher than a suburban house," and besides these the Australians captured 462 artillery pieces, 127 tanks, and 708 motor vehicles; the latter a welcome addition to British resources in a campaign which was obviously going to be one of swift movement over great distances.

The Australians had suffered 456 casualties, of whom 130 were killed.

This rapid and convincing success against the Italian Army had exceeded the fondest hopes of the Australians, and had justified the self-confidence which they had shown before the battle. It proved also that the standard of training achieved by the division was obviously very much higher than had been realised.

Mr Churchill conveyed his congratulations to General Wavell in a message which said: "Hearty congratulations on your second brilliant victory, so profoundly helpful to the whole cause. You knocked and it was opened." To beleaguered Britons in the homeland, enduring almost nightly air raids, it was a great boost to morale. Mussolini, in a broadcast over Radio Rome, claimed that Bardia had been attacked by "250,000 Australian barbarians, and 1,000 aircraft." but even worse was to befall his tottering legions.

The Australians did not rest on their laurels, but pressed on with the advance towards the next enemy bastion along the Libyan coast. This was Tobruk; a name that will forever be enshrined in the proud heritage of Australian military lore.

By the morning of 7 January, the 19th Brigade had covered the sixty miles between Bardia and Tobruk and was in position facing Tobruk's eastern defences. The 16th and 17th Brigades, with all the artillery that the Western Desert force could muster plus the remaining sixteen serviceable Matilda tanks of the 7th Royal Tank Regiment, were rapidly moving to join them.

Wavell was particularly anxious that Tobruk should be taken in the shortest possible time. Not only because of its value as a port, which would help to overcome the acute problems of supplying troops along the lengthening lines of communication, but also because of the menace which had begun to show itself on the other side of the Mediterranean, as a result of the

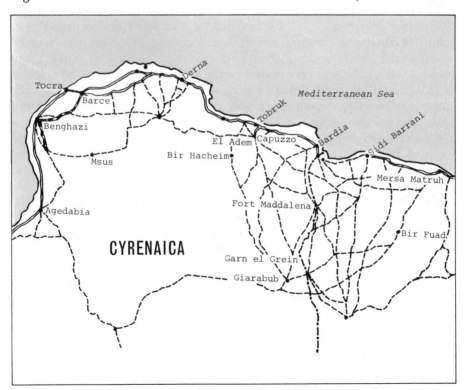

Italian attack on Greece. Churchill had promised assistance to the Greeks if they should have to call for help, and so looked for a rapid success in the Libyan campaign. He wrote, "The 2nd and 7th British Armoured Divisions, the 6th Australian Division, the New Zealand Brigade group soon to become a division, with perhaps one or two British brigades, should suffice to overpower the remaining Italian resistance and to take Benghazi (after Tobruk). With the capture of Benghazi this phase of the Libyan campaign would be ended."

The likelihood of German intervention in the Greek campaign, in an effort to shore up the wilting efforts of their Italian allies, made it obvious that a British expeditionary force would be raised from within General Wavell's command. This prospect weighed upon him, as his over-extended resources already were committed to fighting the Italians on two fronts, but at least the grip on Tobruk was beginning to tighten. Convoys of trucks ground along the rutted desert tracks, bringing the ammunition and other supplies for the assault, and the 16th Brigade came into the line beside the 19th Brigade on 10/11 January. To the north and north-west, the 7th Armoured Division took up position to cut off the fortress from its main escape route to Benghazi.

The defences which the Australians had to assault are described in the *Official War History* as ". . . a semi-circle of concreted underground posts behind barbed wire entanglements five feet high. Outside this was an uncompleted anti-tank ditch. Patrols discovered that for four miles east of the El Adem road it was very shallow and on the western face of the defences there was no ditch at all, though a deep wadi served the purpose. Again the posts were two deep, each inner post being mid-way between two outer posts, and each outer post protected by its own anti-tank ditch and wire. The outer posts were generally 600 to 800 yards apart and the inner line 500 yards behind the outer. Whereas there were eighty posts along the seventeen mile perimeter at Bardia, there were 128 along the thirty mile front at Tobruk."

The plan of attack was very similar to the one launched against Bardia, and was paid the compliment of being copied by Rommel. Eighteen months later, he used almost identical tactics in order to recapture the fortress from South African and British troops, and was promoted to field-marshal for his victory.

The armour was to "demonstrate," but if possible not be committed to the attack, while the infantry were to break the enemy perimeter and then fan out within it. In the meantime, the Australians engaged in very active patrolling, which continually harassed and confused the Italian outposts around the outside of the perimeter.

General O'Connor had instructed Mackay to launch the attack on 20 January, but a delay of twenty-four hours was granted to allow Allen more time for his preparations and in the hope that the British armoured troops would be able to restore more of their tanks to working order. Desert warfare was extremely hard on the comparatively primitive tanks used by the British at that time. The battlefield was almost obscured by a tremendous duststorm which blew up on 18/19 January, but it cleared in time for the assault to commence at 8 a.m. on 21 January.

The Australians had learned the value of speed at Bardia and this time they moved so quickly on to the Tobruk defences that they not only surprised the Italians but their own adjoining units as well. Both the 16th and 19th Brigades reached their objectives, with few losses, by midday, but during the afternoon the Italians brought their coastal and anti-aircraft guns into action and there were several hours of bitter fighting around the middle of the perimeter in the vicinity of Fort Pilastrino, where Italian block houses provided spirited resistance. The Italians also fought bravely from some thirty-seven tanks, well dug in and firing from twin machine-guns.

By dusk, however, the Australians had the situation well in hand and were ranged along the escarpment overlooking the town and harbour. Droves of prisoners, including several generals and the Italian commander, had been taken, and Brigadier Robertson added an admiral to the list when he accepted his surrender on 22 January. By that time, resistance had virtually ceased, and the operation was crowned by an exuberant Australian hoisting his Digger's slouch hat on the flagpole outside the admiral's headquarters.

The booty included nearly 30,000 soldiers of all ranks, 2,000 sailors, 236 guns of a calibre of 75 mm. and over, eighty-seven tanks, and about 200 vehicles. The Australians paid for them with remarkably light casualties; a death-roll of forty-eight, and 306 wounded.

Churchill expressed the Allied joy in a telegram to General Wavell, saying: "I again send you most heartfelt congratulations on the third of the brilliant victories which have in little more than six weeks transformed the situation in the Middle East, and have sensibly affected the movement of the whole war. The daring and scope of the original conception, the perfection of staff work and execution have raised the reputation of the British and Australian Army and its leadership, and will long be regarded as models of the military art."

With the enemy on the run, General O'Connor acted fast to strike the next blow. He used the 17th and 19th Brigades of the 6th Division to attack Derna, and sent the 16th Brigade south with the armour, in the hope of trapping a large enemy force at Mechili. The Italians, however, moved even faster, and escaped them, so O'Connor despatched the 7th Armoured Division, now suffering from considerable wear and tear, to Msus, and the 4th Armoured Brigade to Beda Fomm.

Apart from spasmodic mopping-up operations as the Australians approached Derna, no resistance was met from the Italians. They withdrew on 30 January, allowing the two Australian brigades to occupy the town on the following day.

O'Connor judged that the Italians were preparing to quit the Cyrenaica area of Libya, and early on 1 February reports were received that they were withdrawing substantial forces to Barce, where tanks were spotted being entrained at the railway station. He ordered the Australians to continue their advance and to capture Benghazi, in the hope that this wide out-flanking movement along the coastal road would cut off the enemy escape, and turn the Italian retreat into a complete rout of their army.

The 19th Brigade, under Brigadier Robertson, carried out his orders to the letter. The first troops entered Benghazi on the evening of 6 February, and the brigade made a formal entry on the following morning. In order to maintain pressure on the fleeing Italians, the bulk of the brigade pressed on south and reached Ghemines on 8 February. To General O'Connor's astonishment, they were able to report that their advance guard had penetrated fifteen miles beyond Ghemines on that day.

On the morning of 7 February the Italians surrendered at Beda Fomm to the British armour which had cut off their retreat, after a desperate last ditch battle in which thirty Italian tanks attempted to break out.

The desert victory was now complete. The 6th Australian Division, the 7th Armoured Division, and the Indian 4th Division had destroyed no less than ten Italian divisions between them, and had captured an enormous number of prisoners and huge quantities of enemy weapons and stores. They had dealt a staggering blow to the Italian Army, from which it never really recovered either morally or physically.

General Wavell issued a Special Order of the Day on 14 February, in which he summarised the achievements of O'Connor's command. He said: "On the capture of Benghazi, which has resulted in the occupation of the whole of Cyrenaica, I wish to express my thanks and my admiration to all those who took part in these operations—not only those at the front who have fought so gallantly and so skilfully, but also all those who by their work on the lines of communication or at the base have made possible the rapid advances which have so confounded our enemies.

"The Army of the Nile, as our Prime Minister has called us, has in two months advanced over 400 miles, has destroyed the large army that has gathered to invade Egypt, taking some 125,000 prisoners and well over 1,000 guns besides innumerable quantities of weapons and materials of all kinds. These achievements will always be remembered.

"Much hard work and fighting still lies ahead of us before peace is won. The spirit of quiet resolution that during these operations has animated all ranks in all places—the combatant under fire in the fighting line, the driver making his way over bad tracks in a dust storm, the mechanic working long

ARTILLERY. *Top left*, Howitzer of the 2nd Australian Siege Battery in action, 1917. *Top right*, An Australian field gun bogged on Westhoek Ridge during the Passchendaele operations. *Centre:* Australian field guns fire on Vichy French positions at Wadi Damour, Syria. *Bottom:* Gunners of the 7th Division pound Japanese positions at Balikpapan, Borneo.

hours on repair and maintenance, the pioneer unloading stores, the signaller, the engineer, the medical personnel, will continue and carry us through all dangers and difficulties.

"You have done great deeds and won much glory. We are fighting for freedom and truth and kindliness against oppression and lies and cruelty, and we shall not fail."

Major-General Iven Mackay was knighted for his contribution to these operations, in which he had shown leadership and judgement of a very high order, but the fruits of victory were to wither very soon. After protracted negotiations with the War Cabinet and with the Greek Government, it had been decided to send an expeditionary force to Greece. The 6th and 7th Australian Divisions and the New Zealand Divisions were to provide its main fighting component, together with a Polish brigade and a British armoured brigade.

This decision precluded the possibility of pushing on to Tripoli and completely defeating the Italian army in North Africa, a proposal that had strong supporters both among the British Cabinet and senior officers in Egypt. Wavell himself rather doubted the ability of his army to pursue the campaign. Supply difficulties were acute, and further operations would have strained Royal Navy and R.A.F. support to the limit.

General O'Connor had been keen to press on to Sirte with his forces, and, if the situation warranted it, to capture Tripoli also. There was in fact nothing that could have stopped his forces, for what remained of the Italian army was in a state of complete demoralisation and virtual disintegration. Indeed the Italian and German General Staffs were astonished that the British did not pursue their move further westwards, and it was to be a long and bitter struggle before a similar opportunity would again present itself.

But the opportunity was set aside in favour of the Greek adventure, and ominous events began to crystallise in Africa. Hitler sent a note to Mussolini on 5 February, expressing his displeasure at the performance of the Italian Army and offering German assistance, providing that what remained of the Italian Army held on to their positions and did not retreat further to Tripoli—a retreat that would have been inevitable if O'Connor had continued to attack.

Mussolini grasped at the offer, and the Germans moved with amazing speed; seven days later the commander designate of the *Deutsche Afrika Korps*, Lieutenant-General Erwin Rommèl, arrived in Tripoli. On 13 February the advance guard of his troops, comprising a reconaissance battalion and an anti-tank battalion of the 5th Light Division, disembarked there. On the same day, they were moved up to Sirte with an Italian division, and on 17 February they had their first clash with British and Australian troops, the latter being the losers in a minor skirmish. The first German

ARMOUR. *I op left*, Australians inspect a tank of the type which failed them at Bullecourt. *Top right*, An Australian-manned Matilda moving towards the Bougai. lle attack. *Bottom left*, Men of the Royal Australian Regiment advancing with a tank in Korea. *Bottom right*, A Centurion tank and an armoured personnel carrier manned by Australians preparing for a sweep in Vietnam.

troops were rapidly followed by others of all arms, including the X German Air Corps.

The well-trained, superbly equipped, and supremely confident Germans were about to attack British forces whose recent victories were as nothing against the debilitation and confusion caused by the preparations to send troops to Greece. O'Connor's XIII Corps Headquarters was replaced by I Australian Corps Headquarters, under General Blamey. They in turn were withdrawn on 4 March in order to prepare for the Greek expedition. General Sir Maitland Wilson, who had been appointed G.O.C. Cyrenaica, was also withdrawn, and given command of the force going to Greece. In his place, Wavell appointed Lieutenant-General P. Neame, V.C.

General Neame was to be the first of a line of unsuccessful British generals in the North Africa campaigns. Indeed, the leadership of the British Army in the confrontation with Rommel was to reveal, once more, how abysmally destitute it was of competent senior officers. It was a lack which would cause history to repeat itself. As in the first World War, Australian and New Zealand troops would suffer from British strategic and tactical incompetence, while any successes they gained were invariably lumped together as "British."

Even some British commanders were outspokenly critical about their own army's leadership, training, and organisation. As early as 1935, in a lecture at Cambridge, Wavell referred to, "That home of orthodox soldiering; the sealed box of the Aldershot Command."

Auchinleck, after commanding the British forces at Narvik, and following the dismal showing of the British Army in both Norway and France, was acutely outspoken in a report he made to Churchill; so much so that the Prime Minister suppressed its release until after the war.

Among other comments, Auchinleck said: "The comparison between the efficiency of the French contingent and that of British troops operating under similar conditions has driven this lesson home to all in this theatre, though this was not altogether a matter of equipment. By comparison with the French, or the Germans for that matter, our men for the most part seemed distressingly young, not so much in years as in self-reliance and manliness generally. They give an impression of being callow and under-developed which is not reassuring for the future, unless our methods of man-mastership and training for war can be made more realistic and less effeminate."

This immaturity could largely be blamed upon the stultifying barrack-room discipline of the British Army, and that in turn could be blamed upon the static outlook of the Imperial General Staff, which like the Bourbons had "learnt nothing and forgotten nothing." As in 1915-18, the Australians were to suffer from the continuance of this attitude.

But when the 6th Division was sent to Greece, and replaced in North

Africa by the 9th Division, there was one ray of intelligent leadership to illuminate the otherwise largely depressing countenance of British command. This was in the presence of Major-General L. J. Morshead, the commander of the 9th Division.

Morshead was the classical example of the Australian civilian soldier; a man who had had to earn his living in the less sheltered world outside the army, while maintaining a continuous interest in military affairs.

A schoolteacher by profession, he had been commissioned as a militia officer before the first World War, and had his baptism of fire as second-in-command of a company of the 2nd Battalion in the 1st A.I.F. With them he had stormed ashore at Anzac Cove on 25 April 1915, fought all day to gain a foothold on the ridges above the cove, and participated in the deadly struggle to hold the hill which the Anzacs named "Baby 700." He led a platoon that fought almost to the last man, and was one of the very few officers to survive the first day on that particular sector.

Six months later he was seriously wounded and invalided back to Australia, where he formed and trained the 33rd Battalion. He took them to France, and led them with distinction through Messines, Passchendaele, and Villers-Bretonneux. By the end of the war he had been wounded twice, mentioned in dispatches six times, and decorated with the C.M.G., D.S.O., and Légion d'Honneur. The *Official War History* described him as "A fighting leader . . . the nearest approach to the martinet among all the young Australian colonels. He had turned out a battalion which anyone acquainted with the whole force recognised, even before Messines, as one of the very best."

Between the wars he had abandoned teaching for commerce, and had risen to be Sydney manager of the Orient Line. He had maintained his interest in the army, and as well as commanding a militia brigade for seven years had visited British Army training schools and manoeuvres during a tour of Britain in the 1930s. When the second World War broke out he was given command of the 18th Brigade of the 6th Division; the brigade which was diverted to Britain en route to Egypt. It became the nucleus of the 9th Division, and arrived in the Middle East in January 1941. Morshead took command of the division when its previous leader, Major-General H. D. Wynter, was obliged to go on sick leave.

In the volume of the Australian *Official History* which covers Tobruk and Alamein, Barton Maugham says that: "Morshead was every inch a general. His slight build and seemingly mild facial expression masked a strong personality, the impact of which, even on slight acquaintance, was quickly felt. The precise, incisive speech and flint-like, piercing scrutiny acutely conveyed impressions of authority, resolution, and ruthlessness. If battles, as Montgomery was later to declare, were contests of wills, Morshead was not likely to be found wanting. Unsparing, unforgiving, unspoken in criticism, he was yet quick to commend and praise when he thought men had fought as they should; such men he respected, admired, and honoured. 'Ming the Merciless' was the unduly harsh nickname by which he first came to be known in the 9th Division, softened later to just 'Ming' as a bond of mutual affection and esteem grew up between the general and his men."

When Morshead and his 9th Division took up their positions in Cyrenaica, a khamsin was about to blow across it in the form of Rommel and his *Afrika Korps*. Fortunately for the British in Egypt, Morshead's arrival was very much a matter of the right man at the right time in the right place.

Rommel himself was beginning to demonstrate the dash and vigour which soon bewildered and impressed the British to such an extent that he was regarded as virtually unconquerable; an attitude which finally developed into an odd hero-worship of this general whose steely courage and determination had had much to do with the defeat of the French, might easily have defeated the British, and if unchecked would have led to their serfdom under Nazi rule.

Reinforcements poured into Tripoli, including the remainder of the German 5th Light Division. Fully equipped with tanks, it completed disembarkation on 11 March 1941 and probed forward into the desert. On 24 March, the Germans drove the British out of their outpost positions at El Agheila, but Wavell was unperturbed. He said that "there is no evidence yet that there are many Germans at El Agheila, probably mainly Italians with a small stiffening of Germans."

But this first small bite had given Rommel an appetite. He urged his troops forward, and as the thump of their tank-cannon and crackle of small arms fire resounded across the desert the local commanders began to feel the first stirring of alarm. These were not Italians, to be rounded up like sheep, but Germans; as determined as the British and Australians themselves and given an added edge by the fanaticism of their cause; tigerish in attack and wolf-like in battlefield cunning.

The British frontier force was still in the condition of depletion and confusion consequent upon the withdrawal of the Australian 6th Division. Morshead's 9th Division was not yet fully established, and in any case lacked a good deal of equipment and contained units which were not yet fully trained. It was supported by the 2nd Armoured Division, under Major-General Gambier-Parry, which was about two-thirds under strength. The 20th Brigade of the Australians had to rely upon its own feet for transport, so when the first signs of German activity appeared Morshead drew them back from the advanced defensive position of Marsa Brega to the hills east of Benghazi. He feared that a swift German advance might overrun them and that they would be unable to withdraw quickly enough.

On the night of 1 April, Rommel made a bold decision. "It was a chance I could not resist," he said later. "I gave orders for Agedabia to be attacked and taken, in spite of the fact that our instructions were not to undertake any such operation before the end of May." It was a decision characteristic of the man.

The 5th Light Division advanced in strength, and clashed with the British armour. The British resisted stoutly throughout a day-long battle, but it was an uneven contest. Most of their tanks were no match for the Germans, and tank after tank "brewed up" in the ghastly spouts of black smoke and oily flame which were the funeral pyres of their crews. The British withdrew, and the Germans pressed after them remorselessly until the British retreat rapidly turned into rout.

It was becoming a case of "order, counter-order, disorder." General Neame was issuing orders from his headquarters in Barce, without having any clear idea of what was going on at the front. Gambier-Parry, seeing the few remaining tanks of his division literally melting away before his eyes, was concerned to save what he could. Wavell, in Egypt, began to realise that the situation was falling apart, and asked General O'Connor to return to the front from Cairo and take over from Neame. O'Connor was reluctant to supplant a brother-officer, but agreed to act as adviser. So he and Wavell flew to Cyrenaica on 3 April, and found a situation of "increasing misfortune and confusion."

It could not be saved by the most expert advice. The Germans entered Benghazi on 4 April, and British fortunes were going from disaster to disaster as Rommel pressed home his attack with great vigour along the coastal road and as far inland as Msus and Mechili. The 9th Australian Division had repulsed a German attack between Tocra and Regima on 2 April, before being ordered to withdraw east of Benghazi. They withdrew unit by unit through the passes between the hills, holding off attacks from the Germans fanning out from Benghazi.

But the situation was becoming increasingly desperate. The German drive inland to Msus and Mechili was obviously designed to cut off the British retreat, and Neame and O'Connor ordered Indian and Australian units to Mechili in an attempt to hold the position. Throughout 4/5 April it was becoming harder to make any appreciation of the German movements, and by 6 April they seemed to be everywhere. One of O'Connor's last orders was for the 9th Australian Division to withdraw to Tobruk by the coast road, and shortly after this he and Neame were taken prisoner. He had been appointed G.O.C. British troops in Egypt in recognition of his services in the Cyrenaica campaign, and but for the collapse of the front which he had taken from the Italians would still have been in the Cairo office which he had left only three days before.

The Australians made a fighting retreat across Cyrenaica, harried by the German armour and aircraft. The remnants of the British armour made last-ditch stands at Derna and Mechili, enabling a number of infantry and other troops to withdraw successfully but losing the rest of their tanks in doing so. Gambier-Parry was captured at Mechili.

By 7 April, the 9th Division was established in battle order at Acròma, on the west of the Tobruk defences, and on 8 April Wavell flew up to Tobruk with Major-General J. D. Lavarack, commander of the Australian 7th Division. Already he had ordered reinforcements to Tobruk, by detaching from the 7th Division its 18th Australian Infantry Brigade in addition to a British artillery regiment, and conferred with Morshead and Lavarack as to the best way to hold the fortress for at least two months. After that, he hoped to be able to send in a relieving force.

The hope of holding Tobruk seemed to be the only firm element remaining after what had been another disaster. The British ignored an elementary principle of "always hit where you're winning" by not consolidating their Cyrenaica victory and possibly extending their advance to Tripoli. They chose instead to embark upon an adventure that had no chance of success.

In the meantime, Rommel thrust eastwards in a drive of calculated risk, exploiting the weakness of British armour with magnificent judgement. As on the Western Front in 1918, the British front had been cracked by a ruthless German assault. Then, Monash and his men had held firm. Now it was up to Lavarack, Morshead, and the mainly Australian force in Tobruk.

20

"IT HADN'T A DOG'S CHANCE"

WHILE ROMMEL'S TROOPS IN EGYPT DESCENDED LIKE WOLVES ON THE fold, Field-Marshal von List's 12th Army was invading Greece and southern Jugoslavia. Even before his tanks and troops crossed the border, the force which Wavell had been ordered to send to Greece had been cut almost in half. Originally, it had been planned to send the 6th and 7th Australian Divisions, the New Zealand Division under Major-General B. C. Freyberg, one British armoured brigade, and a Polish brigade. The 7th Division, however, was now digging itself into the yellow-brown earth around Mersa Matruh, and Wavell had decided that the Polish brigade must stay in Egypt. When von List crossed the border on 6 April, the New Zealanders and the British armour had arrived in Greece, but most of the Australians, including General Blamey's I Australian Corps head-quarters, were still en route.

Only one man had any real enthusiasm for the expedition. This was Winston Churchill, who not only was fulfilling an Anglo-French guarantee to support Greece and Roumania in case of attack by the Axis powers but saw an opportunity to open a second front in Europe.

His enthusiasm faded somewhat when the supreme difficulties of the operation became apparent during the negotiations with the Greeks and Jugoslavs, and instead of making the final decision himself, he rather subtly shifted the responsibility from London to Cairo.

Wavell accepted it without demur, though it was to strain his resources almost to the point of disaster. In a strategic appreciation, he concluded: "To sum up, we have a difficult choice, but I think we are more likely to be playing the enemy's game by remaining inactive than by taking action in the Balkans. Providing that conversations with the Greeks show that there is a good chance of establishing a front against the Germans with our assistance, I think we should take it."

Mr Robert Menzies, the Australian Prime Minister, attended a meeting of the War Cabinet in London on 24 February 1941, after which Churchill cabled his Foreign Secretary, Mr Anthony Eden, in Cairo. He said: "The Chiefs of Staff having endorsed action on lines proposed in your telegrams from Cairo and Athens, I brought whole question before War Cabinet this evening, Mr Menzies being present. Decision was unanimous in the sense you desire, but of course Mr Menzies must telegraph home. Presume, also, you have settled with New Zealand Government about troops. No need anticipate difficulties in either quarter."

Eden had been busily engaged in the negotiations with the Greek government following the Italian invasion of Greece and Albania, and the operative sentence in this message to him is the last one. Obviously Churchill expected the quiet acquiescence of the Australian and New Zealand governments to the proposals made by Eden and endorsed by him. In effect, it meant that the brunt of the fighting would be borne by two Australian divisions and a New Zealand division; a role to which they would become very accustomed until the Australians were withdrawn after the Battle of Alamein.

If the Greek operation had had a chance of success which was even comparable with that of Gallipoli, this would not have been so bad. In fact, however, almost every one of the local commanders could see that it was inviting a disastrous defeat.

At that time, Australia's political maturity was not equal to its military maturity, and its government was still under the illusion that Britain possessed a magical expertise in military affairs. Menzies, in his memoirs *Afternoon Light*, tries to justify his government's decision when he says, "My Australian colleagues still adhered to their (and my) belief that the decision to send our troops to Greece was strategically correct."

It is easy, of course, to pass judgement after more than a quarter of a century has passed, but expert opinion against the expedition was freely available when it was being planned. In a terse appreciation drawn up for the Australian government, General Blamey warned them that the Germans had: "As many divisions available as the roads could carry. It is certain that with three or four divisions available we must be prepared to meet overwhelming forces completely equipped and trained. Greek forces inadequate in numbers and equipment to deal with the first interruptions of the German army. Air forces available, twenty-three squadrons. German air forces within striking range of the proposed theatre of operations, and large air forces can be brought to bear early in summer. In view of the Germans' much-proclaimed intention to drive us off the Continent wherever we may appear, landing of this small British force would be most welcome to them, as it gives good reason for attack. The factors to be weighed are: For (a) the effect of failure to reinforce Greece on the opinion of Turkey, Jugoslavia, and Greece, and against (b) the effect of defeat and second evacuation, if possible, on opinion and action of the same centres and Japan."

The situation was even worse than he had outlined. The "twenty-three" squadrons, which he mentioned, comprised the entire R.A.F. strength in the Eastern Mediterranean at that time. And he was not to face the twelve divisions of von List with "three or four divisions," but with only two divisions and one brigade of tanks plus artillery.

Menzies, for some reason, did not seek Blamey's opinion, and the Australian government chose to be swayed by British persuasion rather than by the expert knowledge of the general commanding their own countrymen in the Middle East. However it is appraised, the Greek expedition can only be seen as a strategic blunder of the first magnitude, and a complete misjudgement on the part of Wavell. It could perhaps be justified on the score of Britain's political obligation to support the Greeks, but it is appalling that the Australian Government should have permitted Churchill to use Australian and New Zealand troops to do so.

Months later, when the affair was only a painful memory, Blamey wrote to Lieutenant-General V. Sturdee, then Chief of the General Staff, that, "The Greek expedition hadn't a dog's chance from the start. The Greek plan was a bad one and our plan to support them was equally bad. I am sure our proper role would have been to give them all possible assistance and to have seized Rhodes and maintained Crete, with a division in each. With a properly organised formation in each place, they could never have got us out. I feel and always will that the position and possibilities were not adequately explored."

Admiral Sir Andrew Cunningham, in command of the British naval forces in the Eastern Mediterranean, had no illusions whatever as to the possible success of the operation. Fortunately for the Australian and New Zealand troops, he began planning a method of evacuating the army from Greece as soon as he knew that the campaign was to be launched.

As though to add insult to injury, Wavell did not give command of this predominantly Australian and New Zealand force to one of its own men. He could have appointed Freyberg of the New Zealanders; a fighting man who was as brave as a lion, held the Victoria Cross, and bore on his body the scars of the many wounds which he had suffered in the service of the British Empire; a man who in fact was deeply respected by Churchill, since he evoked all of the Prime Minister's ready hero-worship. Or Blamey, whose pragmatic ability to handle military operations had been demonstrated many times, could have taken command. Blamey and Freyberg had in fact discussed the possibility of forming an Anzac Corps, but this did not materialise until too late.

Instead, Wavell gave command of the expedition to General Sir Maitland Wilson, whose attitude towards the Australians was shown in a conversation with Menzies when the Australian Prime Minister visited Barce after the Italians had been driven out of Cyrenaica. He asked Wilson how the Australians were getting on, and in view of their recent successes expected some form of congratulations. But all that Wilson could bring himself to say was, "They're troublesome, you know."

"I understand that the Italians have found them very troublesome," Menzies replied.

"It's not that. They're not disciplined, you know," Wilson told him.

This was too much even for the urbane Menzies, who some years later was to describe himself as "British to the bootheels." He told Wilson tersely that, "These men haven't spent their lives marching around parade-grounds. They come from all walks of life and they've come here to do a job and get it over."

When Blamey was informed of the decision to send an expeditionary force to Greece, the original strength of which was to include two Australian divisions, one New Zealand division, one British brigade, and one Polish brigade, he wrote to Menzies and said that in his view he was entitled as a matter of principle to command a force containing such a preponderance of Dominion troops. He made no apologies for stating that experience had taught him to look with misgiving on a situation in which British leaders had control of considerable bodies of first-class Dominion troops, while Dominion leaders were excluded from all responsibility in control, planning and policy.

Menzies submitted this view to the British War Cabinet, who rejected the proposal that Blamey should have command in Greece but as a compromise offered an eventual appointment as Deputy Commander-in-Chief, Middle East.

Blamey also told Wilson quite bluntly that he thought himself entitled to the command, but Wilson stated blandly that ultimately there would be more British than Dominion troops in the command, and therefore it was essential to have a British Army leader from the outset. This can have been little more than a spur-of-the-moment statement on his part.

Whatever justifications there may have been for a Dominion general being given a senior field command in the Middle East at this time, and there were many, the "Union of British Generals" maintained a very united front. Unfortunately the Australian and New Zealand Governments were not sufficiently strong to force the British War Cabinet to change an unreasonable attitude.

General Blamey's forthright insistence in supporting the rights of men under his command had created a certain amount of animosity among his British colleagues, who at the same time managed to overlook the fact that British combatant troops in the Middle East were vastly in the minority at that time. No other reason than this animosity can be found for the denial of a senior field command to the Australian general, whom Wavell himself described as "by far and away the best man we have out here." But no doubt Wavell himself was too closely bound by ties of class, profession, and tradition to be able to consider offending the "Union of British Generals."

But the troops themselves knew little or nothing of the political manoeuvrings behind the adventure, and were in good heart as they embarked by stages at Alexandria and were carried over the Mediterranean to Greece. The first elements had landed on 7 March, and the 6th Australian Division was still being transported a month later, when the German invasion had begun. As they landed, they were hurried north towards the fighting line.

The beauty of the Greek countryside was a welcome sight to men who had become accustomed to the dusty monotones of the desert, and the Greeks welcomed them as allies; a pleasant contrast to the morose, antagonistic Egyptians and Arabs. The line to be held by the Australians and New Zealanders ran through some of the most spectacular scenery in Europe, amongst the mountains dominated by the beauty and majesty of Mount Olympus. It was hard country for fighting in, but looked like good country to defend.

The New Zealanders were on the right, from the coast to the Pieria Mountains, north east of Servia; the 16th Australian Brigade was in the Veria Pass, and the 1st British Armoured Brigade, about twenty miles forward with the Greek 20th Division, acted as a covering force. The Greek 12th Division was at Veria, and was to be relieved completely by the 6th Australian Division when its 17th and 19th Brigades had disembarked. When the 19th Brigade came forward on 7 April, however, it was concentrated near Kozani. This placed it in a position to reinforce either Veria or the Florina Valley if they were threatened by the Germans.

General Wilson's troops, who were designated "W" Force, were only responsible for that part of Northern Greece which lies east of the Pindus Mountains and west of Salonika. This area was linked with Athens by one main railway, which wound through the mountain passes east of Mount Olympus, and one main road from the Florina Valley. This road snaked through the mountains on the west side of Olympus. These arteries on which W Force communications depended were difficult to travel at the best of times, and could easily be cut by air attack or a flanking enemy thrust.

The German 12th Army had launched its offensive from Bulgaria with ten infantry and two armoured divisions, the disposition of the Greek Army then being fourteen divisions facing the Italians in Albania and seven and a half divisions covering the frontiers of Jugoslavia and Bulgaria. They fought bravely, but courage alone was not enough. It had checked the Italian advance in Albania, but without the support of modern arms and equipment it could not stand against the unlimited resources of the Wehrmacht. At the

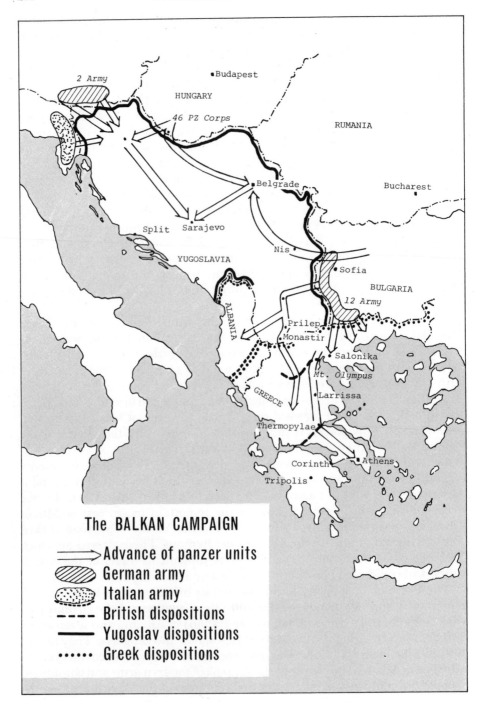

The **BALKAN CAMPAIGN**

⟹ Advance of panzer units
▨ German army
▨ Italian army
--- British dispositions
━━ Yugoslav dispositions
••••• Greek dispositions

points of German invasion on the Bulgarian and Jugoslav borders, the Greeks were overwhelmed in four days. Their so called Metaxas Line crumpled, and the important port of Salonika was occupied.

The rapid collapse of this portion of the Greek army was an ominous portent for the future, and gave plenty of cause for worry to Generals Wilson, Blamey, Freyberg, and Mackay (in command of the 6th Division). Despite the vast differences in terrain, it began to appear that von List in Greece would advance as rapidly as Rommel in Libya, and the main concern of the W Force generals was to ensure that their men would not be outflanked by a German advance and trapped among the mountains.

Three Greek divisions, the 12th, 19th, and 20th, were digging in with Wilson's troops, but they were little more than divisions in name only. The spirit of the men was good enough, but their weapons were ill cared for and obsolete, their training poor, provisions scanty, and transport not much above the ox-cart level. Even their uniforms and boots were ragged or broken.

The German and Italian armies soon joined hands on the northern borders of Greece, and the passes began to fill with bedraggled groups of Greek soldiers in retreat. The Germans began to advance through the Monastir Gap from Jugoslavia, which virtually had collapsed, and seemed likely to outflank Wilson's force. He formed a force to be known as Mackay Force, consisting of the 19th Brigade and the British armoured brigade, under General Mackay, to check this thrust down the Florina Valley, with the Vevi Gap as the main defensive position. The Vermion-Olympus Line was now to be regarded only as a rearguard position, while the bulk of W Force fell back from Veria and took position on a line along the Aliakmon River and through the Olympus and Pindus passes.

The system and distribution of command that General Wilson had introduced was proving to be extraordinarily complex. Blamey, from the Corps headquarters at Gerania, commanded the New Zealanders, part of the Australian 6th Division, and the Greek 12th Division. A Greek general commanded the Central Macedonian Army, and Wilson placed Mackay's force under his own direct control. He divided his staff between his advance headquarters at Elasson, not far from Blamey, and his rear headquarters at Athens, some 200 miles away. In addition, the British air commander was in Athens, quite independent of Wilson, together with a naval staff and a British military mission.

Brigadier G. S. Brunskill, who was Deputy Assistant Quartermaster General of British troops in Greece and Crete, suggested in 1947 that the proper co-ordination of these various commands should have been resolved by the appointment of the Army Commander as Supreme Commander of all British forces in Greece. The air officer commanding should have been his deputy, the British military mission abolished, and the Australian Corps headquarters expanded to command all British and Greek troops on the

Aliakmon Line. As it was, the divided command system developed by General Wilson provided nothing but uncertainty and lack of decision.

The first contact of the British and German forces came on the afternoon of 10 April, when Australian and British artillery opened fire on the German transport columns as they advanced across the plains towards the Vevi positions; a sight that was described by an Australian observer as being like "a dark grey caterpillar on a great green lawn."

That night, German infantry made probing patrols at the Vevi positions, where an Australian battalion had only just dug in after marching across the mountains. It was snowing heavily, which did little to improve the spirit of men almost exhausted by many hours of marching along rough tracks and clambering up hillsides, but next day the German activity increased steadily. Their tanks appeared, and a heavy artillery barrage fell on the Australian positions. Shortly before 5 p.m. this was followed by an attack from two German battalions, which was repulsed by accurate artillery fire. They soon returned, and persisted throughout the night. Prisoners revealed that the Australians were confronted by the élite S.S. Division, the "Adolf Hitler."

By next morning, Australians were reaching the limit of their endurance. Kept awake by constant night attacks and the intense cold, they did not even have the comfort of blankets, because men could not be spared to carry them forward. It was not possible to cook hot food, and one battalion had the impossible task of covering a front of two and a half miles.

Despite these things, the Australian line held for two days against constant German pressure, until the expected major attack developed at 8.30 a.m. on 12 April, supported by intense mortar and machine-gun fire and tanks. All through that day, Brigadier G. A. Vasey's 19th Australian Brigade fought a bitter rearguard action. They caused heavy German casualties but lost many men themselves, as one position after another was overrun by the enemy. It was a classic of its kind, with the Australians holding on literally to the death or until ordered to withdraw, unit by unit, to the assembly points from which they would fall back. Cold, hungry, physically and mentally exhausted by constant effort and danger, they fought a rearguard action which was worthy of the finest troops in the world, and held up the German forces long enough to enable the rest of Wilson's forces to retire to the Olympus-Aliakmon Line. For several days afterwards, soldiers who had been unable to break off the action and retire to their assembly points continued to straggle back through the German lines. Despite their fatigue, and the ruggedness of the country, they were determined not to be taken prisoner.

The withdrawal of W Force was a difficult and dangerous operation for all concerned. Transport was hard to find, and the 16th Australian Brigade used donkeys as pack animals as they retired through the mountain passes from their Veria positions. Snow had been falling on the mountains throughout the previous four days, and it rained steadily in the valleys. When the weather cleared, the troops could see as far as the port of Salonika and to the mountains of Jugoslavia, now falling into German hands.

The British 2nd Armoured Brigade also fought a gallant action, on the day after that of the 19th Brigade. The brigade straddled the Sotir road at Ptolemais, and fought off the advance of German armour up the road. Accurate fire from anti-tank weapons caused many German casualties, but the British armour once more proved inferior to the German tanks and also lost heavily in the encounter.

The new line taken up along the Aliakmon seemed to promise a sturdy resistance to the Germans, especially since General Papagos, the Greek Commander-in-Chief, assured Wilson that his armies would hold the passes west of the Florina and along the Albanian frontier. General Blamey said that his new line was "an immensely strong position," though it was perilously long for two divisions to hold.

On 14 April, however, disturbing reports began to filter through, to the effect that the Greek 12th and 20th Divisions were disintegrating. It was said that they had failed to carry out an orderly withdrawal from their Vermion positions, and it was unkindly suggested that their main object was to reach Athens instead of re-establishing themselves. The 17th Australian Brigade had taken its place on the Aliakmon Line on 13 April, and when Blamey heard reports of a German breakthrough on the left he ordered this brigade to cover the key town of Kalabaka.

The Germans could be seen massing in the valleys below the three main passes covered by the Australians and New Zealanders, and it was reported that they had captured the Kilsoura Pass and were threatening the withdrawal of the Greek West Macedonian Army. It was time for urgent action, and, after consultation with Blamey, General Wilson decided to withdraw a further eighty miles to a line astride the Thermopylae, Brallos, and Delphi passes, at the head of the peninsula on which Athens lay. This move meant the loss of all northern Greece and abandonment of any further co-operation with the main body of the Greek army. To stay on the Aliakmon Line, however, meant that Wilson's force could be outflanked if the Greeks collapsed — as it seemed very likely that they would do.

It was a delicate and serious decision, because a heavily-pressed retirement can turn with disastrous suddenness into a rout. But it seemed the only correct procedure, and General Wilson officially gave control of the withdrawal to Blamey.

Two days before, Blamey had issued a message which gave great heart to the Australians and New Zealanders. It read: "As from 1800 hours, April 12th, 1st Australian Corps will be designated Anzac Corps. In making this announcement, the G.O.C. Anzac Corps desires to say that the reunion of the Australian and New Zealand Divisions gives all ranks the greatest uplift. The task ahead, though difficult, is not nearly so desperate as that which our fathers faced in April twenty-six years ago. We go into it together with stout hearts and certainty of success.''

These were brave words, reviving for a new generation the memory of their fathers' achievements, but it is unfortunate that the Anzac Corps had not been revived when its chances for success were greater. As commander of the newly-named corps, Blamey had as his first task the dangerous and possibly reputation-destroying operation of conducting a fighting withdrawal. He accepted it with his usual determination to succeed.

Now, as the skies cleared of snow and rain, they began to fill with the snarl of German divebombers. On 14 April, the New Zealanders guarding both sides of Mount Olympus had been subjected to intense divebombing attacks by Stuka aircraft, followed by fierce ground attacks on the Servia Pass positions. They had stood firm under all of these. On 16 April, the German intentions became clear, as they switched the attack to the right flank and assaulted New Zealand positions in the coastal pass at Platamon, east of Olympus. This was a vital sector, covering one of the three withdrawal routes to the junction at Larisa. All the Anzac and British formations would have to pass through Larisa on their way to the Thermopylae line, and the Germans obviously planned to cut them off at that point.

Blamey sent Brigadier A. S. Allen, with his 16th Brigade, to reinforce the New Zealanders, who had held off the Germans so far. He instructed the Anzacs to hold until 19 April, and during the next two days they experienced some of the bitterest fighting of the campaign. On the ground, they fought off the troops and tanks of the German 2nd Armoured Division and 112th Reconnaissance Unit, while the Luftwaffe harassed them from above with the nonchalance of a force that enjoys complete command of the air. They bombed and strafed at will, while the steel hulls of the Panzers clanked forward over the rocky ground and pounded the Anzac positions with shells and machine-gun fire.

Trying to clarify the situation of his own New Zealanders in this battle, General Freyberg spoke by radio to Lieutenant-Colonel F. O. Chilton, commanding the Australian 2/2nd Battalion in the line. When the conversation was over, Freyberg turned to Brigadier Allen and remarked, ''You've got a fine man up there. He's as cool as a cucumber.''

Allen later wrote of this engagement, ''It was a fantastic battle. Everybody was on top as there was no time to dig in, and all in the front line, including artillery, Bren carriers, infantry and headquarters, with unit transport only a few hundred yards in the rear. Some confusion could be expected with every weapon firing and aircraft strafing from above. We had to hold this position until after dark, and thanks to the morale of the force it was done.''

During the night of 18 April, the remnants of this rearguard withdrew east of Larisa. Equally vital rearguard actions were fought by the 6th New

Zealand Brigade at Elasson and Brigadier Savige's 17th Australian Brigade at Kalabaka, though these were not as intense as the battle at Pinios Gorge.

By 18 April, it had become obvious that the Greek army could not hold together for much longer. The Macedonian Army of General Tsolakoglou had virtually disappeared, and the retreating Epirus Army, which had fought the Italians to a standstill in Albania, had supply problems which were insurmountable under the existing conditions.

On 16 April, at a conference with Wilson, General Papagos had told him that the British force should be evacuated. Wavell had flown into Athens, and the disunity of the Greek government was sharply accented by the suicide of the Prime Minister. At 2 a.m. on 21 April, Wavell drove north to visit Blamey, and told him that the force must be evacuated.

This was a blow to Blamey, Freyberg, and Mackay, who had been encouraging their subordinates by telling them that the line would be held at Thermopylae. Brigadier G. A. Vasey, who was famous for his explosive language, had passed this on to his 19th Australian Brigade as they settled down astride the Brallos Pass in an operations order which stated: "Brallos Pass will be held to the last f—g man and the last f—g round, and if you can't shoot them in the bloody stomach shoot them in the f—g arse." His brigade major, faced with the task of issuing confirmatory orders in writing, translated this into: "Brallos Pass will be held, come what may."

Apart from the three main rearguard actions, the Anzacs had been under heavy air attack during their withdrawal. The divebombers swooped on the columns of men and vehicles through every break in the clouds, and the German armoured cars dogged them like wolves. At one time it seemed that the withdrawal would have to be halted so that the Anzacs could turn and fight, but they managed to press on southwards while their engineers blew the bridges and cratered the roads behind them, to hold up the German advance.

On 22 April, Blamey issued his last order as G.O.C. Anzac Corps, when he gave instructions for the withdrawal of all units to various evacuation ports and handed over the conduct of the evacuation to Wilson's headquarters. Brigadier Barrowclough, with his 6th New Zealand Brigade, was entrusted with the defence of Thermopylae Pass while all other units moved through on their way south.

Large-scale embarkation began on 24-25 April, from beaches round the coast. Now that the Germans seemed so close to trapping their prey, they pressed on even harder, and a series of bitter rearguard actions were fought as the Anzacs fell back to the beaches. The beaches and ships were bombed, but the Royal Navy continued their calm and steady work of embarking the troops. On 26 April, German paratroops captured the Corinth Canal, cutting off further Anzac retreat to the southern beaches, but the units north of the canal were ordered to other beaches and ships sent to pick them up. If the Luftwaffe had attacked the Corinth Canal bridge, instead of concentrating on vehicles along the roads, the evacuation would have been even more difficult.

Of the 62,600 Australian, New Zealand and British troops sent to Greece, 50,662 were reported to have been re-embarked. 26,000 of these were landed in Crete, while the rest were taken to Egypt.

In approximately eighteen days between the first contact with the Germans and the last day of evacuation, the Australians suffered 320 killed, 494 wounded, 2,065 prisoners; the New Zealanders 291 killed, 599 wounded, 1,614 prisoners; and the British Army 146 killed, 87 wounded and 6,480 prisoners. German losses were 1,160 killed, 3,775 wounded and 345 missing.

The Germans had deployed against the two Anzac divisions and the British brigade no less than two infantry divisions, two motorised divisions, and three armoured divisions, during the course of a fighting withdrawal covering some 300 miles, for the most part along a single road. It was an outstanding military achievement, and one for which General Blamey, as the principal field commander, must be given a major share of the credit.

On the bloody balance sheet of the Greek campaign, however, there was one item which could be reckoned as being of supreme importance to the Allies. This was Hitler's announcement, in a meeting with his commanders-in-chief on 27 March 1941, that, "The beginning of Operation Barbarossa (the invasion of Russia) will have to be postponed up to four weeks as a result of the Balkan operation." Had it not been for this, the Germans might have defeated Russia before they were halted by the winter conditions of 1941.

Against his own wish, General Blamey was flown out of Greece on 24 April, and reported to Admiral Cunningham and General Wavell on his arrival in Egypt. The day after his return, he was appointed Deputy Commander-in-Chief, Middle East, an appointment to which he was richly entitled because of his extremely wide experience; because the Australians now formed the main body of Wavell's front line troops; because of his outstanding leadership in Greece; and because, with the exception of O'Connor in Cyrenaica, the British commanders had certainly not demonstrated any great proficiency in the field so far.

Unhappily, the appointment with its imposing title was to carry little significant influence, particularly after Wavell's replacement by Auchinleck. It did however establish some sort of precedent, whereby leaders of Dominion armies should be considered for the higher Middle East appointments; a principle against which the British Army generals were strongly opposed. For no other reason, it appears, than that they considered it an intrusion into what was technically a British command. Considering that a very high percentage of front line troops were from the Dominions, it was a principle that did not appear to possess very great substance beyond being another example of what Blamey cynically described from his Great War experience as the "Union of British Generals."

*   *   *

Although the Greek campaign was now officially regarded as ended, numerous daring escapes were still being made by Anzac and British troops who crossed the Mediterranean in craft which often were far from seaworthy. Some of them landed on Crete, the island which was the next step in German conquest. The proposal to invade Crete was put to Field-Marshal Goering on 15 April by General Lohr, Commander of the Fourth Air Fleet, who recommended the use of parachute and airborne troops.

The German attack was entrusted to General Student's XI Corps. This included General Sussman's 7th Airborne Division, General Meindl's 1st Assault Regiment, which was to be glider borne, and the air group of General Conrad, whose main task was to transport the Corps.

General Student first planned to launch simultaneous attacks on Maleme, Canea, Suda Bay, Retimo, and Heraklion, but his air commander, General von Richtofen, was unable to guarantee co-ordinated air support over the

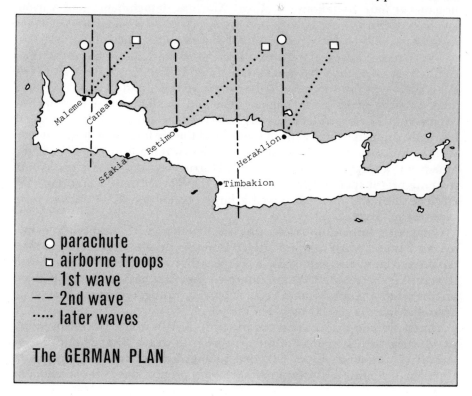

○ parachute
□ airborne troops
— 1st wave
– – 2nd wave
····· later waves

The GERMAN PLAN

four areas at the same time. So Student decided to make airborne attacks on Maleme and Canea in the morning, and Retimo and Heraklion in the afternoon.

A further four groups were to make two seaborne landings; the first on the beaches at Maleme during the first day, and the second one east of Heraklion on the second day. Fear of the Royal Navy, which held vigorous control of the sea, caused this plan to be changed. Instead, both landings would be made on the second day of operations.

After the 7th Air Division and the 1st Assault Regiment had been dropped, General Student proposed to land part of the 5th Mountain Division, under Major-General Ringel, on captured airfields. The rest would follow by sea.

The initial assault, therefore, was to be performed by 750 men in gliders, 10,000 by parachute, 5,000 landed by transport aircraft, and 7,000 by ship. Churchill described these troops as the "flower of German manhood."

In support of the German land operations was General von Richtofen's VIII Air Corps, which contained 430 bombers and dive bombers, 230 twin and single engined fighters, and 50 reconnaissance aircraft. The XI Air Corps had 500 transports and 75 gliders.

Against this formidable invasion, the island was held by the British 14th Brigade of four battalions; a Royal Marines detachment; and various ancillary British troops, together with 7,750 New Zealanders, 6,500 Australians, and 10,200 Greeks; a total of well under 30,000 men.

The Greeks however were as ill-equipped and ill-organised as their comrades-in-arms had been on the mainland. The Australians and New Zealanders were all survivors of the Greek débâcle, and in most cases had landed on the island as incomplete units and lacking a large part of their equipment. Their artillery mainly consisted of captured Italian guns, hurriedly shipped from Egypt to Crete, and the air force which was to help them against assault by a huge modern air fleet was made up of four depleted squadrons; a total of thirty Blenheims, Hurricanes, and Gladiators. About the only bright spot was the existence of the Royal Navy, whose superbly efficient ships and men had saved a large percentage of the Anzacs from captivity in Greece.

Composite formations were thrown together with minimum delay, rearmed as and when supplies arrived from Egypt, and deployed into their rapidly prepared positions. It was a prospect that could hardly have enthused General Freyberg, when Wavell informed him that he had been appointed to command the forces on Crete, following strong representations from Churchill that he should be given the job.

The island had been garrisoned by 3,380 British troops since November 1940, when two battalions of infantry from the 14th Brigade and a contingent of anti-aircraft units landed to supplement the Greek garrison. Once again confusion assumed extraordinary proportions in the subsequent defence planning, with no less than six officers holding command between December 1940 and the end of April 1941. In that month, Major-General E. C. Weston arrived from England to form the "Mobile Naval Base Defence Organization," the principal function of which was to defend the Suda Bay installations.

Weston had hardly had time to settle into his new command before he was superseded by Freyberg, who launched into the fury of preparations which were essential if the island was not to fall to the Germans like a rotten apple. He sent Brigadier Puttick to defend the airfield and a long beach at Maleme, with the 5th and 10th New Zealand Brigades and the 4th New Zealand Brigade in reserve. Suda and Canea, where the harbour and base facilities had to be held, were entrusted to Major-General E. C. Weston, commanding the Royal Marine detachment, one British infantry battalion, two composite Australian battalions, and several mixed units to be used as infantry. The airfield and beaches at Retimo would be defended by the 19th Australian Brigade, under Brigadier G. A. Vasey, and the harbour and airfield at Heraklion by the 14th British Brigade and one Australian battalion, commanded by Brigadier Chappell.

The Greek units were given supplementary operational roles in each of these sectors, but without any great hopes that they would perform as effective fighting units. More weapons, especially artillery, were being brought in from Egypt, but in nothing like the quantities required.

With so little in the way of equipment, and without even proper communications between the various sectors, the defenders could only dig in and wait grimly for the inevitable. It came at first as a series of air attacks from 13 May onwards, with the Germans carrying out heavy and systematic bombing and machine-gunning of the four sectors. In the early morning of 20 May, which dawned clear and still, a heavier than usual air attack by bombers and fighters developed over the Maleme airfield and Suda Bay sectors, and soon it became obvious that it was more than the daily softening-up process to which the defenders had grown almost inured.

The next development has been described by General Freyberg himself. He wrote: "I stood out on the hill with other members of my staff, enthralled by the magnitude of the operation. While we were still watching the bombers, we suddenly became aware of a great throbbing in the moments of comparative quiet, and, looking out to sea with the glasses, I picked out hundreds of planes tier upon tier coming towards us. Here were the huge, slow-moving troop carriers with the loads we were expecting. First we watched them circle counter-clockwise over Maleme aerodrome and then, when they were only a few hundred feet above the ground, as if by magic white specks mixed with other colours suddenly appeared beneath them as clouds of parachutists floated slowly to earth."

Before the parachutists had landed, and even before the dust from the bombing had settled, seventy-five gliders had disgorged their human cargoes, mostly west of the airfield. All through that first day, the New Zealand 5th and 10th Brigades took a heavy toll of the Germans both in the air and after they had landed. Maleme airfield became the critical focal point for the enemy assault. Savage close-quarters fighting routed the German units in some areas, but by evening they had a weak grip on the western edge of the airfield and on Hill 107, by which it was overlooked, although both were still within range of the New Zealanders' guns. Another enemy force had become established in the vital central area east of the airfield, along the slopes which commanded the prison and reservoir adjacent to Galatas. These threatened to cut through the centre of the New Zealand Division positions on the coastal shelf and the foothills.

In the Suda Bay-Canea area, a mixed force of Australians, British and Greeks had dealt severely with numbers of enemy parachutists and glider-borne troops. By the first evening they were well contained, and only small isolated groups were still at large.

At Retimo, the Germans announced their intentions at about 4 p.m., by bombing and strafing in the vicinity of the airfield, but the Australian camouflage was so effective that little damage was inflicted upon them or their positions. Unlike the other sectors, they had not been equipped with either heavy or light anti-aircraft artillery, nor had they received armour-piercing small arms ammunition. Consequently the Germans were able to fly with comparative impunity over the Australian positions whose sole means of defence were their rifles and machine-guns. They still managed to destroy seven of the 161 troop carriers counted over Retimo, together with two bombers. Many more aircraft had to limp back to their bases in Greece, on fire or otherwise damaged.

The town of Retimo is surrounded by rugged mountainous country split by deep ravines sloping steeply down to the coast, at the foot of which a white shingle beach borders the sea. The strategically important airfield was five miles to the east, a little inland from the beach, and was overlooked by a narrow ridge varying from 100 to 200 feet in height.

The original Australian garrison of four battalions had been deployed so that two protected the airfield and the other two covered Georgioupolis Bay, some seven miles to the west. Eventually the corridor between the two forces was cut, and the latter battalions were drawn into the Suda Bay-Canea defence area. Colonel I. Campbell, C.O. of the 2/1st Battalion, had by then assumed command of the Retimo formations, which included a force of 2,300 Greek troops and 800 Crete policemen.

Colonel Campbell's disposition of the relatively few troops under his command, and the manner in which he directed the counter-attacks after the enemy landings, revealed a clarity of thought and courage of decision which elevated his leadership far above the ordinary.

He knew that protection of the airfield was his prime concern, and deployed his troops along the foothills so that they could sweep the field with aimed fire while remaining under cover themselves.

Apart from the common disabilities under which all troops served in Crete, Campbell was also in the unusual position of retaining command of his own battalion whilst taking charge of the whole Retimo garrison, which in numbers, at least, was a brigade. His battalion had lost its second-in-command in Greece, so with the other Australian battalion being short of officers he formed a staff consisting only of his Adjutant and Quartermaster. His Intelligence Officer had been invalided back to Egypt, and his Intelligence Sergeant was sick.

The Retimo sector was also the only one in which the Germans outnumbered the Empire troops. At Maleme, the Germans on the first day were about four against five, and at Heraklion roughly one to two. This did not worry the Australians at Retimo, who ever after their experiences in Greece were confident that they could handle the "invincible" Germans.

During the first few hours after landing, the enemy received a violently hostile welcome. The Australians engaged them in desperate fighting among the ravines and vineyards, exacting a terrible toll in dead and prisoners, but by nightfall the Germans had established themselves on some of the key heights overlooking the airfield. Campbell asked for reinforcements, but Freyberg replied late that night, "Regret unable to send help, good luck."

Campbell understood that the fate of Retimo rested with him, so resolved to collect every man he could muster for a counter-attack at dawn. It came off magnificently, despite initial setbacks in the first charge. An attack by most of the 2/1st Battalion, under Captain Moriarity, dislodged the Germans from the vital Hill A and surrounding points overlooking the airfield, and from this success Campbell directed his two battalions, with supporting Greeks, to clear the Germans from the area. They did so with complete success, and even captured the German local commander, Colonel Sturm, who was found to be still carrying his orders.

By nightfall, the Australians were back in their original positions, many of them equipped with captured weapons. Out of the original 1,500 parachutists dropped in the area, they had killed, wounded, or captured many hundreds.

Colonel Campbell informed Freyberg that the situation at Retimo was well in hand, and received the reply "You have done magnificently." During the critical eighteen hours from the time of invasion at Retimo, he had conducted what in retrospect was a model for the whole defence of Crete. Clear and concise in thought, positive in direction, he had ordered five counter-attacks against the numerically superior Germans entrenched on the hills surrounding the airfield, until he was rewarded by success.

In the ensuing days, between the initial defeat of the German landing and the capitulation of Crete, Campbell and his men fought an almost lone battle. Cut off by poor communications from the rest of the island, and comparatively unaware of the course of battle, they fought on until it was too late. A signal from Freyberg, informing Campbell of the order to retire to the port of Sfakia for evacuation, failed to reach him.

He and his men made persistent efforts to dislodge the Germans from their positions at Perivolia and open up the road to Suda, but on 29 May he decided that further fighting would only result in unnecessary loss of life. His men had done far more than could be asked of them, were almost out of ammunition, and had been on half rations for three days. So he tied a towel to a stick, walked a lonely path down a track towards the Germans, and surrendered his force.

Their courage and spirit in the defence of Retimo is unsurpassed in the annals of Australian arms. For a loss of 120 dead and 182 wounded, they had inflicted casualties totalling 700 killed and taken 500 prisoners. It was a superlative performance by the two depleted Australian battalions and their Greek comrades, darkened only by the destiny which decreed that the majority would have to spend the next four years as prisoners of war.

The garrison at Heraklion had become involved with the enemy at about the same time as Retimo, on the first day of the invasion. This force, of about 8,000 men, contained three battalions of regular British infantry who had not been in Greece, and therefore were among the freshest troops on the island; an Australian battalion from Greece; a composite British battalion; and three raw Greek battalions.

After bombing and strafing the target areas for an hour after 4 a.m., the Germans sent in 240 troop carriers. These dropped their parachutists mainly west of the town and in the immediate vicinity of the airfield. Their intelligence had let them down badly in this instance, for the Germans believed Heraklion to be lightly defended and the 2,000 parachutists had no suspicion of the reception that awaited them.

Brigadier Chappel, the area commander, launched immediate counter-attacks. Within twenty-four hours, 1,000 of the Germans were lying dead within the British perimeter, and the remnants of the two main groups were struggling to make contact with one another. However, they succeeded in retaining control of an area to the east of the British force, and more importantly to the west of Heraklion astride the Retimo road, thus severing connections with the Australians in that sector.

The British commander, once the threats to the harbour and airfield had been stabilised, did not pursue a particularly aggressive policy in clearing the two groups still at large despite his overwhelming numerical superiority. He was content to maintain his existing positions, until he and his men were evacuated eight days later.

Despite these initially decisive local successes at Retimo and Heraklion, the key to the German conquest of Crete remained with the New Zealanders on the Maleme front. During the second day they were subjected to increasingly strong pressures from the Germans, who gained a tenuous grip on the airfield by landing their first transport at 8.10 a.m., in spite of intense machine-gun fire from the New Zealanders. This aircraft unloaded and took off again, to be followed as the day wore on by more and more transports bringing in reinforcements and supplies. With a courage and determination befitting their own military tradition, the Germans had achieved their first objective of capturing an airfield, insecure though their hold might be.

The New Zealanders planned to mount a counter-attack that night, for what would be the most crucial engagement of the battle for Crete. But the measures taken to implement it proceeded with surprising lack of decision during the day and evening. The Germans themselves realised that they were in a critical position, and the diarist of Major-General Ringel's Mountain Division recorded: "On the evening of the second day of the invasion, the situation seemed to be balanced on a knife edge. If 11/100th Mountain Battalion had landed with (only) light casualties, the (German) defences of Maleme airfield would be considerably strengthened, but a heavy, concentrated counter-attack would force the (German) defenders to fight for their lives."

The New Zealand leaders, wearied by the weeks of action since they had landed in Greece, and hampered by poor communication between units, delayed until the early morning of 22 May, but the crucial moment had passed and their counter-attack lacked drive and co-ordination. The troops themselves had been fighting almost continuously for forty-eight hours whilst under constant air attack, and were themselves nearing the end of their physical endurance. They made some progress, but by late in the afternoon it was clear that no vital ground had been regained.

The Germans made a strong attack late that afternoon, and cut the coast road between the 4th and 5th New Zealand brigades. At a conference that night, Brigadier Puttick decided that to save the 5th Brigade from being cut off he would withdraw, and abandon all the ground which they held around Maleme airfield.

This was a vital decision, affecting the ultimate fate of the island. It surrendered the airfield which the Germans so urgently needed, and in effect signalled the beginning of the end in Crete.

General Ringel now had command of all German troops on the island, and on 22 May he received instructions from General Student to secure Maleme, clear Suda Bay, relieve Retimo, and advance to Heraklion. The Royal Navy had destroyed Student's planned seaborne reinforcements, by smashing up two convoys during the night and morning of 21/22 May, but had paid for them by losing the cruisers *Gloucester* and *Fiji* and the destroyer *Greyhound* to air attack.

On 23 May, Churchill sent a characteristic message to General Freyberg, saying, "The whole world watches your splendid battle, on which great things turn." But the valour of Freyberg's troops was not sufficient to counter the weight of enemy troops and material which now were pouring into the island. The position on the Maleme front deteriorated rapidly, and the New Zealand Division withdrew to a defensive arc around Galatas, supported by the remains of Vasey's 19th Australian Brigade. The Germans maintained a relentless pressure, and the second critical phase of the battle for Crete was reached on the 24/25 May, when they forced the depleted New Zealand Division and their Australian comrades out of Galatas.

The worst effects of this withdrawal might have been lessened by employment of the "Force Reserve" to stabilise the front. Consisting mainly of British units, and stationed in the Suda Bay area under the nominal command of Major-General E. C. Weston, this force was not effectively employed. Poor communications, and confusion in the chain of command, prevented it from exerting any decisive influence and resulted in bitter recriminations during subsequent post-mortems on the Crete affair.

On 26 May, Freyberg cabled Wavell: "I regret to report that in my opinion the limit of endurance has been reached by the troops under my command at Suda Bay. No matter what decision is taken by the Commander-in-Chief, from a military point of view our position here is hopeless."

The worst was yet to come. The tiny port of Sfakia, on the south coast of the island, was chosen as the embarkation point. Harried by the triumphant Germans, the Australians and New Zealanders joined with remnants of the British infantry and Royal Marines in fighting a series of savage rearguard actions to cover the retreat down the Suda Bay road and into the White Mountains, which the defeated troops had to cross on their way to Sfakia.

Thousands of men, many of whom were from base and non-combatant units whose lack of spirit contrasted sharply with the enduring courage of the fighting men, straggled across the dry and savage mountains and down to the coast. The Royal Navy once more performed herculean efforts in evacuating the troops, under almost constant air attacks from the Luftwaffe, until the night of 30 May. Then, the Army commanders notified Admiral Cunningham that they did not expect the Navy to attempt to continue with the evacuation.

More than 6,000 men, of all ranks and arms, were left behind, including the 2/7th Battalion of the 6th Australian Division, which sacrificed itself in order to act as rearguard and hold back the German pursuit. The majority of those abandoned on Crete were obliged to surrender, though a number refused to give in and found some kind of hiding in the mountains. Some of these fought with the partisans, others eventually gave themselves up, but about 600 managed to find their way across the Mediterranean to Egypt and Palestine.

The Allied losses totalled 15,900 men, including prisoners of war, of which the Australians suffered 274 killed, 507 wounded, and 3,109 taken prisoner. The Germans lost 4,000 killed and 2,594 wounded, with 220 aircraft destroyed. Most of the 5,312 men of the British Army left on Crete belonged to base units, whereas the Australians suffered the highest ratio of loss from fighting troops, including three infantry battalions and other front line units.

Could Crete have been held? Many military experts have said that it should have been, although General Freyberg, to the very end of his life, said that it was impossible. The inertia which characterised the garrison role of the British troops on the island for six months prior to the battle, and the delay in counter-attacking by the New Zealanders during the critical first twenty-four hours after the landing at Maleme, perhaps contributed most to its loss. The overwhelming German air superiority was of prime importance in the defeat, because their aircraft were able to act as artillery and pound the defenders with unendurable bombing and strafing.

For the Germans, despite heavy losses among their elite paratroops, the vanquishing of both Greece and Crete at a cost of roughly 13,000 men killed and wounded was a strategic and propaganda triumph of the first order. For the Allies, possibly the most important effect of the battle for Crete was that German losses dissuaded Hitler from an "island-hopping" campaign into Cyprus and then across the short sea barrier into Palestine or Syria, where the Vichy French might not have resisted him. Such an advantage was dearly bought by the Australians and New Zealanders.

It is very doubtful whether "world opinion" was much influenced by the British upholding their political obligations to Greece, especially since their attempt to do so exemplified the "too little and too late" character of British operations at that time. A resounding victory in Libya, such as might have been gained if the Anzac troops had been used to drive the Italians out of North Africa, would certainly have been far more effective in the propaganda sense than the reception of a sound thrashing in the Balkans. Whatever delays and casualties were imposed on the enemy in these two campaigns, they certainly did not balance the decimation of the 6th Australian and New Zealand Divisions, which at the time were by far the most effective and best led infantry in the Middle East command.

The suggestion has been made that British tactical competence reached its lowest ebb in the first World War, during the disasters of the Somme. The same, however, might be said of their military operations in Greece, Crete, and along the Mediterranean coasts during 1941, especially since the loss of Greece and Crete was followed by Wavell's catastrophic attempt to relieve Tobruk with British and Indian units.

It is no wonder that Australians in the whole Middle East theatre referred to it cynically as the "Muddle East."

21

"FIGHTING OUR FRIENDS"

T HE LONG LINES OF PRISONERS WERE STILL TRUDGING INTO GERMAN compounds while Cairo headquarters were laying plans for what, on the face of it, seemed to be yet another frustrating and profitless adventure. This was the northwards thrust into French Syria; a campaign which to a large extent has been "swept under the carpet" by those who do not like to remember that Allied troops were used in a fierce campaign against the French. The French, however, have not forgotten, any more than they have forgotten the disabling of the French Mediterranean Fleet by the Royal Navy, for reasons very similar to those which impelled the Syrian campaign.

The British Government feared that Syria, which was controlled by the "neutral" government of Vichy, might become a base for German operations in the Middle East, or from which they might inspire Arab rebellion. Political unrest in this area had simmered for centuries, against a background of Turkish, British, and French occupation. None of these countries had any right to be there, and the area had a long history of exploitation, broken promises, and doubtful motives. With British prestige on the decline and German influence at its peak, the Syrians seeking independence, French national pride rubbed raw, and a condition of extreme animosity between the Free French and Vichy French, the whole territory was ripe for explosion.

In May, the Iraqi army actually attacked British airfields near Baghdad, and had been supported by German aircraft flown in from Crete and refuelling at French airfields in Syria. The Iraqis were defeated, but the danger obviously was acute.

When plans were completed for the invasion of Syria, the 7th Australian

216

Division was given the spearhead role. Less one brigade, which was with the 9th Australian Division in the defence of Tobruk, the division was withdrawn from garrison duty at Mersa Matruh in order to prepare for the operation.

It was commanded by Major-General H. D. Lavarack, who had been Chief of Staff for the four years up to the outbreak of war. He had stepped down from this post in the hope of being chosen to lead the 6th Division, the first sent overseas. The command had gone to Mackay instead, on Blamey's recommendation to the Australian Cabinet.

Lavarack, however, was regarded as one of Australia's most promising military leaders; a judgement which seemed to be confirmed by Wavell when Rommel was in full cry after the British forces in Cyrenaica. Wavell invited Lavarack to join him in a meeting with Morshead, to plan the defence of Tobruk, and then appointed him as commander of all forces on the Western Desert frontier. Lavarack acted quickly and with considerable judgement to stabilise the situation, but when the crisis was past he was replaced by a comparatively junior British officer; General Beresford-Peirse. Another example, perhaps, of the "Union of British Generals."

The 21st and 25th Brigades of the 7th Division were led by Brigadiers J. E. S. Stevens and A. R. Baxter-Cox. Stevens had served in France during the first World War, and had been an active soldier in the militia between the wars. Eventually he became commander of the 6th Division in the Pacific theatre. Baxter-Cox, a West Australian, had a similar record.

The divisional artillery was commanded by Brigadier F. H. Berryman, who had served as Mackay's senior staff officer in the Western Desert, and also was destined for senior command in the Pacific campaigns.

Whether by chance or choice, Lavarack, the professional soldier, had more regulars on his staff than either of the other two Australian divisions in the Middle East. His Chief of Staff, Colonel J. A. Chapman, had been on loan to the British Army when the war broke out, as an instructor at the Staff College, Camberley.

During late May and early June, the 7th Division took up positions along the borders of Palestine and Transjordan, together with the 5th Indian Brigade and Free French Brigade. The attack was to be three-pronged, with the 21st Brigade driving up the coast road to Beirut; the 25th Brigade moving up the centre to take the key points of Metulla, Fort Merdjayoun, and then the air base of Rayak; and the Indian and French advancing on the right into the Hauran, the high wheatlands east of Lake Tiberias and the upper Jordan. They would form a "bridgehead," whence the Free French would drive into Damascus—hopefully to be welcomed as liberators.

The attack was to be in two phases: the first to capture Beirut, Rayak, and Damascus; the second an advance on Palmyra, Homs, and the Syrian port of Tripoli.

Once more, General Maitland Wilson was given command of the Australian forces, and he and Wavell instructed Lavarack to make the main drive along the coastal road to Beirut. Even during the preliminary planning, however, Lavarack contended that an advance on the right was more likely to be successful. The coast road ran through rugged country, ideal for ambushes, and through many tunnels. The road through the centre travelled through valleys and along mountainsides, and could easily be cut. On the extreme right, however, the route was suitable for fast movement across flat desert terrain.

The Vichy French forces were believed to number 35,000 regulars with eighteen good battalions, mostly of coloured colonial troops but including a regiment of the Foreign Legion. They had a half-division of armoured cars and cavalry, about ninety medium tanks, sixty fighter aircraft, and about forty bombers.

This force was to be attacked by six Australian battalions, one British and two Indian battalions, and six Free French battalions of unknown quality. They had no armour, and little air support until halfway through the campaign.

The comparative weakness of the invading force was excused by Wavell's

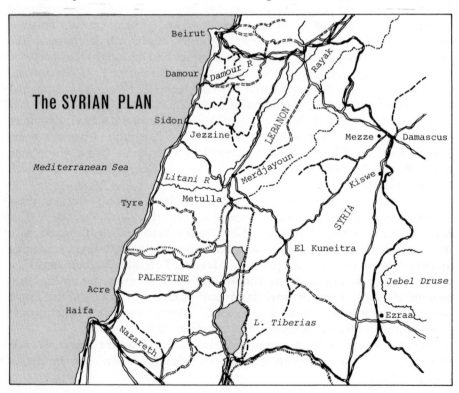

planners with the premise that, "The success of the operation largely depends on lack of resistance or at least acquiescence by the French," based on a conviction that when they were attacked they would "withdraw into the Lebanon, thereby leaving the rest of the country open to invasion." As so often in the "Muddle East," the planners were to be proved wrong, and Lavarack certainly considered that they were approaching the problem with undue optimism.

However, the Australians were by now fairly well accustomed to implementing unsound plans of attack. The main difference on this occasion was that they would be entering an area filled with seething hatreds, in which a man hardly knew whom his enemy might be and no man trusted another. The Vichy French, intolerably conscious of the way in which French military glory had been trodden into the dust during 1940, almost welcomed an opportunity to release their fury against their traditional enemies, the British. For the Australians, unused to the bitterness of European politics, it was to be a strange and hurtful experience. Many of them thought that it would be almost a "walk over," since they had the erroneous idea that the French would welcome them. Others felt that they would be "fighting our friends," because they thought that the French still regarded them as allies. It was to be a campaign without honour or glory in the public sense, because the planners were intent on keeping the whole affair as secret as possible so that "world opinion" would not know that the British were attacking their previous allies, and so that the situation might not be exacerbated even more.

In the Middle East, where a whisper in Cairo resounds as far as Damascus, it was inconceivable that the Vichy French should not be well aware of what was being planned. So when the Australian troops crossed the border early on 8 June 1941, they found the frontier posts fully manned and offering solid resistance. Instead of the passive reception which they had been told to expect, they received volleys of machine-gun and rifle fire which caused immediate casualties.

For the troops of the 21st Brigade, going up the coastal road, the major objective was the crossing of the Litani River. Seventeen miles north of the border, this was a natural defensive barrier. The task was to have been made easier by British Commandos making a diversionary seaborne landing on its far side, but an ill-planned attack proved abortive. They did not save the main bridge across the Litani, which would have been of such great assistance to the Australian advance, but by the end of the first day the brigade had overcome a series of enemy posts and occupied the town of Tyre, with contact being made against the enemy positions along the river.

Meanwhile, on the central sector, Brigadier Cox's brigade had crossed the border near Metulla. Its first objective was Fort Merdjayoun, but like their comrades on the coast they had met determined opposition from the well prepared French positions. On the right, the combined Indian and

British force had established a bridgehead for the Free French to move through in high expectation of a triumphal entry into Damascus.

During the second day, West Australians of the 2/16th Battalion used some of the commando boats and crossed the Litani under heavy fire. Despite shelling from French destroyers, acting in support of the strong defensive positions, they had established a beachhead on its north side by late afternoon. During that night, engineers built a pontoon bridge, and by 5 a.m. on 10 June men and vehicles were beginning to pour across. The crossing of the Litani, which presented such a natural line of defence, was a feat that the troops of the 21st Brigade regarded with justifiable pride.

From the Litani they moved on up the coast, clearing the enemy from their positions along the rugged terrain on their right flank and entering Sidon on 15 June.

In the Fort Merdjayoun sector, the deadlock was unbroken, after abortive attacks against well entrenched French troops. On the right, the Free French had made good progress against little opposition until 10 June, when they reached the Vichy outposts of Kiswe along the Nahr El Awaj, the outer perimeter defence line for Damascus.

Vichy French resistance already was causing concern to British leaders. Not only did the defenders outnumber the invading troops, but possessed armour as well, and operated in terrain that was favourable to them whether in attack or defence.

On the coast, the Vichy French began a long withdrawal north from Sidon, and the Australians occupied several villages and gained control of important lateral roads inland. The position at Merdjayoun took a turn for the better when it fell on 12 June, following a series of attacks by the Australians which included fierce hand to hand engagements. Following the fall of this key fort, General Lavarack decided that he would push north to Jezzine, which joined a lateral road from Sidon, and thus assist the coastal advance which had generally progressed according to plan. He retained one battalion of infantry in a defensive role at Merdjayoun, and thrust other units north east along two routes known as "A" and "B".

The road to Jezzine was a tortuous ribbon through steep, rocky mountains. Three miles south of the town, the Australians ran into fierce defensive action from well-entrenched positions, but a brilliantly executed attack cleared the road and won the town on 14 June.

On the right, the Free French had now been halted by Vichy positions at Kiswe, and it was decided that only a carefully organised attack with artillery support would break through these. Arrangements were made for this to be launched on 15 June, in conjunction with the 5th Indian Brigade, but while preparations were being made the Vichy French counter-attacked with tanks along the Kuneitra road from Damascus. They outflanked the British and Free French positions facing Damascus on the Kiswe front, and also threatened Fort Merdjayoun along routes "A" and "B", which were comparatively lightly held. The Australians were obliged to fall back, and both Kuneitra and Merdjayoun were recaptured by the enemy. Kuneitra was retaken again on 18 June, but a counter-attack on Merdjayoun, on 16/17 June, was a failure, and the Australians suffered heavy casualties.

The confused situation in these two sectors also threatened the Australians at Jezzine, where the enemy launched a strong attack at dawn on 17 June. After bitter fighting which lasted all day, they were repulsed with heavy losses.

The purpose of the Vichy French thrust had been to retake Kuneitra and Merdjayoun, and establish a line south of Kirbe and Fort Khiam, whence a battalion was to fan out eastwards towards Banias and westward towards Metulla. They had three battalions facing the Australians at Merdjayoun, five or six aimed against the Australians on the coastal sector, one and a half at Jezzine, and two at Jebel Druse.

Merdjayoun, however, remained the most critical sector for the whole campaign. The Australians lost heavily in the bitter fighting that raged around the fort, and from 17 to 24 June, when it finally fell, four full-scale attacks were made under the direction of Brigadier Berryman. His three Australian battalions drew five of the enemy's into the area, and there was a danger of them gaining control of the vital mountain passes and being able to thrust into Palestine, with disastrous results.

It was about this time that General Blamey visited the front, and expressed his dissatisfaction in no uncertain terms.

Wilson's headquarters were in Jerusalem, well away from the front, so Blamey drove there during the night and asked to see him. Told that Wilson was asleep, Blamey instructed his ADC to wake him up. When Wilson finally appeared, he found that Blamey was in fighting mood. The Australian insisted that the main advance should be directed through Damascus, in accordance with Lavarack's original contentions. This, according to Blamey, would hasten the end of the campaign and save casualties. When Wilson finally agreed and said that he would ring Lavarack in the morning, Blamey insisted that it should be done there and then. It was, and the attack on Damascus was duly launched on 19 June by the 5th Indian Brigade and Free French forces, but the Indians were severely mauled in heavy fighting around Mezze and the Free French failed.

The operational control of the campaign passed to 1st Australian Corps on 18 June, when General Lavarack assumed command of all land operations in Syria. Major-General A. S. Allen, promoted from command of a brigade in the 6th Division, assumed control of the 7th in succession to Lavarack.

Lavarack's first move was to switch the newly arrived 6th British Division, which in fact was little more than a brigade as it comprised only two British battalions, one Indian battalion, and one Australian, into the Damascus sector. He supplemented this force by two more Australian battalions, including the 2/3rd. This unit fought a furious battle at Mezze, during which its headquarters was captured by the enemy, but in the end it succeeded in cutting the Damascus-Beirut road, recapturing its headquarters, and smashing the key Vichy French positions which protected Damascus. Brigadier Lloyd, Commander of the 5th Indian Brigade, paid high tribute to the Australians when he wrote, "The battalion acted with the greatest gallantry and dash throughout, the initiative and keenness of the junior leaders being marked. The success, in spite of very reduced numbers and fatigue, against an enemy in masonry forts and on ground well known to him, was remarkable and worthy of the highest praise."

As a result of this battle, the Free French were able to enter the city on 21 June. Colonel Casseau, leader of the Free French forces, and Colonel A. S. Blackburn, the senior Australian officer and a V.C. winner from Gallipoli, accepted the formal surrender of Damascus.

Since the main concentration of effort had now been directed to the Damascus sector, the Australian 21st Brigade on the Sidon-Jezzine front resorted to defensive patrolling, but another success was won by the 2/3rd Battalion. They attacked the heights of Jebel Mazar, against superior forces well entrenched, and took the position. This evoked more praise, this time from Brigadier C. E. N. Lomax of the 16th British Infantry Brigade. He wrote, "Throughout the operation, all ranks of the 2/3rd Australian Infantry Battalion displayed the very highest courage and determination, and their dogged endeavour has very justly called forth the unstinted praise and admiration of all ranks of 16 Infantry Brigade."

Meanwhile, heavy fighting had broken out on the Jezzine sector, where the struggle continued for the heights commanding the road leading north. The mountainous terrain, which rose to 1,000 feet in a series of cliffs and rocky shelves, provided perfect positions of defence, but was a difficult and exhausting battlefield for the troops of both sides. Brigadier E. C. Plant, a Gallipoli veteran who had succeeded Baxter-Cox as commander of the 25th Brigade, reported, "The country was as bad as Gallipoli and worse, the hills were bigger; there were more boulders, and in the Kharat area no scrub at all."

Following the fall of Damascus, Brigadier Stevens moved his brigade north with aggressive patrolling along the coastal sector, while big plans were being made for a final blow to be delivered in a campaign which had confounded all expectations that it would be cheap and easy. Obviously it now had to be settled fast, because there was a constant danger that the Germans might intervene.

Reinforcements were arriving to supplement the depleted formations that had been involved from the outset. These included the 17th Australian

Brigade, under Brigadier Savige, which brought the 7th Australian Division almost up to full strength. The Australians were to become solely responsible for the coastal and Jezzine sectors, while British forces would take over the Merdjayoun and Damascus sectors.

Other new formations included "Habforce," of approximately brigade strength, which was to advance from Iraq with the intention of capturing Palmyra and then cutting the road between Damascus and Homs. The 5th Indian Division under General Slim, also from Iraq, was deployed along the Euphrates with the objective of capturing Aleppo.

Now that Damascus had been taken and the situation at Merdjayoun stabilised, the emphasis returned to the coastal sector. The capture of Beirut, which contained the main French base and was the seat of Government, became the prime objective, but the Vichy French positions along the Damour River presented a considerable obstacle to this ambition. They were to face the Australians with the strongest natural defensive line on the coastal sector, but once they could be overrun the route to Beirut would be open.

The approach to Damour represented the tactician's conception of an almost perfect line of defence. The Australian *Official War History* says that: "North from the line of posts which the 21st Brigade occupied, the coast road travelled along a narrow shelf between the sea and a series of precipitous east-west ridges intersected by wadis until it reached the Damour River. This stream wound through a wide cleft in the coastal range. South of it the main road curved along the coastal ledge and then bent inland to a point about a mile from the sea where it crossed the Damour River on a stone bridge. Immediately north of the bridge a road branched off eastward along the bottom of the ravine, crossed to the south bank of the river about two miles inland, and then began to zigzag up the face of the range towards Beit ed Dine, climbing 3,000 feet in a bee-line distance of about six miles. North of the river the coastal plain, about half a mile wide, was thickly planted with orchards and banana groves. A stone-walled channel about twenty yards wide ran east and west through the groves about a mile north of the river. Just beyond it lay Damour, a town of some 5,000 people. From the inland edge of this cultivated area the ridges rose steeply, sometimes climbing 600 feet within a little more than a mile from the orchards, but these ridges were lower than the heights overlooking the ravine from the south. For some two miles from the plantations the mountain ridges were almost bare, but from about the 1,000-foot contour upwards trees and shrub were thicker."

Brigadier Stevens proposed to his divisional commander, General Allen, that the two brigades allotted the task of smashing the French defences should box Damour in. His own 21st Brigade would form two sides of this box, the sea the third, and the newly joined 17th Brigade the fourth; out-

*Greece, Crete, and Syria. Gavin Long.

flanking the town by circling round through the hills on the right and cutting the road leading northwards out of Damour. After a conference at Allen's headquarters, this was agreed upon, with the attack to go in on 5 or 6 July.

While Australian units from other sectors were moving to their new concentration on the coast, Lavarack ordered the British in the Damascus and Merdjayoun areas to maintain aggressive patrols as a diversion from the main attack at Damour. This began at midnight on 5/6 July, as units of the 21st Brigade set off down their respective paths through the ravines and over the extraordinarily rough terrain.

The battle lasted for five days, and in planning and execution was a complete Australian victory. Clambering up and down the steep, rocky hillsides, the Australians fought a series of bitter actions with seven Vichy French battalions, and in many cases were forced to drive them out of their positions with bombs and bayonets. The French resisted with what seemed at first to be an unbreakable determination, but as one after another of their strong points was taken they finally realised that their situation was hopeless.

Aggressive action on other fronts, launched during the battle for Damour, met with varying success, but sufficient pressure was exerted on the Vichy French authorities to force them to sue for an armistice. Hostilities ceased at midnight on 11 July, thus ending a campaign that had lasted approximately five weeks.

The Australians suffered the heaviest losses among the Allied participants, with 416 killed and 1,130 wounded. The British and Indians together lost approximately 600 killed and wounded, while the Free French forces, who did not perform with particular distinction, lost some 100 killed and wounded. The Australian casualties in the Syrian campaign equalled the combined total for Greece and Crete, excluding prisoners of war; a fact which emphasises the severity of an operation which at first was regarded as a "sideshow."

Two Australians won the Victoria Cross during the campaign; Lieutenant A. R. Cutler, now Governor of New South Wales, for sustained bravery at Merdjayoun; and Private J. H. Gordon, for exceptionally gallant action in the bitter fighting on the Jezzine sector.

The Syrian operations concluded six months during which Australian soldiers in the second World War had been well and truly blooded, beginning with Bardia and continuing with Tobruk, Benghazi, Greece, and Crete. And while the 6th and 7th Divisions had been carving their place in history, the 9th Division had been making its own name by its indomitable defence of Tobruk.

22

THE GREAT SIEGE

FIELD-MARSHAL LORD WAVELL'S BIOGRAPHER HAS SUGGESTED THAT, "His greatest stroke of all was executed in adversity. By Tobruk he forced the Germans on to the defensive and probably saved Egypt. By holding Tobruk and aggressive action on the Egyptian front he gained five months' stability for the formation of the 8th Army."

The writer was unduly modest. The siege of Tobruk was as vital to the Middle East as the siege of Stalingrad was to the Russian front for without it there would be no Alamein. It is interesting to observe, in contemporary military literature, a tendency to play down the importance of Tobruk's role in the ultimate fortunes of the Middle East conflict. Perhaps this is due to an embarrassing realisation of the completely disproportionate role played by the Australian forces, who brought ultimate victory in the crucial Libyan desert battles.

The whole situation was summed up by Wavell when he ended his conference with the Australian generals, Lavarack and Morshead, in a battered Tobruk house on 8 April, 1941. He had told them that a stand was to be made and that Lavarack would take command of all forces in the fortress and Cyrenaica, and concluded by emphasising that, "There is nothing between you and Cairo."

That was simply and precisely the situation which he entrusted to the Australian 9th Division. If they failed, the Middle East would be lost. The Germans would drive like an arrow from Cairo across Arabia to the Persian Gulf, and seize the fountainhead of Britain's oil supplies. They would be able to turn north from there, and attack Russia from the south as well as from the west. India would be menaced. They could link up with the Italians in Ethiopia, and invade East Africa. The whole structure of Britain's imperial power could collapse as though its keystone had been knocked away, and Germany would in fact and at last be invincible.

After making his decision, Wavell pencilled for Lavarack on three sheets of notepaper the following brief and not very reassuring instructions:

1. You will take over command of all troops in Cyrenaica. Certain reinforcements have already been notified as being sent to you. You will be informed of any others which it is decided to send.

2. Your main task will be to hold the enemy's advance at Tobruk, in order to give time for the assembly of reinforcements, especially of armoured troops, for the defence of Egypt.

3. To gain time for the assembly of the required reinforcements it may be necessary to hold Tobruk for about two months.

4. Should you consider after reviewing the situation and in the light of the strength deployed by the enemy that it is not possible to maintain your position at Tobruk for this length of time, you will report your views when a decision will be taken by G.H.Q.

5. You will in any case prepare a plan for withdrawal from Tobruk, by land and by sea, should withdrawal become necessary.

6. Your defence will be as mobile as possible and you will take any opportunity of hindering the enemy's concentration by offensive action.

Lavarack made a quick assessment of his resources in men and material, to establish what the results were of the "Tobruk Derby" as the Australians dryly termed the hurried retreat into the fortress.

He had intact the 9th Division's three brigades of infantry, the 20th, 24th and 26th, together with the 18th brigade of the 7th Division. This gave him a total of twelve infantry battalions, plus their ancillary units. However, the division had come to Cyrenaica after little more than basic training, and in fact had been despatched to the area in order to have its training rounded off in what had been expected to be a comparatively quiet area. It had been cut off without its own artillery, which was provided by four Royal Artillery regiments. It had no transport, and a minimum of equipment and ammunition. Its first few weeks in Tobruk were spent in assembling parts of Italian guns into what later became known as the "Bush Artillery."

An assortment of British and Indian troops, remnants of the forces lost in Rommel's recent attacks, were also quickly organised into some semblance of control and responsibility. The initial fighting strength of the front line units totalled 14,270 Australian and 9,000 British troops, plus about 5,700 base troops of mixed Australian, British and Indian origin and 3,000 Libyan labourers. There was also a large number of Italian and German prisoners.

The non-effective formations, together with units of the 2nd British Armoured Divisions which had withdrawn into the perimeter after losing their tanks, were reduced as quickly as possible by evacuation. By 30 June, the total strength of the garrison had been substantially reduced to 14,326 Australians and a little under 8,000 British.

Lavarack appointed Major-General Morshead as fortress commander, and he made his intentions very clear when in a briefing of his brigadiers he said, "There's to be no Dunkirk here. If we should have to get out, we shall fight our way out. There is to be no surrender, and no retreat."

A junior officer expressed the feelings of the Australians in a different way. They felt keenly about the forced retreat into Tobruk, an action which they did not consider to be worthy of their division despite its rawness, and he observed, "We can't let it be said that the 9th had lost what the 6th (Australian Division) had won."

The men of the 9th Division were not impressed by the reputation of the Germans, who at that stage in the war had yet to be defeated in a land battle. There was to be no looking over the shoulder, no negative mental attitudes of mind. They were in Tobruk, and if the Germans wanted it they would have to come and get it.

Wavell had suggested to Lavarack that the outer, or "Red Line" of defence, which had a total length of thirty and a quarter miles, was too extended to hold with the forces at his disposal and that he should base his defence preparations on the so called inner defence line. This imaginary line consisted of a most elementary and disconnected series of weapon pits and tank traps, with little or no defensive value.

The outer defence positions, constructed originally by the Italians, at least offered a continuous system of about 150 posts protected by barbed wire and tank ditches. They provided well-sited observation points and very effective fields of fire. It was important, too, to keep the enemy's artillery as far away from the harbour as possible, so that he could not prevent it from being used for supply and reinforcement.

In order to spread out the thin Australian resources as widely as possible, the perimeter defences were manned by seven of the garrison's twelve infantry battalions, with each battalion having a reserve company dug in half a mile to the rear.

The Italians had held this system of posts with twenty-five to fifty men in each, but the Australians were obliged to man each post with no more than ten to fifteen infantrymen. To back them up, Morshead developed a system of "defence in depth." Behind the first lines of defence, minefields were sown thickly, to prevent deep penetration by enemy tanks. Further back, a mobile reserve was kept in preparation for counter-attack, and an inner series of defences was constructed and christened the "Blue Line."

Morshead's instructions were that if the enemy penetrated the Red Line, the men in its posts were to hold on and keep fighting at all costs, while the Blue Line absorbed the attack. If they pierced the Blue Line, and the mobile

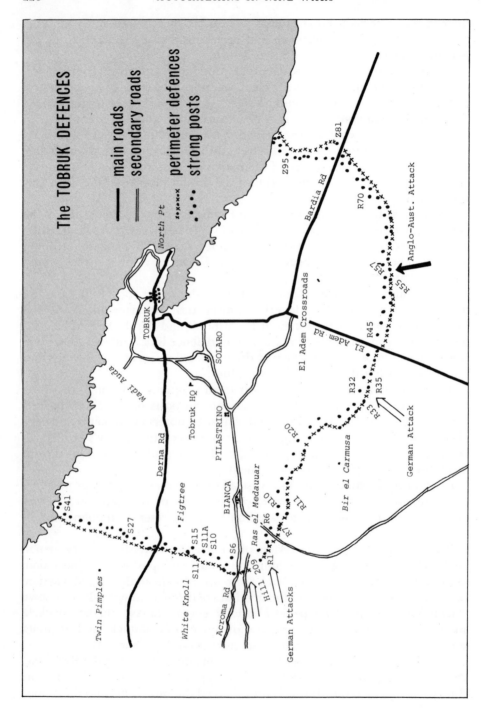

The TOBRUK DEFENCES

——— main roads
——— secondary roads
×××××× perimeter defences
•••••• strong posts

reserve was unable to check them, then every other man in the garrison who was able to hold a rifle, whether he was a combatant soldier or not, would have to be prepared to sell his life dearly.

All this defence work needed time, which Rommel was not going to allow them. He was forced to capture Tobruk as quickly as possible, because he could not leave it as a threat to his rear. It was a seaport, which eventually would allow the British to bring in reinforcements to cut German communications in a thrust towards Egypt, or the garrison could make a sortie for the same purpose. To the hard-driving German general, encouraged by all the plaudits of the Nazi propaganda machine and spurred by centuries of Prussian military tradition, the solution was simple. Cut out Tobruk like a cancer, clean up the coast, and sweep on to Cairo and all the glory which Germany knew how to heap on her triumphant military commanders.

He acted almost immediately. Stragglers were still limping into Tobruk when he began probing the perimeter for soft spots against which to drive his first major assault; the "Easter Battle" which would test the resolve of the Australians and British to the full.

It was heralded by a shower of leaflets dropped on the fortress on 12 April, proclaiming: "The General Officer commanding the German forces in Libya hereby requests that the British troops occupying Tobruk surrender their arms. Single soldiers waving white handkerchiefs will not be fired on. Strong German forces have surrounded Tobruk and it is useless to try to escape. Our dive bombers and Stukas are awaiting your ships which are lying in Tobruk."

The Germans had misjudged the character of the occupants. Morshead's operational summary noted tersely that, "Owing to the prevailing dust and the necessity to ration water for essential purposes there were no white handkerchiefs available," while the Diggers' response was couched in simple soldierly language.

Enemy activity increased throughout Easter Sunday, 13 April 1941, and the main assault came at 11 p.m. After an hour of heavy mortar and machine-gun fire on the forward posts of the 2/17th Battalion, a party of thirty Germans penetrated the barbed wire east of Post 33, and dug themselves in despite heavy fire from the Australians. R.A.F. reconnaissance had spotted a huge build-up of men and vehicles behind the German lines, and this German penetration had been intended as a gap through which they might flow into the perimeter.

Since the intruders could not be dislodged by firing from Post 33, the post commander, Lieutenant F. A. Mackell, decided upon more direct methods. He led a patrol of six men out to attack them, in a feat which won the Victoria Cross for Corporal J. H. Edmondson; the first award to an Australian in the second World War.

Lieutenant Mackell's description of this savage action has been reprinted many times, but bears repetition because it set a standard for the courage, spirit, and resolution which were to become commonplace amongst Tobruk's defenders. He told Chester Wilmot, who was in Tobruk as a war correspondent, that: "About a quarter to twelve we set out. Corporal Jack Edmondson, five men and myself, with fixed bayonets and two grenades apiece. The Germans were dug in about a hundred yards to the east of our post, but we headed northwards away from it, and swung around in a three-quarter circle so as to take them in the flank. As we left the post there was spasmodic fire. Then they saw us running and seemed to turn all their guns on us. We didn't waste any time. After a 200-yard sprint we went to ground for breath; got up again, running till we were about fifty yards from them. Then we went to ground for another breather, and as we lay there, pulled the pins out of our grenades. Apparently the Germans had been able to see us all the way, and they kept up their fire. But it had been reduced a lot because the men we'd left in the post had been firing to cover us. They did a grand job, for they drew much of the enemy fire on themselves.

"We'd arranged with them that, as we got up for the final charge, we'd shout and they would stop firing and start shouting, too. The plan worked. We charged and yelled, but for a moment or two the Germans turned every-

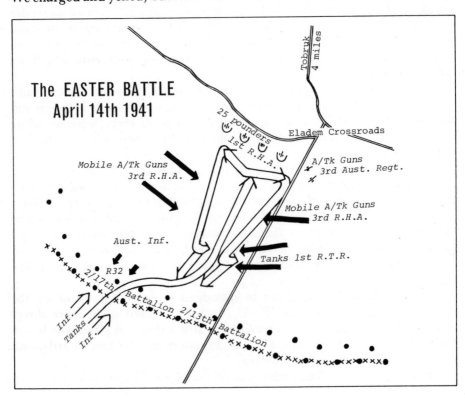

thing on to us. It's amazing that we weren't all hit. As we ran we threw our grenades, and when they burst the German fire stopped. But already Jack Edmondson had been seriously wounded by a burst from a machine-gun that had got him in the stomach, and he'd also been hit in the neck. Still he ran on, and before the Germans could open up again we were into them. They left their guns and scattered. In their panic some actually ran slap into the barbed wire behind them and another party that was coming through the gap turned and fled. We went for them with the bayonet. In spite of his wounds Edmondson was magnificent. As the Germans scattered, he chased them and killed at least two. By this time I was in difficulties, wrestling with one German on the ground while another was coming straight for me with a pistol. I called out "Jack," and from about fifteen yards away Edmondson ran to help me and bayoneted both Germans. He then went on and bayoneted at least one more."

The Australians killed at least a dozen Germans, took one prisoner, and captured all their weapons, but Corporal Jack Edmondson had been mortally wounded. As his comrades sadly carried him back he quietly smoked a cigarette, and died early next morning of his terrible wounds.

The repulse of this German party was followed by larger infantry attacks in the same area during the early hours of 14 April, as the enemy endeavoured to develop their tactic of establishing a bridgehead for the tanks to exploit. The Australians brought up reinforcements, sent out aggressive fighting patrols, and took a number of prisoners, while the British artillery shelled the area heavily from their emplacements within the perimeter.

At 5.20 a.m., the first wave of fifteen German tanks broke through, towing anti-aircraft and anti-tank guns and followed by fifteen to twenty men behind each tank. This force headed towards Post 32, which housed the Australian company commander's headquarters.

In accordance with Morshead's instructions, the forward infantry let them pass and lay in wait for the enemy infantry, while the British gunners pounded the advancing tanks with heavy and accurate shellfire. The first wave was soon followed by thirty-eight more tanks, followed by infantry and artillery working together in the synchronisation developed in the Polish, Belgian and French campaigns. They made a grim picture of modern warfare as they came through the torrent of fire poured on them by the British eighteen-pounders, while the rising sun sent a red-tinged wash of light across the scarred desert soil. As they passed through into the perimeter, the Australian infantry closed in behind them and dealt mercilessly with the infantry, artillerymen, and machine-gunners following the tanks. British and Australian anti-tank gunners sent projectiles slamming into the steel hulls as soon as they were in range, and the attack began to falter to a halt.

As soon as Morshead was certain that this was the main enemy thrust, he sent up his slender tank reserves to support the artillery. By 7 a.m., the

Germans realised that they had fallen into a trap, and half an hour later were beating a hasty retreat to the gap in the perimeter, where the Australians were mopping up in a series of bitter hand to hand engagements.

Captain J. W. Balfe, in whose company area the Germans had forced the perimeter, vividly described the German exit. He said, "There was terrible confusion at the only gap as tanks and infantry pushed their way through it. The crossing was badly churned up and the tanks raised clouds of dust as they went. In addition, there was the smoke of two tanks blazing just outside the wire.

"Into this cloud of dust and smoke we fired anti-tank weapons, Brens, rifles, and mortars, and the gunners sent hundreds of shells. We shot up a lot of infantry as they tried to get past, and many, who took refuge in the anti-tank ditch, were later captured. It was all I could do to stop the troops following them outside the wire. The Germans were a rabble, but the crews of three tanks did keep their heads. They stopped at the anti-tank ditch and hitched on behind them the big guns, whose crews had been killed. They dragged these about 1,000 yards, but by then we had directed our artillery on them. They unhitched the guns and went for their lives. That was the last we saw of the tanks, but it took us several hours to clean up small parties of infantry who hadn't been able to get away."

By 8.30 a.m. all fighting had ceased, and when the dust of battle had settled, it was established that the Germans had lost seventeen tanks. 150 dead were left inside the perimeter, together with 250 prisoners and considerable quantities of weapons and equipment. Twelve supporting aircraft had been destroyed.

The defenders had lost twenty-six killed and sixty-four wounded, and two tanks.

The Germans were incredulous. They had never encountered such tactics nor such a determined opposition, and for the first time in the war their methods had failed. The extreme efficiency of the Royal Horse Artillery gunners, and the way in which the Australian infantry had held their ground and fire until they saw the German infantry and gunners as prime targets, had beaten the German blitzkrieg tactics.

A captured German, who had served in the European campaigns, said, "I cannot understand you Australians. In Poland, France and Belgium, once the tanks got through the soldiers took it for granted that they were beaten. But yo· are like demons. The tanks break through and your infantry still keep fighting."

General Rommel watched the operation from close to the perimeter wire and he expressed his opinion in no uncertain terms to Major-General Streich, commander of the 5th Light Division which had carried out the attack. He wrote later, "I was furious, particularly at the way the tanks had left the infantry in the lurch."

Believing that the 8th Machine-Gun Battalion was still fighting inside the perimeter, he ordered the Italian Ariete Division to attempt its rescue. According to Rommel, they fled in disorder when confronted by the Australian and British fire, but there is no record of this particular engagement in the garrison's records.

General Lavarack, whom Wavell had relieved of his short-lived command of Tobruk and Cyrenaica shortly before this action, issued a special Order of the Day to the garrison which was in the form of congratulations and farewell. He wrote: "I wish to congratulate all ranks of the garrison of Tobruk Fortress on the stern and determined resistance offered to the enemy's attacks with tanks, infantry and aircraft today.

"Refusal by all infantry posts to give up their ground, a prompt counter-attack by reserves of the 20th Brigade, skilful shooting by our artillery and anti-tank guns, combined with a rapid counter-stroke by our tanks, stopped the enemy's advance and drove him from the perimeter in disorder. At the same time the R.A.F. and our A.A. defences dealt severely with the enemy in the air.

"Stern determination, prompt action and close cooperation by all arms ensured the enemy's defeat, and we can now feel more certain than ever of our ability to hold Tobruk in the face of any attacks the enemy can stage. Everyone can feel justly proud of the way the enemy has been dealt with. Well done Tobruk!"

Wavell's decision to remove Lavarack, and merge his Cyrenaica Command into a new Western Desert Command in Egypt, was strongly resented by the Australians. Lavarack's contribution to stabilising the Tobruk and Western forces after the rout of the British troops in the area, with the loss of three of their generals, has never been given proper acknowledgment in military literature.

For Morshead, however, a new and brilliant era in his military career lay ahead; one which would call for all the tenacity he possessed. Events had moved so fast that it was only six weeks since he had been a brigadier, attached to the 6th Australian Division as an observer during its victories in the first Western Desert campaign, and he had been present at the capture of Tobruk. He was then given command of the 9th Division, whose role was foreseen as the garrisoning of Cyrenaica and completion of its training, but the collapse of the British front had given him grave responsibilities almost overnight.

The significance of his role and the responsibility he bore was epitomized in Wavell's Easter message to him which read, "Enemy advance means your isolation by land for time being. Defence of Egypt now depends largely on your holding enemy on your front. Am glad that I have at this crisis such stout-hearted and magnificent troops in Tobruk. I know I can count on you to hold Tobruk to the end. My wishes to you all."

During the first emergence of Rommel and his *Afrika Korps*, Morshead had shown his mettle as a commander of Australian troops. Anticipating Rommel's intentions to outflank the Australians stretched along the coast, he sought the permission of General Neame, then G.O.C. British forces in Cyrenaica, to withdraw the 20th Brigade from the El Agheila area. Neame refused consent, and was adamant that the brigade should remain in position. Morshead was equally adamant that they should withdraw, and believed that it was courting disaster for the brigade to be left in such an exposed position.

So he went direct to Wavell, who at first tended to support Neame. Fortunately Sir John Dill, the Chief of the Imperial General Staff, was with Wavell at the time, and he supported Morshead.

Morshead was able to execute a brilliantly controlled withdrawal of the brigade, which fought a series of effective rearguard actions as they fell back towards the haven of Tobruk. His leadership is all the more remarkable in that the men of the brigade were comparatively raw troops fighting their first actions, and if he had not had the courage to take his case to the Commander-in-Chief they must inevitably have succumbed to the same disaster which fell on the rest of the British troops in Cyrenaica.

Morshead's reputation as a martinet became almost a source of wry pride to the subordinates who called him "Ming the Merciless," after a comic strip character of that era. But they respected his judgement because he was almost invariably proved right, and because they knew that he had been through the same hard school as they themselves were experiencing. He had had three years of front line service, as commander of an infantry battalion, before he was thirty.

"We will never yield a yard unless they take it from us," he told his troops, and he was never content to leave the Germans or Italians in possession of any ground which had been taken from his men.

He refused to tolerate inefficiency, as one of his senior staff officers realised when he was sent back to Palestine after making a mistake which, under less arduous conditions, might have earned no more than a rebuke. He was no less demanding upon himself. Early in May 1941, he gave a characteristic example of self-criticism when he said, "I didn't handle my tanks well. I should have kept them concentrated and used them all together. I didn't know as much about handling tanks then as I do now."

He set a difficult standard to follow, and was ruthless in his criticism of detail, whether in staff work or in the field. He visited all sectors of the Tobruk perimeter regularly, and did not hold back in his opinion of positions which did not meet with his approval.

All ranks who served under him, however, knew that his judgements stemmed from personal experience and observation, not from theory and report. He could be a hard taskmaster, but this very quality gave the troops a feeling of security; a sense that their commander was taking every possible care of them. They saw the wiry, energetic body of "Ming" striding among them and took comfort from his brisk self-confidence. It was apparent that he had no conception of defeat, so there seemed to be no reason why they should let it enter their minds. They were delighted when Radio Berlin later referred to him as "Ali Baba and his 20,000 thieves," at the time when the 9th Division was rushed from Syria to Egypt in July 1942, to bolster the collapse of Auchinleck's "Crusader" operation. When the same broadcast referred to them as "The Rats of Tobruk," they seized upon it as a divisional nickname, and any man who served in the division will still proudly refer to himself as a "Rat."

Morshead was the very man to command a siege, in which a general of the more conventional kind would have been ineffective. "I was determined that we should make No Man's Land our land," he said after the siege, and ordered aggressive patrols into enemy territory. In this, he was following the tradition set by Australian troops in South Africa and on the Western Front, during the "peaceful penetration" of German trenches. His action helped to create that mental attitude of invincibility which eventually made Tobruk into a cancer indeed; a cancer eating into Rommel's flank and becoming an obsession with him, distorting his tactical judgement and causing him to waste more and more men in constantly frustrated attempts to cut it away.

Morshead's combination of toughness and competence was supported by a highly capable band of devoted officers, who possessed all the technical skills needed to implement his brand of aggressive leadership.

His Chief of Staff was a regular officer; Colonel C. E. M. Lloyd, universally known as "Gaffer." Big and bluff, Lloyd had an habitual dislike for humbug, and with it an extraordinary capacity for responsibility and decision. Commissioned in 1918, he had not had the same amount of active service during 1914-18 as that of the majority of 2nd A.I.F. leaders, but between wars had devoted himself to obtaining a Law degree at Sydney University in addition to carrying out the routine staff duties of a regular officer. Ultimately, Lloyd rose to the key administrative appointment of Adjutant General of the Australian Military Forces, with the rank of major-general.

The senior brigade commander, Brigadier G. L. Wootten, who led the 18th Brigade, had seen extensive active service during the first World War. He was one of the first cadets at Duntroon, and went straight from there to Gallipoli. He finished the war as a Staff Officer at Haig's G.H.Q., having won the D.S.O., and been mentioned in dispatches five times while serving at the front. He gained a brilliant pass in the course at Camberley Staff College in the early 1920s, but then left the army to study Law. On the outbreak of the second World War he was appointed C.O. of the 2/2nd Battalion, and succeeded Morshead as commander of the 18th Infantry Brigade. His distinguished leadership at Tobruk was to be followed by outstanding services in the Pacific, notably at Milne Bay and Buna, where he was instrumental in defeating strong Japanese forces. In April 1943 he followed Morshead as G.O.C. of the 9th Division, and in this capacity led the division to fresh triumphs at Lae, Finschafen, and Borneo. He has been described by a contemporary as a "ruthless leader with unlimited capacity, who as a field commander enjoyed brilliant successes and never knew failure."

The 20th Brigade was commanded by Brigadier John Murray, who had seen considerable service in 1914-18. He won the D.S.O. and M.C. and rose to second-in-command of the 53rd Battalion. A big man with a genial temperament, Murray was a popular figure among both his staff and men. He became G.O.C. of the 4th Division in the Pacific in 1942.

Brigadier A. H. L. Godfrey, of the 24th Brigade, was the most junior of the four infantry brigade leaders and an immensely popular figure. He led the 24th with great distinction, adding the D.S.O. and bar to the M.C. he had won in the first World War. His death in action at Alamein was a grievous loss to the A.I.F.

The 26th Brigade was led by Brigadier R. Tovell, who had enlisted in the 1st A.I.F. as a private and rose to be brigade-major of the 4th Brigade, winning the D.S.O. in the meantime. He was a chartered accountant by profession, who like the other three infantry brigadiers had taken an active interest in the citizen forces between the wars.

The field and anti-aircraft artillery commanders were both British regular soldiers. Though there were severe shortcomings in the training and leadership of the British armoured and infantry formations, it was fortunate for the Tobruk defenders that the British artillery was unmatched by any other army. The field and anti-tank artillery was commanded by Brigadier L. E. Thompson, whose astute deployment of the four British and two Australian artillery regiments assured the fortress of maximum coverage from the units at his disposal.

Another Englishman, Brigadier J. N. Slater, commanded the twenty-four heavy and sixty light anti-aircraft guns that ringed Tobruk. His men met the relentless German and Italian air attacks with unflinching courage, so that the vital port facilities continued to function with a minimum of disruption.

Under this inspired and expert leadership the garrison settled down to await Rommel's next onslaught, which they knew would not be long delayed. Beginning on 16 April, the Italians launched a number of attacks with infantry and tanks of the Ariete Division against the Western perimeter defences, but these were repulsed with heavy losses and considerable numbers of prisoners taken.

Morshead's policy of active patrolling of No Man's Land gave the enemy little respite, and this "offensive defence" brought in no less than 1,700

MOVING UP. *Top:* Men of the 2nd Division on the Western Front, 1917. *Bottom:* Men of the 2nd A.I.F. wading the Song River on their way to attack Japanese positions on the Huon Peninsula.

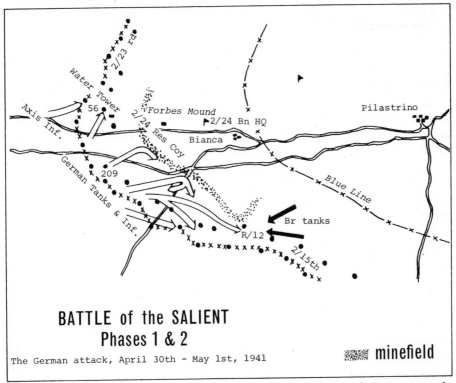

BATTLE of the SALIENT
Phases 1 & 2

The German attack, April 30th - May 1st, 1941   ▨▨▨ **minefield**

prisoners during ten days. In the last three weeks of April, the enemy made fifty raids on the harbour, using nearly 700 aircraft for a loss of sixty-seven. Their aim, of course, was to deny the use of the port for evacuation, reinforcement, and supply.

By 26 April, Rommel had consolidated his forces on the Egyptian frontier, and was now in a position to give Tobruk his undivided attention. A heavy build-up of German forces in the Acroma area gave visible proof of enemy intentions. These were confirmed by a map found in a shot down German aircraft. It was marked with a red arrow running from Acroma to Hill 209 (Ras el Medauuar), key to the Western defence perimeter of Tobruk.

.All through the long day of 30 April, the Australians manning the slopes of Ras el Medauuar could see clouds of dust billowing up from the tracks of enemy vehicles as they came from the direction of Acroma. Enemy infantry piled out of them within 4,000 yards of the perimeter wire, and, as the day faded intó evening, heavy but spasmodic artillery fire fell on the outer defence line of the fortress, slowly growing in intensity. Enemy patrols pierced sections of the wire, creating a confused and uncertain situation, but it was clear that a heavy attack was developing. It was the prelude to what would become known as the Battle of the Salient.

INFANTRYMEN I. *Top left*, A Digger of the 53rd Battalion waiting the signal to go over the top at the Battle of Fromelles, 19 July 1916. *Top right*, 2nd A.I.F. soldiers running up an exposed hillside in Syria. *Bottom left*, An Australian patrol on the Wau-Mubo track, New Guinea 1943. *Bottom right*, 2nd Lieutenant David Sabben makes a cautious return to the battlefield of Long Tan after the heroic action by an Australian company.

The uncertainty of the evening continued through the early hours of 1 May, as parties of German infantry, supported by their artillery, harassed the Australian perimeter outposts. The Germans had learnt their lesson in the Easter Battle, and were intent on creating a wider bridgehead before attempting to make their armoured thrust. By morning, despite the most determined Australian resistance, they had overcome seven of the perimeter posts. The Australian defence evoked the admiration of General Rommel, who when visiting his battle headquarters saw a bunch of Australian prisoners being escorted to the rear. "Shortly afterwards," he wrote, "a batch of some fifty or sixty Australian prisoners was marched off close behind us, immensely big and powerful men, who without question represented an elite formation of the British Empire, a fact that was also evident in battle. Enemy resistance was as stubborn as ever and violent actions were being fought at many points."

Four miles of the perimeter defences, on either side of Ras el Medauuar, were targets for the German attacks, and the confusion of the situation was aggravated by a heavy mist that hung over the battlefield until it cleared just after dawn.

By 8 a.m., the Germans had established the first phase of their plan; the creation of a breach for their armour to exploit. Forty tanks poured through it towards the heart of Tobruk, while another forty helped the infantry to clean up the stubborn Australian outer defence line and to widen the bridgehead.

The spearhead tanks were soon trapped by a minefield in front of the 2/24th battalions reserve company's position. The halted or damaged tanks offered wonderful targets to the infantrymen, but all the Australian anti-tank guns had been knocked out and the armour was comparatively immune to the heavy small arms fire rained upon it. Five had been destroyed and another eleven immobilized, but most of the latter were dragged away by the Germans under the fortuitous cover of a sudden duststorm.

General Morshead was reluctant to commit his only infantry reserve, the 18th Brigade, until he was certain that the salient front was to be the prime area of German attack. His decision was not helped by conflicting reports received from reconnaissance aircraft which first reported that 200 enemy tanks were approaching from the direction of Acroma, and then reported only forty tanks in the area. Communications with the perimeter posts were severely disrupted and attempts to restore them were largely unsuccessful.

The German tanks that had been frustrated by the minefield reassembled, and thrust in a south-easterly direction; attacking the perimeter posts one by one as they advanced. During the afternoon they were engaged by artillery fire and a heavily outnumbered force of British tanks, but the action was broken off after an inconclusive engagement in which several British tanks were damaged.

This was the action that General Morshead referred to when he criticised his own handling of tanks. Whether the use of all his armour in one bold move against the Germans, however, instead of holding a third in reserve and the rest of them piecemeal, would have resulted in a more rapid repulse of the Germans, is purely a matter of conjecture. He had many factors to consider, including the uncertainty of German intentions, broken communication with the perimeter outposts, and the fact that his tanks were inferior to those of the Germans, in size, weight of weapons, and condition of repair. During the morning, when the German armour threatened to outflank the minefields, Morshead was left with little alternative but to divide his tanks. But in the afternoon, when the Germans massed their armour, one bold move might have despatched them with greater expedition.

The Germans were forced to withdraw later in the afternoon having once again suffered heavily from the deadly accuracy of British artillery fire. As they did so, British tanks followed up to assist the Australian outposts which had been left in the wake of the enemy advance. For the most part they were still holding out, although they had been surrounded by enemy armour and infantry for many hours.

A vivid description of the fighting on the perimeter was given by Sergeant Ernest Thurman, who was in command of Post R8. He told Chester Wilmott, "Soon after one o'clock twenty-four tanks advanced on R8 and R9, but they were slowed down by our anti-tank rifle fire. Riding on the back of some were engineers brought along to delouse minefields. We sniped them with our Brens and they jumped to the ground. We also held up the infantry who were following some distance back, and the tanks came on alone. Two mediums kept going till they were only fifty yards from us, but then they stopped, apparently afraid of a minefield that didn't exist. They raked the top of the post with machine-guns and cannon, and the crews even stood up in their turrets and threw stick bombs into our communications trench. But we still kept firing at both tanks and infantry. We'd take a few pot-shots and then duck before their machine-gun bullets thudded into our sandbags. This duel went on until about four o'clock when our artillery came down on them. Shells thundered round the post and the tanks cleared out towards (Hill) 209. By this time half a dozen of my men were wounded and our Bren was out of action. As we couldn't have held out against another attack even by infantry, we withdrew to R10. From there we held off another German attack and, by keeping R8 covered with heavy fire, stopped the Germans occupying it."

Now that the situation was beginning to crystallise a little, Morshead ordered his first infantry counter-attack. At 7.30 p.m. that night, the 2/48th Battalion advanced from its position on the Blue Line against Hill 209; the key to the defence of Tobruk and the centre of the German penetration. After four hours of close-quarters fighting, the Australian attack petered out.

The battalion had been subjected to a heavy air attack as it formed up on the start line, and lack of time for reconnaissance of enemy positions, together with negligible tank and artillery support, had made the attack a doubtful proposition from the start. Nevertheless it had the effect of forcing the Germans on to the defensive, and also prevented them from "de-lousing" the minefield which had frustrated their advance during the morning.

After twenty-four hours of fighting, Rommel's forces controlled an arc of the perimeter spanning about three and a half miles, and had inflicted casualties equivalent to half a battalion as well as destroying four British tanks. This result had cost them about forty-five tanks, although all but twelve were recoverable, plus heavy casualties amongst his infantry and machine-gunners.

His successes were very far short of his intentions, as outlined in his order for the operation: "The *Africa Korps* will force a decision in the battle around Tobruk during the night 30 April-1 May, by an attack from the west."

The strength of the German attack can be gauged from the fact that they had used about ninety tanks, one and a half machine-gun battalions, a brigade of engineers, artillery and other ancillary units, and two Italian

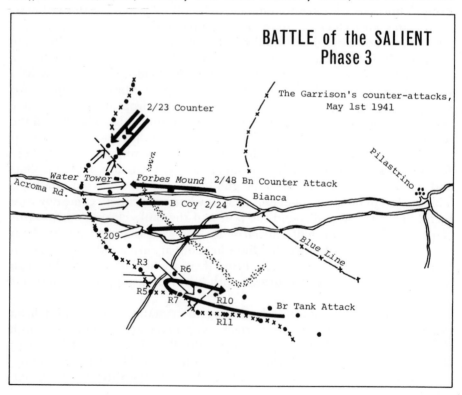

BATTLE of the SALIENT
Phase 3

The Garrison's counter-attacks,
May 1st 1941

2/23 Counter

Water Tower Forbes Mound 2/48 Bn Counter Attack
Acroma Rd.

Bianca

B Coy 2/24

Pilastrino

209

Blue Line

R3

R6

R5

R7 R10   Br Tank Attack

R11

infantry brigades, most of whom had been directed against the positions of the 2/24th Battalion. This formidable force had planned to force the perimeter on either side of Medauuar, taking it from the rear. The Italians would then have rolled up the flanks of the perimeter, while the Germans pushed on to Bianca and the harbour.

Its three main objectives, of seizing the outer defence ring at Medauuar, consolidating their positions at Bianca, and enforcing capitulation after capturing the harbour, had succeeded in only the first being achieved.

The garrison stood ready for a renewal of the attack on 2 May, but a violent sandstorm blew all day and caused a complete stalemate, apart from isolated thrusts by enemy infantry, which were quickly broken up, and heavy artillery duels. The Australians, in order to create a switch line between the outpost S8 and Bianca, made a deliberate withdrawal on the sector held by the 2/10th Battalion, thus consolidating their overall positions in the area.

Towards late afternoon the storm cleared, and the enemy appeared about to renew his aggression. About 100 vehicles and tanks were revealed on the forward slopes of Medauuar, but the enemy concentration was broken up by heavy artillery fire and nothing more serious developed.

Next day, observers peering cautiously from the outposts could not see any sign of enemy preparations to resume his offensive, and Morshead ordered Brigadier Wootten to counter-attack that night with the three battalions of his 18th Brigade; the 2/12th from the right flank and left along the perimeter towards Ras el Medauuar; the 2/10th in the centre; and the 2/9th from the south east along the perimeter in that direction.

The attack went in at 8.45 p.m., in darkness lit only by an insipid moon in its first quarter, veiled by a slightly overcast sky. For the next seven hours the Australians attacked the enemy salient in a series of assaults right up to their emplacements, and supported by heavy artillery fire. But by 3 a.m. very little ground had been recovered, and forty minutes later Morshead ordered the attack to be broken off.

The diary of a German officer recorded "Australians have penetrated the defences between R1 and R7. Immediately counter-attack and cover with tanks. Italians argue and gesticulate wildly. I start by going as far as the gap and then turn right. No officer knows the position. Near R7 an Italian tank is burning. The Australians have gone back leaving 26 dead behind them. Of 150 men occupying R7 there are more than 100 dead or wounded."

Brigadier Wootten correctly summed up the situation however when he commented, "in view of the enemy's defensive strength and disposition it appears that any further large scale infantry operations will require the support of many more guns and tanks." In fact, the task entrusted to the three battalions required a force of two or more brigades with supporting arms. But the Australians had given the enemy a bloody nose, and had shown

Rommel that he could not advance into Egypt while such an aggressive enemy was poised on his left flank. He was still obliged to tie up his best troops and the bulk of his armour outside Tobruk, a fact which in itself was a victory for the defenders.

After Rommel's second unsuccessful attack, congratulations flowed in to the garrison. They included messages from Menzies, Wavell, and Churchill, who with characteristic flourish said, "To General Morshead from Prime Minister England. The whole Empire is watching your steadfast and spirited defence of this important outpost of Egypt with gratitude and admiration."

Wavell's message crystallised the strategic significance of the victory. It said, "Your magnificent defence is upsetting the enemy's plans for the attack on Egypt and giving us time to build up force for counter offensive. You could not be doing better service. Well done."

For General Rommel, this second rebuff in three weeks was an unprecedented event for the German army, whose campaigns so far had been one long story of unbroken success. The Germans lost 954 men, killed, wounded and prisoners, besides their tank losses, while the garrison for its part suffered 797 casualties. General Morshead, after uncertainty during the initial confusion of the attack, had fought an almost perfectly directed battle. The minefields which he had caused to be planted had had the exact effect which he had planned.

For the moment, the battle had gone off the boil; largely because the German High Command, preparing for the invasion of Russia, had warned Rommel not to overstretch his resources.

Morshead returned to his policy of aggressive patrolling of the enemy positions, and soon the whole length of the perimeter was kept simmering as the Australians probed and prodded the enemy positions. It was becoming an unusual siege; one in which the defenders were perhaps even more aggressive than the attackers.

Next, Morshead moved Brigadier Wootten's 18th Brigade into the salient sector, with instructions to resume a counter offensive to regain lost ground. Between May and August a bitter war of attrition was waged between the two forces. One by one, the enemy-held positions were recovered, sometimes changing hands several times before being finally secured, with the dusty earth around them becoming littered with all the debris of battle and the sprawled corpses of Germans and Australians.

Casualties in these actions were heavy, and the strain on the troops increased as the conditions and privations of siege life took their toll. The temperatures soared as a brassy sun beat down from early morning until evening; dust and flies were everywhere; water was eked out by the mugful, warm and unrefreshing; rations were scanty; even the little clothing they wore was falling apart.

A German battalion commander paid tribute to the Australians by writing: "The Australians, who are the men our troops have opposite them so far, are extraordinarily tough fighters. The German is more active in the attack, but the enemy stakes his life in the defence and fights to the last with extreme cunning. Our men, usually easy going and unsuspecting, fall easily into his traps especially as a result of their experiences in the closing stages of the campaign in France. The Australian is unquestionably superior to the German soldier (1) In the use of individual weapons, especially as snipers (2) In the use of ground camouflage (3) In his gift of observation, and the drawing of the correct conclusions from his observation (4) In every means of taking us by surprise. Enemy snipers have astounding results. They shoot at anything they recognise. Several N.C.O.'s of the battalion have been shot through the head with the first shot whilst making observation in the front line."

Wavell made two attempts to carry out his promise to relieve Tobruk, but both of them were unsuccessful. The first began on 15 May, when two mobile columns including about fifty tanks set out from the Egyptian frontier towards the fortress while a formation of infantry and field artillery made a diversionary attack along the coast. By prearrangement with the garrison, an attack was made against the Germans around the perimeter, to keep Rommel's mind off the relieving forces.

The mobile columns fought their way through Halfaya Pass, which naturally was named Hellfire Pass and changed hands over and over again during the course of the war, but after that were stopped dead by the Germans and driven back again.

By 16 June, Wavell was in possession of considerable reinforcements of troops and armour, and mounted another offensive to which his staff gave the optimistic name of Operation Battleaxe. The blade, unfortunately, was blunt. The force started off from the Egyptian frontier, but was decisively beaten in its first encounter with the Germans. Nearly 100 British tanks were left crippled or burning in the desert as the Panzer groups herded the remnants of the offensive back across the frontier, and for Wavell it was the last throw of the dice in the Western Desert. Soon afterwards he was relieved by General Sir Claude Auchinleck as Commander-in-Chief in the Middle East, and "the Auk" began to face the enormous problems posed by the British Army deficiencies in technique, leadership, and equipment.

He and his staff believed that Wavell's failures had been because of operations planned too hastily and carried out with troops who were not seasoned to the desert—though Rommel's men had not been in North Africa for much longer than they had. He decided to wait for cooler weather before making the next attempt to relieve Tobruk, and use the time in bringing troops and armour to a high state of readiness.

In the meantime, Morshead fought on. In August, Brigadier Godfrey and his 24th Brigade made an unsuccessful attempt to drive the enemy out of their foothold in the Medauuar salient, but even before that General Blamey had begun to urge that something more constructive be done about relief or evacuation of the 9th Division.

Reports coming from Tobruk showed that the defenders, though still in good heart, were beginning to suffer in health from the inevitably poor hygiene of more than 20,000 men being crowded together in trenches, dugouts, tunnels, tents, and shattered buildings, under the full blaze of a midsummer desert sun. They rarely had a chance to wash themselves or their clothes, they were bedevilled by the flies and dust which carried the intestinal diseases rife throughout the Mediterranean countries, and they were under constant strain even when withdrawn from the front line for a "rest," because the port and town were battered almost round the clock by German guns and aircraft. The harbour was full of the wreckage of bombed ships, and by that time it was only possible for ships to use the port during darkness.

With the approval of the Australian Government, Blamey asked for the garrison to be relieved in July, when the front was fairly quiet. He told Auchinleck that if this was not done, the 9th Division might deteriorate to such a degree that they might not be able to withstand a full-scale German offensive, and that by the time the British winter offensive took place they might not be able to take any part in it.

Auchinleck and his staff were against it, and sought British Government support. It was impossible to send a land force until November, they said, and an attempt by sea might incur serious losses. But Blamey was now fighting for the welfare of his countrymen, and hammered at Auchinleck while his government sent insistent notes to the British War Cabinet. At last, during the darkest nights of August, the men of the 18th Brigade filed aboard the ships which had brought the Polish Brigade to relieve them, but as soon as they were clear of Tobruk the British refused to consider any further relief. General Auchinleck, Admiral Cunningham, Air Marshal Tedder, and Churchill himself opposed it.

In an atmosphere of increasing acrimony, Blamey worried at his point like a bulldog with a bone, while the Australian Government became increasingly demanding. They all but told the British that it was time for someone else to bear the brunt of fighting in the Middle East, and at last the British gave in. During September and October more and more Australian troops were carried out of Tobruk, and Morshead handed over his command on 22 October 1941. But the 2/13th Battalion, under Lieutenant-Colonel F. A. Burrows, had to be left behind, because the convoy coming to take them out had to turn back after a savage air attack which sank its destroyer escort.

This battalion was to play a vital part in Auchinleck's "Crusader" offensive, launched in November. It started a few days before the date planned by Rommel for his own offensive, so both sides were at a peak of preparation. To begin with, Rommel began to beat the British in his old familiar style. In a two day battle at Sidi Rezegh his Panzer groups knocked out two-thirds of the British tanks, and began a thrust into Egypt behind the British line of advance. General Cunningham, commanding the British offensive, wished to break off the attack, but Auchinleck insisted that it should be continued and replaced him with Lieutenant-General Richie.

Sidi Rezegh was retaken by General Freyberg's New Zealand Division, and British troops of the Tobruk garrison had thrust out of the perimeter to make contact with them. Rommel, in an all-out counter-attack with his armoured divisions, attempted to break up this contact at El Duda, but a night attack by the 2/13th Australian Battalion kept the narrow corridor to Tobruk open.

During the next few days, Rommel concentrated for a renewal of the battle, but the German High Command decided that Royal Navy attacks on supply convoys were making it too difficult to reinforce and supply his troops. On 7 December 1941, while ships of the U.S. Navy were sinking under Japanese bombing in Pearl Harbour, the *Afrika Korps* began to withdraw. After 242 days, the siege of Tobruk was ended.

23

REST AND RETURN

THE RANCOROUS EXCHANGES BETWEEN BLAMEY AND AUCHINLECK, AND what had almost amounted to a political crisis between the Australian and British governments over the relief of the 9th Division, cast something of a shadow over their achievements. Under happier circumstances Mr Churchill might have made one of his eloquent appraisals of their deeds, but in the circumstances the division retired unsung to a well-earned rest in Palestine.

From 8 April to 25 October 1941, the division had lost 749 men killed in action, 604 prisoners, and 1,996 wounded. The enemy casualties before Tobruk are not known, but almost certainly would have been considerably higher.

Auchinleck's dispatch after the withdrawal summarised the garrison's achievements, when he wrote, "Our freedom from embarrassment in the frontier area for four and a half months is to be ascribed largely to the defenders of Tobruk. Behaving not as a hardly pressed garrison, but as a spirited force ready at any moment to launch an attack, they contained an enemy force twice their strength. By keeping the enemy continually in a high state of tension, they held back four Italian divisions and three German battalions from the frontier area from April until November."

Supporting the Australians were the British units in the garrison, especially the artillery and tanks, and also the dogged courage of the Royal Navy and British Merchant Navy, who kept the garrison supplied from the sea under the most savage air attacks, delivered upon them all the way along the coast. The backbone of the defence, however, was the Australian infantry.

The Australians were now to enjoy their longest break from land operations in the Middle East, as the 9th Division rested, reorganised, and trained its reinforcements. They were stationed in Palestine, an area which after the collapse of the Vichy French in Syria was quiet and peaceful.

General Blamey had now left the Middle East, having been recalled in November 1941 for consultations with the Australian Government. The British command may have heaved a sigh of relief when they heard that he was to go, because he had been a constant thorn in its side in his insistence that the 2nd A.I.F. should be treated as a complete national army instead of as a handy group of reinforcements to be dispersed of as required.

His outspoken comments offended the ages-old tradition of the British Army, in which subordinates were expected to follow the dictum of "Theirs not to reason why; theirs but to do or die." Blamey, like other Australians, was quite prepared to do or die, but first he wanted to know the reason why.

The British responded in various ways, subtle and otherwise. When he was given the specially-created post of Deputy Commander-in-Chief, Middle East, they upgraded several of their own officers to full general, so that Blamey would not be their senior following his own elevation to that rank. He described himself as a "fifth wheel," because he was quite conscious of the fact that his position was mainly that of an adviser, with no real authority, even though he sat on all conferences and discussions. It is hard to estimate what influence he did bring to bear on these councils, but he was adamantly opposed to the British practice of splitting divisions into smaller groups to be used piecemeal, which offended all the tenets of military doctrine. He could not prevent the British from employing it upon their own divisions, but certainly he prevented them from doing it to the Australians. Obviously General Montgomery was of the same mind, because he put a stop to the practice when he took command of the 8th Army.

Blamey was bitterly critical of the quality of British leadership in the field, but his frequent clashes with Wavell did not affect the personal and professional respect which they held for each other. The same could not be said of his relations with other British leaders. Auchinleck and Blamey were on very stiff terms, and he regarded General Wilson as an interfering incompetent. After the fall of Syria, largely because of the Australian offensive, Wilson became concerned by numerous cases of indiscipline among off-duty troops in the area. The British tended to blame all infractions of military law upon the Australians, and Wilson wrote to Blamey, "I am asking your commanders to let it be known that in future all cases of assault will be tried by general court-martial. Perhaps if they get a whack of penal servitude with the first two years to be served in the Middle East, it might have a deterrent effect."

It would be absurd to pretend that there were not some pretty tough characters in the A.I.F., but Blamey had the accusations investigated and found that they were largely untrue. He answered tersely, "I am afraid that the question of the discipline of the A.I.F. is one entirely for my action."

Among his reasons for desiring the relief of the 9th Division in Tobruk had been a desire to bring the Australian divisions together by forming an Australian Corps comprising the 7th and 9th Divisions, under General Lavarack, and an Anzac Corps, of the 6th Australian Division and the New Zealand Division, under General Freyberg. World events were to prevent this, because Japan's entry into the war upset the strategic balance on the battlefronts. The Australian Government asked his advice on which two of the divisions in the Middle East should be returned for the defence of Australia, and he recommended the 6th and 7th.

His own return home had caused some consternation. He castigated those who were prepared to treat him as a returning hero, and made a blunt press statement in which he criticised the complacency of Australians while their men overseas were fighting and dying. "Australians are like a lot of gazelles in a dell on the edge of a jungle," he said, and was not only expressing his own feelings but also those of the men overseas. The men in Tobruk claimed that they held a two minutes' silence every week; one for the industrial strikers in Australia, and another for the national heroes, the footballers.

Their feelings were fully justified. A study of Australian newspapers and magazines of the period shows how little impact the war had made upon Australian civilian life up until that time. As late as mid-1941, the Nippon Yusen Kaisha Line was still advertising holiday cruises to Japan, and other advertisements reflected life in a lotus land.

Blamey returned to the Middle East, but not for long. The huge menace of Japan, swarming across the Pacific to Australia's northern outposts, demanded the presence of a man who seemed quite prepared to take on all comers—including his own government. Early in 1941 he had brought his second wife, whom he had married in 1939 after the death of his first wife in 1935, to the Middle East. The ostensible reason for Lady Blamey's presence in the campaign area was so that she might do Red Cross work, but her presence created a storm. The government demanded her return to Australia "at a reasonably early date," and Menzies claimed that her presence in the Middle East "had occasioned much adverse criticism in Australia."

General Blamey advised the government that his wife was "not prepared to submit to the humiliation of returning under orders," and after renewed demands for her return he placed the matter in the hands of solicitors in Cairo. It was quietly allowed to drop.

*　　*　　*

Somewhat envious of the two divisions who were being shipped back to Australia, where they would enjoy some home leave before being thrown into the cauldron of the Pacific campaigns, the 9th Division relaxed in Palestine. Training and other military duties were compensated for by opportunities for relaxation on the coastal beaches and to see something of the Holy Land through which their Light Horse forebears had harried the Turks, but on the whole it was an unsatisfactory existence for thousands of young and youngish men in top physical condition. As though listening to distant thunder, they read of the continuing battle in the Western Desert, where the Germans were slowly gaining the upper hand once more now that British resources were being strained by the need to fight on yet another front. Supplies and reinforcements destined for the Middle East were being diverted to the Far East, and Auchinleck was robbed of the equipment, including motor transport, needed to exploit the German withdrawal from Tobruk. He had pressed on as far as Benghazi, but by that time Rommel had received reinforcements of men and armour, and on 21 January 1942 he struck back with a devastating counter-attack which, during the next five months, drove the British back to Tobruk in a series of battles such as Gazala, Bir Hacheim, Knightsbridge and El Adem. Rommel now seemed truly invincible.

Churchill signalled Auchinleck, asking to be assured that Tobruk would not be surrendered, but the British seemed unable to withstand the devastating blows of Rommel's armour. Again and again, tank battles resulted in British defeats. The 8th Army was streaming back across the desert towards Egypt, and on 20 June the German tanks were bombarding Tobruk harbour from the top of the escarpment overlooking the town. Tobruk was held by 35,000 men, including two South African brigades, one British brigade, an Indian brigade, and a tank brigade. Under the command of Major-General H. B. Klopper, of the South African army, they were more numerous, more experienced, and better equipped than the defenders of Tobruk in 1941. Nevertheless Klopper surrendered the fortress at dawn on 21 June.

For the Germans, it was a gigantic victory. They took all the garrison prisoner, besides enormous quantities of ammunition, stores, weapons, vehicles, and other equipment of every kind. British prestige took a staggering blow, and Rommel had the extreme satisfaction of taking Tobruk at last. Looking ahead, he could see the victory over Egypt, denied to him by the Australians in 1941, lying just over the horizon.

His triumphant army surged towards the frontier, as Auchinleck prepared to make a stand on the El Alamein line from the sea to the Qattara Depression. Mersa Matruh fell to the Germans, and it was only by a furious battle at Minqar Quaim that the New Zealand Division escaped being caught with other formations in the port, and broke through to join the remnants of the British forces at El Alamein. These comprised the 1st South African Division, 5th Indian Division, 9th and 18th Indian Brigades, and the British 50th and 7th (Armoured) Divisions.

They were joined by the only complete and rested division now on the battlefront; the 9th Australian. As Auchinleck suffered blow after blow in the Western Desert he had at last called the Australians back into action, firstly to cover the defence of Cairo and then the coastal sectors at El Alamein. Even during this brief period of movement, Major-General Morshead had had a sharp exchange with Auchinleck.

It was for the same old reason; the British desire to split the division. Auchinleck and his staff had developed new theories of combating Rommel by the splitting of divisions into mobile brigade units, a policy that was strongly opposed by the Australians and New Zealanders and was to prove totally ineffective. When Auchinleck ordered a brigade of the 9th Division up to the front as a mobile unit, Morshead protested, but Auchinleck told him, "I want that brigade right away."

"You can't have that brigade," Morshead answered.

"Why?"

"Because they are going to fight as a formation with the rest of the division."

"Not if I give you orders," Auchinleck said sharply, and the flinty-eyed Morshead gazed at him steadily. "Give me the orders, and you'll see," he told him.

"So you're being like Blamey!" Auchinleck exclaimed. "You're wearing his mantle!"

The 9th Division was saved from this kind of disintegration, but was placed in British XXX Corps, under the command of Major-General Ramsden; a man junior to Morshead, and one who had not distinguished himself in leadership. His own division had been badly cut up in Rommel's advance.

Auchinleck was planning to thwart Rommel's intentions by launching a counter-attack just south of the coast road with the intention of taking the ridges of Tel el Eisa and Tel el Makh Khad. The 9th Division was to capture Tel el Eisa, and the 1st South African Division was to take Tel el Makh Khad.

The Australians were to seize a series of enemy held features, including a double humped hill which lay between the sea, the coast road, and the railway and dominated observation southwards to the vital Miteiriya Ridge, named by the Australians as Ruin Ridge, and much of the territory held by the 8th Army. Conversely it also shielded the coast road against observation from the west. After capturing this objective, the 9th Division was to wheel south to the Tel el Eisa Ridge.

The attack went in at 3.40 a.m. on 10 July, and to surprise the enemy one battalion attacked the first Italian position without artillery support. By dawn they had captured the positions without casualties, and then turning south overran the railway station, taking German prisoners after heavy hand-to-hand fighting. Enemy counter-attacks with tanks followed all through the day, but during the first twenty-four hours the 26th Brigade took 1,150 prisoners and knocked out eighteen tanks. The South Africans meanwhile had reached their objective, cleared it of the enemy, and retired back to their positions in the Alamein Box.

The Germans reacted quickly to this thrust, and Rommel wrote later, "I was compelled to order every last German soldier out of his tent or rest camp up to the front, for in the face of the virtual default of a large proportion of our Italian fighting power, the situation was beginning to take on crisis proportions."

On 11 July, he ordered his 21st Armoured Division to smash the Australian attack by capturing the Alamein Box and then coming in behind to cut them off at Tel el Eisa. "The attack was to be supported by every gun and every aeroplane we could muster," he recorded.

Late in the afternoon of 12 July, in a battle that lasted for three hours, the Germans launched their first assault with men from the 104th Motorised Infantry Regiment, but they were met by a withering fire from the Australians and left over 600 dead on the battlefield. Next day, the 21st Armoured Division made two assaults against the Australian positions. In accordance with Rommel's plan, however, the main attack was directed towards the South Africans in the hope of outflanking the Australians, but this line held firmly and the enemy's efforts were in vain. On 14 July the 21st Armoured Division plunged into action against the Australians, but were thrown back by a most determined defence. The Panzers were driven back by a torrent of artillery and anti-tank fire, but the action was one of the bitterest experienced by Australians in the Western Desert.

Auchinleck was now throwing in a counter-attack at Ruweisat Ridge, to break up German concentrations in the north. This manoeuvre forced Rommel to reduce the scale of his pressure against the Australians, and to begin with the New Zealand Division, with support from the Indians, were very successful. They reached the top of the ridge, but expected support from the British 1st Armoured Division was not forthcoming. When the Germans counter-attacked with their armour, the New Zealanders suffered dreadful casualties and were driven back. Once more, the British armoured formations had shown their astounding lack of leadership and battlecraft, perhaps because they were still led by men with the "cavalry" mentality of the type which had been so disastrous to Britain in the first World War.

The sudden collapse of this sector caused Auchinleck to make another extraordinary decision. Without Morshead's knowledge or concurrence, he ordered the Australian 20th Brigade to a position behind the 5th Indian Division, against which he expected an enemy counter-attack. When he heard what was happening, Morshead protested vigorously and the order was countermanded.

The Germans continued to attack against the 9th Division's positions all through 15 July, but lost ten tanks and sixty-three prisoners. On the following morning the 2/23rd Battalion launched a brilliant attack against one of the enemy held features, and in a fast-moving operation took 601 prisoners including three colonels.

This action completed the 9th Division's first phase of operations in the first battle of El Alamein. It had taken and held the high ground west of El Alamein, suffering comparatively light losses but inflicting some 2,000 casualties on the enemy and taking 3,078 prisoners.

Auchinleck was anxious to exploit these initial successes, and the 24th Brigade took over the offensive role from the 26th, with the objective of capturing Makh Khad Ridge and then moving southwards to Ruin Ridge. The brigade opened its attack at 2.30 a.m. on 17 July, and advanced rapidly. The Australians captured their first target of Makh Khad Ridge, before pushing on to Ruin Ridge (Miteiriya Ridge) where they destroyed enemy positions and took prisoners. But as the 2/43rd Battalion lacked anti-tank guns, and the British tank regiment supporting it was stopped dead by German fire, the Australians withdrew to the Makh Khad Ridge positions. The brigade's operations on this first day had captured 736 prisoners and a considerable amount of equipment. The continued Australian pressure had prevented Rommel from launching an attack in the centre, relieving Auchinleck of his concern for that sector.

The intensity of fire on the El Alamein line can be gauged from the fact that the 2/28th Battalion suffered more casualties from German 88-millimetre airbursts, on 18 July alone, than it had done from artillery shelling during its entire six months in Tobruk.

There was a brief stalemate while both sides regrouped, and then Auchinleck ordered a renewal of his offensive. His first instruction called for envelopment of the enemy from both flanks, in an attack which was to go in at the end of July following constant pressure on all sectors until the main attack began. This, however, was rescinded within twenty-four hours, by a counter-order which set the stage for a main attack directed against the central Ruweisat Ridge area, with supplementary thrusts along the southern sector designed to outflank the enemy. In the northern sector, an offensive would begin to prevent Rommel from concentrating against the main thrust in the centre.

Morshead was extremely critical of the role that his 9th Division was given in this attack. It was required to advance on a two brigade front, 6,000 yards west and then 4,000 yards south, supported by armour. But, by this time, the Australian infantry's confidence in British tank formations was almost zero. Morshead had little more confidence in the ability of his corps commander, General Ramsden, but held initial discussions with him and then asked for a conference with Auchinleck.

He outlined his opposition to the plans for his division, saying that in his view the wide dispersion and difficulty of support in the proposed deploy-

MUD. *Top:* 1st A.I.F. men trudging up to the front during the Passchendaele operations, 1917. *Centre:* It took two days to walk the eight miles between Buna and Sanananda in 1943. *Bottom:* Dragging a trailer load of supplies up the track from Finschhafen to Sattelberg, 1943.

ment of his men would be much more difficult than either Auchinleck or the corps staff could appreciate.

Auchinleck is said to have been infuriated by Morshead's opposition to his plans, but the blundering inability of British commanders left the Dominion leaders with no alternative but to protect their troops from "Charge of the Light Brigade" tactics which were likely to destroy them. The New Zealanders, who lost 904 men on the Ruweisat Ridge because of lack of surport from the armour, were "sourly discontented," and their temporary commander, General Inglis, wrote to General Freyberg that, "I have flatly refused to do another operation of the same kind while I command. I have said that the *sine qua non* is my own armour under my own command."

The New Zealanders had borne the brunt of two ill-planned and ill-concerted battles in a week and suffered heavy casualties as a result, so they and their commander could hardly be blamed for their discontent.

However, the Australians launched their attack in concert with the New Zealanders at dawn on 22 July, and for the next four days bitter and confused fighting raged for control of the blood-soaked ridge as the troops of both sides fought themselves to a standstill. The West Australians of the 2/28th Battalion were cut off on the night of 26 July, and suffered 600 casualties as they withstood attack after attack from the Germans. At four minutes past nine on the morning of 27 July, they sent a brief but vivid message: "We are in trouble." Forty minutes later Lieutenant-Colonel McCarter, the battalion commander, signalled Brigadier Godfrey's headquarters with a message that revealed the gravity of the situation. "There are tanks all around us. You had better hurry up. Rock the artillery in."

For the next three hours, Morshead tried to move the armour into the battle, but its leaders used one excuse after another for their apparent reluctance to go to the help of the Australians. At about midday they reported that they had found a gap in the minefields, but Morshead's laconic report was, "What they did with it, we never knew. Anyhow our battle had already been finished, three hours before."

The last message from the West Australians was received at 10.03 a.m., saying simply, "We have got to give in."

Attacked on all sides by tanks and armoured cars, they had fought until their anti-tank guns were destroyed and at last were overwhelmed by the sheer weight of the enemy. They had wiped out one German battalion and knocked out eight enemy tanks during their bitter resistance.

With this action, Auchinleck's last offensive drew to a close. He had succeeded in exhausting the enemy for the time being, but his own men were no better off, and he had no alternative but to rest and regroup until his depleted divisions were built up to fighting strength again.

Morshead, writing an appreciation for future operations, wrote: "It is

COMMANDERS, 1939-1970. *Top row, from left*, L. J. Morshead; S. G. Savige; T. Blamey. *Second row*, I. G. Mackay; G. Vasey; Gordon Bennett. *Third Row*, Edmund Herring; G. F. Wootten; D. MacArthur. *Bottom row*, J. D. Lavarack; I. B. Ferguson (C.O. of 3rd Battalion Royal Australian Regiment in Korea); S. P. Weir (Brigadier commanding the 1st Australian Task Force, Vietnam).

vital that on the next occasion our armour restores our lost faith in them. Until we can be certain about our armour we must have more limited and less exposed objectives than those in recent operations. The only justification for recent objectives was that our armour would effectively operate."

Though Auchinleck's offensive had not achieved its objective, it had stopped Rommel once more and checked his most recent threat to Egypt. The only ground gained by Auchinleck's forces had been the 9th Division area, in which the ring of hills in the Tel el Eisa region was to prove an invaluable jumping off point for the crucial battle to be fought within the next three months.

24

A VICTORY AT LAST

WELL, MORSHEAD, YOU'VE STEMMED THE TIDE AGAIN," WINSTON Churchill said when he visited Egypt after the repulse of Rommel's thrust at the El Alamein line. It was perhaps the most telling tribute to the Australians for their courage on the hills and ridges of Tel el Eisa.

Churchill was in Egypt to observe the situation for himself. For more than eighteen months, the British seemed to have been at the mercy of Rommel. He had definite advantages in his short supply line across the Mediterranean as against the voyage of almost two months round the Cape, which the British must make to supply and reinforce their army, but also appeared to have something else fighting on his side. Partly this was the mystique of German military might, but largely it was sheer inability on the part of the British so far to provide weapons equivalent to the German armour, to develop leaders who could match Rommel's speed and savagery, and to train troops to handle blitzkrieg warfare. Many British formations were magnificent. The Royal Air Force and the Royal Navy had displayed unparalleled courage and devotion to duty. The average British soldier had plenty of fighting ability. But, overall, there was something lacking.

It was Churchill's intention to supply it. Impatient with the 8th Army's failure to do no more than hold the enemy at El Alamein, he flew to Egypt with Sir Alan Brooke, the Chief of the Imperial General Staff. In his diary, Brooke recorded a conversation with Smuts, in which the South African leader "has a good opinion of the Auk, but considers that he selects his subordinates badly and that several changes are desirable."

Brooke and Churchill considered offering command of the 8th Army to

255

General "Strafer" Gott, whom Alan Moorehead described as "the one great name left on the British side, the one man who had survived death, capture, or major error." But Brooke thought that Gott had reached a point of exhaustion. They considered General Wilson, suggested by Anthony Eden because they had soldiered together in the first World War. Brooke was anxious to give the command to General Bernard Montgomery, but thought that if this was done, Auchinleck would put a damper on his urgent self-confidence. Finally, it was decided that Auchinleck should be relieved by Alexander—"an intensely distasteful decision . . . but his subordinates' ill-coordinated attempts to solve the problems of a mechanised desert campaign had resulted in neglect of the cardinal principle of war—concentration," Brooke wrote; the very point which Blamey and Morshead had hammered home on other occasions, to Wavell as well as Auchinleck. Churchill and Brooke continued to discuss the right man for the 8th Army command, with Churchill backing Gott.

Distasteful though the decision was, it was the right one. Auchinleck had a fine grasp of military operations, but his choice of some senior subordinates was almost farcical. And, despite his own competence, he lacked the temperament required to handle an army that comprised a large percentage of troops from the Dominions, each possessing their own individual characteristics and a sense of independence that neither he nor many of his British Army contemporaries understood.

Major-General F. W. von Mellenthin, Chief of Staff to the 4th Panzer Army, gave a penetrating insight into Auchinleck when he wrote: "Auchinleck was an excellent strategist, with many of the qualities of a great commander, but he seems to have failed in tactical detail, or perhaps in ability to make his subordinates do what he wanted. He saved Eighth Army in Crusader and saved it again at the beginning of July; however, his offensives later in the month were costly, unsuccessful, and from the tactical point of view extremely muddled. I am unable to say how far this was the fault of Auchinleck, or that of his corps commanders, Ramsden and Gott."

Churchill's new broom created a largely inactive Middle East command, comprising Persia and Iraq, which Auchinleck was offered and declined. He was then appointed Commander-in-Chief, India. The critical command was that of Egypt, Palestine, and Syria, which were designated Near East Command.

General Alexander was chosen for this new appointment, although he had previously been selected to command the British Army in the projected North African landings.

Brooke agreed, against his better judgement, that Gott should be given command of the 8th Army, but Gott's aircraft was shot down while he was flying to Cairo to be informed of his promotion. Gott had achieved an enviable reputation for leadership, and his death was regarded as a great blow. It is now believed, however, that he was responsible for a number of serious tactical errors, which contributed substantially to the 8th Army's failures in the Western Desert.

The 8th Army command immediately was given to Lieutenant-General Montgomery, who had been named to succeed Alexander in command of the British troops in the Anglo-American invasion of Algeria. His appointment to the 8th Army brought together two men who stand amongst the greatest captains in British military history.

As personalities, it would be difficult to find two men more diametrically opposed. Perhaps it was for this very reason that they complemented each other so perfectly.

Alexander, then aged fifty-one, was the third son of the Earl of Caledon, and the personification of the English aristocrat; handsome, faultlessly dressed, trim moustached, and a product of Harrow. His army career had been marked by almost continuous service with troops, from the time he left Sandhurst until he received his first staff appointment at thirty-nine.

During the first World War he commanded a battalion of the Irish Guards on the Western Front at the age of twenty-four, was severely wounded, and awarded the D.S.O. and M.C. Between the wars he helped to organise the Latvian Army, commanded a brigade on the north-west frontier of India, and served on other overseas stations of the British regular army.

In 1939 he went to France in command of the British 1st Division, and was one of the few leaders to survive the French débâcle with any personal credit. After Dunkirk he was appointed to the vital Southern Command, which in the event of invasion would have taken the major brunt of German attack. In March 1942 he was hurried out to Burma, to extricate the remnants of the British forces reeling back to India with the Japanese at their heels. Now, in August 1942, he was Churchill's hope for the restoration of confidence and morale in the Middle East theatre.

His capacity to grasp detail and judge the overall situation of both military and political problems, allied to a suave and charming personality, made him the perfect selection for what was a critical appointment. He also possessed a gift for languages, and spoke fluent French, Italian, German, Russian, and Urdu.

Montgomery, with his falcon features, staccato voice, and brusque manner, was the complete contrast. He is probably the most professional soldier the British army has ever turned out, and despite some critics' opinion that he was occasionally over cautious he enjoys the rare distinction of never having lost a battle.

Other critics say that he is a supreme egotist, but if so then this is a trait which helped to establish the "Monty legend," put fire in the bellies of the

British troops, and at last gave the British press, public, and army a figure who was as colourful and grandiloquent as Rommel. The awe-stricken hero worship of the latter, who like the other German generals obeyed Hitler when he was winning but tried to turn against him when he was losing, was one of the phenomena of the war.

Many stories were told about Montgomery; for example that he once fired an officer who had been assigned to his headquarters before the man had time to unpack his bags. "You are a good officer but you are not good enough for me," he told him. The classic, of course, is of his first address to corps and divisional commanders in the Middle East. He prefaced his lecture with the curt instruction, "I do not approve of smoking or coughing. There will be no smoking. For two minutes you may cough; thereafter coughing will cease for twenty minutes, when I shall allow another sixty seconds for coughing." This was his famous "No bellyaching" lecture when he told his leaders that in future there would be no bellyaching at the orders issued; they would be carried out.

Montgomery had a distant relationship with Australia. His father had been Bishop of Tasmania, and it is said that as a lad of twelve he watched 857 Tasmanian volunteers embark at Hobart with their horses for the South African War, and there and then decided to become a soldier.

After leaving Sandhurst in 1908, he joined the Royal Warwickshire Regiment, served on the Western Front, was wounded twice and awarded the D.S.O.

In France during the second World War, he commanded the British 3rd Division and like his chief, Alexander, was one of the few leaders to emerge from that campaign with their reputation intact. After Dunkirk he was appointed to a corps command in England, and in 1941 promoted to South-Eastern Command.

Shortly after taking over the 8th Army he visited the 9th Australian Division, to meet its senior commanders and inspect the terrain it was holding. Whilst at 24th Brigade headquarters he asked for an Australian slouch hat with a Rising Sun badge, claiming as his entitlement the fact that his father had been the Bishop of Tasmania! He assumed his new headgear without denting the sides or wearing it at the usually rakish angle of the Australians, which made him look rather ridiculous. Morshead, noticing Brigadier Windeyer's quizzical expression, murmured to him that despite Montgomery's apparent idiosyncrasies, "He was like a breath of fresh air, and things would be different now."

Very early in his command, Montgomery issued instructions which were to have a profound effect on future operations. Probably the three most far reaching were, firstly, that there were to be no more withdrawals. The El Alamein line was to be held until he was ready to attack.

Secondly, divisions were not to be broken up. The battle groups and mobile columns, which had been so much in vogue during Auchinleck's reign, ceased to exist. This direction particularly pleased the Australians and New Zealanders, for both Morshead and Freyberg had fought a constant battle to retain the identity and control of their divisions. Auchinleck was not the only one guilty of this process. Both Wavell and Maitland Wilson broke up divisions, and General Blamey was frequently at loggerheads with them on this matter.

Thirdly, the word "box" was to be abolished. "Boxes" were defensive areas instituted by Auchinleck, and there were three between Alamein and the Qattara Depression. Each box was an island of defence, an area of ground wired and mined all around, with prepared trenches, weapon pits, and so on. The troops used them as fortresses around which the tide of battle swirled or swamped, but to Montgomery they exemplified the defensive mentality which he was determined to destroy.

Though Montgomery quickly imposed his personality on the 8th Army and inspired a new found confidence in its leadership, his selection of corps commanders raised the ire of Australians once more. Two new and inexperienced leaders, Lieutenant-Generals Oliver Leese and Brian Horrocks, were brought from England to lead XXX and XIII Corps respectively.

General Blamey was quick to draw to the attention of Mr John Curtin, then the Australian Prime Minister, the inequity of such appointments when a man of General Morshead's experience and outstanding ability already was in the theatre of war. Representations were made on a government to government level regarding the appointment of Dominion officers to higher command, including discussions by Morshead with Alexander and Montgomery. Montgomery, however, expressed the traditional British Army opinion that as Morshead was not a regular soldier, he did not possess the requisite training and experience. When asked whether the 9th Australian Division had ever failed to do what was required of it, Montgomery agreed that it was superb, and then made the rather extraordinary admission that he knew nothing of Morshead's background or experience. At last he agreed that if General Leese became a casualty, Morshead should succeed to command of XXX Corps; a concession which could be regarded as nothing more than a sop to the Australians.

Morshead's qualifications for appointment to corps command should have been fairly obvious, and Montgomery's view that only a professional soldier was competent for senior command was laughable after the chaotic leadership demonstrated by so many of his colleagues since Rommel had begun to chase them around the desert.

Obviously, the British army attitude towards Australians was not about to change. As has been demonstrated on the Western Front in 1918, the most inspired leadership was provided by the Australian Corps under

Monash which was almost completely composed of citizen soldiers, so that a very successful precedent had already been established. Unfortunately, the Australian and Canadian victories in 1918 had been largely labelled British so perhaps Montgomery was unaware of their significance.

General Brudenell White's comment in 1918 was very relevant. "The British Army had to have a success—and that the value of the victory would be lost if it was made out as a victory for the Australian and Canadian troops. There was not any fear that we should not get the credit for this, it was only the present credit that we had to contribute to the British Army." "It was a sacrifice we should make for the whole." In actual fact the same situation prevailed in 1942, that is, the British Army had to have a success.

The turn of the wheel had now gone the full cycle; the trouble was that the Australian's "sacrifice for the whole," was to be to their own disadvantage. The full recognition of their achievements had not been and was not acknowledged.

Monash, White, and Chauvel had suffered in the same way. But an interesting sidelight on Morshead was provided by Major-General D. N. Wimberley, commander of the newly arrived 51st Highland Division, who observed, "He gave me a higher feeling of morale than anyone else I had met so far." This was not unnatural, because Morshead was one of the few Allied leaders in the Middle East who could take much pride in his record up to then.

Despite this clash between Australian and British leaders, 8th Army soon settled into its role of reformation and re-establishment with the full intention of achieving Montgomery's objective "to hit the enemy for six right out of North Africa," and Churchill's urgent desire for a victory over Rommel. In these operations the 9th Division was to play a critical and crucial part.

Montgomery's first test came on 30/31 August 1942, when the enemy launched an attack against British positions at Alam El Halfa Ridge, but a carefully conducted defensive battle repulsed the Germans and Italians with heavy casualties. The 20th Brigade of the Australian 9th Division launched a complementary diversionary raid in battalion strength against the enemy's vulnerable supply routes near the coast road, in the early hours of 1 September. The operation, code named Bulimba, developed into extremely heavy fighting for three hours, during which the Australians killed about 150 and took 140 German prisoners, for a loss of thirty-nine killed, 109 wounded, and twenty-five missing.

From this temporarily violent interlude, the front simmered down to a comparatively peaceful tempo while both sides toiled unceasingly to build up reserves of men, materials and armour for the great battle which loomed ahead.

The Australian 24th Brigade moved surreptitiously forward on their front, to occupy and hold ground which was to be used as a springboard in the forthcoming offensive. The South Africans, positioned on their left, also moved forward, with both operations being achieved without hindrance from the enemy.

All through September and October vast reservoirs of men arrived from Britain and the Dominions to reinforce the 8th Army, while guns, tanks and transports were disgorged into Egypt at an unprecedented rate. By the eve of the Battle of El Alamein, on 23 October 1942, Montgomery's army comprised eleven divisions, totalling about 220,000 men, supported by 1,200 tanks and over 1,000 field and medium guns. Its components were:

XXX Corps (Lieutenant-General Leese)
9th Australian Division (Lieutenant-General Morshead)
51st Highland Division (Major-General Wimberley)
2nd New Zealand Division (Lieutenant-General Freyberg)
1st South African Division (Major-General Pienaar)
4th Indian Division (Major-General Tuker)
23rd Armoured Brigade Group (Brigadier Richards)

XIII Corps (Lieutenant-General Horrocks)
7th Armoured Division (Major-General Harding)
44th Division (Major-General Hughes)
50th Division (Major-General Nichols)

X Corps (Lieutenant-General Lumsden)
1st Armoured Division (Major-General Briggs)
10th Armoured Division (Major-General Gatehouse)

In addition there was one Greek brigade, positioned between the 4th Indian Division and the 50th Division, and a Free French brigade on the extreme south of the line.

By contrast the Axis forces numbered twelve divisions (four German and eight Italian) with additional independent groups including the tough Ramcke Parachute Brigade. In all they were about 180,000 strong, with slightly under half of them being Germans. The *Afrika Korps* comprised the 15th and 21st Armoured Divisions, 90th Light Division, 164th Light Division, and the Ramcke Brigade. The German armour consisted of 218 tanks, and the Italians had two armoured divisions containing 278 tanks, of very dubious quality.

In terms of overall manpower the 8th Army held a numerical superiority, and in fact they enjoyed an overwhelming advantage in that more than half of the Axis forces consisted of Italians. The disparity in the armoured formations was even more acute, with the British possessing more than 1,000 tanks while the enemy had only about half this number, including the Italians. Rommel was fully aware of his own weaknesses, and in an attempt to stiffen his line he interlaced Italian units with Germans.

In the air, the Desert Air Force under Air Vice Marshal Coningham had thirty-seven squadrons, totalling 500 aircraft, of which a surprisingly high percentage were of the South African Air Force. No less than fifteen squadrons were South African, the balance being thirteen R.A.F., in which of course a large number of Dominion airmen served; seven American; and two Australian; plus a number of reconnaissance and ambulance units. Against them, the Axis had about 350 aircraft based in North Africa, with support from Crete and Italy readily available if required.

Montgomery's plans were revealed on 15 September, when XXX Corps Commander, General Leese, addressed the divisional commanders. The main battle was to be fought in the northern sector by Leese's Corps, which rather significantly comprised the Australian, Highland, New Zealand, South African, and Indian Divisions, in that order from the coast southwards. The four Dominion divisions were all veterans of the desert, while the 51st Highland Division, which had recently arrived in the Middle East, was placed between the two Anzac Divisions but attached to the Australians for training. The Highlanders, who were immensely popular with their mentors, had the self-imposed duty of avenging the defeat and surrender of their comrades when the original 51st Highland Division had been overcome by Rommel during his lightning drive at St Valery in the French campaign of 1940.

The task of XXX Corps, Leese explained, was to drive twin-pronged corridors through the enemy defensive area. The infantry would be closely followed by the armoured divisions, but in the event of the infantry not being able to clear the corridors, the armour was to fight its own way into the open. At this statement, Australian and New Zealand contempt for the deficiencies of British armoured formations erupted when Generals Freyberg and Morshead called out almost simultaneously, "They won't!"

Leese, who had been in the Middle East only a short time, was somewhat shattered by this expression of no confidence from the two most senior, experienced, and successful infantry commanders in the Army. "Perhaps you don't know the Army Commander very well. What I have said is his order," Leese countered rather tentatively, to which the two recalcitrant infantry leaders repeatedly quite definitely, "They won't!"

As it transpired they were very nearly to be proved right when the battle was under way.

From the outset, the critical role in the plan was entrusted to the 9th Australian Division, whose sector confronted the strongest enemy defences. General Montgomery gave the Australians this task because he considered that their temperament and talents were the most suited for the severe fighting that was inevitable on that sector.

On 6 October, he issued a fresh order which somewhat changed the emphasis in the tactics to be adopted. The standard of training attained by some of his divisions was causing him concern, but, so that none of the planning, training or preparation should be wasted, his second plan was virtually built on the framework of the first.

His new instructions called for the armoured divisions to position themselves at the western ends of the corridors, to hold off the enemy armour, while the infantry methodically destroyed their German and Italian counterparts in what Montgomery termed the "crumbling process."

The main difference in the two plans was that in the first the British armour would have passed through the corridors, fanned out to deploy along Rommel's supply routes, and thus invited the Panzer divisions to battle— and hopefully to destruction. The second plan, however, was for the British to draw the Panzers towards them at the end of the corridors, while standing fast to give greater protection to infantry performing the "crumbling" operations. Montgomery reasoned that Rommel would not remain inactive while the Axis infantry was being destroyed, so would be forced to use the Panzers on ground very much to the advantage of the British armour.

As the Australian and New Zealand infantry divisions would be spear-heading the whole offensive, the amended plan had considerable virtue so far as Morshead and Freyberg were concerned.

Montgomery changed his plan because of his nagging doubts as to the reliability of the British armoured divisions, for despite their tremendous numerical advantage they had been a dismal failure in almost every operation in the Western Desert. In his memoirs, he wrote: "My initial plan had been based on destroying Rommel's armour; the remainder of his army, the un-armoured position, could then be dealt with at leisure. This was in accordance with the accepted military thinking of the day. I decided to reverse the process and thus alter the whole conception of how the battle was to be fought. My modified plan now was to hold off, or contain, the enemy armour, while we carried out a methodical destruction of the infantry divisions holding the defensive system."

While the careful planning and training of the previous two months was reaching its climax, the morale of 8th Army was soaring to meet its crucial test. Montgomery had inspired everyone, from private to general, with the enthusiasm and confidence which had been singularly lacking for so long.

In his original instructions for the battle he had declared, "We must raise the morale of our soldiery to the highest pitch; they must be made enthu-siastic, and must enter this battle with their tails high in the air and with the will to win." In this ambition, he had been brilliantly successful in a remark-ably short time; a classic demonstration of how a born leader can carry his men to victory.

D-Day was set for 23 October. Zero hour for the artillery was 9.40 p.m., and the infantry would begin their advance at 10 p.m. The crimson dawn of that day heralded a clear sky and harsh sun, which as the day wore on tormented the restless assault troops who had been instructed to keep under cover in their forward slit trenches. Besides the heat and flies, the exuberant spirit and aggressive eagerness of the troops also had an unsettling effect on them as they lay in the cramped confines of their positions, waiting for the battle which for many of them would be a baptism of fire.

The sun set in a cloudless sky, with the desert lit by brilliant stars and almost a full moon. The men relaxed a little, and emerged for a proper meal before what General Morshead described as the "hard and bloody battle" as he wrote to his wife that night. He revealed his inner feelings as he recorded, "It is now 8.40 p.m. and in exactly two hours time by far the greatest battle ever fought in the Middle East will be launched. I have settled down in my hole in the ground at my battle headquarters which are little more than 2,000 yards from our start line. I have always been a firm believer in having H.Q. well forward, it makes the job easier, saves a great deal of time, in fact it has every possible advantage. At the present time I can see and hear all the movement forward to battle positions, it is bright moonlight, tomorrow being full moon. A hard fight is expected, and it will no doubt last a long time. We have no delusions about that. But we shall win out, and I trust put an end to this running forward and backward to and from Benghazi.

"The men are full of determination and confidence. Going round them, talking with them, and addressing them, I have noticed an air of quiet and confident purposefulness that augurs well, even though these grand fellows have never once failed to respond fully.

"In the preliminary and opening stages of a battle a commander can do little or nothing. He merely waits and hopes. It is only as the battle develops that he can really act. From then on he is a very busy man."

The three brigades of Morshead's division, the 20th, 24th, and 26th, were commanded by Brigadiers V. Windeyer, A. Godfrey, and D. Whitehead respectively, with Godfrey being the only brigade leader remaining from Tobruk days. Murray and Lovell, who had commanded the 20th and 26th Brigades during the siege, had been returned to Australia to take up more senior appointments.

Windeyer, now a judge of the High Court of Australia, had an outstanding academic background as a Sydney barrister, lecturer, and author of works on legal history and practice. He had taken a keen interest in the citizen forces being a product of the Sydney University Regiment, which he had commanded in 1937. When war broke out he voluntarily stepped down a rank in order to transfer from the militia to the A.I.F., but was seconded from his battalion to the staff of the 7th Division. Two months later he was promoted to command the 2/48th Battalion, then being raised in South Australia, and he led it with distinction through Tobruk and the Battle of Tel el Eisa.

Whitehead, known as "Torpy" (from the Royal Navy's Whitehead torpedo) was a civil engineer. He had served with the machine-gunners during 1914-18, and had commanded machine-gun and infantry battalions during 1940-42. Like Windeyer and Godfrey who also was a 1st A.I.F. veteran, he had served at Tobruk and Tel el Eisa. Godfrey was tremendously popular with his men, with whom he enjoyed the reputation of always being in the forefront of the fighting; a practice which was to cost him his life at El Alamein.

In command of the divisional artillery was Brigadier A. H. Ramsay, another survivor from Tobruk days. A teacher and university lecturer by profession, he had served in the ranks of the 1st A.I.F. and had continued to serve in the militia between the wars, being commissioned in 1930. He had commanded the artillery at Mersa Matruh while Rommel was attacking the Tobruk coastal area, and Morshead thought highly of him. He had proposed that Ramsay should succeed him if he became a casualty.

These men, apart from Windeyer who had fallen sick and had been temporarily replaced by Brigadier H. Wrigley, also waited through the silent hours between sunset and zero hour. Everything possible had been done, and there was nothing to do but wait for the trial by battle.

As zero hour approached the sky filled with noise as the bombers of

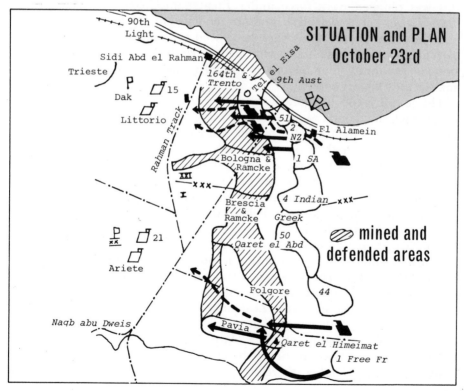

Desert Air Force flew overhead on their missions of destruction. Then, at exactly 9.40 p.m., the forty-mile front erupted in the heaviest artillery barrage since the first World War. The reverberating thunder of 908 field and medium guns, raining their missiles on the enemy positions at a rate of nearly 2,000 rounds a minute, was almost deafening, but at 9.55 p.m., the artillery ceased firing as suddenly as it had begun, and there were long moments of breathless silence. Two searchlight beams darted suddenly into the sky, and crossed like swords at exactly ten o'clock. As they did so, the British barrage crashed out in an even louder roar, and the infantry rose out of their trenches to walk forward at a steady, deliberate pace of seventy-five yards a minute.

The 26th and 20th Brigades were to be the 9th Division's spearhead while the 24th, under Godfrey, made a successful thrust to the north between the railway line and coast. Whitehead's 20th Brigade was entrusted with the main Australian responsibility. It had to advance along a deep and narrow front, protecting the army's right flank which was the exposed open shoulder of the attack. Although the brigade did not achieve all its objectives, it secured most of them with outstanding success. A critical phase of its operations came when a 3,000-yard gap opened on the northern front, but this was plugged by a force under Lieutenant-Colonel F. MacArthur-Onslow, who set up defensive positions modelled on the German pattern of anti-tank and machine-guns, each post wired and mined. The task entrusted to Whitehead was in fact a commitment beyond the reasonable bounds of brigade capability, but fortunately MacArthur-Onslow's force held fast against the enemy probings.

The 20th Brigade, temporarily under the command of Brigadier Wrigley, had a much rougher passage in the latter stages of the attack. As on the other divisional fronts in XXX Corps, the brigade's first objectives were fairly easily taken. From then on, they encountered fierce opposition. British intelligence appears to have miscalculated the siting of enemy positions, for their maps indicated that the first lines of defence were strongly held. In actual fact, they were comparatively lightly held outer lines, to act as "feelers" for the main positions behind them. These were strongly fortified and in considerable depth.

The 2/13th Battalion of the 20th Brigade, under Lieutenant-Colonel R. Turner, suffered heavy casualties in some of the bitterest fighting of the night. Their task was to penetrate 2,600 yards on a front of nearly a mile, which was a tremendous burden for a single battalion.

The Highlanders and New Zealanders, on the two sectors left of the Australians, met with varying degrees of success. The South Africans, on the southern extremity of XXX Corps front, fell short on one objective but attained their goal on the left flank.

By dawn of 24 October, therefore, the right and left extremities of XXX

Corps front had achieved their objectives. Although some indentations remained on each divisional sector, roughly eighty per cent of the ground allotted to the infantry had been seized.

Only the New Zealanders had managed to secure and clear a corridor to a depth sufficient for the armour, but as day dawned it was too late for exploitation. None of the three armoured divisions had fought their way through into the open, and only on one sector, the New Zealanders', had they attempted to do so. As in the case of the infantry, however, the tasks given to the armour had been too ambitious.

On the southern sector of the Alamein line, XIII Corps, under General Horrocks, had had a comparative minor role to play. The 7th Armoured Division, 44th British Infantry Division, and the Free French Brigade had been committed to limited offensive operations, with the intention of holding two enemy divisions in the area while the main battle progressed further north.

The most succinct analysis of the first night's operations was contained in the XXX Corps report, which stated: "An outstanding lesson of these operations is that the depth and frontage of the advance ordered for night 23/24 October, and in one or two other instances, was in fact too great against the opposition which was to be expected."

All through the next day, the "crumbling" process was continued by the infantry, particularly in the Australian and Highland sectors. They were required to seize those objectives not taken on the first night. On the New Zealanders' front, where a corridor had been cleared for the armour, the first crisis of the battle emerged.

The 10th Armoured Division showed some reluctance to break into the open, despite the advantageous position created by the New Zealanders, and in the early hours of 25 October a conference was held between Montgomery, Leese, and General Lumsden, the X Corps commander.

Lumsden, according to Montgomery, had shown "a certain infirmity of purpose" in his handling of the 10th Armoured Division's operations. The heavy casualties which it was suffering in the region of Miteiriya Ridge began to cause signs of wavering. Lumsden and the 10th Division commander, General Gatehouse, asked permission to withdraw all their regiments to the ridge, because of the dangerous situation to which they would be exposed in daylight. But Montgomery was adamant that his plans for the armour should be carried out, and was incensed when he discovered that Gatehouse was directing his armoured formations from a headquarters 16,000 yards behind the front. "I spoke to him in no uncertain voice and ordered him to go forward at once and take charge of his battle; he was to fight his way out, and lead his division from the front and not from the rear," Montgomery says in his memoirs.

The implication is perhaps somewhat unfair, because Gatehouse had a fine reputation as a front line soldier. But, like Morshead, he had a fellow-feeling for the troops under his command, particularly when they were suffering such heavy casualties as the 10th Armoured Division was enduring.

Nevertheless the British armour had not carried out Montgomery's instructions, and he had made it clear that his orders were to be implemented without question. Probably he and his infantry leaders also doubted the capacity of the tanks to carry out their allotted role, as Morshead and Freyberg had done when they exclaimed, "They won't!"

During the same morning, General Freyberg persuaded Montgomery and Leese that to continue the crumbling operations in the New Zealand sector was going to be unnecessarily costly. Consequently, Montgomery made a decision that was to have a profound effect on the outcome of the battle. He instructed the main crumbling operations to be switched from the New Zealanders to the Australian sector. The 9th Division was to work northwards to the coast, and, it was hoped, catch the enemy unawares.

General Morshead was told that his division would be required "to draw everything they could on to themselves for a few days, by the twin threats of cutting off the enemy troops in the coastal pocket and of opening up the coast road behind the minefields."

By a curious coincidence, Montgomery's order had been foreshadowed by Morshead, who the day before had ordered Brigadier Whitehead to prepare for an attack on Trig 29; an enemy strongpoint about twenty feet high that dominated the northern flank.

The 26th Brigade launched their attack at midnight, against the 125th Panzer Grenadiers holding Trig 29. Their objective was not only the seizure of the tactically important hillock, but also the spur and forward slopes of the high ground running to the eastward, and the whole project was galvanised by the commander of the 2/48th Battalion, Lieutenant-Colonel H. H. Hammer, whose troops would spearhead the attack together with the 2/24th Battalion.

He proposed to advance to the objective under strong artillery support with two companies forward. Then as the barrage lifted, a third company would rush forward in twenty-nine carriers and other vehicles. By good fortune, the Australians had captured three German officers earlier in the evening. These included the acting commanders of the 125th Regiment and its 2nd Battalion, and they were carrying maps showing the disposition of the German minefields and other defences.

Hammer's operation was performed with tremendous verve and courage, and some of the fiercest fighting of the whole battle took place as his troops assaulted the strongpoint. By dawn, they had taken the position and consolidated against the first of many bitter counter-attacks, but the post was never surrendered. They captured a total of 173 German prisoners and sixty-seven Italians, but lost heavily themselves. Fifty-five were killed and

236 wounded. The dead included Private P. E. Gratwick, who won a post-humous Victoria Cross for his feat of assaulting two enemy posts by grenade and bayonet and killing the occupants, before losing his own life while attacking a third position.

The tactical importance of Trig 29 can be gauged from Rommel's reaction when he returned to the battlefront at dusk on 25 October from a visit to Germany, and later recorded: "Our main aim for the next four days was to throw the enemy out of our main defence line at all costs and to reoccupy our old positions, in order to avoid having a westward bulge in our front. Attacks were now launched on Hill 28 by elements of the 15th Armoured Division, the Littorio (Armoured Division) and a Bersaglieri battalion; supported by the concentrated fire of all the local artillery and A.A. Unfortunately the attack gained ground very slowly. The British resisted desperately. Rivers of blood were poured out over the miserable strips of land!"

Various British writers, describing the role of United Kingdom troops in the battle, have repeatedly interpreted Hill 28 as being in the 51st Highland Division sector, but it has been conclusively established that Trig 29 in the Australian sector was described as Hill 28 in the German records. It was therefore principally the Australians who poured out Rommel's "rivers of blood;" a phrase which during the next few days was to be no idle metaphor.

From Trig 29, the Australians held a commanding observation post extending 4-5,000 yards in every direction, and they were subjected to a devastating methodical artillery barrage, besides three infantry and tank attacks within the first twelve hours of its capture.

General Morshead's personal contribution to the battle, which has never been given the acknowledgement it deserves, was initiated at a conference at his headquarters on 26 October, attended by Montgomery, Leese and Lumsden. "On the previous day," Morshead wrote later, "I had received orders to 'go north,' and to have my firm plans ready today. The Army Commander (Montgomery) fully approved my plans without alteration."

Morshead's magnificent 9th Division was to attack again on the night of 28 October, in order to keep the enemy looking northwards. In the meantime further thrusts were made, near the boundary of the Australian and Highland Divisions, by the 1st Armoured Division. They attacked the two features of the Kidney Ridge area known as Woodcock and Snipe; an engagement which was a fierce and costly affair. At about the same time, the New Zealanders and South Africans completed their conquest of the middle and southerly parts of the Miteiriya Ridge. XXX Corps Operation Instruction of 26 October stated: "After a policy of mopping up, and the completion of the capture of the final objective by all divisions on October 27th, it was decided to plan the further attack northwards on the night of October 28/29th."

Morshead's ambitious plan proposed to employ all three brigades of the 9th Division, together with the 23rd Armoured Brigade (less two regiments) and the artillery of the 51st Highland, New Zealand, and 10th Armoured Divisions, plus three medium artillery regiments. With his own artillery, this assembly would give him about 360 guns in support.

While this was being prepared, Montgomery caused consternation in London by withdrawing the New Zealand and 1st Armoured Divisions from the front to rest and refit, and ordering the 10th Armoured Division to relieve the 1st. A major regrouping took place on the night of 27/28 October, to allow the Australians to get into position for their momentous attack. When Churchill learnt of the withdrawal of the troops from the front, he assumed all manner of imputations against the generals conducting the battle; none of them very complimentary. He ranted at Sir Alan Brooke, stating that Montgomery was fighting a half-hearted battle, and was only pacified after a conference in which both Brooke and Smuts assured him that, in sending in fresh troops to replace those who had borne the first brunt of the battle, Montgomery was doing exactly the right thing.

On the morning of 28 October, Montgomery decided that a new break out thrust would be made when the 9th Division had completed its northern "crumbling" thrust, and that on completion of their operations, the New Zealanders would take over the sector and continue the advance along the coast.

The Australian 20th Brigade launched their attack at 10 p.m. on 28 October, advancing north from Trig 29 against heavily defended positions and losing heavily in the process. The Australians were to enlarge their hold on Trig 29 and strike for the coast road, with Brigadier Richards' 23rd British Armoured Brigade in support, and then swing south-east to demolish the substantial enemy forces caught in the resulting trap.

The Germans thwarted the Australian drive to the coast, but lost over 300 prisoners and suffered crippling losses in killed and wounded. The 20th Brigade attack had penetrated the German line at a very sensitive spot, and provided just the type of crumbling operations for which Montgomery regarded the Australians to be so superbly suited by nature and training.

The savagery of the fighting was hinted at in Rommel's diary, after one of the main enemy positions had fallen to the Australians at 3.15 a.m. He wrote: "The battle raged at this point with tremendous fury for six hours until finally 11/125th Regiment and XI Bersaglieri Battalion were overrun by the enemy. Their troops, surrounded and exposed to enemy fire from all sides, fought on desperately."

The key to the strongly fortified German defence system in this area was known as Thompson's Post, a grim buttress in the bitter war of attrition which the Australians had to wage against the German 90th and 164th Light Divisions and the Bersaglieri—the crack troops of the Italian Army.

The Germans mounted three counter-attacks next day, with strong artillery and tank support, but all were beaten off with appalling casualties. The Australian operations were quickly having the desired effect of drawing "the enemy on to themselves," and Rommel showed increasing concern with the northern sector by withdrawing still more German mobile forces from the south. He was obliged to group all his German divisions in the northern sector, leaving the Italian divisions to defend what he regarded as the less vulnerable central and southern fronts. In fact, he was beginning to lose control of the battle, because he was acting in the way which Montgomery had planned.

Montgomery planned to deliver his knockout blow, which he called "Supercharge," on the night of 31 October-1 November, at the junction of the 9th German Light and Italian Trento Divisions. Morshead's northern crumbling thrust maintained the momentum of 8th Army's attack at a time of threatened stalemate, and the Australian attack during those last days and nights of October was the decisive factor in the victory of El Alamein.

The 9th Division's third assault northwards was to take place on the night of 30/31 October, with the 26th Brigade leading the advance and Brigadier Richards' 40th Royal Tank Regiment of the 23rd Armoured Brigade in support. The objective was to continue the relentless pressure on Rommel until the final break out was achieved on the night of 1/2 November, and it was in effect an elaboration of Morshead's plans for the attack mounted on 28/29 October. If successful, it would open up the main road from Rommel's original front, and/or strike north from the division's left flank and cut off all enemy forces to the east. Morshead decided to do both.

The 2/32nd Battalion launched the Australian onslaught at 10.10 p.m., with support from a heavy artillery barrage. The infantry achieved their first objective, the railway line, with comparative ease, despite stiff opposition from the Germans of whom 175 were taken prisoner. But as the advance continued to the prime objective, the enemy positions astride the main road, the Australian casualties mounted rapidly. The battalion commander, Lieutenant-Colonel J. Balfe, was seriously wounded in a personal encounter with six Germans.

Meanwhile, the second phase of the Australian operations was being implemented by three other battalions; the 2/24th under Lieutenant-Colonel C. G. Weir; 2/28th under Lieutenant-Colonel H. H. Hammer; and Lieutenant-Colonel A. V. Gallasch's 2/3rd Pioneers, following up in the wake of 2/32nd to get to their start lines. Balfe's battalion had not succeeded in mopping up all the German posts bypassed in its advance, and these engaged in sharp encounters with the following Australians before being disposed of.

The 2/24th and 2/48th Battalions formed up behind the screen of the 2/32nd in an area which became known as the Saucer. Their intention was to fan out eastwards some 2,250 yards, to seize the enemy defences astride the railway line and 1,200 yards north of the track. When this had been done, the 2/24th would wheel south-west from the road and dispose of Thompson's Post, while the 2/48th would advance to the coast through two features known as Cloverleaf and the Egg. The Pioneers on the other hand were to pass through the 2/32nd ånd advance northwards towards the coast, and consolidate facing east and west. The attack was to be supported by the 360 guns which Morshead had secured for his command, under the control of Brigadier Ramsay.

The men of the 2/24th and 2/48th Battalions began their eastward attack at 1 a.m. on 31 October. The start was confused by an intense bombardment in which "shorts" from their own barrage were mingled with the enemy's fire, but in the inferno of noise from German, Italian, British, and Australian batteries, pierced by the staccato of enemy machine-guns, the Australians began to move forward. It was an attack to weaken all but the strongest heart. The two battalions had been cut down by previous fighting to about half their original strength, but the 450 Australians showed superb courage and battle discipline as they moved steadily into the churned-up battlefield. They charged one enemy strongpoint after another, capturing them at bayonet point but losing many of their own men in the storm of fire.

Both battalions lost many of their officers and senior N.C.O.'s, and Sergeant W. H. Kibby won for the 2/48th its third posthumous Victoria Cross. He had been an inspiration to his comrades since the offensive was first launched, and in this particular action, after his company commander and all the platoon leaders had been killed when caught on open ground near the end of their advance, Kibby took command of a dozen survivors and organised an attack on the final objective. They were pinned to the ground twenty yards from the enemy posts until Kibby jumped up and destroyed the machine-guns with grenades. Even as he threw them he was mortally wounded.

Lieutenant-Colonel Hammer's battalion was now reduced to forty-one men, from a nominal roll of thirty officers and 656 other ranks when they went into the battle on 23 October, and their comrades of the 2/24th were reduced to fifty-one survivors by the end of the night attack. Their commander, Lieutenant-Colonel Weir, was seriously wounded while leading fifteen of his men in an attack on Thompson's Post, which was earlier reported to have been evacuated by the enemy. The two battalions inflicted equally savage losses on the enemy, and drove 300 prisoners before them as they retired to their starting lines in the Saucer behind the screen of the 2/32nd Battalion.

Although the night's "crumbling" had not achieved all its objectives, the Australians had driven a thin tongue-like salient into the enemy defences cutting both the railway line and coast road. It had been done at the cost of virtual annihilation of two magnificent battalions, the 2/24th and 2/48th.

The Pioneers were waiting in the Saucer for their orders to go forward, which they received just before dawn at 4.25 a.m. The farthest objective of their advance called for a movement of 3,000 yards, over ground they were supposed to seize and hold. The battalion advanced through heavy fire and reached their first objectives 1,500 yards from the Saucer. One company consolidated, while the second passed through. It was stopped 200 yards further on, and as the sun rose the Pioneers became uncomfortably aware of their precarious situation.

Lacking anti-tank or machine-guns, which were at Tel el Eisa waiting for the coast road to be cleared, they found themselves in a depression overlooked by Germans on three sides.

Rommel's reaction to the Australian assault had prompted him to pull another German Division, the 21st Panzer, into the line opposite the Australians. They now had three German divisions confronting them, and had most thoroughly satisfied Montgomery's wish that they should "draw everything on to themselves." Rommel was so worried by the situation that he set up his command post east of the mosque at Sidi Abd el Rahman, in order to supervise the 21st Armoured and 90th Light Divisions' attack on the thin Australian wedge.

The Pioneers were given a chance to surrender, but the two companies greeted the German envoys with some choice Australian invective, and the advice, "If you want us, come and get us." The Germans surrounded the position, and it was overrun later in the morning.

The first main German counter-attack was launched at 11.30 a.m. on 31 October, by fifteen tanks. This was broken up by a battery of Rhodesian gunners, who were supporting the Australian operations, and further German counter-attacks in the afternoon were thwarted by the artillery and by Valentine tanks of the 40th Royal Tank Regiment.

The 26th Brigade, still holding out in the Saucer, was too depleted to withstand a determined German assault, so Morshead ordered that it be relieved by the 24th Brigade under Brigadier Godfrey. The relief was completed by 3.30 a.m. on 1 November, but the 2/32nd Battalion, which was originally part of the 24th Brigade, and the Pioneers, were not relieved.

At midday on 1 November, Rommel began pressing home counter-attacks by elements of the 21st Panzers and 90th Light Infantry. These continued throughout the afternoon, but two fresh Australian battalions, the 2/23rd and 2/28th, together with the remnants of the Pioneers and the 2/32nd Battalion, presented an unbreakable front.

Morshead's decision to send in the 24th Brigade to relieve the 26th Brigade was a tactical decision that has been described as "his finest hour."

Lieutenant-General Sir Henry Wells, then Chief of Staff of the 9th Division, later wrote a description of the circumstances in which he said that by noon on 1 November General Morshead could perceive four critical elements in the situation.

The retention of the 26th Brigade area, on the right flank of the 9th Division front, could be vital to the success of further 8th Army operations and especially to "Supercharge." Intelligence reports left no doubt that Rommel intended to overrun and capture the 26th Brigade area. After almost continuous operations for eight days and nights, with heavy losses and very little sleep, it was doubtful whether the remnants of the brigade could withstand assaults by combined infantry and Panzers. So, despite the risks involved, immediate relief of the brigade was essential.

These risks were numerous, and could even prove critical if the relief was discovered or delayed. The coastal sector, held by the 24th Brigade, would remain for a time undefended. This brigade would have to move out, 9th Division Cavalry Regiment would move in and screen the area while the 26th Brigade was being reorganised, and then the 26th Brigade would have to take position on the coast while the cavalry moved out for other employment.

This in itself would have to work like clockwork, while battalions of the 24th Brigade would be taking over a very confused defensive position in the Saucer. German attacks could be expected at any time from daylight onwards, before the relievers had had time to settle into their positions. Battalion commanders would have no opportunity to familiarise themselves with the positions, and would have to lead their troops straight into them.

Sir Henry Wells says he is certain that Morshead's decision was correct. Otherwise, the depleted and exhausted units of the 26th Brigade could have collapsed under fierce German attacks. Rommel would have broken through, rolled up the right flank, and smashed on southwards into the right flank of the 8th Army, driving it south of its main lines of communication — the bitumen road and the desert railway — and winning the battle.

Sir Henry writes: "I have not altered the conclusion reached at the time of the battle, namely that it was this decision — probably the most important made during the battle — which in all probability saved the right flank and possibly the battle."

The holding of the right flank, however, enabled Montgomery to launch "Supercharge" as he had planned, and to continue with successive attacks further south until the New Zealand Division penetrated Rommel's line and the armoured units broke through.

It is decisions such as Morshead's which show the born soldier; the man who combines the intelligence to plan an operation and the perception to assess the risk involved with the iron courage needed to make the command decision; knowing that if it fails his soldiers will be massacred and he himself disgraced.

Rommel, in an attempt to break the Australian hold, urged on his crack

infantry and armoured troops in a series of furious attacks which released
the "rivers of blood" he had foreseen. It was the blood of his own troops as
well as that of the Australians, who stood fast even when the German tanks
churned right up to their positions, closely followed by *Afrika Korps* infantry.
It was a hell in which the bursting shells from 9th Division artillery howled
down and exploded among the attacking infantry and armour, mingled
with the crash of grenades, the vicious hammering of Schmeisser machine-
pistols, the spouting boom of mines and the roar of rifle-fire. The desert in
front of the Australian positions was a dreadful chaos of shattered tanks,
tangled wire and slashed sandbags, corpses, weapons, and equipment, all
lying in and out of shell craters and trenches and hazed by the drifting smoke
and dust.

The relief of the 26th Brigade was carried out with a speed and efficiency
of which only the most battlewise troops are capable, and the fresh troops
prepared to meet the German onslaught. A vicious artillery barrage fell on
24th Brigade tactical headquarters, and Brigadier Godfrey was killed with
several of his staff. The death of the successful and popular commander
was a sad loss to his men and in fact to the Australian forces as a whole.

The Australian line held fast until they had taken the sting out of the
German attack. As firing slackened on their own front, shortly after midnight, they were able to relax a little, and then at 1 a.m. on 1 November
they saw the desert night to the south of them lit with the great fans of
exploding shells and heard the thundering roll of gunfire. Operation
Supercharge had begun; Montgomery's great assault on the German lines
which had been weakened by the major withdrawal of forces to fight the
Australians.

Even so, it was to be a savage battle. The first great blow was delivered by
General Freyberg's command of the New Zealand Division, a Highland
Brigade, 9th Armoured Brigade, and a brigade from 50th (British) Division,
with the 1st Armoured Division, which now included the 2nd and 8th
Armoured Brigades and 7th Motor Brigade, to follow up the 9th Armoured
Brigade's attack, cross the Rahman track and defeat the enemy armour.
To support Freyberg's break out were 13 field and 3 medium regiments
of artillery with a total of some 360 guns.

Rommel's men fought desperately. He briefly held the Allied advance
and planned a controlled withdrawal in order to establish another line, but
Hitler sent the *Afrika Korps* a message ordering them to choose between
victory or death. A tactical victory, at that time, was impossible, so they
had no choice but to die under Freyberg's onslaught. The armoured might
of X Corps poured through the hole blasted in Rommel's defences, so
that by late afternoon on 4 November the enemy was in full retreat, and
a major victory won.

"Ring out the bells!" Alexander cabled to Churchill. 30,000 prisoners,

350 tanks, and 400 guns had been captured. Four German and eight Italian divisions had been shattered. Rommel and the disorganised remnants of the *Afrika Korps* were in full flight, and were only saved from complete destruction by a break in the weather which turned the desert into mud, and bogged down the pursuing tanks and vehicles. But the Anglo-American force which was to land in the Western Mediterranean was already on the water, and before long the Axis forces in North Africa would be squeezed in the jaws of assaults from both east and west.

For the Australians, wearily reorganising after a battle in which they had withstood twenty-five furious German counter-attacks, there was to begin with no great cause for elation. They had seen out the final phases of El Alamein by active patrolling to check the enemy retreat along the coastal road, but for the moment were almost too numbed to realise that they had played a critical role in defeating the famed *Afrika Korps* in the field.

During the three main phases of the battle, they had in the first borne an equal share of the heavy fighting in the first assault made by XXX Corps formations. In the second, they had borne the heaviest burden in the long "crumbling" operations which had allowed Montgomery to prepare

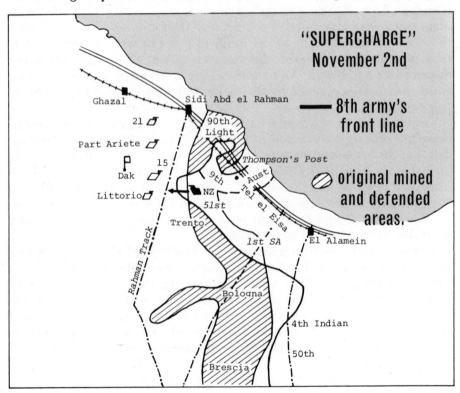

Operation Supercharge, and in the third, though not engaged with the same intensity, they had still been committed on a three-brigade front.

Soon, messages of congratulation began to pour into Morshead's headquarters, including those from the Governor-General of Australia, President Roosevelt and General Blamey. Montgomery and Alexander called on him to convey their personal appreciation, and General Leese wrote: "I would like to write a line to congratulate you on the magnificent fighting which your division has carried out, and to thank you personally for your great co-operation and sound judgement during the battle — I am quite certain that this breakout was only made possible by the Homeric fighting over your divisional sector. When it was no longer possible for the crumbling process to go on in the south, the Army Commander decided to continue with his crumbling policy in the north. This led to five days bitter fighting on your front. During this time your division attacked four times, and were counter-attacked incessantly by enemy infantry and tanks. The main mass of heavy and medium artillery was concentrated in your division front, and we now know they concentrated the whole of the Panzer Troops against you. The final break could never have been carried out unless the Army Commander was certain of the valiant resistances that would be put up by your division. If the Germans could have broken your division, the whole gun support of the attack would have been disorganised and its success vitally prejudiced."

The 9th Division was gradually pulled out of the Alamein line for rest and refit, and on 17 December a new shoulder flash was created for its uniforms. Shaped like a T, it commemorated the division's defence of Tobruk.

Their casualties from 23 October to 5 November totalled 620 killed, 1,994 wounded, and 130 prisoners of war; more than twenty per cent of the Allied casualties suffered in the Battle of El Alamein though the Australians were only about six per cent of Montgomery's forces. Their share of the fighting had been completely out of proportion to their strength.

On 22 December, General Alexander reviewed the 12,000 officers and men of the 9th Division at Gaza, in a spectacular parade which was watched by senior officers and diplomats from many nations. Addressing the division, General Alexander said: "The Battle of Alamein has made history, and you are in the proud position of having taken a major part in that great victory. Your reputation as fighters has always been famous, but I do not believe you have ever fought with greater bravery or distinction than you did during that battle, when you broke the German and Italian Armies in the Western Desert. Now you have added fresh lustre to your already illustrious name. There is one thought I shall cherish above all others; that under my command fought the 9th Australian Division."

But perhaps the most eloquent testimony to the contribution made by the division in this historic battle was on its twenty-fifth anniversary in 1967, when Field-Marshal Lord Montgomery wrote: "When all did so well it would seem hardly right to single out any for special praise. But I must say this—we could not have won the battle in twelve days without that magnificent 9th Australian Division."

For the 8th Army, in which the 9th Division had fought, the way ahead was to be hard but victorious, with the final triumph in North Africa followed by the invasions of Sicily and Italy and the long, hard grind up beyond Rome. The New Zealand Division, with which the Australians briefly had been joined in a resurgent Anzac Corps, played an heroic part in these battles, and in some ways it seems a pity that the 9th Division could not have shared in the Eighth Army's conquests since it had done so much to get them off to a flying start. But, as they climbed up the troopship gangways to leave the Middle East, the 9th Division veterans knew that they had even more important work ahead; the defence of their own country against an enemy who was far more vicious than the Germans, and who compared with the Italians was as a tiger against a domestic cat.

BOOK III

The Fight for the Homeland

❋ ❋ ❋ ❋ ❋ ❋

"*Our troops should have it impressed upon them that killing Japanese is their duty. Not only must we defeat the enemy, but we must destroy him.*"

MAJOR-GENERAL H. GORDON BENNETT

"*Some of us may forget that of all the Allies it was Australian soldiers who first broke the spell of the invincibility of the Japanese Army . . .*"

FIELD-MARSHAL VISCOUNT SLIM

25

THE WORST DISASTER

THE GERMANS HAD CALLED THEIR NORTH AFRICAN CAMPAIGN "A gentleman's war." Perhaps because the area was largely devoid of a civilian population to enslave and murder as they did in Europe, and because they respected their antagonists in a manner which they could not feel for the "sub-men" of the Balkans and Russia. A certain chivalry was displayed by both sides, prisoners were treated as well as circumstances allowed, and the captured wounded were cared for.

The Japanese, who combined an antique and merciless warriors' code with a highly-developed technology, were a very different proposition. But when Australians from the Middle East returned to the acclaim of their countrymen, they found that their nation was still very much a "dell on the edge of the jungle," as General Blamey had described it. For generations, Australians had been accustomed to regarding wars as events which took place on the far side of protecting oceans. Their men sailed away to take a gallant part, and then returned to be absorbed by a civilian population which was almost unchanged by the campaigns in which they had suffered and died.

The Royal Navy was still the ruler of the waves and a sure shield of the British Dominions, despite doubts expressed on many occasions in the Australian Parliament during the 1930s as to the Royal Navy's ability to reinforce Singapore expeditiously should the increasingly belligerent policies of Japan develop into war. But all this had been very distant from the man in the street.

Now, matters were very different. People were beginning to realise that Japan was possessed of a huge fleet, an air force which despite stories of the

281

inability of Japanese pilots to see properly was capable of sinking American and British battleships, and a most savagely efficient army.

The realisation took a long time to sink in. When the A.I.F. formations returned, a large proportion of the nation's military force still consisted of militia enlisted for home service only, and contemptuously referred to as "chokos" (for "chocolate soldiers") by A.I.F. veterans. Trade Union members had no compunction in downing tools on account of trifling disagreements with management, and the public as a whole tended to treat the war as an interesting nuisance. It took the fall of Singapore, referred to by Winston Churchill as "The worst disaster and largest capitulation in British history," to bring it home to Australia, following soon after the first enemy attack on Australia when Japanese aircraft raided Darwin and other north-west ports.

The divisional headquarters and two brigades of the 8th Division, raised in mid-1940 and commanded by Major-General H. Gordon Bennett, had been sent to Malaya in 1941, and it had been agreed with the Dutch government to send the remaining brigade to assist the Dutch in Ambon and Timor if war should break out with Japan. The 2/22nd Battalion had been sent to Rabaul, and smaller units despatched to Nauru, Ocean Island, the Solomons, New Ireland, the Admiralty Islands and New Caledonia. Even though this wide deployment was later regarded as a fatal dispersal of the available forces, it was at least some attempt to deal with the situation.

Malaya, as it was then termed, was to be the scene of yet another British débâcle in the style of Dunkirk, Cyrenaica, Greece, and Crete, and for much the same reasons but as though magnified a hundredfold by the tropical sun. It was a campaign in which the British had virtually no chance of success. Inept military leadership, poorly-equipped troops untrained in jungle warfare, lack of air support, an apathetic European civilian population conditioned to the almost feudal style of pre-war colonial life, and a civil administration incapable of backing up a military campaign, were amongst the main causes of defeat.

Worst of all, perhaps, were the British General Staff's absolute failure to understand Japanese military competence, and the British government's inability to recognise Japanese imperial ambitions—despite the most clear demonstrations of both since the Japanese Army had given the Russians a sound thrashing in 1905. It was perhaps typical of the arrogant British outlook of those days, in which nations east of Suez were not taken entirely seriously.

Field-Marshal Wavell, in a dispatch written two days after the fall of Singapore, summed it all up by saying: "The trouble goes a long way back; climate, the atmosphere of the country (the whole of Malaya has been asleep for at least 200 years), lack of vigour in our peacetime training, the cumbrousness of our tactics and equipment, and the real difficulty of finding an answer to the very skilful and bold tactics of the Japanese in this jungle fighting."

Amid the confusion and humiliation of the disaster, the six infantry battalions of the Australian 8th Division fulfilled their tasks with prodigious valour, and their commander, Major-General H. Gordon Bennett, emerged as perhaps the most controversial figure in Australian military history.

Bennett was as tough and uncompromising as Blamey, which is perhaps why the two clashed head-on more than once. Short, red-headed, and square-jawed, he had been the youngest battalion commander in the 1st A.I.F., the youngest brigadier in the entire British Army between 1914-18, and the possessor of a legendary reputation for personal bravery on Gallipoli and the Western Front.

Ian Morrison, correspondent of the London *Times* during the Malaya campaign, wrote of him: "In my opinion the best of the senior military leaders was Gordon Bennett. He was a rasping, bitter, sarcastic person, given to expressing his views with great freedom. As a result he quarrelled with a good number of people. But he did have a forceful personality. He was imbued with a tough, aggressive, ruthless spirit. As a soldier he was unconventional, but one wanted an unconventional soldier to deal with what was an unconventional situation. He was passionately proud of his men and devoted to their interests. His men knew it and had confidence in him."

However, his escape from Singapore within hours of the surrender, and subsequent safe arrival in Australia, caused him to be condemned for "leaving his men in the lurch," especially by those whose sons or husbands could not escape and fell into Japanese hands. His action aroused all the human passions as to whether it fell within the scope of accepted military ethics, but his magnificent service in the previous war would surely entitle him to any benefit of the doubt concerning the nobility of his motives. He was determined to defend the honour of his division in any post-mortems held on the disastrous Malayan campaign, and to pass on to the military leaders of his country the lessons on Japanese tactics learnt in Malaya. With Australia about to face its darkest hour, he also hoped to be given the opportunity of playing an active role in leading Australian forces in the defence of their country and in the eventual counter offensive. For these tasks, his character and experience would have been invaluable.

Like so many of Australia's military leaders, he was the descendant of sturdy pioneering stock. He was born in what was then the village of Balwyn, near Melbourne, on 15 April, 1887. George Bennett, his father, was the local schoolmaster; a man who believed in the virtues of strict but impartial discipline, and contributed his energy and talents to many community affairs. The grandparents had emigrated from England during the gold rush of the 1850s, and had mined in the Walhalla district with mixed success.

Bennett's father married twice. His first wife left him two daughters and two sons, and the second, the daughter of British emigrants who ran a shipchandling business at Port Melbourne, produced seven children of whom Henry was the eldest. George Bennett's public spirited and Christian virtue were typical of those which formed the communal strength of early Australian settlements. They inspired all the members of his family with a strong moral sense and a powerful national pride and patriotism.

In George Bennett's school, the cadets had an important place in the curriculum. During the South African War a war map was maintained in the classroom, and a daily lecture given on the progress of the campaign. When Mafeking was relieved, the school was given a half holiday. As each of the Australian contingents going to the war marched through the streets of Melbourne, the boys of Bennett's school were there to cheer them on their way.

At thirteen, Henry Gordon Bennett won a scholarship to Hawthorn College, where he showed a talent for mathematics and descriptive writing. Like Monash, he was not interested in sport. His volatile temperament made him too impatient to master the co-ordination required in ball games, but he won an enviable reputation for his ability to use his fists. These, added to his father's moral precepts, became powerful instruments of justice against boys who picked on the school weaklings.

After three years at Hawthorn, he joined the A.M.P. Society as an actuarial clerk; winning the position from many others in the entrance examination. For the next five years he studied to complete his actuarial qualifications, and apart from this had no particular spare-time interest until, at twenty-one, he was accepted as a recruit officer with the 5th Australian Infantry Regiment in May 1908. This began an association with military affairs that was to last thirty-six years.

From the moment he was granted his commission to the outbreak of war in 1914, he devoted all his spare time to the profession of arms. His work with the insurance society took most of his time, but soldiering was developing into his great love. During those six years he spent at least three nights a week, every weekend, and all his annual leave on military training. Such devotion brought its due rewards. By 1912, at twenty-five, he had been promoted to major and was adjutant of his regiment.

During the three years before the first World War, two events had a lasting influence on his future. The first was a brush with a regular staff officer, Captain T. A. Blamey. It came about when Blamey was in charge of Cadet Corps training in Victoria, and apparently Blamey made some criticism of the training of cadets in George Bennett's school. Both father and son re-acted with some vigour, but the professional soldier was not impressed by the opinion of a militia officer. With men like Blamey and Bennett, the trifling incident smouldered between them for the rest of their lives.

KILLERS AND THEIR PREY. *Top:* An Australian anti-tank gun crew in Malaya, and *Centre:* One of the six Japanese tanks which they destroyed. *Bottom:* Private Body, Corporal Cummings, and Lieutenant Bell firing a captured machine-gun at a Japanese patrol sixty yards away.

The second event was one of softer passions. Bennett met Bess Buchanan, who would become his wife, companion, and staunch champion, but even this encounter had its frustrating elements. His prospective father-in-law refused the hand of his daughter on the grounds that she was too young, but relented sufficiently to allow their engagement when Bennett sailed with the first convoy of Australian troops in 1914. Bess Buchanan presented her soldier fiancé with a miniature portrait of herself, on ivory in a gold frame, which he wore throughout the two World Wars in his tunic or shirt pocket. It saved his life on the Western Front in 1917, when a German bullet smashed the glass and frame, but was deflected from his heart.

As an original member of the 6th Battalion, Major "Ginger" Bennett helped to shape the quality of his unit of magnificent but raw material. First in Australia and then in Egypt the men gradually acquired all those skills of soldiering whose final tempering must come in the fires of active service.

Their test was to come on Sunday, 25 April 1915, when they landed at Gallipoli. For Bennett, the bloody beaches began years of front line soldiering in battles which have few parallels for prolonged savagery.

By August 1915, at twenty-eight, he had been promoted to lieutenant-colonel and the command of his battalion. His reputation for tenacity and courage during battles on the Peninsula had become legendary, and his distinguished service was recognised by the award of the C.M.G.; a rare honour for a battalion commander.

After the evacuation, he went to Egypt for the reorganisation of the A.I.F., and then led his battalion to France. Apart from an initial period of routine trench warfare, the hell of Pozières was Bennett's first experience of a major battle in France. The quality of his leadership was so clearly apparent that on 20 November, 1916, at twenty-nine, he was promoted to brigadier with command of the 3rd Brigade, thus becoming the youngest officer to hold this rank in any of the British armies. Between the date of this appointment and the end of the war, he added further lustre to his reputation by holding temporary command of the 1st Division on several occasions.

During this period, he had another clash with Blamey. Blamey, as Chief of Staff for the 1st Division, issued orders for the capture of three villages which Bennett had reported as being taken on the previous day. When Bennett questioned the strange order, Blamey said it had been issued for the purpose of war records: a "staff answer" which annoyed the fighting soldier who already had done the job. He held it against Blamey, too, that his honeymoon leave to marry Bess Buchanan, who at last had received her father's permission and had travelled to England to marry him, had been reduced from fourteen days to ten. General Birdwood had promised him fourteen days, but when the leave voucher came through with "10 Days" marked upon it, Bennett was certain that Blamey was behind this deprival.

INFANTRYMEN II. *Top left*, The men in this forward Section Post, just off the Sanananda track, could hear the Japanese talking in their positions thirty yards away. *Top right*, Private Neil Bextram, of Delta Company, 6th Battalion, Royal Australian Regiment, rests after the company's return to the scene of its heroic lone stand against a crack North Vietnam battalion at Long Tan. *Bottom:* Diggers of a 2nd A.I.F. unit at Gorari, New Guinea, which killed 500 Japanese in hand-to-hand fighting—and then had the task of burying them.

Bennett's leadership of the 3rd Brigade, in all the offensives launched by the Anzac and Australian Corps on the Western Front during 1917-18, brought him to the end of the war as still the youngest brigadier and with the C.B. and D.S.O. added to his honours.

During the uneasy peace, he maintained a lively interest in the militia, and commanded the 2nd Division with the rank of major-general for five years before being placed on the unattached list. In civil life he established himself as a successful businessman, and as the crisis of the 1930s grew in intensity he became a scathing critic of Australian defence policies. This did not endear him to government ministers, nor to the small and devoted band of regular staff officers who held together the thin fabric of Australia's military forces despite tremendous financial difficulties.

When the second World War broke out, he offered his services at once, but was passed over for command of the 6th and 7th Divisions. His volatile personality, and verbal attacks on regular staff officers, would have done nothing to advance his cause, and General Brudenell White himself, as Chief of Staff, observed that Bennett had "certain qualities and certain disqualities" for higher command.

The sudden death of Brudenell White gave Bennett his opportunity. General Vernon Sturdee had been appointed to lead the 8th Division, but on White's death he was promoted to Chief of the General Staff. On 24 October, 1940, Major-General Gordon Bennett was given command of the division, and threw himself into the task with a vigour and enthusiasm which was all the greater for having been bottled up so long. He landed in Singapore with the advance 22nd Brigade in February 1941.

*　　*　　*

The intention in sending the 8th Division to Malaya was so that it might help to garrison that rich and important British possession until sufficient units of the Indian Army had been trained to relieve them. After that, the Australians would join their three sister divisions fighting in the Middle East. It soon became apparent, however, that such a design was purely theoretical, and that Malaya was like a termite-eaten floorboard; superficially strong, but incapable of resisting any pressure.

Bennett's critical and experienced eye quickly assessed the true state of affairs. The regular British and Indian units maintained an extraordinary peace time training programme, in which barrack square discipline and spit and polish reigned supreme, with no recognition of the possibilities of jungle warfare. The only exception to this disastrous attitude was a battalion of the Argyle and Sutherland Highlanders.

Bennett, however, discerned the values as well as the threats of the jungle terrain. He initiated a programme of training which was unprecedented in Malaya command, so that when the Japanese swarmed down the peninsula the 8th Division contained by far the best trained troops on the British side. For most of their British colleagues, however, the threat of war in Asia appeared remote, and the unreal tempo of life was allowed to continue undisturbed; accentuated by propaganda which was designed to create a false impression of the strength of Malaya Command in the hope of deterring Japanese aggression. The British only succeeded in fooling themselves.

After Bennett's arrival, he made persistent appeals to his government for the two remaining brigades and ancillary units of the 8th Division to be sent forward, and after considerable indecision the 27th Brigade arrived in July 1941. The 23rd Brigade was held back so that some of its units could be used on outpost garrison duties, and the remainder used to implement the government's promises to help Holland in Ambon and Timor.

The role of the 8th Division in Malaya was to be responsible for the defence of Malacca and Johore, while the 9th and 11th Indian Divisions, comprising III Indian Corps, would cover Northern Malaya. Bennett established his headquarters at Johore Bahru, on the northern end of the causeway linking Singapore Island to the mainland, on 29 August 1941. His two brigades took up their positions on the east coast, where they created strong defensive systems. The 22nd held the first line of defence, at Mersing, while the 27th was in reserve at Jemaluang.

The 22nd Brigade was led by Brigadier H. B. Taylor, who had served with distinction in France as an infantry officer during 1914-18 and between wars maintained an interest in the Militia, which he had first joined in 1913. By 1939 he had risen to command the 5th Militia Brigade, prior to which he had successively led the Sydney University Regiment, 18th Battalion, New South Wales Scottish Regiment, and the 56th Battalion. In civil life he had become a Doctor of Science in 1925, and he was appointed Deputy Government Analyst of New South Wales in 1934. His career was characteristic of the Australian military tradition, combining as it did a distinguished war record and long experience in the citizen forces with high attainment in civil life. A man of forthright conviction, he had already clashed with Bennett during brigade exercises and the patched up argument continued to simmer between the two leaders.

His counterpart in the 27th Brigade was Brigadier D. S. Maxwell, a giant of six feet three inches who had served as a trooper on Gallipoli and was later commissioned in the infantry. He was decorated for bravery in the bitter fighting at Mouquet Farm, and on demobilisation in 1919 completed a degree in medicine at Sydney University. His interest in military affairs lapsed until August 1939, when despite his profession he returned to the infantry as second in command of the 56th Battalion. Three months later he was promoted to command of the battalion, and took over the 27th Brigade in July 1941 when its original leader, Brigadier N. Marshall, retired because of ill health. Though junior to a number of other officers who were qualified for promotion to brigadier, Maxwell was a most popular figure; highly regarded as a leader and equable in temperament.

Brigadier C. A. Callaghan, a successful Sydney businessman with a distinguished 1914-18 record and continuous militia service between wars, including command of the 8th Infantry Brigade between 1934-38, commanded the divisional artillery. The Chief of Staff Officer was Colonel Thyer, a regular officer who had served with distinction in the 1st A.I.F. and gained a wide reputation as an exponent of infantry tactics during his peace time service.

The division command had all the elements which had proved so successful in other Australian divisions; seasoned front-line soldiers who had returned from civil life, backed by regular soldiers in the vital staff appointments. In the 8th Division, however, Bennett's volatile temperament prevented the leadership from blending into a smooth and cohesive team. His brigade commanders clashed with each other and with Bennett, while his own "anti-regular" complex did not obtain the fullest possible co-operation of regular soldiers on his staff.

The rank and file of the 8th Division consisted very largely of men from the country. Many of them were powerful physical specimens, alert, and accustomed to using their own initiative. Their relations with the Malays, Chinese, and Indians of the local population were generally agreeable. A certain amount of friction arose between them and men of the British units, but no more than had occurred in other theatres of war.

Major-General Bennett was not particularly impressed by the calibre of leadership in either the British or Indian formations; an opinion that was reasonably justified in view of the attitudes then prevailing, and one that was to be tragically confirmed within a very short space of time.

The G.O.C. Malaya was Lieutenant-General A. E. Percival, who had won three decorations during considerable service in 1914-18. He rose to command of a battalion, and had temporary command of a brigade. Between the wars he served in West Africa, and during 1936-38 had acted as senior staff officer in Malaya. He was one of a relatively small group of officers who had graduated from the Naval Staff College as well as the Army Staff College at Camberley, and attended a course at the Imperial Defence College. When the second World War broke out he went to France with the B.E.F., but returned to London in April 1940 to become one of the three Assistant Chiefs of the Imperial General Staff. At his own request he was transferred from this "office job" to command of a division in England, and on 16 May 1941 he was appointed to the Malayan command.

Technically, Percival possessed sound credentials for the position of General Officer in Command, Malaya, but he had flaws which were described in the book *Malayan Postscript* by the *Times* correspondent Ian

Morrison, who wrote: "Percival was a man of considerable personal charm, if one met him socially. He was an able staff officer with a penetrating mind, although a mind that saw difficulties to any scheme before it saw the possibilities. But he was a completely negative person with no vigour, no colour, and no conviction. His personality was not strong, as a leader he did not appeal either to the troops or to the general public."

The other senior British commander in Malaya was Lieutenant-General Sir Lewis Heath, who assumed command of III Indian Corps at about the same time as Percival's arrival in the country. During 1914-18 he had served in Mesopotamia, where he sustained a permanent injury to one arm, and more recently had commanded the 5th Indian Division in operations against the Italians in East Africa. During the latter campaign he gained an enviable reputation for leadership, which, as in the case of other commanders in the East Africa campaign, was to become a little tarnished when opposed to more resolute resistance than that provided by the Italian Army. Up to the time of his appointment in Malaya, Heath had been senior to Percival; a factor which, combined with his stronger personality, allowed him to sway the G.O.C.'s judgement. In Bennett's view it was Heath's policy of "withdrawal and passive conformity to the Japanese offensive" which led to the ultimate fall of Singapore.

* * *

The war clouds began to gather in July 1941, when the isolated French forces in Indo-China were obliged to permit a Japanese occupation of that area. This brought Japanese bases to within 300 miles of Kota Bharu, in the north-east corner of Malaya, and within 750 miles of Singapore. Lieutenant-General Yamashita organised his XXV Japanese Army, comprising four infantry divisions strongly supported by tanks and aircraft, and the weapon long poised by the Japanese fell at half-an-hour after midnight on 8 December 1941.

Japanese operations were well co-ordinated. Thousands of miles away, on the other side of the International Date Line, the dawn of 7 December was breaking on the Pacific as their bombers prepared to attack Pearl Harbour. Seventy-five minutes before those bombs fell, Yamashita unleashed his assault forces against Kota Bharu. They were engaged immediately by the Dogras of the 8th Indian Brigade.

From this moment onwards, events moved with extraordinary rapidity. The American Pacific Fleet was pulverised as it lay at anchor in Pearl Harbour, the largely obsolete and numerically weak squadrons of the R.A.F. in Malaya were substantially destroyed on the ground, the two Royal Navy leviathans, *Prince of Wales* and *Repulse*, were sunk on 10 December, thus virtually eliminating British sea influence from the Pacific, and the Indians were already making heavy weather of the ground fighting.

It has been suggested that the Japanese applied no new concepts to the principles of land warfare, but there can be no question that their method of enveloping the flanks and rear, while employing all the natural advantages of the jungle, introduced a third dimension to the art of war which completely dislocated the tactics of their opponents. European military thinking, schooled on the 1914-18 traditions of static siege warfare followed by the rapid manoeuvres of blitzkrieg tactics in France and the Western Desert, was completely unprepared for the lesson about to be taught.

There is irony in the recollection that the Australians were the first to develop such tactics, in their "peaceful penetration" raids on German lines in 1917-18. Even worse is the fact that the Quetta Staff College had conducted studies of a possible enemy attack on the Malayan Peninsula, and long before the war had forecast tactics similar to those used by the Japanese. The methods required to counter such tactics had been worked out, and published in British Army training manuals. They had seldom been practised in training, nor were they much used in combat.

Worse again is the fact that, in October 1940, a conference in Singapore had recommended the establishment of more than 500 aircraft to defend Malaya, but the Chiefs of Staff had maintained that about 300 would be

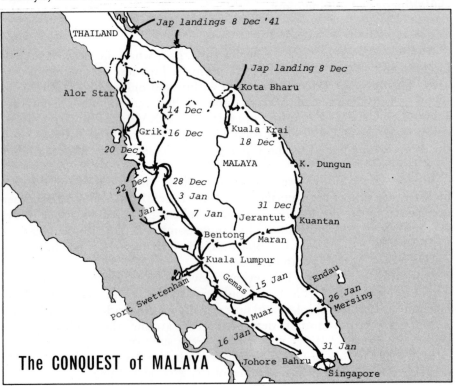

The CONQUEST of MALAYA

sufficient. In the event, only about half that number was available, mostly obsolete, to face a modern Japanese air fleet of more than 600. Command of the air, which every campaign in the war so far had shown to be an absolute essential, was in Japanese hands from the very beginning.

The burden carried by the two Indian Divisions, in resisting the Japanese during the early stages of the Malayan campaign, was too great for them. Many of the soldiers were only partly trained, they were for the most part poorly led at both divisional and regimental level, and they were being faced by tactics which baffled their officers.

Within the first week, the 11th Division had virtually ceased to exist as a co-ordinated force. The whole defensive concept for Northern Malaya was thrown into a state of confusion. General Percival's dispositions were primarily based on the twin concepts of defending the air bases and protecting the naval base at Singapore, but with the Air Force largely destroyed on the ground, one prop had been knocked from his defensive posture at a calamitous cost in ground troops.

Bennett was gravely perturbed by the fast-deteriorating situation. He had made persistent calls on the Australian government for reinforcements, but to no avail. Now, he urged that one of the Australian divisions from the Middle East be sent to Malaya, and despatched one of his staff officers north to investigate the collapse of the British and Indian units engaged so far. The observer's report confirmed Bennett's worst suspicions, and among other things said tersely: "The troops are exhausted, having been engaged for sixteen days. The constant withdrawal has sapped their spirit and they no longer have any heart in the fight. Their officers too have lost their spirit, and the withdrawals have become a habit." To add emphasis to the situation, the divisional commander and the three brigadiers of the 11th Indian Division were replaced on 20 December.

With the Japanese main effort now being directed down the centre and the west coast of the peninsula, Bennett was forced to change the disposition of his defence line from the east coast in order to counter the emerging enemy threat. He ordered his troops to prepare defensive positions at Segamat and Muar.

Christmas Day passed relatively quietly, shadowed by the threat that drew steadily closer to the Australians. Bennett was confident they would render a good account of themselves and was passionately proud of his men. "Our troops should have it impressed upon them that killing Japanese is their duty," he wrote. "Not only must we defeat the enemy, but we must destroy him."

By New Year's Eve, the fighting had reached the Slim River, where the 11th Indian Division was to be annihilated. It was barely 100 miles north of the Australians forward positions, and now Bennett, with Brigadier Maxwell of the 27th Brigade, and Lieutenant-Colonel "Black Jack" Gallaghan of the 2/30th Battalion, planned a major ambush of the Japanese at Gemas and went about their preparations accordingly.

Meanwhile, there had been discussions between the British and American governments. Although Australia was not directly represented in this conference, the Australian Prime Minister, Mr John Curtin, had made some urgent and cogent appeals for greater aid to the Pacific warfronts.

The conference instituted a command called ABDA (American-British-Dutch-Australian), and, at President Roosevelt's wish, Churchill gave supreme command to an Englishman: General Sir Archibald Wavell. Churchill's own staff were not enthused with this appointment, because an English commander inevitably would be held responsible for disasters to American as well as British troops.

Wavell, who had carried an appalling burden in the Middle East during 1940-41, with such limited resources to support him, was now saddled with even greater responsibilities and probably even fewer prospects of success.

The promise of reinforcements from Britain, India and Australia, including the despatch of the battle hardened 6th and 7th Divisions from the Middle East, gave heart to those fighting in Malaya. It also revealed a major change of thought by the British who, not unnaturally, had been preoccupied by events in Europe and Africa up until that time.

Bennett, by now more critical of British leadership than ever, proposed to Percival that when the III Indian Corps had been withdrawn into Johore all the land forces in that State should come under Bennett's command. Percival refused, saying that fusion of the Australians and Indian formations would create administrative difficulties, and that replacement of the 22nd Australian Brigade in their strong defensive positions on the east coast by troops unfamiliar with the area would weaken the overall position. But when Wavell visited Singapore for the first time, on 7 January 1942, and saw the condition of III Indian Corps, he did not consider them to be in a fit condition to continue effective resistance and agreed with Bennett's proposal.

A group called Westforce was formed under Bennett's command. It comprised the newly-arrived Indian 45th Brigade, the 8th and 22nd Brigades of the Indian 9th Division, and the 27th Australian Brigade. Bennett wanted the 22nd Australian Brigade brought over from the east coast to join them, and as might be expected he argued bitterly with Percival over this splitting of the 8th which was directly contrary to the "A.I.F. Charter." Wavell, however, supported Percival, and decided that the 22nd Brigade must become part of Eastforce, together with Indian units and under the command of III Indian Corps.

The battle line now showed itself in the west as from Segamat to Mount Ophir and thence to the mouth of the Muar River, and in the east from Endau on the coast through Kluang to Batu Pahat on the west coast—in effect behind Westforce. By these dispositions, Percival and Wavell hoped to hold the lower portion of the peninsula, and particularly the airfields, until the arrival of components of the 18th British Division and Australian I Corps (6th and 7th Divisions) in Java and Sumatra, whence if necessary they could be employed to reinforce Malaya.

Bennett took command of Westforce on the night of 13 January, and deployed the three battalions of 27th Brigade on the main road forward of Segamat. The raw 45th Indian Brigade was somewhat reluctantly entrusted with the other vital sector, on the coast road near the mouth of the Muar River.

On the same day, Wavell had offered Bennett the newly arrived 53rd British Brigade, but Bennett asked for these troops to be deployed in Australian positions in the east, relieving the 22nd Australian Brigade so that the two A.I.F. brigades might be brought together.

Wavell requested Percival that this should be done, but Percival subsequently denied any knowledge of such a request. The British troops, out of condition after a long sea voyage and completely without tropical training, were consequently placed in the Batu Pahat area behind the Muar front.

It was a misunderstanding which was to be calamitous. It may be too much to claim that if the jungle-trained 22nd Brigade Australians had held this position, there would have been a different outcome to the campaign. It is at least likely, however, that if the stinging defeat inflicted by the Japanese on the Segamat road had been followed up by another reversal at Muar, the Japanese advance on that critical front would have slowed down. This could have had a stiffening effect on the whole Malayan command, and postponed the Japanese surge towards Singapore for long enough for British reinforcements to arrive.

As it was, the 2/30th Battalion of the Australians took up ambush positions at Gemas to await the victorious armies of Yamashita. The spot chosen was a length of the main road leading to a bridge over the Gemencheh River about seven miles west of Gemas. Dense jungle grew for about 500 yards on both sides of the road, which included a cutting twelve feet high and forty yards long, ending about sixty yards from the bridge. From this point to the bridge was low scrub offering little or no concealment. The northern approaches to the bridge consisted of straight road for about 250 yards with open ground on each side.

Lieutenant-Colonel "Black Jack" Gallaghan, the tough commander of the battalion that set the trap, placed one company manning the ambush position and the other three companies three miles further back.

At 4 p.m. on 14 January, the enemy vanguard approached the bridge riding bicycles five or six abreast. They had not seen the retiring Indian forces for about 100 miles, so they rode along casually, chattering cheerfully together, and omitting the precautions usual for a vanguard. The first 300 cyclists were allowed through, to be dealt with by the Australians waiting in the rear, but when the next several hundred were tightly packed on the bridge and its approaches, the bridge was blown.

Timber, bikes and bodies were hurled skywards, and murderous fire from the ambush company caused havoc among the Japanese on the other side. Unfortunately the line back to the artillery had been cut or damaged, so that the planned bombardment of the congested enemy forces on the other side of the bridge did not materialise.

Supporting Japanese forces soon appeared, and backed up by aircraft attack hurled themselves at the Australians, who held for forty-eight hours. Finally, outnumbered and suffering from the impact of aerial strafing, they withdrew in good order to the prepared positions at Segamat. They had fought off the 1st Tank Regiment, with an infantry battalion and machine-gun and artillery in support, which after the initial heavy casualties had been reinforced by the 11th Infantry Regiment.

For a loss of seventeen killed and fifty-five wounded, the Australians had killed about 1,000 of the enemy and destroyed five tanks. The action caused the Singapore *Straits Times* of 16 January to record that: "The news gave good reason to believe that the tide of battle was on the turn, with the A.I.F. as our seawall against the vicious flood."

The Japanese described the Australians as fighting "with a bravery they had not previously seen," and Colonel Tsuji, Director of Military Operations for the 25th Japanese Army, stated that the action "completely changed the aspect of the combat zone."

However, the curtain had barely fallen on this drama before the Japanese coming down the coast road began probing the defences at Muar. Tactically, the Muar River provided a natural defensive barrier, but the inexperienced Indian troops of the 45th Brigade proved no match for men of the Japanese Guards Division who attacked them.

Bennett had disposed two companies of Indians on the northern side of the river, as part of his policy of "aggressive defence." Despite this deployment, and the withdrawal of every boat and ferry to the southern side of the river, the Japanese soon overran the Indians. Then, using boats found in nearby rice paddies, they paddled across the river and collected the larger boats, which they took back to the northern bank so that their comrades might cross.

They worked steadily during the afternoon and night of 16 January, despite heavy fire from Australian gunners, and by dawn of the following morning the enemy had sufficient craft to continue his advance. The 45th Brigade headquarters at Bakri was immediately threatened. Late on 16 January, the Japanese were reported to have made a seaborne landing at Batu Pahat, thus threatening Bennett's whole defensive position on the coast. Two Indian battalions, one each on the Muar and Parit Jawa roads, were pressed back, so Bennett sent in two of his Australian battalions, the 2/19th and 2/29th, to help restore the rapidly deteriorating situation. The 2/19th had been brought over from the 22nd Brigade on the east coast and the 2/29th was from his main front, at Segamat, so this development left him without reserves.

The 2/29th had barely taken up their positions forward of Bakri, late in the afternoon of 17 January, when they had to face two determined Japanese attacks. Both were beaten off with heavy casualties, and were followed during the night by an intense artillery duel. At dawn the Japanese attacked with tanks, ten of which were destroyed by the Australians, and then followed up with another infantry assualt, which was also repulsed. On the evening of 18 January, the Japanese launched two more infantry attacks, which met with the same fate as their predecessors. Meanwhile, however, the enemy had succeeded in setting up a road block between the two Australian battalions which caused a number of casualties including the loss of Lieutenant-Colonel J. C. Robertson, commander of the 2/29th Battalion.

General Nishimura, the Japanese commander of the 5th Guards Division, described this series of engagements as "severe and sanguinary."

On 19 January, Japanese forces coming up the Parit Jawa road engaged the 2/19th Battalion for the first time, and received a taste of their own medicine in some bitter hand to hand fighting that lasted for about two hours and resulted in 140 being killed for the loss of ten Australians killed and fifteen wounded. The Indian troops, who had been deployed on the flanks of the two Australian battalions, had for all practical purposes ceased to exist. When a Japanese air attack on brigade headquarters killed every staff officer and disabled Brigadier Duncan, the 45th Indian Brigade was virtually eliminated as an organized fighting formation.

But Lieutenant-Colonel C. G. W. Anderson, leader of the 2/19th Battalion, assumed command of the brigade, which now largely comprised the two Australian battalions and remnants of the Indians, with supporting artillery. He was to inspire the bitterest resistance in the whole campaign, to which General Percival in his book *The War in Malaya* gave due recognition by saying, "The Battle of Muar was one of the epics of the Malayan campaign. Our little force by dogged resistance had held up a division of the Japanese Imperial Guards, attacking with all the advantages of air and tank support for nearly a week, and in so doing saved the Segamat forces from encirclement and probable annihilation. The award of the Victoria Cross to Lieutenant-Colonel Anderson of the A.I.F. was a fitting tribute both to his own prowess and to the valour of his men."

The 2/29th Battalion was withdrawn to a position behind Bakri with the other Australians, while at the same time meeting heavy attacks from the Japanese infiltrating from the south and north-west. Anderson delayed the withdrawal of his force towards Parit Sulong, a village eight miles away, until the remnants of an Indian battalion of Jats had come in from the north-east, together with a number of Australians who had been cut off from the 2/29th.

Anderson's men were not only about to begin a deadly fight for their own survival, but would also prevent the Japanese from enveloping Bennett's main force, defending the trunk road and railway at Segamat. The position was imperilled even more when Japanese moving up from Batu Pahat dislodged British troops defending Bukit Pelandok, so that Anderson's men were cut off and the whole of Westforce threatened.

Bennett's formations were now falling back to Yong Peng, and Colonel Anderson realised that he would have to act with speed and determination in order to break through and rejoin the main force. He organised his men into a battalion of five rifle companies, with three companies of Indian troops in support. Besides these he had artillerymen, medical corpsmen, and fragments of various auxiliary units.

The column was assembled for its fighting retreat down the road, with trucks, troop carriers, jeeps, ambulances, and 25-pounder guns all ready to roll. At 7 a.m. on 20 January, Anderson gave the order to move off, and the first company drove down the road towards Parit Sulong. Soon afterwards they encountered the first Japanese position, well entrenched on both sides of the road and behind a block on the road itself, and had to attack at close quarters to clear it out of the way. Colonel Anderson personally destroyed two machine-gun posts with grenades, and shot two Japanese with his revolver.

This first encounter characterised those to come. One road block after another was overcome by savage assaults with the rifle and bayonet, grenades, and even axes. Between these desperate encounters, in which they lost steadily in killed and wounded, the column of Indian and Australian troops moved steadily down the road with every sense alert for ambush. The Japanese had brought up air support now, and at any moment the skies might fill with the snarl of engines as fighters and bombers swooped low over the column to strafe it with machine-gun fire or hit it with bombs.

The most distressing problem was that of the wounded, whose numbers mounted with every air attack and every clash with the Japanese. There were two doctors with the column, but medical supplies were almost exhausted and they could not do much to relieve the suffering.

By dusk on the first day, the men of the column began to feel that they had a chance of breaking through, but then they learnt from a villager that a strong Japanese force was waiting for them at Parit Sulong, directly across the road ahead. At nine-thirty on the following morning the leading com-panies scouted up to the village, and saw Japanese troops by the roadside. A burst of firing from the rear told them that the tail of the column, now only about 1,500 yards long, was being attacked, and Japanese aircraft swooped overhead like vultures waiting for the kill.

Anderson rallied his men, and they attacked the village at 11 a.m. They hit hard for four hours, but could not shift the Japanese troops who were determined to destroy the column at all costs. Anderson called off the attack during the afternoon, conscious that his resources were dwindling fast and that his mortar bombs and 25-pounder ammunition were almost exhausted. The troops had had little to eat for two days, and Anderson radioed Bennett to ask for food and medical supplies to be dropped from the air. So that monitoring Japanese would not understand his reply, Bennett used Australian idiom in his answer: "Look up at sparrowfart." Sure enough, next daybreak brought two old Albacores escorted by three R.A.A.F. Buffaloes, to drop bombs on the Japanese and supplies for Anderson and his men.

The plight of the wounded had now become so serious that the two Australian medical officers urged Anderson to ask the Japanese for two ambulances to be allowed through, carrying men who were dying for lack of treatment. Anderson, though sceptical, agreed, providing that only those whose condition was considered hopeless should be sent forward. Two ambulances, with volunteer drivers, duly approached the Japanese lines in the early evening, but the response was as Anderson had foreseen. The drivers were seized, and the Japanese commander said that he would hold the wounded as hostages against Anderson's surrender. The ambulances were placed on the Parit Sulong bridge as road blocks.

Staring towards their dark shapes, and wondering what could be done, the Australians were amazed to see them begin to glide slowly towards them. As they rolled back down the gentle slope, a fury of firing burst out from the Japanese, but the ambulances ran back into the Australian positions. It transpired that two of the grievously wounded men had managed to release the brakes and move the steering-wheels so that the vehicles ran back down the slope of the bridge.

Of such was the calibre of these Australians, but it was to be only a temporary reprieve. The Japanese began to close in during the night, and Anderson was compelled to realise that the position was hopeless. A relieving force was supposed to be on the way, striking across from the main Westforce positions at Yong Peng, but it did not arrive and it was later revealed that it had never even started.

The task had been given to the British 53rd Brigade, part of the 18th Division. Its orders were to clear the Japanese out of Bulik Pelandok and attempt the relief of Anderson's column, but nothing was done. Although it must be allowed that the brigade was newly arrived in Malaya, its complete failure to act is a reflection upon leadership which seems to have been lacking in military competence and moral fibre.

At 9 a.m. on 22 January, Anderson ordered another attack against the bridge at Parit Sulong. It was a last desperate attempt, and was beaten back by a storm of fire from Japanese troops protected by the defences which they had thrown up. He was compelled to admit defeat, and decided to destroy his column's guns and vehicles and lead the remnants of his force through the jungle. As the smoke of burning vehicles rose into the still, humid heat of the Malayan morning, he was forced to a dreadful decision; to leave the wounded behind. There were about 110 Australian and 40 Indian wounded by now, and the question was whether the 800 effective survivors should be sacrificed in order to protect them, or should escape in order to strike another blow at the Japanese.

Such decisions require a moral courage equivalent to the physical courage with which Anderson had fought so far, and he made the one which, in the climate of warfare, was correct. As his grim-faced men took to the jungle, the barbaric Japanese swarmed forward and took their vengeance on the helpless wounded. They stabbed, hit, and kicked them, and rounded off their bestial savagery by roping or wiring together those still alive, soaking them in petrol and setting them on fire.

The rest of Anderson's force fought their way through, and a total of about 800 Australians and Indians rejoined Westforce. Of their fighting march through the jungle, Anderson wrote later: "The well trained Australian units showed a complete moral ascendancy over the enemy. They outmatched the Japs in bushcraft and fire control, where the enemy's faults of bunching together and noisy shouting disclosed their dispositions and enabled the Australians to inflict heavy casualties at small cost to themselves. When the enemy was trapped they fought most gamely. In hand to hand fighting they made a very poor showing against the superior spirit and training of the A.I.F."

When the two Australian battalions remustered at Yong Peng, the 2/29th Battalion had only 130 men remaining, its commander and most of its officers having been killed, and the 2/19th only 271, including 52 wounded. But there was to be no respite, as both battalions were ordered to be ready for battle within a few days. The Japanese had paid even more heavily for their victory, and Bennett estimated that in five days of fighting some 3,000 of their élite Guards Division had been killed.

Meanwhile, the 22nd Brigade on the east coast, under Brigadier Taylor, had been in contact with the Japanese since their landings at Endau on 15 January. Eastforce, now comprising two battalions with supporting artillery, inflicted heavy casualties on the Japanese in a series of engagements, but developments at Muar had sealed the fate of Johore and a fighting withdrawal to Singapore began. Using their ambush tactics, the 2/18th Battalion inflicted heavy casualties on a force of 1,000 Japanese on 27 January between Jemaluang and Mersing in the vicinity of Joo Lye Estate.

This action was described by the Japanese as "an appalling hand to hand battle."

Further disaster befell the Indians in their retreat towards Singapore, and the 15th Brigade was virtually annihilated as it withdrew along the coast road from Batu Pahat. In the centre, Brigadier Maxwell's 27th Brigade with British troops in support fought some bitter engagements while falling back from Ayer Hitam, and "Black Jack" Gallaghan's 2/30th Battalion again distinguished itself in a severe action near Simpang Rengam, on the Namazie Estate.

The inevitable curtain fell on the disastrous mainland campaign when on 30/31 January the last troops marched across the Johore causeway into "Fortress Singapore," whose collapse was to sound the death-knell of British influence east of Suez.

The two Australian brigades were allocated the western area, which Generals Wavell and Bennett regarded as the sector most likely to receive the full impact of the Japanese assault. Percival dissented, believing that the northern area, which lay eastwards from the causeway, would be the scene of the Japanese invasion. Later, however, he recorded his belief that the west was the danger area, and that he had placed the Australians in these positions for that reason. "I had specially selected for it the A.I.F., because I thought that of the troops which had had experience of fighting on the mainland it was the freshest and most likely to give a good account of itself."

The two brigades, now sadly depleted by their heavy fighting, were reinforced by 1,800 raw replacements hurried from Australia. In January, the last reinforcements likely to arrive for some time disembarked in Singapore. They were the rest of the British 18th Division, 7,000 Indian reinforcements, the 44th Indian Brigade, and the 2/4th Australian Machine-Gun Battalion—a well trained and expertly commanded unit which fought with tremendous courage in the battle for Singapore and suffered heavy casualties.

The 27th Brigade was responsible for a front of 4,000 yards, extending west from the causeway, and the 22nd Brigade held a front of 16,000 on its left. These responsibilities were grossly disproportionate to the strength of the brigades, and would have been an unreasonable burden even for fresh troops well equipped and properly supported. Their artillery consisted of three regiments, three anti-tank batteries, and one fixed battery.

By contrast, Percival had the 11th Indian Division and the British 18th Division packed into the northern area, on a front of only about 1,700 yards. This sector was also allotted the greater strength of artillery support; eight regiments and three fixed batteries. The self-interest evident in such deployment was accented by the fact that Australian reinforcements were employed to prepare defensive positions in this area, and not in the one to be held by their countrymen.

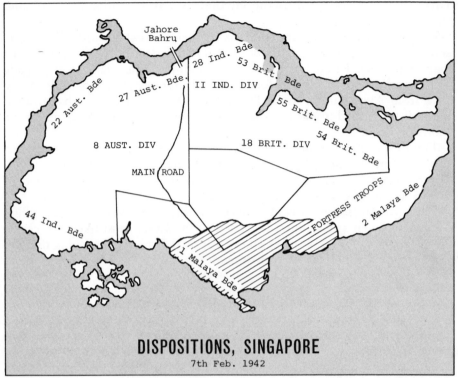

DISPOSITIONS, SINGAPORE
7th Feb. 1942

The battle for Singapore began at dawn on 8 February 1942, when the Japanese opened up with an artillery bombardment of tremendous intensity which was maintained throughout the day. Lieutenant-Colonel A. L. Varley, commanding the Australian 2/18th Battalion, recorded in his diary: "During my four years' service in 1914-18, I never experienced such concentrated shell fire over such a period. Pozieres was the heaviest shelling I experienced in that war. In 2½ days I lost 50 out of 56 men. The German shells seemed more effective in causing casualties. On this occasion 80 shells were counted falling in D Company area in one minute. Lieutenant Jack Vernon's platoon area had 67 in 10 minutes and this was typical of the whole area. Battalion H.Q. had 45 shells in 7 minutes; half an hour's spell then another similar dose and so on throughout the whole area all day. Our signal communications were cut and repaired and cut again."

The full weight of artillery available to the Japanese 5th, 18th and Guards Divisions had been concentrated against the key positions of Brigadier Taylor's 22nd Australian Brigade sector; the focal point for the initial enemy assault, and yet one of the most lightly-held stretches of Singapore Island coastline facing the Japanese across the Straits of Johore.

The vanguard of the invading forces landed at about 10 p.m. During the

ATTACK. *Top:* Men of the 9th Division at El Alamein. *Centre:* Australians during the attack which captured Tobruk from the Italians. *Bottom:* At Giropa Point during the final assault on Buna. An Australian-manned General Stuart tank supports infantrymen with automatic weapons.

night about 13,000 men swarmed ashore, followed by anothu 10,000 shortly after dawn. They flung themselves against positions defended by two battalions of Australians; about 2,000 men.

The Australians fought to the last, and in fact repulsed several of the landings with severe casualties. But the front was so sparsely held that the Japanese, when denied one area, could adopt the tactics so successfully employed all the way down the peninsula and infiltrate through the mangrove swamps. Hidden in the darkness and amongst the dense masses of close-growing mangroves, they could assemble for suicidal charges which overwhelmed the Australians by sheer weight of numbers.

By dawn, the outnumbered forward posts had been overrun or annihilated, and the brigade withdrew four miles to a new perimeter behind Tengah airfield, where they prepared to meet a fresh onslaught. The 2/20th Battalion had sustained no less than 334 killed and 214 wounded in the night's fighting, out of a total of 1,005 men committed to battle. One forward company of 145 was completely destroyed. Fifty-seven men were killed, twenty-two wounded, and the rest taken prisoner. The 2/18th Battalion, being the other formation to receive the brunt of the Japanese attack, also sustained heavy casualties during the early phases of the landings.

The withdrawal of the 22nd Brigade front created a serious gap between it and the 27th Brigade under Brigadier Maxwell, whose men prepared to receive their first invaders at 9 p.m. on 9 February. General Percival belatedly realised that the full force of the Japanese invasion was being directed against the Australians, and not, as he had anticipated, along the more compactly held British and Indian northern area.

The key to the island defence now became the Kranji-Jurong Switch line, facing west and forming a defensive position between the headwaters of the Kranji and Jurong Rivers. Conscious of the threat of the Japanese being able to seize the vital Bukit Timah road, and advance along it towards the city of Singapore, Percival redeployed British and Indian troops to reinforce the Australian front. He also prepared a plan to withdraw his troops from their widely held defensive positions to form a perimeter around the city itself.

The Japanese, now well ashore with both their 5th and Guards Divisions, attacked heavily against the Kranji-Jurong positions on 10 February, and, in the confused fighting, took advantage of an unfortunate situation created by Brigadier Taylor, who misunderstood an order and withdrew part of his brigade too far.

The 22nd Brigade continued to hold its advanced position in the Pandan area, despite attempts by the Japanese all through 12 February to dislodge it. As Percival later recorded, "It had fought a gallant action for forty-eight hours, and done much to hold up the enemy's advance in this area."

With the Japanese pressing on all sectors, and having captured the city's

PAPUA-NEW GUINEA OPERATIONS. *Top:* Australian infantry wade through the swamps at Cape Endaiadere during the advance on Buna. *Bottom left,* Pause for a breather in the Finisterre Ranges on the way to assault Bogadjim. *Bottom right,* The "Golden Stairs," rising towards Imita Ridge on the Kokoda Trail, which had to be climbed by heavily-laden bearers and infantrymen going forward and the wounded coming down.

water supplies, the end came on 15 February, after Percival had called a conference of his senior commanders and civil authorities who made the unavoidable decision to capitulate. To fight on would have meant a massacre of the civil population, already suffering from merciless air attacks.

The two brigades of the Australian 8th Division had fought with all the desperate courage of which human flesh is capable. The six infantry battalions and their supporting units had suffered casualties totalling 1,789 killed and 1,306 wounded in roughly a month's fighting. Their efforts at Gemas and Muar, and while resisting the initial assault on Singapore, inflicted the heaviest casualties sustained by the Japanese during the entire Malayan campaign and were epics which deserve the highest recognition in the annals of military history. But the profession of arms is the most unforgiving of all, and no matter what the circumstances there is rarely honour for the vanquished.

Unfortunately the 8th Division's reputation was tarnished during the final days when the Japanese were pressing into the suburbs of Singapore, and immediately after the capitulation, by the behaviour of some of their replacement troops. These became uncontrollable, and as well as looting from abandoned stores they fought for places on ships evacuating civilians. The fact is that they should not have been on the island at all. They had been in the army for only a few weeks, possessed neither discipline nor unit pride, and were commanded by officers mainly as raw as themselves. Thrown into the chaos of a lost campaign, they behaved as might have been expected. When the Provost-Marshal asked Gordon Bennett what should be done about them, he gave a typical answer, "Shoot them!"

Nearly 134,000 British, Indian, and Australian troops were captured by the Japanese; a staggering defeat which can be matched only by the German defeats at the hands of the Russians. More than 15,000 were Australians, and of these nearly a third were to die of starvation, disease, or at the brutal hands of the Japanese. The story of Japanese treatment of their captives is too well known to need repetition.

Some Australians escaped, including 65 Army nurses sent out on the ship *Vyner Brooke*. Twelve of them died when the ship was destroyed, and twenty-one more were murdered by the Japanese when the party of survivors was found on Banka Island.

Major-General H. Gordon Bennett, with two of his staff officers, escaped to Australia. Intent on telling the story of what Australians had done in Malaya, and hoping that his experiences would help to prevent such disasters in the future, he ran up against a wall of rejection. Much of it was emotional, perhaps based on the ancient feeling that a defeated commander should die with his troops. It is difficult, however, not to feel that it held a certain element of "kicking a man when he's down;" especially in Blamey's unsympathetic treatment of him and curt reply of "I won't touch him" when

Bennett's application came through for another fighting command. Instead, Bennett was given command of III Corps in Western Australia. This was regarded as quite important in 1942, when there was a definite danger of Japanese invasion, but it was too tame for Bennett and he resigned from the army in 1944.

But men such as Bennett are apt to act without considering the consequences; a trait of character which can make them magnificent fighting soldiers but may be less desirable in a leader who must consider not only the men under his command but also the political outcome of his actions. For Bennett, the consequences were disastrous. Two Courts of Enquiry determined that his decision had been unwise, and although he received no formal punishment there must have been punishment enough in the scarcely-veiled pleasure of those whom he had offended in the past, and in his eventual oblivion. It was a sad by-product of "Britain's worst disaster."

26

GULL FORCE, SPARROW FORCE, AND BLACK FORCE

S IR ALAN BROOKE WROTE, "THE WHOLE SCHEME (IS) WILD AND HALF-baked," of the ABDA Command which was the Allies' response to the onslaught of the Japanese. The fact is that the planners in London and Washington had no conception, at first, of the monstrous efficiency of Japanese preparations for war. It was rammed home in one defeat after another. Hong Kong had fallen even before Singapore. ABDA naval forces in the Indonesian area were chopped up piecemeal by the Japanese, in a series of actions which culminated in the heroic fight of the *Houston* and *Perth* against the Japanese fleet. American troops in the Philippines were being overcome by General Homma's XIV Army, and falling back to their final dogged defence of Corregidor. The Japanese were thrusting into Burma, sweeping aside the Dutch colonial troops in the East Indies, and menacing Australia itself by landings on the islands across the nation's northern sea frontier. And all this had happened within two months of the first bombs dropping on Pearl Harbour, in a series of strokes which surpassed the German blitzkrieg of 1940.

Australia's dispersal of her comparatively inconsiderable forces was equally "wild and half-baked" in military terms. The 23rd Brigade, which should have formed a third of Bennett's 8th Division, was divided into three separate locations in Australia's outer defensive system. The 2/21st Battalion was sent to Ambon, the 2/22nd to Rabaul, and the 2/40th to Timor. These were the units, among others, for which Bennett had begged in vain. When one considers the fight which the Australians made in Malaya, it is just possible that these troops might have provided the stiffening needed to prevent the Japanese invasion of Singapore. As it was, they were thrown away in costly actions which made no great difference to the Japanese advance on Australia.

As the Chief of the Australian Staff, General V. A. H. Sturdee, pointed out in a paper prepared on 15 February 1942 concerning the future employment of the A.I.F., the splitting of the 23rd Brigade "violated every principle of concentration of forces, in efforts to hold numerous small localities with totally inadequate forces which were progressively overwhelmed by vastly superior forces."

Rabaul was attacked early on 23 January 1942, by a Japanese force of 5,300 men. There was brief but bitter fighting in some sectors, but communications with headquarters soon broke down and elements of the garrison of 1,400 Australians began to retire in some disorder. The base commander, Colonel J. J. Scanlan, was a veteran of the first World War, and in a New Year's Day message to the men of his command had ordered them to fight to the last and concluded with the words "There shall be no withdrawal."

Such sentiments were in the finest traditions of the 1st A.I.F., but a lack of preparation for possible withdrawal was to be the main reason why more than two-thirds of the garrison became prisoners of the Japanese, who massacred 160 of them in the Tol plantation soon after they had laid down their arms. Some of the subordinate commanders, however, showed magnificent leadership, and led about 400 men to safety. They suffered terrible privations as they marched over steep, jungle-clad mountains of New Britain before being evacuated by ship to New Guinea and eventually the Australian mainland. The last of them were embarked on 9 April, some two and a half months after the fighting had officially ceased at Rabaul. The rich but neglected territory had fallen even faster than Singapore, and the Japanese attack was so overwhelming that a local businessman and army veteran, Captain Murray, was forced to flee in his pyjamas and without his false teeth.

The 2/21st Battalion, with supporting units, disembarked at Ambon as late as 17 December, 1941, and became known as "Gull Force." They joined the local Dutch garrison of about 2,600 men, and were placed under the operational control of the Dutch commander, Lieutenant-Colonel J. R. L. Kapitz. It was not a happy arrangement from the outset, and proved extremely vulnerable when the Japanese invaded Ambon on 31 January. The Australian defensive positions were widely dispersed, along the southwestern portion of Laitimor Peninsula and also at Laha airfield on the Hitu Peninsula. They were on either side of the Bay of Ambon and of the Dutch garrison which was responsible for the upper part of the island, from Paso to Hitu-Lama. The Japanese directed their main attack against the Dutch held sectors which were quickly overcome, thus severing the two main Australian forces. The bulk of Gull Force, located on the Laitimor Peninsula, clashed several times with the Japanese, but surrendered on 3 February when further resistance was considered hopeless. The garrison at Laha, comprising one company, repulsed several determined enemy assaults. They inflicted heavy casualties, and a Japanese observer vividly described the action as "like fighting against the blast of a furnace." "The desperate resistance of the Australians after the breakthrough of the Japanese death band was not to be despised," he remarked, but Japanese admiration for a gallant defence was not tinged with mercy. Survivors from the Australian company were executed by the Japanese on 6 February, as a reprisal for the sinking of a minesweeper by a Dutch mine in the Bay of Ambon on 1 February.

The Japanese forces used in this action were the 228th Infantry Regiment of the 38th Infantry Division, which had played a leading role in the conquest of Hong Kong. Their next objective was Koepang in Dutch Timor, defended by the 2/40th Battalion which had landed on 12 December 1941. It was supported by about 500 Dutch troops and the 2/2nd Australian Independent Company, which after a brief period at Koepang was sent on to Dili, the capital of Portuguese Timor. The Australian-Dutch force was known as "Sparrow Force," and was under the initial command of Lieutenant-Colonel W. Leggatt; a lawyer and citizen soldier who had had a distinguished war record in 1914-18.

Brigadier W. C. D. Veale was subsequently despatched by the Australian government to take command of Sparrow Force. He arrived in Timor on 12 February and established his headquarters at Champlong, but communications between his own and Leggatt's headquarters broke down very soon after the Japanese landings. In essence, Leggatt remained operational commander for the duration of the fighting.

Early on 20 February, the Japanese made simultaneous landings against the Australian positions at Dili, and in Dutch Timor on the south-east coast at the mouth of the River Paha, which was undefended.

About 1,000 Japanese paratroopers landed at Babau, between Leggatt's force and the base which they had established at Champlong. Cut off on one side, the Australians also were threatened with envelopment by the seaborne units, now making a two-pronged thrust up from the River Paha and striking towards Penfui airfield and Koepang itself.

The Australian response was immediate and vigorous. They attacked the Japanese wherever they could find them, and were attacked in turn. For four days, the opponents mauled each other in actions which ranged from patrol skirmishes to full-scale attacks, with Australians and Japanese coming face to face while Japanese aircraft ranged overhead and seized every opportunity to strike.

At last the Australians realised that they could neither break out nor hold off the Japanese assaults any longer. With eighty-four killed, and 132 wounded who could not receive proper attention, Leggatt called an officers' conference. He had hoped to break into the interior and carry on guerilla warfare, but with his men exhausted after ninety-six hours of continuous fighting, and food, water, and ammunition gone, this plan had become impossible.

They decided to give in to the Japanese demands for surrender, and went into the brutalities of enemy captivity. The Japanese, however, had paid heavily for their victory. They admitted the loss of all but seventy-eight of their paratroopers, with comparable losses in their infantry. Fourteen enemy aircraft were claimed by the British 79th Light A.A. Battery, which had been attached to Leggatt's force.

The headquarters force under Brigadier Veale, about 250 men, was able to make good their withdrawal into the hinterland. Veale set up new headquarters at Mape, just inside the border of Portuguese Timor, while Major Spence and his 2/2nd Independent Company began a guerilla campaign based on Dili. Brigadier Veale was withdrawn to Australia in May 1942, and Spence succeeded him in command of Sparrow Force.

Major B. J. Callinan, previously second-in-command, took over the Independent Company, and led it with a courage, brilliance, and tireless energy which not only kept it a jump ahead of the Japanese for twelve months but tied up as many as 30,000 men of their 5th and 48th Divisions, and killed 1,500 of them for the loss of only forty men of his command.

The 2/2nd Independent Company had been raised early in 1941, and consisted very largely of West Australian countrymen. Tough, self-reliant, expert marksmen, and accustomed to the harsh inland climates of the West, they were ideal material for the commando-type training which they received and for the task which lay before them.

Their first test came at Dili, where the Japanese landed 6,000 troops. The 300 men of the Independent Company, backed up by a handful of Dutch troops, hit them hard as soon as they reached the airfield, slaughtered about 200, and made a smart withdrawal before they could be overwhelmed by the vastly superior enemy.

This action set the pattern for the next twelve months. The Australians had all the ingredients for successful guerilla warfare; a rugged hinterland into which they could disappear at will, a civilian population prepared to help them and occasionally to fight with them, and a calculating courage backed by expert bushcraft. With these essentials, they hit the enemy almost as and when they pleased, ambushed them at will, raided their airfields and bases, and slipped through the net of two major offensives designed to wipe them out.

At a time when the Japanese held the initiative, this tiny force threw a spanner in their works. While they were meeting their first major reverses from the Australians in New Guinea and at the hands of the Americans on sea and land in the Solomons, they were still obliged to use thousands of men to guard their flank against this harassment, which could have become a major menace if it was reinforced.

At first, it was assumed in Australia that the Independent Company had also been overwhelmed in the Japanese invasion of Timor, but after months of trial and error a group of signallers managed to improvise a transmitting set which contacted Darwin. Their signals were received almost suspiciously at first, but when their identity was established beyond doubt they began to receive much needed supplies from the air and from daring sorties by small craft of the R.A.N.

In August 1942 they were reinforced by the 2/4th Independent Company under Major Walker, while Blamey and MacArthur gave serious consideration to the idea of attempting a landing in brigade or divisional strength to open a large-scale campaign against the Japanese on Timor. The idea was dropped because of the strain on available naval and air resources and the heavy commitments of the A.I.F. in New Guinea.

The Japanese made several demands for the force to surrender, and used the British Consul at Dili, Mr David Ross, to carry them to Callinan. When they sent him yet again, in July 1942, he decided to stay with the commandos, and remained with them until they were evacuated to the mainland. He was able to give first-hand advice to the Advisory War Council on the situation in Timor.

Though technically neutral, the Portuguese authorities gave active help and co-operation, and quietly provided the Australians with many facilities and supplies. The Timorese natives played an important part in the early Australian successes, but, as time passed and the Japanese began to revenge themselves upon the villagers, they began to turn against the Australians. The operation ended in February 1943, when the last of the Australians were evacuated aboard the U.S. submarine *Gudgeon*.

The third Australian formation to encounter the Japanese after the fall of Singapore was known as "Blackforce," because it was under the command of Brigadier A. S. Blackburn, V.C.; a 1st A.I.F. veteran who had been among the first ashore at Gallipoli and had won his Victoria Cross at Pozières.

His force, most of whom had served in the Syrian campaign, was stationed in Java, and consisted of the 2/3rd Australian Machine-Gun Battalion, the 2/2nd Australian Pioneer Battalion, and the 2/6th Australian Field Company, with supporting transport and ancillary units. He organised his troops into a brigade of three infantry battalions, supported by a squadron of British tanks and part of an American field artillery battery. They were concentrated near Buitenzorg, to be used as a mobile strike force after the Dutch had taken the initial shock of the Japanese force.

General Wavell's shortlived ABDA command was dissolved in late February, and control of the forces in Java was handed over to the Dutch. They consisted of five regiments of Dutch colonial troops, about 3,500

British troops who were mostly anti-aircraft artillery, nearly 3,000 Australians, and an American artillery unit.

The Japanese landed two and a half divisions on 28 February, and began a rapid advance all along the coast. Dutch resistance was almost non-existent, with the native troops of the colonial regiments falling back before the Japanese and the morale of the whole population at the lowest possible ebb after news of the gigantic defeat at Singapore. Blackforce stood fast against the Japanese in western Java, and halted them for several days, but the front was collapsing all around them and they were ordered to fall back on Bandoeng. The Dutch surrendered on 8 March 1942, and Brigadier Blackburn realised that to fight on alone would only bring disaster to his own men. They went into captivity, and almost a third of them were to die or be killed by the Japanese before the end of the war.

In almost exactly three months, the Japanese had achieved enormous success. Except for the Australians in Timor and the Americans holding out in Corregidor, the Japanese were undisputed victors along a line from Rangoon in Burma to Rabaul in New Britain.

27

BLAMEY'S RETURN

THOSE CLOSE TO WINSTON CHURCHILL DURING THE YEARS OF THE second World War have written admiringly of his many virtues as a wartime leader, but despairingly of his tendency towards "diversions and dispersions;" of the impetuosity with which he conceived them, and the obstinacy with which he fought for them against the advice of his military staff. In Prime Minister John Curtin, however, who had succeeded Menzies in 1941, he met an obstinacy as stubborn as his own—and it was fortunate for the 2nd A.I.F. that Curtin was able to withstand the Churchillean blend of blandishment and arrogance.

While the 6th and 7th Australian Divisions were eastward bound from Egypt, the rapid Japanese victories in Malaya and the East Indies made it clear that it would be pointless to land these troops in Java and Sumatra, as originally had been intended. With Australia being encircled by the Japanese, Lieutenant-General V. A. H. Sturdee, Chief of the Australian General Staff, advised Curtin to bring the two divisions home to Australia to hold the continent against a possible invasion and to form the nucleus of an offensive in due course.

General Wavell, however, was desperate for fresh troops to shore up the collapsing British defences in Burma, and asked Churchill to have one or both of the divisions sent to Rangoon. Churchill agreed, and was backed up by President Roosevelt of the U.S.A. But Curtin already had made up his mind, and refused to comply.

For the first time in history, an Australian Prime Minister had to place the defence of his own homeland before the demands of British grand strategy; an action which brought down upon him all Churchill's powers of argument and persuasion backed up by pressure from Roosevelt. But Curtin could see the dangers as they could not, and in an increasingly acrimonious exchange of cables insisted upon the Australians returning home. It was, of course, the right decision, as by the time the two divisions reached Burma they would have been too late to make any difference.

Before this, on 20 February 1941, Curtin had cabled to Lieutenant-General Thomas Blamey in Cairo, saying, "It is desired that you arrange to return here as speedily as possible." Blamey wound up his Middle East affairs without delay, and on 7 March flew from Cairo to Capetown with his wife. He was farewelled by a host of senior officers, including Freyberg and Morshead, and was touched by the reception of a handwritten note from Auchinleck. The British commander wrote:

"*My Dear Blamey,*

I feel a very genuine regret at your going, and I know I shall miss you a lot. We may have had differences of opinion at times, but I have valued greatly your shrewd and sound advice on many matters, and it has been a great support to me to know that I could turn to you when in doubt or trouble. You have done much in and for the Middle East in the months that are past, and you will be missed and not easily forgotten. The departure of you and all your fine officers and men will leave a gap not to be filled easily, and will cause me much sorrow, for I have formed a real affection and tremendous admiration for the A.I.F. I have seen a good deal of them thanks to your assistance; I only wish I could have seen more. I feel it is a great privilege to have had them under my command and I know very well how much I owe to them and to you.

I wish you and them the best of luck in the future and a speedy victory against the Japanese. I wish I could go with you to help you beat them. Perhaps we may meet again over there. I hope so."

On 15 March Blamey boarded the liner *Queen Mary* at Capetown, and found her packed with American troops en route to Australia. While the ship was still five days from Fremantle, he was informed that General Douglas MacArthur had been instructed to leave his fighting command in the Philippines and fly to Australia, to take command of the Allied Forces in the south-west Pacific area. Blamey's reaction was, "I think it's the best thing that could have happened for Australia. MacArthur will be so far away from his own government that he won't have any interference from them, and as far as our government is concerned he won't take any notice of them."

When Blamey landed at Fremantle on 23 March, thirty-six years after giving up his position as a promising junior master at Fremantle Boys' School, he was still uncertain about what post he would be given. This was settled at once, by a letter handed to him containing his appointment as Commander-in-Chief of the Australian Military Forces.

It was to be a mammoth task. Civilian morale was shaken, and many people expected invasion at almost any moment. There was a rumour that Western Australia was to be abandoned to the Japanese, and that the government was preparing a line to defend the eastern States. Most of the nation's best and most experienced troops were still on the high seas, and the army in Australia still reflected its long peacetime neglect. Worst of all, Blamey had to contend with the iniquitous "two-army system" which still prevailed. The men of the regular army and the volunteers of the 2nd A.I.F. served under completely different terms from the men of the militia forces.

Australia had suffered her Pearl Harbour, in the Japanese bombing raids on Darwin and other north-west ports; and her Dunkirk, in the loss of her brigades who in Malaya and the East Indies had been isolated by the collapsing British and Dutch armies just as the British, in France, had been isolated by the collapsing French army in 1940. She was fortunate in having a man like John Curtin to lead her and to work himself to death in the effort, and a soldier like Blamey to devote all his ruthless drive and organisational powers into giving her a powerful new striking force.

Curtin had no doubt that, in the coming deadly struggle against the Japanese, Australia would have to sever many of her traditional links with Britain and ally herself more closely with America. In his cable to the British and U.S. Governments concerning the appointment of MacArthur as commander of the south-west Pacific area, he indicated complete willingness to work with the American general in the words: "His heroic defence of the Philippine Islands has evoked the admiration of the world and has been an example of the stubborn resistance with which the advance of the enemy should be opposed. The Australian Government feels that this leadership of the Allied Forces in this theatre will be an inspiration to the Australian people and all the forces who will be privileged to serve under his command."

MacArthur, like most of the Allied commanders of the second World War, has been subject to a good deal of post-war criticism, but his arrival in Australia after a hazardous escape by torpedo-boat and aircraft from the beleaguered fortress of Corregidor gave a much-needed boost to Australian morale. Though he was sixty years old, he was lean, fast-moving, and energetic, with features which in the words of the Australian *Official History* combined "the intellectual, the aesthetic and the martial." Like most great leaders, he had a flair for publicity and for saying the right thing at the right time; his final words of "I shall return," on leaving Corregidor, were much quoted as an example of Allied determination to win. By such statements and by deliberately building himself into a symbol of proud defiance, he helped to inspire the Australian people with a vigorous offensive mood which was greatly helped by the arrival of American forces.

MacArthur established his first headquarters in Melbourne, and created five separate commands for the Allied forces in the south-west Pacific. The Allied Land Forces were to be led by General Sir Thomas Blamey, the Air Forces by Lieutenant-General G. H. Brett, and the Naval Forces by Vice-Admiral H. E. Leary. Major-General J. F. Barnes was to command U.S. Forces in Australia, and to Lieutenant-General J. M. Wainwright went the command of U.S. Forces in the Philippines. The latter command was to be short-lived, because the Japanese already were poised for their final assault and Wainwright was to see out the war in captivity.

MacArthur's own staff were all American officers, despite a prompting from the U.S. Chief of Staff, General George Marshall, to include Dutch and Australian officers. MacArthur said that the Australian Army did not have enough staff officers to meet its own needs, "therefore there was no prospect of obtaining qualified senior staff officers from the Australians."

This was perhaps disingenuous. The resources of the Australian Army were stretched to the limit, but there is no doubt that it possessed many staff officers whose academic competence was at least the equal of the Americans, and who in addition had far more experience of active service. MacArthur himself, despite his bold defence of the Philippines, had made tactical errors, and had had fairly limited active service experience in the first World War. Many senior Australian officers, who had served with combat troops in both world wars, had experience which far outweighed that of American officers who in some cases had never heard a shot fired in anger.

Since the Australian troops were to shoulder the burden of the land campaigns for a long time to come, and in the interests of Allied unity, it is a pity that MacArthur did not appoint at least one senior Australian officer to his staff. Such an appointment could at least have prevented some of the friction and misconceptions which ultimately were to bedevil American-Australian relationships.

On 9 April 1942, Blamey detailed the way in which the Allied Land Forces, comprising the Australian Army and American troops, were to be reorganised and deployed, both to meet the threat of invasion and to gather strength for the eventual offensive.

The basis of this organisation was the division of Australia into areas of responsibility. First Army was to be responsible for Queensland and New South Wales; Second Army for Victoria, South Australia, and Tasmania; III Corps for Western Australia; and the 6th Division, less two brigades which had been disembarked to reinforce the Ceylon garrison, for the Northern Territory.

First Army, under Lieutenant-General Sir John Lavarack, consisted of the 1st, 2nd, 3rd, 5th, 7th, and 10th Infantry Divisions and the 1st Motorised Division. It was formed into two corps; I Corps, under Lieutenant-General S. Rowell, and II Corps under Lieutenant-General J. Northcott.

Second Army was commanded by Lieutenant-General Sir I. Mackay, who after his distinguished service in the Middle East and Greece had been recalled in August 1941 to take up the new appointment of G.O.C. Home Forces. Second Army consisted of the 32nd and 41st American Divisions, the 2nd (Australian) Motorised Division, and the 12th (Australian) Brigade.

III Corps, under Lieutenant-General Gordon Bennett, consisted of the 4th Division, 1st Armoured Division, and the 19th Brigade.

Major-General E. Herring commanded the 6th Division, and the slender forces in New Guinea were named New Guinea Force, under Major-General B. M. Morris.

On paper, the situation looked quite good. In fact, however, only about 46,000 of the men in Australia at that time, until the disembarkation of 9th Division, were experienced combat troops. These were the veterans of the 6th and 7th Divisions. Of the remainder, about 63,000 were A.I.F. volunteers, who were in various stages of the high standard of training expected of them but who had not yet seen active service. 280,000 men were militia soldiers, whose standards of training and discipline varied extremely widely from one unit to another, and who initially had been mustered for defence duties only. The two American divisions, including base troops and some airmen, totalled 33,000, and most of these had no combat experience and also were of varying quality.

Men alone do not make an army, and staffs of every formation all the way up to General MacArthur faced severe shortages of almost every type of equipment. Ships, especially naval vessels, were scarce. Aircraft, and even the airfields from which to fly them, were far below the needs of the situation. Tanks, armoured vehicles, artillery and its ammunition, and most other weapons had to be eked out where they would do most good.

It was a challenge which Blamey and his battle-wise commanders faced with the same determination and energy which had carried them to victory in the past. Officers and N.C.O.s of the veteran A.I.F. divisions were seconded to militia units, to speed up their training with the benefit of their own experience, and the bulk of the Australian Army, which for so long had existed in a comparative backwater, began to come alive with the knowledge that the country depended upon it for its survival.

28

BREAKING THE SPELL

ON 7/8 MAY AND 3/6 JUNE 1942, TWO GREAT NAVAL BATTLES DEMON-strated the potency of the American alliance. They were Coral Sea and Midway, in which the Americans took their revenge for Pearl Harbour and drove the first two nails into the coffin of Japanese military ambition.

The battle of the Coral Sea was unique in that it was the first large-scale naval action fought out between aircraft of opposing carriers, without their supporting cruisers and destroyers ever having the opportunity to engage each other.

The Japanese plan was to send an invasion force from Rabaul, where they had been organising since its capture in January, to seize Port Moresby. Had they been able to land, they would no doubt have succeeded without much difficulty, because Australian land forces in that area were still comparatively weak.

With Port Moresby as a forward base, they intended to mount further seaborne operations against the islands of Fiji, Samoa, and New Caledonia, on all of which the Americans were preparing air and sea bases with frantic haste. With these in their hands, they would have made American reinforce-ment of Australia extremely difficult, and would have launched air and sea raids against the Australian east and north-east coast in preparation for the inevitable invasion. Rear-Admiral F. J. Fletcher, commanding a fleet of two carriers and eight cruisers including *Hobart* and *Australia*, saved Australia from this fate.

In the battle, which was joined by American and Australian aircraft from Queensland bases and Japanese aircraft from Rabaul, the Japanese force was compelled to turn back to Rabaul. Its commander, Major-General Horii, sought for another approach to Port Moresby. Early in March, he had sent troops to occupy Lae and Salamaua, on the north coast of New Guinea, and they had taken these places without much resistance from the small units stationed there. Now, they began to prospect inland and down the coast to Gona and Buna, with the objective of finding a way across the long peninsula of which the backbone was the precipitous and jungle-clad Owen Stanley Range, separating them from Port Moresby.

General MacArthur also sought for ways in which an offensive could be mounted in New Guinea, with the objective of forcing the Japanese from their toeholds. For the time being, the outlook was not good, with less than 7,000 troops manning the Port Moresby defence area and trained reinforcements in short supply. It would have been unwise to leave Port Moresby open, but to allow the Japanese to remain unscathed would have granted them moral superiority.

So a series of commando-type raids were decided on, and the 5th Independent Company was sent to New Guinea. With the New Guinea Volunteer Rifles, they marched through the jungle to Wau and probed into the Markham Valley. Their raids were designed to harass the Japanese and gain information, and succeeded very well. In one operation, on 28/29 June, seventy-five men raided the Japanese base at Salamaua, killed over 100 Japanese, and brought back valuable documents and equipment at no cost to themselves.

Major-General Horii, and his superior General Hyakutake of the Japanese XVII Army, had, however, not been idle. They planned a new and double thrust against Port Moresby, in which one group was to attack by land, crossing the Owen Stanley Ranges to descend upon the port from the interior, and the other was to seize Milne Bay on the eastern tip of the peninsula and use it as a pivot for a seaborne offensive along the southern coast.

In mid-July, they took the first step by seizing Gona and Buna as jumping off points for the overland offensive. They were just ahead of MacArthur, who had planned to establish a base at Buna for an offensive towards Lae and Salamaua. Gona and Buna were occupied only by outpost troops, who fell back after signalling the Japanese invasion.

Milne Bay, however, was a different proposition. Australian and American troops had been there since late June, in order to build a forward air base. After Buna and Gona fell, and the Allied command could begin to see the Japanese intent, the embryo base was reinforced by the 7th Brigade Group, of three militia battalions under Brigadier J. Field.

Field, a mechanical engineer and university lecturer, had been commissioned in the militia eighteen years before, and had led the 2/12th Battalion of the A.I.F. during the Libyan campaign. His command of the

7th Brigade had been confirmed only a few weeks before his arrival in New Guinea, and his selection as a leader for "Milne Force" was perhaps fortuitous. Apart from his competence as a soldier, his professional skill was of great value in helping to develop, from the ground up, the requisite two airfields, roads, bridges, wharf facilities, and a system of defences.

His assignment was about as unenviable as any commander could be given. The Milne Bay area is a narrow strip of territory between the mountains and the sea, no more than a few hundred yards wide in some places and nowhere wider than about two miles. Then untamed except for a mission establishment and some plantations and native villages, the terrain was the coastal New Guinea blend of eternally sodden ground which becomes tangled mangrove swamps along the shore. It is bombarded by gigantic downpours of rain, and the swamps and jungle are home for billions of malaria-carrying mosquitoes and countless other insects.

Besides the 7th Brigade militia, the garrison included Australian artillery and American engineers and artillery units, which in mid-August were progressively reinforced by the veteran 18th Brigade of the A.I.F., commanded by Brigadier G. F. Wootten who had served with marked distinction in the siege of Tobruk. With other reinforcements en route, command of the

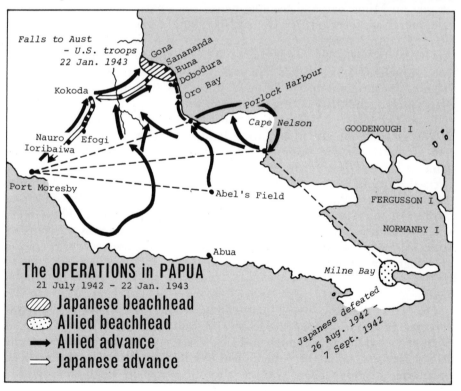

Falls to Aust
- U.S. troops
22 Jan. 1943

Gona
Sanananda
Buna
Dobodura
Oro Bay

Kokoda

Porlock Harbour

Cape Nelson

GOODENOUGH I

Nauro   Efogi
Ioribaiwa

Port Moresby

Abel's Field

FERGUSSON I

NORMANBY I

Abua

The OPERATIONS in PAPUA
21 July 1942 - 22 Jan. 1943

Milne Bay

Japanese defeated
26 Aug. 1942
7 Sept. 1942

🚧 Japanese beachhead
⋯ Allied beachhead
→ Allied advance
⇒ Japanese advance

area now passed to Major-General C. A. Clowes, a regular officer who won the D.S.O. and M.C. in the first World War and had led the Anzac Corps Artillery during the Greek campaign.

His directive was: "In conjunction with the Allied Air Forces, to deny to the enemy the area occupied by Milne Force and vital outlying sea and island areas and to protect and assist the Allied air forces operating from Milne Bay."

By 28 August 1942, he commanded 8,824 soldiers; 7,459 Australians and 1,365 Americans. The infantry, all Australians, numbered about 4,500. They were supported by 75 and 76 Squadrons of the R.A.A.F., flying Kittyhawk aircraft and commanded by Squadron-Leaders L. D. Jackson and P. Turnbull; two fighter aces whose men were to play a vital role in the forthcoming battle. The air group included Squadron-Leader "Bluey" Truscott, who with Wing-Commander "Paddy" Finucane had formed one of the deadliest pairs in R.A.F. Fighter Command during 1941.

The Japanese thrust had begun on 21 July, when the advance guard from Gona had begun to move inland to explore a track leading to the village of Kokoda, in the Owen Stanley Ranges. The second prong was launched when the seaborne force left Rabaul in mid-August, though air attacks on Milne Bay had been launched since early in the month. These two operations were part of General Hyakutake's overall strategy, which was still aimed towards the creation of an iron ring around north-east Australia. It was being countered by Allied strategy directed by the U.S. Joint Chiefs of Staff, which had ordered the recapture of the Solomon Islands, the expulsion of the Japanese from New Britain, New Ireland, and New Guinea, and the securing of those areas.

In accordance with this, U.S. Marines had landed on Guadalcanal early in August, and the Americans were fighting a series of bloody land, sea, and air battles in the Solomons which had obliged Hyakutake to divert some of his troops from the Port Moresby offensive. Nevertheless he still pressed on, and in the last week of August 1942 his veterans of China, Malaya, and the Philippines were thrown against the inexperienced young soldiers of the Australian militia battalions in New Guinea. These men, who had been regarded with a certain amount of amusement by the combat-seasoned troops of the 2nd A.I.F., were to prove themselves worthy of the great fighting tradition forged by Australians before them.

*   *   *

On 24/25 August 1942, coastwatchers and reconnaissance aircraft reported Japanese seaborne forces steaming towards Milne Bay. They had been expected for long enough, because the tempo of air raids against the Allied garrison, toiling in tropical heat to complete the defences, had been increasing steadily. There was an air raid going on when the advance flotilla of seven barges was reported, so that the R.A.A.F. pilots were unable to taxi their aircraft away from their dispersal points. They lost no time as soon as the Japanese bombers had departed, and swooped on the barges with bombs and cannon fire. Some sank and others were damaged, and the surviving troops were forced to land on an isolated island.

The main invasion fleet was not far behind. It consisted of three cruisers, two troopships of about 8,000 tons apiece, two tankers of about 6,000 tons, and two minesweepers.

To protect the base, Major-General Clowes had deployed his troops so that inexperienced soldiers were interlaced with A.I.F. formations. The 2/10th A.I.F. Battalion was inserted between two militia battalions of the 7th Brigade, which was responsible for the eastern sector, and was to hold the Gili Gili area. The two A.I.F. battalions of the 18th Brigade were responsible for the western sector.

The Japanese convoy anchored in Milne Bay on the night of 25 August. The vanguard of the invasion force, numbering between 600 and 1,000 of the crack Japanese Marines, stormed ashore before dawn on 26 August, supported by light tanks. The Australian militia men engaged them immediately in the areas of K.B. Mission and Cameron's Springs, and although they were handicapped by having neither anti-tank guns nor anti-tank rifles they held them off until daybreak. As soon as the sun rose it could be seen that the Japanese had been working frantically during the night, with dumps of petrol and stores piled up along the shore and empty landing barges still aground. The Kittyhawks pounced immediately, and in a storm of anti-aircraft fire from the Japanese ships and shore positions they shot up everything in sight.

During the rest of the day, both sides consolidated their positions, with Clowes moving warily until he could be sure of the exact Japanese intentions. They attacked again at 10 p.m. that night, in dim moonlight, and confused fighting went on until about four the following morning. The Japanese used the outflanking tactics which had proved so successful in Malaya, with groups wading neck-deep through the sea to get around the Australians on one flank while another strong party splashed through the mangrove swamps in an attempt to turn the other flank.

The 61st Battalion, which bore the brunt of the fighting from the moment of the first landing, was almost exhausted by the morning of 27 August, and was relieved by the first of the A.I.F. battalions. Throughout the night, the garrison had heard landing barges churning steadily to and fro, and when the sun rose they could see that six more ships had arrived. The Australians were still hampered by lack of information, but it was estimated at first that about 5,000 Japanese had landed up until that time. In fact, it was considerably less.

Clowes' tactics had so far blocked their advance from the north shore of the bay, but his critical area was in the vicinity of Gili Gili. This contained an airstrip, the wharf installations, and his supply dumps. He was not only fearful of further landings south of Gili Gili, where the coast was lightly defended, but of a flank attack by troops which had penetrated inland to the north and north-west. Above all, he knew that he had no reinforcements and must make the most miserly use of his resources in men and material, whereas the Japanese had command of the sea and could pour in reinforcements from the main base at Rabaul. Such facts compelled caution, for which eventually he was criticised by General MacArthur. The supreme commander's opinion was that he should have driven the Japanese back into the sea without delay.

In the late afternoon of 27 August, the 2/10th Battalion of the A.I.F. moved forward to the defences around the K.B. Mission. About 500 men in all, they had last been in action against the Germans in the sand and rocks of Africa, and settled down into the muddy positions with confidence that they could deal with the Japanese.

But the Japanese proved to be an even tougher foe than the *Afrika Korps*. At 8 p.m., in darkness and blinding rain, they launched themselves against the Australian perimeter, in an attack accompanied by the sonorous chants which they sang to strike fear into the hearts of their enemies and keep up their own spirits. Supported by tanks, the infantry threw themselves fearlessly against the Australian positions, so that the Diggers soon found themselves fighting the Japanese hand to hand. Once more, they were hampered by a lack of anti-tank weapons, and found that the grenades with which they had been issued often failed to explode and that the "sticky bombs," designed to adhere to tank armour and explode inwards, often failed to stick. The heat and moisture of the dense tropical climate had spoiled them.

Despite a savage resistance, the battle degenerated into a confused affair of group and individual contests, until at about midnight the Australians were ordered to withdraw to the west bank of the Gama River. The Japanese pressed after them remorselessly, and forced them even further back; to the critical vicinity of No. 3 Airstrip defended by the 25th Militia Battalion. Here, the Australians managed to hold them, but with some chagrin were to learn later that they had not been forced back by an overwhelmingly superior force. A comparatively small force of resolute and expertly trained Japanese troops, who synchronised perfectly with their supporting tanks, had made the attack.

The next two days were comparatively quiet, except for artillery exchanges and active patrolling by both sides in the vicinity of No. 3 Airstrip. Clowes ordered Brigadier Wootten to prepare an attack by his 18th Brigade, designed to drive the enemy along the north shore as far as K.B. Mission and to mop up the whole peninsula, but cancelled this on the afternoon of

29 August, when a further seaborne force of a cruiser and nine destroyers hove into sight.

Throughout the next day both sides were in constant contact, with the Japanese endeavouring to consolidate their grip on the airfield area and the Australians keeping them out. They were helped by the two Kittyhawk squadrons, which flew almost continuous sorties and with extraordinary heroism strafed the enemy from treetop height. The pilots took enormous risks, but by acting as flying artillery they caused heavy casualties, kept the enemy pinned down, and destroyed his supplies and equipment.

Early on 31 August, the Japanese launched three determined assaults on the 61st Battalion defending the north-east perimeter, but the militia soldiers made them fall back and leave many of their dead and wounded on the muddy ground in front of the Australian positions. By daybreak, now that Clowes was sure that the Japanese were concentrating their efforts along the north shore or eastern sector, the first of Wootten's brigade moved up to counter-attack.

They fought their way through a series of ambushes, and the young militia men who for so long had been a standing joke now proved themselves more than a match for the Japanese who were prepared to die for their Emperor. And die they did, as the Australians forced them back through the slimy mud and dripping foliage and finally stormed the K.B. Mission at bayonet point just as night was falling.

To the rear, 300 Japanese attacked Australians who had taken up positions along the Gama River. Charging out of the jungle with the maniacal screams designed to terrify the Australians, they struck just as dusk was falling, and for the next two hours there was a confused and savage struggle in slashing rain and with the opponents slithering and splashing in mud which in places was knee-deep. After a severe mauling the Japanese fell back, and later in the night the Australians followed them up to finish them off as they attempted to retire westwards.

Clowes felt that he now had the enemy on the run, and planned to continue his advance and mop up the remnants of the Japanese. But at 9 a.m. on 1 September he received an urgent message from MacArthur, who later was to criticise him for his initial caution. It said: "Expect attack Jap ground forces on Milne Bay aerodromes from west and north-west supported by destroyer fire from bay. Take immediate stations."

All units prepared to repel this attack, which never materialised. Two days later, Wootten's men resumed their counter-attack, but the period of grace had enabled the Japanese to dig themselves into strongly defended positions. The Australians were obliged to winkle them out one by one, in a series of actions which were typified by the one in which Corporal J. A. French won his Victoria Cross on 4 September.

He was leading a section which was held up by fire from three machine-gun posts, so he ordered the other men to take cover and crept close enough to knock out two of the posts with grenades. Then, armed with a Thompson sub-machine gun, he charged the third post; firing from the hip as he ran into a storm of bullets. Mortally wounded by these, he kept moving and firing until he fell, and when the staccato of his weapon ceased there was no other sound. His section found him lying dead in front of the gun pit, and that he had killed all of the three Japanese gun crews.

The citation to his award concluded with: "By his cool courage and disregard of his own personal safety, this N.C.O. saved members of his section from heavy casualties and was responsible for the successful conclusion of the attack."

Another sad discovery during the mopping-up operations was that of the body of Squadron-Leader Turnbull, lying among the remains of his Kittyhawk fighter in the bush near K.B. Mission.

By 6 September 1942, Clowes was confident that his troops had broken the Japanese invasion, but a signal from General Blamey warned him to expect more of the enemy that night followed by another landing on the night of 12 September. Less than an hour later another signal arrived, saying that the Japanese would evacuate Milne Bay that night but return in force on 10 September.

Despite this added confusion of an already chaotic situation, and the sound of Japanese ships entering the bay that night, no more Japanese landed and for the next few days the Australians were engaged in mopping up the tattered and starving survivors. They fought with their customary savagery to the very end, and their refusal to surrender meant that every man had to be killed unless he was too gravely wounded to resist. A few tried to escape through the jungle towards Buna.

Two weeks after the first landing, the battle for Milne Bay was over. When the Australian units called their rolls, 161 men were dead or missing and 212 wounded. From a body count it was estimated conservatively that the Japanese had lost 700 killed, allowing for those who would have died among the wounded and survivors taken off on the night of 7 September. Their wounded must have been far greater in number.

For the first time since their tanks had attacked the Indian troops in northern Malaya, the Japanese had suffered a decisive defeat: partly because of their own error in assuming that Milne Bay would be held only by two or three companies deployed for defence of the airfields. They had expected to overcome these with a combined force of 2,000 marines and infantry, but bit off considerably more than they could chew.

On the one hand, it was a strategic victory, because it ruined the Japanese timetable for their new double thrust towards Port Moresby and denied them the base which they needed for an all-out land, sea, and air attack. On the other hand, it was for the Australians a triumphant moral and propaganda victory. They had dealt the Japanese their first decisive defeat on land, had proved that their militia men could stand up to the savage veterans of the enemy army and navy, and had destroyed the myth of invincibility which had surrounded the triumphs of the Japanese Army in its march southwards and westwards.

After this, it might have been thought that Major-General Clowes could look forward to the fruits of victory; possibly to a higher command. Instead, MacArthur from his headquarters, which were now in Brisbane, chose to criticise his handling of the operations and to upbraid him for failing to send back a regular flow of information—though the information which his own headquarters had supplied to Clowes had been inaccurate.

This tactlessness, which naturally led to Australian resentment, stemmed from MacArthur's refusal to have a senior Australian officer on his staff, and also to some extent from his staff's ignorance of active service conditions. It was the first of numerous occasions on which these two factors were to cause resentment and misunderstandings which could have been prevented by a liaison officer capable of explaining the differences in operational procedures between the two armies.

However, MacArthur was seeking desperately for a large-scale land victory in the south-west Pacific area; not only to sustain his own standing and prestige but to support his constant battle to obtain men, ships, aircraft, and supplies from Washington. Other theatres were given greater priority, and even though Curtin appealed as urgently to the British Government as MacArthur did to his, the response was grudging. They were forced to continue fighting what MacArthur described as his "Poor Man's War," or "Cinderella War," but the fact of course was that the Allies were over-extended on every front.

MacArthur's desperate needs may have caused his ungenerous comment, in a message to General Marshall, that: "The enemy's defeat at Milne Bay must not be accepted as a measure of relative fighting capacity of troops involved. The decisive factor was the complete surprise obtained over him by our preliminary concentration of superior forces." Obviously—and perhaps rightly—he did not want the U.S. Chief of Staff to think that the New Guinea campaign would be a walkover.

Other people felt differently. Field-Marshal Viscount Slim, then commanding the British 14th Army in Burma, wrote in his book *Defeat into Victory*: "We were helped, too, by a very cheering piece of news that now reached us, and of which, as a morale booster, I made great use. In August-September 1942, Australian troops had at Milne Bay in New Guinea inflicted on the Japanese their first undoubted defeat on land. If the Australians, in conditions very like ours, had done it, so could we. Some of us may forget that of all the Allies it was Australian soldiers who first broke the spell of the invincibility of the Japanese Army; those of us who were in Burma have cause to remember."

29

THE KOKODA TRAIL

AT MILNE BAY, THE "CHOKOS" OF BRIGADIER FIELD'S 7TH MILITIA BRIGADE had had their baptism of fire. Further to the west, in the fearful territory of the Owen Stanley Ranges, young soldiers of a smaller militia unit, the 39th Battalion, had been proving the "mettle of their pastures."

Since 21 July, Japanese units had been probing along the Kokoda Trail into the Owen Stanley Ranges. The little-used trail climbed through steep, jungle-clad foothills to Kokoda village, which had the only airfield in the area.

The doctrine at Australian military headquarters in Port Moresby was that the Owen Stanley Ranges were impassable for any large force, and that the enemy intended simply to establish an airfield in the Gona-Buna area. But the Japanese had different ideas. For them, the Kokoda Trail was the back door to Port Moresby, with an airfield which would allow them to supply and reinforce their troops and to fly sorties against the port.

The Kokoda Trail was to become as deeply implanted in Australian history as Gallipoli and Tobruk, and no more eloquent testimony to the sacrifice, endurance, and hardship involved in the Kokoda campaign has been expressed than by Major-General Sir Kingsley Morris, who at the time was A.D.M.S., 7th Division. He wrote, "Time and rain and the jungle will obliterate this little native pad, but for evermore will live the memory of weary men who have passed this way; ghosts of glorious men that have gone, gone far beyond the Kokoda Trail.

"Imagine an area of approximately one hundred miles long. Crumple and fold this into a series of ridges, each rising higher and higher until seven thousand feet is reached, then declining in ridges to three thousand feet. Cover this thickly with jungle, short trees and tall trees, tangled with great entwining savage vines. Through an oppression of this density, cut a little native track, two or three feet wide, up the ridges, over the spurs, round gorges and down across swiftly flowing happy mountain streams. Where the track clambers up the mountain sides, cut steps, big steps, little steps, steep steps, or clear the soil from the tree roots.

"Every few miles, bring the track through a small patch of sunlit kunai grass, or an old deserted native garden, and every seven or ten miles, build a group of dilapidated grass huts — as staging shelters, generally set in a foul, offensive clearing. Every now and then, leave beside the track dumps of discarded, putrefying food, occasional dead bodies, and human foulings. In the morning, flicker the sunlight through the tall trees, flutter green and blue and purple and white butterflies lazily through the air, and hide birds of deep throated song, or harsh cockatoos, in the foliage.

"About midday, and through the night, pour water over the forest, so that the steps become broken, and a continual yellow stream flows downwards, and the few level areas become pools and puddles of putrid black mud. In the high ridges above Myola, drip this water day and night over the track through a foetid forest grotesque with moss and glowing phosphorescent

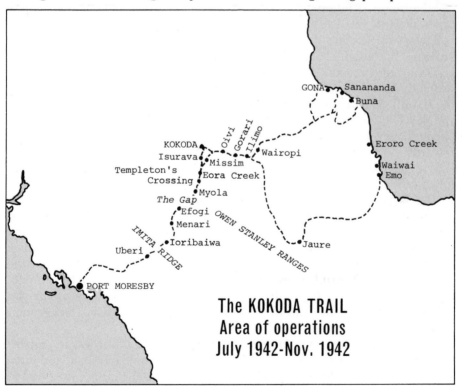

The KOKODA TRAIL
Area of operations
July 1942-Nov. 1942

fungi. Such is the track which a prominent politician publicly described as being 'almost impassable for motor vehicles,' and such is the route for ten days to be covered from Ilolo to Deniki.''

In those days the Kokoda Trail struck out from Uberi for a mile or so along the Goldie River, and turned sharply up a knife edged spur of the Imita Ridge. The engineers were to cut more than 2,000 steps into this narrow and interminable track which seemed to point almost vertically skywards to the thousands of troops who traversed its wearying course. It rose 1,200 feet in the first three miles, then dropped some 1,600 feet, and rose again for 2,000 feet over the last four miles, where the going was always hardest. The rear companies often took some twelve hours to complete this nine miles of horror. To the troops it became known as the "Golden Stairs," and it was their introduction to the Owen Stanley Ranges.

The first soldiers to tread this weary path in action against the Japanese were a company of the 39th Militia Battalion, who set out on 7 July 1942, followed by the rest of the unit on 22 July, when news of the enemy landing near Gona had been received.

After the first Japanese landings in the Gona-Buna area, on 21 July, a force of about 2,000 of the enemy advanced along the trail. They consisted of a battalion of infantry protecting a strong engineer detachment, whose task was to prepare the way for the main force.

There was no one to oppose the landing but elements of the Papuan Infantry Battalion, a native formation officered by Australians, and after reporting the arrival of the Japanese these fell back to join the company of the 39th Battalion. Lieutenant-Colonel W. T. Owen, the commander of the battalion, had been ordered by Major-General Morris, commander of the New Guinea forces, to concentrate his men at Kokoda in order to prevent Japanese penetration south-west of the village and to patrol along the trail towards Buna and Ioma. If he could not stop the advance on Kokoda, he was to fall back on prepared positions in the area and block any further advance towards Port Moresby.

The Japanese moved quickly, and the first clash came on the day after the landing. The Australian militiamen and Papuan infantry fired on advance elements at Awala, about forty-five miles east of Kokoda, but soon were obliged to fall back. During the next few days, the small band of defenders fought a series of delaying actions at Gorari and Oivi, but the Japanese were pressing hard and had forced them back to Kokoda by 29 July. Here, the eighty-odd Australians were attacked by about 500 Japanese infantry, and held them off for two hours in a sharp engagement which left many Japanese dead in the jungle.

Morris was trying to reinforce the men of the 39th, but it was impossible for supporting troops to reach them in time by marching overland and there was not enough transport aircraft to fly them in. So the militia men had to surrender Kokoda to the Japanese, and after sunset fell back through a rubber plantation on the way to Deniki.

They were helped by a heavy fog, and the scene later was vividly recreated by Captain W. H. Vernon, who had attached himself to the company as its acting medical officer. He wrote of: "The thick white mist dimming the moonlight; the mysterious veiling of trees, houses, and men, the drip of moisture from the foliage, and at the last, the almost complete silence as if the rubber groves at Kokoda were sleeping as usual in the depths of the night, and men had not brought disturbance."

They left behind them the body of Lieutenant-Colonel Owen, who had been mortally wounded in a grenade duel on the hardest-pressed sector of the Kokoda perimeter. A survivor of the Rabaul garrison, he had shown outstanding leadership in effecting the escape of several hundred men after the garrison had capitulated, and during this first action on the Kokoda trail he had handled his little force with a confidence which made the Japanese fight for every mile of the way. His courage was recognised by the Americans, who made a posthumous award of the Distinguished Service Cross; the first such award to an Australian in the second World War.

By 6 August 1942, the militia men at Deniki had been reinforced by the remaining companies of the 39th Battalion, bringing the force to a total of thirty-one officers and 433 N.C.O.s and men, plus five Australian officers, three N.C.O.s, and thirty-five native soldiers of the Papuan Infantry Battalion. The force was under the temporary command of Lieutenant-Colonel A. G. Cameron, another survivor of Rabaul and like Owen a most determined and aggressive soldier.

For the militia men who had been through the first engagements with the Japanese, it had been a testing experience. Many of them were very young, with a high percentage being no more than eighteen, and they had been blooded under the most arduous conditions against a savage enemy. Fortunately, the Japanese did not press on with their advance. The formation which had occupied Kokoda had completed its mission, and signalled back to Major-General Horii. When he learnt that the trail was open as far as Kokoda, he ordered the main invasion force to embark for the Gona-Buna area so that the overland attack on Port Moresby could coincide with the invasion of Milne Bay.

Lieutenant-Colonel Cameron, however, did not intend the Japanese to enjoy their victory unscathed. On 7 August, three days after taking over the battalion, he launched it into a three-pronged attack with the aim of retaking Kokoda. For the next week, heavy and confused fighting raged in the jungles and plantations around the little village, which one company of Australians took and held for two and a half days before it was forced out again by an attack by more than 1,500 Japanese. The odds were too great, and the battalion was compelled to retire into its positions around Deniki and Isurawa. Their impact on the Japanese may be gauged by an enemy report which stated: "In the Kokoda area, our Advance Force has been engaged in battle with 1,200 Australians, and suffered unexpectedly heavy casualties."

The menace to Australia's northern frontiers had now been realised by the army and the government, who saw that if the Japanese were not beaten in New Guinea they would have to be faced on the Australian mainland. On 6/7 August, advance brigades of the 7th Division embarked at Brisbane for New Guinea under Major-General A. S. "Tubby" Allen, and on 11 August Lieutenant-General S. Rowell arrived in Port Moresby to take over direction of the operations from Major-General Morris.

Rowell graduated from Duntroon in 1914, at the age of nineteen, and embarked shortly afterwards as a lieutenant with the 3rd Light Horse Regiment. His service at Gallipoli was interrupted by serious illness, and after repatriation to Australia he faced a very clouded future in the army. Eventually he overcame his disabilities, and the penetrating examinations of the medical board, and between the wars earned a reputation as an outstanding staff officer. He was described by one senior British officer as the most eminent of the British and Dominion officers to graduate from the Imperial Defence College during the 1930s.

In 1939, he was appointed Chief Staff Officer of the 6th Division, and served in this capacity throughout the Libyan and Greek campaigns. The successful extrication of the Australian and New Zealand troops from Greece was very largely due to Rowell's organisation as a member of General Blamey's staff, although contemporary history has incorrectly given much of the credit to General Wilson.

General Rowell was also deeply involved in planning the Syrian campaign, but relinquished his duties in the Middle East to take up the appointment of Deputy Chief of the Australian General Staff. When Blamey reorganised the Australian Army in April 1942, Rowell was appointed to command I Corps, and at forty-seven was the youngest Australian officer to have been promoted to lieutenant-general.

News of these developments brought some relief to those sweating and dying in their lonely positions just south of Kokoda, and changes in their immediate area brought reassurance that they had not been left to wither on a remote vine of some higher authority's planting.

Firstly, Lieutenant-Colonel R. Honner was flown from Western Australia to take command of the 39th Battalion. He was a man of cold and rare courage, who had been a schoolmaster and then a lawyer. It is interesting to note how many of Australia's combatant officers had the same type of background; professional men who learnt soldiering in their spare time.

Honner went overseas as a company commander of the 2/11th Battalion, and served in Libya, Greece and Crete. He won the Military Cross in

Greece, and spent three months evading the Germans on Crete after the surrender, before escaping to Egypt.

The second change of command came when Brigadier S. H. Porter, who also had served with distinction in the Middle East, became commander of Maroubra Force, as the troops on the Kokoda Trail had now been named. Porter's command, although of short duration, was to include the 53rd Battalion, which had moved up to defensive positions at Alola. The total force, although nominally comprising two battalions, in fact numbered somewhat less than a full battalion. It totalled forty-five officers and 584 men.

The third and perhaps most heartening occurrence was the arrival of the 21st Brigade of the 7th Division in Port Moresby. It began immediate preparations to enter the Kokoda Trail, and the advance battalion climbed the "Golden Stairs" on 17 August. The second battalion followed on the next day, while the third remained in reserve at Port Moresby. For the Kokoda operation, the combat strength of the 21st Brigade numbered 1,216 of all ranks.

The brigade was led by Brigadier Potts, a West Australian grazier. He had served on Gallipoli, and was commissioned at the age of nineteen. From Gallipoli he went to France, where he was seriously wounded at Vaire Wood during the Hamel Battle in July 1918, where he also won the Military Cross and was mentioned in dispatches. In 1940 he went overseas with the 2/16th Battalion, of which he was second in command in the Syrian campaign. His leadership in his battalion's victories at Sidon and Damour won him the D.S.O.

The inspiration of battle-seasoned commanders, and the commitment of the 7th Division veterans to the campaign, helped to transform the spirit of the battle zone from one of comparative depression to that of optimism, though the young militia men had held grimly to their positions until the reinforcements came.

The great and so far unanswered question is why the 7th Division had not been committed months before to the defence of New Guinea, instead of leaving this vital front to young and inexperienced militia men.

General MacArthur later claimed that he made the decision to fight in New Guinea and not on the shores of Australia, but in retrospect his head-quarters appears to have been slow in recognising the urgent need to reinforce the new battle area. A similar claim has been made for the Australian Chiefs of Staff, but, whatever party was responsible, its action to reinforce the area came only just in time.

*　　　*　　　*

Brigadier Potts took over Maroubra Force from Brigadier Porter on 24 August, and immediately was faced with his first crisis. This was one of supply; the problem which bedevilled all operations on the Kokoda Trail.

Every ounce of food, ammunition, and other supplies had to be man-handled up the trail or dropped from the air. For the wounded, it was a Gethsemane. Those who could walk had to slither back down the interminable stretches of mud and clamber down the flights of rough steps. Those who could not walk had to be carried out on litters borne by the natives to whom the term of "Fuzzy Wuzzy Angels" was justly applied, and many a man owed his life to the strength and patience with which they carried him down the trail.

Brigadier Potts' first experience with the problem came at Myola, which was being established as the main supply centre for the campaign. As the first units of the 21st Brigade pushed up the trail to take up their battle positions, Potts found that only 10,000 ration units had been delivered at Myola instead of the 40,000 which had been ordered.

This jeopardised his plans for a rapid offensive which would throw back the Japanese before they became better established, and subsequent enquiries showed that either the damage or non-recovery rate from air drops had not been correctly reported, or that whole aircraft loads of supplies had been dumped into some other part of the Owen Stanley jungles. The Americans were responsible for air transport, and it was suspected that their then notoriously bad navigation had made them drop supplies in the wrong areas. From then onwards, more and more Australian aircrews were used on flying the "biscuit bombers," as the supply aircraft were called, and a more businesslike approach taken to the problems of supply by land. These two factors gradually began to improve the situation.

Potts had taken over on almost the very day which the Japanese had scheduled for their double thrust towards Port Moresby, and strong reinforcements were pouring ashore at Buna and beginning to push overland along the comparatively easy sections of the trail between the north coast and Kokoda.

By the end of August, Major-General Horii had landed about 13,500 men at Buna, of whom 10,000 were combat troops. A proportion of this force was used to consolidate the base and to build airfields, while a formation of 5,900 men under Colonel Yokoyama began moving up the trail. 2,700 of these were infantry, including marines, and the remainder were engineers, mountain artillery, and base and supply troops. They had brought with them about 1,200 Rabaul natives to act as porters.

The delay caused by the supply failure to some extent influenced Potts' deployment of his troops to meet the Japanese. He had two objectives; to re-capture Kokoda, and then to push the enemy back to the coast.

He proposed to achieve the first of these objectives by retaining the 39th and 53rd Battalions in their present positions, and maintaining active patrolling to screen the arrival of the two 21st Brigade battalions in the area. When these troops were available, he planned to occupy Naro, Deniki, and

Fila, and from these positions conduct a two pronged attack on Kokoda. One thrust would advance down the main track, and the other would cut the track between Oivi and Kokoda. The 39th Battalion would hold the Deniki area, and the 53rd Battalion would cut the Kokoda-Yodda track and demonstrate against the airfield.

After this, Potts intended to leave the 39th and 53rd Battalions to mop up around Kokoda, and drive the Japanese over the Kumusi River back to Buna with his 21st Brigade.

For the conduct of these operations, Potts considered three plans: (a) to retain the 39th and 53rd Battalions at Isurava and Alola, leaving the 2/14th and 2/16th Battalions at Myola until his supply position was assured (b) to relieve the battle weary 39th Battalion with one of his 21st Brigade battalions, leaving the 53rd Battalion in position with the other A.I.F. battalion in reserve (c) to leave the 39th and 53rd Battalions in their present positions and commit the two 21st Brigade battalions on high ground to the east and west of the main track.

After considering all the factors involved, Potts selected the second plan. The first would have invited disaster for the depleted 39th Battalion if a strong enemy attack developed, and his still uncertain supply position dissuaded him from the third course of action.

He began to relieve the 39th Battalion on 26 August, but the Japanese started to attack on the main front and from the right towards the sector held by the 53rd Battalion. For the next two days, the Australians on the main front beat back a succession of persistent assaults by an enemy force which clearly outnumbered the defenders but could not dislodge them from their positions.

On the right, however, the position was more serious. Militia men of the 53rd Battalion faltered in their first action, fell back, and exposed the flank, thus endangering the principal Australian positions at Alola and Isurava. Not the least of their setbacks was the loss of their commander, Lieutenant-Colonel K. H. Ward, who was killed in an ambush on 27 August.

This weakness cast a heavier burden on the remaining three battalions, and Potts was in the desperate position of trying to shore up his right flank with reinforcements arriving piecemeal after a forced march from Myola.

While this crisis was reaching its peak, and with the outcome at Milne Bay still uncertain, General MacArthur and his staff developed an atmosphere that almost bordered on panic and which was wryly described by General George Vasey, Deputy Chief of the Australian General Staff, who said, "G.H.Q. is like a bloody barometer in a cyclone—up and down every two minutes. They're like the militia—they need to be blooded."

The American agitation stemmed from three factors. Firstly, an ignorance of the terrain and conditions of the battlefield which was so complete that Major-General H. Casey, MacArthur's engineer staff officer, suggested to

General Rowell that the Australians should blow up The Gap on the Kokoda Trail, to frustrate the Japanese advance. He imagined that it was some kind of rocky mountain pass, whereas it was merely a name for a section of the trail.

Secondly, they had little faith in Australian troops and their leaders. In their own lack of combat experience, they accused them of lacking aggression.

Thirdly, their own staff work had been so poor that they had completely underestimated the potential strength of the Japanese offensive, in an overconfident optimism which was to recur again and again.

The "G.H.Q. barometer" fell again when they heard of the beginning of the second phase of the battle of Isurava. On 28 August, the Japanese launched an all-out attack on the 2/14th and 39th Battalions on the main front, while on the right flank the 2/16th Battalion endeavoured to repair the damage caused by the 53rd Battalion's retreat. At dawn on 29 August, suicidal waves of Japanese threw themselves against the Australian positions, screaming their war cry of "Banzai! Banzai!" and led by officers wielding two-handed samurai swords. The hurricane of fire from Australian gun pits cut them down in khaki swathes, but as one wave fell another would rise out of the Japanese positions and charge forward.

Five Japanese battalions made the attack, and though they suffered incredible losses from the Australian fire they gradually began to gain ground. By mid afternoon they began to turn the Australian flanks, and a Japanese officer reported, "The Australians are gradually being outflanked, but their resistance is very strong and our casualties are great. The outcome of the battle is difficult to foresee."

It was essentially an infantryman's battle, without armour, artillery, aerial support, or any other factor to weigh the scales in which the courage and determination of the combatants were weighed against each other's. The Australians knew that they were fighting against a truly merciless enemy, and that to be taken prisoner was an unthinkable fate. Consequently they matched the Japanese with a savagery equal to their own, and like them would sooner die than surrender. The mud was churned up by the heavy boots of Australians and the two-toed rubber shoes of the Japanese as the confused battle swayed one way and another, with slashing rainstorms soaking the thin uniforms of men who crouched among the dripping foliage with every sense quivering for the movement which might herald another frenzied charge.

Characteristic of the wild courage displayed was that of Private B. S. Kingsbury, whose platoon was ordered into a counter-attack. He leapt out of his position and rushed forward ahead of his mates, seeming to be unscathed by furious machine-gun fire as he fired his Bren gun from the hip. The Japanese fell away before him, and the rest of his platoon charged on

Action in the Vale of Tempe, Greece (*detail from Australian War Memorial painting by W. Dargie*).

as he fell to a sniper's bullet. His bravery was recognised with a posthumous Victoria Cross.

Major-General Horii's optimistic timetable had allowed for a march of two days from Kokoda to the "mountain range," and a further five days for a triumphant advance from the "mountain range" down into Port Moresby —hopefully to meet the other claw of the pincers, which should be closing around Milne Bay. But he had to watch the battle, from the heights north of Isurava, with growing impatience at the delay caused by an outnumbered opponent.

The Australians claimed to have killed 550 Japanese during the first day's fighting, but were losing heavily themselves, and to Brigadier Potts it was obvious that the situation was deteriorating so quickly that he must choose between three courses—since his force was insufficient to handle all of them. He could deal with the threat to the right flank, even though this might be a diversion to conceal the real attack on the main front; hold the right flank and attack to the left of the 2/14th Battalion's position, thus taking the Japanese in the flank and rear; or withdraw the 2/14th and 39th Battalions and try to hold the Japanese advance.

His only reserves were two companies of the 2/16th Battalion, but he decided on the second course of action. This was unsuccessful, and after a company of the 2/14th had been driven off the high ground with heavy losses after four attempts to regain it, he broke off the attack.

On 30 August, Major-General Horii's impatience amounted almost to frenzy. He issued fresh orders, which made free use of the word "annihilate," for the renewal of the attack on the tightening Australian perimeter at Isurava and Alola. Despite their casualties of the previous day, the Japanese swept upon the Australians in some of the heaviest fighting of the entire campaign. There were no distinctions of rank and position as the Australians fought savagely to keep their perimeter intact. Cooks, clerks, and commanders fought side by side with the veterans of the A.I.F. battalions and the young militia men who were having such a terrible blooding, but it was impossible to check the plunging onslaught of an enemy who were swarming past on either side as well as attacking from the front. They moved south along the high country and by 11 a.m. had bypassed the left flank and were threatening the rear and the brigade headquarters. Machine-gun fire began to slash at the 2/16th Battalion's positions, from across the valley at Alola, and it could be seen that the Australians must now fight to the death or fall back in the hope of checking the Japanese further down the trail.

The 2/14th Battalion, which had borne the brunt of the enemy attack by five battalions, was reduced to 160 effectives. Its commander, Colonel Key, was missing, together with all his headquarters staff. Brigadier Potts' total force was now reduced to about 750 effective fighting men.

The long, bitter, and costly withdrawal to Ioribaiwa began, with Colonel

Australian action at Buna (*detail from Australian War Memorial painting by G. R. Mainwaring*).

Caro's 2/16th Battalion acting as rearguard. For thirty-six hours they held firm so that their comrades might make their way back down the trail, and threw back repeated assaults urged on by Horii in his determination to break the spirit of the Australians.

Caro's men had been ordered to hold on until 6 a.m. on 2 September, and they held fast to the very minute. Then they too fell back, and the remnants of the 21st Brigade fought a running withdrawal action. They made the Japanese fight for every step of the way, and with the help of native carriers made sure that none of their wounded were left behind. Ironically, Brigadier Potts was forced to relinquish his main base at Myola just as supplies were beginning to be received in effective quantities.

By 6 September the two militia battalions had been pulled out of the battle area, and the fresh 2/27th Battalion of the 21st Brigade had moved up to relieve their two sister battalions. The 2/14th and 2/16th retreated through them near Efogi, but on 8 September the Japanese made an all-out attack at Efogi. They tore savagely into the Australians, and when they were unable to penetrate the main perimeter resorted to their well-practised tactics of outflanking the defence and almost surrounded the A.I.F. battalions. The 2/27th Battalion was forced off the track, but the remnants of the other two battalions managed to extricate themselves by following a narrow track through rough country which wound back to the main track at Menari. Again they refused to abandon their wounded to the savage vengeance of the Japanese, and though exhausted through constant fighting and exposure they helped or carried them through the jungle.

On 10 September, Brigadier Potts was relieved of the command of Maroubra Force, which was taken over by Brigadier Porter. As Potts trudged wearily back to Port Moresby, unheralded and unsung, he was coming to the end of distinguished service in two world wars. He was to be made the scapegoat for the initial defeat of the Australians on the Kokoda Trail, and did not receive another field command until the last months of the war. By that time, the true facts had emerged and his decision to fall back from Isurava had been vindicated by knowledge of the overwhelming force which had attacked him.

*   *   *

Brigadier Porter had been ordered to hold the line until it could be reinforced, and so took up positions on the main Ioribaiwa feature. Luckily, help was quite near at hand. The 25th Brigade of the 7th Division began disembarking at Port Moresby on 9 September; seasoned troops under an eager and aggressive commander, Brigadier K. W. Eather.

Eather, like so many of his contemporaries, had learnt his trade in the citizen forces between the wars, and had led the 2/1st Battalion with punch and confidence during the Libyan campaign. The brigade which he now led was a well-honed weapon tempered in the desert battles and strengthened with properly trained replacements. So far as soldiers can ever be said to be anxious to go into battle, they were keen to match their skill against the vaunted Japanese.

Their mobility and efficiency can be gauged by the fact that two battalions were in their battle positions at Ioribaiwa within four days of landing in New Guinea. They relieved the battered 21st Brigade, whose total losses by that time amounted to twenty-six officers and 473 men.

Brigadier Eather now prepared to carry out his orders, which told him he must halt the enemy advance on Port Moresby "by offensive action as far forward as possible," and regain control of the Kokoda Trail through the Isurava-Deniki area with the object of recapturing Kokoda. He was also warned that he must regain and hold the Nauro, Menari, and Efogi air-dropping areas, as these would be vital to the supply of his advance.

General Horii, with the golden prize of Port Moresby now only thirty miles away, had not rested on his laurels while the Australians prepared to strike back. He had maintained a continuous pressure on the Ioribaiwa area, and the 25th Brigade became the anvil on which he dealt what he expected to be the final blows of the campaign. If and when they broke, it would be Singapore all over again; a hard-driven retreat back into a seaport which almost inevitably would fall.

Through reinforcements, brought up from the coast, Horii still had upwards of 5,000 effectives to throw against the two 25th Brigade battalions, which totalled somewhat more than 1,000 officers and men. Even after the most desperate fighting the Australians were being driven back, and, at 8.15 a.m. on 16 September, Brigadier Eather had to signal General Allen: "Enemy filling whole front and flanks. Do not consider can hold him here. Request permission to withdraw to Imita Ridge if necessary. Porter concurs."

Soon afterwards, in a telephone conversation with Allen, Eather reported that the Japanese were moving around his flanks and that he did not think he could hold them at Ioribaiwa. Allen gave permission for the withdrawal to Imita Ridge, but with the emphatic qualification, "There won't be any withdrawal from the Imita position, Ken. You'll die there if necessary. You understand that?"

"Yes," Eather replied. "I understand that."

Allen repeated the conversation to General Rowell. The latter, no doubt thinking of the reaction of MacArthur and the General Staff if Eather was defeated, remarked laconically, "Our heads will be in the basket over this, Tubby."

The Australians began the three mile withdrawal at eleven-thirty that morning, and were digging in on Imita Ridge twenty-four hours later. From their new positions, they looked north across the broad, deep Ua-Ule Creek Valley to their old defences at Ioribaiwa.

The forces of Major-General Tomitaro Horii now enjoyed the rare distinction of having penetrated further south than any of the Imperial troops except those on Timor. From the saddle of the white charger which had carried him up the trail, Horii could now survey the south coast of New Guinea and the placid ocean across which Australia lay such a little distance away. To celebrate the occasion, he issued an Order of the Day which mingled hopes of victory with a cry of anguish for the sacrifices of his troops.

"Repeatedly," he proclaimed, "we were in hot pursuit of the enemy. We smashed his final resistance in the fierce fighting of Ioribaiwa, and today we firmly hold the heights of that area, the most important point for the advance on Port Moresby.

"For more than three weeks during that period, every unit forced its way through deep forests and ravines, and climbed scores of peaks in pursuit of the enemy. Traversing knee deep mud, clambering up steep precipices, bearing uncomplainingly the heavy weight of artillery ammunition, our men overcame the shortage of our supplies, and we succeeded in surmounting the Stanley Ridge. No pen or word can depict adequately the magnitude of the hardships suffered. From the bottom of our hearts we appreciate these many hardships and deeply sympathise with the great numbers killed and wounded.

"We will strike a hammer blow at the stronghold of Moresby. However, ahead of us the enemy still crawls about. It is difficult to judge the direction of his movement and many of you have not yet fully recovered your strength.

"When we next go into action, this force will throw in its fighting power unreservedly."

As his soldiers heard this order read to them, which being Japanese they possibly did not treat with the degree of cynicism reserved by most combatant troops for the words of the higher command, their achievements thus far had caused a command crisis which was unprecedented in the history of Australian arms. Australia, like Britain, was now faced with defeat at her own doorstep.

MacArthur continued to be bitterly critical of the efficiency of Australian leadership and the quality of the troops, and was still convinced that they outnumbered the Japanese on the Kokoda Trail. Following his representations, a meeting of the War Cabinet on 15 September decided to send General Blamey to take over command in New Guinea. He must "energise the situation," MacArthur said.

Blamey was placed in an invidious position, and when he arrived at Port Moresby on 23 September he did not conceal the fact that the arrangement had been forced upon him. General Rowell quite naturally regarded the appointment as a lack of confidence in himself, and later recorded, "The C-in-C suggested that I should become a deputy to him, but I demurred at this as it would have merely made me a staff officer with all vestige of command authority removed.''

Blamey, however, had been given a job to do, and it was not in his nature to allow personal feelings to prevent him from doing it. A sharp clash of personalities developed very quickly between the two strong-minded commanders, and Blamey relieved Rowell of his command on 28 September.

It was a bitter disappointment for Rowell, who had shown all the resolution which could be asked of a commander in his position and should at least have been allowed to see the outcome of his plans. Like Potts, he was to drift into the military wilderness for a while, until he was rescued by the British Army's offer of an appointment as Director of Tactical Investigation; an important staff position concerned with the planning for the invasion of Europe, which made good use of his talents. Blamey's relentless attitude towards those who had once opposed him was shown by the way in which, at first, he blocked the offer, but eventually he gave in.

Subsequent events in the New Guinea jungles confirmed Rowell's tactical judgement, and after the war his reputation was restored completely by his appointment as Chief of the Australian General Staff from 1950 to 1954.

To succeed him in New Guinea, Blamey summoned Lieutenant-General Sir Edmund Herring to Port Moresby. Herring was one of Australia's most distinguished citizens. As Rhodes Scholar for Melbourne University in 1912, he had been studying at Oxford when the first World War was declared, and joined the British Army. He served in the artillery in France and Macedonia, won the D.S.O. and M.C., and returned to Melbourne to practice law. He became a King's Counsel in 1936.

As a prominent citizen soldier, he was given command of the 6th Division artillery when it sailed for the Middle East, and in 1941 succeeded Sir Iven Mackay as divisional commander. His command of the New Guinea Force continued until August 1943, when he was promoted to G.O.C. I Australian Corps. He retired from the army in the following year, and from 1944 to 1954 was Chief Justice of Victoria. From 1945 onwards he was Lieutenant-Governor of his State:

Apart from Sir John Monash, Sir Edmund Herring is probably the most scholarly of the long line of Australian military commanders who have combined civilian achievements with gallantry in the field. A man of great personal charm and diplomacy, with a fine record of participation in community activities, he was perhaps the only Australian wartime commander to establish a really cordial working relationship with General MacArthur—which was of infinite value in easing tensions between the Allies.

To Eather's men, now firmly established on Imita Ridge and reinforced by the 3rd Battalion of the 25th Brigade, the 3rd Militia Battalion, and the 2/1st Pioneers, the quarrel between Blamey and Rowell would have been of purely academic significance. If the remnants of the 21st Brigade, still trickling back down the Kokoda Trail, heard anything about it, they would no doubt have used a wartime expression just coming into vogue and said that they "couldn't care less." The sick, shivering or burning with the recurrent agues and fevers of malaria or racked with gut-twisting dysenteries, or the fortunate ones among the wounded who had survived the dreadful journey down the trail, would have had other things to concern them. All of them, including the dead who lay in the mud, their rotting bodies sodden by the endless rains, had been defamed by MacArthur's scathing comments on their efforts.

No headquarters officer could possibly have understood what the men had undergone. Strong veteran soldiers of the A.I.F. reached the top of the trail almost exhausted by the climb, and almost at once were fighting for their lives against fanatical attacks by husky Japanese infantrymen inured to hardship since birth and whipped on by officers who deemed it a privilege to die for their Emperor. Many Australians on the Kokoda Trail, especially the eighteen-year-old youngsters of the militia, had had to fight, withdraw through knee-deep mud, and stand to fight again while suffering from one of the most debilitating of all diseases; malaria. Even for exhausted men, rest was often impossible. For the men lying in mud, shivering in thin uniforms soaked with daytime sweat and the rain which came again and again, darkness brought the hours of greatest danger. Eerie cries and whispers from the Japanese, saying "You die . . . you die!" or "Give up, Corporal Jones!" came through the black tangle of jungle, tempting the nervous to loose off a few rounds and betray his position to those who crept ever closer. And when the first light of dawn gleamed dully on the leaves it could bring a shower of mortar bombs followed at once by a shrieking pack of infantrymen, careless of their own deaths if only they could take a few Australians with them.

But the Japanese, after all, were not supermen. They too were affected by malarial parasites and dysenteric amoebae, and they were beginning to suffer from the same problems of supply which had beset the Australians earlier in the campaign. Their own brutality betrayed them, for they treated their Papuan carriers so badly that they deserted or died. They were so hungry that they fought each other for captured Australian rations, they were running short of ammunition, and since landing at Buna they had suffered an estimated 1,500 killed and at least 1,400 wounded.

On Imita Ridge, Brigadier Eather had not been content to stand on the defensive. He had initiated a series of fifty-man patrols which probed into the No Man's Land of the valley between it and Ioribaiwa, and soon began to dominate the area. With enormous effort, 25-pounder guns had been brought up the trail, and when the first of their shells exploded on the Japanese positions it sounded the death-knell of Horii's hopes. With further reinforcements denied to him by the Japanese need to maintain the pressure on Guadalcanal, where the U.S. Marines were fighting a desperate battle for control of the island, he was ordered to withdraw on 26 September.

The Australians could not at first bring themselves to believe that the enemy had pulled out. Since 23 September, they had been pushing slowly forward against determined opposition, and had had to take each Japanese position by bombs and bayonets, but on 28 September they advanced cautiously into a strange silence. Suspecting a trap, they entered Ioribaiwa at last, and found immensely strong defences dug deep in the ground and fortified with fallen trees—but all deserted. If the Japanese had made a stand there, it would have been a deadly task to root them out.

Now it was the turn of the Japanese to be harried down the Kokoda Trail. For the Australians in close pursuit, it was a grim experience. Like living corpses, the Papuan carriers whom the Japanese had starved, beaten, and then abandoned came drifting through the jungle to meet them. They found the bodies of two Australians wired to trees; one with its head hacked off, the other showing the marks of torture. Corpses, rotting food, rusting weapons and equipment, Japanese soldiers moribund from wounds or sickness, and all the dreadful debris of battle lay on or beside the trail. At one spot, they buried the remains of seventy-seven men of the 21st Brigade which still lay in the jungle among the Japanese whom they had fought to the death.

They fought spasmodic skirmishes with the Japanese rearguard, though the enemy seemed to be more intent on retreating than fighting. Eather, however, was cautious, and unwilling to risk his men to a full-scale ambush which might wipe them out. His patrols probed ahead tò make sure that the way was clear, and by 10 October the column had passed through Efogi and Myola and was edging down towards the deep gorge of Templeton's Crossing. Here, they found further signs of Japanese barbarism; the bodies of Australian soldiers from which slices had been hacked for a cannibal feast.

The advancing column had plenty of problems apart from enemy resistance. Wherever possible, the Japanese had blocked the trail by destroying log bridges or blowing in the banks of steep defiles. Supplies could not keep up with the advance, and much of the food and ammunition dropped from the air was lost forever in the jungle. In any case it was difficult to maintain a sufficient flow of supplies by such means. There was a constant wastage of men from dysentery and malaria, and when General Allen moved his headquarters to Myola he found many sufferers in the primitive hospital facilities. He had planned a two-pronged drive on Kokoda, but was forced to amend his plans to a single drive down the trail. MacArthur was urging Blamey to make more speed, Blamey urged Allen, and Allen responded bluntly that, in the circumstances, it was impossible.

Then Eather's men at last ran into the opposition which they expected.

The Japanese had dug in to defend the deep gorge through which the Eora Creek rushed down over Templeton's Crossing; dark and ominous among the overshadowing trees laced thickly with vines and rising from dripping, densely-tangled undergrowth.

It was a suicide stand of the type with which Allied soldiers were to become grimly familiar throughout the Pacific islands and South-East Asia. The Australians had to contend with desperate men who had dug hidden positions in the jungle, or lashed themselves up in the trees, and were prepared to fight to the end. For eight days, the 3rd Militia Battalion and two A.I.F. battalions strove to fight their way across the gorge, to the accompaniment of galling signals from MacArthur to Blamey and thence to Allen. MacArthur implied that the "extremely light casualties" proved that the Australians were not making a serious attempt to dislodge the Japanese, to which Allen replied furiously that fifty dead and 133 wounded at Templeton's Crossing, and a sick-list which now totalled over 700 officers and men, was proof to the contrary.

In conversations with the author, Lieutenant-General Sir Edmund Herring supported MacArthur's contention that the advance should have been pressed on more vigorously, but Colonel Buttrose, whose 2/33rd Battalion spearheaded the brigade offensive from Imita onwards, was equally emphatic that no senior officer appreciated the conditions of the battlefront. He said that the men were physically incapable of pursuing the enemy with any greater speed. General Allen, at Myola, was the first senior commander to see the difficulties for himself.

On 20 October, Eather's 25th Brigade was relieved by fresh troops of Brigadier J. E. Lloyd's 16th Brigade. They had begun the march from Port Moresby almost three weeks before, and as Brigadier Lloyd led his men towards the "Golden Stairs" he passed General MacArthur, who was making his first visit to New Guinea. With characteristic flamboyance, MacArthur said, "Lloyd, by some act of God, your brigade has been chosen for the job. The eyes of the western world are upon you. I have every confidence in you and your men. Good luck and don't stop."

As he passed on out of earshot, Lloyd remarked cynically to his brigade Intelligence Officer, "I think that our greatness should be recorded in the War Diary. Make a note of it!"

MacArthur returned to his Brisbane headquarters, having glimpsed in the distance the type of country in which the troops were fighting. The 16th Brigade plodded on, and on 20/21 October these veteran troops drove the Japanese beyond Templeton's Crossing. They were held up again by strong defences at Eora Creek village.

The track from Templeton's Crossing followed the right hand side of the great Eora Creek ravine, rising high up the mountainside through the dense, saturated jungle until not even the roar of the torrent below could be heard. Nothing could be seen but the rain forest which hemmed in the trail and was broken only by·sheer, upward rearing ridges which cut across at right angles and then plunged down to the creek.

The main stream, after flowing down the ever-deepening valley near Templeton's Crossing, had gouged a precipitous, gloomy gorge that was entered by a tributary flowing in from the south-east. The collision of the waters had churned a huge pit where they met.

The track, after climbing and descending humps and razor-back spurs, passed through the village of Eora Creek; no more than a few native huts. It crossed the first bridge, followed the echoing floor of the valley for a short distance, crossed the second bridge, and wandered north again, over a slight widening of the creek valley before thrusting up the scarred side of a mountain so steep that it was overhung by its topmost crags. As the track crossed the creek, even more forbidding cliffs rose to the right, while on the left of the track and creek junction broken country swept away in an arm of tumultuous hills and crevasses thrusting north-west to the track further on.

From 22-29 October, the Japanese clung tenaciously to their positions in this terrain of which the very confusion made it ideal for defence. The Australians attacked them with a series of frontal assaults along the exposed track and up its sheer cliffs, together with outflanking movements through the dense bush in the same style which the Japanese had used with such success. The action at Eora Creek was the 16th Brigade's baptism of fire in New Guinea, and it added further laurels to those won in the Middle East.

The fighting often developed into murderous personal conflicts, since almost every Japanese had to be killed where he stood, and few campaigns can have demanded such a high degree of skill, endurance, and initiative from every man engaged. They broke the enemy at last, but their eight days of savage fighting and losses of ninety-nine killed and 192 wounded were rewarded by the dismissal of General Allen from command of the 7th Division. MacArthur's continued nagging of Blamey about the slow advance had impelled him to replace Allen with Major-General G. A. Vasey.

As Rowell had grimly predicted to Allen, their "heads had fallen into the basket," at the prompting of an American commander whose own countrymen had not yet enjoyed an offensive success against the Japanese. The Australians, in fact, were the only Allied troops who were driving the Japanese back at that time.

This abrupt punctuation of the distinguished service given to his country by Allen, who had risen from a militia private in 1912 to A.I.F. lieutenant in 1914 including considerable front line service at Gallipoli and the Western Front, leader of the 16th Brigade in Libya and Greece and the 7th Division from Syria onwards, was compensated for by the appointment of Vasey.

A Duntroon graduate and regular soldier who had served at Gallipoli and in France, he became one of the small but devoted band of staff officers who somehow maintained the Australian military structure during the parsimonious peace of 1919-1939. The *beau ideal* of a soldier, tall, handsome, witty and fearless, who had led the 19th Brigade in Greece and on Crete, he was to acquire a high reputation for the development of jungle warfare tactics at a time when the British and American armies were just beginning to tackle this technique, and he kept the Australian Army well in advance in this field.

This Australian superiority was in fact one of the causes of ill feeling between the Australian and American armies. When the Americans fared so badly in their introduction to jungle warfare, Blamey suggested that selected officers and N.C.O.s be exchanged between the armies to expedite jungle training and mutual understanding. MacArthur refused, probably because he disliked the idea of Australians teaching the Americans their job.

Blamey also offered the services of experienced officers and men to Wavell, to help train the British and Indian units who were then faring badly in Burma. Wavell also refused, but when he was succeeded by Auchinleck the offer was made again, and accepted. General Slim asked for 400 Australian jungle warfare instructors, but only 168 were sent, though British officers were attached to Australian combat units for experience and others were trained at Canungra, Queensland; the most advanced jungle warfare training school possessed by any army.

Brigadier Lloyd's men broke the Japanese at Eora Creek on 28 October, but were halted again in the Oivi-Gorari area on 5 November. Meanwhile the 25th Brigade had been pushing along the west bank of the creek, and they occupied Kokoda on 2 November.

The re-occupation of this tiny village, in which General Vasey raised the Australian flag on 3 November, was a moment of great emotion, but even as the flag topped the rough flagpole aircraft were dropping supplies onto the vital airstrip and the work had begun of putting it into condition for aircraft landings. For the first time in the Kokoda campaign, the Australians had an airfield suitable for bringing in ample supplies and evacuating sick and wounded.

This enabled Vasey to perform the pincer movement which lack of supplies had denied to Allen. The 16th Brigade kept up their pressure in front of Oivi while the 25th Brigade came round from Kokoda to hit the enemy from the rear.

During the week of furious fighting which ended on 11 November the Australians kept up a relentless attack on the slowly tightening Japanese perimeter. They forced them to give ground yard by yard, until at last 600 Japanese lay dead among the wreckage of their defences while the survivors streamed back towards the deep gorge in which the Kumusi River thundered down to the sea. It had been a terrible battle, in which the

Australians had been forced to kill wounded Japanese because they fought back even with their bare hands, and to fire into corpses because so many Japanese shammed dead and then rose to attack from the rear. The Australians who survived it called it "The Death Valley Massacre."

For the Japanese, it was the end. The suspension bridge across the Kumusi at Wairopi had been destroyed by Allied aircraft, and they tried to cross by swimming or on crude rafts. The raging current swept most of them away, and among those drowned was General Horii himself.

The four months battle for the Kokoda Trail and the safety of Port Moresby was over. It had cost the Australians 1,680 killed and wounded, with a sick list of two to three times that number of men suffering from malaria, dysentery, and scrub typhus.

The campaign had been won for four main reasons. The Japanese had badly miscalculated the position at Milne Bay, which had aborted their double drive on Port Moresby. They had been unable to reinforce their Kokoda force because the dogged American offensive on Guadalcanal had forced them to commit an increasing number of troops to that area. And, in their expectation of a quick and easy passage across the Owen Stanley Range to Port Moresby, they had failed to set up a proper supply organisation. Their troops had had to depend on what they could carry with them.

But the most important reason for the Japanese defeat was the sheer courage of the Australian fighting man, from the eighteen-year-old militia private with only a few weeks' service to the tough veteran of one or another of the A.I.F. battalions. Allied to this was the initiative and adaptability of the Australian soldier, which enabled him to master the rules of this new kind of warfare quickly enough to beat the Japanese at their own game; and of his senior commanders who soon grasped the techniques of manoeuvring troops in territory worse than was ever dreamed of in a staff college exercise.

30

"BUNA OR BUST!"

THE FIRST AMERICAN TROOPS ARRIVED IN NEW GUINEA ON 12 SEPTEMBER 1942, and MacArthur had planned to use Major-General Harding's 32nd (American) Division to back up the Australians. The 126th and 128th Regiments of this division began to develop a track designed to outflank the Japanese at Kokoda, but by the time of Horii's death the Americans had not been used in the campaign apart from flying air support.

This did not prevent MacArthur's communiques from stating that "Allied" troops had won the long battle. Hanson Baldwin, then regarded as the doyen of American military journalists, went even further. In the *New York Times*, he stated that only the intervention of American infantry had saved the Australians from defeat, and continued: "American soldiers were rushed into action, and were instrumental in saving the day. With the Australians, they have since given the Japanese a dose of their own medicine, outflanking them and constantly infiltrating into enemy lines until the Japanese are now fighting desperately for their beach head." He added that the announcement of the presence of American infantry had clarified the apparent mystery of the precipitous Japanese retreat across the Owen Stanley Range.

General Vasey, known as "Bloody George" because of his fondness for that adjective, signalled, "Now it's Buna or bust and we won't bloody well bust!" soon after the Japanese had been beaten at Gorari, and his troops crossed the Kumusi on 16 November, over bridges improvised by the engineers.

The plans for the Buna attack already had been made, involving the first large-scale air movement of troops in the Papua-New Guinea campaigns.

The Australian 16th and 25th Brigades were to press on down the Kokoda Trail, a battalion of the American 126th Regiment to march through Jaure and attack from the south, and the rest of that regiment plus the American 128th Regiment were to fly in to Wanigela and Pongani and attack from there. By the time the Australians had crossed the Kumusi, the Americans were moving on Buna in three separate columns, supported by Australian commandos and artillery. Their entry into battle was watched with eager anticipation by the Australians, still smarting under MacArthur's criticisms, and by the American G.H.Q.

The Japanese, with their usual valour and resilience, had bounced back from their defeat and were preparing to turn their beach heads into a series of "little Tobruks" which would maintain their toeholds on Papua. Reinforcements had been landed, and a total of about 9,000 troops were now entrenched along the track from Soputa to Sanananda, in and around Buna, and at the mouth of the Kumusi. Lieutenant-General Adachi, of the Japanese 18th Army, was now in overall command of the Papua-New Guinea operations. Of the three main Japanese positions, Gona was the first to fall.

As the men of Brigadier Eather's sadly depleted 25th Brigade pushed on after crossing the Kumusi, they must have felt they were entering a new land. Gone were the precipitous mountain trails encompassed by the dark rain forests, to be replaced by the tropical lowlands of steaming vegetation and a rough track winding through flats of coarse kunai grass.

Any optimistic hopes that the Japanese might have evacuated Gona were dispelled on the morning of 19 November, when advance elements of the Australians ran into enemy positions just south of the village. The Japanese had established defences in considerable strength within an area of about 300 yards; square against the sea on the north and along Gona Creek on the west.

The Australians attacked on 22 November, but despite gaining some ground they were forced to retire early next day with heavy casualties. The brigade, already reduced to 736 men of whom most were sick, tired, and hungry, lost 204 killed and wounded in the first assault.

However, they were soon reinforced by the 21st Brigade, now under Brigadier I. N. Dougherty. As C.O. of the 2/4th Battalion, he had fought through the campaigns in Libya, Greece, and Crete. His brigade, which had taken the shock of the Japanese advance between Kokoda and Ioribaiwa, was fresh from a period of rest and refitting in which it had been built up by reinforcements from the Australian mainland. By 4 December, it had completed the relief of Eather's men and assumed responsibility for the Gona area.

As soon as his brigade had taken over, Dougherty kept his men actively engaged in offensive operations. Although several early attacks failed, the

Australians in a succession of grinding assaults finally blasted the Japanese out of their defences and entered the village on 9 December. The Japanese garrison of 800-900 was almost entirely annihilated, and 600 of their dead were buried by the Australians after resistance finally had been quelled.

The gallant 39th (Militia) Battalion, which at one stage had stood alone against the Japanese in their advance towards Port Moresby, also took part in these operations. Their hard bitten commander, Lieutenant-Colonel Honner, signalled the victory to General Vasey in the laconic phrase, "Gona's gone!"

But after the battalion had helped to extinguish the last fires of Japanese resistance, at Haddy's Village to the west of Gona, only seven officers and twenty-five men answered the roll.

These Australian operations secured the left flank of the advance, but along the Sananada Track, and at Buna, it had become confused and stalemated. The American 126th and 128th Regiments, advancing along two coastal trails from the south towards Buna, met only isolated resistance as they approached the main enemy lines, but this soon hardened. General MacArthur, with temporary headquarters in Port Moresby, was looking forward to the infusion of his American troops as a means of expediting progress in the campaign, and he instructed General Blamey that his land forces must attack the Buna-Gona area on 21 November, saying, "All columns will be driven through to objectives regardless of losses."

Major-General Harding obediently launched his troops into the offensive on the morning of 21 November, and for the next nine days utter confusion prevailed. Badly led, poorly trained, and conditioned to the soft life prior to their arrival in New Guinea, the Americans were badly mauled in their first attacks on the main Buna defences.

Bitterly disappointed, MacArthur sent for the commander of I American Corps, Lieutenant-General R. L. Eichelberger, on 29 November. Eichelberger arrived at Port Moresby on 30 November, and MacArthur told him grimly, "Bob, I'm putting you in command at Buna. Relieve Harding. I am sending you in, Bob, and I want you to remove all officers who won't fight. Relieve regimental and battalion commanders if necessary. Put sergeants in charge of battalions and corporals in charge of companies — anyone who will fight . . . I want you to take Buna, or not come back alive, and that goes for your Chief of Staff too. Do you understand?"

"Yes, sir," replied Eichelberger, and set off with the promise of high American and British honours if he accomplished the task. He arrived at Buna on the following day, and was appalled by what he found. General Harding's command structure was chaotic, the morale of the troops was low, and a general malaise hung over the whole operation.

He moved with ruthless speed and decision. He relieved Harding and two regimental commanders, replacing them with members of his own staff, and ordered an attack to be launched on 5 December, with Australian Bren-gun carriers in support.

The Americans mounted their offensive on two fronts; one against Buna village, and the other against the strong defences east of the village, along the airstrip known as New Strip.

The attack achieved some success in the village area, but the main garrison held firm and the airstrip defences could not be cracked despite more vigorous attempts by the Americans. By 10 December they had lost 1,827 men in killed, wounded, missing, and sick, and Eichelberger began to relieve the 126th Regiment with the 127th. The fresh troops gave new impetus to the attack and entered Buna village on 14 December, to find the remnants of the garrison gone. But the airstrip defences still held, and Eichelberger began preparing for a fresh assault.

He and his troops were heartened by the news that Brigadier Wootten's 18th Australian Brigade was coming into the line to take over the responsibility for the airstrip sector, and with the Australians came two troops of General Stuart tanks of the 2/16th Armoured Regiment. These men from the 1st Armoured Division had undergone intensive training in Australia for service in the Middle East, and were widely believed to be the finest division of Australians ever raised. Whether this far reaching estimate of their quality was valid or not, they were certainly the most carefully selected division of men ever recruited, but they were to be appallingly under employed. The Australian withdrawal from the Middle East, and the restricted opportunities for tank tactics in the New Guinea terrain, gave few of them the opportunity of active service for which they yearned. Those who went to Buna, however, were of a calibre that justified their high reputation.

Brigadier Wootten took over the command, including three American battalions, on 17 December. His intention was to capture the Cape Endaiadere-New Strip-Old Strip-Buna Government Station region.

The first objective was the whole coastal area between New Strip and the mouth of the Simemi Creek, where the Japanese were entrenched in a series of powerful strongpoints. Each was a small fortress cunningly concealed and camouflaged; some protected by interlaced coconut logs covered with six feet of earth, some steel roofed, and others concreted.

Wootten launched his assault at 7 a.m. on 18 December, with the Australians spearheading the operation behind seven tanks. Their extraordinary courage as they walked forward into a torrent of fire and disposed of one strongpoint after another captured the imagination of the Americans. General Eichelberger wrote after the war: "It was a spectacular and dramatic assault, and a brave one. From New Strip to the sea was about a mile. American troops wheeled to the west in support, and other Americans were assigned to mopping-up duties. But behind the tanks went the fresh and jaunty Aussie veterans, tall, mustached, erect, with their blazing Tommy guns swinging before them. Concealed Japanese positions, which were even more formidable than our patrols had indicated, burst into flame. There was the greasy smell of tracer fire, and heavy machine-gun fire from barricades and entrenchments. Steadily tanks and infantrymen advanced through the sparse, high coconut trees, seemingly impervious to the heavy opposition."

By the end of the first day, the Australians had cleared the Japanese from their positions on a line which ran from the sea due south to the east end of New Strip, despite having lost about one third of their attacking strength. But Wootten maintained the momentum of his operations with deadly intent, and each day brought further gains despite the depth of the Japanese defences. By New Year's Day 1943, he had reached Giropa Point.

The three Australian battalions of the 18th Brigade, in the operations from 18 December to January, suffered 863 casualties; about forty-five per cent of their total strength. When the 2/9th launched its attack on 18 December it faced an enemy of about twice its own strength and fighting from massively entrenched positions, so that their success was an extraordinary feat of arms. East of Giropa Point the Japanese deployed about 1,500 men, the bulk of whom were completely destroyed by the 18th Brigade offensive.

While they were fighting up the coast towards Buna from the south-east, three battalions of Americans had been trying to overwhelm a force of about 500 Japanese in the Buna village and Government Station area, which they occupied on 2 January. In the final count of the battle for Buna, almost the whole of the American 32nd Division had become involved, and the total Allied losses amounted to some 2,870 battle casualties. Of these, the Australians suffered 913; nearly a third of the total for a third of the total time involved.

The Japanese are known to have lost 1,390 men killed, of which 900 were counted east of Giropa Point, in the 18th Brigade sector, and the balance in the village and Government Station area.

Contemporary American and British historians persist in claiming Buna as a victory for the U.S. forces; a classic illustration of claims made to satisfy national pride when credit for the victory should at the very least be shared with the Australians. In fact, Buna was a shattering setback for the Americans, who were anxious to obtain a quick and decisive result in their own right. This was achieved only by the intervention of Wootten's men, who broke the back of the Japanese defences on the coast.

With the left and right flank of the Allied advance to the coast now secure, attention was once more concentrated upon Sanananda. Here, from mid-November to mid-December 1942, the 16th Australian Brigade, part of the 126th American Regiment, and finally two Australian militia battalions of the 30th Brigade had successively sapped their energies against a Japanese force which numbered upwards of 6,000 men.

Australians attacking at Kapyong, Korea (*detail from Australian War Memorial diorama by Vernon Jones*).

These had established their main defensive positions astride the Sanananda Track, some distance south of the coast, in terrain which was a mixture of heavy swamp, kunai, and thick bush.

During the first month of operations against Sanananda, men of the 16th Brigade arrived at the last stages of physical endurance after their long and arduous fight over the Owen Stanley Ranges. They launched a series of attacks against the stubborn Japanese but achieved only limited success. When General Vasey pulled them out of the line early in December, the brigade's fighting strength had been reduced to 50 officers and 488 men.

The Americans who relieved them came into the line fresh and full of confidence, and told the Australians, "You can go home now. We're here to clean things up."

But this spirit was soon broken by the malarial swamps and the savage Japanese resistance. They were relieved by Australian militia men of the 30th Brigade, who launched a series of heavy attacks on 7 December. They could not break the stalemate, and two fresh units were brought into the line to support the brigade in a series of further offensive operations from 19 December onwards. These achieved only limited success, and General Vasey reluctantly decided that he would have to wait until Buna had been eliminated before finishing the fight at Sanananda.

The character of the country, and the task before the Australian troops, was described by Major-General F. H. Berryman; an Australian acting as Eichelberger's Chief of Staff. He wrote, "Giruwa-Sanananda appeared to be the main base, with a hospital at Cape Killerton. Against this main area were three major lines of approach. Along the sea shore from Tarakena, but this was reputedly a swamp bound line which in places allowed a passage only a few yards wide, with the sea washing one side and mangrove swamps, deep and stagnant, against the other; along the main road to Sanananda, but this was held in depth by obstinate, entrenched and concealed Japanese; along tracks branching westward from the main road towards the coast west of Sanananda, but these were unfamiliar and the country they traversed was known to be largely covered by rotting marshes."

General Edmund Herring, who was in overall command of operations, on 29 December defined his plans to resume operations against the Sanananda-Cape Killerton positions as soon as Buna had been reduced. His forces would comprise the 7th Australian Division, with an American regiment attached, and three regiments of the 32nd American Division. The Australians were to attack the Japanese base frontally, from along the Sanananda Track, while the Americans moved along the coast from Buna.

After the fall of Buna and the necessary re-grouping and deployment of the Allied forces, Vasey allotted the spearhead role to Wootten and his magnificent 18th Brigade. Wootten attacked on the morning of 12 January, by sending two battalions into an outflanking movement against the Japanese

Australians at Long Tan (*detail from Australian War Memorial painting*).

defences. This resulted in a long day of murderous fighting. The steaming heat, malarial mosquitoes, and foul swamps added to the dangers and discomforts of the troops, who had to struggle through a mass of torn and twisted tree branches mutilated by artillery fire; an obstacle almost as effective as barbed wire. By nightfall it seemed that the Australians had been thwarted once more, but a Japanese soldier captured next morning revealed that all fit troops had been ordered to withdraw, leaving only the sick and wounded to defend the strongpoints.

Wootten pounced immediately. By nightfall on 14 December, his men had captured the road-junction defences which delayed the advance for so long, and from then on General Vasey did not allow the retiring Japanese a moment's respite. Their remaining defensive positions were successively overwhelmed by Australian and American troops, until organised resistance ceased on 22 January.

The defence of the Sanananda positions was a fresh demonstration of the extraordinary tenacity of the Japanese soldiers. They lost some 1,600 killed and 1,200 wounded in defending the swamp-bound terrain of Sanananda, held up the Allied advance for about two months, and inflicted heavy casualties on the Australian and American troops. In this area, the Australians lost 600 killed and 800 wounded, and the Americans 274 killed and about 400 wounded. The toll of sickness, in both armies, was even greater than these figures.

The ending of the Sanananda operations completed the first defeat of a Japanese land force during the second World War. They employed about 20,000 men in the Kokoda, Milne Bay and Buna-Gona operations, and it is known that more than 13,000 of these perished in various ways. Of the balance, some 2,000 were evacuated by sea. The fate of the remainder is not clear. Some no doubt escaped from the battle area to join comrades elsewhere on the coast, but a great many would have died of wounds, disease, or starvation. Their bones must still lie in those fearful swamps and jungles.

The Australians suffered 5,698 battle casualties between 22 July 1942 and 22 January 1943, and the Americans, during their involvement in the Buna and Sanananda sectors, lost some 2,931 men.

The victory was one of the great achievements of the second World War campaigns. The Australian Army, which bore the lion's share of the fighting, developed techniques of tactical leadership that ultimately were used with success by the British in Burma. The ordinary Australian soldier defeated an adversary who had established an almost superhuman reputation.

These successes were gained despite a disadvantage of numbers in the field, and a lack of supplies or support from either the British or the American Governments, whose forces were heavily engaged in other theatres.

Whether the bitter fighting and heavy casualties suffered in the final stages of the campaign, especially at Buna, Gona, and Sanananda, were strategically justified, is open to question. Possibly the Japanese garrisons could have been isolated and starved out, or subsequently overwhelmed by vastly superior forces, in keeping with General MacArthur's subsequent strategy in the Pacific islands. But there is no doubt that the successes were of profound importance to Allied morale, and this alone vindicates his decisions at the time.

The victory in Papua also destroyed the Japanese chances of invading Australia at the moment when, flushed with triumph and at their highest efficiency, they had the greatest likelihood of success. For this, it deserves greater recognition in contemporary history. The Coral Sea Battle and the Solomons campaign are usually recognised as the engagements that checked the course of Japanese aggression towards Australia, but these victories would have had little effect if the Japanese had been able to capture Milne Bay and Port Moresby.

31

THE MOST AUDACIOUS RAIDS

THE HUGE OPERATIONS OF THE SECOND WORLD WAR CAUSED THE average participant to be lost in the anonymity of masses of men. Countless individual deeds went unrecorded, and human courage was so common a currency that only the most outstanding feats aroused comment.

Some formations achieved a measure of glamour because they were given more deadly tasks to perform or had to display unusual fighting ability, such as the British and Australian Commandos, the Chindits in Burma, the Long Range Desert Group, and so on.

Also, there were smaller groups; specially trained and prepared for feats of particular daring. The second World War, the first conflict to be waged in the era of sophisticated technology on most continents and oceans of the world, offered unique opportunities for these.

Most of the combatant countries, whether dictatorships or democracies, had men who offered the particular blend of self-discipline, physical co-ordination, and calculating courage required for these very personal attacks upon an enemy.

The Americans launched the first bombing raid on Tokyo by flying twin-engine bombers off aircraft carriers, with crews which could not return but had to find landing places in China. The Italians, using frogmen and underwater "chariots," sank British battleships in Alexandria and freighters in Gibraltar. R.A.F. pilots burst the Mohne and Ede dams in Germany, and made the pinpoint raid on Gestapo headquarters in Copenhagen which freed its prisoners. German parachutists freed Mussolini, and British raiders kidnapped the German general in command of Crete. Men of the Royal

Navy used midget submarines to cripple the battleship *Tirpitz*, and Japanese seamen attacked Sydney Harbour in the same way.

Less publicised but more audacious than any of these were Operations Jaywick and Rimau. Their magnitude in terms of distance alone made them unique. They were roughly equal to an attack on Norway from Gibraltar, on Finland from London, or Mexico from New York—with the attackers having to make their way by sea and return to base in the same way. In the cases of Jaywick and Rimau, the attackers were in hostile and strongly held territory for the greater part of the journey. Jaywick lasted forty-seven days, from departure from Exmouth Gulf, in north-west Australia, to return to the same port. This represented nearly 5,000 miles steaming, with thirty-three days spent in Japanese-held waters near Singapore.

This almost preposterous scheme was born in the mind of Major Ivan Lyon of the Gordon Highlanders. After the surrender of Singapore, he helped the escape of hundreds of refugees and service personnel from the beleaguered city via Sumatra. When he could do no more, he and seventeen others commandeered an old proa at Padang on the west coast of Sumatra, and set sail for Ceylon.

Thirty-eight days later, while their native sailing vessel was still 300 miles south-east of Ceylon, the party was picked up by a freighter and taken to Colombo. As soon as Lyon was fit to do so, he summonsed all the influence he could muster to support a raid against Singapore from Australia. This was fairly considerable. Of a well-known Scottish family with lengthy military connections, he was the son of a brigadier. Educated at Harrow and Sandhurst, he was commissioned in 1935.

Lyon arrived in Melbourne in July 1942, and through his family connections was able to meet the Governor-General, Lord Gowrie. The latter supported his scheme, and it was backed by the First Naval Member, Admiral Sir Guy Royle, and General Sir Thomas Blamey.

With such support assured, Lyon began recruiting his team. As second-in-command, he chose another escaper from Malaya; Lieutenant D. Davidson, r.n.v.r., who was currently serving at Naval Headquarters in Melbourne. It was an excellent choice, because Davidson had spent five years as a jackaroo in Queensland and New South Wales during the late 1920s and early 1930s, and had then been employed in the teak forests of Northern Siam and Burma. Besides his knowledge of the Far East he was extremely keen on physical fitness and was an expert canoeist, a skill which he acquired on the Chindwin River in Burma.

Lyon and Davidson then selected their colleagues for Operation Jaywick. Most of these were recruited from the R.A.N. naval depot at Flinders, and the balance from A.I.F. volunteers.

Their craft, an old Japanese fishing boat which gloried in the name of *Kofuku Maru* until she was taken over by the R.N. in Singapore on the outbreak of war, had been renamed *Krait* after the deadly Indian snake. Lyon had first seen her in the Indragiri River, when she was being used to collect survivors from sunken ships who had taken refuge on the "Thousand Islands" in the Rhio Archipelago. They were taken to Sumatra, where the "Tourist Route" enabled hundreds to make good their escape to Ceylon and Australia.

The vessel intrigued Lyon, and he was delighted to hear that after she had completed her humanitarian task of survivor collection she was steamed laboriously across the Indian Ocean to Bombay under the command of Bill Reynolds, an old Australian "Eastern Hand." When Lyon was crystallising his plans for the raid on Singapore, he claimed the *Krait* as the ideal craft for the raid because she was a Japanese built ship, and not so likely to arouse suspicion as a newer, faster vessel. After abortive attempts to sail her to Australia, she was eventually shipped as deck cargo to Sydney, and unloaded in November 1942.

In September of that year, at a camp at Broken Bay north of Sydney, the selected volunteers of Z Force began a long and arduous training for their task. Physical fitness, canoeing, stealth in movement at night, an intimate knowledge of firearms, and an ability to kill with hand, cord, knife, parang, or blackjack, all became second nature to them. Davidson, in charge of training, drove his charges to the limit of their physical endurance from early in the morning to late at night, and on occasions all night as well.

They embarked in the *Krait* in January 1943, with the intention of going north to another Z Force camp at Cairns, but the engines of the old tub repeatedly broke down and she took nearly two months to complete the voyage. This upset the whole schedule, because Lyon was hoping to launch the attack on 15 February, the date on which Singapore had fallen, by way of reminding the victors that they would not enjoy their spoils for very long.

Another volunteer had been appointed to command the *Krait* for the operation. He was Lieutenant H. E. Carse, R.A.N.V.R., who had graduated from the Royal Australian Naval College in 1918 and joined the Home Fleet of the Royal Navy just in time to see the once proud ships of the Kaiser's fleet being scuttled in Scapa Flow.

His utter disdain for all authority was one of the main reasons for his retirement from the navy during the 1920s to pursue a variety of occupations which included those of schoolteacher, merchant seaman, pearl fisherman, factory cleaner, camel driver, and S.P. bookmaker. He was, however, regarded as an outstanding navigator, with an intimate knowledge of the tropics from his early navy days and subsequent pearling out of Thursday Island and along the northern coasts.

He volunteered for naval service in 1939, was rejected on health grounds, but accepted when he volunteered again in 1942 and the emergency had made the authorities less meticulous.

Another officer chosen for the party was Lieutenant R. C. Page, an A.I.F. volunteer. Page had successfully completed his second year of medical studies at Sydney University in 1939, but abandoned his medical career for the time being in order to join the army. He was on his way to Dutch Timor with A.I.F. units when the Japanese attacked Darwin, and his ship, much to his disappointment, was recalled. He had a personal reason for wanting to take on the Japanese, because his father, who won the D.S.O. and M.C. in the first World War, had been Deputy Administrator of New Britain and was captured during the invasion of Rabaul. Later he was to lose his life aboard the prison ship *Monte Video Maru*, which was torpedoed off Luzon.

In 1942 Lieutenant Page was twenty-one, and a representative of the finest qualities of Australian youth, with beliefs which he put into words with his comment to Carse that, "A man must be ready not only to fight, but to give his life and give it gladly."

By August 1943, all was ready for the adventure. The final composition of the raiding party had been determined, after a number whose physical or temperamental characteristics were not considered adequate had been dropped. The *Krait* had been overhauled and new engines installed, and the party had reached the peak of its training.

At midnight on 9 August 1943, Carse navigated the *Krait* out of Cairns on the first stage of the operation; the 2,400 mile journey across the north of Australia to Exmouth Gulf, the launching point of Operation Jaywick. Besides himself, those on board were:

Army officers and men: Major Ivan Lyon, D.S.O., M.B.E., Gordon Highlanders; Lieutenant R. C. Page, D.S.O., A.I.F.; Corporal A. Crilley, M.M., A.I.F.; Corporal R. G. Morris, B.E.M., M.M., R.A.M.C.

Naval officer and men: Lieutenant D. M. N. Davidson, D.S.O., Leading Stoker J. P. McDowell, D.S.M., Leading Telegraphist H. C. Young, M.I.D.; Acting Leading Seaman R. P. Cain, M.I.D.; Acting Able Seamen W. G. Fales, D.S.M.; A. M. W. Jones, D.S.M.; A. W. Huston, D.S.M.; F. W. Marsh, M.I.D.; M. M. Berryman, M.I.D.; all of the Royal Australian Navy. (Decorations shown were in most cases awarded after the raid.)

They reached Exmouth Gulf eighteen days after leaving Cairns. It was a major submarine base for the U.S. Navy, and operated under the code name "Potshot." Their voyage had been uneventful except for occasional sightings of Japanese aircraft, which had not molested them, and a near disaster on an uncharted reef, avoided by Carse's navigational instincts.

On 1 September, after four days at Potshot, during which they had replenished their supplies and received four new canoes flown out from England as top priority, they cast off their lines and set sail amidst a generous farewell from their American hosts. But they had barely got under way when the *Krait*'s engine ground to an embarrassing standstill, and it was discovered that the coupling key of the intermediate propeller shaft had sheared. The U.S. Navy engineers worked round the clock to repair the damage, and by mid-afternoon of the following day all was ready again. "Don't forget to have that shaft fixed when you reach Fremantle," the engineers advised them solemnly. The Americans had asked no questions, but no doubt guessed that the *Krait* was not on a training mission. Their main wonder was whether she would even reach the end of the Exmouth Gulf.

But she steamed out of the Gulf into a fresh southerly breeze, the Blue Ensign was struck, and Operation Jaywick had begun. Naturally her crew had speculated at length as to their target, and on the first day out Major Lyon mustered all hands and informed them that it was to be shipping in Singapore Harbour.

He explained that it was proposed to enter the Java Sea through Lombok Strait, and then sail to an island near Singapore. The attack would be launched from this location, with the *Krait* probably hiding in the waters off Sumatra.

The Japanese flag was hoisted, and the *Krait* became to all intents and purposes an enemy fishing vessel. All went smoothly until they were five days out of Exmouth, when the tall mountains on Bali and Lombok heralded the approach to Lombok Straits, which are twenty-five miles wide. The extent of Japanese defences in the area was virtually unknown, and the little ship sailed into the dusk with those on board watching tensely for the first challenge.

It came from nature, and not from man. They entered the Straits, abeam of Nusa Besar, as the last light of day merged with the tropical evening, and the *Krait*'s top speed of six and three-quarter knots began to battle against the full current pouring south from the Java Sea. She struggled gamely onwards throughout the night, with Japanese searchlights playing across the waters from both sides, but when daylight came they found themselves still in the middle of the Strait with Nusa Besar only six miles astern. They felt certain that they would be challenged by Japanese naval patrols, but to watchers from the shore the *Krait* must have looked like an ordinary fishing boat.

It took them sixteen hours to get through the Lombok Straits, but they emerged at last into the Java Sea and for the next ten days steamed through the steep jungle-clad islands scattered over its placid waters.

At last, as they approached the Rhio Islands, signs of enemy activity increased. Aircraft droned overhead, steam-ships were seen in the distance, and they saw many junks and other native craft. Lyon's choice of the old *Krait* was justified again and again as the old fishing-vessel waddled onwards, obviously taken for granted by every other craft in the area.

On the night of 17/18 September, 1943, they unloaded their gear on Pandjang Island, thirty miles from Singapore, and Lyon arranged with Carse for the *Krait* to return at midnight on 1/2 October. Pompong Island was chosen for the rendezvous, since it was regarded as safer than Pandjang though fifty miles further away. In the meantime, Carse was to steam into the South China Sea, and hide the ship among the islands off the Borneo coast.

The attacking parties assembled their three canoes and gear on the afternoon of 20 September. Each canoe was stored with food for a week, which together with limpet mines and arms made up a total weight of about a third of a ton. The teams were Lyon and Huston, Davidson and Fales, and Page and Jones.

They canoed in easy stages towards the target until 23 September, when they made Dongas Island their final assault base. They were now twenty-one days and 2,000 miles from Exmouth Gulf, with the prize of Singapore lying before their eyes barely eight miles away across the Straits. They could see the movements of Japanese shipping in and out of the harbour, and assessed that about 65,000 tons, including three tankers, were lying at anchor in the Roads.

Apparently the Japanese in Singapore felt quite secure against raids of any kind. At night, the raiders could see that the city was not even blacked out, and that the lights along the waterfront would give them a clear guide into the harbour. Their first attempt, however, was aborted by the strong currents, so they changed camp to Subar Island, seven miles west of Dongas.

On 26 September they made their final plans. Davidson and Fales would enter Keppel Harbour, Lyon and Huston the Examination Anchorage, and Page and Jones the oil refinery berths at Palau Bukum. That night they donned their black suits, blackened their faces, and slid their heavily loaded canoes into the water at about 8 p.m.

Singapore Harbour is a huge expanse of water stretching from the straits to the low, gently-curving coast and waterfront of Singapore Island, and protected on each side by numbers of small islands lying closely together. Its surface provides a placid anchorage for large ships, but can be choppy for small craft. The three canoes crept across it towards their targets, through darkness pierced by searchlights sweeping the sky and harbour and lights twinkling from wharves and ships. If they were seen, they were not challenged, but in all likelihood their silhouettes were so low that they escaped notice.

At last, almost unable to believe that they had got so far without being spotted, they let the canvas hulls of their canoes drift against the steel sides of the targets. The enemy was only a matter of yards away, but apparently was somnolent in the seeming security of the tropical midnight. In tense silence, the raiders carried out the motions which they had practised many times, and fixed the limpet mines to the steel, but even when these were clamped fast they were not out of danger. The long paddle back to their island camp still lay before them.

Page, Jones, Lyon and Huston grounded their canoes just as the first streaks of dawn were lighting the sky, and staggered ashore exhausted by the tension and physical effort of hours of paddling. Davidson and Fales reached Batam Island, seven miles from Dongas, and were to be the first crew to reach Pompong, their rendezvous point with the *Krait*. At 5.15 a.m., they were rewarded by the sound of a muffled explosion, and for the next twenty minutes the sound of successive charges rumbled across the waters.

The limpet mines shattered the complacency of the garrison as well as wrecking the ships to which they were attached, and a hornet's nest of Japanese aircraft and patrol boats burst out over the area. Tired as they were, the crews on Subar Island had to push on, and dodged from island to island, battling against adverse currents, until they reached Pompong at 3 a.m. on 2 October. Davidson and Fales had arrived twenty-three hours ahead of schedule, and had been picked up, but the other four men could see nothing of the *Krait*. Unable to go any further from sheer exhaustion, they dragged their canoes ashore and collapsed on the beach—and woke at daybreak to see the *Krait* sailing past them into the waters round nearby islands.

They had landed on the wrong beach, but had forty-eight hours in which to reach the next rendezvous. A party of Malay fishermen was camped on the island, so Lyon bribed them with Dutch gold guilders into selling the food which made it possible for the party to continue. They pushed off again, reached the next rendezvous safely, and were picked up by the *Krait*.

Seven days later, after an uneventful crossing of the Java Sea despite a mammoth sea and air search mounted by the Japanese, the *Krait* neared the Lombok Straits again, and her crew prepared for the second passage through these dangerous waters. Once through, Australia would be only 800 miles away—but the major Japanese sea and air base of Surabaya was only 120 miles away, and there were airfields on both Bali and Lombok islands.

The current was running with them this time, and they made good progress for half an hour after they entered the Strait at 11 p.m. on 12 October. It was a clear moonlight night, with the loom of the land distinct on each side, and suddenly the lookouts saw a dark shape moving towards them.

It was a Japanese destroyer approaching at high speed, her white bow wave glittering in the moonlight. She came close enough for her guns and upperworks to be seen silhouetted against the clear sky, and then turned to sail parallel with the *Krait* and only about a hundred yards away. The crew of the *Krait* crouched under cover, weapons in hand and determined to fight to the death rather than surrender to the horrors of capture by the Japanese.

The destroyer moved ahead, slowed, and then allowed the *Krait* to pass her, while the Australians waited tensely for the sudden glare of a searchlight and a harsh challenge. They waited for ten apprehensive minutes, and then the destroyer suddenly put her helm down and steamed towards Lombok Island.

By midnight the *Krait* was out of the straits, and by daylight was well out into the Indian Ocean with her crew revelling in the fresh, free winds of a strong south-easter. Lyon decided to break radio silence, and sent the coded message: TO AUSTRALIAN COMMONWEALTH NAVAL BOARD FROM KRAIT MISSION COMPLETED FOR ADMIRAL CHRISTIE (COMMANDING U.S. SUBMARINES EXMOUTH) LOMBOK NOW PATROLLED ETA 17AR.

The *Krait* anchored at "Potshot" on 19 October, and received a heroes' welcome from the Americans. The raid had resulted in seven ships totalling approximately 39,000 tons, including the 10,000 ton tanker *Sinkoku Maru* which had been the victim of Page and Jones, being sunk or damaged.

The success of Operation Jaywick inspired Lyon to plan another raid on the same target, using different methods. Called Operation Rimau by the Australians, and *Tora Kohsaku Tai* by the Japanese, it was to be a tragic failure.

Davidson and Page, the latter now promoted to captain, felt strong misgivings at Lyon's proposed method of attack, but loyalty to their leader prompted them to volunteer for the second operation. Able Seamen Fales, Marsh, and Huston also volunteered again, and were joined by Major R. N. Ingleton, Royal Marines, representing South-East Asia Command; Lieutenant B. Reymon, R.A.N.R.; Lieutenants A. L. Sargent and W. G. Carey, A.I.F.; Lieutenant H. R. Ross of the British Army; Sub-Lieutenant J. G. M. Riggs, R.N.V.R.; Warrant Officers J. Willersdorf and A. Warren, A.I.F.; Sergeants D. P. Gooley and C. B. Cameron, A.I.F.; and Corporals A. S. R. Campbell, C. M. Stewart, C. M. Craft, R. B. Fletcher, and Lance-Corporals J. T. Hardy and H. J. Page and Private D. R. Warne, all of the A.I.F.

Originally, Operation Rimau was planned as part of a larger attack in conjunction with raids sponsored by South-East Asia Command, operating out of Ceylon against Saigon as well as Singapore. This plan was abandoned, and Lyon proceeded with his own scheme.

The plan was to sail by submarine from Garden Island, in Western Australia, into the South China Sea. There they would capture a Chinese junk of convenient size, and use it as camouflage wherein to enter enemy waters and launch their "Sleeping Beauties."

These were electrically powered submersible metal boats, rather resembling Eskimo kayaks. Each boat carried one man, who rode it clad in what was then a new type of suit; the prototype of the SCUBA diving gear in common use nowadays. The intention was to ride the Sleeping Beauties to the targets, affix limpet mines, and return to the pirated mother ship.

This would sail to an island for rendezvous with the submarine, which would return the crew to Australia.

The raiders trained on Garden Island, off Fremantle, where many more Australian saboteurs who eventually found their way behind Japanese lines were schooled in their deadly arts. The Sleeping Beauties were tested in Cockburn Sound, where they proved to be technically deficient and hard to handle, but it was decided to continue with the operation.

On 11 September 1944 the party embarked in *Porpoise*, a mine laying submarine, with their equipment of fifteen Sleeping Beauties, eleven canoes, and fifteen tons of supplies apart from arms, ammunition, grenades, limpet mines, and radio sets.

They reached Merapas, the most easterly island of the Rhio Archipelago, on 23 September, and Lyon decided to establish a rear base on the island. They unloaded their supplies during the next two nights, and left Lieutenant Carey, an experienced commando, to guard them.

The submarine then sailed to Pejantan island, about 140 miles to the east, which was to be used as a forward base. The first step was the pirating of a junk, and on 28 September the 100-ton Canton type junk *Mustika* hove into the submarine's periscope lenses, near the small lonely island of Datu about eighty miles from Pejantan.

Her terrified Malay captain and eight-man crew saw the *Porpoise* surface close astern, and a few minutes later Lyon and Davidson led a party of seven armed men aboard. The junk crew co-operated without resistance, and showed the pirates how to sail their prize. A course was set for Pejantan, with the *Porpoise* idling along below the surface in the daytime, and taking the junk in tow at night.

At Pejantan they transferred their equipment from the submarine to the junk, completing the operation during the night of 30 September-1 October. At 3 a.m. the two craft parted company and the *Porpoise* returned to Fremantle.

From that moment onwards, the course of events must to a large extent be conjectured, though Ronald McKie, in his splendid book *The Heroes*, has undoubtedly come as close to the truth as anyone is likely to at this time.

He believes that the *Mustika* sailed for Singapore via Merapas Island, where they left an uncertain number of men to join Carey in guarding their base supplies. In the afternoon of 6 October 1944 they hove to at Laban Island, about ten miles south-east of Keppel Harbour and only four miles from Subar, whence Operation Jaywick had been launched a year before. Here, their luck ran out.

A small patrol boat, run by three Malay water police, sailed close to the junk. In answer to a shouted challenge, for some reason somebody on board the *Mustika* opened fire. He killed two of the police, but the third man was able to take the boat out of range and speed back towards Singapore.

Lyon realised that he would alert the base, and decided to abandon the operation. He sailed the junk south until they reached the island of Kapala Jernih, and that night they blew up the *Mustika* with limpet mines and took to four of the canoes which had been part of their equipment.

100 miles of sea lay between them and Merapas Island, but they had more than a month in which to get there. The rendezvous date with the *Porpoise* was 8 November.

The rendezvous was never kept; partly because, for some never-explained reason, the *Porpoise* did not arrive at Merapas until fourteen days after the agreed date.

By that time, the remnants of the party had been captured by the Japanese. It seems likely that Lyon, Davidson, and some others were killed before they reached Merapas, in a series of running engagements with the Japanese. Those who remained of the four canoe parties landed on Merapas, were discovered by the Japanese on 4 November, and fought their way free again. During the following weeks they were gradually rounded up by the Japanese but sold their lives very dearly. Twelve were killed during the enemy attempts to capture them.

Lieutenant A. L. Sargent, with two others whose identity has never been established, made what must be the most remarkable escape in military history. They paddled their canoe for two thousand miles through the Japanese net, from the Rhio Islands past Sumatra, Borneo, Java, Lombok, Flores, Alor and Wetar to Romang Island, north-east of Timor and only about 400 miles from Darwin. Here their canoe foundered, and they crawled ashore too exhausted to go any further. They were handed over to the Japanese, who took them back to Singapore to join the rest of the eleven survivors.

In February, their "examination" began, on three charges. Firstly that they had infiltrated Japanese-occupied territory wearing jungle-green uniforms without emblems, while being members of the Army, Navy, or Marines. Secondly that while passing through the Rhio Archipelago they had made sketches of ships. Since they were not in proper uniform this was an act of espionage. Thirdly that, while disguised as natives and in a ship flying the Japanese flag, they attacked and killed members of a Malay police patrol serving under Japanese command. Though sailing under false colours was recognised as a legitimate ruse of war, they had not struck the Japanese flag, nor raised their own, before attacking.

During their interrogation, Captain Page was told by an interpreter that a group of Chinese had been accused of sinking or damaging the ships which the Jaywick party had attacked in Singapore, and that they had been sentenced to death. Though Page realised that a confession would not help the cause of his friends and himself, he could not permit innocent men to suffer. He told the Japanese, who were still ignorant of how their shipping had been attacked, the complete details of the Jaywick operation, and the Chinese were released.

The Japanese had showed unusual kindness towards their prisoners, but by the end of May had decided that they must be court-martialled. The trial, on 5 July, lasted for several hours, but the raiders knew that their fate was a foregone conclusion.

The prosecutor eulogised their spirit and courage, which he compared to those of traditional Japanese heroes, but they were sentenced to death.

On 7 July, the eleven survivors were taken from the notorious Outram Road jail to a lonely part of Singapore Island, and ceremoniously executed. Major-General M. Otsuka, Chief of the Judicial Affairs Section of the Japanese 7th Army in Singapore, who was himself to be hanged for war crimes, reported to a staff conference on the "patriotism, fearless enterprise, heroic behaviour and sublime end" of all members of this party. He praised them as "The flower of chivalry, which should be taken as a model by the Japanese," and concluded: "All Japanese soldiers should be inspired by their fine attitude, and on reflection must feel the necessity of bracing up their own spirits in emulation if they hope to win the war."

A few days later the Japanese Commander-in-Chief, General S. Itagaki, who was a ruthless officer of the old order, told the full staff of the 7th Army that: "We Japanese have been proud of our bravery and courage in action, but those heroes showed us a fine example of what true bravery should be. Unless we try much harder to make ourselves better soldiers, we ought to feel ashamed of ourselves before these heroes."

Only a month after their execution, the atom bomb was dropped on Hiroshima. Nine days later, Japan surrendered.

Posthumous awards were made of the D.S.O. to Captain Robert Page and the D.S.M. to Able Seamen Fales and Huston, but wartime censorship and the uncertainty of the raiders' fate kept the story of Operations Jaywick and Rimau from the Australian public until about a year later, when the Minister for the Army, Mr F. Forde, gave a brief description of the operations to the House of Representatives. The full story, so far as it is known, was not told until the publication of Ronald McKie's book. The extreme parsimony with which awards for bravery were made when Australian forces were not under British command has frequently been commented upon. The magnificent success of Operation Jaywick under the conditions described is a classic example of this situation. Many Victorian Crosses have been awarded for less hazardous enterprises. But a mention in dispatches for the captain of the *Krait*, Lieutenant Carse, must surely rank as one of the meanest examples of recognition ever made.

The operations did not alter the course of the war, but their memory remains as a tribute to the courage, spirit, and endurance of the British and Australians who took part in them.

32

THE DRIVE TO SALAMAUA

A LONG AND BLOODY CAMPAIGN HAD BEEN WON, BUT THE JAPANESE were far from beaten. Nor had they given up hope of advancing from the north coasts of Papua and New Guinea to Port Moresby. With their defeat at Buna and Gona, Papua was for the time being lost to them. But they still had a foothold in New Guinea; at Salamaua, along the coast to the north-west of Gona. When the Milne Bay-Kokoda Trail thrusts began in August 1942, they commenced to move inland and occupied Mubo on 31 August.

They had not been forgotten by the Australians. A previous chapter has described how the 5th Independent Company and the New Guinea Volunteer Rifles harried them at Lae and Salamaua, and, even during the Kokoda Trail fighting, Blamey had been planning an offensive to prise them loose.

The Australians in the area, known as Kanga Force, had continued to pester them with minor raids and to report their movements to Port Moresby. When they made their move to Mubo, Kanga Force kept in close contact and on 1 October made an attack designed to show them that they were not yet masters of the area.

Kanga Force was reinforced by the 2/7th Independent Company, and with consummate bushcraft the force survived in an area which was alive with enemy patrols and made frequent forays against the enemy. On 11 January 1943, about 300 men attacked Mubo again. They moved stealthily into position along three jungle trails, caught the enemy unawares, and killed more than a hundred.

By coincidence, they had hit the Japanese just as the enemy had been preparing for a major drive from Mubo towards Wau, as a diagonal approach

to Port Moresby. They had conceded victory to the Americans on Guadalcanal and to the Australians in Papua, but were now concentrating for their
next attempt. The Kanga Force strike made them think that an Australian
counter-attack was beginning in the Wau-Mubo area, and they landed
troops at Nassau Bay, between Salamaua and Gona, to make another thrust
towards Wau and save their main body from being outflanked.

The battle exploded almost immediately. Kanga Force had to retire
towards Wau, but by a further coincidence Blamey had ordered the 17th
Brigade, under Brigadier M. J. Moten, to relieve them, and the brigade
began to fly into Wau on 14 January. Fortunately they and their commander
were veterans of Libya, Greece, Crete, and in some cases Syria, because the
first units to leave the aircraft were sent directly into action against the
advancing Japanese.

These consisted of between 2,000 and 3,000 of their 51st Division, who had
fought the Chinese at Shanghai and garrisoned French Indo-China. They
moved towards Wau along a forgotten track through the jungle from Nassau
Bay, so that Australian patrols were taken unawares. Bad weather and a
shortage of transport delayed the remaining two battalions of the 17th
Brigade, and by 28 January the men of the 2/6th Battalion were in a critical
position. Despite desperate fighting on the approaches to Wau, and the
daring raids by men of Kanga Force, the superior Japanese forces had been
able to push steadily onwards. By 29 January their mortar fire was falling on
Wau airfield as they pressed closely around the outskirts of the little town
which had developed as a centre for the goldfields in the surrounding hills.

By that time, however, General Kenney of the U.S. Air Force had
assembled more transport aircraft and the skies were clearing somewhat, so
the rest of the 17th Brigade was landed in the nick of time. As the aircraft
circled for landing the pilots could see the flashes of gunfire in the jungle
and the spouts of smoke and earth from bursting mortar shells, and the
infantrymen were warned to be ready for immediate action. The landing
wheels had hardly stopped rolling before the men were pouring out of the
aircraft and running to take up their positions, while the machine which had
brought them in was taking off again to make room for another.

Artillery as well as infantrymen were landed on the airfield, and the Australians fought with such determination that by 5 February the Japanese had
been forced to withdraw and were falling back towards Mubo. Their first
probe towards Wau cost them 1,200 men, but this did not cause them to
abandon their plans for another drive on Port Moresby. They determined
to land more men and to advance from the mouth of the Markham River
through the Snake River valley, so a considerable convoy of reinforcements
sailed from Rabaul to make this attempt.

The ships were sighted by reconnaissance aircraft, and General Kenney's
American and Australian fighter and bomber squadrons were sent to attack

them. In the Battle of the Bismarck Sea they swooped on the seven transports and nine escorting vessels, and sank all the transports and four destroyers. About 2,300 troops were drowned, and only 900 reinforcements reached Lae; an important American achievement in view of the operations being planned to drive the Japanese out of the north coast of New Guinea.

General Blamey had now returned to Australia, leaving General Iven Mackay in command in New Guinea. Mackay defined the strategy planned by Blamey when he signalled Moten: "I would be glad if you would give consideration to the question of inflicting a severe blow upon the enemy in the Salamaua area. Should you find your initial stages unsuccessful and come up against conditions and arrangements for defence as they were in the Gona-Buna area, you should not allow your force to become involved in operations amounting to siege conditions as existed in the areas referred to."

Moten moved at once. His 16th Brigade and supporting troops isolated the enemy base at Mubo, and by mid-April his men were deployed close to Salamaua and along the track leading to the major Japanese base at Lae. With Australian troops poised to take the initiative, supported by increasing American and Australian air strength in transport, supply, and offensive operations, it was a satisfactory conclusion to the fifteen months of campaigning which had begun with the massacre of Australians at Rabaul.

Much of the credit must go to Blamey, subsequent to Curtin's dogged refusal to allow Churchill to divert the 6th and 7th Divisions to Burma. Had he done so the picture would have been very different, because the commanders, officers, and men of those divisions played a vital part in defeating the first three Japanese thrusts towards Port Moresby. It was an unfortunate miscalculation by the British Prime Minister, whose overriding concern for Britain's Imperial interests, to the detriment of an Australia fighting for her life, cast a grave reflection on his judgement.

Blamey's influence upon the strategic handling of the early Papua-New Guinea campaigns has been greatly underestimated. He had transformed the Australian Army from a force accustomed to fighting under British Commanders-in-Chief into an integral formation fully capable of tackling warfare under the worst possible conditions. His dismissal of Rowell and Allen, under the pressure of MacArthur's desperate demands for a victory, often has been held against him, but in military life nothing counts but success and there are no second prizes. It may well be that the dynamic and ruthless personality of Blamey was exactly what was needed to send the Australians on to the victory which they gained in Papua.

*   *   *

On 23 April, command of the Wau area and of the operations directed towards the Japanese along the coast was given to Major-General S. G. Savige; a commander of great experience in both World Wars from

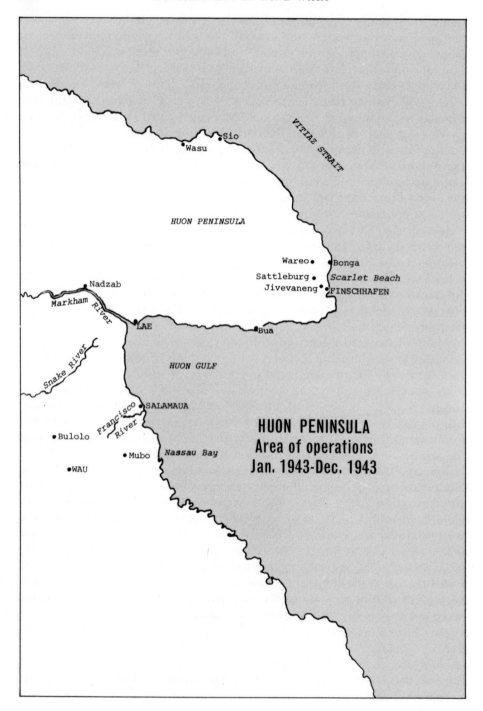

VITIAZ STRAIT

• Sio
• Wasu

HUON PENINSULA

Wareo •   • Bonga
Sattleburg •   *Scarlet Beach*
Jivevaneng •   • FINSCHHAFEN

• Nadzab

Markham River

• LAE   • Bua

HUON GULF

Snake River

Francisco River

• SALAMAUA

• Bulolo

Nassau Bay

• Mubo

• WAU

HUON PENINSULA
Area of operations
Jan. 1943-Dec. 1943

Gallipoli to Syria. But despite his gallant and distinguished military record, perhaps his most lasting monument is his record of service as one of the founders of Legacy; the unique Australian association which is devoted to the care of dependants of those killed on active service, or who have died as a result of disabilities incurred in service.

By March of that year, the plans of the Allied Chiefs of Staff showed that any New Guinea offensive would be largely an Australian affair. Europe still had priority, with Pacific operations confined to the Solomons area for the Americans apart from the I American Corps in the Australian sphere. The Japanese, whose Solomons and New Guinea operations were directed from Rabaul, could deploy upwards of 100,000 men throughout the south-west Pacific. Of these, Adachi's 18th Army of three divisions was concentrated on New Guinea.

Australian reinforcements were secured by the passing of the Citizen Military Forces Act in February, which provided that the militia could be required to serve within an area bordered approximately by the western tip of Borneo in the west and the Solomons in the east. Previously, they had enlisted to serve only within Australia and her territories.

In May, MacArthur directed Blamey and Lieutenant-General Walter Krueger, commander of the American Sixth Army, to prepare for operations designed to recapture the Lae-Salamaua-Finschhafen-Madang area, establish bases and airfields on Kiriwina and Woodlark Islands, and occupy western New Britain.

Savige's 3rd Australian Division already had begun to take the first steps towards this end. During April and May, they fought a series of stiff actions with the Japanese in the jungle area between Wau and Salamaua, ranging from patrol clashes to several bloody attacks on a feature known as the Pimple and on Bobdubi and Lababia Ridges. Their main task was to keep the Japanese in check and to prevent penetration inland, but on 17 May, Blamey indicated the plans designed to seize the Lae area.

Following the fall of Mubo, Savige's command was supplemented by a regiment of American infantry landed at Nassau Bay, south of Salamaua. The initial role of the combined force was to isolate the Japanese garrison there and prevent them from receiving further supplies or reinforcements by land, without actually initiating a direct attack on the enemy base. It was also hoped that control of the coastal area would assist in relieving the critical supply position of the Australians fighting inland, but as it transpired it was a hope that went largely unsatisfied. Herring's instructions to him said: "Your role is still first of all to drive the enemy north of the Francisco River. The capture of Salamaua is of course devoutly to be wished but no attempt upon it is to be allowed to interfere with the major operation being planned. The role of the 3rd Australian Division during the main operation will be to hold in the Salamaua area, if not already in your hands, the maximum number of the enemy." He was to take Goodview Junction, Mount Tambu, and the ridges running down to Tambu Bay.

From the landing at Nassau Bay to the moment when Australian and American troops closed in on Salamaua, the campaign took three months of bloody and almost incessant fighting. The units under Savige spread a net which stretched from Lababia Ridge in the south-east to the upper waters of the Francisco River in the north-east, and contained the Japanese positions at Mubo, Lababia Ridge, the Pimple, Observation Hill, Bobdubi Ridge, Old Vickers Position, Komiatum Ridge, Davidson Ridge, Charlie Hill, Scout Ridge, Roosevelt Ridge, and Bitoi Ridge. Approximately in its centre was Mount Tambu, which was the most bitterly defended of all.

Slowly the net was closed, but the conquest of each Japanese position was a full scale battle on its own; most savagely resisted by the Japanese and most determinedly pressed home by the Australians, who formed the bulk of the Allied Force, and the Americans. Nor were the Japanese content with defence alone. They counter-attacked continually, and the Allied gains had to be held against furious assaults by an enemy who had to be forced back to yet another of the deadly ridges—and then attacked again in a new position.

All the troops engaged, on each side, were becoming experts in this fear-some style of warfare. American and Australian aircraft flew above the ridges, often in abominable weather, to drop supplies or to strafe the enemy positions. New units reaching the front had their initial failures through lack of experience, such as the initial inability of the Australian 58th/59th Battalion to capture Old Vickers Position and Orodubi and the American confusion after the landing at Nassau Bay. But they learnt fast, and ground the Japanese northwards towards the Francisco. With their own dead and wounded, and those who succumbed to the jungle diseases despite the vastly improved medical services, they paid the toll required by their orders that they should draw the enemy towards them from Lae. In this they succeeded most excellently, because the savagely mauled Japanese 51st Division had to be reinforced again and again by fresh troops brought down to the killing ground.

At Mount Tambu, they seemed for a while to be unconquerable. General Herring had ordered fresh troops and artillery to be landed at Tambu Bay, and Brigadier Moten decided upon a policy of encirclement after a series of frontal attacks had failed. The Americans stormed and captured Roosevelt Ridge, seaward of Mount Tambu, and the American and Australian batteries began to pound the positions around the mount. A two-pronged attack began to drive the Japanese off the ridges north and south, and as soon as they found themselves being trapped the enemy withdrew north-wards from Mount Tambu.

At last they were fighting with their backs to the Francisco River, which

Australian troops already had crossed further up, and then their whole resistance began to crumble and they fell back on positions protecting Salamaua. By 20 August, the Australians were looking down from the jigsaw of the ridges to the coastline below Salamaua and the shimmering waters of Huon Gulf. They continued to press the retreating Japanese, but by this time had done all that was required of them. On 22 August, Savige signalled Brigadier Hammer, of the Australian 15th Brigade, "Situation most satisfactory, but on no account undertake any operation which may influence the enemy to evacuate Salamaua."

Four days later General Savige's 3rd Division headquarters was relieved by that of the 5th Division, under Major-General E. J. Milford. He was a regular soldier who had graduated from Duntroon in 1915, and was now on active service for the first time in the second World War. He had commanded the 5th Division since it had been deployed in North Queensland in anticipation of an invasion of the mainland. The 17th Brigade, which had been almost constantly in action since beating off the attack on Wau airfield, was relieved by Brigadier R. F. Monaghan's 29th Brigade.

For the time being, while the attack on Lae was being prepared, the troops east of Salamaua were used for harassing attacks and patrol actions designed to distract the enemy. The assault on Lae·began on 4 September, and from then onwards the Australians surged forwards upon Salamaua, so that the Japanese had to fight on two fronts.

A race between Hammer's 15th Brigade and Monaghan's 29th Brigade began, with Salamaua the prize. Despite the most sacrificial resistance from the Japanese, they cleaned up one enemy position after another. The Japanese fought grimly north of the Francisco River, in an effort to block the advance into the flat country around Salamaua, but on 8 September the remnants of their 51st Division were ordered to withdraw. The Australians heard that the final drive on Salamaua was to be performed by the Americans, while the 29th Brigade was to secure the Kela area, west of the town, and then continue the advance towards Lae, and the 15th Brigade held firm on the coast halfway between Kela and Mission Point. But the 42nd Battalion of the 29th Brigade beat everyone into Salamaua, which was secured on 13 September. The onset of torrential rains, which flooded the creeks and rivers, slowed down any further advance, and the survivors of the Japanese force escaped towards Lae.

On 16 September, 1943, the Australians hoisted over Salamaua the flag which the New Guinea Rifles had taken with them when they were forced to abandon the town in early 1942. Salamaua, for which so much blood had been shed on both sides, was described as "a filthy, rat ridden, pestilential hole."

During the campaign which ended with the capture of the town, the Japanese suffered 8,100 casualties, including 2,722 killed. The Australians, between April and September, lost 358 killed and 776 wounded. Of the Americans, 81 were killed and 396 wounded.

In a special Order of the Day congratulating the Australians, General Herring wrote: "The capture of Salamaua marks the end of a campaign in which the Australians had performed a magnificent job in out-fighting the enemy despite difficult terrain and trying conditions." He addressed his message, "privately to all of you who have borne the heat and burden of the fighting; to the infantry first and foremost." But he did not forget those in support; the gunners, engineers, signallers, medical services, air forces, and service troops.

The overall Australian strategy had been a complete success, since it had kept the Japanese looking towards Salamaua, and wasting their strength in that campaign while the Allies were preparing to attack Lae. As late as 4 September their 51st Division commander, General Nakano, had been preparing to defend Salamaua in accordance with his orders that, "The main body of the Salamaua Peninsula unit will at once build and strengthen positions."

During the year, the entire aspect of the campaign had been radically changed. In February, the Japanese were preparing for their third and last thrust towards Port Moresby. This had been foiled by the Australian defence around Wau, and the destruction of the Japanese supply and reinforcement convoy by the Americans in the Bismarck Sea. Now, they had no more thought of advancing. They were on the defensive; a position which they were to retain until the end of the war.

33

SCARLET BEACH TO X-DAY

WHILE THE AUSTRALIANS HAD BEEN FORCING THE JAPANESE BACK towards Salamaua, great events had been taking place on nearby Pacific battlefields. Two American divisions had invaded New Georgia in the Solomons, and in a savage five-day battle had defeated the Japanese at a cost of nearly 6,000 casualties to themselves and twice that number to the enemy. They had followed up their success by taking Vella Lavella. American units had landed on Woodlark and Kiriwina Islands, and American engineers protected by Australian infantry had been building airfields at Tsili Tsili and Goroka. All these actions were part of the overall Allied strategy designed to break the Japanese hold on the Solomons-New Britain-New Guinea area, and were building up towards the attack on Lae.

This included the first amphibious operation in which Australian troops had been engaged since Gallipoli. General Blamey planned a landing east of Lae, a paratroop landing at Nadzab, and an overland attack down the Markham Valley.

The assault forces were to be made up of brigades from what may have been the finest infantry divisions of any armies in the second World War; the 7th and 9th Australian.

The 7th Division, blooded in Syria and North Africa and victors of the Kokoda Trail, Milne Bay, Gona, Sananada, and Buna, was to have a new role; as airborne troops flown in for the attack down the Markham Valley. They were commanded by "Bloody George" Vasey.

The 9th Division, veterans of Tobruk and Alamein, was to receive its baptism of jungle warfare against a foe which it was prepared to treat with respect but not with awe. They were to make the amphibious landing.

371

Since returning to Australia, they had lost the commander who had led them in North Africa; Lieutenant-General Sir Leslie Morshead. A cliché of military histories is to say that the troops worshipped their commander, but this has rarely been the case. Between Morshead and the men of the 9th Division, however, there did in fact exist a special relationship, founded largely upon their trust in his military instincts and knowledge that he would stand up for them. His promotion to commander of II Australian Corps, with headquarters in Queensland, made them feel a definite sense of loss.

Although he was at the peak of his reputation when he returned to Australia early in 1943, he had to wait some time before receiving another field command. The growing power of the American Army from 1944 onwards, and the corresponding decline in Australian military influence, substantially reduced the opportunities for active leadership by Australian commanders.

Blamey had the difficult task of finding suitable commands for such men as Morshead, Lavarack, and Mackay, to say nothing of the less well-known leaders who had proved their calibre at brigade level. But New Guinea was the principal campaign being fought at that time, it had been commanded with conspicuous success by Lieutenant-General Sir Edmund Herring since mid-1942, and there was no way to make the senior operational promotions which would enable steps up the ladder for all the men who had learnt the warrior's craft so excellently.

Morshead's successor as commander of the 9th Division was Major-General George Wootten, who had led the 18th Brigade at Tobruk, and whose brilliant leadership was instrumental in the victories at Milne Bay and the Buna-Sanananda fighting. Despite his own extraordinarily successful background, Wootten's task of taking over such a magnificent division from a leader the troops so highly respected was not an easy one.

His 9th Division embarked on American landing craft of a U.S. Navy task force, supported by U.S. Air Force fighters and bombers. It was the first major co-ordinated sea, air, and land assault in Australian history, and the convoy was a majestic sight as it steamed through the tropical seas. It was also the most formidable land offensive so far launched against the Japanese in the Pacific. The American naval historian wrote, "Never before had the Solomon Sea witnessed such a fleet; few waters had ever seen one so strange to old seamen's eyes."

Later, an Australian private reflected what must have been the silent question asked by many of the 9th Division men, when he wrote, "Not since our forefathers landed at Gallipoli had an Australian force made an opposed landing by sea. Could we, the 2nd A.I.F., uphold the gallantry shown by those men?"

At dawn on 4 September, the naval escorts bombarded the beaches code-named Red and Yellow, eighteen miles east of Lae, and the landing-craft made for the shore. The men crouched behind their steel sides, loaded with equipment, expecting at any moment to hear the roar of the defenders' fire, but to their surprise the landing was unopposed. The only Japanese reaction was a series of air raids which damaged some of the landing craft and caused casualties among the Australian infantry and American seamen.

The 20th Brigade, under Brigadier Windeyer, landed first, followed within forty-eight hours by the 26th Brigade under Whitehead and the 24th Brigade under Evans. The initial three objectives of the 20th Brigade were appropriately code-named Bardia, Tobruk, and Benghazi.

The landing was the first move in the biggest Allied offensive of the New Guinea campaign. On the following morning, 5 September, three battalions of the 503rd U.S. Parachute Regiment were dropped to Nadzab, to secure the airfield for the transport aircraft bringing in the Australian 7th Division. The spectacular air armada, totalling 302 aircraft, was witnessed by MacArthur and the U.S. air commander, Kenney. They had come along as a gesture of faith towards American troops entering their first operation.

The Americans at Nadzab, like the Australians landing from the sea, met little opposition. Soon, the 25th Brigade of the 7th Australian Division, under Brigadier Eather, was swarming out of its aircraft, followed quickly by the rest of the division. Before flying out of Port Moresby they had suffered the worst disaster of the offensive, when a Liberator bomber crashed on take-off and smashed into the 2/33rd Battalion, killing fifty-nine and injuring ninety-two.

General Vasey's force, advancing down the Markham Valley, entered the area somewhat more slowly. Their advance battalion met their first opposition on 10 September, and, during the next five days, four battalions had to overcome desperate last stands by Japanese positions which had to be reduced by artillery and then overcome by close-quarters fighting. The enemy artillery became more active as they approached Lae, but on the morning of 15 September men of the 2/25th pushed through into the town — but had to retreat again. The enemy had been beaten, but Lae was being shelled and bombed so heavily by American aircraft and 9th Division artillery that it was a dangerous place to be in.

The 9th Division had met some sporadic opposition as they wheeled west along the coast from their landing beaches, but their worst problem was the crossing of the flooded Busu and Butibum Rivers. The latter was crossed on 15 September, and in the afternoon the Australian flag was raised over Lae.

The heavy rains and flooded rivers had slowed down the advance more than the enemy resistance had done, and also had enabled many of the Japanese garrison to escape. A Japanese signal, intercepted on 14 September, had indicated that they would try to break out along the north coast, and the Australians manoeuvred to cut them off. But most of them escaped along

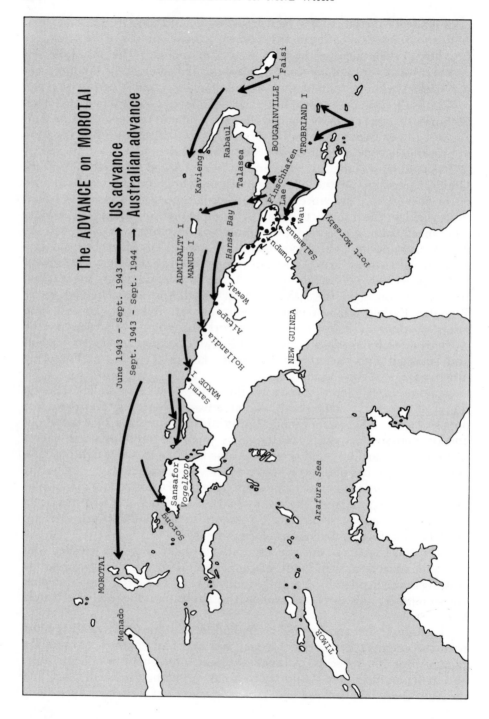

isolated trails farther west, and it is probable that about 6,000 evaded the trap which was closing on them.

The capture of Lae had been far easier than expected, but it had still cost the Australians 115 dead, 73 missing, and about 600 wounded. These casualties would have been far worse but for the Salamaua operations, which had worked perfectly in their intent of drawing off Japanese strength. The blow on Lae was delivered when the Japanese were still falling back from Salamaua; shattered and exhausted by the long battle in that area. They lost a known 2,200 casualties, and no doubt many more expired as they struggled away across the precipitous ranges, short of food and with a long march to the next Japanese base.

This was Finschhafen; just around the tip of the Huon Peninsula on the base of which stood Lae. With better than two almost untouched divisions of fighting-fit soldiers in possession of Lae, Blamey did not lose a moment in following up the advantage. So far, he had carried out two of the steps outlined in MacArthur's operations instructions of 13 June 1943, which read in part: "Forces of the South-West Pacific area supported by South Pacific Forces will seize the Lae-Salamaua-Finschhafen-Markham River Valley area and establish major elements of the Allied Forces therein to provide from the Markham Valley area general and direct air support of subsequent operations in northern New Guinea and western New Britain, and to control Vitiaz Strait and protect the north-western flank of subsequent operations in western New Britain."

Major-General Wootten's 9th Division was to make another seaborne invasion, to seize Finschhafen by sea, while the 7th Division advanced along the Markham and Ramu Valleys to clear up pockets of enemy resistance, mop up stragglers, and act as the left hand claw of the pincers which would crack Finschhafen in the same way as Lae. As a further threat, a battalion was to advance along the coast from Lae to Finschhafen.

General Herring arrived at Lae by P.T. boat on 17 September, to discuss the invasion plans with General Wootten, but a main problem was the Intelligence inability to forecast the likely strength of the Japanese garrison at Finschhafen. Estimates varied from 350 to 5,000.

The 20th Brigade was chosen once more to spearhead the landing, which was to be on Scarlet Beach, four miles north of the town. The whole concept of the operation was marked by exceptional boldness, and was unique in three respects. The proposal to land at night on a hostile shore was fraught with difficulties, particularly as infantry seldom undertook large assaults through jungle after dark; the mounting of an amphibious operation on this scale at such notice had few, if any, precedents; and the nature of enemy dispositions in the Finschhafen area were so vague as to be virtually useless to General Wootten and his planning staff.

The actual time of the landing was a cause of some conflict between the

Australian infantry and the American seamen. The U.S. Navy insisted that it should be performed at twenty-five minutes after midnight on 22 September, thus enabling the landing craft to withdraw before daylight. Brigadier Windeyer of the 20th Brigade doubted their ability to pinpoint the landing area in darkness, and asked for a landing at first light: 5.15 a.m. After much discussion, General Herring and Admiral Barbey, commanding the U.S. task force, compromised on 0445 as H-hour. Of this dispute, the American naval historian remarked tersely: "Barbey suggested a midwatch landing under a bright quartering moon. The Australians demurred and a compromise resulted—H-hour to be in the darkness before dawn, ships to clear the beach before daylight, air attack could develop. The Australians proved to be right. "Uncle Dan's" outfit was not prepared for a neat night landing. The usual SNAFU developed." (SNAFU, in U.S. Navy slang = Situation Normal; All F—d Up.)

The landing craft grounded in darkness flashing with Japanese rifle and machine-gun fire, and with numerous craft dropping their landing ramps on a beach south of Scarlet Beach. Units were mixed up, and there could have been considerable confusion, but the Australians had been instructed that in case of a misdirected landing they were not to attempt reorganisation until the immediate enemy had been cleaned up.

They did this with a will, and assaulted the Japanese defences with such vigour that they killed between 300 and 400 and had cleared the beaches within two hours of landing. The various units sorted themselves out, assembled into their planned line of advance, and pressed on towards Finschhafen.

At the Bumi River, they ran into stiff opposition, but one battalion moved inland and forced a crossing further up. Japanese resistance in the area solidified into something considerably stronger than had been indicated by the vague Intelligence reports, and the 20th Brigade's task was made even harder by the need to watch the landing area, to protect its own flank, to find enough men to tackle each of the Japanese positions, and to block the route of possible Japanese reinforcements being sent down into the area from Sattelberg, further to the west.

Nor were they assisted by MacArthur and his staff playing the same card as at Kokoda, by insisting that Japanese forces in the area were scanty and were in fact being withdrawn. They reneged on a previous arrangement, made with Herring, to bring in another brigade by sea, and said that they must have more information on Japanese strength before the sea-lift was made.

The Australians had no option but to beg whatever American craft they could lay hands on, and ship in a battalion to protect the Scarlet Beach area which was the vital keyhole through which supplies could be landed. Their arrival allowed the 20th Brigade to concentrate for the final assault on

Finschhafen. The Japanese, tricked by the advance of the battalion coming along the coast from Lae into thinking that they were being trapped, put up a savage day-long battle on the outskirts of Finschhafen but then withdrew inland. On 2 October, the 20th Brigade occupied Finschhafen, after eleven days of fighting which amounted to a military classic. They had in fact been vastly outnumbered, because captured documents revealed that more than 5,000 Japanese had been in the immediate area when the Australians landed, including élite Marine infantry. The force and determination of the Australian attack, coming so soon after the demoralising Japanese set-backs at Salamaua and Lae, had caught the Japanese off balance. For a cost of 358 casualties to themselves, the 20th Brigade had captured a vital strategic area which would be the springboard for the next advance.

An important part of the operations was performed by the 7th Division in its advance down the Markham and Ramu Valleys. With the collapse of Lae the advance was widened to take in more ground, and the Japanese were forced steadily out of their positions in a series of stiff encounters. The occupation of this area allowed the Americans to begin work on a big new airfield at Gusap.

But the enemy reacted swiftly. A large concentration began to gather at Sattelberg, with the obvious intention of driving the Australians back into the sea, and it was immediately apparent that Windeyer's troops would be insufficient to hold them. The Americans at last realised the gravity of the situation, and began to transport the 24th Brigade into Finschhafen. On 10 October, General Wootten set up 9th Division headquarters in Finschhafen, with two brigades and support troops established in the area.

Three days before, the men of the 9th Division had been pleased to hear that General Sir Leslie Morshead was to succeed General Sir Edmund Herring as commander of I Australian Corps in New Guinea; not because they had any complaint against Sir Edmund, but because it meant that they would once more be under the direction of their old commander. Sir Edmund, who had rendered sterling service since the turn of the tide against the Japanese, was soon to retire from active army life on his appointment as Chief Justice of the Supreme Court of Victoria in February 1944.

Apart from his outstanding background in the pursuit of his academic, law and military achievements, his great personal charm and breadth of interest were no doubt largely responsible for his cordial relations with MacArthur, as on more than one occasion his diplomacy helped smooth the ruffled feelings of both sides. Indeed, Sir Edmund Herring is probably the most scholarly soldier produced by Australia, apart from Sir John Monash, his great Victorian compatriot of a previous generation.

Soon after Morshead's arrival in New Guinea, the 9th Division was to face some of its toughest trials, as Major-General Wootten pressed forward from Finschhafen to Sattelberg. This was the first step in an offensive designed to drive the Japanese across the head of the Huon Peninsula to Sio, on its north coast. The Sattelberg road was a winding quagmire threading its way up through steep mountain passes which formed ideal defence positions.

Then, on 14 October, an enemy signal was intercepted ordering the Japanese divisional commander to attack all positions from Arndt Point to Langemak Bay at dusk on 16 October. This was confirmed when a copy of orders issued by General Katagiri, the Japanese area commander, were found on the body of a dead officer. These read in part: "After dusk on X Oct., the main strength of 79th Infantry Regiment will attack the enemy in Arndt Point area from the north side. The assault boat *Butai* will penetrate through the north coast of Arndt Point on the night of X day."

From the intercepted information, Allied Intelligence worked out the enemy plans for a three-pronged attack. Firstly, a diversion from the north by the 11/26th Artillery Battalion and two companies of the 1/79th Battalion, which were to occupy the Bonga area. Secondly, a seaborne attack by other elements of the 79th Regiment, supported by a detachment of the 20th Engineer Regiment. Armed with explosives and demolition charges, this group was instructed that: "Ammunition dumps, artillery positions, tanks, enemy H.Q., moored boats, barracks etc. should be the selected objectives." Thirdly, the main attack from the west was to be made by the 80th Regiment, advancing astride the Sattelberg road towards Heldsbach and Australian artillery positions, and from the north by the rest of the 79th Regiment, with the object of driving the Australians north of Arndt Point.

Katagiri's order stated that, "X day will be decided on X minus 1 day at 2200 hours, and a fire will be seen for 20 minutes on the Sattelberg Heights. When the fire is seen answer back at a suitable spot by fire."

Thus forewarned, General Wootten proceeded to forearm, and for the time being fell back onto the defensive. Brigadier Windeyer was ordered to co-ordinate the defence of Langemak Bay, to hold important ground at all costs, defend in depth, maintain a mobile reserve, and organise a coast-watching station and beach defences. Brigadier Evans was instructed to "site and hold at all'costs a post north of River Song on direct track running through (map reference) 620700 to Warco, which track is a possible axis of enemy land attack."

Even before the main attack of the Japanese X-day began, the enemy had been probing down the Sattelberg road towards the Australian positions at Jivenaneng. Several heavy assaults had been thrown back by Australians entrenched along the precipitous hillsides among the dank kunai grass, scrub, and rain forest, and a heavier attack made on the morning of 16 October, by elements of the Japanese 80th Regiment, met with no more success than those which had gone before.

As they fought, the Australians kept a weather eye lifting for the beacon which was to signal the start of the Japanese main attack, but rain and mist along the hilltops were so thick that it was never seen—if indeed it was lit.

The expected seaborne attack manifested itself with the growl of barge engines through the darkness before dawn on 17 October, as they headed south-east from Sio. But it was doomed from the start. Lurking American P.T. boats sprang into action and with torpedoes and gunfire sank more than half the barges. Those that did struggle through received a merciless reception at Scarlet Beach, and only about sixty men managed to set foot on the beach. They were dealt with very soon.

At about the same time, the Japanese 79th Regiment began pressing a heavy attack against the northern Australian flank. This was more successful, because the Japanese had infiltrated through the forward Australian positions and captured some high ground west of Scarlet Beach. Some units withdrew, contrary to General Wootten's orders, but the majority held and slowed down the Japanese advance with a storm of fire.

Wootten had little in the way of a reserve to check the rapidly developing Japanese battle plan, and asked for the 26th Brigade, under Brigadier D. A. Whitehead, to be sent forward urgently. They began their move forward only just in time.

In their battle to reach the Australian beachhead and thus check the drive towards Sattelberg, the Japanese tried all the tactics to which the 9th Division men were now becoming accustomed. Once more they crept through the thick scrub and kunai grass, in order to reach Siki Cove and split the Australians into two groups divided by the Siki River. They succeeded, but only temporarily, because the 9th Division men hit back so hard that the Japanese units were shredded. They tried a furious charge against the guns at Katika, but the Australian artillerymen held firm and worked their pieces with disciplined precision, firing over open sights until the attack was shredded away by the shellbursts. They blocked the Sattelberg road on the seaward side of Jivenanang, so that the Australian battalion was cut off, and attacked from all sides. They were thrown back every time.

Gradually the impetus of their attack slackened, especially when the 26th Brigade swung into action with the support of eighteen tanks. Operating far from their base, the Japanese were running short of supplies and men, but the real reason for their defeat was the way in which the 9th Division units countered every move they made. After the war, General Adachi of the Japanese 18th Army remarked of this battle: "It appeared at one stage that the attack was on the verge of success, but it ended in a complete failure."

The fury of the Japanese attack, and the efficiency with which it was countered, was shown by the "blood reckoning" after the enemy had begun to retreat. The Australians counted 679 Japanese dead, and it was thought that their casualties must have totalled about 1,500. The 9th Division suffered 228 casualties, of which forty-nine were killed, and had held fast to the vital beachhead area.

34

CONQUEST OF THE HUON

O N 25 OCTOBER 1943, THE FIRST ANNIVERSARY OF THE BATTLE OF Alamein, the men of the 9th Division on the Huon Peninsula were visited by Lieutenant-General Morshead, who had commanded the division in action a year before. Times were vastly changed since then, in every aspect and condition of the war which they were still fighting. Only one thing remained the same; the offensive spirit of the division.

Morshead conferred with Major-General Wootten, and it was decided that another brigade would be needed to recommence the offensive against Sattelberg and Wareo and then thrust along the coast to seize Sio. What had begun as a brigade landing was developing into a four brigade operation; a clear indication of the previous underestimate of enemy strength in the area.

The Japanese had no sooner begun to retire from their unsuccessful counter-attack against Scarlet Beach than the Australians followed them up with aggressive patrolling. On 29 October, the 9th Division commenced the grinding assault up the Sattelberg road, supported by tanks, but progress against the strongly entrenched positions on the steep hillsides was inevitably slow. On 5 November, however, they relieved the 2/17th Battalion at Jivenaneng, and the troops which had formed a stubborn island in the swirling Japanese advance could go back for a rest.

Many of the steep hills and ridges around Sattelberg became the scenes of determined attacks and desperate defence—with the roles sometimes interchangeable between Australians and Japanese. Steeple Tree Hill and Green Ridge had to be stormed by the Diggers, who in the same old style had to overcome the enemy virtually man by man as they fought back from entrenchments along the steep heights. A smaller hill, named Pabu, was captured by the 2/32nd Battalion without much difficulty, but very soon became the object of a series of furious counterattacks. It was a wooded knoll standing out of a plain of kunai grass, so that the defenders had a clear view of the Japanese advances and could not understand why such desperate attempts were being made to recapture the position. For several days the Australians on Pabu were shelled, machine-gunned, and attacked at close quarters, but they hung on grimly despite their steadily mounting losses and the knowledge that they were surrounded. It was only later that it was realised that Pabu had been a key position, because it stood astride the enemy track which they used to supply Sattelberg and Wareo from Gusika, on the coast.

The seizing and holding of Pabu devitalised an enemy counterattack against the main Australian advance, delivered on 22 November, because the Japanese could not be properly supplied or reinforced and despite bitter fighting could not make any headway. The 9th Division ground forward along the savage hillsides, supported by air strikes, by the artillery which was dragged arduously into position, and by the tanks which inched up the churned up track. At last the 2/48th Battalion reached the Sattelberg slopes, and after two days of vicious infantry fighting drove the enemy out of the town. On 25 November, the Australian flag was hoisted on a tree by Sergeant Tom Derrick, V.C., M.M.; one of the finest infantrymen of the 2nd A.I.F., but destined to be killed in action during the assault on Tarakan towards the end of the war.

General Wootten's next step towards Sio was to conquer the enemy defences along the ridge running from Wareo, north-west of Sattelberg, to the sea. This operation began on 27 November, and for the next eighteen days the Australians pushed steadily forward. They relieved the battalion besieged at Pabu, captured Gusika on the seacoast, and fought the Japanese in country which ranged from the swampy coastal areas to hillsides so steep that the infantrymen had to drag themselves upwards through the scrub.

With the astounding fanaticism and devotion to duty which characterised their actions until the bitter end, the Japanese fought back all the way — and counterattacked whenever they could organise formations in sufficient strength. But they were being assaulted by some of the world's finest infantry; men as self-reliant and adaptable as their pioneering forebears, as tough as stringybark, as irresistible as a bushfire. They countered the Japanese fanaticism with a deadly and calculating courage, and fought them with that mixture of boldness and cunning which is the mark of the veteran soldier.

They were used to Japanese tactics now, and foiled them with the skills of jungle warfare which they had quickly learnt. An ambush would find that it was itself being ambushed, infiltrators were chopped down before they could organise into an attack, flanking parties ran into well-laid traps, banzai charges were slaughtered before they got within striking distance, and even the most stubbornly entrenched positions had to yield to the deadly persistence of men who crept closer and closer until the final furious assault.

The Australian front-line troops were well supported, by contrast to the plight of the Japanese whose supply and reinforcement organisations rarely seemed adequate to the demands of the combat units. Australian requirements were well catered for now, from preventive medicine which cut down the sick lists to the supply vessels and aircraft which landed stores along the coast or dropped them for the advancing units. Shells, cartridges, and grenades were kept steadily moving all along the line until their final discharge against the enemy. The wounded were treated and cared for as fast as possible, the engineers improved the roads along which the trucks and jeeps and guns must roll, the spotting aircraft flew overhead and were followed by the vicious strikes of fighter-bombers or the torrents of shells poured into positions which they had seen. An Australian officer, Captain Owen, had designed a light, simple, and sturdy sub-machine gun which was the ideal personal weapon for jungle warfare—and had to wait for many years after the war before a grudging government rewarded him for his invention.

The growing strength and efficiency of the advance rolled the Japanese before it, and despite their last-ditch resistance in many places they left every sign of a defeated enemy behind them. The corpses of hundreds of men who had died from wounds, sickness, or starvation lay along the muddy tracks; wrecked or abandoned guns and vehicles rusted in the jungle; weapons, clothing, and equipment lay in the kunai grass; shattered barges and other craft were washed by the waves of the Vitiaz Straits between the Huon Peninsula and New Britain.

On Christmas Day of 1943, men of the 9th Division stood on the heights which overlooked the Straits and watched a huge American invasion fleet steaming through them towards New Britain. Their capture of the heights allowed this fleet to pass through without opposition, and it sailed on to land the 1st American Marine Division on Cape Gloucester, on the western tip of New Britain. After four days fighting they captured the airfield there; another step in the Allied strategy directed towards driving the Japanese out of the entire area.

During the first two weeks of the New Year the Australians pressed forward with increasing speed, with Japanese opposition faltering all the time and the main problem being that of the fantastically difficult terrain. They entered Sio on 15 January, to find the enemy gone and large quantities of equipment abandoned. The battle for the Huon Peninsula was over, and Japanese hopes for the conquest of New Guinea had gone for ever.

The 9th Division had defeated the Japanese 20th Division, in a four months campaign which was estimated to have cost the Japanese a total casualty list of about 8,000. The 9th Division suffered 1,028 casualties, including 283 killed.

*   *   *

While the 9th Division was gaining this decisive victory, the 7th Division had been sweating and suffering in a vital but less spectacular role. After their push down the Markham-Ramu Valley area, during the operations against Finschhafen, the division had been relegated to the rugged hinterland behind the Ramu Valley. After capturing Dumpu on 5 October, they were confronted by an enemy force of some 12,000 men under Major-General Nakai.

General Vasey, commanding the Australians, was given the task of pushing these Japanese right out of the Ramu Valley into the Finisterre Ranges, to ensure the security of the major base being developed at Lae and the complex of airfields being built to supply and support the next Allied offensive.

The 7th Division was thus operating inland from the 9th Division, and General Vasey was confident that if he was given sufficient support he could make an accompanying advance right across the base of the Huon Peninsula, and reach the sea at Bogadjim. This would in fact have cut off the Japanese retreat from Sio.

But the requisite support was not available, and the division's work was that of stabilising the Japanese force opposed to it while the main push went along the ranges closer to the coast. For both sides it became a grim holding operation, with the Japanese holding the tracks which led through the ranges to the coast at Bogadjim and Madang, and the Australians probing for a way through while diverting the enemy from their hard-pressed comrades further east.

The Australian intrusion into the Finisterre Ranges was particularly provoking to the Japanese, because it stood in the way of a road which was planned to run from Bogadjim to Dumpu. This would have enabled a flanking movement against the Australians pressing against the 20th Division, and would have threatened the Lae base and the new airfields. Dumpu had fallen, but the 7th Division advance was blocked by Shaggy Ridge; a precipitous, razor-backed feature along which the enemy was strongly entrenched.

From Dumpu, elements of the 7th Division probed towards Shaggy Ridge, and one battalion established itself across the Japanese lines of communications. On 12/13 October the enemy lashed back with a sharp counter-attack, but this was beaten off and the operations split up into a series of patrol actions in which each side tested the other's strength. Any one of these patrols, thrusting deep into enemy territory and undertaken under conditions of constant tension and danger, would merit a book in itself, but is now virtually forgotten except in the minds of survivors or in battalion war diaries. Often the patrols treading cautiously along the muddy tracks would glimpse a stir of movement among the dense jungle, heralding the vicious chatter of a Nambu machine-gun or the sight of a grenade arching through the leaves. A brief and bloody skirmish would take place between opposing patrols, of which the men might see no more of the enemy than a form flitting through foliage.

These patrol actions provoked the Japanese into another full-scale attack, which was successful in driving some 7th Division units back towards the Ramu River. But it petered out in face of stubborn Australian resistance, complicated by the enemy's usual problem in supplying and reinforcing units which ventured far from base.

For such an active commander as General Vasey this comparatively static warfare was aggravating in the extreme. He felt that he was left out of the mainstream of battle, and when a request for reinforcements was turned down he wrote, "New Guinea Force has just forgotten me, not even moral support from the rear, left alone and don't understand it."

But by 27 December he had obtained sufficient air and artillery support to launch an attack on Shaggy Ridge, and the 2/16th Battalion inched forward along the only line of approach that followed the crest of the ridge. By New Year's Day 1944 they had driven the enemy out of a series of redoubts and captured a feature known as the Pimple. The way was open to the key position of Kankiryo Saddle, and though Vasey was not supposed to launch an offensive he could not resist this opportunity. His orders read, "Contain hostile forces in the Bogadjim-Ramu area by vigorous action of fighting patrols against enemy posts. Major forces will not be committed."

But, with two of his brigades relieved by fresh formations, he launched a three-pronged assault against Kankiryo Saddle on 19 January. By that time, the Americans had landed at Saidor, between Bogadjim and Sio, so the attack was ideally timed to hit the Japanese when they were beginning to worry about their rear. After bitter fighting, they abandoned their positions on 1 February, and the 7th Division began a pursuit which took them down through the sharp steep slopes of the Finisterres towards the sea.

After this, and during the first half of 1944, the 6th, 7th, and 9th Divisions began a withdrawal from the area and a regrouping on Atherton Tableland in northern Queensland. They were replaced by three militia divisions, and these together with an increasing number of Americans continued the pressure which drove the Japanese further and further along the coast until the capture of Madang.

After the war, General Adachi expressed the Japanese view of the 7th Division operations when he said, "It would have been much more advisable for the Australians to have employed about a brigade strength in the Ramu

Valley, as a threat only to Madang, and use the bulk of the forces for the operations along the coastline."

No doubt General Vasey would have agreed wholeheartedly, but there is also the possibility that the Japanese would have performed an outflanking manoeuvre and descended upon the great Allied bases and airfields being developed on the Lae side of the Huon Peninsula. So the comparatively unspectacular operations of his 7th Division, gruelling though they had been to the men engaged in them, had been vital to the overall success of the Huon Peninsula campaign.

35

THE FINAL BLOWS

A POLICY DIRECTIVE ISSUED BY GENERAL BLAMEY ON 23 DECEMBER 1943 foreshadowed the future role of Australian land forces in the words, "The operational role of the Australian military forces engaged in forward operations in New Guinea will be taken over by U.S. Army forces in accordance with plans being prepared."

The directive arose out of decisions made at the Quebec Conference, attended by Churchill and Roosevelt and the Combined Chiefs of Staff, in August 1943. Allied global strategy was still focused on the defeat of Germany first, which involved the gigantic effort of the invasion of Europe. Japan, however, was not forgotten, especially since the U.S. operations in the Pacific were employing by far the greater part of the American battleship, carrier, and landing-craft fleet, and thirteen of its assault divisions. A sea and air war of attrition was agreed upon, along a general line of attack through the southern central Pacific and involving the enemy-held island of Wake, the Gilbert, Marshall, Paulu, and Caroline groups, and eastern New Guinea. The grand design was to conquer Japan a year after the defeat of Germany.

Such plans did not please MacArthur. He foresaw his theatre of operations becoming a stagnant backwater, while the available ships, aircraft, men, supplies, and glory went to the monster task forces under the command of Admiral Chester Nimitz in the central Pacific.

His area strategy had been to complete the isolation of Rabaul in five moves. One, a landing on the west coast of New Britain (which already had been accomplished). Two and three, the seizing of Green Island and the Admiralty Islands, so that sea and air bases could be established to the rear of the Japanese 18th Army's front, which ran along the line Wewak-Madang-

New Britain-Bougainville. Four, the capture of Kavieng in New Ireland. Five, an advance along the north coast of New Guinea to Vogelkop Peninsula, in Dutch New Guinea.

The final move was the most important. It would provide the jumping-off point for the invasion of Mindanao, in the Philippines, and thus fulfil MacArthur's promise of "I shall return." To do this, he would also have to protect his left flank by immobilising the Japanese in Borneo, to forestall a thrust against his lines of communication up through the islands south of the Philippines.

He approached General Marshall, the U.S. Chief of Staff, seeking permission for the offensive. It made strategic sense, because it would provide the southern claw of an American pincer movement and divert some Japanese attention from the main Pacific thrust, but also would demand a share of the men and materials needed so urgently for every theatre of war.

However, Marshall agreed, perhaps influenced by the knowledge that MacArthur still retained an aura of glamour in the eyes of many Americans, and could swing a lot of weight if his vanity was offended.

From that point onwards, the U.S. Army assumed the major role in the south-west Pacific area land fighting, after two years of war against the Japanese in which the principal land victories had been gained by predominantly Australian forces. The A.I.F. and militia divisions in New Guinea, by their drive as far as Madang, had in fact cleared the way for MacArthur's main advance.

After Madang, and while the 6th, 7th, and 9th Divisions were resting and refitting in Australia, the comparative inactivity of the Australian land forces drew considerable criticism from various sources—most of which were unaware of actual Australian achievements up to that time.

This was largely due to the carefully manicured communiques issued by MacArthur's staff, in which Australian successes were ascribed to "Allied effort." When the Americans became the prime contributors to the land fighting, however, the successes were no longer described as Allied, but as American.

This is not intended to be a detraction from the immense efforts of the American people in the second World War. It is, however, a reflection upon the American techniques of overpublicising their own achievements—and upon the Australian government of the day which permitted the deeds of Australians to be thrust out of the limelight.

* * *

On 12 July 1944, MacArthur issued a directive to Blamey. It read in part: "It is desired that Australian forces assume the responsibility for the continued neutralisation of the Japanese in Australian and British territory, exclusive of the Admiralties, by the following dates: North Solomons—

Green Island—Emirau Island: 1st December 1944. Australian New Guinea: 1st November 1944. New Britain: 1st November 1944. In the advance to the Philippines it is desired to use Australian ground forces as follows: 1 division —November 1944; 1 division—January 1945.''

Whether MacArthur seriously contemplated using two Australian divisions in the Philippines is open to some doubt, of the kind expressed by Lieutenant-General R. K. Sutherland, Chief of Staff to MacArthur, who told Blamey, "It is not politically expedient for the A.I.F. to be among the first troops into the Philippines.''

In any case Blamey refused to release the 7th and 9th Divisions to MacArthur, because the American commander proposed to make them components of separate U.S. Army corps. Blamey had stood firm against the British attempts to split Australian divisions into brigades, to be assimilated by British divisions. He had no intention of allowing Australian divisions to be assimilated by American army corps.

During this in-fighting in the upper echelons, the Allies had been making great strides in the area once dominated by the Japanese from their great base at Rabaul. Rabaul itself had been pounded almost constantly since bomber airfields had been established in the Lae-Finschhafen area after its capture by the Australians in October 1943. After the successful American landings in New Britain, the 3rd New Zealand Division had occupied Nissan Island, in the Green Islands, only 117 miles from Rabaul. The Americans landed in the Admiralty Islands in late February, took Emirau Island in March, and fought a savage battle against the Japanese on Bougainville in the same month, ending in an overwhelming local victory for the Americans though large enemy forces still remained on the island.

As the Australian militiamen pressed on Madang, the Americans leap-frogged forward to land at Aitape and Hollandia, about 400 miles further along the coast, and took them in April. In May they took Wakde Island and Sarmi, in July they fought the Japanese out of Biak Island, Noemfoor Island, and Cape Sansapor, and by the end of September they were in control of Morotai, Peleliu, and Angaur.

MacArthur's claim to be allowed to continue his offensive had been splendidly justified, but his tactics had placed him in an awkward position. They were designed to keep the Americans moving towards the southern Philippines in a series of hops which captured successive positions and established a chain of bases leading towards his objective. The problem was that, although the Americans had gained resounding victories with the capture of each position, and had killed many thousands of the enemy, the main Japanese armies were still firmly established in the areas behind the captured bases.

MacArthur's theory was that each of the bases could be held by troops which would safeguard their perimeters, while the Japanese who had been driven away from them would gradually wither into impotence because they could no longer be supplied through their coastal bases.

This meant, however, that the bulk of MacArthur's troops would have to be used to protect his own bases, leaving few to spare for the invasion of the Philippines. Hence his direction to Blamey to relieve the Americans holding the bases, to free them for the invasion.

But Blamey disagreed with MacArthur's theory that the Japanese isolated by his leapfrog progress would "wither on the vine." Far from withering, he pointed out, they were faring very well on the farms which with characteristic industry they had established to feed their troops. They had plenty of native labour, they were good agriculturists, and they were used to looking after themselves on a much simpler diet than that enjoyed by white troops— especially the Americans.

So long as these very considerable pockets of the enemy were allowed to remain undisturbed, and still in possession of huge stocks of arms and ammunition, they constituted a constant menace to the Allied lines of communication, and Blamey felt that they should be tackled wherever possible if this could be done without unduly heavy loss.

He submitted a plan which provided for the holding of the established perimeters with seven Australian brigades. These would be the 6th and 23rd Brigades of the 3rd Division, on Bougainville; the 13th and 29th Brigades of the 11th Division, on New Britain; and the 4th, 7th, and 8th Brigades of the 5th Division, in New Guinea.

This did not suit MacArthur, who did not like the idea of six American divisions being relieved by only seven Australian brigades. After a series of conferences, Blamey agreed to twelve being used. Four would be sent to Bougainville, four to New Guinea, three to New Britain, and one to cover Emirau, Green, Treasury, and New Georgia islands.

Since April 1944, Australian troops in the New Guinea area and in support had been divided into I and II Corps. I Corps, consisting of the 6th, 7th, and 9th A.I.F. Divisions, under Lieutenant-General Sir Leslie Morshead, was refitting on the Atherton Tableland in preparation for a new offensive in the south Pacific. II Corps, consisting of the 3rd, 5th, and 11th Militia Divisions, now comprised New Guinea Force. After long consideration, Blamey had given the command of this force to Lieutenant-General S. G. Savige instead of to Vasey, who had very similar qualifications for the command.

When MacArthur insisted on the use of twelve Australian brigades in the forward areas, 1st Australian Army was created under Lieutenant-General V. A. H. Sturdee, formerly Chief of the General Staff.

II Corps was made responsible to 1st Army, strengthened by the transfer of 6th Division from I Corps, and given the task of relieving the Americans.

I Corps, now consisting only of the 7th and 9th Divisions, was earmarked for the main northern advance, but had its orders changed several times until it was at last determined, in April 1945, that the 7th Division would capture Balikpapan in Dutch Borneo and the 9th Division would capture Tarakan in Dutch Borneo and Brunei Bay in British Borneo.

*   *   *

The 6th Division, now under Major-General J. E. S. Stevens, relieved the three divisions and one regiment which comprised the American 11th Corps at Aitape, during October-November 1944.

The Americans had had little contact with the Japanese since August of that year. They faced three divisions of General Adachi's 18th Army, with headquarters in Wewak; a formation whose original strength of about 100,000 men had been cut down to 50,000 by the Australian offensives in 1942-43. When the 6th Division relieved the Americans, this number had been further reduced to about 35,000—partly by the heavy casualties inflicted by the Americans on an offensive designed to drive them into the sea.

In accordance with Blamey's feeling that a mere static possession of the beachhead was not enough to keep the enemy in check, the 6th Division began work by harassing patrols against the Japanese and assembling information as to their strength and positions. In November, Stevens proposed an offensive which Blamey approved, and accordingly began a two-pronged drive along the coast and through the mountains, with Wewak as the main objective.

With the spirit and vigour which had carried them through Libya, Greece, Crete, and earlier battles in New Guinea, the senior division of the 2nd A.I.F. drove steadily forward in an offensive which gained little world publicity during the months of November 1944 to August 1945. Even though the Japanese were cut off from their main supply routes, they fought back with their customary tenacity—and the Australians quite often felt themselves to be "orphans" so far as supplies were concerned. Much of what was available was going to the great American operations in the central Pacific, and at one stage the Australian advance had to be halted because of a shortage of parachutes for dropping supplies to forward units.

The division fought its way forward through the usual savage New Guinea conditions, battling the jungle itself as well as the Japanese which it concealed. The country was so broken by rivers, creeks and gullies that by the time they had advanced forty-two miles along the coast from Aitape towards Wewak, the vehicles which supplied them had to cross forty-six bridges. In the depths of the mountains, they encountered many small Japanese units which had settled down in native villages and were living on food provided by the villagers, and had to winkle these out one by one. Rain, mud, flooded rivers, hillsides steeper than the roof of a house, scrub entangled with vicious thorns, nights in which the cacophony of innumerable insects and jungle creatures could obscure the pad of a stealthy foot, diseases of many kinds from the fungus infections such as tinea to the ever-present malaria, dysentery, and scrub typhus, leeches, mosquitoes so thick that in some places "a man could hardly breathe for them"—all these and many other of the dangers and discomforts of the jungle had to be taken in stride as the 16th, 17th, and 19th Brigades of the division, preceded by commando troops of the 2/6th Cavalry Regiment, fought their way forward.

Wewak fell on 25 May 1945, and by the time the war ended the 6th Division had compressed the remnants of the Japanese 18th Army into a defensive arc south of their former base and backed by the inland ranges. In ten months of campaigning, the Australians counted more than 5,000 Japanese dead but believed that many more, to a possible total of about 9,000, had lost their lives in the operations. They had taken 269 prisoners, and recovered about 3,000 square miles of enemy-held territory. The divisional losses were 442 killed and 1,141 wounded.

*   *   *

When the 14th American Corps handed over its positions on Bougainville to II Australian Corps, the American intelligence estimate was that about 14,000 Japanese remained on the island. The Australian staff decided that it was more likely to be 18,000, and after the war it was in fact revealed that more than 40,000 Japanese garrisoned Bougainville in October 1944.

They had launched a savage offensive in May of that year, but lost more than 5,000 men to the Americans. After that they had withdrawn beyond the fourteen-mile perimeter which the Americans had established around Torokina, and had virtually ignored the American presence on the island.

The 7th, 11th, 15th, and 29th Militia Brigades relieved the Americans, and General Savige soon gave them the task of taking over the island. Like most islands in that area, the 130-mile length of Bougainville consists of a mountainous spine rising steeply from the coastal flats, smothered with the usual jungle and furrowed with the usual steep valleys and gullies of which many hold fast flowing creeks or rivers.

Savige divided the island into two, and gave the three brigades of the 3rd Division the task of seizing the southern sector, in which most of the Japanese were concentrated. The fourth brigade on the island, the 11th, was given the northern sector; somewhat less than half the island.

With little delay, the four brigades began their drives north and south from their base at Torokina. From December to mid-March, the 3rd Division pressed the Japanese southwards; at first through the coastal swamps and then swinging inland through the lower slopes of the Crown Prince Range. It was drearily unpleasant work, with the advance checked by rivers rushing down in sudden flood as well as by the constant rearguard skirmishing of the Japanese, but the militiamen had been well trained in jungle warfare and were adept at putting theory into practice. They encountered a number of strong defensive posts, but dealt with them one after another by outflanking and surrounding them and then closing in for the final butchery.

Progress could have been faster with better equipment, but only a few landing craft were available. These were used for outflanking landings, and by mid-February the 20th Battalion had secured a crossing across the Puriata River and had driven the Japanese out of more than half of the southern sector of the island.

The enemy, now being compressed back towards their base at Buin in the extreme south, began to react more vigorously. On 29 March, they counter-attacked in full force. In an eight-day battle concentrated into the swampy coastland south of the Puriata, they drove the Australians back a little way at first, but their attack was shredded by torrents of fire from strong emplace-ments around Slater's Knoll. A squadron of Australian tanks came up on 31 March, and when these and the infantry began to attack, the Japanese fell back. They left 620 dead behind them, for a cost of 25 Australians.

The Australians recommenced their advance, which was now contested every mile of the way by a steady flow of troops flung in from Buin. By 11 July, when the advance was stopped by almost constant downpours which flooded the rivers, the Australians were less than fifteen miles from the main Japanese base and the war was nearly over.

In the north, the 11th Brigade had been achieving similar successes; thrusting across the ranges towards Numa Numa on the opposite coast and northwards to the Bonis Peninsula. Tenacious resistance by the Japanese was unable to check the advance of the citizen soldiers who, as Menzies had said of the A.I.F. men years before, had "come here to do a job." Every foot they gained through the swampy wilderness of the coast or the rain forest of the ranges, every Japanese slit trench left behind them with its quota of silent bodies, was another step towards the conclusion of the weary, dangerous task. By the end of the war, they had thrust the Japanese right back into the Bonis Peninsula, in the far north of the island.

When the atom bomb was dropped, the Japanese on Bougainville were in a pathetic condition. Since the Australians had landed, 8,500 had been killed in battle and nearly 10,000 had died of diseases which were carrying off hundreds every month. They were near starving, and almost at the end of their other supplies. More than 23,000 surrendered.

The plans for the final battle of Bougainville were being prepared when the Rising Sun was lowered for the last time, thus saving any addition to the total of 516 Australians who lost their lives on the island. 1,572 had been wounded in action.

Colonel A. R. Garrett, who was G.S.O.I. to the 3rd Division during the Bougainville campaign and later Chief of the General Staff, expressed the opinion to the author that the 3rd Division at the end of the war was the finest division in the Pacific, even including the 6th, 7th, and 9th which had borne so much of the Australian land fighting during World War II. General Bridgeford, the divisional commander, was an outstanding soldier who had brought into his division a substantial leavening of experienced A.I.F. officers from the other veteran divisions, and moulded them into a great fighting unit, despite its origins as a militia division.

*   *   *

On New Britain, Major-General A. H. Ramsay's 5th Division relieved the U.S. 40th Division, at the northern end of an island as mountainous as Bougainville. Enemy strength was estimated as 38,000, but the bulk of these were concentrated into an area of about 200 square miles around the great base which had been established at Rabaul; once the springboard for the victorious drive to the south which had been checked in the Coral Sea, at Milne Bay, and on the Kokoda Trail.

Most of the Americans were on Cape Gloucester, at the opposite tip of the island from Rabaul, but it was soon decided that the relieving Australians would take a more offensive posture. The 6th Brigade was landed at Jacquinot Bay, about ninety miles from Rabaul, and the 36th Battalion took over from an American regiment at Cape Hoskins on the opposite coast of the island and about 120 miles from Rabaul.

From these bases, the Australians began to advance along each coast, plodding along the beaches or the swampy coastal tracks with occasional units being taken forward by sea. Enemy opposition was negligible until the 36th Battalion had advanced about two-thirds of the way to Rabaul, when the Japanese made a series of strong attacks but were driven back each time. On the south coast the 6th Brigade had advanced almost as far, to Wide Bay, before having to tackle strongly organised Japanese opposition, but this too was defeated and the enemy fell back to his positions at the foot of the Gazelle Peninsula, on which Rabaul lies.

From then until the end of the war, the Australian action was concentrated on aggressive patrols designed to keep the enemy within a perimeter around Rabaul, which was now indeed fulfilling MacArthur's intent that it should "wither on the vine."

In the three campaigns of Bougainville, New Britain, and Aitape-Wewak, the Australian forces engaged had fulfilled Blamey's strategy of breaking the enemy's spirit and defensive organisation, and placing him in a position in which the final blow might be delivered at will. It must be remembered that, when the campaigns were in full swing, very few people had any idea that the war would be concluded so abruptly by the dropping of the atom bombs on Nagasaki and Hiroshima. MacArthur could have been right in his belief that the three Japanese garrisons had been rendered impotent and could present no further menace to the Allies. Blamey, however, could also have been right in his feeling that enemy forces totalling nearly 150,000 could not be left undisturbed in the Allied rear, to wax fat and prepare for whatever mischief their ingenuity might have suggested. Without the atom bomb, it is not likely that they would have waited tamely until their home islands had been reduced by invasion.

Before and during these campaigns, an important part was played by an adventurous organisation with the colourless name of the Allied Intelligence Bureau. The foundations of this force were laid by the Australian, Papuan, and New Guinea men who took incredible risks during the Japanese invasion in order to supply the Allied headquarters with information. First known as "coastwatchers," they consisted usually of tiny groups made up of one Australian with local knowledge backed up by a few indigenes. Remaining behind the Japanese lines, they literally watched the coast, and radioed information about Japanese dispositions, ship and aircraft movements, and so on. A number of these men lost their lives—some after cruel torture.

By the end of the war, the Allied Intelligence Bureau comprised 1,659 British and Australians, 1,100 indigenes, 268 Dutch, and 19 Americans. They progressed from the gathering of information to bold commando-type raids behind the enemy lines, and on Bougainville, for example, several groups penetrated into the mountains far ahead of the advancing Australian Army units. They kept a steady flow of information moving back to headquarters, and confused the Japanese by quick in-and-out raids on their communications and outposts. Some of the leaders of these groups had been living on Bougainville for as much as two years before the American landings, in constant danger of discovery or betrayal.

The scope of their operations may be judged by the fact that they killed 7,061 Japanese, took 141 prisoners, and freed 1,054 servicemen and civilians from enemy-held territory, but the full story of their part in the war is yet to be told.

*   *   *

While the militia divisions and the 6th Division were winning their island campaigns, the 7th and 9th Divisions of Morshead's I Australian Corps were carrying out the task for which they had been prepared. This was the invasion of Dutch and British Borneo.

The first objective was Tarakan, where it was intended to establish an airfield for further operations in the Borneo campaign, but damage to the area made this impracticable in time for the landings further north and south. Besides its part in the general encircling thrust towards the Japanese home islands, the invasion was also planned in order to establish a fleet base at Brunei Bay and to rob the Japanese of the oilfields.

At Tarakan, the defence was softened by two weeks of pounding by

U.S.A.F. and R.A.A.F. heavy bombers, and when Brigadier D. A. White-head's 26th Brigade landed on Tarakan Island on 1 May 1945 the initial resistance was not great. But from then onwards it increased considerably, and though the Australians had taken the town and the airfield by 5 May they were still faced with the task of cleaning out the major pockets of Japanese defence. This took them until 13 June, at the cost of 224 killed and 669 wounded. The Japanese lost 1,540, and 229 surrendered—the latter being a demonstration of the steadily declining morale of the Japanese since the days when even the wounded would sooner kill themselves than surrender.

On the other side of the island, around Brunei Bay and Labuan, the landings had been preceded some time before by Australian guerrilla penetration. The A.I.B. had been active here, and the intruders defrayed the Japanese garrison by frequent ambushes which accounted for 1,800 of the enemy. This, together with sea and air bombardment, accounted for the fact that the Australian landings were virtually unopposed. They were carried out by the 20th and 24th Brigades of the 9th Division, under Brigadiers Windeyer and Porter, closely followed by other units of the army and R.A.A.F. About 29,000 Australians were ashore by the time the two brigades were thrusting beyond their beachheads at Brunei Bay and Labuan,

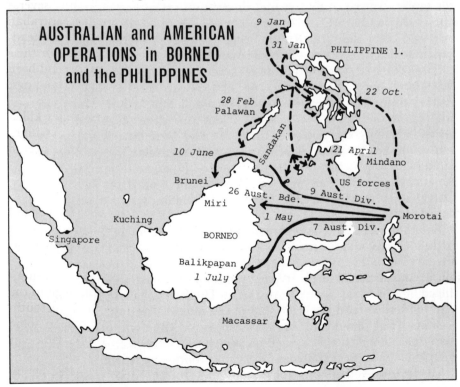

AUSTRALIAN and AMERICAN
OPERATIONS in BORNEO
and the PHILIPPINES

and the leading units soon ran into Japanese resistance on the hills around the town. The brigades' objectives were to secure a perimeter around the area and protect Brunei Bay from counter-attack, but after some fierce fighting the Japanese withdrew entirely by the last week in June.

For the 9th Division it was the end of a long and bloody trail, and for the rest of the war they and the other Australians in the area were kept busy in cleaning up the chaos which had been left by three and a half years of ruthless occupation. In recognition of their efforts the State of Borneo incorporated the famous divisional colour patch into its coat of arms, and the T for Tobruk became an honoured symbol far from its place of origin.

The last major Allied operation of the war, and the largest amphibious operation engaged in by Australian forces, was made on 1 July 1945, when the 7th Division under Major-General Milford landed at Balikpapan.

The assault convoy, of more than 100 vessels, sailed from Morotai on 26 June, commanded by the same Admiral Barbey whose U.S. Navy craft had supported the 7th Division operations in New Guinea.

Probably the operation included the most lavish support ever given to Australian troops. For twenty days before the landing, forty heavy bomber squadrons of the R.A.A.F. and the 5th and 13th U.S. Air Forces had saturated the target. American underwater demolition teams had cleared the beach approaches under fire, extensive minesweeping operations had been carried out, and Rear Admiral Ralph Briggs' cruiser squadron bombarded the Japanese defences before the Australian landings.

The 18th, 21st, and 25th Brigades landed on a 2,000-yard beach between Klandasan and Stalkudo at 9 a.m., and quickly secured their beachhead. As they prepared to advance inland, Generals MacArthur, Morshead, and Milford waded ashore at 1 p.m. From this show of Allied solidarity, General Blamey was notably absent. He had been bitterly opposed to the whole Borneo operation, as being a waste of Australian lives without contributing anything to the ultimate defeat of the Japanese—especially since the Americans already had entered Manila and landed on Iwo Jima and Okinawa, so that the enemy forces in Indonesia were cut off from their homeland.

But the Australian Government had overruled his objections to Mac-Arthur's plans, and the invasion went on. As the three 7th Division brigades advanced into the town of Balikpapan and inland along the coast north and south, MacArthur issued a typically flamboyant communique which read in part: "It is fitting that 7th Australian Division, which in July three years ago met and turned back the tide of invasion of Australia on the historic Kokoda Trail, should this same month secure what was once perhaps the most lucrative strategic target on our East Indies sector, and virtually complete our tactical control of the entire south-west Pacific."

Meanwhile Australian soldiers continued to die, in what was in fact a

THE WOUNDED, 1. *Top left*, One of the best-known Australian photographs of the second World War. A "fuzzy-wuzzy angel" leads Private G. C. Whittington of the 2/10th Battalion, wounded in the Buna fighting, to a base hospital. *Top right*, Corporal L. Allen carrying a wounded and unconscious American soldier out of the fighting on Mount Tambu. *Bottom*, German prisoners were used to help 1st A.I.F. wounded after the Battle of Hamel.

redundant operation. During twenty-two days of fighting, the three 7th Division brigades, as spearheads of a combined force of more than 30,000 landed at Balikpapan, pressed the Japanese hard in a series of bitterly-fought actions which pushed them away from the coast. They killed 2,032 and captured sixty-three of the enemy, at a cost of 229 Australians killed and 634 wounded. When Japan surrendered on 15 August 1945, the Australians were still mopping up isolated pockets of resistance.

OPERATION JAYWICK. *Top:* The fishing boat *Krait. Bottom:* The men who sailed in her. *Front row,* H. E. Carse; D. M. N. Davidson; I. Lyon; H. A. Campbell; R. C. Page. *Middle row,* A. A. Crilly; K. P. Cain; J. P. McDowell; H. S. Young; W. G. Falls; R. G. Morris. *Back row,* M. Berryman; F. W. L. Marsh; A. W. Jones; A. W. G. Huston (Campbell escaped from Singapore with Lyon but did not sail on the operation).

36

A SUMMING-UP

A S IN THE FIRST WORLD WAR, THE AUSTRALIAN CONTRIBUTION TO THE Allied victory had been of a standard far higher than might have been expected of a comparatively small and poor country in terms of population and gross national product. The Australian population in 1940 is estimated to have been 7,077,586, rising to 7,638,628 by 1947, so the population by the end of the war would have been in the region of seven and a half million. At that time, the number of men and women serving in the Australian armed forces was 575,111, constituting one of the highest percentages of any combatant country. Gross enlistments in the armed forces had been 993,000. About one in four of the male population, or eight out of every ten men aged between 18 and 35 years, had served in one of the armed forces by the end of the war.

The death toll had totalled 33,826. 180,864 had suffered wounds or injuries. 23,058 survived imprisonment by the enemy. Early in the Papua-New Guinea campaigns, sickness had been as bad as in a medieval army, and sufferers outnumbered battle casualties by more than three to one. At Milne Bay, it seemed as though the entire force might be rendered helpless by malaria, which strikes with devastating effect within a few days of the first bite by a parasite-carrying mosquito—and recurs at regular intervals with debilitating high fevers and chills. The medical services of the Australian Army tackled this problem as vigorously as the combatant troops were fighting the human enemy, and by strict preventive medicine and mosquito control were able to keep men healthy.

In December 1939 the Turkish dictator Mustapha Kemal, who had commanded troops on Gallipoli, told the English author Rosita Forbes that:

398

"If there had been another half-dozen Australians on Gallipoli we would have lost it. The Australians did not appear to know when they were dead. The only way to stop them was to bury them."

He said that the Anatolian peasants were the world's best fighters because, to them, fighting was a holiday from ploughing, but that the Australians were their equal. He believed that Gallipoli could have been taken in a day if the Anzacs had had reconnaissance aircraft, because the topmost ridge was at first held by only twenty-one Turks.

Captain Sir Basil Liddell Hart, the most noted of British military critics, remarked in his book, *Why don't we learn from history*: "The best fighting force in the fourth year of the war (1914-18) was by general recognition the Australian Corps." Had the Australian Corps been formed earlier in the war, as was the wish of the Australian Government but opposed by the British High Command, it would also have been the best fighting force in 1917. As it was, the individual Australian divisions fighting under other Corps command were by far the most effective units in the British Army, not forgetting the superb Light Horse regiments that rendered such outstanding service in the Middle East. With this reputation as a base therefore, the 2nd A.I.F. had an extraordinarily high standard to maintain.

Between 1940-1945, the Australian Army did not suffer by comparison with its forebears. The Middle East operations of 1940-1941 would not have been possible without the 6th, 7th, and 9th Divisions, which in turn took the brunt of the first Libyan advance, the ill-fated Greece and Crete campaigns, Syria, and Tobruk. There can be little doubt that the defence of Tobruk saved the Middle East from complete collapse. In 1942, the 9th Division played the critical role at El Alamein.

In the south-west Pacific campaigns of 1942-1943, the Australian land forces were the first to halt the Japanese advance and then to take the offensive against a previously unstoppable enemy. The campaigns of 1944-1945 were of dubious value in their contribution to the ultimate defeat of the Japanese, but nevertheless were executed brilliantly from the first step to the last. The contingencies of the second World War kept the Australian Army divided into several theatres for the greater part of the time, but little imagination is needed to picture the striking power that would have been available if the 6th, 7th, 8th, and 9th Divisions, together with the 1st Armoured Division and backed by the militia divisions, had been concentrated into one theatre. The use of such a force in the Papua-New Guinea theatre, early in that campaign, would have given it a very different aspect.

The second World War was the first in which conscripted Australian militia were used overseas, and they proved their mettle in the toughest of all schools, the jungle. The 3rd and 5th Divisions received most recognition, mainly because it fell to them to do much of the fighting, and also because they did whatever was asked of them.

In the quality of their leadership, the Australian soldiers were served as well as those of the first World War had been served by Monash, White, and Chauvel. The stories of such men as Morshead, Herring, Vasey (who was killed in an air crash in March 1945), Wootten, Bennett, Allen, Savige, Mackay, and various others have been partly told in this book. One special characteristic which binds them together is that the majority were civilian soldiers who achieved their commands after long and arduous apprenticeships; first as "spare-time soldiers," who gave up their leisure in order to learn the principles of the military art, then as privates or junior officers who were blooded at Gallipoli, on the Western Front, or in Egypt and Palestine, and subsequently as battalion or brigade commanders in the "Muddle East."

All these civilian soldiers had risen to rewarding positions in business or the professions. Unlike regular officers, to whom war might promise advancement in rank, pay, and pension, they had nothing to gain by war except the deep and intangible satisfactions of serving and protecting their country. Any system that produces men of this calibre deserves to be maintained and encouraged whatever future changes occur within the Australian military structure.

At the same time, the magnificent contribution made to Australia's two World War armies by the small band of devoted regular staff officers is often forgotten. In peace time they had to contend with all the frustrations of national indifference and appalling economic famine. On active service they were generally appointed to the less glamorous key roles on the staff.

*　　*　　*

After the Japanese instrument of surrender had been signed in Tokyo Bay, most of the Australian commanders faded into civilian life as quickly as the most recently joined private who returned to his work or his studies. Among them was General Sir Thomas Blamey, who after receiving the surrender of the Japanese 2nd Army on Morotai had told the Australian Government that he wished to be relieved as Commander-in-Chief of the Australian Army.

On Morotai, Blamey had told General Teshima, "In receiving your surrender I do not recognise you as an honourable and gallant foe, but you will be treated with due but severe courtesy in all matters. I recall the atrocities inflicted upon the persons of our nationals as prisoners of war and internees, designed to reduce them by punishment and starvation to slavery. In the light of these evils, I will enforce most rigorously all orders issued to you, so let there be no delay or hesitation in their fulfilment at your peril."

As it transpired, he himself received little more than "due but severe courtesy" from his own government. After requesting him to remain as Commander-in-Chief for an indefinite period, the Minister for the Army wrote to him on 14 November 1945 to advise that the government had decided to terminate his appointment.

Always a somewhat controversial figure, and never a popular man in the public eye, Blamey had become the target for increased criticism by the Australian press and parliament during 1944-1945. This was partly because of the slowdown in Australian military operations during that period, as American power reached its zenith and rolled on towards Tokyo, and partly because of the death of Prime Minister John Curtin in 1945. While Curtin was alive, Blamey had a loyal supporter in the Cabinet. After his death, Blamey realised that he could expect little sympathy from a Labor Government whose antipathy dated from his term as Commissioner of Police for Victoria—and was not soothed by his forthright comments on its policies.

It is doubtful whether the Australian press, government, people, or army ever really knew what to make of Blamey. The fact may be simply that he did not care what anyone thought of him, that he had no consciousness of what is nowadays termed a "public image," and that he stubbornly forged ahead as he saw fit, in the manner implanted in him by his Cornish ancestry and Nonconformist upbringing. Such men are never well liked, especially by those who lack the same type of self-confidence.

Often he was criticised as being ruthless—though this quality must surely form a part of any leader's character. His dismissal of Rowell and Allen, under MacArthur's urgent demands to "energise" the Kokoda Trail campaign, is cited as proof. For Allen, it was a tragedy, especially since his men had advanced from Ioribaiwa to Kokoda in sixteen days less than it had taken the Japanese to traverse the same distance. Yet Allen had not hesitated to relieve Brigadier Potts, and replace him with Porter, when Potts did not seem to be achieving the desired results with the 21st Brigade in the Ioribaiwa area. In the profession of arms there is only achievement which counts for anything; complete and overwhelming success. Success will wipe out any amount of sacrifice, but there is no forgiveness for the loser. MacArthur knew this very well; it was the principle which he followed for the whole of his military career, and he was still attempting to follow it when his career was ended by President Truman, who forbade him to take the risk which might have involved the United States in war with Russia and China.

The temporary eclipse of Lieutenant-General Sir Leslie Morshead, after his return from the Middle East, is also cited as an example of Blamey's ruthlessness by critics who forgot how Blamey had championed Morshead's qualifications when Montgomery appointed relatively inexperienced British corps commanders in North Africa, to the exclusion of Morshead. Morshead certainly would have been the logical successor to Blamey as Commander-in-Chief of the Australian land forces, but it was Blamey's decision, as commander, to give him I Corps for the offensive aimed at giving the *coup de grâce* to Japan. Few people knew, at that time, that the atom bomb would do it instead.

The relationship between Blamey and MacArthur, cordial to begin with, deteriorated on further acquaintance. The same might be said of relationships between Australian and American troops. The former developed a very human resentment of the great advantages in pay and conditions enjoyed by Americans who were doing the same job; of their arrogant assumption of a superiority which was bestowed by material resources rather than by individual character; and of the way in which they behaved when stationed or on leave in Australian cities.

But Blamey did his utmost to implement every directive given to him by MacArthur, including the order to take active command of New Guinea Force and "energise" the campaign. He did not hesitate to take issue with the American when he thought that MacArthur's strategy was wrong, as in the case of Borneo, but limited his public criticism to the remark, "The best and the worst things that you hear about him are both true," when asked his opinion of MacArthur. This evaluation has been confirmed by leading military authorities, whose summary of MacArthur is that he possessed "great strengths and great weaknesses of military virtue."

MacArthur did not give public expression to his opinion of Blamey, but once told him that he was "A lucky commander," and that he was, "Trying to cover too much ground."

"I don't think it's luck," Blamey replied. "I think it's taking a calculated risk after good reconnaissance, with good officers and good troops."

But other people had the same opinion of Blamey. Curtin suggested several times that he should appoint General Northcott as his deputy, but Blamey always was reluctant to delegate his prime responsibilities and authority. This characteristic created many staff problems in Canberra and Melbourne, especially when he took on the extra load of the New Guinea command.

The firmest wartime relationship at the vital summit of responsibility was that between MacArthur and Curtin. The Prime Minister never faltered in his conviction that Australia must now look to America, instead of Britain, as her prime ally, and supported MacArthur unwaveringly. MacArthur responded with all the sentiment and emotion of which he was capable, and in his reminiscences wrote, "John Curtin, the Prime Minister, died early in July. His death saddened me greatly. I tried to express what I felt in my message to the Australian people; 'He was one of the greatest wartime statesmen, and the preservation of Australia from invasion will be his immemorial monument.' I mourn him deeply."

The wisdom and leadership of Curtin during Australia's most critical era have received less recognition than they deserve. His task was not made easier by the somewhat dubious calibre of some of his senior ministers, nor by the trade union unrest which simmered below the surface of Australia's war effort. Such factors must have contributed to his sudden death when the victory which he had worked for was close at hand, but his true monument may be the fact that he laid the foundations of an Australian-American relationship which has been of great importance since the end of the war.

After his death, the government which he had led showed a remarkably paltry attitude towards senior commanders of the Australian armed forces. It refused to accept Blamey's recommendations on awards to senior officers, even though he pointed out that they had received little recognition or reward for six years of service. He said that the British had shown greater generosity, in this respect, to the Australians who had served under them in the Middle East, than the Australians had shown to their own men fighting on their northern frontiers.

Forde, the Minister for the Army, replied that the Labor Government would not recommend knighthoods for any officers, nor decorations for non-operational services. He stated that this attitude was not activated by ingratitude, but was merely "Labor policy."

However, he did ask Blamey what he wanted for himself. Blamey answered, "I don't want anything. All I want to do after I leave the barracks is to attack your government. I'll do it at every opportunity."

In the end he retained his Buick staff car, which had carried him through 50,000 miles of Australian operational areas.

He spent the last days of his command in pressing the government to accept a number of recommendations for the reorganisation of the Australian Army, but the government's animosity towards its own Commander-in-Chief was so great that not only were these ignored, but an opportunity for revenge was seized when Blamey was invited to attend the first post-war convention of the American Legion, to be held in Chicago on 3 November 1945. He was to be guest of honour, a gesture which had never been made to an Australian before then, and his attendance would have been a fitting punctuation mark to the Australian-American wartime alliance. The Labor Government, however, chose to refuse him permission to attend.

By 1948, when MacArthur invited him to visit Tokyo, he was a private citizen and relatively free from such bureaucratic vengeance, so he was able to enjoy the visit. The government had to content itself with steadfastly refusing numerous suggestions that he should be promoted in retirement to field-marshal, but when Labor was thrown out of power in 1949, Mr R. G. Menzies made immediate representations to the British Cabinet.

The British were lukewarm to his proposal, on the grounds that Blamey was no longer on the active list, but Menzies found this a minor obstacle. He restored Blamey to the active list, and made sure that he was appointed field-marshal in the King's Birthday Honours published on 8 June 1950.

It was almost too late. Blamey fell sick a few weeks later, and with both legs paralysed was admitted to Heidelberg Repatriation Hospital, Melbourne. But his lifelong determination did not fail him, and by 16 September he had rallied sufficiently for the ceremony in which the Governor-General, Mr William McKell, presented his field-marshal's baton in the presence of Mr Menzies and many of Blamey's wartime colleagues. In uniform but in a wheel chair, Blamey was too overcome to deliver his prepared speech but responded informally. Shown his picture in the paper next morning, he remarked, "I look like a broken-down German General with a meerschaum pipe."

He was not to leave hospital again. His doctors and his own will power enabled him to walk once more, early in 1951, but the life of the old soldier was slowly fading away. On 30 May 1951, 20,000 people filed through the Melbourne Shrine of Remembrance, in which his body lay in state for five hours, and then ten generals marched with the gun carriage bearing his coffin from the Shrine to Fawkner Crematorium. Whatever may have been said or written about him during his lifetime, the presence of 300,000 people along the route seemed to show that the people of Australia knew what had been done for them by their most controversial general.

BOOK IV

The Uncertain Years

❋ ❋ ❋ ❋ ❋ ❋

"For," said he, "as flourishing a condition as we may appear to be in to foreigners, we labour under two mighty evils; a violent faction at home, and the danger of an invasion, by a most potent enemy, from abroad."

A Voyage to Lilliput
JONATHAN SWIFT

37

"TRUE FIGHTING SOLDIERS"

THOSE WHO SURVIVED THE FIRST WORLD WAR, AND IN THEIR INNOCENCE had hoped for an era of peace and plenty, had been granted neither. Those who were discharged in 1945, and their sons after them, have lived through a phenomenal era of a constantly developing world economy but a constantly threatened world security. The dreadful shadow of the mushroom cloud has lain over the world ever since 6 August 1945, but the strange thing is that, despite a proliferation of nuclear weapons sufficient to destroy all human life, most campaigns since then have been predominantly those of the infantryman.

The edgy suspicions which almost always have characterised Russian foreign policy very soon came to the surface after the war. On 24 June 1948 they blockaded West Berlin, in the hope of strangling the outpost which clumsy diplomacy had left in their sphere of influence, but they were countered by the British and American air lift which for nearly eleven months supplied the city with its necessities and gave the Russians a wounding propaganda defeat. Australian aircrews and aircraft helped in this operation, and R.A.A.F. Dakotas of No. 86 Wing, despatched to Europe for the purpose, carried 7,000 tons of coal and 7,072 passengers.

For about five years after the war, Australian servicemen formed a large component of the British Commonwealth Occupation Forces in Japan, but this force was nearing the end of its tenure and had in fact lost all its Indian and most British units when the North Koreans invaded South Korea.

The situation on the Korean peninsula had been growing increasingly ominous since the withdrawal of the Japanese. Korea, previously known as Cho Sen or the Land of the Morning Calm, had for centuries been a subject

407

nation. Conquered by the violent and bloody Chinese empress Wu Hou in 684, it was annexed by Japan in 1910, fifteen years after the defeat of China in the Sino-Japanese War, and five years after Russia's capitulation in the Russo-Japanese War. For Japan, Korea was the first step towards establishing a sphere of influence in South-east Asia, and a springboard for her invasion of Manchuria and long drawn out Chinese adventure. She made Korea into a Japanese colony and market, enlisted Koreans into her armies (they were known as the most brutal of the prison camp guards) and lost it entirely in 1945.

The Japanese departure left a vacuum to be filled immediately by Russia, which by her last-minute and almost inactive entry into the war against Japan had been enabled to enjoy the spoils of victory and repossess the sphere of influence which Japan had wrenched from her in 1905. Russia set up a communist republic in North Korea, and South Korea became a democratic republic under the tutelage and protection of the United States.

The Koreans are a Mongolian people, related to both the Chinese and the Japanese. Those of the North are traditionally jealous of the South, who by comparison enjoy a softer life in more favourable conditions of climate and terrain. It did not take long for political differences fomented by the Russians to erupt into a series of clashes of minor or major degree, and on 25 June 1950 an army of North Koreans trained, equipped, and partially led by the Russians invaded South Korea.

The Russians recently had walked out of the United Nations, so that body was able to react with unusual vigour and promptitude. A force which eventually comprised the troops of fifteen nations, predominantly those of the United States, was raised to hold South Korea. Of these, Australians were among the first in action.

Men of No. 77 Squadron, R.A.A.F., based at Iwakuni in Japan as part of the British Commonwealth Occupation Force, were giving farewell parties prior to leaving for home when the news of the invasion broke on the world. Within a week they were back on operations, and among their first missions was the escorting of American light bombers in an attack on the bridges over the Han River.

In Australia, a number of men volunteered to join the 3rd Battalion of the Royal Australian Regiment, which was to be detached to become part of the 27th British Commonwealth Infantry Brigade. The other components of this brigade were a battalion each of the Argyll and Sutherland Highlanders and the Middlesex Regiment.

All ranks of the 3rd Battalion were volunteers, with service in the second World War, and drawn either from civilian life or from the 67th Infantry Battalion, then on occupation duties in Japan. Its most highly decorated member was Private Alex Kroll, who had just failed second year medicine at Melbourne University. During the second World War he had reached the rank of flight lieutenant in the R.A.A.F., and won the D.F.C. and D.F.M. while flying on seventy-six bombing raids over Germany. He was to be critically wounded and crippled for life within a fortnight of landing in Korea, and only his great spirit and courage enabled him to survive.

The Australians, led by Lieutenant-Colonel C. H. Green, were thrown into action at once, and for the first week were engaged in mopping-up operations in the Songju-Waegwan area. On 5 October, with the two British battalions, they were airlifted to Kimpo to take part in the invasion of North Korea.

This was General MacArthur's plan. For five years he had been the virtual ruler of Japan, and under his guidance the country had been making its first faltering steps out of shameful and cataclysmic defeat into a future brighter than anyone could have dreamed of. News of the Korean invasion had brought the old warrior back into action with all his old vigour and flamboyance apparently undimmed. Chest blazing with a huge splash of "fruit salad," non-regulation cap cocked jauntily, he took firm hold of a campaign which was to be his from the start.

Initially the Americans had been caught completely off-balance. Partly trained occupation troops who had been enjoying almost holiday conditions in South Korea and Japan were unprepared for the savage assault by tough North Koreans who had been thoroughly drilled and indoctrinated by the communists. But they rebounded very quickly, and began to fly in enormous quantities of war material and reinforcements. MacArthur planned to thrust the North Koreans far back beyond the 38th parallel of latitude, which was the disputed border between the two sections of the peninsula, and drive right up to Manchuria.

The 27th British Commonwealth Infantry Brigade joined the U.S. 1st Cavalry Division at Kaesong, and was given an immediate objective of Kumchon, about twenty miles north of the 38th parallel. The 8th U.S. Cavalry Regiment was to advance up the centre, along the main road, while the 5th Cavalry made a wide encircling movement on the right flank with the intention of joining the 8th at Kumchon. The 7th Cavalry was to move west and north, bypassing Kumchon on the left to seal off the main road leading north.

The thrust began on 9 October 1950, with the Australians rolling through a battle area completely different from anything they had known before. The earth roads which they followed ran along broad, shallow valleys crossed by many rivers and streams flowing, and then zig-zagged up into the ridges and ranges of the mountainous peninsula. There were many huddled villages or small towns, largely of thatched huts or tiled buildings in the Chinese style. Rice paddies, which virtually are shallow swamps, lay along the valley floors, and sometimes were terraced up the slopes of the foothills. As the Australians went north, the rice paddies were empty except for the dry stalks moving in the cool winds of autumn.

Brigadier B. A. Coad, in command of the Commonwealth troops, found that his men had a comparatively inactive role as they entered the mountains around Kumchon, which was taken by the 7th Cavalry against light opposition. He commented, "I kept on being put on to an axis which did not exist, and we floundered about in those mountains. I was longing for someone to put us on a decent axis and let us go. They did eventually and ordered me to capture a place called Sariwon. We were thirty-four miles from it and it was reported to be the Aldershot of North Korea."

The Argylls took Sariwon without difficulty, and the Australians moved through them to defensive positions eight miles further north. They were sited in rolling country through which the enemy was falling back to Pyongyang before the massive United Nations drive, and after nightfall there was considerable confusion because they did not know that they had been outflanked by the Commonwealth troops and continued to stage troops through the area.

These ran into the Argylls and Americans in Sariwon, and attempted to withdraw northwards. They encountered the Australians, who soon found themselves fighting on both ends of their position with the reserve company turning round to face south.

After the first skirmishing, two Australian company commanders thought of a way in which to pull off a monumental piece of bluff. They were Majors G. M. Thirlwell and I. B. Ferguson, who mounted a tank with an interpreter and had themselves driven towards the enemy. They took the risk of being cut down, but were able to tell the North Koreans that they were completely surrounded, and invite them to surrender.

After a few moments of acute tension, the Koreans began to throw down their arms. 1,982 surrendered, together with a quantity of anti-tank guns, machine-guns, and mortars.

The Australians resumed their advance under the command of the U.S. 24th Division, with the object of capturing Chongju via Sinanju. Pyongyang was taken by Americans and South Koreans on 19 October.

The autumn rains were flooding down now, and though the Australians advanced seventy-six miles in two days they became bogged down in the primitive roads churned up by troop movements. But by 22 October they were on the move again, and the Argylls captured Yongyu while American paratroops dropped further north to cut the escape route to Sukchon. The Middlesex men took up defensive positions around the northern outskirts of Yongyu, and the Australians were advised that the paratroops were about a mile north of the point which they had reached.

During the night, retreating Koreans ran into the paratroops and a heavy engagement broke out. The Australians moved in with the support of Sherman tanks, and launched a bayonet attack on North Koreans dug in on a wooded knoll. They routed the first line of defences and swarmed on to the second line, killing about 270 North Koreans and capturing 239, at a cost to themselves of seven wounded.

Lieutenant-Colonel Green was proving to be a superb leader, and at one stage of the battle found himself at grips with the enemy. In Brigadier Coad's description of the battle, he said: "The battalion deployed and Colonel Green put a company over a small hill where they killed about 70 North Koreans, and moved on. The C.O. then moved up with his tactical H.Q. and was immediately counter-attacked and he had a grim battle with his small party. As the Australians drove them off the hills, they got down into the paddy and were hiding in the paddy, in the ditches, everywhere; sniping and being an infernal nuisance. Then I saw a marvellous sight. An Australian platoon lined up in a paddy field and walked through it as thoug' they were driving snipe. The Australians thoroughly enjoyed it, they did the whole day and they really were absolutely in their element."

The Commonwealth Brigade, being in the vanguard of the advance, was next ordered to secure a bridgehead across the Changchow River and capture Pakchon and Chongju, on the main routes from Pyongyang to the Manchurian border.

The Middlesex made an unopposed crossing of the river, but the Australians, further upstream, ran into stiff opposition at Anju. They pushed on, and moved to a point one mile south of Pakchon, where the main road crossed the Taenyong River. In an engagement which became known as the Battle of the Broken Ridge, they secured a tenuous bridgehead across the Taenyong, and after a day and night of heavy fighting increased the depth of their perimeter and linked up with the Argylls, who had crossed at Pakchon. Besides inflicting heavy casualties, they captured about 225 North Korean prisoners.

Chongju, which lies forty miles from the Manchurian border, was the brigade's next objective as it spearheaded the advance along the west coast. The Argylls, with tanks in support, were in the vanguard until they encountered opposition four miles south of Chongju, when the Australians passed through them.

The entry into Chongju was through a mountain pass, overlooked by enemy concentrations including tanks concealed in undergrowth on a north-south ridge along the road. Despite this, Green ordered his battalion into the attack.

Artillery support sent barrages ahead of them to explode among the enemy positions, but the Australians still had a hard grind as they attacked up the ridges and drove the enemy back from one to another. By the end of the day they had captured several important ridges, but then had to withstand a heavy counter-attack in which the enemy did their utmost to regain the lost ground. They were fought off with heavy casualties during a four hours engagement, and at daybreak the weary Australians began to move forward again. But the North Koreans faded away ahead of them, and it became obvious that organised resistance had almost ceased.

The Argylls passed through the Australians to continue the advance, and that afternoon the Commonwealth troops occupied Chongju, which like every Korean town and village through which the armies passed was a place of corpse-strewn wreckage and desolation, with a few civilians emerging half-dazed from the ruins.

The hills around the town still echoed to the thump of occasional artillery and small-arms fire, and that evening a stray shell hit the tree under which Lieutenant-Colonel Green's tent had been pitched. A fragment pierced the canvas and hit him as he slept, and he died two days later. He was succeeded in command by Lieutenant-Colonel I. B. Ferguson.

After eight weeks in action the Commonwealth Brigade was to go into reserve, and General Hobart Gay of the U.S. 1st Cavalry Division, to which it had been attached for most of the operation, signalled Brigadier Coad: "Congratulations on your splendid, sensational drive into enemy territory. I know it is a proud day in your brigade's record and one which deserves the envy of all soldiers. It is a great pleasure to have such a unit as yours associated with 1st Cavalry. Men of your brigade are true fighting soldiers, who marched thirty-one miles in twelve hours to deal the enemy this disastrous blow."

Chongju was the farthest north reached by Australian troops in Korea, and the nearest they got to the Yalu River or the Manchurian border. Coad considered the enemy nut had been cracked, and asked General Gay to pass a regimental combat team through his brigade to continue the advance. This was done, the Americans advanced sixteen miles without opposition, but on the following afternoon he was for no apparent reason requested to move the brigade back to Pakchon.

MacArthur's "police action," as it had then began to be termed, had been a speedy success. The invading North Koreans had been chased out of the South like thieves from an orchard, and their army had been pursued into its lair and all but annihilated. The next logical step would have been for the matter to be negotiated in the United Nations, but it was too much to expect that the communists should accept such a disastrous defeat.

A large Chinese force, to which communist propaganda gave the name of "volunteers hastening to help North Korean comrades attacked without provocation by imperialistic forces of the U.S.A.," swarmed across the Yalu River. They struck the South Koreans on the right flank of the United Nations forces, and began to drive them back almost immediately. The U.S. 1st Cavalry Division, sent to support them, was soon fighting desperately, and with the 8th Cavalry Regiment was encircled and almost wiped out. On 2 November the United Nations forces began to withdraw, in steadily worsening weather which heralded the full blast of the Korean winter.

YEAR OF VICTORY: *Top:* Lieutenant-General Adachi, commander of the Japanese 18th Army in New Guinea, hands his sword to Major-General H. C. H. Robertson of the 6th Division after signing the surrender documents at Cape Wom airstrip. *Bottom:* An LCVP craft landing troops of the 7th Australian Division at Balikpapan on 1 July 1945.

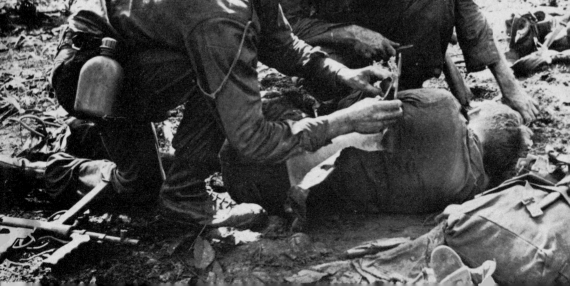

The 27th Commonwealth Brigade's rest period ended abruptly, with orders to hold the north-west corner of a bridgehead guarding the Taen-yong River crossing and the river crossing further south, at Sinanju and Anju. To the right of the Commonwealth bridgehead, the 24th U.S. Infantry Division extended its perimeter to cover the Anju crossing. The South Koreans were further to the east.

The Chinese launched an attack of the kind which was to become all too familiar in the Korean campaigns, with hordes of soldiers in clumsy-looking padded jackets and breeches charging forward in wave after wave which seemed inexhaustible. The uproar of firing was pierced by the screeching bugles which they blew either by way of encouragement or to pass on movement orders, and like a grey tide they washed up and over the American perimeter and forced the infantrymen to retire.

Then the Chinese swung to the west, in an attempt to outflank the Commonwealth Brigade. The Argylls took the first shock, and left many grey-clad corpses before them as they were forced to withdraw. The Australians moved up through them as they fell back, and exerted such solid pressure that the Chinese onslaught faltered and fell back. It was revived by a series of counter-attacks, each of which was beaten back as the Australians recaptured lost ground and several strongpoints. By next morning they were still astride the road to the south, and Lieutenant-Colonel Ferguson sent clearing patrols out to the north. One of them reached a hilltop from which they were cheered by the sight of the enemy retiring northwards.

The Australians had lost twelve killed and sixty-four wounded during the engagement, but had taken a heavy toll of the enemy. They had been supported for the first time by aircraft of 77 Squadron R.A.A.F., and Ferguson remarked, "It was an all-Australian day."

The Commonwealth Brigade had repulsed an attack by a mass of Chinese troops, estimated at about 10,000, which had been launched in the hope of outflanking the United Nations retreat. For the next three weeks, it seemed that this repulse had discouraged the Chinese, and that MacArthur would be able to deliver a counter-thrust which would drive them back across the Yalu River and enable him to carry out his promise of "home for Christmas."

Patrols from the three Commonwealth battalions probed northwards ahead of the main units, and they fanned out from their Chongchon positions in order to re-establish themselves in their former defence lines near Pakchon. Winter had set in with a vengeance, with blizzards driving down from the Mongolian wastes.

By this time the Commonwealth Brigade had experienced almost ninety days of continuous action and movement. The Australians had spent fifty-four days in the front line, and had suffered the heaviest casualties in the brigade. But any hopes of rest and relief were as shortlived as the forward movement of MacArthur's offensive, because the Chinese struck back with

THE WOUNDED, II. *Top:* In beds made from blankets strung on timber hacked from the jungle, wounded Diggers lie in a dressing station after the fighting at Oivi, New Guinea. *Bottom:* When Delta Company of the 6th Battalion, 3rd Royal Australian Regiment, returned to the Long Tan battlefield twelve hours after defeating the North Vietnamese, they found two wounded soldiers still lying there. Here, one receives first aid.

a massive counter-attack which almost shattered several South Korean divisions on the right flank and threatened the 2nd and 24th U.S. Divisions in the centre. The whole United Nations front was forced to withdraw to avoid complete destruction.

Fifteen nations now had troops in or en route to South Korea, and a Turkish brigade was now in alliance with the Australians as they tramped south to Kunu-Ri and then Sunchon, in freezing winter conditions. Thirty-five years after their fathers had fought each other in the dust and heat of Gallipoli, Turks and Australians now stood together in the snow of the east flank of the United Nations front, fighting off the "human sea" which pressed against them from the north. The Australian task, together with the British battalions and the 2nd U.S. Division, was to prevent the Chinese from getting behind them and closing the roads along which the rest of the United Nations forces were pouring to the south.

The Americans suffered most heavily in this rearguard fight, and lost over 4,000 killed, wounded, and prisoners, but the U.S. official battle report paid generous tribute to the Commonwealth Brigade, saying, "Without help from the British 27th Brigade and close Air Force support to break up road blocks near Kunu-Ri, the embattled division could have been lost." Of the Turks, an American liaison officer reported, "When the Turks ran out of bullets they unsheathed their knives. They are as tough as their reputation. They obeyed only one order: Advance. Any other command confuses them."

The 27th Brigade continued its retirement with occasional heavy fighting but in general suffered only spasmodic Chinese attacks. They passed through the newly arrived British 29th Brigade and reached the town of Uijongbu, only fifteen miles north of Seoul, the capital of South Korea.

A pathetic feature of the retreat was the columns of refugees; men, women, and children, who dreaded being left to the mercy of the advancing communists. Most of the Korean peasants lived in abject poverty at the best of times, and now, driven southwards in deepening snow and flogged by shrieking blizzards, their plight was fearful. They were hoping to reach safety in the capital or at least behind the United Nations lines, but the Chinese launched another major offensive on New Year's Eve and threatened the capital itself.

The orderly withdrawal of the Australians had covered 200 miles in nine days, a great deal of it on foot. Though officially placed in reserve to the U.S. 9th Corps, their brigade together with the British 29th Brigade and American units formed a rearguard protecting the northern approaches to Seoul.

When the new Chinese offensive began, the Australians were ordered to move six miles north of Uijongbu, to act as rearguard to the 6th South Korean Division. The South Koreans passed through them, but when they attempted to pull back they found that they had been outflanked by the Chinese, who had established a series of road blocks. Each of these had to be overcome by a short and savage attack, and the Australians fought their way through to rejoin their brigade as it withdrew to Seoul.

The city was in chaos, with hordes of refugees trying to leave among the troops and vehicles of the United Nations forces, but the Americans had decided against trying to make a stand in its immediate area. The Australians covered the retirement of the U.S. 1st Cavalry Regiment and 24th Division, and were the last United Nations troops across the railway bridge before it was blown up by the U.S. Engineers.

The United Nations retreat continued for forty-five miles south of Seoul, and the Commonwealth Brigade dug into defensive positions along "Frost-bite Ridge," seven miles west of Changhowon-ni. For the next month, the British and Australians fought a "Western Front" type of war across the No Man's Land which lay between their lines and the Chinese.

The four Australian companies and one Middlesex company held a front of 3,500 yards, and in temperatures which often fell below zero they sent out patrols which were involved in frequent clashes with the Chinese. On 25 January the U.S. 8th Army, under its newly-appointed commander General Ridgway, launched a new offensive, but the Commonwealth Brigade was held as 9th Corps reserve.

The Chinese counter-attacked strongly on 4 February, and the brigade moved to positions south of Yoju but was not thrown into the fighting until 14 February. Then, it crossed the Han River to support the U.S. 2nd Division in the Chipyong-ni area, where its 23rd Infantry Regiment and a French battalion had been cut off.

American tanks fought their way through to the surrounded troops, while the Commonwealth Brigade cleared its flank among the stark, snow-covered hills. The Australians had twenty-four hours of heavy fighting, and the Argylls and Middlesex occupied hills on each side of them against light opposition.

The brigade was now being strengthened by more Commonwealth units. It had been joined by a New Zealand field regiment and an Indian ambulance unit, and on 19 February the 2nd Battalion of Princess Patricia's (Canadian) Light Infantry came into the line. Probably it was the first time that a formation as small as a brigade and commanded by an Englishman, Brigadier Coad, had contained so many Commonwealth contingents.

As part of the U.S. 9th Corps, the brigade participated in General Ridgway's offensive, and was given the task of trapping a large force of North Koreans moving south-east of Wonju.

This called for a cross-country movement through mountainous terrain in which the roads, where they existed, were no better than tracks. The troops were heavily laden with weapons, ammunition, and supplies, so that the Australians described themselves as "human camels without humps."

The brigade struck off into the mountains, with the Canadians and

Australians in the van, while Ridgway attempted to develop his plan of rolling up the enemy from east and west simultaneously. This was frustrated by heavy rains and the flooding Han River, which slowed up the advance just as the Australians and Canadians came in touch with the enemy on the right flank.

Their immediate objective was to cut the main supply route to Chunchon, a town just below the 38th parallel which was held by the Chinese. To do this they had to drive the enemy off three hills, designated Hills 410, 419, and 614, as well as other features which were more lightly held.

Hill 614 was assigned to the Australians, who had to approach it along a steep ridge so narrow that only one section at a time could approach the enemy strongpoints. It was so steep that the Chinese could roll hand grenades down onto them, but for two days the Australians attacked steadily up this murderous defile until a patrol could get close enough to launch a bayonet attack which overwhelmed the Chinese.

Hill 419 and other neighbouring hills fell more easily to the Australians and Canadians, and the next hard nut to crack was Hill 410, which dominated the road to Chunchon.

Heavy snow was falling as the Australians attacked this feature, and during the afternoon they had to grope forward against a blizzard of both snow and fire and in freezing weather. But they pressed on so determinedly that the Chinese abandoned the position during the night, leaving large quantities of arms and ammunition behind them.

The Argylls and Middlesex now passed through the Australians and Canadians, and on 11 March the Commonwealth Brigade launched an attack on high ground south of Yangdogwon-ni. The Australians were the only troops who had to fight for their objective.

Two days later the brigade went into Corps reserve near Chipyong-ni, and enjoyed ten days leave. The Australians had now been in action for 165 days out of the six months spent in Korea, and had suffered 300 casualties including their first commanding officer.

Towards the end of March they returned to the front just north of Hyon-ni, and were given the objective of Kapyong. The brigade advanced up the Kapyong road against sporadic opposition until the objective was captured by the Australians and Canadians.

Ever since the Chinese "volunteers" had made their appearance in Korea, General MacArthur had favoured an all-out assault which would carry the United Nations forces into the Chinese base areas beyond the Yalu River. He spoke bitterly of the "privileged sanctuary" which the Chinese enjoyed, since the United Nations were not prepared to attack them in their own country and they were able to prepare their offensives without harassment from bombing or ground attack. It was a pattern which was to be repeated fifteen years later, when the American offensives in Vietnam stopped short of venturing to cross the border except for bombing raids.

MacArthur's outspoken criticism of U.S. and U.N. policy brought him into conflict with President Truman, who with good reason feared that the general would take the initiative into his own hands and launch an attack across the Yalu River—with the possibility of drawing the Russians into an all-out war. He summoned MacArthur to a conference at which it soon became obvious that the general would not back down, and so decided to relieve him of his command. On 11 April 1951 he was succeeded by General Matthew Ridgway, whose field command of the U.S. 8th Army was given to General James Van Fleet.

The removal of MacArthur awoke great controversy, but the Australian government and its opposition leaders prepared a tribute in which they spoke of, "His great comradeship with Australian forces and the magnificent part he played in delivering us from the scourge of Japanese aggression and the danger of threatened invasion." There was indeed a special relationship between MacArthur and the Australians, especially since his reputation was founded on the Australian land victories of 1942-1943.

Eleven days after his relief by Ridgway, the Chinese launched the heaviest offensive so far experienced by United Nations troops in Korea. By that time, the offensive begun by Ridgway had driven the enemy back north of Seoul, and the British 29th Brigade, as part of U.S. I Corps, was holding a line on the Imjin River about thirty-five miles north of the capital. The Commonwealth Brigade, in IX Corps, was in support of the 6th South Korean Division, in an area just north of Chongchon-ni on the Kapyong River, thirty-five miles north-east of Seoul. Both these brigades were to play a vital part in the operations, and their gallant stand blunted the full force of the Chinese attack.

The Chinese struck on 22 April 1951, with their 187th Division falling on the British brigade like a tidal wave and driving them into a defensive perimeter at Choksong. The British troops, enormously outnumbered, fought back to such effect that the Chinese were obliged to commit another division to this attack, and it was here that the "Glorious Gloucesters," the 1st Battalion, Gloucester Regiment, earned fresh laurels for their colours. They fought the Chinese until they were exhausted, overwhelmed, and obliged to surrender.

The offensive hit the Commonwealth Brigade while the Argylls were on their way back to Hong Kong for rest, having just been relieved by the 1st Battalion, King's Own Scottish Borderers. The brigade was deployed with the Canadians to the left, on Hill 677, and the 3rd Battalion, Royal Australian Regiment, to the right, on Hill 504. The positions were about three miles apart and separated by the Kapyong River. The Middlesex battalion was in support, about a mile to the rear.

The brigade was supporting the 6th South Korean Division, and from their positions could hear the battle north of them increasing in intensity. The first signs that all was not well on the South Korean front came in the evening of 23 April, when some of their troops appeared and began to establish themselves in the Australian battalion area. More and more appeared, and it was soon obvious that the division had crumbled before the Chinese onslaught.

By 10 p.m., patrols from the Chinese 118th Division were probing the brigade front, mainly on the Australian sector, and these were followed very quickly by larger formations. In most of the Korean fighting so far the Chinese had used "human sea" attacks, which were in much the same style as the banzai charges of the Japanese; wave after wave of men being thrust forward with utter disregard for loss. By midnight, the Australians were fighting off the first of these, and in the stabbing flashes of small arms fire and the explosions of grenades, with flares arching overhead, could see the enemy charging up the hillside and being torn away by the torrent of fire. But as one line fell, so another would rise and follow after them with the eerie brazen screeches of their bugles rising and falling among the roar of explosions. At one time they came dangerously close to battalion headquarters, but were thrown back by a vigorous counter-attack.

Daylight showed the hillside slopes, green with the northern spring, littered with the drably-uniformed corpses of Chinese—and with yet another wave swarming up towards the Australian defences. They launched one assault after another throughout the day, coming close enough for their officers to fire their pistols at the Australians before being cut down.

Even those men among the Australians who had fought the Japanese had seen nothing to surpass the sacrificial fury of the Chinese attacks. The dead began to lie in heaps before the Australian positions, with a squirming form here and there showing where one of the enemy had managed to get within grenade-throw. The Australians were also suffering, and had to drag their own wounded clear even as another wave of attackers came up the hillside, but their casualties were not anywhere near to the enormous numbers of enemy dead and wounded.

This battle, all through the eve of Anzac Day 1951, went on until evening, when the Australians were ordered to withdraw to new positions near brigade headquarters. The Chinese then turned the full fury of their assault on the Canadians, who up until then had had to withstand comparatively minor attacks. They were surrounded for most of 25 April, until communications were reopened during the afternoon.

This marked the end of the battle, which concluded as abruptly as it began. By 4.30 p.m. the brigade front was quiet, the enemy had disappeared, and the 5th U.S. Cavalry Regiment had occupied the old Australian positions.

The battle of Kapyong had been fought and won, and the men of the

27th and 29th Brigades had demonstrated that the best way to counter the Chinese "human sea" tactics was to form determined defensive positions against which they dashed themselves in vain, and not to "butt out" as a number of American and South Korean units had been prone to do up until that time.

The two brigades had been largely responsible for defeating the Chinese spring offensive of 1951. The 3rd Battalion Royal Australian Regiment and the 2nd Battalion Princess Patricia's Light Infantry were two of the three units which received a Presidential citation for the action, the third being 'A' Company of the 72nd U.S. Heavy Tank Battalion.

The citation read: "The seriousness of the break-through on the central front had been changed from defeat to victory by the gallant stand of these heroic and courageous soldiers. The 3rd Battalion Royal Australian Regiment, the 2nd Battalion Princess Patricia's Canadian Light Infantry and 'A' Company, 72nd U.S. Heavy Tank Battalion, displayed such gallantry, determination and *esprit de corps* in accomplishing their mission as to set them apart from and above other units participating in the campaign, and by their achievements they have brought distinguished credit to themselves, their homelands, and all freedom-loving nations."

The 27th Brigade had fought its last battle. At midnight on 25/26 April 1951 its designation was changed officially to 28th Commonwealth Infantry Brigade, and on 26 April the brigade withdrew for rest and refit.

The flag of the old 27th Brigade was presented to Lieutenant-Colonel I. B. Ferguson, commander of the Australians, as a souvenir of the 3rd Battalion's distinguished service in Korea. A senior officer of one of the original British battalions of the brigade described the Australian unit as, "the finest fighting infantry battalion I have ever seen."

The ebb and flow of warfare up and down the Korean peninsula since June 1950 now stabilised into an almost static front, with the United Nations line running from a point on the west coast, about twenty miles below the 38th parallel, north-west to the east coast roughly twenty miles north of the parallel, cutting the parallel some forty miles north of Seoul.

11,000 yards of this front, on what was known as the Kansas Line south of the Widgeon Crossing on the Imjin River, was held by the 1st Commonwealth Division as part of the U.S. 1st Corps.

The 1st Commonwealth Division was formed in June, when the Commonwealth troops in Korea were joined by the 25th Canadian Brigade. This was the first time that British, Canadian, Australian and New Zealand troops had been integrated into a combat division, with medical services ably provided by the 60th Indian Field Ambulance. The division's first commander was Major-General A. J. H. Cassells, who had been serving in Canberra as Chief Liaison Officer, U.K. Services Liaison Staff.

Formation of the division was marked officially by a short ceremony held near Tokchong at noon on 28 July 1951, attended by General J. A. Van Fleet, commanding U.S. 8th Army; Lieutenant-General Sir Horace Robertson, C-in-C British Commonwealth Occupation Forces in Japan; and other senior officers.

On the Imjin front, the division faced the 192nd Chinese Division, which with the 190th and 191st were to be their main adversaries during the next phase. Initially, the Chinese held only lightly defended outposts up to 3,000 yards north of the river, with well-prepared defences some 6,000 to 8,000 yards to the rear, so No Man's Land was unusually wide.

The Australians, as part of the 28th Brigade, held the right of the Commonwealth front, with the British infantry to their left and the 25th Canadians in reserve. The left and right flanks of this sector were held by the 1st South Korean Division and the 1st U.S. Cavalry Division respectively.

The Commonwealth Division's task was to hold their front and to harass the enemy by aggressive patrols and raids, but the area was comparatively quiet until 3 October 1951. The Australians spearheaded a raid across the Imjin early in September, taking a few Chinese prisoners after light opposition, and a bridgehead was formed through which the whole division crossed a few days later, to establish a new defensive line about 6,000 yards north of the river in the Misan Myon area. From this line the division was to launch its first major attack against defended positions.

The preparations for the assault proceeded against a background of peace overtures initiated in a broadcast by W. M. Malik, Soviet representative at the United Nations, on 23 June 1951. But hopes for an early ceasefire, on honourable terms for both sides, sank in a morass of negotiations.

The divisional attack, code named Operation Commando, was designed to advance the whole corps front and to give the enemy an emphatic reminder that the United Nations force packed a solid punch. It was planned in three phases: one, an attack on the right by the 28th Commonwealth Brigade, to secure the dominating feature Point 355. Two, an advance by the 25th Canadian Infantry Brigade, on the left, on D-Day plus 1, to secure a line of high ground about 3,000 yards in front of their position. Three, exploitation to the divisional line by the Canadian Brigade on the left and the Commonwealth Brigade on the right.

At 3 a.m. on 2 October, the King's Own Scottish Borderers moved into the darkness towards their task of capturing Hill 355, with the Australians and the Shropshire Light Infantry in support. Once the hill had been taken, the Australians were to assault Hill 317, while Hill 217, on the left, was to be attacked by the Royal Northumberland Fusiliers, who had been attached to the brigade for that purpose.

The taking of the first outposts alerted the main Chinese line, which was well entrenched in strong defensive positions along and on top of the steep hills. They reacted with a storm of fire which was soon joined by the crash of shells as their artillery support opened up, and the Commonwealth troops had hard going. The advance of the two British battalions was slowed down, but by nightfall the Australians had stormed and captured an elevation on the right, covering the Borderers' line of advance. Next morning, the Australians surged forward again. They forced their way within grenade-throw of another Chinese strongpoint, and took it with bombs and bayonets. This weakened the Chinese grip on Hill 355, and the Borderers were able to take it in the early afternoon.

Next day, the Australians and Fusiliers began their attacks on Hills 317 and 217 respectively. The battlefield erupted into a chaotic uproar. The staccato clamour of small arms and machine-gun fire was punctuated by the crash of bombs or obscured by the scream of jets swooping down to pound the Chinese positions with rockets, while supporting artillery from both sides rolled thunderously in the background and sent barrages down to explode in great spouts of earth and flame. Through this turmoil the British and Australians advanced doggedly towards their objectives, and the Fusiliers stormed and took Hill 217 by three in the afternoon. They hardly had time to settle into their new positions before a Chinese counter-attack swarmed up the hill and drove them out again, to spend a wakeful night on the battlefield before attacking again next morning, taking the hill once more, and being forced to surrender it to yet another savage Chinese attack.

The Australian attack began at 3.30 a.m. on 5 October. Hill 317, a key point in the Chinese winter line, was a pyramid-shaped hill which on its eastern face was so steep that it could be climbed only on hands and knees. From their seemingly impregnable positions the Chinese poured machine-gun fire down on the Australians, who inched upwards with their supporting air and artillery fire bursting ahead of them. As deadly as fate they pressed closer and closer to the Chinese positions, until just before dusk they were close enough to send in a final shower of bombs and follow them up with bayonet-wielding infantrymen leaping in through the smoke and dust. Sixty-eight enemy dead littered their defences, and thirty prisoners were taken.

At first light next morning, 7 October, the Australians attacked the Hinge; a key point in the Chinese Hill 217 position. Despite furious opposition they took it by mid-morning, and held it against a series of counter-attacks which grew in intensity after 8 p.m., following a thirty minutes artillery bombardment. One attack after another was thrown in during the night, but the Australians repelled them without faltering. At 5 a.m. the Chinese gave up, and as the first cold streaks of dawn lit the battlefield the Australians watched in weary silence as Chinese stretcher-bearers began to carry away the 120 dead and wounded who had fallen in their vain counter-attacks. The Borderers took over from the Australians, and soon afterwards occupied Hill 217 without opposition.

"Their sheer guts is beyond belief," said Lieutenant-Colonel F. G. Hassett, now in command of the Australians. Their divisional commander singled them out for special praise, and General Van Fleet sent congratulations to the Commonwealth Division, which in six days of bitter fighting had taken the key defence points, Hills 217, 317, and 355, and advanced their front some 6,000 yards. Out of the casualty list of fifty-eight killed and 262 wounded, the Australians had lost twenty killed and 104 wounded.

The two hills which they had spent so much blood and effort in conquering were lost when the Borderers were forced to withdraw from them by heavy Chinese attacks beginning on 4 November, and after this the 28th Commonwealth Brigade went back into rest camps until January 1952.

During November 1951, the truce negotiations had reached one point of agreement when the communists accepted a proposal that a Demarcation Line between the forces should be based on a withdrawal of two kilometres by each opponent, at a time to be specified in an armistice agreement. After this the front subsided into less violent activity, with the commander of the 1 U.S. Corps ordering operations to be confined to holding existing positions. As the snows of another winter began to fly, the war had reached a stalemate.

There were occasional sharp actions, including an Australian raid on Hill 217 on 26/27 January. In a surprise advance across snow-covered No Man's Land they recaptured the hill, but were forced back again by a vigorous counter-attack.

The year wore on until June, when the 1st Battalion, Royal Australian Regiment, joined the 28th Commonwealth Brigade, and Brigadier T. J. Daly took command; the first Australian to lead a brigade in the Korean War. The 1st Battalion's first operation was a raid on Hill 217 in order to capture a prisoner for intelligence purposes, but they became so heavily involved with the enemy that they failed to achieve their objective. They destroyed four bunkers and inflicted casualties before being forced to withdraw by heavy artillery, mortar, and machine-gun fire, losing three killed and twenty-eight wounded in the process. Eleven nights later, the 3rd Battalion made a similar attack with similar results.

Such operations characterised the rest of 1952; sharp cut-and-thrust actions, patrol activities, and frequent ambushes by both sides. The Chinese had now established heavy artillery concentrations, and their barrages fell on the divisional front with increasing frequency and intensity.

Major-General Cassells was succeeded by Major-General West on 7 September, and went to take up an appointment in Europe. He had done a fine job of welding the various Commonwealth units into a strong fighting force, and his popularity was expressed by a senior Canadian officer's remark that, "If you had searched the whole world you could not have found a better man than Jim Cassells."

The Western Front type of operations continued, typified by a "Snatch" party sent out by the 3rd Battalion on 24/25 January 1953. A sergeant and four men, with two protective groups of thirteen apiece, tried to capture a prisoner from Chinese positions north-west of Hill 355. They saw large groups of Chinese moving between them and their objective, and ambushed one of these and killed about twenty. This action soon brought the enemy swarming towards them, but with characteristic aggression they charged and routed Chinese formations on several occasions. Eventually they were obliged to return to their own lines with thirteen wounded and without a prisoner, but leaving about ninety of the enemy dead behind them.

On 21 March 1953 the 1st Battalion R.A.R. was relieved by the 2nd Battalion, and five days later Brigadier Daly relinquished command of the Commonwealth Brigade to another Australian, Brigadier J. G. N. Wilton.

The Commonwealth Division's last major engagement was in the Battle of the Hook, in which the Chinese made several unsuccessful efforts to capture the area. The 2nd Battalion, which had relieved the French battalion in this sector, was involved in a heavy local action, but at last the war faded out when the truce was signed on 27 July 1953. It had lasted for three years and one month, during which the Commonwealth forces suffered 1,263 killed and 4,817 wounded. Of these, 281 and 1,257 had been Australians.

38

"WE WILL DO THE LURKING"

O N A RUBBER PLANTATION NEAR SUNGEI SIPUT, IN THE STATE OF PERAK, Malaya, Chinese guerrilla fighters executed communist-style justice by tying three English rubber planters to trees and killing them in cold blood. It was 16 June 1948; a day which began twelve years of fighting communist attempts to take Malaysia.

The bullets fired on that day climaxed nearly three years of intense political agitation which had its origin in the Japanese occupation of Malaya. During that period, Chinese guerrilla groups in Malaya were trained and supplied by the British in the hope that they would harass the Japanese. Most of these groups were communist, but the belief was that they would fight a common enemy. As in China itself, in the Balkans, and to some extent in France, the communists had different ideas. The Axis forces comprised only one of the enemies whom they were prepared to fight. The other was Western democracy, and if it was possible to use weapons supplied by Britain and America against the people of those countries, then so much the better.

So the Japanese surrender signalled a new phase of war for the communists in Malaya; one for which they had been training and recruiting in the jungles. The killing of the planters brought it into the open.

On the day they died, the British High Commissioner, Sir Edward Gent, proclaimed a state of emergency in Perak and Johore. This was extended to the whole of Malaya on the following day, and thus became the "Malayan Emergency" which lasted until after that country gained its independence and became known initially as Malaysia and later as Malaysia and Singapore.

The first three and a half years of this emergency were the gravest. Malaya was once more caught off balance. Its civil service was still in the process of post-war reorganisation, and the troops in the country were largely young British National Servicemen, sweating out their period of conscription. The policy of village resettlement, in which the people of jungle villages were pulled back so that they could not supply nor be disaffected by the communists, was far from popular. Military action was largely that of pursuing an elusive enemy through the jungle. The communists became so bold that in late 1951 they assassinated the then British High Commissioner, Sir Henry Gurney. Morale sank to a low from which it was to be restored by General Sir Gerald Templer, who was given the combined responsibilities of military and civil administration.

He made the oft-quoted statement that, "The answer lies not in pouring more troops into the jungle, but in the minds and hearts of the people." He believed that, in what was virtually a civil war, civil and military affairs were inseparable.

However, the number of troops engaged rose to about 50,000 British, Gurkha, and Malayan combat and auxiliary soldiers, handled with ruthless efficiency by General Templer, before the country was secured from communist terrorism.

In this campaign, the R.A.A.F. was once more the first of the Australian services to become involved. No. 1 Squadron, flying Lincoln bombers, was operational for eight years; from July 1950 to July 1958. During this period, the squadron flew 4,000 sorties out of its base at Tengah, on Singapore Island, to attack communist positions in the mainland hills and jungle. It delivered eighty-five per cent of the bomb tonnage dropped during the entire campaign; more than five times the bomb load of all other squadrons in Malaya.

No. 38 Transport Squadron, flying Dakotas, was employed in supplying the British and Gurkha columns with food, ammunition, and equipment, as they penetrated deep into the jungle and in accordance with General Templer's strategy kept the communists constantly on the move, refusing them any chance to rest and reorganise in their previously hidden strongholds.

Australian ground troops of the 1st, 2nd, and 3rd Battalions, Royal Australian Regiment, with supporting arms were committed to the Malayan insurgency campaign between 1955-62. These battalions, after finishing their service in Korea, had been withdrawn to Australia for reorganisation and reinforcement, and as in Korea consisted of volunteer regular soldiers. The government of the day, conscious that a communist threat to South-East Asia constituted an indirect threat to Australia, had decided to send them to back up the British operations.

By 1954, however, General Templer's relentless pressure was taking its full effect. The fabric of Chinese communist political and guerrilla influence had been torn to shreds, and the main cadres had either been split up into relatively ineffective but still potentially dangerous fragments, or had retreated across the border into Thailand.

The task of the Australians during the next four or five years was the unglamorous one of patrolling the areas which hopefully had been pacified by the vast British effort, with occasional skirmishes when a fragmented group was cornered. The pattern of the country was changing, with a slogan of *Merdeka* (freedom) as the British proceeded to bow out gracefully and turn over the country which they had· saved from the communists to those who would rule it henceforward. The success of General Templer's policy was demonstrated by the growing prosperity of Malaysia and Singapore.

A new confrontation was soon to come—expressed in that very word. President Soekarno of Indonesia, flushed with the power which had come to him after the liberation of his archipelago nation from the Dutch, was challenging the Dutch right to rule western New Guinea (which he called West Irian) and the Malaysian frontiers in what had been British North Borneo.

It was Soekarno who gave to his imperialist adventures the title of *konfrontasi*; confrontation with those who possessed what he desired. No one was quite certain how far he would go, and a combination of bluff on his side and weakness on the other enabled him to take over West Irian. As with all demagogues this only gave him an appetite for more, and he began to make demonstrations against Malaysia which boded ill for the peace of South-East Asia. With the communists stirring the pot, he ordered minor raids against the Malaysian coastline and frontiers; of not much more than nuisance value but enough to maintain an atmosphere of tension and apprehension.

Once more it fell to the British, only too anxious to hand over their former possessions to their inhabitants, to protect a nation which was as yet unable to protect itself. British army, navy, and air force units were deployed in southern Malaysia, and to these were added the 3rd and 4th Battalions, Royal Australian Regiment, in 1965 and 1966 respectively.

These units were placed under the command of the 99th British Brigade, or West Brigade as it was more commonly known because of its theatre of operations in western Malaysia. The two Australian battalions, with their own artillery and engineering support, were responsible for all of the Bau district and the southern portion of the Lundu district; a front of thirty-five miles along the border to a depth of thirty miles.

The Australian task was purely defensive, to prevent Indonesian troops infiltrating into their area of responsibility. For some of the men engaged it was a dress rehearsal for their later work in Vietnam, because the Indonesians followed somewhat the same tactics as the "National Liberation Front" forces in that country. Disguised as fishermen or farmers, they would try to slip through in order to stir up dissidence among the inhabitants or to do whatever damage they might. At other times they would appear more boldly, properly uniformed and equipped.

The whole affair was largely one of jungle patrols and scouting; a wearisome business in a languid climate without the climax of a genuine confrontation, though whenever it did come to a clash between patrols the Indonesians showed that they would have been no match for the defenders if they had tried a more definite invasion.

For the Australians the period added to their experience of jungle warfare, and saw the inception of the Special Air Services squadrons whose principle was that, in such campaigns, a smaller force is easier to operate and conceal and can often do much more damage than a larger one; a principle which they were to demonstrate with resounding success in Vietnam.

The "confrontation" campaign faded away soon after Soekarno's violent overthrow by the Moslem generals of his army, who saw clearly that his flirting with the communists could lead only to the eventual surrender of his country. For the Australians, much grimmer work lay ahead.

*　　*　　*

The raw wound of Vietnam is still bleeding, and it is far too soon to predict its eventual effect upon the body of the world. No one, in 1945, would have dared to predict the enormous return to economic power of Japan and West Germany, and it is impossible to predict how the Vietnam conflict may be seen a quarter of a century later. The latest Washington estimates, released in March 1971, show that over a million combatants and non-combatants of both sides have perished so far, with the Americans losing more men killed than in the first World War. Up to date, the Australians have suffered their fourth highest casualty list.

Australia's contribution to the conflict began modestly, with the appointment of thirty advisers, known as the Australian Army Training Team, to help the Army of the Republic of Vietnam (A.R.V.N.) and its irregular support groups. Compared with the more than half-a-million American servicemen and 50,000 South Koreans serving in Vietnam, the Australian effort may be thought of as comparatively minor, though it grew to a Task Force of 8,000 men, including three infantry battalions; a squadron of Iroquois helicopters, one of Canberra bombers, one of Caribou transports and two of Hercules transports, which altogether have mounted 300,000 operational sorties; and naval support including the destroyer *Hobart*, later relieved by the *Perth*.

No war in which Australia has been engaged has aroused such violent civilian reactions and argument, both for and against participation. Numerous intellectuals and politicians, with the aid of many strange bedfellows all the way from those who genuinely believe in the justice of their cause down to a lunatic fringe of anarchists and failed students, choose to ignore the vile cruelties and civilian slaughter by North Vietnam forces and place the entire onus upon the Americans. However they may feel, they can take nothing away from the courage and military expertise shown by their own countrymen in Vietnam—including the National Servicemen whom they have on occasion attempted to disaffect.

The original thirty men of the Australian Army Training Team have since been increased to 100, and these would certainly include some of the toughest and most experienced soldiers in the country. They have been heavily engaged in operations with the front line units of the South Vietnam Army during their eight years of service, and suffered heavy casualties, but have been rewarded with over eighty decorations including four Victoria Crosses.

The first of these was awarded to Warrant Officer K. A. Wheatley, for deeds of a character which exemplify the work of the advisers with the men of a foreign army and isolated from their own kind.

Warrant Officer Wheatley went out with a Vietnamese Civil Irregular Defence Group company on 13 November 1965, on a search and destroy operation in the Tra Bong Valley, fifteen kilometres east of Tra Bong Special Forces Camp in Quang Ngai Province. He was with the right platoon of the company, accompanied by Warrant Officer Swanton. The company was led by Captain F. Fazekas, with the centre platoon; an officer who was to die later in the war in a very similar action.

About forty minutes after leaving their base, and while they were crossing some open rice fields, Wheatley reported that his platoon was in contact with the Viet Cong. The enemy fought strongly, and their resistance increased so much that Wheatley radioed for help. Captain Fazekas organised the centre platoon to fight its way towards him, and led it through heavy Viet Cong fire. While still pushing through the jungle, he received another radio message from Wheatley to say that Swanton had been hit in the chest, and asking for an air strike and aircraft to evacuate casualties.

At almost the same moment, Wheatley's platoon began to break under the impact of Viet Cong fire, and the irregulars started to scatter into the bush. Their medical assistant stayed long enough to tell Wheatley that Swanton was dying, but Wheatley refused to abandon him. He dropped his radio, and began to half-drag, half-carry Swanton out of the open rice paddies towards the shelter of the jungle, about 250 yards away.

He was helped by one of the irregulars, Private Dinh Do, who urged Wheatley to leave his dying comrade as the air about them cracked and howled with machine-gun and automatic rifle fire and the Viet Cong could be seen running through the jungle to intercept them. At last, when they were only about ten yards away, Dinh Do left the two Australians together, and his last sight of Wheatley was of the warrant officer pulling the pins from two grenades and calmly awaiting the enemy. Soon afterwards, Dinh Do heard two grenade explosions followed by several bursts of fire. The two bodies were found at first light next morning.

Warrant Officer Wheatley had had the choice of leaving Swanton to his fate, and escaping through the dense jungle, or of staying with his wounded comrade and accepting certain death. He chose the latter.

"His acts of heroism, determination, and unflinching courage in the face of the enemy will always stand as examples of the true meaning of valour," said his citation for the Victoria Cross, which also said that he had displayed magnificent courage in the face of an overwhelming Viet Cong force which was later estimated at more than company strength.

The same kind of self-sacrificing courage was displayed by the other winners of the Victoria Cross in Vietnam; Major P. J. Badcoe, and Warrant Officers R. S. Simpson and K. Payne. Their courage stands as a symbol of the work of the Australian Army Training Team, and indeed of that of many Australians, both regular soldiers and National Servicemen, who have faced and outfought the enemy in scores of savage little actions whose histories are to be found in the bald language of battalion war diaries.

Apart from the work of the advisers, the first role of the Australians in Vietnam was seen as being largely defensive. When the 1st Battalion, Royal Australian Regiment, landed in Vietnam, they were attached to the 173rd U.S. Airborne Brigade at Bien Hoa, and given the task of securing the air base so that its work could continue without impediment. Together with a brigade of U.S. Marines stationed further north at Danang, the Bien Hoa force stood across the main route to Saigon and also contributed to the security of the capital.

The first Battalion took up their positions during June 1965, and at about the same time the war in Vietnam exploded from what had been a dangerous guerrilla warfare into an all-out Viet Cong offensive which obviously was designed to roll up the ARVN and their allies and take possession of South Vietnam for the communists.

The Government of South Vietnam asked for more effective help, and President Johnson instructed General William Westmoreland to use U.S. troops in counter-offensive action. The Australians, having been placed under American command, became involved almost immediately.

From that time until late 1970, when the first announcements were made of a planned withdrawal of Australians, they were engaged almost continually in a campaign which its opponents branded in such terms as the "cruellest, dirtiest, most unwinnable of wars," though it is hard to know what standards of comparison were used. In terms of human suffering, all wars are the same.

The Australians of the 1st Battalion were professional soldiers, including veterans of Korea and Malaya. They had a businesslike interest in seeing what the Viet Cong were made of, and they soon found that the protection of Bien Hoa involved more than mere static defence. It had been attacked several times by Viet Cong guerrillas, and it was soon realised that the only effective defence was offence. On 14 June, the first Australian patrol set out, and within days the jungle around the airfield was being regularly probed by patrols who aimed to hit the Viet Cong first.

Late that month the battalions rifle companies joined the Americans in an all out search and destroy action which was intended to mop up Viet Cong bases. This was preceded by a massive American bombing raid, and when the Australians found their sector almost empty of the enemy they naturally blamed the Americans for having given them such ample warning that they had simply moved out. Again and again the American strategy was to have a similar result, whereas the Australian feeling was that a stealthy movement into the heart of enemy territory, erupting with sudden violence against an unsuspecting foe, would have far more impressive results. In fact, they wanted to turn the enemy tactics against themselves, and to fight a jungle war in the same way that the 2nd A.I.F. and the militia divisions had fought the Japanese.

In subsequent operations, they were able to prove their theory; by using small patrols spread out and moving quietly through the jungle. If one man encountered the enemy, his mates would close in rapidly to attack them from all sides. This was in great contrast to the Americans, who moved through the jungle in close-knit groups which hoped to defeat any ambush by superior firepower, but often did not even see or hear the enemy who slipped away until they could strike with maximum effectiveness.

In July, the battalion had to fight off a hot attack on Bien Hoa airfield, but despite the volume of fire poured out by the Americans and themselves the Viet Cong still managed to damage parked aircraft with mortar fire.

During the last half of 1965, the Australians joined in more sweeps which were designed to keep the enemy on the move and prevent him from organising attacks on Bien Hoa. Those towards the Iron Triangle and Ben Cat areas, north of Bien Hoa and near the Cambodian border, penetrated for the first time in Viet Cong zones which had been safe havens and in which most villages had been communist-indoctrinated. In many of them, the Australians found weapons and explosives, but usually the men had left and no one remained but women and children.

It was difficult, dangerous, and often unrewarding work, and very often the Australians would see nothing of the enemy except for their defences of trenches lined with punji stakes (sharp bamboos smeared with human excrement) or the food and equipment which they had abandoned in a hurry. They discovered tons of rice in jungle caches, uncovered the tunnels dug by the Viet Cong to hide themselves and their weapons, and suffered casualties from the occasional brief skirmishes with escaping enemy. In

October a platoon led by Corporal Waring surprised a group of guerrillas in a village, moved in quietly, and attacked with a speed which made them run away leaving their dead and weapons behind them. It was one of the proofs of the Australian theory; that they could beat the enemy at their own game.

The battalion ended the sweeps with two dead, thirty-six wounded, and two Military Medals—including one for Corporal Waring. It had not been warfare in the style of Kokoda or Buna, with every step resisted by a determined enemy, but it had been remarkably effective. Unrelenting infiltration by the Australians had kept the enemy on the run so effectively that the sweep areas were declared, somewhat optimistically, to have been cleared.

Reinforced by the 105th Field Battery armed with 105 mm pack howitzers, the 3rd Field Troop of engineers, and a signals unit, the Australian land forces had risen to 1,500, and soon were engaged in further operations of much the same kind. Their object, as before, was to keep the Viet Cong on the move; to clear them out of the villages, to deny them rest, support, and supply, and to capture their stores of food and ammunition.

On one of these sweeps, known as Operation Rice Bowl because it was designed to protect the rice harvest from Viet Cong depredations, the Australians made their first attack against a fixed enemy position. This was at Duc Hoa, west of Saigon, and the Australians were airlifted into the area together with armoured personnel carriers. Well aware that the Viet Cong would receive early warning of the approach of such a force, and either reinforce the frontal approach to Duc Hoa or abandon it altogether, the Australians made a feint towards the position and then made a quick turning movement to attack it from the rear. They caught the enemy completely by surprise, and in a fierce onslaught killed seven and took the village without suffering a single casualty.

This sweep lasted four and a half weeks, and in the process captured 177 Viet Cong "tax collectors" whose job was to force the villagers to hand over a substantial portion of their harvest. For the loss of one man killed and four wounded, the battalion had prised loose the Viet Cong grip on one of the rich rice-producing areas.

From the time that the French began to move back into Vietnam in late 1945 and early 1946, the communist forces of Ho Chi Minh had developed a strengthening grip upon the Phuoc Tuy area and particularly on the districts round the road connecting Saigon with the port of Vung Tau. This was the most important, sophisticated, and fertile territory of the country; closely cultivated in the rich delta soil, focused upon the administrative capital and the trade routes along the river and between the coast and capital.

The communists, known as Viet Minh, began almost surreptitiously at first, but soon progressed to ambushing French vehicles and eventually wiped out a whole convoy and slaughtered all its men. When the French abandoned Vietnam after their disastrous defeat at Dien Bien Phu, the whole area between Saigon and the coast was under the influence of the communists who changed their name to Viet Cong.

In 1966, the Americans determined on a series of onslaughts which would clear them out more definitely than the previous "rice bowl" operations had done. The main Viet Cong forces were still in the mountains, but their food, money, and reinforcements still flowed upwards from the rich lowlands.

The 1st Battalion, Royal Australian Regiment, joined the 173rd U.S. Airborne Brigade and the 1st U.S. Infantry Division in a series of operations beginning in January 1966; lasting until the end of March and titled Crimp, Rolling Stone, Roundhouse, Mastiff, Phoenix, and Silver City.

On 8 January the Australians were air lifted into "Hobo"; a jungle area north-west of Saigon, but the moment their helicopters landed they were fighting for their lives. Their landing zone was ambushed by a company of Viet Cong who killed and wounded several men, but the rest dug in quickly and poured back fire from close range. With the help of air and artillery support they were able to fight out of the trap, and when they did so discovered that they had been landed almost on top of a strongly defended Viet Cong position. They drove the enemy out of it and captured a number of prisoners and a quantity of arms and ammunition.

The American-Australian advance went quickly after that, with the support of scores of armoured vehicles airlifted into the area. As the Viet Cong fell back, the Australians captured what was thought to be the headquarters of their whole guerrilla operation for the area which included Saigon. In a fantastically complex network of bunkers and tunnels, the 1st Battalion men found huge stores of food, weapons, ammunition, and equipment. Cleaning out the tunnels was a task which called for cold-blooded courage on the part of the Australian engineers who had to do it, and one of them died of fumes from one of the booby-traps with which they were bristling.

Each of the operations became a combination of probing patrol actions, sometimes ineffective but sometimes flushing out groups of the enemy or finding signs of his hasty retreat, and all out actions in which the Viet Cong fought back. In February, an Australian outpost was caught in a cross-fire between three battalions of Viet Cong and the 1st U.S. Infantry Brigade, when the Viet Cong launched a night attack on the Americans. The Australians kept their heads down until they saw their chance, and then sprang an ambush of their own on a group of the enemy as they scattered. Corporal W. Brunalli, leading the Australian patrol, had been wounded twice in the cross-fire, but by morning he and his men were still alive and had killed seven Viet Cong and wounded two.

In March, after the combined force had captured huge enemy supplies of food and equipment including vehicles, the Viet Cong launched a massive counter-attack against an American battalion, apparently in the hope of recapturing their stores. The Americans were surrounded, and despite the fire which they poured into the enemy found themselves in danger of being overwhelmed and with their ammunition running low. They called for artillery support which was rendered by Australian gunners of the 105th Field Battery, and even though it was pitch dark the Australians dropped their shells precisely where they would do most good. The enemy attack faltered and fell away, and the Americans found more than 200 of their dead lying in the jungle next day.

On 30 May 1965, the 1st Battalion held its final ceremonial parade before returning to Australia. Its men had been in Vietnam for almost eleven months, and during that time had participated in thirty-three major operations and lost twenty-four men killed in action. After the parade, their commander Lieutenant-Colonel Preece told the Adelaide journalist Ian Mackay that, "What we have done is show that the Viet Cong can be beaten."

Lieutenant-Colonel Preece, who had commanded the battalion for its last six months in Vietnam, was awarded the D.S.O. for his leadership and personal bravery—and when he returned home and led the march of the 1st Battalion through Sydney, he was assaulted by a woman who had smeared herself with red paint.

* * *

While the 1st Battalion prepared to depart from Vietnam, elements of the Australian Task Force reinforcements had been arriving. They included the 5th and 6th Battalions Royal Australian Regiment, which for the first time brought National Servicemen to serve in Vietnam, and altogether constituted what was virtually a miniature army. Under Major-General K. Mackay, C-in-C Australian Forces in Vietnam, and Brigadier O. D. Jackson, commander of the First Australian Task Force, were the two R.A.R. battalions, the 1st Field Regiment, and the 1st Armoured Personnel Carrier Regiment; a headquarters group, artillery, engineers, army service corps troops with an air despatch company, a field ambulance, a dental unit, an ordnance unit and a field workshop, a reconnaissance aircraft unit, military police, and other supporting elements which included a small ships squadron of the Royal Australian Engineers. These were to perform the dangerous work of ferrying men and material up and down the waterways of the Saigon River delta, under constant threat of ambush from Viet Cong hidden in the mangroves and from mines which they placed in the muddy water.

The Task Force also included the 3rd Special Air Services Squadron; one of the Australian Army's commando units which had developed out of such Independent Regiments as the one which harassed the Japanese on Timor for so long during the second World War.

During 1966 and 1967, the Allied forces in South Vietnam were steadily increased in order to implement the basic strategy of isolating the main enemy forces from the centres of population, and providing a protective shield behind which the administration and economy of the country could function.

The Australian Task Force was given responsibility for the Phuoc Tuy region east of Saigon. This area included the port of Vung Tau, with its important logistic installation and air base, and covers the south-eastern approach to Saigon and the access routes to the Rung Sat Special Zone, which includes the delta of the Saigon River.

The force was responsible for seeking out and destroying the enemy within this area, protecting the civilians, helping other Allied units in emergencies, assisting the civilians so far as was consistent with military duties, and providing training teams of officers and warrant officers to advise and assist the South Vietnam armed forces, both regulars and irregulars.

When the Task Force first arrived in the area it was outnumbered by the Viet Cong at least three to one, and certainly until the battle of Long Tan, there was an urgent need to place heavy emphasis on the search for main forces of the enemy.

The Australians have carried out all these duties with zest and efficiency— including the assistance to the civil population which exemplified General Templer's strategy, initiated in Malaysia, of "winning the battle for hearts and minds." In countless ways, from providing medical assistance to rebuilding war-shattered homes, entertaining children and feeding orphans, the Australian soldiers have won over the vast majority of the population of the Phuoc Tuy Province to trust and believe in their cause. Their work in this respect has been quite apart from the selfless and devoted toil of Australian civilian teams, from doctors to agricultural advisers, which is another story.

The first Task Force operation was to sweep the Nui Dat area around the 5th Battalion's positions at Ba Ria; about ten miles north of the main Task Force headquarters camp and logistics area around the port of Vung Tau. About one third of the battalion were National Servicemen, and it was in this sweep that the first conscripted Australian soldier died in action in the Vietnam war. He was Private W. Noack, a South Australian; the only battalion casualty in the month-long sweep which captured a large store of Viet Cong rice but saw little of the enemy. The rice was re-distributed to villagers in the area—from whom it had been taken in the first place.

In July and August, units of both the 5th and 6th Battalions continued to carry out that part of their operational orders which required them to "seek out and destroy the enemy" within the Phuoc Tuy area. For the most part, their contacts with the Viet Cong were fleeting exchanges of shots as their patrols surprised occasional small groups, or the usual discoveries of abandoned positions and dumps of food and weapons.

It seemed strange that the communists were not reacting more vigorously, but it was only the lull before the storm. The area had previously been under the control of the 5th Viet Cong Division, whose commander had 10,000 men of various categories at his disposal, and no doubt he was under pressure to rid this important province of the intruding Australians. Patrol actions became fiercer, but the enemy lost men without inflicting casualties, and then the Viet Cong Regiment 274 made an unsuccessful attempt to ambush a company of the 5th Battalion.

After this, it may be presumed that he decided to try a trap. The bait was a barrage of mortar shells on 6th Battalion headquarters early on 17 August, and the Australians took it by sending out D Company, under Major H. Smith, to clear the area.

They found the mortar positions, but saw nothing of the enemy. Next morning, Major Smith decided to investigate tracks leading into Long Tan rubber plantation, north of Long Tan village. Until the arrival of the Australians, Long Tan had been the headquarters of D445 Battalion of the Viet Cong.

Recent B Company patrol reports had reported some enemy in the Long Tan area, but the D Company men had no idea that they were advancing into a Viet Cong trap of at least 2,500 men. In torrential tropical rain, of the kind which makes it useless to even think of keeping dry, the men of two Australian platoons advanced into the gloomy rubber plantation, moving between the grey trunks beneath the thick canopy of branches through which the rain poured in a blinding cascade.

Suddenly, the plantation erupted all around them. Mortar shells crashed among the trees and a hail of bullets from rifles and automatic weapons snarled and ricocheted between their trunks as the Australians threw themselves down on the sodden ground, drawing together as they attempted to see the enemy and then beginning to return their fire.

It soon became obvious that they were surrounded, but they formed a flimsy perimeter among the rubber trees, sheltering behind their trunks or scratching out shallow rifle pits in the muddy ground. Wave after wave of the enemy charged forward and were shredded by the coolly directed Australian fire, but new attacks formed up behind the cover of their own dead and then made another suicidal charge of the type which Australians had defeated many times before, when they were attempted by the Japanese or Chinese.

But the Australians were suffering too, and their ammunition was running low. The continuing heavy rain, with a low cloud ceiling and the obscuring foliage, hindered attempts at air support, but the remainder of the battalion

did not intend to leave them to the mercy of the Viet Cong. Ten minutes
after nightfall, A Company attacked the enemy rear, having been brought
up in armoured personnel carriers led by Lieutenant-Colonel Colin
Townsend, the battalion commander. The Viet Cong broke and fled,
carrying their wounded and as many dead as they could. In the savage three
hour battle, the Australians lost seventeen killed and nineteen wounded
from D Company's strength of 108 men. The Viet Cong left 245 dead behind
them, and suffered an estimated 350 wounded.

For its epic stand, D Company was awarded the Presidential Unit Citation
"for extraordinary heroism" by President Lyndon Johnson. The action at
Long Tan also showed the calibre of the National Servicemen who fight
alongside the regular Australian soldiers in Vietnam. Their courage and
determination, against any odds, has shown that they have inherited the
finest qualities of the Australian fighting man.

*   *   *

The Viet Cong trap had failed because the prey which they had caught
in it was too fierce for them to hold. It was expected that similar ruses or
even a full-scale offensive would be tried in order to rid Phuoc Tuy Province
of the Australian Task Force, which constituted the most serious challenge
to its communist overlords since they had moved in during the confusion
after the Japanese had surrendered.

In their major task of securing the Task Force's base camp area while its
defences were being developed, the Australians made extensive use of the
3rd Special Air Service Squadron; the first of those which have been
employed so successfully in Vietnam.

From the earliest days in Vietnam, there had been some dissension as to
the most effective size of patrol. The use of small patrols had caused some
concern from Army Headquarters down, and there was an opinion that
such units would fare badly against the highly mobile Viet Cong units
which combined inborn junglecraft with good weapons and an intimate
knowledge of the terrain. A dissenter to this opinion was Brigadier T. F.
Serong of the Australian Army Training Team, whom Ian Mackay in his
book *Australians in Vietnam* quotes as saying, "Conventional soldiers think
of the jungle as being full of lurking enemies. Under our system, we will
do the lurking."

Brigadier Serong was convinced from the start that the war against the
Viet Cong could be won, and in a speech delivered late in 1970 stated that
it had in fact been won, and that the Viet Cong and their North Vietnam
ally had been rendered ineffectual in the provinces of South Vietnam which
they once controlled.

The Special Air Service, which in any army less pragmatic than the
Australian might be regarded as an élite, is of much the same opinion as

Brigadier Serong; that a small patrol can move with far less likelihood of discovery, yet with the aid of modern weapons and explosives can pounce devastatingly on far larger enemy groups when opportunity offers—and vanish again when the damage has been done. When their method was tried in the Phuoc Tuy area, it proved so successful that it was not questioned again.

The intelligence agencies in the area were to begin with fragmented and unreliable. They delivered plenty of information, but most of it was based on guesswork, gossip, and rumour. The Task Force commander was faced with the urgent need to check on enemy dispositions around his still incomplete base area defences. The S.A.S. was given the task of checking the intelligence reports, and though their operations produced a good deal of "negative intelligence" they were invaluable in showing that there were no immediate threats from specific directions.

After that the Task Force command and its G2 (Intelligence) Branch planned S.A.S. operations designed to gain maximum information from their limited resources and to apply the principle of economy of force. One example of this successful procedure was a six weeks constant surveillance carried out by six S.A.S. patrols over 15,000 metres of the eastern approaches to the base. Twice daily reporting by these patrols kept the Task Force command continually informed that there was no enemy movement in that area, thus enabling the force to carry out a large scale sweep, employing all but one company left behind for base defence, without being worried by having an open flank.

An S.A.S. patrol could operate for fourteen days on its own supplies, but when helicopters became the usual means of inserting patrols into their operational areas this period was cut to seven or ten days. Such periods were found to be long enough to achieve patrol objectives without wearing down the soldiers; an important point in the wet season, when skin diseases are endemic and movement in the hot, humid atmosphere is fatiguing in the extreme; or in the height of the dry season when water is hard to find and it is difficult to move through the jungle without noise, especially in defoliated areas.

Most S.A.S. operations were for reconnaissance or surveillance, but raids and ambushes were carried out from time to time. The endurance of S.A.S. men enabled them to move slowly and stealthily deep into enemy territory, and they found that the Viet Cong tended to be noisy and careless when they considered themselves secure in their base areas. In the jungle, the monkey is killed by the leopard; he who moves silently has a supreme advantage over the noisy one. S.A.S. patrols were able to penetrate Viet Cong base areas, execute close reconnaissance, and, when necessary, spring ambushes from ranges which ensure maximum effect.

Close liaison with the R.A.A.F. and constant review of procedures enabled joint S.A.S./R.A.A.F. operations to be highly successful in the infiltration and extraction of patrols. When General William Westmoreland commanded the Allied forces in Vietnam he became intrigued by the S.A.S. operations, and ordered a study of their procedures which culminated in the establishment, with the help of S.A.S., of a training school for his own and other personnel. All U.S. infantry brigades and divisions were ordered to develop and maintain at least one Long Range Reconnaissance Patrol Company apiece, and the success of such companies is believed to be a major advance in U.S. counter-insurgency techniques.

S.A.S. operations have received little publicity, but the Viet Cong have no doubts as to their abilities. They have been mentioned in numerous captured enemy documents, and among their main achievements has been the destruction of the security which the Viet Cong bases enjoyed for so long. The sudden devastating air strikes or artillery barrages which fell upon them were often the result of a close-quarters reconnaissance by a few S.A.S. troopers, penetrating unseen and unheard and then withdrawing to indicate the enemy positions.

Though it is no true measure of the effectiveness of S.A.S. operations in Vietnam, the tally now stands at over 500 Viet Cong killed in S.A.S. ambushes for the loss of one Australian died of wounds during patrol operations. The fact that Australian patrols can operate deep in enemy territory with such relative immunity proves the value of having highly-trained specialists in units such as these, and justifies the time and expense of bringing them to this standard of training.

After the battle of Long Tan, the Australian Task Force continued their work of establishing itself in Phuoc Tuy Province with a determination steeled by the knowledge that its men could meet and defeat the Viet Cong on its own ground. One operation followed another; one camp or base or tunnel complex after another was unearthed and destroyed; firefights flared through the jungle as the Australians encountered the Viet Cong in actions ranging from patrol skirmishes to the repulse of desperate attempts to recapture lost ground.

Yard by yard, the province was secured for the people who ask nothing better than to be allowed to live out their obscure lives in peace. On the waterways winding through the jungle, the Australians trapped and sank the sampans taking ammunition and supplies to the guerillas. Viet Cong leaders who had held the area to ransom were captured. Towns and villages which had had to pay out as much as half their produce and income to the Viet Cong were liberated—not without savage running battles as the claws of the National "Liberation" Army were torn loose. Hundreds of tons of rice, countless rounds of ammunition, weapons ranging from captured American Armalite rifles to Chinese and Russian mortars and sub-machine guns were dug out of the caches and tunnels. In late 1967, the Task Force was reinforced with another battalion, and its work continued with even greater vigour.

And as soon as the combat infantrymen had secured another small section of the province, they set to work to win another battle; the "hearts and minds" campaign which must be won before the enemy has been defeated. Little or nothing has been said about this campaign among all the millions of words poured out by those opposed to Australian participation in the war. It did not suit them to mention the number of villagers who were fed, resettled, and generally looked after by the Australians—any more than it suited them to mention the multitude of civilians massacred in cold blood by the communists before, during, and after the Tet offensive of 1968.

There is a certain monotony in the record of offensive sweeps carried out by Australian soldiers in Vietnam; Operations Beaumaris, Renmark, Portsea, Lismore, Puckapunyal, and the rest. But they were not monotonous for the men who participated in them. Each drive into the jungle brought them into contact with a dangerous and cunning enemy, who fought back with every skill and weapon at his command. Mines and booby traps killed and wounded men just as efficiently as a volley from ambush or an all out attack, and in their dogged work of clearing the Viet Cong out of the province which had been given them to protect the Australians lost a steady trickle of killed and wounded.

For much of the time since the battle of Long Tan, the Australian involvement in Vietnam has been the police work of keeping the peace in Phuoc Tuy. Difficult and dangerous though this has been, it has not brought them into such heavy contact with the enemy as that of the American and South Vietnam armies—yet the task of the latter would have been infinitely more difficult if it had not been for the Australians protecting their rear, and making sure that the Viet Cong did not infiltrate back to take possession of the areas out of which they had been expelled.

Indeed it is generally accepted that the Australian efforts in Phuoc Tuy Province have been more successful than those in any other area in South Vietnam, because in purely military skills the Australians were well prepared. Their understanding of the type of war in which they were to become involved was always much deeper than that of most Americans.

Australian military leaders in South Vietnam have never been impressed by "body counts" as such, but they have understood the implications of pacification of an area. A former commander of the Australian Task Force illustrated this point in discussions with the author when he commented, "No 'kill ratio' is an indication of progress towards our objective or of the capability of our forces. The only yardstick which has any validity is to what degree the security of an area of responsibilities is being advanced. In any case the best way to handle an insurgent is to convert him, and figures of returnees would not be included in any ratio of kills to losses, though they might, in some circumstances, be much more important."

A number of Australians in South Vietnam have been attached to the Americans in I Corps area, which covers five provinces with a total population of about three million. They have assisted in advising the Popular and Regional Forces of about 50,000 men, and in advising South Vietnam government departments at district and province level.

Their work has covered a great variety of military and civilian activities. They have served as advisors on Province Advisory Teams, worked on the Chieu Hoi programme which is designed to attract Viet Cong and North Vietnamese to the Government side, and acted as instructors in the Revolutionary Development Cadre teams; a force of nearly 12,000 men and women employed on government projects for the benefit of people in the rural areas.

These Australians have been integrated into the American establishment on a number of levels, including those of logistics and intelligence. Several have been killed or wounded in line of duty. An American ex-official of I Corps area told the author:"The Australians were highly thought of by their American comrades in arms. Their willingness to play a loyal and enthusiastic role as members of a team, and their versatility in adapting not only to the kind of war involved in pacification but to a foreign military organisation, was what made them so successful."

He said also: "I never saw the Australian Task Force in operation but I heard good things about it from some Americans who had. I believe that one of the reasons for its success was that it stayed in the same area for a long time and therefore was able to apply some of the lessons learned in Malaysia."

It is said that the Americans would have liked the Australian Task Force to have operated elsewhere in South Vietnam, but this has been resisted on two main counts. Firstly, because of Australian reluctance to serve directly under American command due to their different operational methods. Secondly, because the Australians could see no good reason why, after having largely pacified Phuoc Tuy Province, they should move out and allow the Viet Cong to regain their former ascendancy.

The strategy used by the High Command to counter Viet Cong tactics has been the subject of considerable debate. General W. C. Westmoreland, the former Commander-in-Chief in Vietnam has of recent times come under particularly strong criticism. But probably no military commander has ever had to fight a campaign where the politico/military considerations were so delicately interwoven. In Korea General MacArthur was allowed the privilege of invading North Korea although President Truman rightly halted his ambition to cross the Yalu River.

Westmoreland was never allowed this luxury, although he favoured action against the Ho Chi Minh Trail and North Vietnamese sanctuaries in Laos instead of bombing North Vietnam. Had he been allowed to undertake these operations when the American forces were at their peak of strength, it is highly likely that he could have dealt the Viet Cong a blow from which they could not have militarily recovered. But basically, General Westmoreland did reflect the misunderstanding of the war that characterised most of the American leadership.

The great mistake the Americans made was to divide the war into military, political, or other phases, and to assume that once the military phase was finished, the rest would fall rapidly into line. This meant that throughout the early period of the war, political objections were consistently sacrificed for purely military objectives, even in some cases for very minor military gains. It was not until 1967 that the real impact of the "one war" theory began to be felt.

At the time of writing, it seems almost possible that everything done in South Vietnam will have been in vain; that the communists will win by propaganda and the war-weariness of their opponents, and above all by the efforts of those within the democracies who are opposed to the war, all that they could not gain on the battlefield. There can be little doubt that the withdrawal of the Americans and their allies will lay South Vietnam open to a full-scale invasion from the North, with all it implies of cold-blooded communist savagery. Australian soldiers in Vietnam have seen some of that at first-hand.

After that, only history can show whether the forecast made by Sir Robert Menzies, in an address to students of the University of Hawaii in November 1969, has been correct. He said, "I subscribe to the 'domino theory,' sometimes rejected by academic theorists, because I believe it to be obvious in a world of 'real politics'; that if the Vietnam war ends with some compromise that denies South Vietnam a real and protected independence, Laos and Cambodia, Thailand, Malaysia, Singapore and Indonesia will be vulnerable . . . However susceptible to criticism this domino theory may seem to be in a university study in America, it has formidable reality to Australians who see the boundaries of aggressive communism coming closer and closer."

* * *

Australia's defence policy has been the subject of much debate since Britain's declaration of intention to withdraw west of Suez, the beginning of peace negotiations to end the Vietnam War, and the steadily increasing Russian presence in the Indian Ocean. "In a world of real politics," those who oppose the supply of arms to South Africa overlook the fact that South Africa could, at a single stroke, cut Australia's sea communications with Europe by refusing permission for ships bound for Britain to refuel in South African ports. The Russians are angling for the great naval base at Trincomalee, in Ceylon, just as they fished for and won the base at Alexandria in Egypt. And yet there is plenty of opposition to the American presence in

Australia, both economically and, as in the case of the North-West Cape radio station, militarily. Perhaps Australians are still, as Blamey described them in 1942, living "in a dell on the edge of the jungle."

No man in his senses would glorify war—especially a man who has seen war at first-hand. Yet those who have lived in captivity, such as the Hungarians and Czechoslovakians, know that other things can be as bad or worse. There may come a time when Australians are faced once more with a threat of invasion such as the Japanese posed in 1942. If so, then nothing will save her but the same factors which saved her then; the courage and determination of her men in the front line. Without a strongly-based army, navy, and air force, which do not necessarily rely upon the fickle whims of "big and powerful friends," the continent is indefensible.

Despite the protestations of various academics, clerics, students, professional agitators, and the others who make up society's vocal minority, the words of General Sir Charles Brudenell White are as relevant today as when he spoke them in his Armistice Day address of 1928:

"Whether or not war is a defensible process, all I can say is that war is better than dishonour."

BIBLIOGRAPHY

The reader who desires further information on the first and second World Wars can select from a vast body of literature. The anthology *Vain Glory*, edited by Guy Chapman and published in 1936, uses material from nearly 200 sources, and these are only a fraction of the whole. Books on both wars range from the academic to the purely personal statements of participants, and from best sellers to obscure volumes produced by now forgotten publishers. By far the greater part of them, however, are by British, American, French, or German writers. Having regard to Australian participation in both wars, the contribution by Australian writers to the body of war literature is comparatively slight. On the first World War, two of the best are *Jacka's Mob*, by E. J. Rule, which amongst other graphic descriptions contains a vigorous portrayal of the battle of Bullecourt; and *The Desert Column*, by Ion Idriess. *Flesh in Armour*, by Leonard Mann, is a classic novel of the first World War, as is *Her Privates We*, by the Australian Frederic Manning—though he based it on his experiences in the British and not the Australian Army. The collected short stories of Harley Matthews, *Saints and Sinners*, and of William Baylebridge, *Anzac Muster*, give an insight into the character of Australians in the first world conflict.

For the serious student, there is of course no substitute for *The Official History of Australia in the War of 1914-18*, in twelve volumes of which the first was published in 1921 and the last in 1942. Its editor and main author, Dr C. E. W. Bean, had been an official war correspondent and had visited every Australian battlefield. In 1946, he published *Anzac to Amiens*, which might be described as a "digest" of the six volumes of the official history which he wrote.

An almost unobtainable publication of the first World War is *Aussie*, the Australian Army newspaper produced by the 1st A.I.F. Printing Section in France. Consisting entirely of contributions from serving soldiers, it gives a remarkable insight into the character of men of the 1st A.I.F. Some of the cartoons display a grim humour—especially that of the wounded soldier who holds up a hand on which only one finger remains, and says that he's not worried because his peacetime job is playing a one-string fiddle on the music-halls. Two more publications which are rather rare are collections of photographs entitled *From the Australian Front, 1917*, published by Cassell's in Melbourne, and *Australian War Photographs*, which bears no imprint but was edited by Captain G. H. Wilkins, M.C.—later Sir Hubert Wilkins, the explorer.

As after the second World War, several brigade and battalion histories were published; some of them privately printed and circulated. Other

443

novels and reminiscences may be found, and of course the newspapers and magazines of the period carry a good deal of material, but a good deal of it is very obviously written for "home consumption" and to some extent tends to play down the realities of war.

The second world conflict inspired the creation of a larger and perhaps more lasting body of Australian war literature. During the war, the Australian War Memorial published several volumes of contributions by serving members of all three forces, and these contain some graphic articles, stories, paintings, and sketches. John Hetherington and Alan Moorehead, both of whom were war correspondents, published *Airborne Invasion* and *The Australian Soldier* and *Mediterranean Front, A Year of Battle*, and *The End in Africa* respectively. (Moorehead's *Gallipoli*, published in 1957, was highly praised.)

Chester Wilmot, also a war correspondent, was able to give a first-hand picture of the siege and relief of Tobruk, and the noted Australian novelist George Johnston wrote *Australia at War* in 1942 and *Grey Gladiator* and *Battle of the Seaways*, both about the war at sea.

A series of excellent novels and works of personal reminiscences followed the close of hostilities. Rohan Rivett's *Behind Bamboo* was one of the first to document the horrifying experiences of Australians in Japanese captivity, and was followed some years later by Russell Braddon's *The Naked Island*, covering somewhat the same area but including the author's experiences as a soldier in the 8th Division fighting the Japanese in Malaya and Singapore. A third book on rather the same lines is K. Harrison's *The Brave Japanese*, published in the 1960s. Ray Parkin's three fine books *Out of the Smoke*, *Into the Smother*, and the *Sword and the Blossom* cover somewhat similar experiences but told from the viewpoint of a survivor of H.M.A.S. *Perth*.

Ronald McKie, whose fine book *The Heroes* reconstructed the story of Operation Rimau and suggested a solution to the mystery of its failure, published *This Was Singapore* in 1942 and *Proud Echo*, the story of H.M.A.S. *Perth*, in 1953. An interesting follow-up to this story is *The Bells of Sunda Strait*, by David Burchell, which describes the latter's attempt to salvage the ship's bell of the *Perth* during the 1960s.

Among the most notable Australian novels of the second World War was *We Were the Rats*, by Lawson Glassop, published in 1944; a vivid picture of the enlistment, training, and combat experiences of a group of infantrymen, with special relevance to Tobruk. Jon Cleary's *Climate of Courage*, and T. A. Hungerford's *The Ridge and the River*, give insight into the feelings of men fighting in New Guinea.

James Aldridge, another Australian war correspondent, wrote three novels centred on Greece and the Middle East; *Signed With their Honour*, *The Sea Eagle*, and *Of Many Men*, though these concerned British rather than

Australian personnel. Another novel which was very popular was *The 20,000 Thieves*, by Eric Lambert; written very much from the "ranker's" viewpoint, scathing about the military mentality and with hardly a good word to say about officers in general, and with some lacerating scenes of desert warfare and of front-line fighting at Tobruk. It was the first book of a quartet, of which the others are *The Veterans*, *The Dark Backward*, and *Glory Thrown In*.

Biographies of second World War commanders include *There Goes a Man*, by W. B. Russell, the story of Lieutenant-General Sir Stanley Savige; John Hetherington's *Blamey*; and *The Gordon Bennett Story*, by Frank Legg, who is also the author of *War Correspondent*. Some of the best-known writers of Australian birth, such as Paul Brickhill, Ivan Southall, and Russell Braddon, have written fine books about the exploits of British, rather than Australian, units or personalities.

Some excellent unit histories were produced after the second World War, notably *The 2/14th Australian Infantry Battalion*, by W. B. Russell, and *Tobruk to Tarakan*, the story of the 48th Battalion, by John Glenn. Raymond Paull's *Retreat from Kokoda*, and a more recently published paperback entitled *The Knights of Kokoda*, give scarifying pictures of what Australian soldiers had to endure in that campaign.

The definitive works on Australia's part in the second World War, however, are the twenty-two volumes of the Official History. The general editor was Gavin Long, who had been a war correspondent in France and the Middle East. He wrote the volumes *To Benghazi; Greece, Crete, and Syria; The Final Campaign;* and a summary of the work. Also, he edited, and wrote a portion of, the 105-page article on the second World War which appears in the *Australian Encyclopaedia*, which provides a valuable reference and summary of events. Other authors of volumes of the official history are John Hetherington, A. S. Walker, Sir Paul Hasluck, S. J. Butlin, George Odgers, Lionel Wigmore, G. H. Gill, D. P. Mellor, B. Maughan, D. McCarthy, David Dexter, and Douglas Gillison, of whom some also contributed to the *Australian Encyclopaedia* article.

Some other books of specific interest are *The Coast Watchers*, by Eric Feldt, which is a very full description of the work of those brave men; *White Coolies*, by Betty Jeffrey, which is one of the very few war books written by Australian women, and tells of Australian military nurses in Japanese captivity; and H. Gordon Bennett's own personal record, *Why Singapore Fell*.

Books on Australia's involvement in the other seven conflicts mentioned by the author are comparatively few and in some cases very rare. There is an Australian *Official History of the South African War*, which covers the work and actions of Australian units in South Africa, but a more personal record is *Tommy Cornstalk*. Not a great deal has been written by Australians about the conflicts in Korea, Malaysia, and Vietnam—or not in book form, at least. A useful and lively record, dealing mainly with the military aspect, is *Australians in Vietnam*, by Ian Mackay.

Some poignant war poetry has been written by Australians. Vance Palmer's *The Farmer Remembers the Somme* epitomises the feelings of men who had seen so much that was strange and awful, and returned from it to the placidity of Australian life. Leon Gellert's poems of the first World War have a place in many anthologies, but probably are less well known than C. J. Dennis' *The Moods of Ginger Mick* and *Digger Smith*, which, being written by a man who did not know war at first hand, are very far from realism. Edward Harrington published *Songs of War and Peace* in 1920, but made little impact. Ian Mudie's *New Guinea Campaign* is a fine war poem, and David Campbell wrote *Men in Green*.

A good many books by English writers mention Australian servicemen, from John Masefield's *Gallipoli* and Sir Ian Hamilton's *Dardanelles Despatches* to the works of Sir Winston Churchill. Some give accurate pictures, others are mere caricatures of the "dinkum Aussie cobber" type, and some make sour references to such Australian characteristics as neglecting to salute British officers.

A study of any or all of the works mentioned above will enable the interested reader to broaden his knowledge of the background, actions, and attitudes of the Australian people and their fighting men in their nine wars from Waikato to Long Tan. A concise bibliography of the works principally referred to in the preparation of this book is as follows:

Bartlett, N.	*With the Australians in Korea*	Australian War Memorial, Canberra
Barclay, Brigadier C. N.	*The First Commonwealth Division*	Gale & Polden
Bateson, Charles	*The War with Japan*	Ure Smith, Sydney
Bean, Doctor C. E. W.	*Official History of Australia in the War of 1914-1918*	Australian War Memorial, Canberra
	Anzac to Amiens	Angus & Robertson, Sydney
	Two Men I Knew	Angus & Robertson Sydney
Bryant, Sir Arthur	*Turn of the Tide*	Collins, London
Braddon, Russell	*The Naked Island*	T. Werner Laurie, London
Buchan, John	*History of the Great War*	Nelson, London
Clutterbuck, Brigadier Richard	*The Long, Long War: the Emergency in Malaya*	Cassell, London

Callinan, Bernard	*Independent Company*	Heinemann, London
Connell, John	*Auchinleck*	Collins, London
	Wavell—Soldier and Scholar	Collins, London
Gibbs, Philip	*Realities of War*	Heinemann, London
	The Battles of the Somme	Heinemann, London
	Bapaume to Passchendaele	Heinemann, London
Hetherington, John	*Blamey*	Cheshire, Melbourne
Johnston, George H.	*New Guinea Diary*	Angus & Robertson, Sydney
Laffin, John	*Anzacs at War*	Abelard Schuman, London
Legg, Frank	*The Gordon Bennett Story*	Angus & Robertson, Sydney
	War Correspondent	Rigby, Adelaide
Lloyd George, David	*War Memoirs*	Ivor Nicholson and Watson, London
Long, Gavin	*MacArthur*	Angus & Robertson, Sydney
Long, Gavin (*editor*)	*Australia in the War of 1939-1945 (Official History)*	Australian War Memorial, Canberra
Mackay, Ian	*Australians in Vietnam*	Rigby, Adelaide
McKie, R. H.	*The Heroes*	Angus & Robertson, Sydney
Masel, Philip	*The Second 28th*	The Griffin Press, Adelaide
Mellenthin, Major-General F. W. von	*Panzer Battles, 1939-1945*	Cassell, London
Monash, General Sir John	*War Letters (ed. F. W. Cutlack)*	Angus & Robertson, Sydney
	The Australian Victories in France, 1918	Hutchinson, London
Montgomery, Field-Marshal Viscount	*El Alamein to the River Sangro*	Hutchinson, London
Moorehead, Alan	*Gallipoli*	Hamish Hamilton, London
	The Desert War	Hamish Hamilton, London
Morison, S. E.	*History of U.S. Naval Operations in World War II*	Oxford University Press
O'Malley, R., and Moore, A.	*As You Were*	Australian War Memorial, Canberra

447

Owen, Frank	*The Fall of Singapore*	Michael Joseph, London
Paull, Raymond	*Retreat from Kokoda*	Heinemann, Melbourne
Percival, Lieutenant-General A. E.	*The War in Malaya*	Eyre & Spottiswood, London
Slim, Field-Marshal Viscount	*Defeat into Victory*	Cassell, London
Stewart, I. McD. G.	*The Struggle for Crete*	Oxford University Press
Terraine, John	*The Western Front, 1914-1918*	Hutchinson, London
	Douglas Haig, the Educated Soldier	Hutchinson, London
Wilmot, Chester	*Tobruk*	Angus & Robertson, Sydney
Woollcombe, Robert	*The Campaigns of Wavell, 1939-43*	Cassell, London

INDEX OF MILITARY FORMATIONS

KOREA, MALAYA, VIETNAM

GENERAL INDEX